REVOLUTIONARY BROTHERS

ALSO BY TOM CHAFFIN

*Giant's Causeway: Frederick Douglass's Irish Odyssey and
the Making of an American Visionary* (2014)

*Met His Every Goal? James K. Polk and the
Legends of Manifest Destiny* (2014)

The H. L. Hunley: *The Secret Hope of the Confederacy* (2008)

*Sea of Gray: The Around-the-World Odyssey of the
Confederate Raider* Shenandoah (2006)

*Pathfinder: John Charles Frémont and the
Course of American Empire* (2002)

*Fatal Glory: Narciso López and the
First Clandestine U.S. War against Cuba* (1996)

REVOLUTIONARY BROTHERS

*Thomas Jefferson, the Marquis de Lafayette,
and the Friendship That Helped Forge
Two Nations*

TOM CHAFFIN

ST. MARTIN'S PRESS
NEW YORK

First published in the United States by St. Martin's Press, an imprint of
St. Martin's Publishing Group

www.stmartins.com

Designed by Kathryn Parise

The Library of Congress Cataloging-in-Publication Data is available upon request.

ISBN 978-1-250-11372-6 (hardcover)
ISBN 978-1-250-11374-0 (ebook)

Our books may be purchased in bulk for promotional, educational, or business use.
Please contact your local bookseller or the Macmillan Corporate and Premium
Sales Department at 1-800-221-7945, extension 5442, or by email at
MacmillanSpecialMarkets@macmillan.com.

First Edition: November 2019

10 9 8 7 6 5 4 3 2 1

À Bernard Obellianne, cher ami et compagnon de route:

"Les Fleuves m'ont laissé descendre où je voulais."

—ARTHUR RIMBAUD

CONTENTS

PART THREE

In Common Cause, 1781–1782

117

PART FOUR

Parisiens, 1782–1785

163

PART FIVE
Revolutionary Tide, 1786–1789
263

PART SIX
Diverging Paths, 1790–1824
391

I am what time, circumstance, history, have made of me, certainly, but I am also so much more than that. So are we all.

—James Baldwin

INTRODUCTION

Trails Long and Severe

We have gone through too many trying scenes together, to forget the sympathies and affections they nourished. Your trails have indeed been long and severe.

—Thomas Jefferson to Lafayette, Nov. 4, 1823

Life can only be understood backwards; but it must be lived forwards.

—Søren Kierkegaard

Rolling southeast on France's A61, we'd set out that morning from Toulouse. In the distant Pyrenees visible to our south, snow already covered the range's higher elevations. But in the gently rolling landscape before us, the summer's heat stubbornly persisted into late September. With my friend Bernard Obellianne at the wheel of his Citroën Berlingo, we were in the Haute-Garonne, looking for the ghosts of Thomas Jefferson and the marquis de Lafayette.

Bernard has lived in the South of France—*le Midi*—for most of his life. And that morning and over the next few days, our hope was to find our way to some of the places visited by Jefferson during the spring and summer of 1787, when—putting aside ambassadorial toils in Paris—he departed for the South of France to, as he put it, "see what I have never seen before."

Our first stop that morning—l'écluse du Sanglier, a nearby canal lock—belonged to one of the curiosities that brought Jefferson to these parts—the Canal du Midi, or as it was known then, the Canal royal en Languedoc. A jewel of seventeenth-century civil engineering, the canal, then 150 miles in length, was built to link France's Mediterranean and Atlantic coasts and thus spare the country's merchant ships the time, costs, and exposure to Barbary pirates of the voyage around the Iberian Peninsula. Over the past few years, before and since that morning, I've visited other places associated with this book's story: In front of the Hôtel de Ville—Paris's City Hall—I've lingered in the plaza where, on a morning in July 1789, a triumphant Lafayette, commanding the National Guard, stood before thousands of cheering compatriots and greeted a humbled Louis XVI.

In that same city, on a sidewalk several blocks southeast of the Arc de Triomphe, I stepped away from the Champs-Élysées' crowds to try to imagine the Hôtel de Langeac, Jefferson's town house, which once stood at that avenue's intersection with the rue de Berri.

In the late 1780s—in that long-ago demolished residence in a once leafy district now dense with shops and restaurants—Jefferson and Lafayette talked politics over meals that included vegetables cultivated in the diplomat's own garden, from seeds sent from Virginia.

At Monticello, Jefferson's beloved mountaintop Virginia estate, I stood in the room where Lafayette likely stayed during his visits there. I also visited nearby Montalto, the mountain from which Jefferson, in 1781, spotted British troops approaching Charlottesville and feared that, with Lafayette unable to rescue him as he had weeks earlier, enemy forces would soon come looking for him at Monticello. On Paris's rue d'Anjou, not far from the Élysée Palace, I visited Lafayette's final Paris residence, the apartment in which he breathed his last. And, in the city's Picpus neighborhood, in a far corner of a walled cemetery, I stood before the grave where Lafayette and his beloved wife, Adrienne, lie beneath a marble slab festooned with American and French flags.

Of course most of the historian's labors, the research and writing, are necessarily conducted in the great indoors. Even so, while working on historical narratives, I've long found that, as circumstances allow, visits to scenes of depicted events can be of value. In some instances they provide physical details that allow sharper description of places or, on occasion, the correction of factual errors—errors of geography and the like—perpetuated in diaries, letters, and other contemporary documents. In other cases such visits can better one's sense of the character, physical scale, and proximity of a depicted place to others relevant to the story.

———————

While most Americans possess at least an inkling of knowledge about Jefferson's life, fewer know Lafayette's story. That gap becomes more striking when one considers that the United States virtually teems with places that bear Lafayette's name—parks, schools, streets, squares, towns, and counties. There are also scores of places named La Grange, after the Château de la Grange-Bléneau, his estate near Paris. Indeed, contrast the ubiquity of his name in American life with how little many Americans know about this derring-do but complex figure—and it might be fair to consider Lafayette among the best and least known of our Founding Fathers.

That blind spot among Americans owes much to the fact that Lafayette was French and did not linger here after helping us to win our independence. In our civic memory he materializes in October 1781, at the American Revolution's decisive Battle of Yorktown, and stays long enough to accept, with General Washington, the surrender of General Cornwallis's British forces. Then he disappears. And though we know vaguely that, years later, he returned to hear some tributes and have some places named for him, we've never truly known what became of him after Yorktown—or who he was in the first place.

We Americans and our French friends often see things differently, viewing behavior through national stereotypes, sometimes exasperating one another. For complex reasons on which I try to cast new light herein, the French have never been as enamored of Lafayette as Americans believe they should be. Typifying such indifference, a bronze statue of the hero—a gift of American schoolchildren that stood for decades in the Louvre's courtyard—was removed in the 1980s to make room for I. M. Pei's glass pyramid.

Even so, the Lafayette connection, in Franco-American affairs, continues to inspire reciprocal goodwill. In my own experiences visiting and briefly living in France, I've witnessed it serving, at least among Americans, as a sort of consolation for perceived Gallic irritants—for everything from haughty Parisian waiters to seemingly arbitrary rules. After enduring such aggravations, Americans sometimes remark to one another that, say what you will, France was our first foreign ally—and, without the French, we wouldn't have won our independence.

Inevitably, that's when Lafayette's name comes up.

With slight variations, the story usually goes something like this: Oppressed North American colonists yearn for freedom from onerous British overlords. They rebel but prove no match for Britain's army and navy. When we're down for the count, France—guided by Lafayette and liberal Enlightenment values—rides in to our rescue. Revolution accomplished! For good measure, two centuries later Americans repay the debt—liberating France twice in the course of three decades from German invaders.

Lafayette, we are here!

Certainly it's a nice story. And to paraphrase Hemingway, it would be even prettier were it true. Alas, however, from the infancy of the American republic, cherished legends concerning Lafayette—and, for that matter, Jefferson—have often crowded out more complex, sometimes less ennobling, truths.

Beyond that, among many Americans, Lafayette's and Jefferson's respective roles in the French Revolution remain largely unknown. For those and other reasons, I believe that a forthright retelling of their shared story—their solitary, convergent, and divergent paths through two revolutions and their final reunion—is long overdue.

Over the years each of the two men has drawn the attention of many talented biographers. Likewise, numerous gifted historians have explored the American and the French Revolutions. This book, however—the first sustained account of the Jefferson-Lafayette friendship and collaboration—is not intended as a joint biography or as a history of the American and French Revolutions. It seeks to capture another quarry: the story of a single, and singularly extraordinary, friendship, and its role in the making of two revolutions—and two nations.

On that late September day in *le Midi*, Bernard and I visited three of the Languedoc Canal's locks. The waterway had numbered among the main sights that Jefferson wanted to see during his spring 1787 tour of France's South; and, afloat upon it, he reveled in the mechanics of its operations, indulged his lifelong fascination with watersheds, and savored its scenic beauties: "Of all the methods of travelling I have ever tried this is the pleasantest." While scenic, even in its heyday, the canal—twenty-four feet wide, six feet deep—could accommodate only low-draft, flat-bottom boats. And with the coming of the railroad to France in the 1850s, commercial traffic vanished from its waters. These days, travel along the canal is strictly recreational—mainly houseboat voyagers and bicyclists, savoring the lovely plane-tree-shaded path that threads its length.

Otherwise—as Bernard and I remarked to each other that day as we lingered by the second lock that we visited—l'écluse de l'Océan—the canal seems to have changed little over the past centuries. Except for the absence of commercial cargo on its waters and the fact that modern engines now operate its locks, the waterway would seem to be much as it was during Jefferson's day.

However, as we were leaving, walking by the lock's two-story canal tender's house with its terra-cotta roof, Bernard noticed something that had escaped us earlier—an object definitely added since Jefferson's passage: Affixed to the house's wall was a handsome metal plaque honoring Jefferson. Installed by a private foundation in 2009, it featured a bas-relief bust of the Virginian.

The plaque's raised-letter text, curiously without reference to the canal or Jefferson's passage through it, declared him a *"SYMBOLE DE L'AMITIÉ FRANCO AMÉRICAINE."* Noting his roles as author of the Declaration of Independence and U.S. president, it further praised Jefferson as a "lover of France" who, after living on French soil, became a promoter of the country's architecture, culture, and values. "With his friend La Fayette he assisted in the drafting of the Declaration of the Rights of Man and of the Citizen."

Sometimes history's truths hide in secret places.

In other instances, you're given a sign.

PART ONE

The Road Rises,
1743–1777

ONE

La Victoire

Lanky and redheaded, the nineteen-year-old French nobleman stood as if in a trance on the three-masted ship's quarterdeck. Twenty-five feet long, with an eighteen-foot beam, *La Victoire* was as stubby as it was crowded. And as the sea rolled beneath the young man's feet, a northeasterly wind swelled his ship's sails, nudging it down the final hours of its four-month, four-thousand-mile Atlantic crossing.

Just before noon, on June 13, 1777, the marquis de Lafayette reached for his telescope. Scanning the western horizon, unmindful of the summer morning's merciless brightness and searing heat, he longed for his first sighting of South Carolina's coast. For the past few days he and his crew had spotted birds associated with land. He had grown so convinced of their imminent landfall that, as a precaution against hostile ships possibly lurking close to the shore, he had taken to ordering the ship to sail without lights at night. Increasing their discomfiture, the voyage had been badly planned, and they were running low on food and water.

Ironically, however, those privations only sweetened that morning's renewed spirits. As Lafayette scanned the horizon, his shipmates—each man at his station—optimistically prepared for their long journey's conclusion. Even so, amid the morning's gathering joy, if Lafayette still appeared anxious, all understood his reasons: If expectations proved sound, he was about to set foot upon the terra firma of a lifelong dream.[1]

———

Since childhood Lafayette had hungered for martial glory. What he never contemplated was realizing that dream in the uniform of a foreign army. With a general's commission in hand, he would soon report for duty in the Continental army, the military arm of the United States of America, an improbable republic declared two years earlier. The ill-equipped, poorly trained army was now slogging through the third year of a dispiriting insurgent war against the superior forces of Great Britain, against whose empire its former North American colonists were now rebelling.

In reality much of the brave, leveling rhetoric of that young nation's self-described "Patriots"—from "Give me liberty or give me death" to "All men are created equal"—carried a hollow, abstract resonance for the young, wealthy French nobleman. His Enlightenment education, venerating safely distant ancient republics, disposed him in principle to share such sentiments. But in day-to-day life Lafayette also remained a loyal subject of his own country's monarch, Louis XVI, whose absolutism made Britain's king George III appear, by comparison, a zealot of democratic principles.

Other considerations, however, drew Lafayette to the Patriots' cause. Fourteen years earlier, in the Seven Years' War, the same British forces that the Americans now faced had defeated those of the marquis's native land. Personalizing that sting, his father, fighting for France, had died in the conflict. Lafayette was just two years old when his father—Michel-Louis-Christophe-Roch-Gilbert du Motier, from whom he inherited his title—died. But in the coming years, as the fallen soldier's only son grew up in an extended family that revered military service, Lafayette père acquired, in the mind of that son, an almost mythic scale.[2]

———

Marie-Joseph-Paul-Yves-Roch-Gilbert du Motier was born on September 6, 1757, in south-central France's province of Auvergne—three years after his parents' marriage in Paris. The boy's father had generational ties to Auvergne. His mother, Marie Louise Jolie de La Rivière, was the daughter of a rich nobleman from Brittany.

Auvergne lay inside the Massif Central, landlocked mountains indented by deep-valley forests teeming with tall oaks, chestnuts, firs, and beech trees; high plateaus; and sublime uplands crowned with domed, rocky outcrops. Lafayette spent his childhood at the Château de Chavaniac, an eighteen-room mansion set on a hillock amid the area's volcano-sculpted mountains. The Lafayette family, its lineage deeply embedded in France's history, could lay claim to celebrated figures. But recent generations, though retaining noble titles and landholdings, had scant ties to Versailles's reigning Bourbon dynasty. Recalled Lafayette, the family by then "left the provinces only to make war and played no role at court."

Jacques-Roch du Motier, the older brother of Lafayette's father, died in 1734, at age eighteen, fighting Austrian forces in the War of the Polish Succession. Two years later Éduoard du Motier, a recently titled marquis—father of the two brothers—died in an equestrian accident while serving as a bodyguard for Louis XV. From Éduoard—Lafayette's paternal grandfather—Lafayette's own father, Michel-Louis-Christophe-Roch-Gilbert du Motier, had inherited the marquis title. And after his death at age twenty-six—in August 1759, killed by a British cannonball during the Battle of Minden in the Seven Years' War, in what is today's northern Germany—the title fell to his son, Gilbert, then just weeks shy of his second birthday.

An extended configuration of the Lafayette clan, overseen by Gilbert's paternal grandmother, was, by then, living at the Château de Chavaniac. And by February 1762—apparently traumatized by her husband's death—Gilbert's mother, Mary Louise Jolie de La Rivière, a native of Paris, had returned there to live with her family. Her son, Gilbert, thus spent his formative years living amid a ménage of aunts, cousins, and servants, all dominated by his formidable paternal grandmother.

During Gilbert's lifetime his name was often spelled "La Fayette" and variations thereof. It was an age, after all, that had yet to standardize spellings; and many, including some who knew him, were unaware of how Lafayette spelled the family name. But he himself, when referring to himself, spelled it as one word, though whether as "LaFayette" or "Lafayette," his autograph—its *F* indecipherable as to lower- or uppercase—makes it impossible to render any final conclusion.

For five years during the 1760s, Lafayette saw his mother only during her occasional visits to the Auvergne. While the thought of a mother leaving a child to be raised by others may seem harsh to modern sensibilities, in the world of eighteenth-century French nobility it was accepted practice: Infants were often turned over to wet nurses; and older children to governesses, tutors, and grandparents: "Although my mother loved me a great deal," Lafayette remembered, "the thought of taking me away from my grandmother La Fayette never crossed her mind."

At Chavaniac, beyond what he learned from the family's hired tutors, Lafayette grew up transfixed by stories, doubtless embellished, of the glorious deeds of his father, uncle, and other relatives who had perished in service to France. Gilbert also relished adolescent explorations of the wildernesses that lay within his childhood's reach. In the Auvergne's highlands, canyons, and forests, he cultivated a fertile imagination—one that made room for a legendary creature, the Beast of the Gévaudan, reputed to roam south-central France.

Its size and predations exaggerated in local folklore, the "beast" was likely a large lynx, some other known species of forest mammal, or even a human being. Whatever the legend's origins, the chimerical creature had reputedly killed livestock and even women and children. And while Lafayette never claimed to have actually seen the beast, his contemplations of it—his ponderings of its powers and size—inflamed his imagination. And along with tales of his relatives' military exploits, the Beast of the Gévaudan nourished an early taste for romantic adventure: "I recall nothing in my life that preceded my enthusiasm for glorious tales or my plans to travel the world in search of renown." Moreover, he recalled, himself "burning with the desire to have a uniform."[3]

By 1767 Lafayette's mother had decided that it was time for her son to join her in Paris. Soon returning to Chavaniac that December, Marie Louise Jolie and Gilbert commenced a two-week journey to Paris and her Luxembourg Palace apartment. Later recalling his first months in Paris, he remembered being "separated with the utmost chagrin from a grandmother, two aunts, and a cousin, whom I adored." Even so—though taken aback by the lack of deference shown him in Paris, compared with that accorded him in the Auvergne—the city stamped an indelible impression on him.

In 1768 Gilbert was enrolled in Paris's Collège du Plessis, a secondary school run by the University of Paris, on the rue Saint-Jacques, not far from the Lafayette family's residence. Most of his Plessis classmates came from families whose social status derived from the Nobility of the Robe, a category derived from government or judicial service.

Nobles among Lafayette's family, by contrast, belonged to the Nobility of the Sword, a more prestigious ranking, derived from military service to the court. At the Collège du Plessis, Lafayette—heretofore having spent much of his free time in rural isolation—now reveled in the company of other boys. Moreover, he blossomed into a popular and gifted student (excelling in Latin) and quickly established himself as a leader among his classmates.

With his growing proficiency in Latin, he also commenced his lifelong love of the writings of Cicero, Plutarch, Virgil, Horace, and other classical writers who celebrated the heroes of ancient Rome and Greece. But—at least initially for Lafayette, as was the tendency among other students of his generation and court milieu—those readings tended to foster a republicanism more ornamental than active, rarely producing antimonarchist actions. "One comes away from the study of the Latin language with a taste for republics," observed a contemporary. But, he added, upon graduation those same young men realize that they "must lose and forget" such tastes—"for their safety, for their advancement and for their happiness."

Even so, attesting to the imaginative powers of such readings, Lafayette—like other young Frenchmen in his circle—tended to view the American leaders and emissaries they met, at least initially, as latter-day avatars of classical Greece or Rome. As a Lafayette friend recalled after meeting Benjamin Franklin, Silas Deane, and other American diplomats in Paris, he could not help but view the exotic, foreign-speaking emissaries as "some wise contemporaries of Plato, or republicans from the time of Cato and Fabius."

In April 1770, upon the deaths of his mother and, weeks later, an even wealthier grandfather—both heavily invested in land, the latter in Brittany—Gilbert became rich. Indeed, his combined inheritances made the twelve-year-old orphan one of the wealthiest souls in all of France. In 1774, when he was sixteen, those riches grew still more: In an arranged marriage he wed fourteen-year-old Marie-Adrienne-Françoise de Noailles, the daughter of a wealthy, well-connected Parisian nobleman. For Lafayette's relatives, who arranged the union, the Noailleses promised social entrée; for the Noailleses—with five daughters to marry off—the groom offered solid finances, funds that lessened the family's burden, at least in Adrienne's case, of their dowry-provision obligations.

Adrienne's father, Jean-Paul-François de Noailles, duc d'Ayen, a chemist and courtier, favored the union. But given the couple's youth when the marriage arrangements were made—Adrienne was only twelve—her mother, Henriette-Anne-Louise d'Aguesseau, duchesse d'Ayen, insisted that the wedding be delayed for two years. In the interim Gilbert moved into a separate wing of the Hôtel de Noailles, the family's capacious Paris town house. There, for two years, he lived not as a family member, but as a tenant—albeit a pampered one, paying rent and for his own food, fuel, and servants. All the while, hoping to keep the couple's union unconsummated until their marriage, Gilbert's future in-laws did their best to keep watchful eyes upon him.

Before and after the couple's eventual wedding, on April 11, 1774, Lafayette, through the Noailleses, expanded his social ties into court society's upper tiers. In contrast, however, to the ease of his adjustment to the Collège du Plessis, his entry into those circles proved difficult. His provincial origins discomfited him, and his former ease collapsed into awkwardness and self-conscious reticence.

Acquiring what became a lifelong indulgence, he spent lavishly on clothes. Otherwise, adapting to the high-spending, high-living ways of young men and women of Versailles and Paris court society, he took up—at least during those years—heavy drinking and high-stakes wagering on card games and horses. In time his closest friends even formed their own club, the "Society of the Wooden Sword." Named after a favorite cabaret, its members included Adrienne's friend, Vienna-born Marie Antoinette. Then barely twenty and recently arrived at Versailles, Marie Antoinette, with her husband, Louis XVI, would, upon the death of Louis XV in 1774, assume France's Bourbon throne.

In the end, however, despite Lafayette's strivings, he often felt undone "by the gaucheness of [his] manners which, without being out of place on any important occasion, never yielded to the graces of the court or the charms of supper in the capital." The comte de La Marck, a Belgian nobleman who often socialized with the Noailleses, regarded Lafayette as a hopeless arriviste—disdainfully recalled that he "danced without grace [and] sat badly on his horse." He also recalled an episode in which Lafayette, assisted by his in-laws, secured an invitation to an evening of dancing hosted by Marie Antoinette; but when Lafayette's moment arrived to dance with the queen, La Marck noted that the scion of Chavaniac proved himself to be so "maladroit . . . that the Queen could not stop herself from laughing."

Making matters worse, Lafayette's native wit often rendered it difficult for him to abide the intellectual pretensions of generational peers in such elevated circles. On one occasion, as the comte de Provence, the elder of Louis XVI's two brothers, boasted ad nauseam of the capacity of his memory, an irritated Lafayette could not resist a tart retort: "Memory," he shot back, "is a fool's intellect." Until that moment, as Lafayette was aware, he had been under consideration by the comte de Provence for a court sinecure arranged by his in-laws. But the experience apparently left him unchastened, for it was not the last time that an impolitic impulse would cost him royal favor.[4]

TWO

"My Heart Was Enlisted"

Even as Lafayette struggled at the Hôtel de Noailles with his new life's social demands, he still pined for military glory. In April 1775, that goal suddenly seemed within reach when his father-in-law—through a purchase from the minister of defense, as was that day's tradition—obtained for him a commission as second lieutenant in a regiment sponsored by the marquis de Noailles, an uncle of Adrienne's.

Alas, however, France was then fighting no wars; and, over the coming months, as Lafayette contemplated his command's scant prospects for battlefield engagement, and the fact that his appointment was largely honorary, he grew disconsolate. In the end, however, the commission did prove fortuitous.

On August 8, 1775, while in the northeastern French town of Metz for training exercises, Lafayette attended a dinner honoring a visiting young English prince—the Duke of Gloucester, a younger brother of Britain's king George III. The prince, accompanied by his wife, was en route to Italy, where, hoping to restore the prince's fragile health, the couple planned to spend the winter. Along the way, with the permission of Louis XVI, Gloucester was conducting a ceremonial inspection tour of selected French military fortifications.

Already drawn to the views of political radicals such as John Wilkes,

Gloucester had compounded his brother's disfavor by marrying an illegitimate granddaughter of the former prime minister Sir Robert Walpole. Emblematic of the enmity between the siblings, during the dinner at Metz, the duke mocked the monarch's suppression of the Patriots in Britain's rebellious North American colonies and voiced support for them.

Hosting the meal was Lafayette's commanding officer, Charles-François de Broglie. Fifty-six years old, Broglie was a former ambassador to Poland and by then serving as governor of Metz. A man of small physical stature who won the affections of few, he was nonetheless described by contemporaries as possessed of "sparkling eyes" and a "restless spirit."

During the reign of Louis XV, Broglie had served in the court's "Secret Ministry"—tasked with implementing policies with which the king preferred not to be publicly associated. Similarly, as France's envoy in Poland during the Seven Years' War, Broglie came to be associated with pro-French intrigues. Upon Louis XV's death Broglie ingratiated himself with the successor court; and, since 1774, he had been consumed with avenging Britain's defeat of France in the Seven Years' War—even planning, with royal encouragement, a (never-attempted) invasion of England.

In fall 1776, a year after hosting the dinner attended by Lafayette, Broglie organized an expedition to support the Patriots. Joining him were Silas Deane, a secret agent in Paris for the U.S. government, Johann Kalb, a Prussian-born military officer, and Pierre Beaumarchais, a mysterious agent with ties to the French government. Their plot entailed the departure, from France's port of Le Havre, of three ships to America—each carrying supplies and recruits for the Patriot cause, among the latter sixteen officers selected by Kalb. In mid-December, however, upon learning of the plot, David Lord Stormont, Britain's ambassador in France, alerted royal officials. Embarrassed ministers at Versailles, forced to act, disrupted the plot.

Prior to his August 1775 dinner for the Duke of Gloucester, Broglie had introduced Lafayette to a circle of European supporters of America's Patriots. Further influencing Lafayette, Broglie, by the time he and Lafayette met, had grown obsessed with America's Patriots—viewed French assistance to them as a means of achieving his goal of avenging England for its earlier victory over France.

For Lafayette, Broglie's August 1775 dinner marked a turning point. Then and there, like other callow aristocrats of his generation, he became infatuated with the American cause. Over the evening, Lafayette recalled, he "listened with ardent curiosity" and "pressed the duke with questions"; and by the dinner's end "he had conceived the idea of going to America." Moreover, in the days ahead, his conversion to the American cause remained firm: "When I first learned of that quarrel, my heart was enlisted, and I thought only of joining my colors to those of the revolutionaries."

Also attending Broglie's dinner was Johann Kalb, the fifty-year-old Prussia-born officer sympathetic to the American rebels. A contemporary recalled Kalb as "a tall, raw-boned man." Born in Bavaria of peasant stock, he had married well and, buoyed by his wife's fortune, soon affected aristocratic pretensions—becoming von Kalb in Prussia, de Kalb in France. In 1768 he had visited America for four months as a covert French government agent—assessing whether anti-British feeling in the colonies had reached a level sufficient to risk open French support of a rebellion there. By the trip's end Kalb concluded that Britain's government would mollify discontent in the colonies before it flared into open revolt.

By 1776, however, Kalb believed that the time was ripe for French assistance to America's Patriots. Although more than three decades Lafayette's senior, Kalb and the marquis established an easy rapport. Rendering the Prussian all the more useful to the young French officer, Kalb, unlike Lafayette, spoke English; he also knew Silas Deane, the American agent in Paris. Soon enough Lafayette and Kalb—the latter acting as translator—became regular callers at Deane's Paris apartment near the Pont Royal, on the rue de l'Université—increasingly watched by British spies.

———

The forty-year-old Deane, a former Connecticut congressman, had arrived in Paris that same summer (June 1776)—assigned by the congress's Committee of Secret Correspondence to arrange financial assistance and munitions shipments from the French government for the Patriot war effort. Given Deane's assignment, his congressional overseers had ordered him to conceal his labors. "On your arrival in France, you will for some time be engaged in the business of providing goods for the Indian trade," read his instructions (likely penned by Benjamin Franklin)—the first to an American agent dispatched to a foreign country:

> This will give good countenance to your appearing in the character of a merchant, which we wish you continually to retain among the French, in general, it being probable that the court of France may not like it should be known publickly, that any agent from the Colonies is in that country. . . . It is scarce necessary to pretend any other business at Paris, than the gratifying of that curiosity, which draws numbers thither yearly, merely to see so famous a city.

Acting on his orders, Deane, after arriving in Paris—covertly guided by French officials—soon enlisted in his web of intrigue forty-four-year-old Pierre Beaumarchais, the shadowy figure who had been involved in Broglie's failed conspiracy—otherwise a quixotic businessman, watchmaker, inventor, and playwright. (Two of his plays provided source materials for Mozart's opera *The Marriage of Figaro* and Rossini's *The Barber of Seville*.) With Deane's connivance, Beaumarchais established a front business, Roderigue Hortalez et Compagnie, through which surplus French army guns and ammunition were transferred to the Continental army. Deane also recruited European officers for the Continental army—though all the commissions he arranged remained subject to the Continental Congress's approval.

In December 1776 Deane would be surprised by the arrival in Paris of Benjamin Franklin—also dispatched there by the Continental Congress. Franklin arrived with news that, along with himself, Deane and Arthur Lee had been appointed by the congress as commissioners, assigned to negotiate formal commercial ties with France. The latter was a Virginian-born physician, lawyer, and politician then in his midtwenties and living in London.

As in England, where Franklin had been posted as a business agent for the

Pennsylvania colony, in Paris—first as a commissioner and later as U.S. minister—he was renowned as much for his scientific as his political accomplishments. Thus, in Paris, maintaining a visible social life, Franklin won broad public acclaim, and likewise, in Philadelphia, enjoyed similarly robust support within the Continental Congress. Deane, by contrast, due to the nature of his Paris assignment, maintained a shadowy life there; deepening his isolation, he didn't speak French, and perhaps inevitably soon fell into disfavor among many Continental Congress delegates.

For Lafayette, however, Deane proved indispensable. "When I presented myself to Mr. Deane," he remembered, "I was just nineteen years old, and I spoke more of my enthusiasm than of my experience." Soon thereafter, on December 7, 1776, Deane offered Lafayette a commission as major general in the Continental army. He agreed, however, to serve gratis. Beyond that, the arrangement struck with Deane pointedly implied that the young nobleman would bring to the Patriots' cause goods purchased from, as Deane put it, "his considerable Estates." Rarely if ever had a commission from Deane made reference to its subject's wealth. Financial matters aside, however, for Lafayette and others recruited by Deane, the challenge would be getting to America. And the origins of the obstacles surrounding that difficulty lay in recent French history.[1]

Chastened by defeat thirteen years earlier in the Seven Years' War, in 1776 the kingdom of France feared being drawn into a new confrontation with Britain. The Seven Years' War—fought on a global stage but known in its North American theater as the French and Indian War—had cost France most of its empire in the Western Hemisphere. Still resenting that defeat, in July 1776 Louis XVI and his ministers had quietly agreed to provide clothing, guns, and ammunition for Britain's rebellious North American colonists. But those transfers—to preserve appearances of French neutrality—were kept secret. Louis had no desire, through open support for the American rebels, to disrupt officially amicable relations between France and Britain.

Unbeknownst to most of Broglie's contemporaries, his disrupted plot of autumn 1776 also aspired, with Silas Deane's connivance, to elevate Broglie to commander in chief of the Patriots' army—thus supplanting the then-beleaguered George Washington. Moreover, unlike the exclusively military role that Washington played, Broglie also aspired to become the American republic's stadtholder, a leader vested with absolute control over civil and military affairs. In Broglie's view a succession of battlefield defeats suffered by Washington in 1776 had left an opening for bold new—*French*—leadership.

No convincing evidence indicates that Lafayette ever knew of Broglie's stadtholder aspirations—though Kalb (soon Lafayette's partner) as the expedition's second in command surely did (though he apparently never disclosed them to Lafayette). Beyond that the degree of the French government's involvement with the plot remains unknown. To the extent, however, that Broglie's plot may be viewed as a (albeit-long-shot) gambit by Versailles to supplant Britain in America's rebelling colonies, it beggars belief to imagine that, had he sailed from Le Havre, America's Patriots would have granted him unfettered powers; the rebellion of King George's former subjects, most of whom were Protestants, was by then too far advanced for them to ponder swapping one king for another—and a Catholic one at that.

Even so, Broglie's failed scheme sheds light on incipient French support for the Patriot cause. The American historian Charles J. Stillé, an early chronicler of the plot, observed in 1887 that Broglie—and for that matter, Kalb and the plot's other French recruits (those privy to Broglie's stadtholder dreams)—would all have been aware of the degree to which Broglie's ambition clashed with the professed idealism of the cause they were rushing to join. Thus, by Stillé's lights, Broglie's failed plot illustrates how, among French officers, the American rebellion appealed to both idealistic and pecuniary incentives. Observed Stillé: "We can only explain it by remembering that these Frenchmen were mere soldiers of fortune, ready to serve any cause, provided the rank and pay were satisfactory. If they had any special interest in the war it was that it would humiliate England."[2]

After French officials foiled Broglie's plot, Deane and Kalb began conspiring with Lafayette—by then embarked on his own clandestine plans to reach America. Indeed, by late fall 1776, the three were meeting several times a week in Deane's Paris apartment. By then Kalb, through his work with Deane in Broglie's failed plot, knew Deane far better than did Lafayette. And thus, by

December, with Kalb acting as both intermediary and translator, Lafayette and Deane were finalizing terms for an officer's commission in the Continental army for the young nobleman.

Through a surrogate, Lafayette soon also purchased and outfitted his own ship, which he renamed *La Victoire*. Advantages do accrue from great wealth. Lafayette likewise recruited to his project several officers who had planned to sail with Broglie to America. Also booking passage aboard *La Victoire* was Edmund Brice, a young Maryland-born American who, after traveling to London to study painting, was recruited by Deane's secretary, William Carmichael, to accompany Lafayette's party.

Mindful of the ill fate of Broglie's plot, Lafayette confided his latest plans to only a handful of allies: "The secrecy of those negotiations and of my preparations was truly miraculous. Family, friends, minister, French spies, English spies, all were blind to them." Among Lafayette's secrets was his decision that Charlestown (today's Charleston), South Carolina, would be *La Victoire*'s destination.

Unlike many, more northerly American ports, Charlestown remained under Patriot control. From there Lafayette would make his way overland to the infant republic's capital in Philadelphia. To offset the marquis's costs, *La Victoire* would return to France without him but carrying a load of Carolina rice for the French market. In addition to *La Victoire*'s thirty-man crew and commander (a Captain Le Boursier), Lafayette would also bring to America twelve other European officers recruited by Deane—including several who had hoped to sail to America with Broglie. Like Lafayette, all twelve would be obliged to find their way, on their own, from Charlestown to Philadelphia.

In early 1777, however, as the scheduled date for *La Victoire*'s departure approached, an unforeseen disruption thwarted his long-planned sailing. Learning of Lafayette's plans were his conservative father-in-law, Jean de Noailles, duc d'Ayen; and Britain's ambassador in Paris, Lord Stormont. Each disclosed the plot to Louis XVI's government. Alerted, ministers at Versailles—France's capital just outside of Paris—did everything in their powers to block his ship's departure.

Countering the government's action, Lafayette and his allies arranged for *La Victoire*, by then docked at Bordeaux, their original port of departure, to sail to Puerto de Pasajes, on Spain's Bay of Biscay. And from there—on April 20, 1777—after making his way from Bordeaux to the ship, Lafayette joined the other volunteers and sailed for Charlestown.

Over the coming days, as *La Victoire* settled into its Atlantic crossing, Lafayette's wife, Adrienne, numbered among those stunned to learn of his departure. Though aware of his earlier thwarted plans, she assumed he had abandoned his resolve to join the fight in America. His unexpected sailing thus left her alone with their firstborn child—their two-year-old daughter, Henriette—and pregnant with another. Subterfuges likewise kept even *La Victoire*'s captain ignorant of the vessel's true mission and destination. Before sailing, Captain Le Boursier had registered a French port in the West Indies as his destination. But not until they were well at sea did Lafayette reveal to him their true destination. Le Boursier protested, but in the end the ship's owner prevailed.[3]

Mere months earlier *La Victoire*, with its 268 tonnage, had plied the seas as the merchant ship *La Bonne Mère*. After its purchase by Lafayette, with its new name painted across its stern, the craft had been hastily, if incompletely, refitted for its new military mission. "A sluggish ship, with two defective cannons and a few muskets, [it] could not have escaped from the smallest privateer," Lafayette later recalled, echoing a worry that haunted that era's sailors. Privateers were armed ships authorized by their home governments to prey on the merchant fleets of enemy countries—to attack, seize the cargoes, and imprison the crews of such vessels. And, as Lafayette was well aware, by 1777 British privateers had become a serious menace in both European and New World waters. Indeed, aware that his own ship's meager armaments would be no match for any English privateer they encountered, he had instructed *La Victoire*'s captain to blow up the vessel before risking a confrontation or capture.[4]

Such mordancy comported with Lafayette's singular lack of enthusiasm for all things maritime—including a proclivity for seasickness and, on this outing, a complement of quarrelsome shipmates. One of them, Charles-Louis, vicomte de Mauroy, took particular pleasure in needling Lafayette. De Mauroy was yet another major-general minted by Deane. But unlike Lafayette, he had no personal wealth. To break the voyage's tedium, Mauroy relished taunting Lafayette with his views on their destination—opinions decidedly less rosy than those held by Lafayette and *La Victoire*'s other officers. As Mauroy later sniffed, most of those men "were in a laughable state of enthusiasm."

To Mauroy, the continent to which they were sailing, far from being an unspoiled Eden, was already being ruined by greedy Europeans. "Fanaticism, the insatiable desire to get rich, and misery—those are, unfortunately, the three sources from which flows that nearly interrupted stream of immigrants who, sword in hand, go to cut down, under an alien sky, forests more ancient than the world, watering a still virgin land with the blood of its savage inhabitants, and fertilizing with thousands of scattered cadavers the field they conquered through crime."

Of his own exchanges with Lafayette, Mauroy recalled, "Whereas everyone around him took care to flatter his fondest hopes, I wanted by my objections to prepare him for the disappointments he would perhaps experience, and which would make too painful an impression upon him if he experienced them at the very moment when his imagination was the most inflamed on the subject of the Americans." During one argument, flustered by Mauroy's cynicism, Lafayette reputedly exclaimed, "Don't you believe that the people are united by the love of virtue and liberty? Don't you believe that they are simple, hospitable people who prefer beneficence to all our vain pleasures, and death to slavery?"

But Mauroy had a ready retort: "If the savages of the new continent," he answered, "had united to live together, if some man of genius, virtue, talent, and constancy . . . had given North America its laws, such a people could present to us the tableau you have just described, but it was people who were already civilized . . . who brought to a savage land the views and prejudices of their respective homelands."

Lafayette soon wearied of the shipboard routine. "I will not write a journal of my voyage for you," he griped in a midvoyage letter to Adrienne. "One day follows another here, and what is worse, they are all alike. . . . In truth, the people who write volumes about an ocean voyage must be cruel babblers."[5]

Distracting himself from the seasickness of the crossing's first weeks and the thinning supply of rations that bedeviled its final days, Lafayette turned his energies to useful labors—to studying books on military strategy and to learning English. Those latter efforts were further advanced by conversations with another of Silas Deane's recruits—Johann Kalb, the Prussian-born, English-fluent officer who had acted as his interpreter with Deane. Upon their arrival in Charlestown, Lafayette looked forward to gauging the success of his shipboard language study.

On that morning of June 13, 1777, as Lafayette scanned the western horizon, he spotted a sight that swelled his heart—a green ribbon of coastline. After four thousand miles and eight weeks at sea, he and his shipmates were approaching landfall. As the men prepared for their return to terra firma, a cacophony of huzzahs rose from *La Victoire*'s decks and riggings. All the while Lafayette, indifferent to the commotion, remained on the quarterdeck—still peering into his telescope.

Moments later, however, a less welcome realization darkened spirits aboard the ship. As a northeasterly wind blew *La Victoire* closer to the shore, its men suddenly realized that they were off course: navigational errors had caused them to overshoot Charlestown, placing them along South Carolina's coast but north of their intended destination. Still worse, they soon spotted another ship, apparently a British privateer, standing between them and the shore.

Lafayette was startled. Weeks earlier he had vowed to scuttle *La Victoire* before risking its capture. But now, confronted with that very quandary—and after eight weeks at sea and, they reckoned, mere miles from landfall—he revised that earlier resolve. "Hasty preparations were made for defense," he recalled. Crewmen assigned to the two cannons on the ship's main deck dashed to their posts. Other officers and crew, meanwhile, many brandishing small arms and knives, likewise rushed to their assigned stations—preparing to resist any boarding by men from the privateer.

Battle stations, however, barely were reached when closer proximity revealed the approaching vessel to be not an English but an American privateer. Their sense of relief, however, proved short-lived. As *La Victoire* neared the shore, two other ships—both frigates—were spotted—both standing in the path of *La Victoire*'s landward approach. And as the vessels hove into view, confirming Lafayette and his crew's worst fears, both were identified as British ships. Unlike *La Victoire*'s earlier false alarm, this predicament seemed unlikely to end as a case of mistaken identity.[6]

On Friday June 13, 1777, as late afternoon gave way to evening, and the two English privateers stood between *La Victoire* and South Carolina's marsh-fringed shoreline, the marquis de Lafayette conferred with Captain Le Boursier'.[7]

Prevailing winds, they concluded, likely offered their best option for escape: The same northeasterly breeze that had hastened *La Victoire*'s shoreward movement might yet impede any northward pursuit of the French ship by the two still-distant British frigates. Through his first mate, Captain Le Boursier ordered the square-rigged vessel's crew to trim their sails and tack northward into the wind.

Yes, provisions were running low. Even so, they would have to sail north until they found a suitable anchorage.

The ploy worked. Recalled Lafayette: "The same strong northeasterly wind, which brought the French vessel to the coast, had driven the cruisers to the south, and thus left an open passage for [our] vessel, which otherwise probably would have been captured."[8]

THREE

"Beyond the Reach of Pursuers"

Tacking north over the next few hours, on June 13, 1777, *La Victoire* passed Cape Romain and the Santee River delta. Finally Captain Le Boursier spotted an opening in Winyah Bay. Before midnight, having entered the bay but spotting no harbor, the shipmates were growing fearful of running aground on one of the estuary's shallow bars.

Off North Island, near Georgetown on the mainland, Le Boursier ordered the ship's anchor dropped and its launch lowered into the water. Hoping to find dry land and a pilot who could guide *La Victoire* to safe harbor, Lafayette, seven other officers, and two shipmates then squeezed into the jolly boat. The other officers and crew remained aboard *La Victoire*.

By the light of a waxing moon, the launch sliced through the bay's shallow waters. As their oars drew them farther into the estuary, they quickly found themselves inside a spartina marsh threaded by labyrinthine tidal streams. As the men pondered their options, faint voices floated over the lapping moonlight-flecked waters.

Taking a chance, they began rowing toward the voices, and soon encountered a party of enslaved men, combing for oysters in an oyster boat. To them

Johann Kalb—the only person aboard the launch fluent in English—explained their plight.

Answering Kalb, the men in the oyster boat said that they knew of no nearby harbor or pilot. They did, however, offer to guide the weary travelers to their master's nearby summerhouse. Perhaps he would know what to do.

Accepting the offer, the men of *La Victoire*, rowing their launch, followed the slaves in their oyster boat toward a distant light on the shore. Leaving the boat, the weary sailors—on foot now, continuing toward the light, spotted a ramshackle wooden house. As they approached it, dogs began barking and a voice called out, demanding to know their identity and what they wanted.

The voice was that of Benjamin Huger, an energetic thirty-year-old rice planter; and the house that the voyagers had stumbled upon was Huger's beach house. Like other South Carolina rice planters—on the mainland and on the lee of local barrier islands—Huger feared the malaria that thrived during the summer in rice fields and their standing waters. To avoid the fever, he lived during those months in his beach house; there, along North Island's western shore, Atlantic breezes freshened salt marshes and beaches where the island met Winyah Bay.

After Johann Kalb, speaking in English, explained the men's plight, Huger welcomed them inside and invited them to stay and rest. Fortunately for the visitors Huger, besides being able to offer them shelter, was also a major in a local Patriot militia. Equally welcome was the news that Huger was a grandson of an exiled Huguenot, a French Protestant who had found his way to South Carolina. Providing still more commonality, Huger had been educated in Europe and had firsthand familiarity with his guests' native land.

Once under Huger's welcoming roof, Lafayette recalled, he knew he "had attained the haven of his wishes, and was safely landed in America beyond the reach of his pursuers." That night, for the first time in eight weeks, he and the other men slept in beds unmoored to the sea's ceaseless rocking. And when the following "beautiful" morning dawned, Lafayette reveled in his new circumstances.

In the third-person voice often deployed in his memoirs, he recalled: "The novelty of everything around him, the room, the bed with mosquito curtains, the black servants"—enslaved persons—"who came to ascertain his wants, the beauty and strange appearance of the country as he saw it from his window, clothed in luxuriant verdure, all conspired to produce a magical effect."[1]

Beyond those solaces, however, Lafayette still had to get to Charlestown and, ultimately, to Philadelphia. He still had a war to fight. More immediately, however, the rest of his men—still aboard *La Victoire*, still swinging at anchor in Winyah Bay—were still awaiting his return; and where in the world could he and his compatriots find safe harbor for their ship and fresh provisions for their continued journey?

On June 14, the day after his guests arrived, Huger, aware that the Philadelphia merchant Charles Biddle was in Georgetown and that Biddle spoke French, invited him to come and meet his visitors.

Huger's invitation, however, masked an ulterior motive. Outward pleasantries aside, his visitors' predicament was dire. And the stakes were too high to risk linguistic confusion. Johann Kalb, whose native language was German, had a functional command of French and English. But Huger wanted a native English speaker—one he knew and trusted—who could convey, in fluent French, to his guests, what he wanted to tell them.

As Biddle interpreted, Huger explained that, aside from Charlestown, there was no suitable nearby anchorage for their ship. But he warned that British naval activities off Charlestown's harbor rendered it risky for them to try to reach that port aboard *La Victoire*. Instead Huger advised them to go to Charlestown via an overland route. Huger, meanwhile, would arrange for a local pilot to sail *La Victoire* to the port. Pursuant to Lafayette's original plan, Huger would also arrange for the ship's return voyage to France bearing a cargo of rice.

On the following morning—on June 15, two days after they had reached North Island—Lafayette, Kalb, and the party's other members began their seventy-five-mile overland journey to Charlestown.[2]

Although Huger attempted to provide the men horses for the trip, he was unable to arrange mounts for the entire party. Thus the majority of the men were forced to make most of the trek on foot. Over the coming days, as the party crossed salt marshes, swamps, and maritime forests of live oaks, loblolly pines, and magnolia, the journey proved arduous. Adding to their concerns, Huger had warned them of "marauding negroes." To wit: Rumors of slave revolts haunted Low Country planters; and the party, most of them on foot, had thus elected to carry guns in lieu of extra clothes on their march to Charlestown—a decision that soon caused unanticipated vexations.

Stretching over two days and three nights, the march exceeded the men's worst expectations. Humidity on a level unknown in northern Europe bedeviled them, as did mosquitoes, red bugs, ticks, and snakes, some venomous; and during the day, stunted prickly vegetation—from palmetto bushes to cabbage palms—afforded scant protection from the scorching summer sun.

Moreover, as Charles-François, chevalier du Buysson, among the party's officers, recalled, the dearth of extra clothes—including footwear—on difficult, often boggy terrain, presented unique problems. "Some of us were wearing riding boots, but we were not able to walk in them, and we were forced to take them off and finish the trip barefoot, which was an uncomfortable means of travel on burning sand and in the woods," recalled the twenty-four year old officer, whose Gallic surname was soon contracted into the shortened "Dubuysson." "For the next two weeks my legs were swollen to the size of my thighs"—once again, a consequence of having "chosen to carry arms rather than clothing." On June 17, when the party reached Charlestown, they appeared, in Dubuysson's words, haggard and ragged, "looking very much like beggars and brigands." He continued: "We were received accordingly. We were pointed at in scorn by the local populace when we said we were French officers, motivated solely by the desire to attain glory and defend their liberty, and we were treated as adventurers"—mercenaries—"even by the French, who are very numerous in Charleston."

In Charlestown the new arrivals discovered that any welcome they might otherwise have expected had been squandered by the French volunteers who preceded them there. Most had found their way to Charlestown via the French West Indies. Many were patently unqualified for any military service— and, indeed, many of them remained in Charlestown. Further subverting goodwill, Dubuysson complained, "most of these Frenchmen are officers who are deeply in debt, and some of them have been discharged from their units. Many of them come from the French colonies, whose governors get rid of as many of the bad ones who arrived from France as they can, by giving them letters of recommendation to the Anglo-American generals."[3]

Though Lafayette and the other officers would have had no way of knowing it, days earlier, even Charles Biddle—the Philadelphia merchant enlisted as an interpreter by Benjamin Huger—had entertained doubts about the foreigners' value to the Patriot's cause. Though Biddle would later come to regard Lafayette's men as "officers of great merit," upon first meeting them he recalled having "a very unfavorable opinion of them. . . . I supposed they were only barbers or tailors."[4]

On June 18, the day after Lafayette reached Charlestown, *La Victoire* sailed into the harbor; true to his word, Huger had arranged for a pilot to sail the ship to the city; the vessel's arrival was made all the more dramatic—and conspicuous— by a close encounter with the two English frigates attempting to blockade the harbor. Watching nervously from ashore, Lafayette witnessed the drama. "I even sent orders, by land and sea, for the captain to put the men ashore and burn the ship," he recalled. Once again, however, Lafayette's run of good luck carried the day: "A gale [had] momentarily driven off the frigates, and my vessel arrived in broad daylight, without encountering either friend or foe."[5]

The volunteers by then were bathed, shaved, and in clean clothes; and with the arrival of *La Victoire* and its cargo of war matériel, Charlestown's citizenry now understood that these particular French visitors were hardly beggars, brigands, or debt-ridden wastrels (nor, for that matter, barbers or tailors!). Among those soon extending welcomes were South Carolina's governor, Robert Rutledge; the state militia's Gen. William Moultrie; and Gen. Robert Howe, commander of the Continental army's southern operations.

Over the coming days those and other dignitaries feted the men with dinners and tours of local battle sites and military fortifications. To Lafayette's added satisfaction, a five-hour dinner in his honor hosted by Moultrie and Howe confirmed that his shipboard language studies had not been for naught: "We drank toasts and conversed in broken English," he gushed to Adrienne.

But Lafayette also knew that he was a man who had—without notice— abandoned a pregnant spouse already with one child. Piercing his bravado, the longings and guilt that issued from that act soon spilled into his letter: "I miss you, dear heart," he lamented. "I miss my dear friends, and I cannot be happy when I am far away from you and from them. I often ask you, dear heart, if you still love me, but I ask myself the same question much more often, and my heart always answers yes. I trust it is not deceiving me."

Since leaving France Lafayette had yet to receive a letter from Adrienne—though, as he wrote, "I hope to find some of them at Philadelphia." He pined to hear from her: "Write to me often, please, and make them long."[6] In the meantime, he promised, he would continue to find obliging ships—even, if necessary, English ones—willing to carry to France his letters to her.

Mostly, however, he detailed to Adrienne the welcome he and his men were receiving. As their spirits brightened, he wrote, they could now appreciate the city's virtues: "Charleston is one of the most beautiful and well-built of cities, and its inhabitants are amongst the most agreeable I have ever seen."[7]

Amid Charlestown's inhabitants, Lafayette no doubt would have noticed that enslaved men and women comprised the majority of the city's population. Indeed, the 1790 U.S. census, the first conducted there, would count among its total 67,000 residents some 51,000 slaves. Presumably, however, Charlestown, did not present Lafayette his first glimpse of enslaved African peoples.

In mainland France, to the extent that the institution of slavery existed, its presence was nowhere near as prevalent as in South Carolina. By 1777, however, it did thrive in the country's overseas Caribbean colonies. As a consequence many mainland ports hosted a robust slave trade. And the city of Bordeaux, through which Lafayette had passed before sailing to America, as well as other major French entrepôts, teemed with enslaved men and women.

Lafayette's reaction to the slavery, and quite possibly the slave auctions, that he saw in Charlestown remains unknown; his writings from those months barely mention slavery—and only in passing. Apparently, however, the human bondage he witnessed during those weeks failed to dim his view of South Carolina—and indeed America—as a land of freedom. To be sure, as his time in Charlestown drew to a close and he prepared for his overland journey to Philadelphia, Lafayette professed to delight in all he saw and heard.

To Adrienne he rhapsodized over the ongoing confirmation of his earlier view—expressed to his *La Victoire* shipmate vicomte de Mauroy (among others) before he set foot in America—of the country's prevailing national character:

He thus praised "a simplicity of manners, the desire to oblige, the love of country and of liberty." Moreover, ignoring the ubiquitous enslavement he had witnessed—from North Island to Charlestown—he assured his spouse that "sweet equality . . . reigns over all." It was an oversight that, for the time being, Lafayette would share with another tall redhead, an American, whom he would later befriend.[8]

FOUR

The Pursuit of Happiness

By the late 1770s, as Lafayette was hastening across the globe to throw himself upon history's grinding gears, Thomas Jefferson, having exhausted his own appetites for such exertions, had retreated back to the relative calm of his Virginia mountains. Indeed, on June 14, 1777, as *La Victoire*'s men, after weeks at sea, were adjusting to American climes, Jefferson, seated high in a handsome carriage, was rolling across Virginia's countryside, homeward bound.

The principal author, the previous summer, of his fledgling nation's Declaration of Independence, Jefferson was done for the time being with Philadelphia and its Second Continental Congress. Instead the thirty-four-year-old lawyer and planter was representing his native Albemarle County in Virginia's legislative assembly—just as he had since 1769, when he attended his first session of Virginia's House of Burgesses. And so today, as he had so many times before, he was hastening northwestward—away from Williamsburg and back to Albemarle.

On the eighth day of a two-month assembly session, Jefferson had been granted a leave of absence to attend to personal matters. Normally the 120-mile Williamsburg-to-Albemarle trip consumed three days, with overnight stays in two taverns; and Jefferson's coachman, one of more than two hundred slaves whom he owned, would be driving.

Today, however, Jefferson himself, whip in hand, gripped the reins. A bondsman later recalled, "Whenever he wanted to travel fast he'd drive: would drive powerful hard himself." Jefferson's coachman and another "servant" (another enslaved man) were the passengers, though one of them was riding postilion and was mounted on the team's lead left-hand horse, the better to keep it on course.

Urging the horses onward, Jefferson braced his legs against the phaeton's narrow iron foot bar, a cramped posture made even more uncomfortable by his physique: When standing, he exceeded six feet two.

Six horses pulled Jefferson's carriage, a phaeton in that day's nomenclature of horse-drawn conveyances. Thanks to its springs, added on his orders beneath the carriage's upholstered bench, the ride was, if not smooth, certainly smoother than it otherwise would have been, given the state of most Virginia roads.[1]

Beneath the horse hooves' rumble, the carriage's wheels clanked over the spring landscape at a devil's pace. As Jefferson settled into the journey, blooming smooth azaleas and redbud trees gilded the route's edge; the music of cardinals and mockingbirds filled the air. Jefferson was nothing if not a connoisseur of flora and fauna. (Then and during his entire lifetime, he kept mockingbirds as pets.) And under any other circumstances the wildlife would have claimed his attention, but today his eyes stayed fixed on the road: Rolling, then increasingly hilly, it stretched northwestward from Williamsburg to Albemarle County. By now, having made this trip countless times, he knew this route like a long-memorized poem.

Thomas Jefferson was born on April 13, 1743—fourteen years before the birth of his future friend Lafayette. Jefferson's mother, Jane, was born in England; his father, Peter, descended from Welsh and English ancestry. Thomas was the third of the couple's eventual ten children—six of whom lived into adulthood. Neither parent could be considered an aristocrat, a designation usually reserved in Virginia for planters holding tracts near its Atlantic coast—or, more specifically, its Tidewater region, the area abounding in tobacco and wheat cultivation that surrounded Williamsburg.

Albemarle County, by contrast, lay in Virginia's Piedmont—a highland area set amid the state's vast northwestern uplands. (Virginia still included the area carved out in 1861, to create the modern U.S. state of West Virginia.) Then and later in Virginia, the Tidewater, in wealth and politics, overshadowed the Piedmont. Indeed, just as Lafayette's own native highlands—the Auvergne—lay outside France's dominant realms, so Jefferson's Piedmont, even within Virginia, constituted an outlier region. And thus, like Lafayette in Paris, Jefferson never felt entirely at ease amid the elite social milieus of the cities of his age.

Again like Lafayette, however, Jefferson did enjoy advantages: His father, Peter, considered a "gentleman," was a well-off planter, surveyor, and frequent public officeholder. Jefferson's mother Jane, meanwhile, was a Randolph, a member of a storied Virginia family. Jefferson was born at Shadwell, the Albemarle County plantation (named for the London parish where Jane Jefferson was born) developed by Peter Jefferson in the early 1740s. Before Jefferson's third birthday the family moved to Tuckahoe, a plantation owned by the Randolphs, to care for the children of a recently deceased cousin of his mother. The Jeffersons lived there until 1751, when they returned to Shadwell.

Thomas Jefferson lionized his father for his "strong mind, sound judgment." But Peter Jefferson's formal schooling was limited—"quite neglected," conceded his son. Even so, according to Jefferson, his father "read much and improved himself."

Testifying to that self-betterment were the public offices that Peter held during his life—sheriff, justice of the peace, and Burgesses delegate. Magnifying his reputation in the eyes of Thomas, Peter, and a friend, in 1749, surveyed a ninety-mile stretch of the North Carolina–Virginia border. A descendant, writing with Homeric flourishes, rendered Peter a latter-day Odysseus: "Colonel Jefferson and his companions had often to defend themselves against the attacks of wild beasts during the day, and at night found but a broken rest, sleeping . . . in trees. . . . living upon raw flesh, or whatever could be found to sustain life." Indeed, Thomas's feelings for his father partook of a veneration not dissimilar to that of Lafayette fils for Lafayette père.[2]

At Shadwell, Peter Jefferson owned a book collection comprising about two dozen volumes in which Thomas spent hours poring over works of history, science, and literature. Resolute that his oldest son receive the formal education that he lacked, Peter enrolled him, at age five, in a school at Tuckahoe devoted to studies in English. And when Jefferson was nine, Peter enrolled him in yet another school—this one run by William Douglas, a Scottish cleric and scholar—devoted to instruction in Latin.

Peter died in 1757, but surviving family elders were determined that Thomas's education continue. In 1758 they enrolled him as one of five students in a log-cabin boarding school in Albemarle County run by James Maury, a prominent Anglican cleric and scholar. There the young student received instruction in classical languages and French.

Jefferson's classroom studies over those years, his readings in Shadwell's books, and his rambles through local forests, inculcated in him the interests in nature, music, science, and literature that enlivened his future years. Indeed, according to Henry S. Randall, the first of Jefferson's biographers to interview and otherwise enjoy the family's cooperation, he was already a skilled musician while at Maury's: "His favorite amusement, indoors, was playing on the violin, and he was already a proficient on that instrument for one of his years."[3]

In spring 1760 Jefferson, at seventeen, moved from Albemarle to Williamsburg, where he entered the College of William and Mary. There he fell under the tutelage of William Small, a professor of mathematics with infectious interests in other fields that he happily shared—including rhetoric, literature, science, and philosophy, particularly Enlightenment philosophy. Later, fondly recalling Small, Jefferson wrote: "He, most happily for me, became soon attached to me & made me his daily companion when not engaged in the school; and from his conversation I got my first views of the expansion of science & of the system of things in which we are all placed."[4]

During his college years Jefferson joined a club called the "Flat Hat Society"—his equivalent of Lafayette's Society of the Wooden Sword. By Jefferson's recollection, however, his Flat Hat Society had fewer members than Lafayette's college club and scarcer purpose—"confined to the number of six students only, of which I was a member, but it had no useful object."

Through Professor Small, however, Jefferson won entrée into more numerous and elite Williamsburg circles—including gatherings at the Governor's Palace and the Raleigh Tavern, center of the city's upper-crust life. Through those he befriended two other future mentors—Francis Fauquier, a writer and merchant who, for ten years, served as the colony's acting governor; and George Wythe, a brilliant lawyer, Burgesses member, and classicist.

In 1762 Jefferson graduated from William and Mary, but, clerking for Wythe and reading law, he stayed in Williamsburg for another five years. In 1767, after joining the Virginia bar, he returned to Albemarle County. There, living with his widowed mother, he established a law practice. Williamsburg and its salons, however, still exerted their pull, as legal work often returned him there. And in December 1768, following his election to the Burgesses, Jefferson relished having an excuse to spend even more time in Williamsburg. Indeed, over his entire lifetime, whether living at Shadwell, Monticello, Philadelphia, Paris, Annapolis, New York, or Washington, memories of Virginia's capital furnished his ideal for the sort of social gatherings—lively, witty, learned—that he aspired to re-create.

In May 1769 Jefferson attended his first session of the House of Burgesses. But then and afterward, there and as a member of other assemblies, legislating for him remained part-time work. Typically, for instance, the Burgesses met for no more than a half dozen weeks each year, and between 1767 and 1774, lawyering consumed most of Jefferson's time.

However, in both the law and politics—unlike, say, Patrick Henry, his colleague in legislatures and at the bar—Jefferson had no reputation as a spellbinding orator. A visitor later suggested that he lacked "exterior grace." As a lawyer he preferred cases tried before judges rather than juries. The private labors of writing—whether briefs for clients and judges or laws for legislative assemblies—pleased Jefferson more than formal gatherings. Similarly, he found interactions with individuals or small groups—clients, judges, fellow attorneys, or legislators or legislative committees—more satisfying than speaking before larger gatherings.

Throughout those years, however, whether writing or speaking, Jefferson crafted an unadorned but subtly persuasive style. An elderly man who during his youth often heard lawyer Jefferson argue cases was asked how he ranked as a speaker: "Well," he replied, "it is hard to tell, because he always took the right side."[5]

Jefferson's legal career, combined with income from inherited lands, proved lucrative—yielding an approximate annual income of five thousand dollars: three thousand from the former, two thousand from the latter.[6] It was just as well—for during those years, those enterprises and his budding career in public office provided welcome distractions from sadness and disappointments.

The death, at age twenty-five in October 1765, of Jefferson's sister Jane devastated him. Almost three years older, she was his eldest sister, a confidante, and a favorite among his siblings. Jane never married, and among all his brothers and sisters, she reputedly most shared Jefferson's curiosities about the world—particularly his interests in nature and music.

For Jefferson, Jane's death added to what was for him a gathering emptiness at Shadwell. Mary, his second-oldest sister, had by then been married for six years to John Boling, a Virginia farmer and lawyer; and Martha, the fourth sister, had the previous July wed Jefferson's lifelong friend Dabney Carr. Upon their marriages both sisters had left Shadwell. All of Jefferson's surviving brothers and sisters, Randolph, Lucy, Anne Scott, and Elizabeth—all younger than he—remained at home. But none could fill the emptiness Jane's passing left for Jefferson at Shadwell.[7]

Turmoil, meanwhile, roiled his romantic life. During the early 1760s two young women caught Jefferson's attention: Three years younger than him, Rebecca Lewis Burwell was the sister of a William and Mary classmate and member of a prominent Virginia family; and Elizabeth "Betsey" Moore, three years older than Jefferson, was the granddaughter of a royal governor. In both cases Jefferson's infatuation went unrequited, ending in his humiliation and the marriage of each of the women to rival suitors. Indeed, Jefferson pursued Betsey even after her marriage to his friend and college classmate John Walker—an infatuation that resulted in several alleged incidents whose retelling caused him later embarrassment.

Little is known of the other romantic and sexual pursuits of Jefferson's bachelor years. Even so, a 1764 letter suggests that he possibly found emotional and sexual release through masturbation or sexual intimacies with married women, prostitutes, or slave women. Writing to a friend after his hopes for a life with Rebecca Burwell had come to naught—and applying lawyerly sophistry to a biblical injunction—he confided: "You say you are determined to be married as soon as possible: and advise me to do the same. No, thank ye: I will consider of it first. Many and great are the comforts of a single state. . . . For St. Paul only says that is better to be married than to burn." Moreover, he added, for young men there exist "other means of extinguishing their fire than those of matrimony."[8]

On February 1, 1770, while Jefferson was away from Shadwell, a fire destroyed its main house. Afterward Jefferson's mother, Jane, expressed her desire to remain at the estate, and plans soon commenced for construction of a new main house. For his part, however, Jefferson was by then already embarked on plans for his own estate.

Upon Peter Jefferson's death in 1757, his will had directed that his wife retain possession of Shadwell for her life's duration. After her death, the document directed, Jefferson and his sole living brother, Randolph, would each inherit one of the two plantations that Peter had owned—Shadwell, in Albemarle; and Snowden, in Buckingham County, about forty miles due south. The will specified that as the elder brother, Thomas would have his choice of the two.

Jefferson chose Shadwell, but not for the site of its main house. For most of his life he had delighted in an untrammeled corner of Shadwell's twelve hundred acres. As a boy, often in the company of his friend and future brother-in-law Dabney Carr, he had regularly ridden to and lingered at the top of a small nearby mountain. The dome-shaped elevation, rising to 867 feet, lay about three miles west—a quick ride—from Shadwell's main house.

So smitten was Jefferson with the mountain as the site for his own estate that in May 1768, he contracted to have part of its top cleared, the work to be completed by Christmas. By then, having acquired an interest in architecture, he had resolved to design himself and have constructed there a house inspired by the Italian Renaissance architect Andrea Palladio. Attesting to Jefferson's affection for Palladio's work, in selecting a name for his estate he borrowed the Italian word for "little mountain"—Monticello.[9]

After the 1770 Shadwell conflagration, Jefferson's mother eventually moved into a rebuilt, albeit smaller version of the plantation's original mansion. For Jefferson, meanwhile, the fire added fresh impetus to complete work on a brick building rising at Monticello. As construction moved forward, he recorded its progress in what became a series of bound notebooks that he called his "Memorandum books." Throughout most of his adult life Jefferson recorded his life's quotidian details—from observations of nature to personal finances, and births and deaths, to details of travel—in the books. And before the end of 1770—on November 26—he inscribed in its pages a signal triumph: "Moved to Monticello."[10]

Two years later, however, only one of Jefferson's envisioned buildings for Monticello had been constructed—and even that remained unfinished. That lone edifice, some landscaping, and spartan slave quarters were the sole fruits of his resolve. But he *was* able to commence 1772 with a bride to bring to his mountain.

Thomas Jefferson may have first met Martha Wayles Skelton as early as October 1768, when he began doing legal work for her father, the planter John Wayles. By 1771 romance was abloom. Unlike Jefferson's past courtships, however, his relationship with Martha—sweetened by shared interests, particularly in music—developed quickly and with ease. By all accounts Martha was brainy, well read, musically talented, and pretty—"a little above middle height, with a lithe and exquisitely formed figure."[11]

The two married on New Year's Day 1772. Thomas was twenty-eight—late for marrying in his world. Martha was five and a half years younger. She came from a family of wealth but of dubious social standing. Her father, John Wayles, was born poor in England. During his youth he immigrated to America, where he accumulated a fortune as a slave trader, planter, and lawyer. As an attorney he specialized in debt collections—not a practice bound to endear him to local planters, many of whom perpetually teetered on the edge of insolvency.

When Jefferson and Martha married, John had already outlived three wives. With his first two spouses, he had four children who survived into adulthood. After the death in February 1761 of his third spouse, he began having children with Elizabeth Hemings, an enslaved woman of mixed race formerly owned by his late wife. Reputedly Elizabeth had been born in 1735 to an enslaved woman from Africa. She, in turn, had been impregnated by a white English sea captain. Before moving to the Wayles plantation, Elizabeth had been owned by the parents of Martha Eppes—John's first wife and Martha's mother—having entered the Wayles household as a parental wedding gift.

Elizabeth was about twenty-six years old when, according to her grandson Madison, she "was taken by the widower Wayles as his concubine." Between 1762 and 1770, John Wayles would father five children with Elizabeth Hemings: Robert, James, Thenia, Critta, and Peter. In 1773, a sixth child came from the union—Sarah, known as Sally.[12]

Martha, half a decade younger than her new husband, was recently widowed. When thinking about his new bride, however, Jefferson apparently sought to avoid thoughts of her first spouse. In the bond he took out for their marriage license, he erroneously listed her as a "spinster." The entry was later crossed out; above it, in another hand, was written the correction "widow."[13]

Martha's first husband, the attorney Bathurst Skelton, had died just six months before her marriage to Jefferson. The couple had had a son, John Skelton, who died as an infant in June 1771. Nine months after Thomas and Martha's wedding, the couple—on September 27, 1772—celebrated the birth of their first child, also named Martha, but soon called Patsy.

Little is known of Jefferson's wife, and no writings by her, or contemporary paintings or drawings of her, are known to exist. Even so, available evidence suggests that Martha's move to Monticello commenced for the couple a period—rare in Jefferson's life—of domestic happiness.

While Jefferson was often dark and brooding, Martha's temperament was effervescent and optimistic. They also continued to revel in their shared musical interests. As Jefferson played the violin or cello, Martha would accompany him on the harpsichord or piano—the latter of which, anticipating their life together, he had purchased for her in 1771.

Jefferson's law practice, meanwhile, continued to prosper. Beyond that, the death, in May 1773, of Martha's father, John Wayles, and Jefferson's resultant inheritance—adding to from his own father's death—increased his wealth still more. Jefferson, who numbered among the executors of his father-in-law's estate, already owned some five thousand acres and around fifty slaves. But even after the sale of a substantial portion of the Wayles properties to satisfy creditors, he still doubled his wealth—adding another five thousand acres and 135 slaves to his holdings.

Numbering among the slaves who moved to Monticello after John Wayles's death were Elizabeth Hemings and her children—including her most recently born daughter, Sally, then a toddler but destined to play a singular role in Jefferson's life.[14]

During the same period in which Thomas and Martha buried John Wayles, another event occurred that, for Jefferson, carried a personal sting. In May 1775—mere days before the death of Martha's father—Jefferson's closest friend, Dabney Carr, died.

The deaths in 1757 of Jefferson's own father and, sixteen years later, his father-in-law, bestowed upon Jefferson wealth sufficient to gradually discontinue most of his legal practice. Moreover, by the time of John Wayles's death, Jefferson's legislative work was acquiring an increasingly radical, anti-British bent.

Reflecting growing dissatisfaction with British authorities, Jefferson's evolving radicalism aligned with political winds rising across Virginia and throughout Britain's other twelve insurgent colonies. Or—from Britain's perspective—London's other *twenty-five* North American colonies. Indeed, it bears emphasizing that London in 1775 regarded *all* of its twenty-six North American colonies as still under British dominion; moreover, while precise figures remain impossible to determine, even within the rebellious thirteen colonies, estimates of those loyal to Britain range from a fifth to a third of the population. As the historian Maya Jasanoff has observed, "Loyalism cut right across the social, geographical, racial and ethnic spectrum of early America—making loyalists every bit as 'American' as their patriot fellow subjects."

———————

Since the early seventeenth century, when Britain established its first colonies on North America's mainland, successive waves of settlers—defying an official royal ban issued in 1688 against such movement—pushed increasingly westward, away from the Atlantic seaboard, ever deeper into the continent's interior, encroaching upon lands occupied by Native Americans. In those domains conflicts increasingly flared into wars between Indians and the white newcomers. In time, as the whites sought to vanquish the Native Americans militarily, the aggressors and their descendants came to call on, and expect, support from Britain's army. Eventually such assistance from the king's North American garrison dovetailed with campaigns by London against European rivals in the Western Hemisphere—mainly the kingdoms of France and Spain.

By 1763, with the Treaty of Paris, those two rivals lay defeated. The Seven Years' War bestowed upon Great Britain a world empire. The conflict, however, had radically depleted Britain's treasury, and to replenish those funds, Britain's government soon began raising the taxes required of colonists in America. The recent war, British officials argued, had been fought at least in part to guarantee the security of American colonists. Beyond that, they held, ongoing conflicts between Indians and the colonists required the continuing presence of—and the costs of maintaining—Britain's garrison in America.

Inevitably, however, those actions by Parliament sparked grievances. American colonists chafed at what they considered unfair tax policies. Additionally, they argued that such policies usurped the colonists' own assemblies, bodies such as Virginia's House of Burgesses—and, more fundamentally, violated their notions of the "rights of Englishmen."

———————

In 1774 Thomas Jefferson penned a resolution, adopted by the House of Burgesses, calling for a day of fasting and prayer in protest of the recent "Intolerable Acts," a series of punitive tariff measures enacted by Parliament to punish Massachusetts for the Boston Tea Party. Shortly thereafter, in his treatise *A*

Summary View of the Rights of British North America, he argued that Parliament had no rights to govern the thirteen colonies. He wrote the essay for Virginia's House of Burgesses, hoping that it might win adoption as formal instructions for delegates it was dispatching to Philadelphia, site of the First Continental Congress.

The Virginia assembly, however, adopted another, more moderate, set of delegate instructions. By then, however, a group of Jefferson's allies had published *Summary View* as a pamphlet that eventually circulated in both North America and England. While Jefferson's name did not appear on the booklet, its authorship was hardly a secret and won him wide acclaim. Delegate George Washington, purchasing multiple copies, called it "Mr. Jefferson's Bill of Rights." Moreover, in Philadelphia, read before and debated by the congress, *Summary View* consolidated Jefferson's reputation as a talented writer and advocate of radical politics.[15]

The First Continental Congress adjourned in late October 1775—after meeting for only seven weeks, but not before calling for a second congress to meet the following year. Responding to parliamentary acts perceived as hostile to American colonists, the 1775 assembly had called for a boycott of British goods, but declined to call for an outright break with the mother country. Few, however, expected the next congress to exhibit such forbearance.

Months earlier, meanwhile, in March 1775, a convention in Richmond—acting as an ad hoc state legislature after the House of Burgesses was disbanded by the royal governor—elected Jefferson to serve as one of Virginia's delegates to the Second Continental Congress.

But when he arrived that June in Philadelphia, the newly convened congress was already in session. Among its other duties the Philadelphia assembly faced the task of overseeing a war that was going badly for the nascent republic. The delegates knew, however, that the likeliest way of arresting that trend would be to win a foreign ally or allies to assist their fight. And, from their earliest days as a collective body, the delegates focused on Britain's traditional enemy, France.

But to entice France—or, for that matter, any other country—as an ally, the delegates also knew that they needed a governing document for their nascent republic, as well as another official paper to announce their break with Great Britain and their creation of a new, independent nation-state.

To create a governing document, the Second Continental Congress appointed a committee of thirteen members to draft what became known as the Articles of Confederation. To draft their republic's birth announcement, its Declaration of Independence, the assembly's members named a committee comprising five delegates—among them Thomas Jefferson. After several meetings that latter committee, in turn, initially called on forty-one-year-old John Adams of Massachusetts to draft the actual document. Adams, however, demurred—suggesting that Jefferson was the superior writer. Beyond that, Adams added, political advantage accrued from the young delegate's Virginia origins.

Jefferson was wounded that the Second Continental Congress eventually modified his original draft of the Declaration of Independence, omitting what he regarded as many of its key elements—including a section condemning, and holding King George III responsible for the slave trade. Truth be known, however, beyond the circle of his fellow delegates to the Continental Congress, Jefferson's role as the principal author of the Declaration of Independence was not widely known until the 1790s. Like Thomas Paine's *Common Sense*, which also appeared in 1776; the later *Federalist Papers*; and Jefferson's only book, *Notes on the State of Virginia* (1787), Jefferson's authorship of the Declaration of Independence remained, for those years, officially consigned to anonymity. Indeed, for official purposes the document was, strictly speaking, as the historian Robert M. S. McDonald described it, "a group statement issued by the Continental Congress—'The unanimous declaration of the thirteen united States of America.'"

Jefferson relished his legislative work. But when away from Albemarle—whether in Philadelphia or Williamsburg—he often longed for home and the company of his spouse, Martha, and, in recent years, that of their now four-year-old daughter, Patsy.[16]

More to the point—on May 28, 1777, as Jefferson raced across Virginia in his phaeton—he did so with added urgency. In fact he had barely completed the 120-mile Williamsburg-to-Monticello trip when Martha gave birth—at ten o'clock that evening. Not quite three weeks later—on June 14, a day that Lafayette began by awaking to the mosquito-netted comforts of planter Benjamin Huger's South Carolina island home—Jefferson and Martha's infant son breathed his last. Characteristically the two left behind no account of the birth, the child, or their grief. They buried him without a name—the infant appearing in his father's Memorandum book only as "our son."[17]

FIVE

To Philadelphia

On June 26, 1777, nine days after reaching Charlestown, the marquis de Lafayette and his cohort began their eight-hundred-mile trek to Philadelphia. There, if all went as planned, each of the thirteen men signed to become officers by the Continental Congress's Paris agent Silas Deane would have his commission formally accepted and be dispatched to a command in Gen. George Washington's Continental army.

Thereafter, orders from a superior officer would govern each man's daily movements. In the meantime, lacking during the interim a formal chain of command, each of the putative officers remained free to chart his own course to Philadelphia. In the end they set out from Charlestown in three parties—one by sea, the other two by land.

In contrast to most of the men's bedraggled arrival in Charlestown, the party of ten or so men that included Lafayette began its journey to the young republic's capital in regal style, in a line of three splendid horse-drawn carriages.

Beyond Lafayette and Kalb, the other officers in the overland party included Charles-François Dubuysson des Hayes, Jean Thevet Leser, Louis Silvestre Valfort, Edmund Brice, Jean-Joseph Charles Sourbader de Gimat, and Charles Frederic de Bedaulx. Lafayette and Kalb rode in the first coach, its enclosed compartment undergirded with four metal springs to soften the trip. Two lower-ranking officers rode in the second carriage, and three aides-de-camp in the third, followed by a baggage cart.

The entourage also included several men without rank—including two servants of Lafayette. One rode at the lead attired in the elegant uniform of a hussar. The other, also on horseback, rode beside Lafayette's carriage and "performed the functions of a squire." Cryptically—in a reference found nowhere else in firsthand accounts of the journey—Dubuysson, serving as aide-de-camp to the Prussian Kalb, recalled that the retinue, when departing from Charlestown, "ended with a Negro on horseback."

The terrain—coastal plains and, in time, forested uplands—often proved inhospitable. By the fourth day esprit de corps gave way to disconsolacy. "Some of our carriages were in splinters," recalled Dubuysson. "Several of our horses, nearly all of which were old and weak, either died or went lame." The cost of replacing the horses depleted their funds, and to lighten their load, they abandoned much of their baggage, even as thieves filched many of their remaining belongings. "We traveled a great part of the way on foot," Dubuysson remembered, "often sleeping in the woods, starving, prostrated by the heat." Fever and dysentery afflicted several in the party.[1]

Pressing on, however, Lafayette remained undaunted; a July 17 letter to Adrienne, from Petersburg, Virginia, teemed with optimism: "The farther I advance toward the north, the more I like both this country and its inhabitants. There are no courtesies or kind attentions that I do not receive, although many people hardly know who I am."

Six days later the party reached Annapolis, Maryland. There, he hastily penned another letter to his wife, necessarily short due to his hope of getting it onto a Europe-bound ship about to weigh anchor. "I have less than a quarter hour in which to write," he explained. "The vessel is ready to sail."

In the brief missive Lafayette—already caught up in the cause he had traveled so far to join—lamented the dispiriting "bad news here" from distant northern New York that was the talk of Annapolis: "Ticonderoga, the strongest post in America, has been taken by the enemy," he wrote. On July 5—hours after the first anniversary of the self-proclaimed nation's Declaration of Independence—the American garrison at the fort had abandoned it to British forces.

"We must try to make up for that," Lafayette vowed to Adrienne, all the more reason he felt "hurried" to reach Philadelphia. With a personal flourish, he wrote, "I love you more tenderly than ever," adding "that it took the pain of this separation to convince me how very dear you are to me."

His longing for Adrienne aside, however, as Lafayette and his party's journey neared its end—having passed through the two Carolinas, Virginia, Maryland, and soon enough, across Delaware and into Pennsylvania—he felt a swelling elation. "While studying the language and customs of the inhabitants," and their "new methods of cultivation," he noted that all were set amid "vast forests and immense rivers [that] combine to give that country an appearance of youth and majesty." Moreover, he assured his spouse, "the journey is a bit fatiguing, but, though several of my companions have suffered a great deal from it, I myself have not felt it at all."

But not all in the party shared his good cheer. "It is safe to say that no campaign in Europe could be more difficult than this journey," Dubuysson later recalled. "On this journey our misery increased each day, and our solace was the expectation of arriving at last in Philadelphia." Even so, as he allowed, inspired by "Lafayette's enthusiasm," "I . . . made up my mind to complete the journey. We were all animated by the same spirit."[2]

On July 27, thirty-one days after leaving Charlestown, the men reached Philadelphia. There they found lodging and, "after cleaning ourselves up a bit," Lafayette, Kalb, and Dubuysson went out looking for an official authorized to accept their credentials.

Because it was a Sunday and the congress was not in session, the three eventually found their way to the home of John Hancock, a delegate from Massachusetts and the congress's president. But as it quickly became clear, Hancock had no time for the foreigners who, interrupting his Sunday, had appeared at his door without advance notice. Declining to accept their credentials, Hancock suggested that the foreigners call on congressional delegate Robert Morris. The Liverpool-born Morris represented Pennsylvania. More saliently he sat on the Committee of Secret Correspondence, recently renamed the Committee on Foreign Affairs.

It was, after all, Morris's committee that had dispatched the increasingly distrusted Silas Deane to Paris, and because Deane was in turn responsible for these foreigners who had turned up at Hancock's door, by his—Hancock's—lights, it seemed only fair that Morris should receive them.

Later that day the three found Morris. After accepting their papers, he told them to meet him the next morning at the door to the State House (later renamed Independence Hall). There the Second Continental Congress would be in session.

After a night's rest Lafayette, Kalb, Dubuysson, and their companions, on July 28, arrived at the appointed time at the assembly's door. "We had to wait a very long time," Dubuysson recalled. Eventually Morris did appear, but only to refer them to yet another member of the congress. "This gentleman speaks French very well," said Morris, introducing them to Massachusetts delegate James Lovell. Added Morris, "He is in charge of all dealings with people of your nation. Thus it is with him that you will deal in the future."

Morris reentered the State House, leaving the suitors outside with Lovell. In their eagerness to foist the arrivals from France onto their colleague, Hancock and Morris had concealed their true feelings. But Lovell labored under no such restraints. He accepted the newcomers' papers, but just as quickly, speaking in French, he dismissed them as "adventurers" and found his way into a harangue: "Gentlemen, have you seen Mr. Deane's commission? We empowered him to send us four French engineers."

In the end, complained Lovell, Deane had dispatched to Philadelphia a host of recruits ill suited to the army's needs—including Philippe-Charles-Jean-Baptiste Tronson Du Coudray, a haughty, soon unpopular artillery specialist—and "some men who claimed to be engineers, but were not." Du Coudray had in fact been on the lone ship of Broglie's otherwise thwarted expedition that, in fall 1776, had managed to leave Le Havre. (In September 1777, two months after Lafayette reached Philadelphia, Du Coudray would die in a drowning accident.) Continuing to berate Lafayette's group, meanwhile, Lovell added that though other Frenchmen had continue to arrive with offers to serve, "This year we have plenty, and all of them are experienced."

While understanding the caution, even the anger, that fueled Lovell's diatribe, Lafayette, Kalb, Dubuysson, and the others were nonetheless stung by his invective. Over the next few hours they composed and then sent to the congress a letter defending their qualifications, motives, and honor; the missive demanded their promised commissions, or if those were not forthcoming, reimbursement for their expenses.[3]

Among the papers Lovell accepted that day from the erstwhile foreigners was a letter of recommendation on Lafayette's behalf from Deane for the Committee of Secret Correspondence. Penned the previous year in Paris, the letter catalogued the factors that "induce me alone to promise him the rank of major general in the name of the United States."

The letter praised Lafayette's "personal merit, his reputation, his disinterestedness, and above all his zeal for the liberty of our provinces." But it also extolled the marquis's "high birth, his alliances, the great dignities which his family holds at this court [and] his considerable estates in this realm." While vouching for Lafayette's personal virtues and his wealth and prominence, Deane's letter nonetheless acknowledged a gaping shortcoming in the nobleman's case for a military command—the absence of any actual war experience in his young years.

In fact Lafayette himself was keenly aware of that drawback. Indeed that lack of experience, under other circumstances—especially combined with Deane's growing reputation for sending ill-qualified recruits to America—likely would have doomed him to a humiliating rejection. But fortunately for the young nobleman, the papers he gave Lovell contained another, more recent letter of endorsement; and that other letter, in addition to Deane's signature, also bore that of a man held in high esteem by the congress—Benjamin Franklin.

In their letter—written in Paris that May, after Lafayette had sailed but before he arrived in South Carolina—Franklin and Deane, acknowledged what many called his "imprudent" behavior. But they also noted that the marquis was "exceedingly beloved" in France, and concluded with a frank assessment of the diplomatic benefits that would accrue to the Patriots from an association with the novice officer: "The civilities and respect that may be shown him will be serviceable to our affairs here" and "pleasing to his powerful relations" and "the whole French nation."[4]

The following morning, July 29, brought two unexpected visitors to Lafayette's lodging. And when he answered their knock and began conversing with them, it became clear that they had come to talk with him, and him alone. The first of the two was James Lovell of Massachusetts—the same Lovell who had shown Lafayette disdain the day before. Accompanying him was another French-speaking delegate, William Duer, who represented New York. Duer, Dubuysson later recalled, "had instructions to sound out Lafayette. He spoke to him in private, promised him wonders, and learned from him everything he wanted to know."

Lovell apologized for his curtness the day before. Possibly he was chastened by the recruits' letter of rebuke to the congress. More likely, he was acting on the assurances from that body's revered Paris legate Benjamin Franklin. Whatever their reasons, Lovell and Duer had come to make amends—but only to Lafayette. His cohort's other members would be dealt with individually.

On July 31, during a second meeting of the three men, Lafayette exacted from Lovell and Duer assurances that he would be granted his promised rank of major general. But—departing from the terms of the commission negotiated with Deane—the marquis agreed to serve without pay and with no command. His dream of commanding a division, at least for the time being, lay dashed.

But then again, two hours after Lafayette accepted the terms, the congress, meeting at the State House, formalized the commission. Along with the documents certifying his status as major general came a splendid shoulder sash of red silk—emblematic of the lofty rank he had coveted since boyhood frolics in the green volcano-fractured mountains of the Auvergne.[5]

In submitting to Lovell's and Duer's terms, Lafayette had forsaken his long-held dream of commanding troops in the field. But even as he accepted the compromise, he also had implicitly agreed to betray the aspirations of the twelve men who, gambling their fates, had accompanied him to America.

Lafayette left no record of whatever remorse he felt for the separate deal he accepted from Lovell and Duer—a bargain he arguably had no practical alternative but to accept. But by Dubuysson's recollection, pangs of guilt did afflict the young marquis. Indeed, by Dubuysson's account, Lafayette's remorse was already surging when his general's sash arrived. "He was very sorry to have accepted the sash," claimed Dubuysson. "He wished to send it back, but they persuaded him to keep it, with more promises, and sent him a carriage and four horses to stop his complaints."

Moreover, according to Dubuysson, well after Lafayette succumbed to the Americans' blandishments, he continued to press his case for the twelve men he was leaving behind. "I must do him justice," Dubuysson wrote. "He was too good a heart to allow his forgetfulness to last very long. He did his utmost to obtain positions for us, but in vain, as he has no influence." Even so, those failed efforts proved cold comfort to Lafayette's disappointed compatriots. "As for us," Dubuysson lamented, "we were left at Philadelphia, and the Congress at once sent us 18,000 livres' worth of American paper money to pay our debts, without making any other reply to us."[6]

SIX

~~~

City Tavern

Later that day—near midnight, on July 31–August 1—a few blocks from the State House, attendees of a just-concluded formal dinner were spilling out of the long second-floor dining room of Philadelphia's City Tavern. Gen. George Washington, the evening's honoree, was about to do the same when, out of the corner of an eye, while bidding adieu to other guests, he spotted the young officer. Although dashing in his uniform, the tall young man nonetheless appeared ill at ease. If anything the red sash across his chest—a decoration bestowed earlier that day—only pointed up his boyish looks.

Washington, forty-five years old that night, had been introduced to the young man, the marquis de Lafayette, earlier that evening. For Lafayette, a month shy of his twentieth birthday, meeting the general was the realization of a long-fantasized moment. If anything, Washington in the flesh seemed even more impressive than the figure Lafayette knew from the printed page: "Although he was surrounded by officers and citizens, the majesty of his figure and his height were unmistakable."[1]

The commander in chief was tall and muscular. When asked his height, he allowed, with reflexive modesty, to being six feet tall—a figure actually two inches shy of his true height. He had blue eyes and a straight nose. Recalled a surgeon who served in a Continental regiment: "There is a fine symmetry in the features of his face, indicative of a benign and dignified spirit."

Washington wore his brown hair long but swept away from his forehead and gathered in back into a queue (or "cue"), a style popular among that era's officers. As was the fashion, he lightly powdered his hair. But—defying both fashion and later misconceptions about him—Washington, according to his biographer Ron Chernow, never, then or later, wore a wig. His handsome uniform only magnified the sense of projected strength and dignity: Two gold epaulettes accented the blue officer's coat that he wore over buff-colored pants and shirt. A small sword, boots, spurs, and three-cornered hat with a black cockade—a rosette-styled arrangement of ribbons—completed the effect. To the aforementioned surgeon who had observed Washington, "the serenity of his countenance, and majestic gracefulness of his deportment impart[ed] a strong impression of that dignity and grandeur, which are his peculiar characteristics."[2]

Earlier in the evening Washington and Lafayette had exchanged pleasantries, but that was all. In truth, however, for months the Continental army's commander in chief had known, for better or for worse, of Lafayette's expectations and imminent arrival. But the evening's earlier encounter had been too brief for substantive conversation. Lafayette, for his part, apparently had not told his companions from *La Victoire*—still smarting from being spurned by the Continental Congress—about his plans to attend this dinner.

The tavern, a handsome two-story brick building, sat on the west side of Second Street, just above Walnut, on which, a few blocks away, stood the Pennsylvania State House. In fact, when the Continental Congress was in session, its delegates routinely met at the tavern at four o'clock for dinner and conversations. Thomas Jefferson, during his days in the assembly, had numbered among those who regularly dined there. Among such establishments, Jefferson's Massachusetts colleague John Adams ranked it "the most genteel one in America."[3]

Conversations among delegates at City Tavern could be lighthearted. At that July 1777 dinner, however, an expected British campaign to capture Philadelphia weighed upon the delegates. Weeks earlier—even as the congress was digesting news of Fort Ticonderoga's fall, word had reached Philadelphia that a British fleet carrying eighteen thousand soldiers had sailed from British-occupied New York City.

Washington and other Patriot leaders assumed that the enemy troop movements presaged some ambitious campaign—but toward what objective? Where were the ships and the soldiers bound? Their whereabouts became a mystery. Speculation soon settled on three places as the next major British target—Philadelphia; Albany, New York; or Charlestown, South Carolina.

———————

At last—on July 31, 1777, the day now ending for Washington at City Tavern—the mystery had appeared solved. Shortly before nine o'clock that morning a messenger had galloped into the camp of Washington's army, near Warwick Township, Pennsylvania, twenty miles northwest of Philadelphia. The courier bore a letter reporting that British ships had been spotted off Chesapeake Bay's far northern end, fifty-five miles southwest of Philadelphia. As many had guessed, the young nation's capital was the British army's next destination.

Washington issued orders commanding most of his regiments to prepare to march to Philadelphia. Such marches, however, took days. And urgency dictated that he consult with his civilian counterparts in Philadelphia as soon as possible. He thus ordered a mount readied for himself and notified the commander in chief's guard, the security detail that always accompanied him, to prepare to ride right away to Philadelphia. It was after 10:00 p.m. when he and his detail reached the capital; and they went immediately to the City Tavern.[4]

Thus, hours later that evening, when Washington saw Lafayette lingering in the tavern, he was saddle weary from a long day's ride. Even so, like all American leaders, Washington hoped for eventual assistance from the kingdom of France in winning the war against Great Britain—and was thus loath to appear aloof to any Frenchman. Moreover, Washington took pride in his well-earned reputation as an artful conversationalist. Beyond remembering names and faces, he also had a winning knack for gaining the goodwill of interlocutors by remembering elements from past conversations or seeming to confide in them observations on current affairs.

As Lafayette later recalled, Washington thus, before leaving City Tavern, approached and "spoke to him very kindly." He "complimented him upon the noble spirit he had shown and the sacrifices he had made in favor of the American cause."

George and his wife, Martha, had no children, and as the general and Lafayette conversed, something about the young Frenchman—so alone and seemingly vulnerable, with his halting command of English—appealed to a paternal longing. Acting on that sentiment, Washington told Lafayette that "he should be pleased if he would make the quarters of the Commander-in-chief his home, establish himself there whenever he thought proper, and consider himself at all times as one of his family."[5]

Aware of Lafayette's background, Washington added "that he could not promise him the luxuries of a court, or even the conveniences, which his former habits might have rendered essential to his comfort." But he assumed that because the young man had joined the Patriots, he would "submit with a good grace to the customs, and privations of a republican army."

As Lafayette listened to Washington's offer, he was still exultant after renegotiating, earlier that day, the terms of his commission as major general. And now with this latest stroke of good fortune, "his joy was redoubled by this flattering proof of friendship by the Commander-in-chief." The fortunes of *La Victoire*'s other aspiring officers, whose plight Lafayette apparently never mentioned to Washington, had dimmed that day with each passing hour.

His own star, by contrast, was waxing ever brighter.[6]

PART TWO

Converging Paths,
1778–1780

SEVEN

"To Learn, and Not to Teach"

In the same way, gentleness is most impressive in a man who is a capable and courageous warrior; and just as his boldness is magnified by his modesty, so his modesty is enhanced and more apparent on account of his boldness. Hence to talk little and to do much, and not to praise oneself for praiseworthy deeds but to dissimulate them politely, serve to enhance both these virtues in anyone who knows how to employ this method discreetly.

BALDESAR CASTIGLIONE, *THE BOOK OF THE COURTIER*, 1528

At City Tavern, Washington invited Lafayette to join him the next day, August 1, 1777, for a tour of defenses along the Delaware River. As Philadelphia braced for attack, hopes for thwarting the city's capture focused on forts and gun batteries along the river that flowed by it. A week later, at noon on August 8, Lafayette got his first glimpse of the Continental army. At an encampment eight miles north of Philadelphia, near Germantown, Pennsylvania, he joined Washington for a review of troops. Lafayette refrained from critical comment that day, but found the scene at once impressive and dispiriting: "About eleven thousand men rather poorly armed, and much worse clad, presented a singular appearance," he recalled. "In the midst of a great variety of clothing, sometimes even of nakedness, the best garments were a sort of hunting-shirts, loose jackets made of grey linen, very common in the Carolinas."

Also present that day were four other generals—the American-born British aristocrat William Alexander, better known as Lord Stirling, Nathanael Greene, Henry Knox, and Adam Stephen. Since arriving in Pennsylvania, Lafayette had heard enough to form opinions of several generals; and he found two he saw that day wanting: Lord Stirling, he had concluded, was "more brave than judicious" and Stephen was "often intoxicated."

Washington required no outsider to alert him to his army's shortcomings. For two years he had pressed Congress for better funding and recruits. Watching silently as Lafayette took in the scene, he imagined how his troops must appear to someone accustomed to a better-equipped, better-trained force.

Finally, no longer able to contain himself, Washington commented to Lafayette, "We should be embarrassed to show ourselves to an officer who has just left the French army."

"I am here to learn, and not to teach," the young officer answered.

Word of the marquis's humility quickly circulated among Continental army officers, and regardless of his artful reply's sincerity, he was also mindful of its likely impact: "That tone," he later reflected, "produced a good effect, because it was unusual for a European."[1]

By then Lafayette had already accompanied Washington to the army's newest encampment, close to Little Neshaminy Creek, near Warwick Township. Not far from there he moved into a two-story stone dwelling called Moland House that for the past few weeks had served as Washington's headquarters (and which survives today). Commented Timothy Pickering, the Continental army's adjutant general, "There has been an addition to the general's family lately—the Marquis Lafayette, of one of the first families in France, a young gentleman of modest manners."[2]

Modesty aside, Lafayette, before, then, and later, continued to seek an actual command. After all, had he been content to settle for mere honorary glory, he could have stayed in the army of France. Alas, however, he also knew that, by that fall of 1777, the chances of his obtaining any post, honorary or otherwise, in his native land's military had waned. Two years earlier the Ministry of Defense initiated reforms to improve the French army's fighting capabilities. As a consequence, merit more than royal court ties now governed army promotions. At least for now, Lafayette's search for military glory would have to be confined to American shores.

Washington, meanwhile, over that same fall of 1777, was perturbed. He had assumed that the terms of Lafayette's service had been settled by the Continental Congress. But—mindful of how French goodwill could assist the American cause—he also had no desire to offend the wealthy, well-connected young nobleman.

Personal memories also likely shaped Washington's ambivalences: Yes, Lafayette was seeking a position for which, based on actual experience, he was patently unqualified. But had not Washington, as a young, aspiring, but inexperienced soldier, once chased a similarly lofty rank? In 1755, after all, during the French and Indian War, Washington had sought the rank of major in a British expedition tasked with capturing the French outpost Fort Duquesne, site of today's Pittsburgh. Washington's request was declined. But in the end he participated in the expedition, at a lower rank. And though it had ended badly, the expedition afforded Washington the opportunity—his first military experience—to demonstrate bravery and tactical prowess.

But while Washington had personal affections for Lafayette, he was also irked at him. To the Virginia delegate Benjamin Harrison, Washington complained that Lafayette had agreed to serve in a "merely honorary" capacity: "True, he has said that he is young, & inexperienced, but at the same time has always accompanied it with a hint, that so soon as I shall think him fit for the Command of a division, he shall be ready to enter upon the duties of it." Moreover, Lafayette "has actually applied to me . . . for Commissions for his Two Aid, de, Camps."

By then, beyond Lafayette, other officers from foreign shores had found their way to Washington's camp, and—to be fair—many proved worthy additions to his army. From France came François-Louis Teissedre de Fleury; Charles-Armand Tuffin, marquis de La Rouerie; and the Irish-born French officer Thomas Conway. From Poland came Tadeusz Kościuszko and Kazimierz Pulaski; and from Prussia, Friedrich Wilhelm von Steuben—baron von Steuben—and Johann Kalb. Indeed, on September 15, 1777—months after Lafayette had received his own general's sash, his mentor Kalb—thanks to Lafayette's continued advocacy—was commissioned a major general.[3]

Unbeknownst to American leaders that summer of 1777, officials in London had formulated a strategy intended to quash the American revolt once and for all. A divide-and-conquer approach, it sought to split the newborn republic into isolated regions. More specifically, by controlling the Hudson River, it sought to separate New England, cradle of the insurgency, from the rest of the country. By choking off the rebels' supplies of New England goods and recruits, British strategists believed, their forces could impose grave consequences upon Washington's army and Philadelphia.

Earlier that summer, implementing part of the strategy, Gen. John Burgoyne and his army, departing Montreal, moved south along Lake Champlain's eastern shore. Upon reaching the the lake's southern end, they crossed to its western shore and, in early July, captured Fort Ticonderoga. From there plans called for them to continue south and capture Albany. A trade entrepôt, Albany sat 150 miles north of New York City, on the Hudson's western bank, at the head of the river's navigable waters; adding to its geographical importance, Albany also sat ten miles south of the Hudson's confluence with its largest tributary, the Mohawk River, whose waters reached into New York's west.

At Albany, according to the plan hatched in London, Burgoyne's forces were to be joined by those of Gen. William Howe, up from British-occupied New York City. The combined British forces would then proceed south—presumably toward Philadelphia, inflicting damage there and at other Patriot strongholds. Still another force, meanwhile, comprising British and Indian elements, was to move down the Mohawk River and capture Albany.

Unfortunately for the British, however, whatever coherence their plan possessed on paper vanished in the field. Most critically—due to faulty communications and logistical problems—Burgoyne's and Howe's armies failed to coordinate. And if that state of affairs confused British military planners, its outward manifestations—abrupt appearances and disappearances of British forces—perplexed George Washington even more. Indicative of such uncertainties, the British ships that had suddenly appeared in Chesapeake Bay's northern end in late July—the reports of which had caused Washington to rush back to Philadelphia—had quickly disappeared back to sea.

"The conduct of the Enemy is distressing, and difficult to be understood," Washington complained on August 3 to an associate. In the meantime, he noted, his own troops were "marching & countermarching in the disagreeable road of suspense and incertainty. I wish, we could but fix on their Object."[4]

As Washington pondered the enemy's movements and his own army's battle readiness, Lafayette prepared for his first glimpse of war. For weeks a major battle had seemed inevitable—and in late August its likely setting became apparent. On August 22, at his Moland House headquarters, Washington received word of the British armada's reappearance in the Chesapeake.

The next day, beginning his army's march toward the enemy's location, Washington stopped near Germantown, north of Philadelphia, and established headquarters at Stenton, a two-story brick mansion. There he penned instructions for a procession, intended to bolster civilian morale, by his army through Philadelphia en route to the Chesapeake.[5]

The level of detail in those orders suggests that his army's poor presentation during its early August review still weighed on Washington: The soldiers were to march in a single column, he instructed; beyond specifying the parade route, he also prescribed the order of march for the regiments and the distances to be kept between each unit.

Washington likewise selected the songs that should accompany the procession—even the tempo at which they should be played: "The drums and fifes of each brigade are to be collected in the center of it; and a tune for the quick step played, but with such moderation, that the men may step to it with ease; and without dancing along, or totally disregarding the music, as too often has been the case." He also emphasized the seriousness with which he regarded the parade: "It is expected that every officer, without exception, will keep his post in passing thro' the city, and under no pretence whatsoever leave it; and if any soldier shall dare to quit his ranks, he shall receive Thirty-nine lashes at the first halting place afterwards."

The following day, August 24, delayed by a morning rain, the procession began at 10:00 a.m. Over the next two hours fifteen thousand men passed through Philadelphia's streets. Washington, mounted on his white horse, with Lafayette riding at his side, led the procession. Behind them followed other members of Washington's cohort, including his two young aides-de-camp—and Lafayette's new housemates and friends—John Laurens and Alexander Hamilton, both twenty-two years old and fluent in French.

A son of the Continental Congress delegate and wealthy South Carolina planter Henry Laurens, John Laurens—possessed of sharp blue eyes and an aquiline nose—had proved himself a talented officer in Washington's army. Increasingly, the younger Laurens was becoming a critic of slavery, a topic on which he would soon influence Lafayette. Indeed John Laurens later advocated the enlistment of slaves into the Patriot war effort, with promises of their later freedom.

Unlike John, however, Hamilton was born into humble circumstances—on the Caribbean island of Nevis. As a young man he "was slight and thin shouldered . . . with a florid complexion, reddish brown hair, and sparkling violet-blue eyes." Hamilton's mother was of British and Huguenot ancestry, her husband an immigrant from Scotland. Because his mother had failed to legally end a prior marriage, Alexander carried the stigma of being born out of wedlock. Moreover, his father soon abandoned the family, and Alexander's mother moved with her two sons to the nearby island of Saint Croix.

There she died of fever in 1768, thus orphaning the boys who were soon separated from each other. Through hard work and voracious reading, however, Alexander acquired skills that won him a clerkship at a local import-export firm. And by his seventeenth birthday, his curiosity about the larger world had taken him to Boston and later New York. In the latter, he enrolled in King's College (now Columbia University) and collected influential mentors and friends.

Publishing pro-Patriot political essays during those years, Hamilton also became known as a gifted writer. In 1775, interrupting his studies, he joined a volunteer New York militia artillery company. Although it was as a militia captain that Hamilton attracted the Continental army's attention, it was his gifts as a writer that cinched his ties to Washington, for whom he soon drafted many of his orders and official correspondence.

Laurens and Hamilton were each young men of considerable talents; and both soon grew close to Lafayette. Moreover, their presence in the Continental army—like that of other French-speaking officers—helped to ease Lafayette's transition into his new army life.

———

Following Washington, Lafayette, Hamilton, and Laurens in the August 24 Philadelphia procession came the regiments of Washington's army, each marching in the order set forth by the general. In lieu of proper uniforms, each soldier tucked a green sprig into his hat. Along the parade route, cheering onlookers filled the sidewalks and leaned from windows. Numbering among those observers, John Adams found a great deal of what he saw wanting. "Much remains yet to be done," he wrote to his wife, Abigail. "Our soldiers have not yet, quite the Air of Soldiers. They dont step exactly in Time. They dont hold up their Heads, quite erect, nor turn out their Toes, so exactly as they ought." Even so, he allowed, he did find the regiments "extremely well armed, pretty well cloathed, and tolerably disciplined."

Even Lafayette, downplaying his earlier reservations about the troops, later claimed to have been impressed. "With their heads adorned with green branches, and marching to the sound of drums and fifes, these soldiers, despite their nakedness, presented a pleasing spectacle to the eyes of all the citizens," he later recalled in his memoir's usual third-person voice, his own vanity much on display: "The general shown at their head, and M. de Lafayette was at his side."[6]

———

For a commander contemplating a naval landing to capture Philadelphia, Delaware Bay, the estuary of the Delaware River, would seem to have been the logical destination for an invasion armada. But, aware of the defenses deployed on that river, Britain's General Howe instead decided to land his army at Chesapeake Bay's northern end and from there march overland to Philadelphia.

After surveying the northern Chesapeake shoreline for two days, Howe selected a landing site near a settlement called Head of Elk, named for its location at the navigable head of the Elk River. By any measure, Howe's armada was impressive—comprising more than 260 ships carrying eighteen thousand soldiers, plus another five thousand men, counting officers, servants, and camp followers. Opposing them, under Washington's command, was a force of seventeen thousand men.

Howe's men completed their landing on the twenty-seventh and began their inland march the next day. Over the next ten days, fighting intermittent skirmishes with the Patriots, the British forces expended most of their energies on their northeasterly drive toward Philadelphia.[7]

By September 10 Patriot and British armies, facing one another, were both encamped midway between Head of Elk and Philadelphia. A tributary of the Delaware, Brandywine Creek, flowing northwest to southeast, separated the two armies. Washington's forces were positioned along its northern bank while Howe's were six miles south of its opposite bank.

Steep wooded slopes cradled Brandywine Creek, which could only be crossed, Washington's scouts reported, at seven obvious fords. Upstream, to the northwest, it forked into tributary streams, and above those, the scouts informed him, no crossings were possible. Early on the morning of September 11, reports arrived in Washington's camp that Howe's army had resumed its eastward march toward Philadelphia. Acting quickly, the commander in chief ordered forces to the stream's southernmost fords—principally at a place called Chadd's Ford. Nearby ran a road to Philadelphia, rendering it, by Washington's lights, Howe's likeliest crossing point.

On September 11 a morning fog had given way to a sweltering sun by the time fighting commenced near Chadd's Ford. Cannon fire and musket shots soon filled the air. However, the troops the Pariots confronted comprised only half of the enemy's total numbers. Unbeknownst to the Patriots, they were actually engaging not General Howe's army but troops under the Hessian general Wilhelm von Knyphausen.

Howe's troops were by then marching north, soon to surprise an American division, under Gen. John Sullivan, along the Brandywine's northern reaches. The Patriots had not only underestimated the enemy's troop strength, but their intelligence concerning local terrain was flawed. Howe's troops—outflanking the Americans—had located a ford on the Brandywine north and west of the line where scouts had assured Washington no crossings were possible.[8]

Although Washington had refused to allow Lafayette to command a division, the untested young officer did fight in the eventual battle near the creek. At Chadd's Ford, in a Pennsylvania Continental unit led by Gen. Thomas Conway, the marquis, under heavy British fire, rode into the action. Along with other French members of Conway's division, Lafayette was soon urging the Patriots to charge the enemy with fixed bayonets—a tactic common to European armies but then rarely used by the Patriots. But as he urged his comrades onward, Lafayette became a battle casualty: He later claimed that he did not initially feel the musket ball as it pierced his left leg below the calf. Only when he noticed blood coming from his boot did he realize he had been hit.[9]

EIGHT

Renown

On September 11, 1777, upon noticing the scarlet stream seeping from his boot, Lafayette's first impulse was to stay in the fight. Assisted by his aide-de-camp Jean Gimat, the young officer, five days into his twentieth year, managed to find and mount a horse. Moments later—amid the cries of battling soldiers, clinking swords, whinnying horses, and the smoke, smell, and sound of musket and cannon fire—General Washington arrived on the scene with fresh troops.

Lafayette, as he later recalled, "was about to join him when loss of blood forced him to stop and bandage his wound." Dismounting, he removed his left boot and, in short order, his silk general's sash; but as he wrapped it around his left leg—and blood darkened the already red fabric—he realized the wound's severity. The Patriots' line, meanwhile, was failing to hold; moments later, "retreating soldiers, cannons, and wagons flowed pell-mell along the road" toward the settlement of Chester, Pennsylvania, twelve miles to the northeast. Washington, meanwhile "took advantage of the remaining daylight to delay the enemy's advance. Several regiments had done well but the rout was complete."

By the day's end ninety-three soldiers lay dead on the British side. American casualties were far higher—with credible estimates ranging from two hundred to five hundred killed. Beyond that, what became known as the Battle of Brandywine Creek ranked, until the American Civil War, as the largest and longest battle ever fought on U.S. soil—of the longest duration, with the most combatants, and spread across the largest area.[1]

Writing to Adrienne the next day, September 12, Lafayette minimized his wound: "The ball," he wrote, "hit neither bone nor nerve, and all I have to do for it to heal is to lie on my back for a while." His apparent blitheness notwithstanding, the wound had been serious enough for Washington to dispatch his personal surgeon to tend to it. From Chester, Lafayette was taken by boat to Philadelphia. Afterward, as the city braced for its inevitable British capture (that occurred on September 26), Lafayette was moved from one safe locale to another, and eventually to Bethlehem, Pennsylvania.

There he spent four weeks recuperating under what he described to Adrienne as the "truly touching" care of the Moravian Fellowship. From the writings of the philosopher and historian Abbé Guillaume Thomas François Raynal, Lafayette was familiar with the Protestant sect, then associated with pacifism and therefore exempt from military service. "The people here lead a gentle and peaceful life; we shall talk about that when I return."[2]

But although Brandywine had been a disaster for the Patriots—Lafayette, thanks to Washington, now had his long-coveted battle experience. On the night of September 11, mere hours after the engagement, Washington penned a report on the battle for the Continental Congress. The dispatch, soon appearing in newspapers, recounted the defeat. But it also included a sentence that commenced Lafayette's American fame: "The Marquis La Fayette was wounded in the leg, & General [William] Woodford in the hand," Washington wrote, adding vaguely: "Divers other officers were wounded, & some slain; but the numbers of either cannot now be ascertained."

As Lafayette recuperated, thanks to Washington's report, his fame—his renown—spread across America: "No longer considered as a stranger, never was any adoption more complete than his own," he recalled. Weeks earlier

Lafayette and his companions had been scorned as "adventurers" and worse. Increasingly, he now found himself surrounded by "citizens . . . all interested in his situation and extreme youth."[3]

Like Lafayette, his friend John Laurens had fought bravely at Brandywine. But unlike Lafayette, the South Carolinian came through unscathed: "It was not his fault that he was not killed or wounded," Lafayette allegedly quipped afterward. "He did everything that was necessary to procure one or t[he] other."

Indeed, Lafayette's exaltation soared so high that even the news that reached him, as he recuperated in Bethlehem, of the loss of *La Victoire* did not dampen his spirits. That August he learned that, while he was presenting his bona fides to the Continental Congress, the ship that had brought him to America had been lost. He had assumed that the vessel was, by then, homeward bound with a cargo of rice for the French market. Instead, it had foundered and sunk off the South Carolina coast.

Even so, in his September 12 letter to Adrienne, Lafayette was downright jaunty—even while recounting the moment he was wounded: "While I was trying to rally them [Patriot troops], the English honored me with a musket shot, which wounded me slightly in the leg."

Otherwise his brief letter turned to inevitable subjects. He wrote of the Patriot army's Brandywine defeat and hopes for better days. "This battle will, I fear, have unpleasant consequences for America; we must try to repair the damage, if we can." He also expressed his longing to hear from Adrienne: "You must have received many letters from me, unless the English are as hostile to my letters as to my legs. I have received only one from you so far, and I long for news." The one letter—now lost—he had received from Adrienne had been brought from France in August by the Polish-born Kazimierz Pulaski, who that month had arrived at the Continental army's Neshaminy Creek headquarters.[4]

Equally telling of Lafayette's heightened spirits were other letters written from Bethlehem over those weeks—to François-Claude-Amour de Bouillé, marquis de Bouillé—a military officer and Lafayette cousin then serving as governor of France's Caribbean colony of Martinique—and to a government minister at Versailles. To the two Lafayette proposed expeditionary raids, with himself leading American troops, against British interests in the Caribbean and India respectively. Lafayette later recalled—with irony and again in the third person—his martial scheming as he recuperated among his pacifist caregivers: "The good Moravian brothers loved him and deplored his warlike folly. . . . [Even so] while listening to their sermons he planned setting Europe and Asia in a flame."[5]

While in Bethlehem, Lafayette also initiated what grew into regular correspondences on multiple other subjects with a wide array of other French and American officials. To the former, for instance, he sought to counter disparaging reports that he assumed *La Victoire*'s spurned warriors, upon returning to France, would be circulating.

Toward that end Lafayette reassured officials at Versailles of the virtues of the Patriot cause and its prospects for victory against the British. Likewise, to Patriot officials—particularly delegates to the Continental Congress—he became a prolific and increasingly valued commentator on Franco-American relations as well as the respective merits of arriving French officers.

While Lafayette's proposed invasions found no sponsors, his zeal did not go unnoticed. The comte de Maurepas—Louis XVI's aging naval minister to whom Lafayette had proposed the raid on British interests in India—playfully commented to an associate that the young marquis would eventually sell "all the furniture of Versailles to support the American cause; because, once he gets something in his head, it's impossible to resist him." More concretely, Lafayette's correspondence over time won him a vital diplomatic role in America's quest for independence: His steadfast enthusiasm for the Patriots, antipathy toward Britain, and insider's knowledge of French and, increasingly, American political and military matters was making him a key, arguably *the* key, intermediary between America and France. He wasn't quite wrestling with the Beast of the Gévaudan. But his growing fame was transforming him into an auspicious figure in the public life of his adopted country.[6]

NINE

"Soldier's Friend"

Following the September 11, 1777, defeat of Washington's army at Brandy-wine Creek, his troops suffered two other major setbacks against General Howe's forces, both just north of Philadelphia—at Germantown, on October 4; and near White Marsh Township, in a series of skirmishes between December 5 and 8. Even so, that same autumn did bring other—splendid—news to Washington's camp: In pitched battles on September 19 and October 7, in Saratoga, New York, American forces led by Gen. Horatio Gates had defeated British divisions under Gen. John Burgoyne. Patriot forces suffered 90 dead and 240 wounded, but British casualties numbered far higher—440 killed and close to 700 wounded. Even more stunning, on October 17 Burgoyne had surrendered his entire army to the Americans—resulting in 5,800 prisoners.

On October 19, meanwhile, Lafayette, recovered from his Brandywine wound, arrived at Washington's latest encampment north of Philadelphia. On November 25, near the town of Gloucester, New Jersey, though formally still without a command, he led a regiment of about three hundred Patriots, mostly militia, against a three-hundred-man British force. The attack, as Lafayette immediately informed Washington, resulted in from twenty-five to thirty British deaths and a similar number of wounded. On the same November 26 that Lafayette wrote to Washington, the commander in chief penned a letter to Continental Congress president Henry Laurens: "The Marquis de Lafayette," he wrote, "is more & more solicitous to be in actual service & is pressing in his applications for a Command." Unsentimentally he repeated earlier expressed fears of Lafayette's potential to damage American relations with France: "I still fear a refusal will not only induce him to return in disgust—but may involve some unfavorable consequences."

But then again, Washington conceded, the aspiring commander *had* demonstrated undeniable élan under fire—and the Continental army *did* need leaders: "There are now some vacant Divisions in the Army, to one of which he may be appointed, if it should be the pleasure of Congress. I am convinced he possesses a large share of that Military ardor which generally characterises the Nobility of his Country." On December 1 the Continental Congress, responding to Washington's suggestion, passed a resolution appointing Lafayette to command a Continental army division.[1]

But while Lafayette relished the command, his hopes of leading anyone into battle would have to wait. On December 19, seeking a winter encampment, Washington's entire army repaired to a site twenty miles northwest of Philadelphia. Named after a long-defunct foundry beside a local stream called Valley Creek, the forested plateau was called (however misleadingly) Valley Forge.

In the wake of the Battle of Gloucester, a report by Washington to the congress on the engagement, with a praiseful mention of Lafayette, had appeared in numerous American newspapers. And his behavior during the brutal winter encampment at Valley Forge—further testing the young aristocrat's mettle—soon added to his growing reputation. There, as Lafayette remembered: "The unfortunate American soldiers lacked everything—coats, hats, shirts, and shoes. Their feet and legs turned black with frostbite, and often had to be amputated." Compounding their woes: "The sight of the misery halted enlistments," encouraged desertions, and reinforced perceptions—among the public as well as enemy forces—of a faltering Patriot cause.

Mortified, using his own funds, Lafayette purchased shoes and clothes for the men of his division, a unit comprised of Virginians. His largesse soon earned him the epithet "the soldier's friend." Moreover, as he recalled: "In his dress, his food, and his habits he adopted American customs, but he was even more simple, frugal, and austere than anyone else. He had been raised in a genteel fashion, but now he suddenly changed his whole way of living, and his temperament became adapted to privation and fatigue."[2]

A January 1778 letter to Adrienne gave vent, simultaneously, to bewildered despair—guilt at leaving her behind—and longings for home and hearth. "My destiny is strange indeed. In a camp, in the middle of the wood, fifteen hundred leagues [5,179 miles] from you, I am confined by the winter," he lamented.

Whatever remorse still haunted Lafayette for having, six months earlier, abandoned his pregnant wife and their infant daughter, Henriette, was now compounded by more recent news. In a letter—since lost—that reached him at Valley Forge, he had learned of the birth of their second daughter, Anastasie.[3]

On January 24 the marquis, learning that his winter confinement at Valley Forge was about to end, received orders to lead an attempted invasion of Canada—today's Quebec. The word came from Washington's rival Horatio Gates. In issuing the command Gates was acting as president of the Continental Congress's Board of War, a civilian position that, in theory, rendered the ambitious general Washington's superior. Gates in turn had close ties to Gen. Thomas Conway. A courageous if imperious soldier, the forty-two-year-old Conway was a former officer in an Irish brigade of France's army; he was also at the center of a clique later known as the Conway Cabal, reputedly with designs to replace Washington as commander in chief. Although Washington and Lafayette were both wary of the Canada expedition—of its political origins and chances of success—Lafayette, with Washington's blessings, accepted the command.[4]

After selecting twenty French officers for the mission, Lafayette and his men, on February 7, began their four-hundred-mile, ten-day northerly ride toward Albany. In the end, however, the mission—star-crossed by weather and logistics-related snafus—proved a disaster. The winter transit to Albany proved brutal, and, once there, they found only half of the 2,500 expected reinforcements awaiting them. On February 24 the congress, responding to desperate letters from Lafayette, canceled the invasion and summoned him to leave Albany and return to Pennsylvania to resume command of his old division. It was March when the order reached him, but before leaving upstate New York, by prior arrangement, he ventured to nearby Fort Stanwix, where he recruited for the Continental army forty-seven Oneida Indian warriors.

All the while, tormented by self-recrimination for the failure of the Canada invasion, Lafayette assuaged his guilt with fatherly counsel from Washington that had reached him in Albany: "I am persuaded that every one will applaud your prudence in renouncing a Project in pursuing which you would vainly have attempted Physical Impossibilities," he wrote. "Your Character stands as fair as ever it did and . . . no new Enterprise is necessary to wipe off this imaginary Stain."[5]

In early April, Lafayette arrived at Valley Forge. There welcome news soon greeted him: In Paris on February 6 France and the United States had signed a treaty—actually two treaties, one commercial, the other military. The commercial treaty accorded each country, in trade with the other, most-favored-nation status, and opened to American ships several ports in France and the Caribbean. The military treaty—to go into effect if France and Britain went to war, a probable eventuality—stipulated a strategic alliance between the two countries.

The signatories' mutual desire to preserve the independence and freedom of the United States underlay the alliance: "Neither of the two Parties shall conclude either Truce or Peace with Great Britain, without the formal consent of the other first obtained," read a key article of the pact. "And they mutually engage not to lay down their arms, until the independence of the United States have been formally or tacitly assured by the Treaty or Treaties that shall terminate the War." Moreover, the French government also promised to abstain from claiming any English territory on the North American mainland and agreed that any such conquests made by its forces would belong to the United States.

"The news of the [treaties]," Lafayette recalled, "excited a great sensation in America, and above all, in the army." But still other good news soon arrived: On April 22, effectively ending the Conway Cabal, its namesake general resigned from the Continental army.

Moreover, on July 4 Gen. John Cadwalader, a friend of Washington's, shot and wounded Conway in a duel sparked by an insult against Washington. Eventually recovering, the resilient Conway soon returned to Europe and resumed his military career—once again in the army of France.[6]

TEN

Stargazer

Are those powers . . . which being intended for the erudition of the world, like air and light, the world's common property, to be taken from their proper pursuit to do the commonplace drudgery of governing a single state, a work which may be executed by men of an ordinary stature, such as are always and every where to be found?

THOMAS JEFFERSON TO DAVID RITTENHOUSE, JULY 19, 1778, LAMENTING THE ASTRONOMER'S PARTICIPATION IN PENNSYLVANIA'S GOVERNANCE

After burying his infant son at Monticello, on June 14, 1777, Thomas Jefferson ordered his phaeton and six horses readied for his return trip to Williamsburg. The following summer, on August 1, 1778—again interrupting his state legislature toils in Williamsburg—he was again at Monticello. There Martha gave birth to another child. They named the infant Mary, but she was soon called Polly.

The couple had buried two children in the mid-1770s. And now, with the family's latest member, their firstborn daughter, Patsy, now five years old, had a new little sister. By then, inherited wealth had unburdened Jefferson from the necessity of practicing law. The infant Polly thus joined a household that reveled in domestic pleasures—gardening, dining, games, reading, and music-making. Even so, although Jefferson's responsibilities as a legislator were officially part-time, politics and legal matters continued, during the late 1770s, to consume much of his time.

Jefferson had played a major role in steeling the Patriots for their fight as citizens of an independent nation. Nonetheless, after drafting the Declaration of Independence in the summer of 1776, he left Philadelphia and his seat in the Second Continental Congress in late August. Indeed, even before writing the Declaration, he had already been elected to a seat in Virginia's House of Delegates, the successor body to the House of Burgesses. There, he had resolved to redirect his energies to reforming his native state's government. However, soon after he settled into that work, an opportunity—as unforeseen as it was alluring—reached him: Congress asked him to join Benjamin Franklin and Silas Deane on its commission in Paris.

The offer reached Jefferson on October 8 via a courier dispatched from Philadelphia to Williamsburg. At thirty-three, Jefferson was a longtime admirer of French civilization who had never been abroad. He was tempted. But after keeping the messenger waiting for three days, he declined the offer. In a letter to the congress's president John Hancock, Jefferson attributed his decision, vaguely, to "circumstances very peculiar in the situation of my family." But politesse also lurked behind his explanation. By then—and more acutely later—Jefferson's perceived aloofness from national affairs was creating resentments in Philadelphia. Thus, left unremarked upon in the letter to Hancock, was Jefferson's reengagement with his legislative work in Williamsburg.

Jefferson by then had grown obsessed with reforming Virginia's governance to reflect the values shaping the national revolution—new attitudes concerning, among other matters, voter suffrage, equality of citizens before the law (albeit in both cases, exclusively for propertied white men), and separation of church and state. By the summer of 1776 he believed that the moment had arrived to overhaul the entire legal code of his native Virginia—the realm he always had in mind when he referred to his "country."[1]

Appropriately, then, Jefferson, had been the first delegate named to a "committee of revisors" created by the House of Delegates in 1776. The panel's members varied over the years, but its original numbers included, along with

Jefferson, other gifted legal minds such as George Mason, Edmund Pendleton, and George Wythe—the latter two of whom had earlier served in the Continental Congress; and however daunting its task, within three years the panel had drafted more than 130 bills.[2]

Throughout the war George Washington, as the Continental army's commander in chief, was obliged to address the military and civil concerns of a realm stretching from Massachusetts to Georgia. Jefferson, by contrast, for several years after leaving the congress, rarely felt burdened by matters outside Virginia—or, for that matter, the vagaries of waging a war. By contrast, as Washington, Lafayette, and other Patriots confronted British forces at places such as Saratoga and Brandywine Creek, or shivered at Valley Forge, the civilian Jefferson remained in the more comfortable climes of Williamsburg and Monticello—usually safely indoors, poring over law books and penning revisions of Virginia's laws.

Moreover, with the arrival in 1778 of news of the U.S. military alliance with France, Jefferson concluded that the conflict was effectively over; to a friend in Europe that June, he wrote: "If there could have been a doubt before as to the event of the war, it is now totally removed by the interposition of France; and the generous alliance she has entered into with us."

Jefferson routinely recorded sundry astronomical phenomena—"as early as possible in the morning and again about 4. o'clock in the afternoon." But now—with the new treaties' signings—there seemed, by his lights, even more time for such observations. In fact the occasion of Jefferson's letter—to the Italian naturalist Giovanni Fabbroni—was to convey that he now had more time "to indulge my fondness for" such pursuits.[3]

On July 19 Jefferson penned a letter commencing an episode that, over the coming months, further revealed his aloofness from the war effort. Of Virginia's congressional delegate John Harvie he inquired about finding some needed craftsmen for Monticello among British army prisoners then being held in Cambridge, Massachusetts.

The prisoners had been captured in fall 1777 during the Battle of Saratoga. Afterward about eleven hundred of them had been released—"paroled"—into Canada upon promising to not return to the war. About 4,100 detainees, however, had been marched to Cambridge—roughly half of whom were "Hessians," hireling soldiers recruited by the British from a half dozen German principalities. Overall, an estimated thirty thousand Hessians contributed to the British war effort.

The soldiers captured at Saratoga became known—after the Convention of Saratoga, the negotiated document that stipulated their captivity's terms—as the "Troops of the Convention." In Cambridge, rank-and-file Convention soldiers were housed in ramshackle Continental army barracks. Captured officers resided in local private homes. By fall 1778, however, the arrangement was showing signs of wear.

The Cambridge barracks were no match for the Massachusetts winter. Moreover, the prisoners' presence was raising local fears of a British army raid to secure their freedom. And, as word of those discontents reached Virginia, Jefferson and other Albemarle businessmen saw an opportunity: By transferring the prisoners to Albemarle, they believed, the county could gain, in fees paid by Congress for their upkeep, a new source of revenue; beyond that—if Jefferson's hunch proved correct—local planters might gain a new pool of skilled craftsmen.

Congress liked Jefferson's idea; and, in September, Delegate Harvie informed him that the prisoners "may be sent to Virginia this Fall or Winter." Even better, Harvie added, "some Tradesmen of the Professions you want may be found amongst them." As plans for the transfer proceeded, Harvie offered the use of land he owned as the site for the camp—and Congress authorized twenty thousand dollars to compensate him for the costs of its construction.

That winter, without warning, the prisoners learned that they were about to be marched from Cambridge to Virginia, and that they would be required to leave behind most of their possessions. Soon adding to their misery, jeers from local citizens attended their departure. Even worse, over the next eight weeks, as the prisoners made their 641-mile wintry trek, conditions proved harsh, provisions scarce.

Reaching Albemarle in January 1779, the captive officers once again found comfortable local housing. Rank-and-file soldiers, by contrast, confronted a gloomy complex of unfinished cabins constructed on an isolated snowbound landscape: "Never shall I be able to forget this day, which was terrible in every way," wrote one Hessian officer of the grim scene, by then called Albemarle Barracks. Many prisoners eventually camped in the site's forest, seeking "shelter in the woods like wild animals."

Unfinished sections of free-standing wooden walls ringed Albemarle Barracks. Forty-eight huts, many also unfinished—each built to house eighteen men—sat on a grid of four rows. Their construction, mainly by slaves owned by Harvie, had begun that fall but had halted with winter's onset. The camp's advocates had stressed its remoteness as an asset: Amid the foothills of the Blue Ridge mountains, ten miles from the main road, the camp, they had argued, would be difficult for British raiders to reach.

That remoteness, however, aggravated the site's problems. Beyond frigid temperatures and rain, from which its buildings provided scant protection, water was not readily available, provisions were scarce, and from the start, overcrowding bedeviled the camp. Eventually, as its population swelled to 3,700 prisoners, Albemarle Barracks became Virginia's largest settlement, with a population twice that of Williamsburg. Appalled members of Congress soon threatened to relocate the prisoners. Moreover, even as local planters, including Jefferson, defended the arrangement, local residents began to complain. Like their counterparts in Cambridge, they argued that the camp rendered their environs a likely target for a British raid.

When spring arrived the prisoners were ordered by their own officers to improve the camp. In time they constructed new housing, planted gardens, and procured livestock; they also built and operated stores, a coffee shop, taverns, a church, and a theater. As a new laxity settled over the arrangement, some officers even rented fine houses in town. Jefferson himself arranged estates for at least two officers and their families. Indeed, one of them—for Gen. William Phillips, soon to loom large in the lives of both Jefferson and Lafayette—came with slaves to attend to the needs of himself and his family.

As he had hoped, Jefferson, in the end, did find new craftsmen for Monticello. And among the Hessians he also found gifted musicians whom he and Martha could accompany. More broadly, amid the enemy officers Jefferson found cultivated guests for gatherings at Monticello, as well as hosts for social outings that he and Martha could attend.

Among the new musical accompanists that soon arrived at Monticello was Friedrich Wilhelm von Geismar, a young Hessian officer who joined Jefferson in spirited violin duets. Later, in 1799—after Jefferson arranged an early release for Geismar to return to Prussia to tend to his ailing father—the officer, to express his gratitude, left behind for Jefferson all of the sheaves of sheet music he had brought to America.

The British commander, William Phillips, and the Hessian general, Friedrich Riedesel, and their families likewise numbered among Thomas and Martha's new friends. An August 1779 letter from Phillips soliciting the Jeffersons' company at an upcoming performance typified the concord between Jefferson and the nominal prisoners: "The British Officers intend to perform a Play next Saturday at the Barracks," Phillips wrote, requesting "the honour to attend to you and Mrs. Jefferson in my Box at the Theatre." Reciprocating the cordiality, Jefferson made clear that he viewed their bond as transcending both politics and war: "The great cause which divides our countries is not to be decided by individual animosities."[4]

If, in hindsight, Jefferson's fraternization with enemy officers appeared naive, his own past—to be fair—included scant military experience or guidance for thinking in such terms. Jefferson, after all, was on the cusp of his thirty-second birthday when, in April 1775, Anglo-American tensions burst into open warfare at Lexington and Concord.

To be sure, there were soldiers in the Patriot army Jefferson's age and older, and as his biographer Dumas Malone noted, Jefferson's skills as a rider and writer might well have allowed him to contribute to that army—the latter as perhaps a military aide in the vein of James Monroe or Alexander Hamilton. But then again, those men were younger than Jefferson when the war came—Monroe sixteen and Hamilton, twenty. And, as Malone noted, Jefferson was "somewhat too old and rather too prominent for that sort of post."

Beyond that, Jefferson had no particular qualifications to merit service as an officer. Lafayette, by contrast—though untested in battle when he arrived in Philadelphia—did have formal education and training in military matters.

Equally important, Lafayette was obsessed with military service and Jefferson was demonstrably devoid of such interest. Tellingly, although Jefferson had since 1770 been the official leader of the Albemarle County militia, there was, as Malone noted, "significance in the fact that he was rarely called 'Colonel,' though many of his fellows often were designated thus, without having any better claim to the title than he had."[5]

In time, as the Patriots' strategic fortunes worsened and the military struggle for their independence increasingly shifted south, George Washington grew frustrated with those who, in his view, appeared aloof from the war effort. In a 1778 letter to Benjamin Harrison, president of Virginia's House of Delegates, he chastened state governments that he deemed wanting in their commitments to the larger nation-state: "America never Stood in more eminent need of the wise— patriotic—& spirited exertions of her Sons than at this period," Washington wrote. "The States separately are too much engaged in their local concerns."

To Harrison, Washington faulted Virginia for depriving Congress of its most talented statesmen: "Where is Mason, Wythe, Jefferson, Nicholas, Pendleton, Nelson, and another"—presumably Harrison—"I could name?" Meanwhile, intruding upon his contemplations of celestial bodies, the war that Jefferson was convinced had reached its end would soon enough imperil his days— eventually, indeed, find its way to Monticello's doorsteps.[6]

ELEVEN

"No One Better Situated"

On May 6, 1778, crisp musket blasts fired in rapid succession into the air, cascading down the ranks of the assembled soldiers and melding into a single roar at Valley Forge. Following the splendid *feu de joie*—literally, fire of joy—as Pvt. Elijah Fisher of the 4th Massachusetts Regiment recorded that spring day, "the Artillery Discharged forty-four Cannon and it was followed with three Chears for the Thirteen United States of Amarica [*sic*]."

Other toasts and huzzahs rose. For the occasion—the celebration of Congress's approval of the two American treaties with France—General Washington, having ordered the posting of extra sentries, even permitted the soldiers to exceed their usual rations of drink. Recalled aide-de-camp Tench Tilghman, "The troops must have more than the common quantity of liquor and perhaps there will be some little drunkenness among them."

Lafayette, meanwhile, had donned a neckerchief of white—the color of France's House of Bourbon. Breaching protocol, with joy and in tears, he embraced the commander in chief, declaring: "The king my master has acknowledged your Independence, and entered into an alliance with you for its establishment."[1]

Both George Washington and Lafayette had yet another reason for exultation: Regular drills implemented throughout the army over the past months at Valley Forge by the Prussia-born general baron von Steuben had brought a new polish and discipline to the troops.

The day's celebration aside, Washington had, in fact, known of the treaties' "good tidings" as early as April 27.[2] Indeed, by one early account, it had been Lafayette who brought Washington the news. True or not, however, Lafayette's renown was waxing: Circumstances beyond his control had forced the scrubbing of his "irruption into Canada." But the skills he displayed while attempting the mission were undeniable. Moreover, at Brandywine, Gloucester, Valley Forge, and—yes—Albany the young major general had displayed bravery, resourcefulness, and leadership skills.

Indeed, in spring 1778, after Lafayette's return from Albany, Washington's reservations about his fitness for command had melted with the winter's snow. More to the point, Washington appeared ever more inclined to entrust the twenty-one-year-old officer with challenging missions.

Most assumed that the treaties with France would propel Lafayette into a new role; and a rumor soon spread that he was about to be named ambassador to the United States by the kingdom of France—the first foreign state to extend diplomatic recognition to the new republic. That post, however, went instead to Conrad Alexandre Gérard, a career diplomat who had helped negotiate the recent treaties in Paris with Deane, Franklin, and Arthur Lee.

On March 17, four days after France's ambassador in London informed British officials of the treaties, Britain, as expected, declared war on France; and, over the coming weeks, British military planners adjusted their war strategy to take into account the Patriots' new ally.

In fact, well before learning of the Patriots' alliance with France, officials in London had come to view the American rebellion as belonging to an international war. Moreover, they assumed—correctly, as it turned out—that France's entry into the war would prompt Spain, traditionally a French ally and British antagonist, to join the fray. Along with France, Spain—which would join the war in April 1779—had numbered among the countries Britain defeated in the Seven Years' War.

Further internationalizing Britain's war with its former colonies, in December 1790 Anglo-Dutch differences over trade with the United States would bring the Dutch Republic into the contest as another U.S. ally—albeit to scant military effect.

During the American war's early years, British strategists saw their task solely as defeating a colonial rebellion. Consequently, from Lexington and Concord to the campaigns contesting Boston, New York, and Philadelphia, their forces had fought in large part on Patriot-selected terms and battlefields.

As it became clear, however, that the war was acquiring an international character—likely with multiple parties fighting in multiple theaters—London officials concluded that new circumstances required a new strategy: They decided to shift resources southward—toward the American South and the Caribbean. In the latter all the European combatants held valuable, and militarily vulnerable, island colonies. Britain's trade with its West Indies colonies, for instance, produced more wealth for London's coffers than all of its mainland American commerce. Indeed, in early 1778 George III briefly considered a plan that would have shifted to the Caribbean *all* British forces in its thirteen rebellious mainland colonies.

By March, however, British strategists had settled on a less drastic southward reallocation of resources: Without abandoning their presence in more northerly realms, in late 1778 British forces invaded Georgia, and in 1780 they entered, successively, South and North Carolina. Moreover, plans soon emerged to dispatch five thousand Redcoats to raid France's profitable island colony of Saint Lucia; and another three thousand to secure British holdings in western Florida.

Simultaneously British military commanders resolved, in future actions, to conceive of the conflict as primarily a naval war. Until then British ships had been used, when at all, to blockade Patriot ports and to convoy land troops between various battle theaters. Henceforth, however, given the formidable navies possessed by France and Spain, British strategists resolved to deploy their ships for both offensive and defensive actions against vessels of their new European adversaries.[3]

In time, as British strategists shifted many of their forces to the Caribbean, they realized that they lacked adequate resources to defend both Philadelphia and New York against the expected French forces dispatched to America. In the end they decided to abandon Philadelphia and concentrate both their naval and ground forces on defending New York. General Washington, meanwhile, learning of British troop movements around Philadelphia, suspected an evacuation might be in the offing. But he also worried that the movements might be a ruse intended to distract from preparations for a new offensive in Pennsylvania.

Spring 1778 had brought to Valley Forge the welcome news of the alliance with France. Even so, for Washington's troops the arrival of spring brought no immediate clashes with the enemy. As the Patriots awaited an expected British withdrawal from Philadelphia, lacking more specific intelligence, their best course was to wait and watch. Toward that latter end, Washington, on May 18, ordered Lafayette to leave that morning to gather intelligence of British intentions. He was to lead a force of more than two thousand men—the largest he had yet commanded—comprising Continental army soldiers, several hundred Pennsylvania militiamen, and the forty-seven Oneida warriors he had recently recruited. The mission, Washington cautioned, "will require the greatest caution and prudence."[4]

On May 20, two days after Lafayette's detachments set out—while on an elevation north of Philadelphia called Barren Hill, overlooking the Schuylkill River—a British force of sixteen thousand soldiers surrounded his army on three sides. Outnumbered, he deployed a feint—dispatching patrols whose appearance and sniper shots conveyed, falsely, troop strengths greater than his force's actual numbers, as well as an intention to stay and fight. In the end Lafayette quietly led his army down a narrow road off the hill to a ford on the Schuylkill, and they crossed the river to safety. By the day's end, with only seven casualties, his entire army had escaped the attempted encirclement.

The withdrawal had involved both cunning and luck, but certainly Lafayette had violated Washington's admonition to exercise the "greatest caution and prudence." Even so, setting the tone for American public reaction, Washington reported to the Continental Congress that Lafayette had "made a timely and handsome retreat." Indeed, while earlier acts by Lafayette had won him plaudits, Barren Hill projected his name far beyond Patriot army encampments. His fame was now reaching even his native land: "Like his master, Washington," recalled a friend in France, "he might be conquered, but he could not be discouraged."[5]

Praise for his leadership at Barren Hill aside, a heavy heart burdened the young general. Weeks earlier, on May 6 at Valley Forge, even as Lafayette donned his white Bourbon neckerchief to celebrate the treaties with France, sad personal news haunted him. Days earlier—in a rare instance in which a letter from Adrienne reached him—he learned of the death the previous October of the couple's first daughter, Henriette.

Preoccupied with duties, however, not until five weeks later, on June 16, did Lafayette answer Adrienne's sad dispatch, albeit with faint confidence of his words ever reaching her: "I neither know when my letter by this opportunity will leave America nor when it will arrive." Yet still he wrote: "How dreadful our separation is!" and lamented: "The distance from Europe to America seemed more immense than ever; the loss of our poor child is almost always on my mind."

That same May, meanwhile, a prisoner exchange had returned a familiar but long-absent face to the Continental army. Maj. Gen. Charles Lee, Washington's forty-six-year-old second in command, was a thin, gangly man with a booming voice, flinty gray eyes, and a ready smile that betrayed, to the uninitiated, little hint of a troublesome personality.

The England-born Lee, in addition to his considerable successes as an American general, had also served with British forces in the French and Indian War. In the current conflict, he was captured in New Jersey in December 1776, seven months before Lafayette joined Washington's army, and sotto voce griping among officers at Valley Forge now attended Lee's return. A talented commander, Lee was also complex, imperious, and frequently rude. Moreover, he affected slovenly dress and preferred canine over human company. To a contemporary he was "a perfect original, a good scholar and soldier, and an odd genius; full of fire and passion." Since late 1776, growing mutual distrust had aggravated Lee's relations with Washington—and the coming weeks would insert Lafayette into the two men's rivalry.

The British had captured Philadelphia in September 1777. But as they approached that event's first anniversary, it dawned on their commanders that the triumph had failed to yield the same sort of psychological advantage associated with enemy occupations of European capitals. Likewise, during those months, Washington's army was frustrating the Redcoats. Neither in Pennsylvania or in New Jersey were they able to lure the Patriots into a decisive battle. By spring 1778, British strategists were bracing for a joint Franco-American strike against British-occupied New York. Given that, even as the Redcoats shifted resources to the south, they bolstered their New York presence by withdrawing their troops occupying Philadelphia and relocated them to New York.

Patriot forces had a general but uncertain knowledge of British intentions. According to reports that reached Washington, the Redcoats—under the command of forty-eight-year-old Gen. Henry Clinton, replacing William Howe—were soon to depart Philadelphia. After crossing the Delaware River and marching thorough New Jersey—covering seventy miles in the heart of enemy territory—they were to make their way to New York.

By the time Charles Lee had returned to Valley Forge, the evacuation by land of Clinton's forces had become a certainty. The precise date of their departure and their route across New Jersey, however, remained unknown to the Patriots. As it turned out, the British evacuation commenced on the morning of June 18: Roughly ten thousand troops were escorting three thousand departing Loyalists and a supply train of about fifteen hundred wagons. When the news reached Washington, his twelve-thousand-man-strong Continental army decamped from Valley Forge to pursue the departing Britons.

Before and after leaving Valley Forge, Washington discussed among his field officers whether to seek an open engagement with the enemy or merely to harass them with guerrilla actions—and otherwise be content with relishing their abandonment of the nation's capital.

Washington and Lafayette favored landing a strong blow without bringing on a risky general engagement. Most of the officers, however, including Lee, favored less bold action. On June 24, at Hopewell, New Jersey, Washington— still on Clinton's trail—learned that the Redcoats were approaching the town of Monmouth Court House (today's Freehold). Following a council of war with his officers, Washington, with Lee still urging caution, decided to reinforce the troops shadowing Clinton. When Lee—finding the assignment beneath his stature—initially balked at Washington's offer that he lead the Continental vanguard, Lafayette offered himself for the assignment.

After the enthusiastic young Frenchman led the vanguard close to the British—and too far from the main army for Washington to provide support— Washington had Lafayette pull back and sent the more experienced Lee (who now decided he did want the assignment) to take command.

On June 27, as Clinton's army approached Monmouth Court House, Washington's troops were six miles behind the Redcoats. Gathering his generals, Washington gave Lee discretionary orders to attack the following morning as Clinton's army broke camp. Washington, meanwhile, commanding six thousand men, would wait in the rear and, in the wake of Lee's vanguard offensive, follow with a larger force to support Lee.

The following morning, Lee moved toward Clinton's forces, finding them at around ten o'clock. But as Clinton reinforced his rear guard with more than four thousand troops, Lee's vanguard soon faced a vigorous counterattack. Toward noon, as his troops faltered, he ordered a retreat. Soon thereafter Washington, riding forward, encountered Lee and his retreating troops. Furious, the usually mild-mannered commander in chief gave Lee a choice: Either go to the rear and organize the main army as it came up, or remain forward and fight a delaying action while Washington went back to position the rest of the army. Lee remained forward, where he and General "Mad Anthony" Wayne fought a brutal defensive battle, giving Washington time to rally the main army in a strong defensive position.

The Battle of Monmouth Court House—lasting the rest of the day and fought in unrelenting, sometimes over 100-degree heat—proved to be a major engagement. Five thousand American soldiers faced a British force of two thousand. Moreover, Lafayette later recalled: "Cannon fire was exchanged all day." The following morning Washington's troops, to their surprise, awoke to discover that, during the night, the enemy's forces had decamped.

The battle was over.

Both sides suffered casualties in the hundreds at Monmouth Court House, and while tactically a stalemate, the battle provided a morale-boosting triumph for the Americans—marking the first time that Patriot forces had advanced against a British army. Beyond that, for Washington's forces, following their debilitating winter at Valley Forge, the engagement signaled their emergence as a worthy adversary against their British counterparts. Moreover, their performance had offered a dramatic demonstration of the discipline instilled during six months of drills conducted by Steuben—and, to a lesser degree, Lafayette—during their winter encampment.

Many Patriots viewed the exchange as a clear victory for American arms. Observed the historians Mark Edward Lender and Garry Wheeler Stone: "It was a battle that gripped the public imagination, with many Americans believing it heralded an early end to the conflict." Washington, Lafayette, Henry Knox, and Nathanael Greene had all proved themselves able commanders. For Lafayette the battle also marked a triumph in his rivalry with Washington's second in command. Weeks later during a court-martial Lee would defend his retreat at Monmouth Court House as a tactical maneuver intended to lure the Redcoats "into the maw of Washington's main force."

Ending his American military career, Lee was court-martialed on three separate charges, including disobeying orders. By contrast Lafayette recalled that he and Washington, following the Monmouth Court House engagement, "passed the night on the same cloak." Among other topics the two discussed that evening, recalled the marquis, was General Lee's abhorrent behavior.[6]

At age forty-eight in 1778, the French officer Charles Hector d'Estaing had already completed three decades of military service stationed all over the world, including turns as both a general and admiral. In addition to multiple medals for valor and service, the Seven Years' War veteran also had earned a reputation as vain and difficult. By that summer of '78—commanding a fleet of sixteen ships, twelve ships of the line and four frigates—he was sailing toward America.

D'Estaing's original plan was to sail to Delaware Bay. There, while Washington attacked retreating British land forces from the north, d'Estaing's fleet would ambush Royal Navy ships as they sailed for New York. In the end, however, the British evacuated Philadelphia before d'Estaing could reach Delaware Bay.

Plans were revised: D'Estaing, who had reached Maryland's coast on July 4, was to sail toward New York. There it would attack Howe's fleet—at anchor at Sandy Hook, New Jersey, in New York Bay—as well as British land forces on New York Island, today's Manhattan.

However, on July 11, upon reaching New York and anchoring offshore, d'Estaing discovered that his ships' hulls were too deep to clear a sandbar protruding from Sandy Hook, at the harbor's entrance. On July 22, after eleven days of failed attempts to enter the harbor, d'Estaing abandoned the effort. At Washington's suggestion he ordered his ships to sail for Newport, Rhode Island. By then d'Estaing had agreed to an alternate strategy—to attack a five-thousand-man enemy garrison occupying Newport and most of the rest of Rhode Island proper (today's Aquidneck Island) an assault to be coordinated with a Continental army militia force at nearby Providence, commanded by John Sullivan.

Over the rest of the summer, however, allied and British land and naval forces fell into what became a prolonged standoff: As tactical, logistical, and intelligence mishaps dogged both sides, substantive triumphs on sea and water eluded both forces. During those months Lafayette—acting variously as a Patriot commander and liaison between the French and American forces—spent much of the season shuttling between the war's New York and Rhode Island theaters.

Emblematic of the troubled—often interculturally so—waters that Lafayette navigated during those months was an episode sparked by an order that reached him in early August. Prior to a planned joint attack by Patriot and French forces at Rhode Island, Washington, in early August, sent Lafayette to Newport at the head of a two-thousand-man army. Before the planned assault, however, allied commanders became embroiled in a dispute over which forces, French or American, would have the honor of the first landing. The exchange, reflecting rival assertions of national pride, was eventually mediated by Lafayette. The two armies would land simultaneously on August 10.

On August 9, however, Sullivan—having learned that the British, apprised of the imminent assault, were already abandoning Newport—ordered his army forward to attack that day without alerting d'Estaing. The admiral and his fellow French officers became irate; and, conversing aboard his flagship, the *Languedoc*, confronted a delegation dispatched by their American counterparts. John Laurens—Washington's French-speaking aide-de-camp who had been assigned to d'Estaing since his arrival—soon reacted with unbridled chauvinism; writing to his father, Henry Laurens, John complained that the French officers had "conceived their troops injured by our landing first, and talked like women disputing precedence in a country dance, instead of men engaged in pursuing the common interest of two great Nations."

D'Estaing eventually agreed to resume cooperation with the Americans and ordered four thousand French troops to land on the island. Hours later there suddenly appeared on the horizon thirty-six British ships. Responding to a call for reinforcements from Newport's British garrison, the vessels belonged to the fleet of Adm. Richard Lord Howe.

The following morning—leaving three frigates behind and promising Sullivan to return to complete Rhode Island's capture—d'Estaing's fleet set out to sea in pursuit of the British ships. The French ships made a promising start in attacking their British adversaries. But before d'Estaing could secure victory, a violent storm arose, and by the next morning both fleets lay scattered and damaged. Not until August 20 did d'Estaing's fleet limp back to join Sullivan's army on Rhode Island.

Upon realizing, however, that d'Estaing intended to stay in port only long enough to assess the damage to his ships, Sullivan became incensed. Compounding ill feelings, on the evening of August 21—with Sullivan soon accusing the French officer of desertion and worse—d'Estaing sailed from Newport toward Boston for repairs.

D'Estaing's departure and an indignant letter that Sullivan soon dispatched to him left Lafayette in a "predicament." Although the marquis wore the uniform of the Continental army, Franco-American frictions had roused his native loyalties. Writing to d'Estaing, Lafayette disavowed Sullivan's actions: "Would you believe that they dared summon me to a council where they protested against a measure taken by the French squadron?" he asked. "I told those gentlemen that my country was more dear to me than America, that whatever France did was always right."

By August 26 Lafayette had prevailed upon Sullivan to allow him to go to Boston and meet with d'Estaing. Leaving that evening, he rode the sixty miles between Rhode Island and Boston in seven hours. Over the coming days Lafayette assuaged d'Estaing's wounded feelings, persuaded him to return to Rhode Island, and helped arrange for needed repairs for his ships. More broadly, Lafayette prevented a premature fraying of the Franco-American alliance, and, by the thirtieth, was back in Rhode Island.[7]

Throughout that summer, meanwhile, as d'Estaing's fleet lay anchored off New York and later sailed to Rhode Island, Lafayette via couriers had been dispatching letters to the French admiral, offering his services to his native country's naval force: "However pleasantly situated I am in America," he wrote on July 14, "I have always thought and I have written and said everywhere here, that I would prefer to be a soldier under the French flag." In that and five other letters written between July 14 and 30, Lafayette reiterated his desire to serve the admiral.

The marquis knew that during the Seven Years' War, d'Estaing had been briefly held as a prisoner of war by the British—and harbored bitter feelings toward John Bull. Moreover, Lafayette was distantly related to d'Estaing, a native of the Auvergne. In his first letter to the admiral, seeking to ingratiate himself, he thus began by emphasizing their shared antipathy for all things English—and the need for revenge, by Frenchmen, for France's defeat in the Seven Years' War: "I like to think that you will strike the first blows against that insolent nation because I know you value the pleasure of humiliating her and because you know her well enough to have an aversion for her." He then turned to their common origins: "I have the honor to be as much related to you by this sentiment as by ties of blood and our common title of 'Auvergnat.'"[8]

D'Estaing often found what he called Lafayette's "extreme impatience" exasperating, but he welcomed the marquis's impulsiveness as a contrast to what he considered the Americans' "incalculable slowness." Indeed, in a report sent that autumn to France's Ministry of the Marine, the admiral thus praised Lafayette: "No one," he wrote, "was better situated to serve as a link" between France and America. In that assessment he embraced a view not unlike that held by George Washington himself—presumably unbeknownst to the admiral—of Lafayette as an officer of unique capabilities among the Continental army. Indeed, in 1778 Washington—albeit in a backhanded compliment—had written to a congressman: "I do most devoutly wish that we had not a single Foreigner among us, except the Marquis de la Fayette, who acts upon very different principles than those which govern the rest."[9]

By the summer's end, meanwhile, as Lafayette waited in Rhode Island for a British attack that never came, he resumed his pleas to Washington and d'Estaing to be placed at the head of various expeditions. Likewise, he implored the American commander in chief to allow his return to his headquarters at White Plains. In a September 25 letter, however, Washington ended, at least for the immediate future, both of those hopes. "I should be very happy [to have] you with the grand army again," he wrote. In the meantime, he preferred that Lafayette remain on Rhode Island, due to its proximity to Boston.

Not that Washington, by then, was certain that the enemy intended to fight another day. To Lafayette, he speculated as to whether the British "mean to quit the United States altogether" and posed a suggestion: "If you have entertained thoughts my dear Marquis of paying a visit to your Court—To your Lady—and to your friends this Winter," it might be a good time to go. In suggesting a visit to France, Washington knew that the pain of Lafayette's separation from Adrienne had been sharpened that summer by news from her of the death of their daughter Henriette.[10]

Moreover, Washington was also thinking that the new U.S.-France alliance, coupled with Lafayette's increasing exchanges with French civil and military officials—in France and the United States—heightened a need for clarification of his official role in the current war. Indeed, even after Conrad Alexandre Gérard's appointment, in early 1788, as France's ambassador to the United States, speculation persisted about a new role for Lafayette: Would he continue to wear the uniform of the Continental army? Or would he now—with his native land having abandoned its conceit of neutrality—wear the uniform of Bourbon France?

———

On October 13 Lafayette wrote to Congress. Enclosing a letter of support from "his Excellency, General Washington," he requested a leave of absence. "As long as I thought I could dispose of myself," he wrote, "I made it my pride and pleasure to fight under American colours." But, he added, circumstances had changed. "Now, sir, that France is involved in a war, I am urged by my duty as well as by patriotic love, to present myself before the king, and know in what manner he judges proper to employ my services." He thus asked permission for "going home for the next winter."[11]

In October, Congress granted Lafayette's requested leave. In doing so, Henry Laurens, president of the Continental Congress, assured him of the "high Esteem and Affection in which You are held by the good People of these States."

Laurens added that Congress had commissioned for Lafayette an "Elegant Sword" that would be presented to him by the American minister at Versailles (Benjamin Franklin). Additionally, Laurens informed Lafayette of a letter, soon sent by Congress to King Louis XVI, that extolled Lafayette's "devotion to his sovereign" and his winning of "the confidence of these United States, your good and faithful friends and allies, and the affections of their citizens." On January 11, 1782, the returning hero sailed for France. In honor of the crossing the 151-foot frigate on which he sailed from Boston had been accorded a new name—*Alliance*.[12]

TWELVE

"À Hunting with the King"

In April 1777 tawdry, even illegal, circumstances had attended Lafayette's departure from France. Thus, to preserve his good standing in the Bourbon court, his return two years later required that he participate in a round of precisely planned appearances and symbolic acts: some were designed to save face for the laws and the monarch his exit had defied; others to celebrate his heroism in a cause, popular across the kingdom, that the Bourbons now openly supported, and with which they now sought public identification.

The *Alliance* reached the port of Brest on February 6, 1779. Because Lafayette had been away from France for twenty-two months, "I thought only of rejoining my family and friends, of whom I had heard nothing for eight months," he later recalled. Even so—according to plans, bypassing Paris—he went straight to Versailles, where he was immediately arrested. Later, jocularly recalling the scripted ritual of state, "I was questioned, complimented, and exiled."

His sentence—his "exile"—was a week of house arrest in Paris, in "the confines of the Hôtel de Noailles," his in-laws' luxurious Paris town house—a bastion "thought preferable to the honors of the Bastille, which was first proposed." He continued his description:

A few days later I wrote to the king to admit my error, which had such happy results. He granted me an audience to receive a mild reprimand, and when my freedom was restored I was advised to avoid those places where the public might consecrate my disobedience. On my arrival I had enjoyed the honor of being consulted by all the ministers and, what was far better, being kissed by all the ladies. The kissing stopped the following day, but I retained the confidence of the ministry much longer and enjoyed both favor at Versailles and popularity at Paris.

Culminating the orgy of reconciliation, for eighty thousand livres, Lafayette was allowed the honor of purchasing the command of a regiment of the king's dragoons.[1]

Before the marquis's return emblematic of the French public's newfound adulation for him, the aging philosopher François-Marie Arouet, better known by his nom de plume Voltaire, had been asked, at a private gathering in Paris—in the home of the socialite Madame de Choiseul, by one account—to meet Adrienne. "I wish," Voltaire reputedly said, on bent knee before her, "to make my obeisance to the wife of the hero of the New World. May I live long enough to salute in him the hero of the Old." Dying nine months before Lafayette's return, Voltaire did not live to see his wish fulfilled. But in the coming years, when revolution came to France, Lafayette's admirers conflated Voltaire's reputed tribute into a succinct epithet—"The Hero of Two Worlds."[2]

Adrienne was nineteen when, in February 1779, the twenty-two-year-old Lafayette returned to Paris; and, by all accounts, joy—as it always did after such separations—suffused their reunion. According to her biographer André Maurois, Adrienne "loved her husband not only because it was her duty to do so, and because she admired him, but"—to use her term—"'Voluptuously.' Whenever he came back to her unexpectedly, she was near to swooning. The self-denial with which she spared him all jealousy, brought its own reward."

Moreover, their extended time apart and the understanding that he would again be departing for a lengthy stay abroad compelled a fuller discussion of plans and contingencies than in the past: "A closer intimacy from now on made her a partner in all his plans for the future. He welcomed this complete agreement between them."[3]

In letters to Washington, Lafayette often wrote of Adrienne, always with affection. Reciprocally, Washington, in a letter to Lafayette during that period, paid tribute to the couple's devotion: "I have a heart susceptable of the tenderest passion, & that it is already so strongly impressed with the most favourable ideas of her, that she must be cautious of putting loves torch to it; as you must be in fanning the flame."[4]

Adrienne became pregnant soon after Lafayette's return. And on Christmas Eve 1779—at Benjamin Franklin's home in the village of Passy, on Paris's western edge, where the couple often visited—she gave birth to a son. Because Lafayette was in Paris, she sent him a note informing him of the event, a missive that also playfully alluded to his newfound status as a transatlantic hero: "Accept my congratulations, Monsieur le Marquis. They are very sincere, and very deeply felt. America will be illuminated, and, in my opinion, Paris should be too. The number of those who resemble you is so small that any addition to their ranks is a public service."

It was two o'clock in the morning when Adrienne's note reached Lafayette, but he already knew the name he would give their firstborn son—George Washington. Painful memories, meanwhile, haunted Adrienne of how her husband had been away for much of the brief life of their first daughter as well as the birth of their second. Thus, in the same note, she also expressed hopes that, during his visit, he would find time to savor fatherhood's pleasures: "They are so sweet that nothing else is near so good."

Compounding Adrienne's concerns, according to Maurois, "She had endured some months of suffering in order to give him this son, and had a right to his presence. Had he not written to her from America: 'Once we are reunited, no one shall ever part us again'? He spent a week with her, then resumed the round of correspondence and visits."[5]

———

Predictably, however, socializing, politicking, and scheming dominated Lafayette's time during his 1779 visit to France. Indeed, with his usual alacrity, those pursuits often blurred into one. Writing Benjamin Franklin in March to impart the latest war news, he began by mentioning en passant, "I am just Coming from Versailles where I went à hunting with the king."

In fact, after returning to Paris—when he and Adrienne were not socializing with Louis XVI, Marie Antoinette, and members of court society—Lafayette was settling into a close friendship with Franklin.

The Pennsylvanian had been in Paris since late 1776. With Silas Deane and Arthur Lee, Franklin had served as one of the Continental Congress's three commissioners in Paris. The three eventually negotiated the U.S.-France treaties of commerce and amity of 1778. After that success Deane and Lee, incurring Franklin's disfavor, would be successively recalled from Paris. But the 1778 treaties had heightened Franklin's status. That September, after France and the United States established formal diplomatic relations, Congress elevated him to the rank of minister plenipotentiary—ambassador—to the court of Versailles. Indeed, among the papers Lafayette carried with him aboard the *Alliance* was Franklin's official notification of that promotion.

Franklin was seventy-three years old when Lafayette returned to France. For both men that return was fortuitous: Franklin, garrulous and possessed of bountiful enthusiasms and libertine tendencies, had scant rapport with the two other American diplomats then based in Paris—Arthur Lee and (replacing Silas Deane) John Adams, both conservative Anglophiles of formal bearing.

By contrast Lafayette, upon arriving in Paris, immediately savored Franklin's company. Reciprocally Franklin was drawn to the younger man's impulsiveness and spirit of adventure. Moreover, to Lafayette's advantage, no individual of that time and place was better situated than Franklin to assist the returning nobleman.

Beyond his substantive achievements, Franklin, in Paris society and among the general populace, enjoyed a cultlike popularity. His image adorned clocks, snuffboxes, fans, statuettes, and medallions; fashionable women, inspired by the fur cap that Franklin wore in lieu of a wig, adopted the "coiffure à la Franklin." Lafayette's association with the estimable Franklin therefore had the effect of magnifying the young officer's growing celebrity.

Over the coming months, the two, in multiple collaborations, constituted an unlikely duo. Among their projects was a children's book they envisioned co-authoring that was to depict alleged British war atrocities of the American Revolution. Though never completed, the two did compile a list of twenty-six illustrations to be commissioned for the work. A caption, in Lafayette's hand-writing, for one of the envisioned images recorded dubiously: "Prisoners Killed and Roasted for a great festival where the Lanape indians are eating American flesh; Colonel Butler, and English officers, sitting at table."

Tellingly, it was Franklin whom Congress entrusted with overseeing the creation—by Lafayette's own cutler—of the honorary silver sword it had awarded the marquis. The weapon's hilt depicted four moments in his military career: Gloucester, Barren Hill, Monmouth Court House, and Rhode Island. According to John Adams, he wore the sword whenever he ventured out; it was at once propaganda for the American cause and tangible proof that he had achieved his long-coveted glory.[6]

While in France, Lafayette, in addition to his interactions with Franklin, regularly met and corresponded with other high-level U.S. and French officials. Inevitably he proposed invasions that he envisioned leading or coleading—among them one that Franklin helped plan, a joint naval and land attack by French forces along England's coast. Franklin had spent eighteen years living in London as the commercial agent for several American colonies and knew England and Ireland well. To raise money for America's Patriots, the two men's proposed expedition envisioned robbing countinghouses at the ports of Liverpool and Bristol. The raids were to be led by Lafayette and the Scottish-born American naval captain John Paul Jones, already renowned for his raids off the coasts of Nova Scotia and England. Indeed, Lafayette grew so convinced that the English expedition would be approved that he spent much of the spring and summer of 1779 at Le Havre awaiting orders to sail. In the end, however, like so many of Lafayette's other envisioned invasions, the proposal was rejected.

Undaunted, in February he nominated himself to command a new America-bound French flotilla then being planned. But to Lafayette's disappointment, that command fell to a fifty-four-year-old general—Jean-Baptiste-Donatien de

Vimeur, comte de Rochambeau—a seasoned officer (albeit commanding armies on land) whose experience included battles and multiple wounds during the Seven Years' War.

In his letter to the foreign minister, Charles Gravier, comte de Vergennes, seeking the command that ultimately went to Rochambeau, Lafayette had also outlined a lesser but face-saving assignment for himself. If the requested flotilla command was declined, he wrote, "I must leave immediately with the resources I request." More pointedly he nominated himself to "instruct General Washington" concerning the soon-to-arrive French forces. On March 5, 1780, granting that reduced mission, Vergennes ordered Lafayette to "hasten to join General Washington" and "inform him confidentially that the king . . . has resolved to send to their aid six ships of the line and 6,000 regular infantry troops at the onset of spring." Although denied the renown of leading his native land's forces to American shores, Lafayette savored the consolation he had secured: He would be the Frenchman who informed his adoptive American father of the welcome news.[7]

THIRTEEN

Burdens Wrong to Decline

On June 1, 1779, as the marquis de Lafayette was marking the sixth month of his return to France, a nervous Thomas Jefferson was seated in the state's House of Delegates in Williamsburg. Though he was never comfortable as an orator, his speaking duties that day were not onerous—confined to procedural matters.

Even so, on that day—a Tuesday—he had sound cause for his nervousness: The assembly, in a joint ballot with the recently established senate, was about to elect a successor to the state's departing chief executive, Patrick Henry.

When the ballots were counted, Jefferson had 55 votes, his rivals, John Page and Thomas Nelson, Jr., 38 and 32 respectively. With no candidate securing a majority, a second ballot was taken. This time, even after most of Nelson's votes shifted to Page, Jefferson eked out a 67-to-61 majority. But it was hardly an auspicious moment: Virginia faced an uncertain future, and for the new thirty-five-year-old governor, the moment lacked the aura of personal triumph that, a decade earlier, in December 1768, had attended his first election to the House of Burgesses.[1]

The war, meanwhile, then entering its fourth year, had grown unpopular across Virginia. From the Tidewater to the Piedmont, inflation undermined the value of circulating money, and though most of the fighting remained in the North, the British capture, in December 1778, of Savannah, Georgia, had opened a new southern theater; and Virginians feared enemy incursions into their state.

Those anxieties, in turn, provoked among state officials a painful self-consciousness of the Virginia militia's lack of battle readiness. Virginians also knew that the Continental army was deployed in places too distant to thwart a British invasion of their state. More particularly, the proximity of Williamsburg, the state capital, to the Chesapeake and its rivers rendered it vulnerable to an attack by sea.

Equally dispiriting for Jefferson, he entertained no illusions about the weak powers of the office he had assumed: Under Virginia's state constitution, drafted and adopted in 1776, the governor could not veto legislation and was required, in most decision making, to share executive authority with a cumbersome, eight-member "Council of State." Further diluting gubernatorial powers, the legislature appointed commissioners to oversee vital matters such as trade, war, and the navy.

Given those restrictions, Jefferson viewed his new office as more a challenge to be stoically endured than a welcome opportunity. On June 17, answering a congratulatory letter from Virginia political ally Richard Henry Lee, he lamented, "In a virtuous government, and more especially in times like these, public offices are, what they should be, burdens to those appointed to them which it would be wrong to decline, though foreseen to bring with them intense labor and great private loss."[2]

After his election as governor Jefferson knew he faced the certainty of spending most of the next year at Williamsburg—with no expectation of visits by his family in the near future. And after moving to the governor's residence in the summer of 1779, he began missing his family and the society that regularly gathered at Monticello. On June 25, to his friend the British general William Phillips, he wrote of his longing for the day when he concluded his gubernatorial duties and returned "to the same agreeable circle" that he so longed for at Monticello. That return, he avowed, "will be the most welcome of my life."

As governor, Jefferson had assumed responsibilities for the British prisoners that had been transferred to Albemarle County. And in that same June letter to Phillips, he also granted permission for Phillips—along with the Hessian general Riedesel, and both men's families—to travel to Berkeley Springs, a hotsprings resort 120 miles north of Charlottesville, in today's West Virginia. "No impediment," Jefferson assured him, "can arise on my part to the excursion proposed by your family and Genl. Riedesel's to the Berkeley springs for your amusement."

In permitting their trips, Jefferson seems to have entertained no suspicions that the two commanders might use their travel through Virginia's interior to scout routes for an invasion of the state. After all, Phillips by then had already been allowed unsupervised trips to Williamsburg, Richmond, and possibly other locales. Unbeknownst to Jefferson, however, even as he was granting the two generals permission to visit the resort, British soldiers, slipping away from Albemarle Barracks, were headed north. By July 17, when Jefferson learned of the breach, a trickle of escapees had become a stream—"not less than 400 in the last fortnight," as he alerted Washington that same day. According to the reports that had reached Jefferson, the Convention troops' escape had occurred, with "the connivance of some of their Officers," and the soldiers, to conceal their identity, were traveling with forged documents: "I mention this to your Excellency as perhaps it may be in your power to have such of them intercepted as shall be passing through Pennsylvania & Jersey."

On July 27, ten days after Jefferson had alerted him to the escapes, Washington wrote to Theodorick Bland, the warden at Albemarle Barracks. "I must entreat that you will use every possible means to have them recovered—and to prevent any farther desertions," he demanded. Ordering an end to Albemarle Barracks' lax security, Washington instructed that its inmates "must be well guarded and pretty much restricted—or the whole of the Army by degrees will slip through our fingers." In the meantime, "the men who deserted should suffer a close confinement, at least for a good while, both to convince them of their error, and as an example to Others."

Jefferson's friend William Phillips denied any culpability for the escapes. He had, he assured Bland, always taken "every care and caution" to prevent such incidents. As to the whereabouts or intentions of the northward-bound soldiers, "I cannot possibly know any thing concerning them after they have left the troops of convention," he wrote. "From that instance they are no longer considered upon our muster-rolls; nor is it a matter that concerns me." Moreover, Phillips added, because the prisoners of war had violated terms negotiated, in good faith, by him and other British officers at Saratoga, he regarded them as having forsaken "the cause of Great Britain for that of America." They were, in his eyes, "miscreants, who will embrace any cause, and change from party to party, from fear of punishment or hope of reward."[3]

By 1779 in his late forties, Phillips was a man of small physical stature rendered plump by decades of officer's life. Above his angular facial figures, his hairline, receding and mostly gray, nonetheless retained some of the darker strands of his youth. And if he seemed, in his letter concerning Albemarle Barracks, too brusquely dismissive of rank-and-file soldiers, Phillips was also no stranger to their milieu.

Unlike most British officers in the American war, Phillips had not been born into privilege. In his youth, hard work and talent, rather than social and political connections, had won him entry to the royal military academy at Woolwich and powered his subsequent rise through the ranks. His leadership during the Seven Years' War won him a reputation as a resourceful officer. Though on occasion short tempered and vain, he also had a winning smile and was known for his dedication to his troops. Phillips was also, as Jefferson had come to know firsthand, a gifted conversationalist.[4]

Jefferson eventually dismissed suspicions that Phillips or Riedesel had encouraged the Albemarle Barracks desertions. By then, Riedesel, his family, a military aide, and several servants, their travels approved by Jefferson, had already departed for Berkeley Springs. While taking the baths there, Riedesel learned of negotiations for a prisoner swap, to occur in British-occupied New York. There he and Phillips were to be traded for captured American officers. The deal's final terms remained unnegotiated. Even so—leaving his wife at the resort with plans to travel together later to New York—Riedesel hastily returned to Albemarle. Arriving in September, he arranged for the sale of his furniture and a new house—already built and paid for—into which he and his family had planned to move. By late November, Phillips and Riedesel, along with their families, servants, and aides—"forming a caravan of twenty persons, and twenty horses"—were New York–bound.

As they neared New York, however, a snag in negotiations stalled their entry into the city. Word of the delay reached the travelers as they were dining at a New Jersey inn. Jumping from his seat, Phillips—known for his explosive temper—banged his fist on the table: "This might have been expected of men who are all rascals!" he exclaimed.

The party eventually found its way to Patriot-held Bethlehem, Pennsylvania, to wait out the delay. In late November, however, under a negotiated parole—in which the two generals agreed not to rejoin the war effort until or unless the exchange's final terms were reached—both were permitted, with their entourage, to continue to New York.

During the delay Jefferson wrote to Riedesel, regretting the holdup but expressing hopes for "the possibility that we may again have a pleasure we should otherwise perhaps never have had; that of seeing you again." The prisoner exchange's final terms, freeing both men to return to the field, occurred in late 1780. The following year, Riedesel, his wife, and their children—including a newborn daughter, America—moved to Canada, where he assisted in colonial administration. The families of the two officers never returned to Charlottesville. In 1781, however, General Phillips did return to Virginia—but not on a social call.[5]

FOURTEEN

Blast Like an Earthquake

In January 1780, fulfilling thirty-six-year-old Governor Jefferson's wishes, Virginia's capital was moved from Williamsburg to Richmond, then a town of fewer than 770 inhabitants, fifty miles northwest of the old capital. Situated along the fall line of the James River, Richmond linked Virginia's inland and Tidewater worlds. And, by most thinking, Richmond—a hundred miles from the Atlantic—was less vulnerable to enemy attack than Williamsburg.[1]

In Richmond the Jefferson family and several enslaved servants soon moved into a wooden house, rented at the government's expense, on Shockoe Hill, not far from today's governor's mansion, near the intersection of Twelfth and Franklin Streets.

Though not Monticello, Shockoe Hill did seem, for the sitting governor, more like home by the following June, when the legislature elected him to a second term. But if Jefferson had begun his first term under troubling conditions, he commenced his second leading a state facing even graver threats. To Col. William Preston of Virginia's militia Jefferson—pleading for help in gathering troops and ammunition—wrote, on June 15: "While we are threatened with a formidable attack from the northward on our Ohio settlements and from the southern indians on our frontiers convenient to them, our eastern country is exposed to invasion from the British army in Carolina."[2]

While addressing new external threats, internal state problems that antedated his governorship also burdened Jefferson. Indeed, the provision of the soldiers and supplies needed to counter the British threat required a strong central government and a healthy state economy—neither of which Virginia could claim in the summer of 1780. A shortage of specie and dangerous levels of grossly depreciated paper currency in circulation continued to bedevil Virginia's economy and its government's finances. Moreover, an enemy naval blockade off the state's coast added to gathering woes.

Also troubling, by that summer word had found its way to Richmond of the capture, on May 12, of Charlestown, South Carolina, following a six-week siege by British forces under Gens. Henry Clinton and Charles Cornwallis. Given the engagement's duration, casualties on both sides had been relatively light— seventy-six British and eighty-nine Patriot deaths. More dramatic was the number of Patriots captured—2,571. Also dispiriting, the enemy had managed to seize 343 artillery pieces and a substantial haul of other weapons and ordnance.[3]

Unaware that General Clinton, leaving General Charles Cornwallis's forces in the South, had already sailed back to New York, Jefferson, on June 11, fearing imminent invasion, wrote to Washington, requesting ordnance and equipment: "Our intelligence from the Southward is most lamentably defective. . . . Charlestown has now been in the hands of the enemy a month, [but] we hear nothing of their movements which can be relied on. Rumours are that they are penetrating Northward," he wrote. "There is really nothing to oppose the progress of the enemy Northward but the cautious principles of the military art."[4]

Soon answering, Washington wrote that he could spare no reinforcements from the war's northern theater. Instead he urged Jefferson to do all he could to reinforce Gen. Horatio Gates's army. In the wake of Charlestown's capture, Gates, the hero of Saratoga, had been dispatched south, into the Carolinas.

On August 15, 1780, Jefferson wrote to Gates, offering his army five hundred regular troops. At roughly the same time Jefferson, leaving Richmond, ventured back to Monticello "to take some little recess from Business after a very long and laborious confinement." The following day, August 16, he learned that Gates's army had suffered a rout at Camden, South Carolina. Adding to his worries, he learned that many militia members of Gates's army, including soldiers from Virginia, had deserted. In the wake of the debacle, Nathanael Greene replaced Gates as commander of troops in the south.[5]

As the days of Jefferson's second gubernatorial term passed, his self-doubts grew. Even as allies beseeched him to seek election to a third term, he worried that he could not provide the leadership Virginia needed. "The application requisite to the duties of the office I hold is so excessive . . . that I have determined to retire from it at the close of the present campaign," he confessed to Richard Henry Lee on September 13. Jefferson attempted to persuade his friend John Page—an assembly member and former lieutenant governor—to seek the post.[6]

But John Page and others persisted in pressing Jefferson to seek a third term. On December 9, Page praised the governor as possessing "greater Abilities than can be fou[nd in] any other Person within this State," adding:

> I know your Love of Study and Retirement must strongly solicit you to leave the Hurry, Bustle, and Nonsense your station daily exposes you to. I know too the many Mortifications you must meet with, but 18 Months will s[oon] pass away.[7]

That October, a British fleet comprising six warships, carrying 2,200 soldiers under the command of Gen. Alexander Leslie, arrived off Virginia's coast at Hampton Roads. On the twenty-first, Leslie's troops landed at Portsmouth and briefly attacked nearby coastal installations. Reacting, Jefferson mobilized local militia units. Before the Patriots could reach the port, however, Leslie, acting on orders to reinforce Cornwallis, withdrew from Portsmouth. Even so, as the year neared its end, another, more formidable enemy fleet arrived off the state's coast. On Sunday, December 31, Jefferson learned that on the preceding morning, a fleet of twenty-seven vessels had entered Chesapeake Bay. Immediately he suspected them to be enemy ships—an invasion force commanded by the thirty-nine-year-old British general Benedict Arnold.

A former American general, the Connecticut-born Arnold had played key roles in the Patriot victories at Fort Ticonderoga and Saratoga. Although disappointed not to win greater recognition after each of those triumphs, in June 1778 he had been appointed commander of Philadelphia—a post in which he directed both military and civil affairs there following the British evacuation. In Philadelphia he soon met, courted, and—in April 1779—married Peggy Shippen, the daughter of a prominent local Loyalist.

When the couple wed, the bride was eighteen, the groom thirty-eight. Their two-decade age difference notwithstanding, Shippen was smitten with the general. Indeed, despite the cane that Arnold used to support a leg two inches shorter than the other—the result of a wound at Saratoga—he nonetheless cut a dashing figure. Resplendent in his officer's uniform, he also exuded infectious charm and teemed with tales of past military adventures.

Due to Arnold's habit of paying from his own pocket expenses incurred in the course of his military duties—and the army's perpetually laggard reimbursements for such expenditures—he was frequently in debt. Moreover, disputes arising from those and other transactions had resulted in a tangle of military investigations into his spending. Beyond that, Peggy's affinity for extravagances—culminating in Benedict's purchase for her of an expensive mansion outside Philadelphia—compounded his financial woes. Indeed, the couple's financial difficulties by then were so severe that they were forced to sell the mansion (which still stands as a museum) before they had time to move in.

It was particularly troubling for Arnold during the period that he was courting Peggy that he faced allegations by civilians over alleged kickbacks from a concession he arranged for a local merchant. After pressing Washington to convene a formal court of inquiry on the charges, he was, in January 1780, found guilty on two charges of dereliction of duty and publicly reprimanded. The rebukes infuriated Arnold, but by the late summer he had a new command: In August, Washington, seeking to make amends with a man he considered a gifted officer, offered Arnold the prestigious position of supervising the American fortifications at West Point, north of New York City.

Embittered at what he considered the army's ingratitude for his demonstrated valor—and suspecting French malevolence in its alliance with America—Arnold had also decided by then to betray his country. With enemy forces that summer, he entered into an agreement to—in exchange for money and a command in the British army—facilitate the British seizure of the vital Hudson River redoubt and the capture of George Washington. The former he planned to accomplish by leaving West Point undermanned for a British raid that he would arrange; the latter, by luring Washington to a conference near the fort. Serving as Arnold's British intermediary in his scheming was Maj. John André, a former beau of Peggy's during the British army's occupation of Philadelphia.

In late September, following a dinner that Arnold shared close to West Point with Washington and Lafayette, Arnold and André's plot—due to a miscommunication among the fort's putative conquerors—unraveled. In October 1780 André was captured and hanged by the Patriots. Arnold, however, managed to cross to enemy lines and soon received his promised command. Indeed, on December 20—after weeks of beseeching Henry Clinton for command of a major expedition—Arnold sailed from New York, Virginia-bound for raids there, at the head of a fleet of twenty-seven ships carrying sixteen hundred men.

On Tuesday, January 2, Jefferson, commencing 1781, learned that Benedict Arnold's fleet lay anchored at Jamestown, a berth suggesting nearby Williamsburg as the expedition's likely target. The next day, however, weighing anchor and catching a strong headwind, the fleet began sailing up the James—a movement that suggested Petersburg or Jamestown as its destination. Near dusk, however, the mystery lifted: The fleet anchored at Westover, twenty-five miles downstream from Richmond; its troops disembarked and began marching overland toward the capital.

Jefferson ordered all militia units in adjoining counties to the capital—even as he suspected that most lacked sufficient time to beat the British to Richmond. To General Friedrich Wilhelm von Steuben, meanwhile, Jefferson hastily wrote a letter, beseeching him "to consider the militia of every place as under your command from the moment of their being embodied, and to direct their motions and stations as you please." The Prussia-born general had been sent south by Washington the previous November—ordered to find his way to the Carolinas and there assist Gen. Nathanael Greene. But after Greene and Steuben, by arrangement, conferred in Virginia, Greene—aware of the growing perils facing the state—ordered Steuben to remain there.

Bracing for Arnold's raid, Jefferson ordered wagons outfitted to remove from Richmond the state's records and military supplies. Firearms and ammunition were to be moved to a foundry and laboratory in the town of Westham, six miles up the James—and, like Richmond, on the river's north bank.

Jefferson himself soon rode to Westham. There, between 7:30 and 11:00 p.m., he supervised the unloading of wagons bearing the weapons and gunpowder. Afterward, having sent word for his family to meet him at the Randolph's plantation Tuckahoe, he rode there for the night. The following morning—Friday, January 5—he sent his family on to a house at nearby Fine Creek, one of the properties he had inherited from his father. Hours later, while passing through Manchester—across the James from Richmond—he saw Arnold's troops nearing the capital. From there, in rain and snow, he rode to find General Steuben.

———————

That afternoon at one o'clock, Arnold led his troops unopposed into Richmond. Recalled the British officer John Simcoe: "The heights in rear of the town were gained; then the lower town." The few militia members still in the capital, "panic-stricken, fled from the place." Jefferson's enslaved servant Isaac Jefferson likewise recalled surprise among the town's inhabitants: "As soon as the British formed a line three cannon was wheeled round all at once & fired three rounds." Until the invaders fired, he remembered, "the Richmond people thought they was a company come from Petersburg to join them: some of em even hurraed when they see them coming: but that moment they fired every body knew it was the British."

British army regulations prohibited wholesale looting by soldiers; moreover Arnold—on December 20, the day his troops sailed from New York for Virginia—had issued strict orders to his troops forbidding "depredations in the country where the expedition was bound to." Beyond his desire to avoid damage to private property owned by Loyalists, Arnold was also mindful of how such acts might needlessly alienate other civilians who might be potential re-cruits to the British side.

Nonetheless, in addition to damaging public buildings, Arnold's troops, in-advertently or through willful violations of his orders, also destroyed several private businesses—including a print shop and a lumber warehouse; in at least a few instances there was also looting.

Meanwhile, learning of the state property's removal to Westham, Lieuten-ant Colonel Simcoe dispatched a detail there to burn the foundry. As the con-flagration reached the munitions stashed inside, an explosion rocked the countryside—a blast recalled by Isaac Jefferson, six miles away in Richmond, as "like an earthquake." The destruction in Virginia's capital resumed the fol-lowing morning; and that afternoon, twenty-four hours after its arrival, Arnold's army departed the capital. Marching away from the smoke cloud that hung over Richmond, the soldiers left behind a warscape of ruined buildings and streets. Toward nightfall, a slashing rain began to fall.

The morning of January 6, 1781, the day that ended with the enemy's departure from Richmond, found Jefferson still on the road. Having slipped across the James before Arnold's army reached the capital, he was still trying to find Steuben, under whose command he had placed the state's militia. Replacing an exhausted mount at Manchester, Jefferson spent the rest of the day riding from place to place. By the next day, Sunday, January 7, he had returned to Manchester, across the river from Richmond—in time to gaze upon the British forces as, departing the capital, they reembarked and sailed back down the James.

The next morning, recrossing the James, Jefferson returned to Richmond. Two days later, on January 10, attributing his delay to "unremitting exertions," he apprised Washington of Virginia's plight and the threat it now faced from the "parricide Arnold": "To what place they will point their next exertions we cannot even conjecture," he warned. "The whole Country in the tide waters and some distance from them is equally open to similar insult."[8]

PART THREE

In Common Cause,
1781–1782

FIFTEEN

"The Latitude of His Plans"

In early 1780, as the twenty-two-year-old Lafayette prepared to leave Paris, he remained piqued at having been passed over to command France's expeditionary force to America. In February at Versailles, he vented that displeasure in a cocky display of lèse-majesté. As witnessed by John Adams, he appeared before Louis XVI "in the Uniform of an American Major General, and attracted the Eyes of the whole Court more than ever." Moreover, "he had on . . . his American Sword"—festooned with representations of his battlefield triumphs and awarded by the Continental Congress—"which is indeed a Beauty, and which he shews with great Pleasure, upon proper Occasions."

On March 11 Lafayette sailed from Rochefort aboard the thirty-two-gun French frigate *Hermione*, reaching Boston on April 28. John Adams had witnessed his auspicious adieu at Versailles, but it fell to John's spouse, Abigail, to record the hero's return to American shores: *Hermione*'s arrival, she wrote, occasioned "universal joy of all who know the Merit and Worth of that Nobleman. He was received with the ringing of Bells, fireing of cannon, [and] bon fires."[1]

Setting off for Philadelphia, on May 10 Lafayette stopped en route at George

Washington's current encampment, at Morristown, New Jersey. There, he shared with the commander in chief the plans he brought of the French reinforcements soon to arrive. Lafayette savored being the bearer of good news, but was horrified to observe how months of missed soldier's pay, inflation, desertions, and paltry recruiting had degraded Washington's army. He was likewise appalled to see how worsening material privations bedeviled the troops still with Washington—including shortages of food, blankets, and clothing.

Magnifying Lafayette's perturbation was his knowledge that four thousand uniforms he had purchased in France had failed to reach the *Hermione* before it sailed. Hoping to make up the loss, he soon wrote letters soliciting clothes for the ragged troops, to Massachusetts delegate Samuel Adams, New York governor George Clinton, and other leaders in those states.[2]

It had been almost two years since Lafayette had last been in a battle. And from the first days of his return, anticipating the arrival of French forces, he was convinced that, with much of the British army diverted from New York to the southern Atlantic coast, the time was ripe to plan a joint Franco-American assault on the enemy's New York garrison. In May, British general Henry Clinton's army, recently based in New York, had marched into and captured Charlestown, and thereafter stayed in the South, conducting raids in Virginia and North Carolina.

On May 16 General Washington, writing to Lafayette, concurred with the idea of attacking New York: "It will be proper for the French fleet and army to pursue, on their arrival . . . the enemy at New York." Moreover, he added that, "it ought to be our first object to reduce that Post, and that it is of the utmost importance not to lose a moment in repairing to that place." Four days later, similarly imploring Foreign Minster Vergennes, Lafayette wrote: "If the French troops arrive in time, chances are good that New York is ours; if the English troops have time to reunite their forces, it will be necessary to consider fighting that army of fifteen thousand men if it goes into the field."[3]

Washington soon dispatched Lafayette to Newport to welcome the French fleet and serve as its liaison to the Continental army. But when the fleet finally landed on July 10, it was clear that any operation to recover New York would have to wait. Beyond the shortages of weapons and ordnance that still afflicted the Continental army, the arriving French force, expected to comprise 7,500 men, numbered but 5,100. Moreover, many of the French soldiers, suffering from illnesses acquired during the crossing, needed weeks of recuperation. And amid signs that the British were planning an attempt to retake Newport, those arriving troops deemed sufficiently fit were immediately put to work improving the island's defenses.[4]

In August 1780, after Lafayette's return from Newport, Washington assigned him to command a 1,850-man light infantry corps. Light infantry units, which tended to be created on an ad hoc basis, were made up of elite soldiers adept at fighting in close skirmishes; they performed as advance units that attacked ahead of their army's regular infantry. Lafayette's corps, organized before his return from France, had been created to participate in the eventually canceled New York campaign. And while plans for its future deployment remained unclear, he nevertheless relished his command of the unit.

Lafayette arranged for the elite corps' officers to purchase at cost uniforms from a merchant in France; to adorn their outfits he provided at his own expense feathers, epaulets, and cockades. He also purchased for each officer a handsome sword. For himself he asked France's consul in Philadelphia to find a horse "of a perfect whiteness and the greatest beauty"—an animal the diplomat soon purchased but for which, embarrassing the marquis, he refused to be reimbursed.[5]

Throughout late 1780, meanwhile, as Lafayette drilled his light infantry corps, George Washington worried over Patriot setbacks in the war's southern theater. In early November he had dispatched Friedrich von Steuben to Virginia to assemble an army of Virginia troops to send to the Carolinas to assist Nathanael Greene. Replacing Horatio Gates, Washington had appointed Greene his new commander of forces in the South. In mid-November, Steuben and Greene met in Richmond to discuss strategies. However, as Benedict Arnold continued his depredations across Virginia, Greene, with Jefferson's encouragement, ordered Steuben to remain in Virginia and mold the recruits already gathered around him into a capable army.

Over the coming months, however, Steuben's efforts against Arnold proved ineffectual. Moreover, the Prussian-born and -trained officer proved personally unpopular among Virginian's citizenry and state officials. And in late April 1781, culminating a season of disappointments, Steuben's army, at the Battle of Blandford, near Petersburg, Virginia, suffered a decisive defeat at the hands of British forces.[6]

Months before Steuben's defeat at Blandford, George Washington knew that he needed a new commander in Virginia—and Lafayette was his logical choice. Indeed, on February 20, 1781, appalled by Arnold's raids in Virginia, Washington had placed Lafayette in charge of a Continental army detachment of twelve hundred men, with orders to leave immediately for Virginia. Likely consoling Lafayette for not having had the opportunity to lead his earlier light infantry unit in battle, the new detachment, as described by Washington, "chiefly" consisted of light infantry.

Washington instructed Lafayette to march his detachment to Head of Elk, Maryland, the settlement near Chesapeake Bay's northern shore. From there he was to arrange a southbound convoy—or failing that, to go by land—and find a strategic location along the eastern shore of the Virginia section of Chesapeake Bay. He was further ordered to correspond and coordinate with General Steuben, then still commanding more than a thousand militia forces in Virginia. Finally, the marquis was ordered to liaise with four Chesapeake-bound French warships that had sailed from Newport two weeks earlier.

Writing to Jefferson, Washington explained that the French ships had sailed to the Chesapeake "in hopes of finding there and destroying the Fleet under the direction of Arnold." And in his orders to Lafayette, Washington—expressing still more strongly his disdain for the traitor—added that if Arnold himself "should fall into your hands, you will execute [him] in the most summary way."[7]

From Washington, Lafayette also soon received orders that, while in Virginia, he was to pursue not only Arnold but Thomas Jefferson's former houseguest, the British general William Phillips, who had by then returned to—and was conducting raids across—the state.

To Washington, Phillips—with his repertory of feints, sacrifices, captures, and gambits—was just another British combatant in the war; just another piece (perhaps a bishop) on the sprawling chessboard of the war's southern theater: "Whether General Phillips remains in Virginia or goes further southward," he instructed, "he must be opposed by a force more substantial than Militia alone."

Seemingly unbeknownst to Washington, however, in ordering Lafayette's pursuit of Phillips, he was setting the young man on a very personal errand—a mission that, for the marquis, tapped into motivations that transcended the usual causes that drive soldiers. To Nathanael Greene, Lafayette soon confided: "I will not only mention that General Phillips's Battery at Minden Having killed My father, I would Have No objection to Contract [, to restrict,] the Latitude of his plans."

Lafayette's alignment with the Patriots always partook of an element of revenge—a quest to retaliate against Britain for France's defeat, and his father's death, in the Seven Years' War. But now, with orders to pursue Phillips, his quarry suddenly included the man whom he held personally responsible for his father's death. More than ever, destiny seemed to be taking this son of the Auvergne to places and situations inconceivable to him when he arrived in America.[8]

After the final terms of the prisoner exchange that had freed Phillips and Riedesel were reached in 1780, both eventually became eligible to resume military duty. Phillips in particular had pined for a new command; and, in March 1781, he had received new orders: Henry Clinton ordered him to lead an army of 2,200 men to reinforce Benedict Arnold, by then trapped by Patriot forces in Portsmouth, Virginia.

Sailing ahead of Phillips to Virginia, however, had been another British fleet. On March 16, near the Capes of Virginia, that British fleet, under Adm. Mariot Arbuthnot, surprised a French fleet commanded by the chevalier

Destouches. The French admiral commanded the ships that the Patriots, including Lafayette, had been awaiting to reinforce their efforts to vanquish Benedict Arnold. After a brief but indecisive sea battle, both fleets withdrew—Arbuthnot to New York; Destouches, back to Rhode Island. The way was now cleared for Phillips's landing at Portsmouth to reinforce Arnold.

Leading a flotilla of thirty-one transports and three small warships, Phillips sailed from Sandy Hook on March 20. By April 15 he had landed at Portsmouth. Four years earlier, Phillips had surrendered his forces at Saratoga to Arnold and other Patriot officers. But now Phillips was Arnold's commanding officer. By Phillips's lights as a professional soldier, Arnold's betrayal of his country had been contemptible; moreover, the predicament that brought Phillips to Portsmouth—to rescue Arnold's army—hardly attested to the traitor officer's tactical acumen. Even so, months earlier, Arnold had conducted astonishingly successful raids on Richmond and other Virginia locales, and for those Phillips admired the Connecticut-born officer.

———

After Arnold's January raid on Richmond, he had been ordered to bring his army of sixteen hundred to Portsmouth and camp there for the winter. During their Portsmouth encampment—in anticipation of the expected French naval forces—Arnold's men were ordered to rebuild the port's fortifications, damaged during Gen. Alexander Leslie's raid there the previous October. Beyond that, they were instructed to transform Portsmouth into a secure base for future British operations in Virginia.

After reaching Portsmouth, however, Phillips concluded that its fortifications, even rebuilt, would still be vulnerable to cannonballs from the French ships. He also decided that he could ill afford to risk leaving his 3,500 British troops there as he had planned. Instead, he decided to combine his ships and troops with those under Arnold and head upstream. Thus, on April 18, leading the newly enlarged flotilla, Phillips set sail up the James River. As both Lafayette and Jefferson soon learned, Jefferson's onetime houseguest—no longer a prisoner and newly emboldened—was Richmond-bound.[9]

SIXTEEN

"Flattered by the Command"

On February 21, 1781, the day after being ordered to Virginia, Lafayette had penned the first of the many letters he would write over the coming years to Thomas Jefferson. The marquis's delight with his new orders, he noted to the governor, were heightened by his earlier command of a Continental army division of Virginians. Due to those ties and the fact that Virginia was his adoptive father's native state, "I Am the More flattered By the Command Which His Excellency General Washington Has Been Pleased to Intrust to Me."[1]

Responding in a March 2 letter—the first of many that Jefferson, in turn, would write to Lafayette—the governor delighted at the prospect "of lopping off this Branch of the British Force. . . . It gives me great Pleasure that we shall be so far indebted for it to a Nobleman who has already so much endeared himself to the Citizens of these States."

Lafayette, as it turned out, reached Head of Elk by March 3—three days earlier than Washington had told Jefferson to expect him. Writing from there to Jefferson, he reiterated plans for his Virginia campaign and detailed a range of requests—from horses to militia troops, weapons to scows—that he hoped the governor could fill.[2]

On March 8 Jefferson answered that while he hoped to muster the needed militia forces, he doubted that he could meet the other requests. Two days later, explaining that expected failure, he added, "Mild Laws, a People not used to war and prompt obedience, a want of the Provisions of War and means of procuring them render our orders often ineffectual."[3]

Virginia's predicament worsened through the spring; moreover, for Jefferson personally, a darkening of another sort fell over his domestic sphere: At 10:00 a.m. on April 15, his and Martha's infant daughter Lucy Elizabeth died. Just shy of six months old when she breathed her last, Lucy was the third child the couple had lost. A meeting of the State Council was scheduled for the following day, but Jefferson decided that circumstances required his presence at home. Beyond that, ill weather suggested that a quorum would be unlikely. "The day is so very bad that I hardly expect a council, and there being nothing that I know of very pressing, and Mrs. Jefferson in a situation in which I would not wish to leave her, I shall not attend to-day."[4]

Three days later, however, on the nineteenth—interrupting the couple's mourning—a report reached Jefferson that eleven square-rigged enemy ships were advancing up the James River. Chastened by January's British raid on Richmond and fearing the ships were Richmond-bound, he reacted immediately. Reminding militia officers of the consequences of their delay three months earlier, he called up units from all nearby counties: "Former experience will I hope induce a more prompt Attendance on this Occasion." Jefferson also ordered department heads in the state's government to remove records from the capital for safekeeping.[5]

After his January raid on the capital, Benedict Arnold's sixteen-hundred-man army had retreated to Portsmouth, at the mouth of the James River. And now, that April, his forces—combined with the two thousand soldiers under Phillips—were sailing toward Richmond.

Acting on Washington's instructions, Lafayette and his twelve-hundred-man army had spent much of that spring marching and ferrying between Head of Elk and the Chesapeake's southerly waters. Along the way they were dogged by erroneous intelligence concerning the whereabouts of friends and foes alike. Searching in vain for enemies to attack and allies with whom to coordinate, the troops fell into a wild-goose chase.[6]

In early March, after a French naval force long expected off Virginia's coast failed to disembark, Lafayette ordered part of his army to double back to Head of Elk. But as British forces continued their raids across Virginia, on April 11 Washington summoned Lafayette to bring *all* of his forces back into the state. And, by the seventeenth, having learned of Phillip's latest movements—and suspecting Fredericksburg or Richmond to be in jeopardy—Lafayette began marching his army south toward Virginia's capital.

In late April, as Lafayette approached Richmond, a flurry of letters deepened his rancor toward the British officer whom he blamed for his father's death. In dispatches that reached Lafayette via courier, William Phillips himself accused the marquis of violating war protocols—of failing to return the captured servant of Phillips' aide-de-camp, of firing on British troops from an American ship flying a flag of truce, and of detaining civilians guaranteed protection by British forces.

Pondering Phillips's successive letters, Lafayette knew that none of the alleged incidents involved forces under his command. But what rankled more was the letters' sanctimony: In the one alleging misuse of a flag of truce, for example, Phillips wrote of "a charge of the deepest nature to make against the American arms" and "the Compassion & Benevolence which has mark'd the Kings Troops." The letter closed with a blustery threat: "Shou'd you, Sir, refuse this I hereby make you answerable for any desolation which may follow in Consequence." Another missive—the one alleging the capture of noncombatant civilians—concluded with a gibe about the "the barbarous spirit, which seems to prevail in the Councils of the present civil power of this colony."

However galling Lafayette found Phillips's haughtiness, he chose to postpone answering him—the better instead to focus, for now, on beating him to Richmond. True to that resolve, Lafayette hastened to Virginia's capital. By April 29—commencing at sunrise that day from an encampment at Hanover, Virginia—his troops completed the final twenty miles of their march to

Richmond; and by 5:30 that afternoon, they were quartered in a building among the city's ropewalks—long narrow lanes in which workers twined strands fashioned from hemp into ropes—on Richmond's eastern edge. Set on an elevation above the James, the factory afforded a clear view down the river.

On the afternoon of April 30, the day after Lafayette reached Richmond, with only the width of the James River separating his army from the enemy, he was sharing a meal with several soldiers in a cabin overlooking the river. Interrupting their repast, one of the soldiers, seated before a window, abruptly "called attention to the fact that Generals Phillips and Arnold had advanced along the beach and were making an examination with the spyglass whilst their servants held their horses."

Moments later a banging rattled the cabin door. When opened, it revealed "five riflemen in hunting shirts and moccasins"—each "eagerly solicit[ing] permission to steal down to a point from which they felt sure they could pick off these officers."

Lafayette pondered their proposal, one he had every reason to accept: Arnold was, after all, a traitor, and Washington, Lafayette's adoptive father, had singled out the turncoat for summary execution in the event of his capture. Moreover, Lafayette associated Phillips with the death of his biological father.

Ultimately, however, the marquis declined their offer, "declaring that he would meet the enemy openly in the field but would authorize nothing like assassination." As a witness recalled, "This decision excited great dissatisfaction." Even so, by that age's code of military honor, sound reason underlay Lafayette's decision. Captain and sharpshooter Patrick Ferguson, after all, commanding a company of British marksmen during the Battle of Brandywine, had achieved renown for declining a similar opportunity to kill an unsuspecting George Washington.

Afterward, Lafayette recalled, the enemy forces, having "declined Engaging," soon scurried back down the James River.

That same day, April 30, the marquis did decide that the time had arrived to answer Phillips's war-crimes accusations. The letter Lafayette wrote that day—whether before or after he declined to order shots at Phillips is unclear—made no mention of Minden or his father's death. Indeed, no records indicate that Phillips ever knew that Lafayette fils held him responsible for the death of Lafayette père.

Lafayette promised Phillips to have his allegations investigated. But he concluded the missive by giving the imperious general as good as he had gotten: "The stile of your letters Sir obliges me, to tell you, that should your future favors be wanting in . . . [respect] due to the Civil and military . . . [officials of] the United States . . . I shall not think it consistent with the dignity of an american officer to continue the Correspondance [*sic*]."

Days later, Lafayette wrote to Washington of his "Rapid March" to Richmond—conducted, he pointedly noted, "not without trouble." He then gleefully recounted a report that had just reached him: "General Phillips Has Expressed to an officer . . . the astonishment He felt at our Celerity" and "flew into a Violent passion and Swore Vengeance against me and the Corps I had Brought with me."[7]

More concretely, beyond provoking Phillips's temper, Lafayette had spared Jefferson the ignominy of a second enemy raid, in a period of four months, on the capital he was duty-bound to protect. Equally gratifying, Lafayette was now acting under orders that entrusted him with safeguarding his adoptive father's native state. To complete that mission, however, he would need assistance from Virginia's governor to obtain badly needed militia forces and horses. But as he was about to learn, the increasingly beleaguered Jefferson was—even less so than when they first discussed the possibility—in no position to assure provision of those requested resources. Over the coming weeks, however, shared days in the crucible of adversity would provide ample opportunities for the two men to take the other's measure.

SEVENTEEN

Rumours Gone Abroad

On May 1 Lafayette learned that Phillips's and Arnold's armies, prevented from seizing Richmond, had "retired" to Petersburg, twenty-five miles south of the capital. Recalled army officer Ebenezer Wild of that day: "Between 5 & 6 o'clk the army was paraded on a large plain N.W. of the Town, where we were reviewed by the Marquis [La Fayette] and Baron [Steuben]."

Two days later Lafayette's army—newly heartened after saving the capital and learning of the enemy's retreat—departed Richmond to pursue the British forces. Before they left, Lafayette—in a nod to his resolve to move with greater stealth, and to the "exceeding[ly] warm weather"—ordered the men "to cut their coats short for their greater ease in marches."[1]

In late spring of 1781—even after Lafayette's timely arrival had spared Richmond from a second British raid—Jefferson's worries persisted. In the days before Richmond's rescue, the governor had confided, in his May 1 letter to assembly members, that he had contemplated temporarily moving the capital to a safer location. Immediate military threats to Richmond, meanwhile, lifted with Lafayette's arrival there.

But even before Lafayette's subsequent departure from the capital, Jefferson worried about the impact of "rumours . . . gone abroad" that Richmond had suffered a second raid and was even under enemy occupation. In a May 1 letter, he worried that the false reports might lead delegates to stay away from the legislature's next session, scheduled for the following Monday, the seventh. To prevent that, Jefferson specifically addressed members from counties close to the capital—those within easy reach of couriers and who, in turn, could get to Richmond on short notice: He wanted them to know that Richmond was free of enemy troops.

When May 7 arrived, neither assembly chamber, as Jefferson had feared, could muster a quorum. Therefore, on May 10, before adjourning, those members present resolved that the assembly would convene again on the twenty-fourth, but this time in Charlottesville.[2]

By rushing to Richmond, Lafayette had spared Virginia's capital a second raid. But neither Richmond nor the rest of the state were out of harm's way. British forces across Virginia—by then seven thousand well-equipped soldiers—numbered twice those of the ill-supplied Patriots. Beyond that, the enemy dominated the state's rivers and access to the Atlantic, and there was still no assurance of the arrival of either the Continental army or French reinforcements.

Attempting to reduce their disadvantages, the Council of State—on May 10, in a session attended by Jefferson and Lafayette—met and formally advised Jefferson to spend state funds to conscript another 622 men for Lafayette's army. Many Virginians, however, weary of the war, were already resisting both conscription and impressment policies—among the latter, particularly laws that sanctioned the seizure of horses for Lafayette's army.[3]

On May 15 Governor Jefferson left Richmond for Charlottesville. There, on the twenty-fourth, he and other assembly members gathered in the state's new temporary capital. Not until May 28, however, did the House of Delegates achieve what the Senate gathered in Charlottesville never attained—a quorum. As legislators shuttled between Albemarle County's wooden courthouse and meals at the town's Swan Tavern, they discussed worsening developments in a war in which each new week brought Virginia fresh perils. Most recently Phillips's and Arnold's forces—seemingly put on the defensive after retreating down the James weeks earlier—had headed back up the river; and on May 20, at Petersburg, had linked up with Charles Cornwallis's army, recently arrived from North Carolina.

Moreover, in many of the state's more westerly counties, mere resistance to conscription laws had grown into active sedition: "Those mutinyous rascals in Augusta and Rockbridge amount to a majority, a great majority," reported one correspondent.

By then Lafayette's army—leaving Richmond exposed to attack—was positioned about fifty miles east of Charlottesville, awaiting the coming of Anthony Wayne and an army of eight hundred soldiers. Together the two officers hoped to repulse an expected attack on Charlottesville by Cornwallis's forces. Meanwhile, throughout the state, militia units remained vexed by shortages of recruits, supplies, and horses. Beyond that, reported another correspondent, a lengthening shadow of demoralization seemed to be falling west-to-east across the state: "The people at present are really panic struck and have lost much of their military ardor."

For two months the assembly had balked at Jefferson's requests for stronger laws to compel militia service. On May 29, however, it finally acted. Acknowledging that "a powerful army of the enemy" was wreaking havoc in the state and that "our forces at present in the field are inferior to those of the enemy," the body authorized the governor to "order into service such a number of militia" necessary "to oppose the enemy with effect." The legislature also bolstered Jefferson's powers to compel conscription.[4]

House members likewise discussed what some, including Jefferson, considered the war's second front—the fight in the state's west against British-allied Indians. By royal proclamation in 1763, Britain had banned American colonists from settling west of the Appalachians. But, among many white Americans, the War of Independence had breathed fresh life into hungers for western land. Political leaders now saw in those domains additional territory for the young republic; large landowners, meanwhile, saw opportunities to acquire new landholdings and increase their personal wealth.

Jefferson's interest in western lands and Native Americans, even then, had been nourished by his extensive readings in Indian ethnology; and when opportunities arose, he was prepared to flatter tribal leaders friendly to the Patriot cause. Toward that end, in late May he interrupted the assembly's other business to welcome a visiting tribal chief, Jean Baptiste Ducoigne. The native leader—of mixed blood and hailing from the Ohio country—belonged to the dwindling Kaskaskia tribe. When Ducoigne called on Jefferson, revelatory of his esteem, he had already named a son after the governor.

In Charlottesville, Jefferson and his colleagues smoked a pipe with Chief Ducoigne. Jefferson, at the chief's request, likewise commissioned a medallion extolling his esteem for the chief—one similar to those, as president, he later supplied to the explorers Lewis and Clark to ease their passage through Indian territories in the Far West. The governor also delivered a speech. Like similar pronouncements by Jefferson and other U.S. leaders then and later, the oration made no reference to policies already being orchestrated to dispossess tribal peoples of their traditional lands, and to move them, by increments, to realms ever more westerly. Indeed, for now, the governor asked of his visitor only his neutrality in the present conflict: "This quarrel, when it first began, was a family quarrel between us and the English, who were then our brothers," he declared. "We, therefore, did not wish you to engage in it at all. We are strong enough of ourselves without wasting your blood in fighting our battles."[5]

Jefferson's second term as governor was to end June 2; and, once the House of Delegates obtained a quorum, he intended to set a date for the members to vote on his successor. Amid their crush of work, however, a misunderstanding occurred. Absent an explicit statement to the contrary from Jefferson, the legislators, misgauging the depth of his unhappiness in the office, assumed he was willing to serve a third term.

Presuming therefore that the ballot would be a pro forma affair—a rote renewal of the office's current occupant for another term—they scheduled the ballot for the same day, June 2, that Jefferson's second term was to end. Compounding the confusion, no one apparently noticed that June 2 fell on a Saturday. And when the error was noticed, the ballot was rescheduled for the following Monday, June 4.

The war, meanwhile, and its demands on Jefferson, indifferent to the official limits on his term in office, continued unabated through the weekend. Thus that Sunday, June 3—technically one day after the end of his second term—found him still writing official letters as the state's chief executive.

As he labored, however, Jefferson was also experiencing relief. Even as his by-then eight-room mountaintop house was undergoing one of its many renovation projects, he was reveling anew in Monticello's familiar comforts. Beyond that, at thirty-eight, he was finding solace in the knowledge that his burdens of office were about to lift. Indeed, on the eve of his anticipated permanent return to his beloved "agreeable circle," he could barely contain his happiness.

Two years earlier, under different circumstances, he had assured the same British general—William Phillips—who was now threatening Virginia that the cessation, then distant but now mere hours away, of his gubernatorial duties "will be the most welcome of my life." Even so, the letters Jefferson wrote that day—missives that under normal circumstances would have been forgotten as an insignificant deviation from legal niceties—soon assumed grave importance.[6]

EIGHTEEN

The Enemy at Monticello

During the final weeks of May 1781, General Cornwallis, upon learning that Jefferson and Virginia's state assembly were in Charlottesville, dispatched a cavalry detail, a detachment of dragoons, commanded by twenty-six-year-old Lt. Col. Banastre Tarleton, to ride there and capture the state officials.

Jefferson, by contrast, unaware of Tarleton's mission, was feeling anything but imperiled. Indeed, on Sunday, June 3—anticipating his release the following day from his gubernatorial travails—he settled into a welcome reverie. Even as Jefferson savored his new freedom, however, Tarleton's men were riding toward Charlottesville—eventually stopping that night near Louisa, Virginia—a village forty miles east of Charlottesville. Concluding a long day of riding, the soldiers had halted to rest themselves and their horses. There, observing the soldiers, John "Jack" Jouett, Jr., a twenty-six-year-old Charlottesville resident, overheard their conversations and deduced their mission.

Jouett's father ran Charlottesville's Swan Tavern, where Jefferson and the legislators had frequently gathered. Viewing himself as a latter-day knight-errant, the young man wore a feathered cap, commanded an encyclopedic knowledge of local roads, and was considered—not without cause—one of the area's most skilled riders. Then and there, slipping out of the tavern, Jouett decided to ride to Charlottesville to warn the state's leaders. Leaving Louisa at ten that evening, he commenced the forty-mile journey to Charlottesville, avoiding routes where he might be spotted by Tarleton's soldiers.

Jefferson that weekend had taken comfort in assuming that Lafayette—as he had weeks earlier when he saved Richmond from a British raid—would soon arrive in Charlottesville ahead of the enemy. He also believed that Monticello—discreetly located, with commanding views from which to monitor troop movements—offered a safer refuge from the enemy than did Charlottesville. Indeed, since late May, fleeing the latest British visit to Richmond, a clutch of state legislators had already taken refuge at Monticello. Crowding the eight-room mansion, in disarray with its current renovation, the legislators included Benjamin Harrison and Thomas Nelson, Jr., speakers of the state house and senate respectively.

Knowing that Jefferson and the legislators were at Monticello, Jouett had decided to hasten there first and afterward ride to Charlottesville. He reached Jefferson's mountain in the wee hours of Monday morning, June 4. While ascending the estate's wooded slope on horseback, however, despite repeatedly ducking he suffered multiple cuts to his face from low-hanging tree branches. By 4:30 when Jouett—later immortalized as "the Paul Revere of Virginia"—knocked on Jefferson's door, his face was bleeding from wounds that left scars for the rest of his life.

———————

By all accounts Jefferson remained preternaturally, even eerily, calm that morning. Informed of the approaching troops, he expressed skepticism about the warning—insisting that, regardless of its accuracy, there was still time for breakfast. Indeed, according to one version, before breakfast and sending Jouett off, he even offered the young man a glass of Madeira. After breakfast Jefferson ordered a carriage readied to take his family to a neighbor's farm. Martha remained frail from difficulties that attended the birth, the previous November, of their short-lived daughter Lucy Elizabeth. Even so, after bundling up their two-year-old Polly and eight-year-old Patsy, Martha was soon in the carriage waving good-bye to her husband. Imprudently, meanwhile, the legislators decided to return to Charlottesville, a decision that rendered them vulnerable to capture by the British troops.

After his family and the legislators departed, Jefferson rode to the top of a nearby mountain, that he called Montalto, on which he owned property. On its northwest side Montalto—410 feet higher than Monticello's 867 feet—offered a commanding view of Charlottesville. Through his silver-plated, mahogany-encased folding telescope, he surveyed the surrounding area. Confirming his skepticism concerning Jouett's report, he saw no signs of British troops. Before leaving, however, when he took one last look, a distant movement caught his attention: It was Tarleton's cavalry riding toward Charlottesville.

Hastening back to Monticello, Jefferson commenced gathering and stuffing into saddlebags and pockets, among other items, personal papers and documents from his careers in the law and government. Amid the packing, another unexpected visitor—the second that morning—appeared at Monticello. Christopher Hudson, a twenty-three-year-old officer en route to join Lafayette's forces, had also spotted Tarleton's cavalry. And, unaware of Jouett's Monticello visit hours earlier, Hudson had hurried there to alert Jefferson. Only now, as Hudson would soon inform Jefferson, Tarleton's dragoons were already ascending Monticello's slopes.

Once atop the mountain and inside the mansion, "I found Mr. Jefferson perfectly tranquil & undisturbed," Hudson later recalled. "I was convinced his situation was truly critical since there was only one man (his gardener) upon the Spot," the Patriot officer remembered. "At my earnest request he left his house."

Mounting Caractacus, his favorite horse, Jefferson "plunged into the woods of [an] . . . adjoining mountain." As he later recalled: "Knowing that I should be pursued if I followed the public road, in which too my family would be found, I took my course thro' the woods along the mountains." It was a close call: Ten minutes later Tarleton's cavalry reached Monticello. (In his Memorandum book, Jefferson later encapsulated the entire drama of June 4 in five words—"British horse"—cavalry—"came to Monticello.")

As the soldiers entered the house, two enslaved servants, Martin Hemings and another known as Caesar, were busy hiding the Jeffersons' silver in a storage area accessed by the removal of floor planks. As they heard the soldiers' arrive, Martin handed the last of the silver pieces to Caesar. With Caesar still below—and moments before the soldiers entered the room—Martin carefully replaced the planks. According to family legend, Caesar, meanwhile, not wanting to take any chances, "remained in the dark and without food for three days and three nights"—though Jefferson, for his part, later put the entire enemy occupation of Monticello at "about 18. hours."

Frustrated at missing Jefferson, Tarleton's forces, not lingering at Monticello, soon rode off for Charlottesville. Soon thereafter, they captured seven legislators, a group that included the surveyor, frontiersman, and explorer Daniel Boone. Still other assemblymen, meanwhile, who had evaded the enemy, hastened into the Blue Ridge Mountains, bound for the town of Staunton. Forty miles northwest of Charlottesville, Staunton had been designated—during the final hours of the state assembly's Charlottesville session—Virginia's latest temporary capital.

Jefferson, meanwhile, after fleeing Monticello on horseback, eventually caught up with the carriage carrying his family. Hours later they stopped for dinner at his friend John Coles's Albemarle County plantation, then spent the night at the plantation of another friend, forty miles to the southwest. On June 7, learning that the dragoons had departed Monticello, Jefferson returned there alone for a brief inspection. Tarleton, as it turned out, had given orders that nothing was to be taken or damaged at the estate. Thus Jefferson, upon his return, found scant evidence of the British forces' presence there; and later praised the "Sacred care" they had shown his property.

Relieved, he soon rejoined his family, and after several more stops in their flight, they finally landed, on June 14, at his Poplar Forest plantation, inherited from his father-in-law, John Wayles. There, on the five-thousand-acre spread that few knew Jefferson owned—as he recuperated from a riding accident suffered soon after their arrival—he and his family remained for most of the summer.

On June 12, meanwhile, meeting in Staunton, the state assembly had elected Jefferson's friend Thomas Nelson, Jr., to succeed him as governor. Thus—as the war continued to rage across Virginia and another man occupied the state's highest office—Jefferson, still hiding from enemy forces, bided his time at Poplar Forest. Amid his worries, however, he found consolation in one proposition—the certainty that the agonies of his own time in the governor's post lay consigned to an ever-more-distant past, or so he reasonably assumed.[1]

NINETEEN

"A Good School for Me"

As Lafayette, in April 1781, sparing Governor Jefferson fresh embarrassment, was saving Richmond from a second enemy raid, Gen. Charles Cornwallis, still in the Carolinas, was nearing the end of a dispiriting months-long campaign for military dominance in those climes, most recently against the cagey Rhode Island–born American general Nathanael Greene.

On March 15 Cornwallis had confronted Greene's army at the Battle of Guilford Courthouse, near today's Greensboro, North Carolina. From that engagement, both officers had hoped to snag a decisive victory. But after heavy fighting, Greene's army of 4,500—though outnumbering the Redcoats two-to-one—eventually retreated. Cornwallis's tactical triumph, however, proved a Pyrrhic victory. Official British casualty reports recorded heavy losses: 93 dead and 413 wounded. Moreover, for Cornwallis the battle confirmed his view—fatal in the long run to British hopes in the thirteen colonies—that to subdue the Carolinas he had to invade Virginia, the source of supplies and reinforcements filtering south to Greene.

At forty-two, Cornwallis, soon Lafayette's nemesis, was tall with an appearance of resoluteness offset by a walleye—the vestige of a boyhood sports accident, a hockey-stick blow to the eye. To new acquaintances the misalignment could suggest disengagement, but the better acquainted knew that Cornwallis's biography included robust military service stretching back to the Seven Years' War.

Like Lafayette, Cornwallis was an aristocrat who, early on, had yearned for military glory; and like Lafayette, he had found those first urges frustrated. Upon graduating from Eton and Cambridge, he obtained an officer's commission, only to find himself—again, similar to Lafayette's early frustrations—consigned to duties far from any battlefield.

In 1758 Cornwallis enrolled in a military academy in Turin, Italy. Upon completing his studies, his longings for combat experience were realized only after—once again like Lafayette—he arranged his own transportation to a battle theater. To be sure, Cornwallis, like General Phillips, fought in the Seven Years' War; indeed, perhaps unbeknownst to Lafayette, whose writings never mention the coincidence, Cornwallis's first combat experience had been at the Battle of Minden in which Lafayette's father had lost his life.

In 1760 Cornwallis won election to the House of Commons. Two years later—after his father's death and his inheritance of the title of earl—he rose to the House of Lords. In Parliament, often siding with Britain's discontented American colonists, Cornwallis numbered among only five peers to vote against the Stamp Act of 1765—legislation that played a major role in driving a wedge between Britain and the colonies. Even so, when war came to America, Cornwallis resumed his military career. Promoted to lieutenant general, he contributed, in New York and Pennsylvania, to early British victories. And, in 1776 and 1780, under Henry Clinton, he participated in British attempts—the first a failure, the second successful—to capture Charlestown, episodes that created tensions between the two headstrong officers.

Cornwallis and his commanding officer, Henry Clinton—at fifty-one, nine years Cornwallis's senior—shared a bond that reached back to their military service in Europe and, more recently, in June 1776, to the failed British siege of Charlestown (the Battle of Sullivan Island). Notably, their shared European experiences created for both men—as for many British officers who had served in the Seven Years' War—a pride often manifested as disdain for younger British officers who could not make that boast.

Those bonds notwithstanding, by spring 1781 the two men had grown apart—particularly since 1778, when Clinton, replacing William Howe, had assumed command of all British troops in America. Indeed, by that season a barely disguised mutual contempt poisoned their interactions. For Clinton, headquartered in New York, three strategic priorities dominated his thinking: safeguarding the British occupation of New York, completing the conquest of the Carolinas and Georgia, and recapturing Philadelphia.

Geography shaped Cornwallis's view that the key to British victory in the South lay in Virginia, not the Carolinas. "Until Virginia is in a manner subdued, our hold of the Carolinas must be difficult, if not precarious," he emphasized to Clinton on April 10, three weeks after the Battle of Guilford Courthouse. "The rivers in Virginia are advantageous to an invading army." By contrast, in Cornwallis's view, North Carolina's smaller if "numberless rivers and creeks" offered "a total want of interior navigation."

Moreover, Cornwallis—like other British commanders then and later operating in the American South's hinterlands—never generated the same levels of support from Loyalist populations that followed British occupations of Savannah, Charlestown, and the region's other coastal cities. Clinton eventually rejected Cornwallis's requests to bring his troops to Virginia as "dangerous to our interests in the southern colonies." However, by the time Clinton's answer reached Cornwallis, he and his fourteen-thousand-man army—leaving that April—had already departed North Carolina.[1]

On May 20, in Petersburg, Virginia, relieving the increasingly unpopular Benedict Arnold of his command, Cornwallis assumed control of all British forces in Virginia. Leading his expanded army, Cornwallis relished the idea of defeating the young French general who had prevented a second British raid on Richmond. "The boy cannot escape me," he allegedly vowed. He also soon learned that an arriving Continental army detachment, under Gen. "Mad" Anthony Wayne, was to soon enlarge Lafayette's force. But that intelligence, Cornwallis claimed, left him unfazed: "I am superior to La Fayette, even after Wayne joins him."

By May 26 the British general's army, by then on the James River's north bank, was encamped thirty miles southeast of Richmond—at Westover plantation, seat of Virginia's dynastic Byrd family. Writing again to Clinton, Cornwallis vowed, "I shall now proceed to dislodge La Fayette from Richmond, and with my light troops to destroy any magazines or stores in the neighborhood." Uncertainties, however, undermined Cornwallis's professed zeal: "Wayne has not yet joined La Fayette, nor can I learn positively where he is, or what is his force," he admitted. Moreover, Cornwallis worried over reports that his old adversary from the Carolinas was Virginia-bound: "Greene's cavalry are said to be coming this way, but I have no certain accounts of it."[2]

There was, in fact, no need to "dislodge" Lafayette from Richmond. Still awaiting General Wayne's army—and unbeknownst to Cornwallis—Lafayette, withdrawing in late May from Virginia's capital, had moved west. Before leaving, as time allowed, he tried to transfer all valuable public and private property remaining in Richmond to Point of Fork, fifty miles up the James.[3]

Washington, meanwhile, even as Cornwallis and his expanded army were roaming across Virginia, still believed that the British general would soon return to the war's Carolina theater to bolster Redcoat troops there. Anticipating that southward shift, Washington thus believed that the British threat in Virginia was about to lift. Against that background, in late May, he met in Wethersfield, Connecticut, with the comte de Rochambeau, commander of the French forces, then still in Newport.

The two planned a campaign against the enemy's New York garrison. Washington had, after all, long viewed New York as Britain's strategic center; attack and capture it, he believed, and Britain was finished in the thirteen colonies. Moreover, Washington believed, a collateral advantage would accrue from allied actions against the New York garrison: To defend the city the British commander in chief, Henry Clinton, would be compelled to move his forces, then in the south, to New York. That movement would in turn relieve the Continental army's Nathanael Greene and his army, still facing challenges in the Carolinas.

In Virginia, meanwhile, the reinforcements that Lafayette had long awaited— the Continental army regiment of Pennsylvanians under General Wayne— eventually, on June 10, found their way to the marquis's encampment—on that particular day in central Virginia's Orange County, seventy miles northwest of Richmond.

The thirty-five-year-old commander's "Mad" sobriquet had been bestowed not for conduct in battle but for his actions in a civil dispute earlier that year. Even so, Wayne's often-daring war exploits, then and later, rendered it an apt moniker—and it thus stayed with him. For Lafayette, Wayne's arrival marked a milestone: The marquis now commanded two thousand regular troops and about three thousand state militia raised by recent drafts.[4]

Aware of Lafayette's reinforcements, Cornwallis, in the coming days, moved cautiously, soon retreating with his forces toward Richmond and encamping there on June 16. Savoring his reversal of roles from prey to hunter, Lafayette boasted of his advantage to France's U.S. minister, Anne-César, chevalier de la Luzerne: "Lord Cornwallis seemed not to like these hilly terrains and withdrew toward Richmond."

The altered circumstances, Lafayette confessed, had given his own troops a refreshed taste for strategic feints: "We make it seem we are pursuing him, and my riflemen, their faces smeared with charcoal, make the woods resound with their yells; I have made them an army of devils and have given them plenary absolution." Indeed, he believed, the contest had grown personal: "It seems to me the enemy wants to make us think that the southern states belong to them. . . . My conduct toward him [Cornwallis] is calculated upon the same political motives; when he moves from one place to another, I try to let my movements give his the appearance of a retreat. Would to God there were a way to give him the appearance of a defeat."[5]

On June 21 Lafayette was encamped twenty-two miles southwest of Richmond, when he learned that Cornwallis, ending a five-day encampment there, had left Virginia's capital. Immediately Lafayette ordered his light infantry to seek out and, if possible, attack Richmond's late occupiers. To Nathanael Greene he confided, "What Lord Cornwallis Means I do not know But this Retreat will not Read well in Newspaper[s]."[6]

In fact, over the next four days—shadowing but never engaging Lafayette's army—Cornwallis continued his march toward Williamsburg, where he expected to receive new orders from Henry Clinton. Reaching Virginia's former capital on June 25, Cornwallis soon received his expected new orders: Worried about a joint Patriot and French assault on New York, and also contemplating a British recapture of Philadelphia, Clinton instructed Cornwallis to find a defensible port on Chesapeake Bay and to secure it as a base for the eventual transport of three thousand of his troops to New York or Delaware Bay.

Acting on the new orders, on July 4 Cornwallis left Williamsburg, bound for nearby Jamestown. There he crossed the James River en route to his ultimate destination—Portsmouth, Virginia, a port to the north where the Elizabeth River flowed into Hampton Roads, an estuary linked to the Chesapeake.[7]

It was as the Redcoats were en route from Jamestown to Portsmouth—crossing the James—that Lafayette and Wayne saw their opportunity to award Cornwallis Lafayette's fantasized "appearance of a defeat." The moment arrived on the morning of July 6—on Jamestown Island, as Wayne led a vanguard of five hundred men: Assuming—wrongly—that most of the Redcoats had already crossed the James, Wayne's vanguard commenced a surprise attack on what the Patriots assumed was a rear column. "The Marquis intended to attack our rear-guard, and luckily stumbled on our army," Cornwallis soon crowed to Clinton.

Having concealed most of his seven-thousand-man army in nearby woods, Cornwallis had drawn Wayne's smaller unit into a trap. What became known, after a local plantation, as the Battle of Green Spring stretched through the day and ended with inconclusive results: Lafayette lost 28 men, Cornwallis, 11. To Clinton, Cornwallis soon reported that his army had given Wayne's Pennsylvanians "a trimming." Had not night fallen, he boasted, they would have fared even better: "A little more daylight would have given us the whole corps."

Lafayette, for his part, remained resolute—but with a heightened respect for his nemesis: "This devil Cornwallis is much wiser than the other generals with whom I have dealt," he soon confided to a brother-in-law serving under Rochambeau. "He inspires with me a sincere fear, and his name has greatly troubled my sleep. This campaign is a good school for me. God grant that the public does not have to pay for my lessons."[8]

TWENTY

To Do Some Very Good Things

As early as May 1781, Washington and Rochambeau had decided to launch a joint attack by Patriot and French forces against New York's British garrison. In addition to inflicting damage on the attack's immediate target, the two hoped that the assault would prompt British commander Henry Clinton to transfer troops, then in the south, northward to assist New York's defense.

Weeks later, in June, Washington learned that Adm. François-Joseph-Paul, comte de Grasse had sailed from Brest with a fleet intended to increase French might in the war. In fact de Grasse was actually bound for the Caribbean with orders to attack British interests in its sugar-producing islands. Washington and Rochambeau, however, with no knowledge of the size of de Grasse's fleet or its destination, continued to plan their New York campaign.

In July, Rochambeau marched his seven thousand men from Rhode Island to Washington's latest encampment, at Mt. Kisco, a village just north of New York on the Hudson River. The two generals soon commenced their campaign against New York, but, still dogged by troop shortages, their attacks proved ineffectual. On August 11, however, Washington received news that, mitigating recent disappointments, soon led to new plans: Admiral de Grasse, his fleet's whereabouts until recently a mystery, was now sailing toward the

Chesapeake. Indeed, following its capture of Britain's Caribbean colony of Tobago and a stop at France's nearby colony of Saint-Domingue (today's Haiti), De Grasse's Chesapeake-bound armada now included twenty-nine ships and more than three thousand soldiers.[1]

In the weeks after the Battle of Green Spring, on Jamestown Island, Cornwallis's army had moved northeast some twenty-five miles. By early August it was encamped near the tobacco-exporting town of Yorktown, astride the York River near the Chesapeake Bay's southern end. There and at Gloucester Point, just across the York, responding to what by then had become a series of confusing instructions from Clinton, Cornwallis had ordered the construction of fortifications to protect British ships expected for the transfer of three thousand of his troops to New York.

In Cornwallis's lingering at Yorktown and Gloucester, Lafayette, meanwhile, soon spotted an opportunity. "If the French army could all of a sudden arrive in Virginia and be supported by a squadron, we would do some very good things," he confided, on August 14, to France's U.S. minister Luzerne. "I am thirty miles from Yorktown and Gloucester by water and thirty-five by land, and we can move there from either direction."[2]

Unbeknownst to Lafayette, Washington, thinking along similar lines, was already planning to send reinforcements to Virginia—for a combined Patriot and French land force that would coordinate with de Grasse's Chesapeake-bound fleet. "You will hear further from me as soon as I have concerted plans and formed dispositions for sending a reinforcement from hence," Washington wrote to Lafayette on August 15. "In the meantime, I have only to recommend a continuance of that prudence and good conduct that you have manifested thro the whole of your Campaign."

More specifically, he ordered Lafayette to position his troops to block any southward retreat by Cornwallis into North Carolina. Furthermore, to preserve the element of surprise, Washington cautioned against actions that might betray to the enemy the French fleet's imminent arrival.

Lafayette's response to Washington, written on August 21, teemed with fresh—and justified—optimism. After all, four summers earlier, upon arriving in the United States, he had been initially consigned to a largely ceremonial role. Now, however, the young officer suddenly occupied the war's center stage alongside its chief Patriot actor: "In the present State of affairs, My dear General, I Hope You will come Yourself to Virginia, and that if the french Army Moves this way, I will Have at last the Satisfaction of Beholding You Myself at the Head of the Combined Armies," he wrote. "When a french fleet takes possession of the Bay and Rivers, and we form a land force Superior to His, that Army must Soon or late Be forced to Surrender as we may get what Reinforcements we please."[3]

More than youthful exuberance animated Lafayette's cockiness. As Washington was aware, the young general's appraisal of his foe rested on inside knowledge. British deserters often provided the Patriots with useful reports, but Lafayette's most valuable information, as he reminded Washington on August 25, came from an even better source: "I Have Got Some Intelligences By the Way of this Servant I Have once Mentioned."

The servant was actually a slave named James owned by the Tidewater planter William Armistead, Jr. Promised his eventual freedom if he would assist the Patriots, James initially worked for Lafayette as a messenger; later, after agreeing to serve as a spy, he made his way to Cornwallis's camp. There he found work as a servant—by some accounts for Cornwallis himself. James's clandestine service for Lafayette, however, soon dovetailed with a proposal from Cornwallis's camp that he spy on the Patriots.

By late summer James found himself functioning as a double agent, ostensibly spying for both sides. In reality, however, as he fed the Redcoats false information concocted by the Patriots, James provided Lafayette accurate reports on the British, abounding in detailed information on enemy positions, troop strengths, and the progress of construction around Yorktown.[4]

Unbeknownst then to Lafayette, Washington was already Virginia-bound. For weeks, even as Washington was otherwise preoccupied with capturing New York, Rochambeau had been pressing him to coordinate in the Chesapeake with the French navy, and by late summer Rochambeau had won Washington over. Thus, on August 19, Washington's army, soon followed by Rochambeau's forces, had begun their long march from New York to the Chesapeake. To conceal their destination from Britain's New York garrison, Washington's generals, over those weeks, had conducted a series of feints—including marching three columns toward the city as if presaging an attack.

Beyond Washington's and Rochambeau's troops, the combined allied force on Virginia's coast was also to include Admiral de Grasse's twenty-nine ships, then Chesapeake-bound, carrying more than three thousand soldiers. Completing their 450-mile transport of men and supplies, Washington's and Rochambeau's armies reached the Chesapeake in mid-September. When they arrived, de Grasse's fleet had already been swinging at anchor inside the bay since August 30. Days later, however, the French admiral learned that his fleet's Chesapeake presence would not go uncontested.[5]

That summer, as Washington, de Grasse, and Rochambeau contemplated the Chesapeake, the bay had been on the mind of another military commander. In New York, Adm. Thomas Graves, Britain's ranking naval officer in America, had deduced that de Grasse, sailing from the Caribbean, was likely bound for the Chesapeake. Moreover, Graves also learned that another French fleet—the one previously anchored at Newport and now commanded by the French admiral Jacques-Melchior Saint-Laurent, comte de Barras—had recently departed Rhode Island. Moreover, like de Grasse's fleet, de Barras's ships were also likely Chesapeake-bound. Determined to confront both French fleets, Graves, commanding nineteen ships of the line, departed Sandy Hook on August 21 and reached the Chesapeake on September 5.

Fatefully, however, Graves was not aware that de Grasse's fleet, having reached the Chesapeake a week earlier, had beaten him to Virginia. Having taken on additional troops in Saint-Domingue, de Grasse also brought a force of 3,200 soldiers, larger than Graves had anticipated. Under other circumstances, two frigates under Cornwallis's command might have warned the British admiral of de Grasse's fleet. Unfortunately for Graves, however, both of those vessels lay bottled up inside the bay by the French flotilla.

Consequently, on the afternoon of September 5, when Graves arrived at the Chesapeake's mouth, he was unaware of the French fleet's presence. Spotting de Grasse's ships swinging at anchor, Graves immediately began forming his ships into a line for an expected confrontation.

De Grasse, for his part—with ninety officers and 150 sailors away on ferrying duties—was unable to deploy his full force against Graves. Even so, determined to engage the arriving British ships, he sailed into the bay with twenty-four ships of the line. That afternoon and intermittently over the next two days, the two fleets, though never fully engaging, nonetheless battled to a standoff. Two of de Grasse's ships suffered damage. Five British ships were damaged, and one was scuttled.

As Graves and de Grasse battled in the open sea, Admiral Barras, meanwhile arriving from Newport, reached the Chesapeake. Slipping behind the offshore combatants, his eight ships of the line soon lay anchored inside the bay, thus trapping Cornwallis's land forces. Portentously for Cornwallis, de Barras's arrival brought French naval power in the Chesapeake to thirty-six ships of the line.

Graves, meanwhile, took stock of his predicament—and the ramifications of a defeat of his vessels. After all, he commanded the only British fleet in the Americas, and its destruction would leave Britain's Caribbean colonies vulnerable to French naval forces. Judging the risks of further engagement too great, on September 12 Graves departed for New York, leaving Cornwallis's army to fend for itself.

Worsening Cornwallis's plight, a fleet of more than sixty ships assigned to him had been rendered militarily useless. Anticipating relief from the Royal Navy, he had ordered the removal from the fleet's warships of all their guns for use on land, and all their sails stripped for use in fashioning tents and bandages for the wounded. For the British general who had declared Virginia a key to victory, the odds against that triumph seemed to be growing longer with each of autumn's shortening days.[6]

TWENTY-ONE

Yorktown

Standing on Malvern Hill, a rise overlooking Yorktown, Lafayette gathered his thoughts. By late afternoon on October 14, as he prepared for the allied attack that evening, he could not help but hope, even expect, that the assault would deliver not just victory in the war's southern theater, but the long-awaited final triumph over Britain's effort to vanquish the American rebellion. Certainly over the past weeks, Lafayette and his men had trained hard for the coming assault.

Moreover, by all accounts, their deportment bore witness to their desired readiness. "His men look as if they are fit for business," recalled Maj. Ebenezer Denny, a recent recruit to Lafayette's forces. "They are all chiefly light infantry, dressed in frocks and over-alls of linen."

Even so, knowing he faced a formidable adversary, the twenty-four-year-old marquis was nervous. For him personally, after all, the attack—one way or the other—would likely conclude a cat-and-mouse game begun nine months earlier. For good measure, then, Lafayette and the forces he commanded were spending these waning daylight hours readying themselves for the moment when he gave the order to attack. And if Lafayette and his troops were on edge, they had endured a rough past few months.

For Lafayette personally there had been the incessant riding between army camps scattered across Virginia's sweltering, malarial Tidewater; most recently, during those rides, he had played the dual roles of, as he put it, "quarter-master and commissary"—"stealing salt, impressing cattle, and crying out for flour."

By early September, Lafayette had been bedridden in Williamsburg with fever, in the home of a local militia officer, St. George Tucker. On September 8, between spells of sweat-drenched sleep, to an aide he dictated a letter to France's minister Luzerne: Weeks of exertions, he lamented, "have ended up, very stupidly, giving myself a fever and a migraine. . . . I do not know if I am withering of old age, but for the past two days my twenty-four years have been well toiled."

Days later, from Jamestown, Anthony Wayne dispatched wishes of good cheer: "Try my Dear Marquis, to shake it off," he urged. As it turned out, the patient was already rallying. On September 9 Lafayette managed to mount a horse and review his troops.

As Lafayette drifted in and out of his fevered sleep, meanwhile, events beyond St. George Tucker's house were bringing a gathering momentum to the Patriot war effort. On September 12, after his Chesapeake Bay duel with French naval forces, British admiral Thomas Graves—stranding Cornwallis's army at Yorktown—had retreated with his fleet back to New York. Two days later, at Williamsburg, Washington's and Rochambeau's forces, completing their march from New York, arrived at Williamsburg to join those of Lafayette and other Patriot officers.

The following day, venturing to Tucker's house (which survives today), Washington visited Lafayette. It had been twenty-one months since the two had last seen each other; and, as recalled by Tucker, as Washington entered his room, the marquis "caught the General round his body, hugged him as close as it was possible, and absolutely kissed him from ear to ear once or twice . . . with as much ardor as ever an absent lover kissed his mistress on his return."[1]

By September 28 a combined allied force of more than fifteen thousand soldiers had Cornwallis's army of nine thousand men trapped. Allied land forces, positioned just outside Yorktown, were poised to strike from the northwest, south, and west. Offshore French naval forces blocked any escape by sea.

Three divisions comprised the Continental army presence at Yorktown— each led by experienced commanders: Lafayette, Steuben, and Benjamin Lincoln. Though captured and paroled in May 1780 by British forces in Charleston, Lincoln had, months later, rejoined the Patriot war effort courtesy of the same prisoner exchange that returned William Phillips to British service. Lafayette's Continental army division, though made up mostly of light infantry, consisted of three brigades—the one he had brought from New York and commanded for the past months, and two others recently created by Washington—one led by John Laurens, the other by Alexander Hamilton.

Hamilton's presence at Yorktown represented a long-sought chance for the sort of renown to which his friends Laurens and Lafayette had grown accustomed. Then twenty-six, Hamilton had served as a Washington aide-de-camp until that February when, after frictions with the commander in chief, he resigned the position. A year earlier, he had married Elizabeth Schuyler, the twenty-three-year-old daughter of Continental army general Philip Schuyler, scion of a wealthy Albany, New York–based Dutch-American family; and it was from his new father-in-law that Hamilton, days after his break with Washington, sought consolation: "I am no longer a member of the General's family," he wrote to him on February 18. "I have felt no friendship for him and have professed none." By the following September, however, with Lafayette's help, Hamilton, at Yorktown, was leading his first field command.[2]

As September waned and the allied forces continued to advance toward the Redcoats at Yorktown, General Cornwallis's forces—aware of their disadvantage and without firing a shot—moved back from a wooden palisade constructed to secure their outer defense. Tightening their net, the allies soon rolled siege guns beyond the enemy's now unmanned outer palisade. Further dampening the Redcoats' morale, as their supplies dwindled, they were forced to watch helplessly as the allies, soon encamped two miles from Yorktown, dug trenches ever closer to their position.

On October 6 more than a hundred allied cannons exploded into life, blasting from three hundred yards the innermost British fortifications. The next day's cannonade broadened to also target Cornwallis's helpless sail-and-gun-denuded fleet stranded in the York River. The allies' siege of Yorktown and the smaller British garrison at Gloucester continued over the next week, and by October 14 Washington's orders for the inevitable infantry attack—the coup de grâce—were in place: Facing Yorktown, French forces were assembled on the left, Americans on the right.

As recalled by Major Denny, the daylight hours of October 14 passed much like those of the past two weeks. "Our batteries . . . kept a constant fire upon the redoubts through the day." But the evening, unlike recent nightfalls, brought a stony silence. "The night was dark and favorable. Our batteries had ceased—there appeared to be a dead calm."

In the moonless night Lafayette's division led the allies' first wave of infantry assault. Within that division Lafayette's former aide-de-camp, Col. Jean-Joseph Sourbader de Gimat, led a vanguard battalion, followed by battalions under Hamilton, John Laurens, and Lafayette. Wielding fixed bayonets and axes, the attackers soon breached Cornwallis's inner fortifications. "You will understand that my heart was beating rapidly for the reputation of my light infantry," Lafayette recalled.

To the left of Lafayette's division, he recalled, a French column "with bayonets fixed to their guns" advanced against a British fortification. But, as he also described it, "the American attack" against the same redoubt "was no less prompt. They"—the Americans—"had not a single gun loaded and conducted themselves equally well." "Owing to the conduct of the commanders, and bravery of the men, the redoubt was stormed with an uncommon rapidity."

Afterward, according to Major Denny, silence returned. "The business was over, not a gun was fired by the assailants; the bayonet only was used; ten or twelve of the infantry were killed."

Allied cannon fire resumed that evening, and that night and over the next two days, it continued to reduce the British fortifications to rubble—in the process sending surviving soldiers of Cornwallis's army searching for whatever shelter they could find. "Shot and shell raked the town in every direction," Denny recalled. "Bomb-proofs"—enclosed bunkers constructed beneath ramparts—were "the only place of safety."

After sunrise on October 17 Cornwallis emerged to assess the scene. Shortly thereafter, a drummer appeared on a British parapet, beating out a crisp parley—the traditional drum pattern signaling a desire for a truce. Simultaneously a British officer appeared waving a white handkerchief. As the firing ceased on both sides, the officer and the drummer, leaving the British fortifications, began walking toward the Allied forces.

Negotiations began at two o'clock that afternoon and concluded two days later. During the interval Cornwallis, while visiting the Patriots, was stunned to find *his* undercover agent, James, appearing at ease in Lafayette's quarters.[3]

Another two days later, Lafayette, writing to Adrienne on the Patriot victory at Yorktown, recalled that he counted among the battle's "finest moments the time when M. de Saint-Simon's division"—forces from his native land—"remained united with my army." Moreover, he reported, "my health is excellent; I did not experience a single mishap during our operation." To another correspondent Lafayette was magnanimous toward Cornwallis ("I respect and admire [him] wholeheartedly")—attributing his defeat to poor decision-making by his commander in chief, Henry Clinton. Even so, Lafayette conceded, by acting as Clinton had ordered, "He [Cornwallis] established himself at Yorktown just where we wanted him."

Noting that, at Yorktown, the British general had been repaid for "the indignities" he inflicted on the Patriots at Charlestown, Lafayette reflected to Adrienne: "I do not wish to carry vengeance any further."[4]

TWENTY-TWO

Taps

W here is Mason, Wythe, Jefferson, Nicholas, Pendleton, [and] Nelson?" George Washington had lamented in 1778. As the Continental army that year—ragged, ill-equipped, and outnumbered—struggled against a resolute enemy, the commander in chief found himself bewildered by the seeming indifference and absence, physical and otherwise, of fellow Virginians to the concerns of the national government in Philadelphia.

Three years later, in October 1781, Jefferson wrote Washington to congratulate him on the Yorktown victory—a triumph unimaginable during those earlier, darker years. In his letter Jefferson could not resist a playful allusion to their shared Virginia origins: "I hope it will not be unacceptable to your Excellency to receive the congratulations of a private individual on your return to your native country, & above all things on the important success which [h]as attended it."

Jefferson assured Washington that his preference would be to visit Mt. Vernon and partake of "the honour of paying my respects to you personally." But, he added, such an outing, for now, would be impossible, owing to "the state of perpetual decrepitude to which I am unfortunately reduced." Though Jefferson's allusion to his "decrepitude" referred to the lingering effects of his midsummer riding accident, it also underscored another anguish bedeviling him.[1]

Jefferson was now retired from the governorship and returned to full-time residence at Monticello. But if he failed to share fully the American public's jubilation over Yorktown, he had good reason. Jefferson's governorship had ended months earlier, but its ramifications still weighed upon him. On June 12, meeting in Staunton, the state assembly had voted to conduct an investigation into Jefferson's conduct—principally allegations of cowardice—during his final year in the office. But because the legislators adjourned before taking up the inquiry, it wasn't until November 26 that, meeting in Richmond, they appointed a committee to investigate the accusations. By December 10 Jefferson, having rejoined Albemarle County's delegation, was again seated in the assembly; and two days later, absolving the former governor of all wrong-doing, the legislators adopted a resolution thanking him "for his impartial, upright, and attentive administration *of the powers of the Executive.*"

Attempting to justify themselves, Jefferson's colleagues noted that *"popular rumours, gaining some degree of credence, by more pointed Accusations, rendered it necessary to make an enquirey into his conduct."* But now that the assembly had a fuller—and exculpatory—view of his actions, *"tenfold value"* would be attached to his conduct as governor: "The Assembly wish *therefore* in the strongest manner to declare the high opinion which they entertain of Mr. Jefferson's Ability, Rectitude, and Integrity as cheif Magistrate of this Commonwealth, and mean by thus publicly avowing their Opinion, to obviate *all future,* and to remove all *former* unmerited Censure."[2]

The Yorktown victory had left Jefferson with lingering regrets about his own experiences during the war. Lafayette, by contrast, possessed few causes for wistful reflection. He had, after all, begun the conflict as a hapless suitor to the Continental army and concluded it a hero acclaimed on both sides of the Atlantic. Even so—though his regrets paled beside Jefferson's—the war, for Lafayette, had ended with at least one unrealized aspiration.

For a few weeks in spring 1781, Patriot and British forces fighting in Virginia had fallen into a stalemate; as Lafayette, in May, awaited reinforcements under

Anthony Wayne's command, so the enemy's armies under Benedict Arnold and William Phillips had awaited the arrival of Charles Cornwallis's army from North Carolina to reinforce their own numbers.

During that interval each side sought to project to the other an exaggerated sense of its actual troop strength. But, aware of their real numbers—and each expecting reinforcements—both armies, in the meantime, also sought to avoid major engagements with enemy forces.

It was during that interval, too—following the arrival on May 9 of Arnold and Phillips's armies at Petersburg, Virginia—that Lafayette required a diversion to protect the passage of a shipment of ammunition that he was sending to Patriot forces in North Carolina. To conceal the transfer, he had ordered an artillery shelling of the British forces at Petersburg.

Meanwhile, a detachment from Lafayette's army, led by Jean Gimat, soon took up a position on the Appomattox River's north bank opposite Petersburg and began shelling the British.

Two days later the bombardment stopped long enough for a British courier to cross the Appomattox with a letter from Arnold proposing an exchange of prisoners. Because Lafayette knew that Phillips was commander in chief of the army at Petersburg, he declined to officially receive the courier's letter. The following day, after another flag of truce appeared, the courier returned with the same letter. This time he also confirmed Lafayette's suspicion—which he had denied the previous day.

The messenger admitted that Phillips was dead.

———

Less than three weeks earlier, declining an offer by marksmen to kill the man he blamed for the death of his father, Lafayette had avowed his preference for meeting Phillips "openly in the field." Now, however—just as Lafayette père had reportedly been killed in an artillery shelling ordered by Phillips—so the British general had apparently died during a shelling ordered by Lafayette fils.

But as Lafayette soon learned, Patriot cannonballs had not dispatched Phillips. Unbeknownst to Lafayette, as his troops were shelling Petersburg, his nemesis—bedridden, delirious, and ravaged by fever—had lain inside a house owned by a Mrs. Boland, the widow of a prominent Petersburg landowner.

Phillips breathed his last on May 13; the precise cause of death—malaria, typhus, yellow fever—is now lost. He was soon buried nearby—in an unmarked grave, lest it become a target for Patriot vandalism.

———

After learning of Phillips's death, Lafayette, writing to Washington on May 17, grudgingly conceded that, following his earlier cantankerous letters from the general, more recent exchanges had displayed, "a degree of Politeness that seemed to apologize for his unbecoming Stile."

In a development of which Lafayette was possibly unaware, it had, in fact, been Thomas Jefferson who had prompted Phillips's newfound politeness. Earlier that month, when Jefferson was still governor, Phillips had sought his help in arranging for the safe passage through Patriot-controlled waters of a British ship carrying relief supplies for the Convention Army prisoners at Charlottesville.

Aware, however, of Phillips's accusations against Lafayette (and Steuben), Jefferson made clear that he would likely decline the request unless Phillips "made an Apology for his rudeness." To Virginia's congressional delegation, Jefferson recounted the episode. "This Gentleman's letters to Baron Steuben first & afterwards to the Marquis Fayette have been in a stile so intolerably insolent & haughty." Simultaneously condemning his former houseguest's rudeness and offering ironic praise, he added that he "personally" knew "Phillips to be the proudest man of the proudest Nation on Earth."[3]

———

Jefferson, meanwhile, though relieved, found cold comfort in his December 1781 exculpation by Virginia's assembly. The following May to his friend, fellow Virginian James Monroe, he recalled his gubernatorial tenure as "a constant sacrifice of time, labour, loss, parental and friendly duties," adding: "The affection of my countrymen was the only reward I ever asked or could have felt." The investigation thus came as "a shock on which I had not calculated." And though it had ended with a full exculpation, the "injuries" caused, he wrote, "inflicted a wound on my spirit which will only be cured by the all-healing grave."

The assembly's exoneration notwithstanding, Jefferson, had he been aware of it—and he possibly was—would likely have found more satisfaction in an earlier assessment of his gubernatorial conduct. Enhancing its value, the evaluation came from a man who, though often working at distances, had come to know firsthand the obstacles Jefferson faced as he labored to cajole a government and a people, otherwise disinclined to sacrifice, to contribute to the war effort.

In a September 1781 letter to George Washington, a missive otherwise teeming with frustrations about Virginia's executive branch—by then headed by Governor Thomas Nelson, Jr.—the letter's author conceded that inevitable obstacles came with the chief executive's office: "The Governor does what He can[. T]he Wheels of his Government are so very rusty that no Governor whatever will be able to set them fiercely agoing [*sic*]," he wrote. Then, almost as an afterthought—anticipating the outcome of the then-current investigation—General Lafayette added, "Time will prove that Jefferson has been too severely charged."[4]

PART FOUR

Parisiens,
1782–1785

TWENTY-THREE

More Mortification Than
Any of My Life

Ly spring 1782, an embittered Thomas Jefferson had resolved that his days
in public office lay behind him. Done with such duties, eventually resign-
ing from his Virginia assembly seat, he savored more time for writing. He
particularly relished working on a manuscript begun two years earlier in response to questions posed by a French diplomat in Philadelphia—on Virginia's
geography, society, ethnography, and politics.

To a visitor during those months, Jefferson, in his Monticello aerie, embodied
the unstudied graces of a philosopher-prince. François-Jean de Chastellux,
marquis de Chastellux, a writer and historian who had served as a major general in Rochambeau's expeditionary force, recalled him as a "man not yet
forty, tall, and with a mild and pleasing countenance, but whose mind and
knowledge could serve in lieu of all outward graces. . . . I found his first appearance serious, nay even cold; but before I had been two hours with him we
were as intimate as if we had passed our whole lives together." As Virginia's
governor, Chastellux noted, Jefferson had occupied that "difficult station
during the invasions of Arnold, Phillips, and Cornwallis." But now, having

concluded those trials, Chastellux found him "finally a Philosopher, retired from the world and public business, because he loves the world only insofar as he can feel that he is useful."

At Monticello, Jefferson was determined to spend the coming years with Martha and their two daughters—Patsy, now nine years old, and Polly, three. Adding to his responsibilities, Jefferson and Martha had taken in his younger sister Martha Jefferson Carr—widow of Dabney Carr—and their six children. Indeed, that May, providing all the more reason for Jefferson to stay put, Martha Jefferson was in the final month of her latest pregnancy.

On May 8, when Martha gave birth to their new daughter, the parents named her Lucy Elizabeth, after the infant they buried a year earlier. Lucy's arrival brought to nine the children the couple were raising. Describing to James Monroe his expanded responsibilities, Jefferson wrote that he now had at Monticello "a family advanced to years which require my attention and instruction" as well as "hopeful offspring of a deceased friend whose memory must be for ever dear to me."[1]

Martha's pregnancies were never easy, and Lucy's birth left her bedridden. Her husband, meanwhile, stayed dutifully close by—"never out of calling," according to a later account provided by Patsy Jefferson—who on the eve of her tenth birthday witnessed the daily scenes. "When not at her bedside he was writing in a small room which opened immediately at the head of her bed."

Over the coming weeks, as Martha's health worsened, family members and enslaved servants passed in and out of her room. During that period, according to an account that entered family lore, an exchange occurred that shaped Jefferson's remaining years: Though weakened and barely audible, Martha spoke to her husband: "She told him she could not die happy if she thought her four children would ever have a step-mother brought in over them." Holding her hand, "Mr. Jefferson promised her solemnly that he would never marry again."

On the afternoon of September 6, four months after Martha, at thirty-three, had given birth, her thirty-nine-year-old husband opened his Memorandum book and penned the saddest entry ever to darken its pages: "My dear wife died this day at 11:45."

Over the coming weeks Patsy and her sister Polly stayed close to their grieving father. "He kept his room for weeks, and I was never a moment from his side," Patsy recalled. Eventually Jefferson began venturing outside: "He walked almost incessantly night and day, only lying down occasionally, when nature was completely exhausted, on a pallet that had been brought in during his long fainting fit," Patsy remembered.

> My aunts remained constantly with him for some weeks, I do not remember how many. When at last he left his room, he rode out, and from time to time he was incessantly on horseback, rambling about the mountain, in the least frequented roads, and just as often through the woods. In those melancholy rambles, I was his constant companion, a solitary witness to many a burst of grief.[2]

Personal misfortunes suffered during the American Revolution compounded Jefferson's woes. There was the agonizing inquiry into his conduct as governor. The war also cost him financially. Tarleton's raiders spared Monticello, but a ten-day occupation in June 1781 by Cornwallis's army at Elk Hill, a farm he owned near Richmond, cost him dearly in property damage and what Jefferson called "carried off slaves."[3]

By 1783, even as Jefferson mourned his late wife and grappled with anguishes resulting from the war, delegates in the newly established Congress of the Confederation were struggling to bring order to their infant nation-state's affairs. The assembly took its name from the new nation's governing document, the Articles of Confederation—adopted by the Continental Congress in 1777 but not ratified by all thirteen states until 1781.

But even after the document's ratification, turmoil still roiled the young republic. Indeed, in June 1783, disgruntled Continental army soldiers, irate over nonpayment for their war service, had staged a "mutiny" in Philadelphia, in which they blocked congressional delegates from entering their usual assembly hall. Shut out, the delegates soon assembled temporarily in Maryland. And it was there—in Annapolis in June 1783—that Jefferson, resuming his public life, joined the Confederation Congress as a Virginia delegate. Taking an active role in the body's work, he drafted legislation to establish a uniform national monetary system. And to create an orderly process for bringing new states into the republic's union, he drew up legislation passed several years later, eventually known as the Northwest Ordinance (1787).

Among the issues before the Confederation Congress, however, none mattered more to its members than the negotiation of treaties of amity and commerce with the nations of Europe. Toward that end the members were, by late 1783, considering possible appointees to a commission that would gather in Paris to negotiate those treaties. The delegates had already appointed to the team New York attorney and politician John Jay, along with Benjamin Franklin, John Adams, and John Laurens.

James Madison and other delegates had long believed that Jefferson would be ideal for the commission—and congressmen from southern states were by then clamoring for the inclusion of a commissioner who understood their region's particular needs. But the delegates were also aware that Jefferson had been offered appointments in Paris twice before—in 1776 and, more recently, in June 1781, when he was offered a spot on the peace commission.

In both instances Jefferson had claimed that domestic responsibilities in Virginia precluded his acceptance. In November 1782, however, after Congress had renewed its offer, Jefferson had accepted the assignment. (Reacting to the news, the retired Washington—apparently still perturbed over his fellow Virginian's wartime conduct—had inquired of Robert Livingston, "What Office is Mr Jefferson appointed to, that he has, you say, lately accepted? If it is that of Commissioner of Peace, I hope he will arrive too late to have any hand in it.") Ultimately, however, Washington's wish came true. A delay in Jefferson's departure, and news that soon arrived of the peace treaty's completion, obviated the posting.

Jefferson, meanwhile, over those years, as he declined repeated offers to go to Paris, felt a growing wistfulness. After declining the posting in 1781, he had conceded to Lafayette that because he had never ventured to foreign climes, he ached to see more of the world; the resultant gap in his experiences "has given me more mortification than al[most] any occurrence of my life." Moreover, by declining the post, he lamented, "I lose an opportunity, the only one I ever had and perhaps ever shall have of combining public service with private gratification, of seeing count[ries] whose improvements in science, in arts, and in civilization it has been my fortune to [ad]mire at a distance but never to see."

In May 1784, therefore, Madison and his colleagues—aware of Jefferson's pent-up wanderlust—decided the moment was right to ask him again. Furthermore—also aware that an ailing John Jay was coming home to become Congress's secretary of foreign affairs—they knew that a spot had opened in the Paris delegation. Thus the congressmen unanimously voted to offer the open post to Jefferson. This time, without hesitation, he accepted.[4]

TWENTY-FOUR

"Your Name Here Is Held
in Veneration"

In November 1781, more than a month after the Patriots' Yorktown triumph, New York and Charlestown remained under British occupation. Moreover, the terms of the war's formal conclusion—a conflict that now involved Spain, France, and the Dutch Republic—had yet to be negotiated. Even so, Cornwallis's surrender had largely concluded the fighting in the seven-year-long war. And for Lafayette—whose post-Yorktown months had proved more gratifying than Jefferson's—the pause in fighting, whether temporary or permanent, presented an opportune interval to visit France.

Thus, after the marquis bade adieu to his troops and informed Washington of his desire for the visit, Congress, on November 23, readily acceded to his request. Indeed, in Congress's letter—drafted by James Madison—granting the leave, the delegates showered praise on both Lafayette and those who had served under him. Moreover, they beseeched him to "make known to the officers & troops whom he commanded," Congress's "particular satisfaction & approbation."

But the delegates also made clear that they did not expect Lafayette to be idle while in France. He was instructed to deliver letters to U.S. negotiators already in Paris, to update Congress on war-related matters, and to assist efforts to arrange more French aid for the young republic.[1]

On Christmas morning 1781—again, as in 1779, sailing aboard the frigate *Alliance*—Lafayette departed Boston Harbor. Joining him for the crossing was a coterie of other homesick, French-born Continental army officers.

On January 17, 1782, arriving at the port of Lorient, they again stepped on French soil. Four days later the marquis was back in Paris. There he headed directly to his in-laws' town house, the Hôtel de Noailles, where Adrienne and his children still resided. Clanking over the rue Saint-Honoré's cobblestones, his carriage halted before the building's gated entrance. It was early afternoon on a chill winter's day, and as he stepped to the sidewalk, several *dames de la halle*, women who operated stands in the city's markets, greeted him. Having heard through the grapevine of his arrival, they surrounded the returning hero, offering laurel branches.

Inside the Hôtel de Noailles, Lafayette was reunited with his two children—Anastasie, now four years old, and George, now two. As they embraced, Lafayette was struck by how different each seemed since his last visit two years earlier. To Washington he wrote of finding them "grown up so Much that I find Myself [a] great deal older than I Aprehended [*sic*]." But as he gathered the children in his arms, he was also crestfallen to learn that Adrienne was away for the afternoon, at the Hôtel de Ville—Paris's City Hall.

Three months earlier Marie Antoinette, after eleven years of marriage, had finally produced a male heir to the Bourbon throne. The queen and Adrienne were old friends, and shared experiences over the years had nurtured sisterly bonds between the two young women; and though the queen was four years older than Adrienne, the two even shared the same birthday. That day, however, Louis XVI and Marie Antoinette were marking another birth—that of their son, Louis-Joseph, born the previous October—and to celebrate they were hosting a banquet. The event, Lafayette learned, was to last several hours; afterward Adrienne was to join a procession of noble ladies, likely to take several more hours, to accompany the royal couple from the Hôtel de Ville to the Château de la Muette, a residence of the royal couple on Paris's western edge.

Hours later, Lafayette, still at the Noailles residence, heard the sounds of horse hooves and carriage wheels on the rue Saint-Honoré. Hastening outside to the town house's gate, he craned his neck, hoping to glimpse Adrienne as she passed by in the royal procession.

But instead of passing, the entourage halted in front of the Noailles town house. Earlier that day, learning that Adrienne's husband had returned, the king and queen had tried to persuade her to leave the banquet early. But, steeped in court protocols, Adrienne had declined. She did, however, ask if later that day, the retinue might divert from its usual course and pass before the Noailles mansion—if only so that she might glimpse her husband as the procession rolled down the street.

The royal couple had assented. Beyond that, Marie Antoinette had insisted that Adrienne ride in her carriage—ahead of where in the retinue (the order of its carriages ranked by descending order of social prominence) Adrienne otherwise would have been consigned.

After stopping in front of the Hôtel de Noailles, the passengers in the queen's carriage immediately spotted Lafayette standing at salute—resplendent in his blue-and-white gold-brocaded uniform. Adrienne and Marie Antoinette stepped down from the carriage; and as Adrienne, now twenty-two, embraced Lafayette, the twenty-six-year-old queen congratulated him on the Yorktown victory. Gathering throngs, meanwhile, realizing what they were witnessing, erupted in cheers and applause.

Moments later, by one account, "Trembling and faint with joy, Adrienne fell into her Lafayette's arms, and he carried her into the house." Moreover, "for a long time afterward, Adrienne later confessed, she would grow weak whenever her husband entered a room where she was and, afraid to become a nuisance to him, tried to restrain her feelings."[2]

The next day, when Lafayette was summoned to La Muette to discuss with Louis XVI the war in America, the king declined to promise more aid. "It is Generally thought in this Quarter, that the Exertions of America are not Equal to Her Abilities," Lafayette reported to Washington. Even so, the monarch did express satisfaction with France's newest ally, avowing his "Confidence, Regard, Admiration, and Affection" regarding George Washington.

Over the coming weeks Lafayette found himself awash in praise for America and its victory over France's rival. To Washington he crowed: "The Reception I Have Met With from the Nation at Large, from the King and from My friends Will I am Sure Be pleasing to You and Has Surpassed My Utmost Ambition." Typifying those plaudits was one from France's foreign minister, the comte de Vergennes. Two years earlier, the now sixty-four-year-old minister had rebuffed Lafayette's bid to lead France's expeditionary army to America. But now he was unstinting in praise: "History records few examples of as complete a success [as yours]," wrote Vergennes. "You may rest assured that your name here is held in veneration."

Predictably, Lafayette's court-society admirers included young noblemen who, aspiring to replicate his renown, beseeched him to arrange Continental army commissions for them. On Paris's streets, meanwhile, admirers of both high and low station flocked around him. And, over the coming months—in verses, articles, songs, and plays—writers and musicians expressed admiration for the returning hero. One evening, while Lafayette was attending the opera, a production of Christoph Willibald Gluck's *Iphigénie en Aulide*, a singer onstage was portraying a heroine about to bestow a crown of laurel leaves on the head of Achilles. Instead, breaking character, she suggested the crown more properly belonged to an audience member. The resultant applause ended only after Lafayette, rising from his seat, delivered a brief speech.[3]

Lafayette also found time for more formal honors—among them soliciting his expected official recognition by the French military for his role in securing America's victory. Louis had already honored officers in the French military for their role in that triumph. Lafayette, for his part, still held an officer's rank in his native land's army, but pined for a higher rank in that force. Eventually skipping several ranks, he was promoted from captain to *maréchal*—marshal—a rank equivalent to major general in the American army.

Uniquely, he thus soon held high-ranking officers' commissions in the armies of both France and a foreign nation. And lest that elevation create for France's military a troublesome precedent concerning other Frenchmen who had served in the Continental army, Lafayette's new rank came with a stipulation—that its singular circumstance applied exclusively to him. Such dual commissions would be denied to other French officers.

It was further stipulated that Lafayette's former commission as captain of the king's dragoons would be sold to an in-law, a younger brother of Adrienne, the vicomte de Noailles. Lafayette had paid eighty thousand livres for the commission, but he soon sold it for sixty thousand.[4]

Among the tasks the Confederation Congress assigned to Lafayette was to serve as unofficial adviser to its European diplomats; they, in turn, were instructed to defer to the young Frenchman.

As Lafayette plunged into the role, Benjamin Franklin was the first diplomat with whom he met. By then seventy-six and afflicted with gout, Franklin was increasingly confined to his home in Passy. But he retained affections for the young man developed during Lafayette's visit to Paris five years earlier.

Housebound, Franklin also welcomed Lafayette's willingness to call on officials at Versailles. By January 28, writing to Robert Morris, Franklin was beside himself with admiration: "[The] Marquis whom I have just now seen," he wrote, "has been at my Request with all the Ministers" and "spent an hour with each of them" pressing his case for a loan for the infant nation. And because, Franklin added, Lafayette was "better acquainted with Facts he was able to speak with greater Weight than I could possibly do."[5]

Simultaneously during that period, Lafayette traveled to other European countries and cultivated relationships with other American diplomats in the continent—including John Jay and John Adams. By February 1783, writing from Madrid to John Jay, Lafayette was playfully appointing himself as "your political Aide de Camp," adding, "If I may any how serve America I am Happy and satisfied."[6]

During those same months, distilling and deepening his thoughts on America's economic future—delving into politics, economics, trade, manufactures, and related matters—Lafayette also self-consciously became a writer: In 1786 his essay *Observations on Trade Between France and the United States* appeared as a twelve octavo-page tract.

Lafayette, during those months, also became swept up in that day's Parisian enthusiasm for all things scientific. In July 1782 he joined the city's Establishment for the Correspondence of the Sciences and the Arts—more commonly known as the Salon de Correspondance.

The club devoted itself to the dissemination of "useful knowledge"—broadly defined—for societal advancement. Stretching back to the seventeenth century, such clubs constituted a vital part of the community of scholars and intellectuals, straddling oceans and continents, that was also called the Republic of Letters. He also joined the American Philosophical Society, based in Philadelphia. Typical of such societies of that era, the organization pursued a wide range of interests, from physics and the natural sciences to inventions and the arts.

In that same spirit Lafayette in 1783 embraced Paris's infatuation with the hot-air balloon, a wondrous new invention of two enterprising brothers. In a display that the marquis soon detailed to the American Philosophical Society, Joseph-Michel and Jacques-Étienne Montgolfier—at Versailles, on September 19—sent a balloon gloriously aloft—its basket occupied by a duck, a sheep, and a rooster. Constructed of toile and measuring five feet seven in height and forty-one feet in diameter, the balloon inaugurated the modern age of aviation. Indeed, the spectacle became an instant cause célèbre for scientists, newspapers, and the public at large. Fashionable ladies even adopted *la coiffure à la montgolfière*, their tresses piled high and topped with a small faux balloon.

But some "scientific" achievements were, in retrospect, more authentic than others. Like many Parisians, Lafayette became infatuated with the Austrian physician Franz Mesmer, whose name survives today in the word "mesmerized," a synonym for "astonished" or "spellbound." Less remembered is the term for the public adoration that Mesmer inspired—"Mesmermania."

Forty-three years old when he arrived in Paris in February 1778, Mesmer, in public lectures, demonstrations, and a popular book, touted his alleged ability to cure various ailments—including convulsions, hysteria, and seasickness. By, as he put it, redirecting mysterious currents—"animal magnetism"—that flowed through the human body, all such ailments, he vowed, might be vanquished. One particular and oft-repeated procedure typified his showmanship: Twenty or more paying patients gathered in a room around a "banquet"—a circular, wooden-tub-like contraption, ringed by a rope and about one and a half feet high, from which iron rods protruded. Each "patient," taking a rope section in hand, was then instructed to press the ailing part of his or her body against the closest iron rod.

Wolfgang Mozart and Austria's empress (and mother of Marie Antoinette) Maria Theresa numbered among Mesmer's admirers. But even as public adulation grew, he was eventually denounced as a fraud by Franklin, Jefferson, and other leading lights. Louis XVI—unlike Marie Antoinette—saw Mesmer as a huckster. The king even appointed a royal commission to investigate the physician, and to Lafayette's chagrin, Franklin agreed to serve on the panel. Indeed, even as Mesmer's reputation waned, Lafayette stubbornly persisted in defending the Viennese physician—soon boasting to Washington that Mesmer had "instructed scholars, Among Whom Your Humble Servant is Called One of the Most Enthusiastic."

Indeed, one episode in particular that season attested, in the words of the historian Robert Darnton, to the inability of Lafayette and others in France to, "distinguish from the real and the imaginary." In 1783 Lafayette's name appeared as one of the largest donors on a list of prominent men who had contributed to an eventually confessed hoaxer who claimed to be at work on a pair of "elastic wooden shoes" that would enable him to cross the Seine by walking on water.

The marquis also contributed up to 2,500 livres to become one of a hundred members of Franz Mesmer's Société de l'Harmonie. Ostensibly the society was formed to establish a hospital to be operated by Mesmer and a school to instruct his students. Members, in turn, signed a contract in which they pledged, while employing his methods, not to divulge their secrets, to establish no rival societies, to take on no students of their own, to take on patients only on an individual basis, and to otherwise respect Mesmer's claimed proprietary rights to his methods.[7]

Throughout his Paris sojourn Lafayette, meanwhile, continued to act as a free-lance U.S diplomat—in France and in travels to Spain and Holland. Unbe-knownst to him, however, those forays were rankling more seasoned U.S. emissaries, and their grievances were reaching American shores.

By early 1783 both Jay and Adams were often irked by what they viewed as Lafayette's meddling—intrusions, they complained, that undermined the work of formally accredited diplomats.

To an American associate Adams griped in April 1783 that he found "the Instruction of Congress to their foreign ministers to consult with" Lafayette to have been "very ill Judged. It was lowering themselves & their Servants." A re-cent Lafayette request that he be accorded official credentials to participate as a U.S. delegate in the Paris peace talks, commenced a year earlier, likewise in-furiated Adams. With British troops continuing to occupy New York City, the Massachusetts-born diplomat feared that Lafayette's participation could un-dermine America's formal ministers at the talks.

The young nobleman, Adams inveighed, "has gained more applause than human nature at 25 can bear. [It] has in kindled in him an unbounded Ambition, which it concerns Us much to watch." Moreover, the breadth of Lafayette's ambitions and his ties to the court gave Adams doubts about his fealty to the United States: "This Mongrel Character of French Patriot and American Patriot cannot exist long."[8]

For his part, Lafayette had by then come to view most of America's official ministers in Europe—Franklin excepted—as unmotivated and ill suited for their tasks. In December 1783, writing to an American friend, he complained that Jay and Adams had called "but twice" at Versailles, and at that, only "when I pushed them into it."

Lafayette failed to gain a seat at the Paris peace treaty negotiations. But his sojourn in France was not without accomplishments—including helping to persuade Versailles officials to extend a loan of six million livres to the United States.

Moreover, while in France, he also tended to business matters concerning lands in Brittany that he had inherited while away fighting in America. The property had belonged to a great-grandfather, and while in Paris, Lafayette used his expanded wealth to assist numerous causes and individuals—including his friend the American diplomat John Laurens, imprisoned in London. Following a diplomatic donnybrook, Laurens was later paroled and released without funds there.

Lafayette also spent personal funds to assist the poor of Paris and his native Auvergne; the arts; French and American war veterans who had served under him; and the Irish-born publisher and reformer Mathew Carey, who had emigrated to Philadelphia in 1784. Using four hundred dollars provided by Lafayette, Carey established the *Pennsylvania Herald*, an Irish nationalist newspaper.[9]

The returning hero was also broadening his intellectual horizons. As the Lafayette biographer Louis Gottschalk observed, prior to 1782 the marquis's writings "only rarely" refer to Voltaire, Rousseau, Montesquieu, Diderot, Raynal, and the other major French philosophers whose ideas were shaping the ideas of the country's reformers. Indeed, among the era's only major *philosophes* who, up until then, had influenced Lafayette—and among the few still living when he returned to France in 1782—was the Abbé Raynal.

A former Jesuit priest, Raynal in 1770 had published *Philosophical and Political History of the Two Indies*. Published anonymously, the book comprised articles written by Raynal and various friends. The writings celebrated the New World's indigenous cultures and flora and fauna, but largely ignored the destructive impact of European settlement there. The book did, however, condemn the slavery that Europeans had brought to the New World. Raynal thus became associated with the cause later known as gradual abolition, which promoted incremental reforms—ranging from instruction in agricultural methods to land tenancy—by which enslaved peoples were to be prepared for eventual emancipation.[10]

Before coming to America, Lafayette had read *History of the Two Indies*. Even so, the book's antislavery message apparently failed to make an immediate impression—hence his seeming indifference to the slavery he witnessed upon arriving, in 1777, in South Carolina: "Sweet equality," he had written, "reigns over all." And shortly after reaching Philadelphia, Lafayette had been given a slave by his *La Victoire* shipmate Edmund Brice. A receipt indicates that Brice—in Annapolis, on August 4, 1777, for £180—purchased "a negro Boy for the Marquiss"; moreover, a letter from Henry Laurens to Lafayette in October of that year makes reference to "your black Servant." Lafayette apparently tasked the enslaved man with running errands around Philadelphia and environs. But beyond that, virtually nothing else is known about him—neither his name nor how long he was with the marquis.

This much, however, seems certain: By 1784, having observed slavery longer and more intimately than ever before in his life, Lafayette was rethinking his views on human bondage. Indeed, as early as October 1783, he had dined twice in Paris with famed British abolitionist William Wilberforce—in the latter instance at his by then Paris residence, the Hôtel de Lafayette, with, among other guests, Benjamin Franklin. During those years Lafayette also purchased a revised edition of *History of the Two Indies* that had appeared in 1780. By then he also likely knew its author personally. Lafayette's friend Franklin was close to Raynal, and like Lafayette, Raynal often enjoyed Franklin's hospitality at Passy. Tellingly, in his 1780 revision of *Two Indies*, Raynal lavishly praised Franklin's scientific work.

Moreover, Lafayette, as a Frenchman with firsthand knowledge of America, would have been, like Franklin, a natural interlocutor for Raynal. In the mid-1780s, after all, when Raynal and Lafayette likely first met, the marquis was a returning hero brimming with inside stories of the Patriots' war against the British; Raynal, for his part, deepening his interest in American matters, had in 1781, before the fighting was over, published a book, *The Revolution of America*. Consequently as the marquis, at Passy soirées, unspooled his tales of the New World, the Abbé would have been all ears.[11]

In February 1783 Lafayette's emancipationist activism combusted into a bold proposal that he placed before George Washington. "Let us Unite in Purchasing a small Estate Where We May try the Experiment to free the Negroes, and Use them only as tenants," he wrote to Washington, "and if We succeed in America, I Will chearfully devote a part of My time to Render the Method fasciona-ble in the West Indias [Indies]."[12]

Although slavery had been abolished in France in 1315, the institution, as Lafayette noted, persisted in its Western Hemisphere colonies. Beyond that, French entrepreneurs and ships played an active role in the Atlantic slave trade. Indeed, during the transatlantic slave trade, an estimated 1,381,000 Africans were carried into bondage aboard French ships. The port of Nantes alone, through which thousands of enslaved Africans passed each year, remained, as late as 1792, the focus of almost half of France's slave trade.

Much of Washington's personal wealth was tied to slavery. Moreover, Lafayette knew him well enough to not be surprised by the caution with which he eventually responded to the proposal: "The scheme my dear Marqs which you propose as a precedent, to encourage the emancipation of the black people of this country from the Bondage in wch they are held, is a striking evidence of the benevolence of your Heart." In the meantime, Washington promised vaguely, "I shall be happy to join you in so laudable a work; but will defer going into a detail of the business, 'till I have the pleasure of seeing you."[13]

In other realms Lafayette obtained more tangible satisfactions. On September 17, 1782, Adrienne gave birth to their third child—Marie Antoinette Virginie, named in part after Adrienne's childhood friend, now France's queen. The Virginie in the girl's name had emerged as a compromise between a father seeking a moniker evocative of America—in the end, the native state of Washington and Jefferson—and a mother seeking a Catholic saint as a namesake.

Two months later, to provide more space for his growing family, Lafayette—having reached France's majority age of twenty-five and thus coming into full possession of his wealth—purchased, for two hundred thousand livres, a town house on Paris's rue de Bourbon (today's rue de Lille). Though smaller and less imposing than his in-laws' dwelling, he soon had it remodeled, renamed (Hôtel de Lafayette), and filled with mementos of his affection for America—including, as a "chief ornament" in the new residence a portrait of George Washington. Writing to Benjamin Franklin's grandson, William Temple Franklin, also living in Paris, Lafayette soon also sought—for "the Most Conspicuous part of my Cabinet," his study or office—a replica of the Declaration of Independence. Straying, however, from the republican simplicity the document extolled, Lafayette instructed that his replica be "engraved in Golden letters." When the facsimile arrived, the marquis had it placed in one side of a double frame—the empty space, he vowed, to be filled later by the "declaration of the rights of France"—which by then he was confident he would live to see.

Unfortunately, however, in the coming years, the Hôtel de Lafayette also bore witness to another, less attractive aspect of the European legacy in America. Lafayette arranged to be sent to Paris, to live with the family as a servant, a young man named Peter Otsiquette, the son of an Oneida mother and a French father. Otsiquette was nineteen when he arrived in Paris in 1786. During his two-year stay at the Hôtel de Lafayette, the marquis routinely purchased European-style clothes for the young man. And, according to visitors, Otsiquette was also frequently called upon to entertain guests with ethnically demeaning performances: Garbed in "a belt of feathers over a flesh-colored tunic" and other "Indian" adornments, he would act out "scalp dance[s]" and other equally stereotypical European projections of Native American culture.

Over the coming years the Hôtel de Lafayette became a gathering place for American and French veterans of the overseas war and, more broadly, of American expatriates in Europe. Notably, it also buzzed with regular Monday dinners overseen by Adrienne during which the couple welcomed the extended Noailles clan, as well as the Jays, the Adamses, Benjamin Franklin, and other American and French guests. Attending one such gathering, John Adams's eldest daughter, Abigail "Nabby" Adams, although enjoying herself, nonetheless found its Anglophone guest list disconcerting: "It was intended as a compliment; but I had rather it had been thought so to introduce us to French company."

But if Nabby Adams found reason to complain, her mother, Abigail Adams, delighted in what she regarded as, compared with visits to other Paris families, the warmth and republican simplicity of the Lafayettes' hospitality. "I take no pleasure in a life of ceremony and parade," Abigail noted to a relative in Massachusetts:

> I had rather dine . . . with your family and a set of chosen o[ld] Friends, than with the Marquisses Counts and countesses Abbes and Great folks who dine with us to day. Madam de la Fayette, I will however except. I should always take pleasure in her company. She is a good and amiable

Lady, exceedingly fond of her Children and attentive to their education, passionatly attached to her Husband!!![14]

Venturing out, often alone, Lafayette regularly attended several salons. In Paris as elsewhere, salons generally took place in the homes of socially prominent and outgoing hosts—usually women. Indeed, through salons, hostesses, though possessed of few legal rights, wielded substantial influence in the city's public life. And though by the 1780s, the golden age of Paris's salons had passed, they remained a venue for witty conversations on topics ranging from politics to the arts, fashions to philosophy.[15]

Lafayette and Adrienne shared a close relationship. To Abigail Adams, Adrienne confided that although she had come to disapprove of arranged marriages, in her case her union had led to a satisfying life. "She said to me," Adams remembered,

> that she dissapr[o]ved very much the Manner in which the conjugal connection was formed in this Country. I was married said she before I was capable of Love. It was very happy for me that my friends made so wise a choice. I made it the Study of my Life to perform my duty and I have always been so happy as to find my pleasures result from the performance of my duty.

Adrienne's contentment notwithstanding, her husband, Gilbert, throughout their marriage continued to pursue the company of other women—and it was through Paris's salons and their collateral circles that he established those liaisons. Notably, after Lafayette returned to Paris from America, Charlotte Gabrielle Elisabeth Aglaé de Puget de Barbantane, comtesse de Hunolstein—who had spurned him in the 1770s—now welcomed a dalliance with the hero of Yorktown.

Indeed, their liaison soon became fodder for Parisian gossip and an embarrassment for her husband's family. It also grew increasingly tortured—racked by mutual incriminations. "You are too cruel, my dear," Lafayette wrote her in March 1783. "You know the torments of my heart, you know that it is torn between love and duty." Later that season, at Aglaé's insistence, the two ended the affair; shortly thereafter she entered a convent.

Well before Aglaé and Lafayette's breakup, however, he had plunged into another affair. Diane-Adélaïde de Damas d'Antiguy, comtesse de Simiane, lady-in-waiting to the comtesse de Provence, was twenty-two years old when she met Lafayette. To a friend he described her as "pretty" and "amiable." Without mentioning her name, but with Madame Simiane clearly in mind, he later recalled her—if briskly—in a passage of an early memoir: "Our relationship went from esteem all the way to the contrary sentiment and was finally terminated by a catastrophe unconnected with me."

But his allusion to "a catastrophe unconnected with me" concealed a season of turmoil. In March 1787, *Mémoires secrets*, an underground Paris publication, reported: "Rumor has it that Monsieur the Comte Simiane, husband of the renowned beauty Madame Simiane . . . killed himself a few days ago in a fit of jealously over the Marquis de Lafayette."

The tragedy, however, had hardly "terminated" their relationship: It lasted for decades—albeit surviving correspondence suggests it was sustained less by romance than by a shared passions for politics. Unapologetically monarchist in her views, Madame de Simiane over the years became a reliable private foil to Lafayette's public liberalism.

For Adrienne, meanwhile, whatever pain her husband's infidelities inflicted, she maintained a resolutely cheerful public face—apparently secure in his abundantly evident love of her and their *ménage*: Daughter Virginie later recalled her possessing "an exalted delicacy which removed her from any suspicion of jealousy, or at least of the petty actions which ordinarily follow therefrom."

Lafayette, for his part, apparently suffered no remorse over his strayings. His memoirs barely mention them, a reticence that seemed to owe less to shame or embarrassment than to his view of their insignificance: "I shall spare you also the confession of an unedifying youth, and even of the story of two romances dedicated to beauties who were then very celebrated, in which my head had a larger part than my heart," he wrote. "It is more pleasant for me to speak of the tender and stable affection that I never cease to feel for the woman whom I had the good fortune to marry."[16]

Lafayette, by late 1782, was missing his adopted land and longed to return to America. But before he could arrange his return, his ongoing hunger for military glory overwhelmed that longing. In December 1782, with peace negotiations stalled, he traveled to Brest. There—after his hopes of leading an allied invasion of Canada were once again dashed—he focused on a contemplated Franco-Spanish raid on British islands in the Caribbean; and when that idea too was abandoned, he remained undaunted: "We shall have war," he wrote to his friend Prince Poix: "I shall not return before next winter."

From Brest, Lafayette sailed to Cádiz, arriving on December 23 at the Spanish port. There, joining Admiral d'Estaing, he aspired to help lead Spanish and French forces preparing to join an already-ongoing siege by Spain's army of Britain's tiny Gibraltar colony.

In 1779, when Spain entered the war, Madrid had not formally recognized the United States. Therefore the United States was not a signatory to the Treaty of Aranjuez, between France and Spain, by which Spain entered the conflict. By the pact's terms Spain agreed to ally with France in warring against Britain, and France agreed to assist Spain in efforts to recover various former colonies lost to Britain—particularly Gibraltar, the port at the Iberian Peninsula's southern tip. Since 1779 Spanish and French forces had made multiple unsuccessful efforts to recapture the Mediterranean entrepôt lost to Spain in 1704. Against that background, in late 1782 as negotiators in Paris edged toward a settlement to end the long war, forces were gathering in Cádiz, seventy-five miles northwest of Gibraltar, in hopes of finally seizing the prized port before the treaty's final terms were reached.

To Adrienne, Lafayette wrote: "My dear heart, We reached Cadiz yesterday. . . . We are awaiting certain political decisions: I only wish that they might be the occasion of bringing me back to you. . . . How I long to embrace you." But in Cádiz, a city that otherwise bored him, he also found time for "a beauty with black eyes" as well as an "English lady less beautiful than kind." Likewise, Lafayette found time to assure Madame Hunolstein of his devotions and to write yet another letter to Prince Poix that extolled the virtues of Madame Simiane ("so pretty, charming, engaging, noble and sincere").[17]

Like so many of Lafayette's plans, the Gibraltar project unraveled before it began: When word reached Cádiz of an imminent armistice, the mission was canceled. Lafayette consoled himself with the knowledge that his next visit to the United States would take place after it finally became, in the entire world's eyes, an officially independent country. Likewise, he would also be able to visit George Washington, now retired at Mt. Vernon.[18]

The treaty ending the war went into effect on May 12, 1784. Two weeks later Lafayette left Paris for Brittany. There, from the port of Lorient, on about June 28—accompanied by a young aide, the chevalier de Caraman—he sailed for America aboard *Le Courier de New York*, one of five first-class packets, mail ships, recently placed into service by France's government to provide monthly sailings between U.S. and French ports. Indeed, somewhere on the broad Atlantic that July 1784, Lafayette's westbound *Le Courier de New York* would cross the path of the *Ceres*, an eastbound brig whose list of passengers included Thomas Jefferson.

Aboard *Le Courier de New York*, at Lorient, on the eve of its sailing, as Lafayette and Caraman adjusted their hammocks and otherwise prepared for their departure, the marquis found time to write to Adrienne. Bracing for his sixth Atlantic crossing in a period of seven years, he informed her, he was thus resigned to "what my mental and physical being will always suffer at being confined." But this voyage would come, he added, with one consolation—a new regimen for protecting against his usual seasickness; he planned, he informed her, to "fortify myself with magnetism, camphor, and treacle tablets."

Among those palliatives, however, one in particular seemed obviously untenable by Lafayette's lights: "In recommending that I embrace the mainmast, Mesmer did not know, and I forgot, that it is coated with tar up to a certain height, and hugging it is absolutely impossible without getting tarred from head to foot."[19]

TWENTY-FIVE

Paris Autumn

In May 1784, when Thomas Jefferson accepted John Jay's vacated spot on the Paris commission, the Confederation Congress expected him to leave promptly for France. Nonetheless its delegates assumed he would find time to return to Monticello to pack and tie up his affairs.

But in Annapolis, after accepting the appointment, another idea struck Jefferson. His selection, he knew, was based in part on his knowledge of Virginia and the rest of the South's commercial needs. But it occurred to him that his success in Paris would also turn on his ability to represent *all* of the infant republic's states: "I am now to take my leave of the jostlings of states and to repair [to] a feild [*sic*] where the divisions will be fewer but on a larger scale," he wrote to James Madison.

From his travels Jefferson knew Maryland, Pennsylvania, New Jersey, Delaware, and New York. But there was one region that he had never visited—New England. Thus, forgoing a return trip to Monticello before sailing for France, he decided to conduct a brief tour of New England.

He also decided to bring to Paris his eldest daughter, Patsy, by then eleven years old. In November 1783, en route to join the Confederation Congress in Annapolis, he had left her in Philadelphia to live with and be instructed by, among other tutors, Mary John Hopkinson, the widowed mother of his friend Thomas Hopkinson. Patsy and her father were close, and he believed that living in France would be culturally enriching for her.

Jefferson would likewise bring to Paris his enslaved personal servant James Hemings, by then in his late teens and living at Monticello. Hastily writing to relatives and associates in Virginia, he also made arrangements for the handling of his business affairs during his absence and for the care of the other children living under his roof. For the time being his relatives Francis and Elizabeth Eppes would care for his two younger daughters, Lucy Elizabeth and Polly. James Madison, meanwhile, agreed to assist Jefferson's sister Martha in directing the education—the selection of schools and colleges—of her two sons from her marriage to the late Dabney Carr.

Also agreeing to join Jefferson in Paris, but at a later date—to serve as his private secretary—was his protégé, the lawyer William Short. Twenty-four years old, Short—distantly related to Jefferson through the Wayles family—had, while studying law at William and Mary, recently fallen into Jefferson's orbit. Even more recently he had lived with the family at Poplar Forest after they fled Tarleton's raiders. Having studied French but never been abroad, Short accepted Jefferson's invitation, agreeing to the proviso that his formal appointment would come after his arrival in Paris.

Leaving Annapolis on May 7, Jefferson traveled to Philadelphia to get Patsy. There he also had arranged to meet James Hemings and James's older brother Robert, then in his early twenties. Unlike Patsy and James, however, Robert, would not be traveling to France but would remain with the party only through the New England tour.

From Philadelphia the four rode to New York for a six-day visit. Commencing the New England tour, they stopped in Providence and, over the next few weeks, found their way as far north as Portsmouth, New Hampshire. Their visits, mainly to seaport towns, were conducted in Jefferson's phaeton (which he planned to have disassembled and shipped to France for travels there). And by the tour's end, both Jefferson and Patsy were able to reflect with pride that, except for Georgia and the Carolinas, each had now set foot in ten of the infant republic's thirteen states.[1]

Jefferson had planned to sail from Boston on the American ship the *Active*, aboard which he had hoped to escort John Adams's spouse, Abigail—bound for the English port of Deal; from there she planned to travel to London and reunite with her husband after a long separation. Aboard the *Active*, Jefferson had been assured, "I could with certainty get ashore on the coast of France" from any England-bound ship during its final miles inside the English Channel, before it headed north to enter the Thames Estuary.

But after hastening to Boston, arriving there on June 20, Jefferson learned that the *Active* would be sailing in only a few hours—insufficient time for his phaeton's disassembly. Moreover, warned of crowded conditions aboard the ship, he also arrived too late to persuade Abigail Adams to wait for a later crossing. Resigned to wait for the next scheduled crossing, Jefferson eventually booked passage aboard the two-masted London-bound brig *Ceres*.

Thus, in Boston Harbor after a ten-day wait, on July 4, 1784, the eighth anniversary of the Declaration of Independence, its principal author, with his daughter and an enslaved man, boarded a British ship for his first trip aboard. Delayed, however, not until 4:00 a.m. the following morning did the *Ceres* weigh anchor and sail into the wide Atlantic.[2]

The crossing went smoothly. Fair and sunny weather held, and Jefferson, on his first oceanic trip, suffered minimal seasickness. At noon each day, he took readings of the *Ceres*'s latitudinal and longitudinal positions, the day's temperatures, and distances covered. Along with notations memorializing marine wildlife observed—including sharks and a whale—he recorded the findings in his Memorandum book. Aided by a Spanish dictionary and grammar book, he otherwise spent most of his shipboard time working his way through a copy of *Don Quixote*. Indeed, he later claimed that by the trip's end he had learned Spanish (of which a skeptical John Quincy Adams later commented: "Mr. Jefferson tells large stories.")

However, upon entering the English Channel—and not encountering a France-bound vessel—the *Ceres*'s captain, on July 26, deposited Jefferson's party at Cowes on the Isle of Wight. From there the travelers found passage to Portsmouth, on England's southern coast. After lingering there for four days as Patsy recuperated from a fever, the party crossed to Le Havre on July 31.[3]

Reaching Paris on August 6, Jefferson and his entourage spent their first four days there at the Hôtel d'Orléans on the rue de Richelieu, before moving to a lodging of the same name on the Left Bank's rue des Petits-Augustins (today's rue Bonaparte). During his first days in the city, determined that he and his daughter meet Parisian standards of finery, he shopped and summoned tailors and other craftsmen to their quarters—soon acquiring for himself, among other accoutrements, a sword and belt, a buckle, and lace ruffles. He also spent prodigiously on books—including 751 livres for a subscription to an encyclopedia that revised and reorganized the articles published in Diderot's *Encyclopédie*.

In Paris, Jefferson would live a life of luxury unsurpassed by any other period in his life. Compounding his usual profligacy, now operating in a second language, he indulged a long-standing aversion to negotiating prices. "I do not understand bargaining nor possess the dexterity requisite to make them," he confessed to James Madison.[4]

Tending to Patsy's education, he enrolled her at the Abbaye Royale de Panthémont (also spelled Pentemont), a convent boarding school on the Left Bank operated by Cistercian nuns. Jefferson had little regard for Roman Catholicism—once dismissing it as a "religion which makes" its practitioners "believe that, to keep the Creator in good humor with his own works, they must mumble a mass every day." But he also knew that Panthémont's school enjoyed a reputation as "altogether the best in France." Many English expatriates enrolled their offspring in the school, and Jefferson soon finalized Patsy's enrollment among its fifty or sixty students after receiving the reassurances he wanted to hear: "There are in it as many protestants as Catholics, and not a word is ever spoken to them on the subject of religion."

Patsy was initially so homesick at Panthémont that, as she later recalled, her father visited her there every evening "for the first month or two." But as she made friends and became conversant in French, Patsy thrived, later remembering the school as the "brightest part" of her life.[5]

During Jefferson's Paris residency, images and reputations—his own and his nation's—preoccupied him. Of the latter he was determined that a diplomat of the United States occupy quarters as opulent as those of envoys representing older states. Not until mid-October, however, did he find what he viewed as a suitable residence.

Jefferson expected to conclude his work in Paris "by Apr. 1786." Nonetheless, on October 16, he took out a nine-year lease on a three-story town house in a newly developed residential precinct on the city's Right Bank. Located on the cul-de-sac Taitbout, in today's Ninth Arrondissement, Jefferson soon called the house the "Hôtel Tetebout" and used it as both office and residence. Though unfurnished, the abode did include a courtyard and two gardens. To (by his lights) suitably appoint the house, he soon acquired furniture, carpets, glassware, dishes, silver, linens, a rented pianoforte, and, at auctions, works of art.[6]

Later that fall, with the arrival of his private secretary William Short and David Humphreys, the secretary to the American commissioners, the Hôtel Tetebout sheltered still more residents. Additionally, as Jefferson had anticipated, it also lodged a constant stream of visitors from America. To accommodate them and to otherwise run the house and manage his affairs, he assembled a staff that included a household manager and five domestic servants. After accepting the Paris appointment, Jefferson had eagerly anticipated dining regularly on French cuisine. But as he savored that expectation, an idea had occurred to him that promised to extend that pleasure beyond his stay in Paris: He would bring his enslaved servant, James Hemings, to Paris and have him trained in French cooking.

James's residence in Paris, however, entailed challenges for his Virginia master. Because slavery was illegal in France, Jefferson faced the risk of James's asserting his legal freedom there or perhaps being forcibly returned to Virginia. By French law even Jefferson's status as a diplomat did not did not allow him to retain ownership of James on French soil. Simultaneously, even if James was permitted to stay and chose not to assert his freedom, the presence of a slave in the Jefferson household risked diplomatic embarrassment.

To discourage James from asserting his legal freedom, Jefferson decided to pay him four dollars a month for his work as a servant while in Paris. He also decided to cover the costs of an apprenticeship for James with a caterer— eventually a succession of caterers—hired to cook at the Hôtel Tetebout. In time he also paid for French language lessons for the enslaved servant. More- over, to diminish the risks of embarrassment still further, Jefferson apparently avoided references to James's enslaved status back in Virginia.

Tellingly, shortly after arriving in Paris—answering a query from a more re- cently arrived American slaveholder, puzzled over the status of a bondsman he had brought to France—Jefferson responded with an answer doubtless drawn from his own experience:

> I have made enquiries on the subject of the negro boy you have brought, and find that the laws of France give him freedom if he claims it, and that it will be difficult, if not impossible, to interrupt the course of the law. Never- theless I have known an instance where a person bringing in a slave, and saying nothing about it, has not been disturbed in his possession.

Beyond that, Jefferson could have taken further solace in his likely knowl- edge that the legal process for claiming freedom was "neither simple or inexpensive"—requiring the hiring of a lawyer to press a lawsuit in France's court of admiralty.[7]

Upon arriving in Paris, Jefferson—for four years a widower—also established a pattern, continued through his years there, of befriending married women—among them Anne Willing Bingham; Abigail Adams; Marguerite- Victoire de Corny; the comtesse de Tessé; Maria Cosway; Angelica Church; and Anne-Louise-Germaine Necker, baronne de Staël-Holstein—the last better known as Madame de Staël. Even modern-day human relationships never fully yield their secrets to outsiders—and those of the distant past are even more inscrutable. Available (albeit scarce) evidence, however, suggests that among the married women Jefferson befriended in Paris, the fact that they were mar- ried was only incidental: To wit, his bonds with them—however sometimes conflicted—turned on the genuine pleasures he found in their company, as well as mutual interests and affections. In almost all cases, his ties to them seemed (at least viewed from the outside) entirely platonic. Indeed, with the exception of his bonds with Abigail Adams, the friendships proceeded, on Jefferson's part, with scarce attention, even indifference, to their spouses.

None of Jefferson's platonic friendships with married women in Paris better exemplified those patterns than his ties to the comtesse de Tessé. Two years younger than Jefferson, Madame de Tessé—Adrienne Catherine de Noailles, comtesse de Tessé—was a sister of Adrienne's mother and aunt of Adrienne. She was married to a wealthy nobleman, René de Froulay, comte de Tessé. At her town house on the rue de Varenne, in Paris's Faubourg Saint-Germain, Madame de Tessé (a sister of Adrienne's mother) hosted one of the city's leading salons—gatherings whose attendees over the years included Voltaire, Benjamin Franklin, Madame de Staël, Denis Diderot—and Lafayette, whom she lionized.

A contemporary recalled Madame de Tessé as a "remarkable person" with "small, piercing eyes" and "a pretty face marred at the age of twenty by small pox." Nonetheless the same source recalled her as possessed of a "precocious mind" and "an imposing air [of] . . . grace and dignity in all her movements, and above all, infinitely witty." To most admirers her reputation rested on the salons she hosted in her Paris home. But for Jefferson, his friendship with this quintessential woman of the Enlightenment ripened through visits to her and her husband's country estate in the village of Chaville, southwest of Paris; and true to form, Jefferson seemed to have had little if any relationship with Madame de Tessé's spouse.

The couple's neoclassical-style Château de Chaville with its sixty-five acres of grounds and gardens had once belonged to Louis XV. There Jefferson developed what became his enduring friendship with Madame de Tessé—a bond nourished by shared interests in politics and the arts—particularly architecture, an area in which Tessé became a mentor of sorts. The two also shared an interest in horticulture, and throughout Jefferson's Paris years and later, he obtained imported Virginia plant species for her gardens.[8]

Soon after settling into Paris, Jefferson also ventured to the village of Passy to visit Benjamin Franklin. Jefferson had served with Franklin, in 1776, in the Continental Congress. But when Jefferson arrived in Paris, because the octogenarian diplomat was by then afflicted with gout, he rarely left his house. Jefferson thus seldom saw Franklin outside of trips he and John Adams made to Passy on official business during daylight hours. Beyond that, while ties between Jefferson and Franklin were mutually respectful, the two were never close. During Jefferson's first months in Paris, he saw John and Abigail Adams more often than he did Franklin. Drawing the Jefferson-Adams axis still tighter was the fraught relationship between John Adams and Franklin.

Indeed, if Lafayette approached Franklin with genuine affection and Jefferson with mere cordiality, John Adams regarded the Philadelphian with barely concealed contempt. Adams acknowledged Franklin to be an "extraordinary Man." But after years of working, however intermittently, with the international celebrity, he had grown resentful of Franklin—particularly of his personal ties to the French court. Especially galling to Adams, Franklin—sidelining both Adams and Jefferson—often dealt directly with Foreign Minister Vergennes, with whom Adams had a stormy relationship.

Adams likewise resented what he saw as Franklin's devotion of more time to socializing than working. "I found that the Business of our Commission would never be done unless I did it," Adams complained to his diary. "It was late when he breakfasted," and soon thereafter "a crowd of carriages" began rolling up to Franklin's door. Economists, intellectuals, scholars, admiring strangers, men, women and children—they all, according to Adams, came to Passy, "to have the honour to see the great Franklin, and to have the pleasure of telling Stories about his Simplicity, his bald head and scattering strait hairs, among their Acquaintances."

Except for six months in the latter half of 1779, when Adams returned to the United States to help write the Massachusetts' constitution, he had been abroad since spring 1778, representing the United States in France and the

Netherlands. Indeed, since spring 1782 he had served as U.S. minister to the Netherlands, a post Adams still held as he toiled with Franklin and Jefferson as commissioners in Paris. Even so, like Jefferson that season, John and Abigail Adams's ties to Paris were no match for Franklin's; and like Jefferson, the couple found themselves much less in social demand than Franklin.

Further bonding Jefferson and the Adamses—John and Abigail were both closer in age to Jefferson than was Franklin. Jefferson was forty-three when he arrived in Paris. John Adams was seven years older (and six inches shorter) than his newly arrived friend; Abigail, at forty, was three years younger than Jefferson. Moreover, Jefferson and Abigail, who had met briefly in Boston the previous summer, had struck up an immediate friendship.

Paris would change Jefferson in many ways. There, through frequent conversations, often with women, he deepened his knowledge of the fine arts— particularly of painting, sculpture, and furniture design. Then and later, however, he clung to a disposition that deemed political topics ill suited to women. While living in Paris, to his friend Angelica Church he would write: "The tender breasts of ladies were not formed for political convulsion; and the French ladies miscalculate much their own happiness when they wander from the true field of their influence into that of politicks." With Abigail Adams, however, as would soon become clear, no topic—including politics—was off-limits.

More critically for Jefferson's work in Paris, having first met John Adams when both were Continental Congress delegates, he had known him for almost a decade—sufficient time to learn his strengths and shortcomings. In a February 1783 letter to Madison Jefferson assayed those characteristics as Adams, in Paris, commenced his latest diplomatic assignment.

He hates Franklin, he hates Jay, he hates the French, he hates the English. . . . His vanity is a lineament in his character which had entirely escaped me. . . . Notwithstanding all this he has a sound head on substantial points, and I think he has integrity. I am glad therefore that he is of the commission and expect he will be useful in it.

In contrast to Franklin's unconventional household at Passy, the Adams's more traditional *ménage* in the suburb of Auteuil put Jefferson at ease and strengthened bonds between the two families. Both Jefferson and Patsy, who was twelve years old when they arrived, developed an affinity for John and Abigail's two children—"Nabby," nineteen; and John Quincy, seventeen. Closing the circle, among all the Adamses, affections for the Jeffersons were mutual.

Soon after arriving in Paris, the Adamses and Jeffersons dined together in the home of Thomas Barclay, the Irish-born U.S. consul general in Paris, then in his midfifties, and posted in Paris since 1781. Soon thereafter Jefferson became a regular dinner guest of the Adamses in Auteuil. And after Jefferson established his own permanent residence, joined by William Short and David Humphreys, he often hosted the Adamses.[9]

By late December 1784, Jefferson was taking his first steps into Paris's social and intellectual life—thus soon writing to American friends such as astronomer David Rittenhouse of hot-air balloons, the latest in telescopic optics, the "folly" of Franz Mesmer's theories, and other *Parisien* fixations.

Overall, however, his few first months in Paris proved disappointing for the novice diplomat. Beyond the homesickness and spending-related financial strains that dogged him, Jefferson spent much of that fall confined to his house by various ailments—unspecified common illnesses that he dismissed as "seasoning" and attributed to the local water and fall's dampness. And when he did go out, the demands of work left scarce time for the long walks that had long been the heart of his physical regimen in Virginia.

Jefferson's diplomatic work was proving likewise dispiriting. On August 30, three weeks after his arrival in Paris, he and Adams rode to Franklin's house in Passy for his first official meeting of the American commissioners. And on September 15 the three commissioners ventured to Versailles to present their credentials to Foreign Minister Vergennes—documents that formally authorized them to negotiate a treaty of trade with the kingdom of France.

In the meantime, based on results achieved, most of the letters the American commissioners penned to diplomats of the other states with which they had been tasked to negotiate might as well have gone unwritten. The Confederation Congress had saddled the commissioners with a daunting workload—to negotiate "treaties of amity and commerce," pacts to remove trade barriers, with

Portugal, Spain, Britain, the Austrian Empire, Russia, and Prussia, as well as various Italian, Germanic, and Barbary Coast states. During that era, the Barbary States—city-states on North Africa's coast—deployed privateers against other countries' vessels. If captains of targeted ships failed to pay tributes of gold and silver, the pirates destroyed or captured their vessels and often held their crews for ransom or sold them into slavery.

The two American diplomats were also expected to negotiate pacts to supplement already negotiated treaties between the United States and France, Sweden, and the Netherlands. Tellingly, John Adams, writing to his former Paris colleague John Jay in April 1785—eight months after Jefferson's arrival— praised his new partner in Paris, noting that he was "very happy in my Friend Mr Jefferson." But, Adams also conceded, "our Negotiations in this Place, have not answered the Ends proposed by Congress, and expected by the People of America, nor is there now Scarcely a possibility that they should."

———————

Beyond those irritations Jefferson often found himself discomfited by the rituals and expectations of Versailles court society. On September 8, a month after his arrival in Paris—albeit noting a discomfort that persisted during Jefferson's entire Paris residency—Abigail Adams observed: "Mr. Jefferson who is really a man who abhors this shew and parade full as much as Mr. Adams, yet he has not been long enough enured to it, to Submit with patience, or bear it without fretting." Hairdressing, she noted, was, for him, a particularly irksome obligation. "His Hair too is an other affliction which he is tempted to cut off. He expects not to live above a Dozen years and he shall lose one of those in hair dressing."

That same week, upon the death of an eight-year-old prince in Prussia, an ally of France, Versailles's court had ordered all officials—including foreign diplomats—to observe eleven days of mourning. Reported Abigail:

> Poor Mr. Jefferson had to [hire] . . . a Tailor to get a whole black silk suit made up in two days, and at the end of Eleven days should an other death happen, he will be obliged to have a new Suit of mourning of Cloth, because that is the Season when Silk must be cast of[f]. . . . Fashion is the Deity

every one worships in this country and from the highest to the lowest you must submit.

In Jefferson's work and personal life, meanwhile, his limitations with the French language hindered him. Unlike Franklin, neither Adams nor Jefferson, by most accounts, was ever truly at ease in French. Jefferson had studied the language for most of his life and read it with ease. In Paris, however—even as Patsy Jefferson developed a genuine fluency in French—her father seems never to have obtained a similar competency. Jefferson rarely wrote in the language—particularly as a diplomat; according to the historian Gilbert Chinard, an expert on Jefferson's Paris years, during his entire residency there he wrote only one "document of importance" entirely in French, a letter declining an invitation.

Indeed, when William Short arrived in Paris in November 1784, the young lawyer found himself appalled by how poorly, in his estimation, Jefferson spoke the language. (Years later, recalling her first days in France, Patsy Jefferson noted that "papa spoke very little French and me not a word.") Short soon concluded that at least one of the two men should command French fluency; as Abigail Adams reported, by spring 1785 Short had resolved to find a French family with whom he might live—as, in her words, "This is the only way for a foreigner to obtain it [French fluency]."

Compounding frustrations, by spring 1784 Franklin—the most experienced of the three diplomats though increasingly afflicted by the gout—was talking openly of his desire to return home. By midautumn such talk—along with Jefferson's own frustrations—was deepening his self-consciousness at being an outsider in a foreign capital. Moreover, the Versailles court seemed increasingly uninterested in the American cause. Like other European states, France was preoccupied with growing tensions between Austria and Holland, and what seemed to be the likelihood of another European war. By November, to James Monroe, Jefferson was complaining of being a member of "the lowest and most obscure of the whole diplomatic tribe."[10]

TWENTY-SIX

Hero's Tour

O n the evening of August 4, 1784, when *Le Courier de New York*, carrying Lafayette and his assistant, the chevalier de Caraman, sailed into the East River and docked on Manhattan's South Street, the island and its thirty thousand inhabitants were recovering from years of neglect during its occupation by British forces. Even so, descending the ship's gangplank, Lafayette, now twenty-seven, savored his arrival—his first visit to a city that, as a general, three years earlier, he and his comrades in arms had targeted for military capture.

The next day the marquis explored the island: The Redcoats had marched out just sixteen months earlier, leaving behind a battered city. Along Broadway, Trinity Church's burned-out facade typified the bleakness. At Bowling Green, a bare plinth—on which an equestrian statue of George III, pulled down by a mob, had once stood—bore further testimony to the late discord. Two major fires had destroyed a third of Manhattan's buildings, docks were collapsing, and a sprawling network of trenches, dug for the city's defense, had transformed streets into obstacle courses. For seven years, after all, New York had served as headquarters for British operations in North America, a role that drew to Manhattan soldiers and sailors as well as thousands of Loyalists and runaway slaves.

At least eleven thousand prisoners of war—crowding jails and disease-ridden prison ships in the harbor—additionally swelled the local population.[1]

Initially Lafayette's arrival attracted scant attention. But as word spread, public interest surged. On his first full day in New York, Michel-Guillaume-Jean de Crèvecoeur*, France's consul, hosted a banquet in Lafayette's honor, with Continental army veteran officers in full uniform. Days later in Philadelphia, the state assembly and retired Patriot officers similarly honored him. "In the crowd that surrounded me I delighted to see my former soldiers," he crowed to Adrienne.[2]

At City Tavern Lafayette made a nostalgic return to the dining room where he first met Washington. On August 12 he attended a special meeting of Philadelphia's American Philosophical Society, a gathering called at his request for him to extol the "wonderful effects" of Franz Mesmer's animal magnetism.[3]

After passing through Annapolis and Baltimore, Lafayette and Caraman reached Mt. Vernon on August 17. There for ten days the retired general and his adoptive son reminisced and toasted a constant stream of visiting admirers. "Never was General Washington so great," Lafayette wrote to Adrienne, "as in the simplicity of his retirement." The two men devoted "sweet hours" alone, "speaking of the past and the present, and talking a bit of politics about the future." But if they discussed the proposal broached by Lafayette a year earlier that they purchase "a small Estate Where We May try the Experiment to free the Negroes," no record of the exchange survives.

However, in at least two known instances during his 1784 American visit Lafayette did take up the issue of slavery. On October 14, in Richmond addressing Virginia's House of Delegates, he endorsed a short-lived initiative to abolish slavery in the state. Five weeks later, again in Richmond, he wrote a letter of support for efforts to win the freedom of James, the enslaved man who had assisted him as a double agent, spying on Cornwallis's army. James had been promised his freedom when he entered the war. However, because his service had been categorized as that of spy rather than soldier, his petition for freedom

---

*Through his writings—particularly *Letters from an American Farmer* (1782)—the French diplomat, publishing under the name Hector St. John Crèvecoeur, established himself as an early European chronicler of life on the new American republic's frontier.

had been denied under the terms of a 1783 Virginia statute granting manumission to slaves who had served as soldiers during the war.[4]

Leaving Mt. Vernon on August 28, Lafayette and Caraman traveled to Annapolis and Baltimore. In the latter the two "fell in with" Jefferson's friend James Madison. The thirty-three-year-old Madison, having left the Confederation Congress, had recently been elected to another term in Virginia's House of Delegates. Like many American leaders, Madison had recently grown alarmed by what he feared was a coming diplomatic clash with Spain over its navigational rights on the Mississippi River.

In Baltimore, Madison—knowing that Lafayette had the ear of powerful French officials—broached the delicate topic of Spain's asserted claims. Indeed, the matter was of such diplomatic sensitivity that, in Madison's account of the exchange that he soon sent to Jefferson, he rendered it in cipher:

> The relation in which the Marquis stands to France and America has induced me to enter into a free conversation with him on the subject of the Missisipi [*sic*]. I have endeavored emphatically to impress on him that the ideas of America and of Spain irreconciliably clash, that unless the mediation of France be effectually exerted an actual rupture is near at hand.

Such a rupture, Madison worried, could cause resentments in the United States against both Spain and France—and possibly reverberate to Britain's advantage. To preempt that outcome, Madison recalled to Jefferson, he had expressed to Lafayette hopes that France will "set every engine at work to divert Spain" from such a confrontation. He also reminded the marquis that France itself had "a great interest in a trade with the western country thro the Missisipi."

For Madison, the fact that Lafayette, two years earlier, had traveled to Madrid and established high-level contacts in the Spanish court enhanced his value as freelance diplomat. "He admitted the force of every thing I said," a gratified Madison wrote to Jefferson. Further gladdening Madison, Lafayette also promised that he would write to France's foreign minister conveying his views on the topic, "and let me see his letter at N. York before he sends it."

On September 3 Lafayette and Caraman, accompanied by Madison, returned to Philadelphia. There, amid the usual feting of the returning hero, France's chargé d'affaires, the marquis de Barbé-Marbois, told Lafayette of an upcoming treaty signing at western New York's Fort Schuyler—formerly Fort Stanwix. The treaty would formally establish peace between the United States and the Six Nations of the Iroquois Confederacy. With the exception of the Oneida and the Tuscarora, all the confederacy's member nations had allied with the British in the recent war. Barbé-Marbois planned to attend the signing as an observer and suggested that Lafayette and Caraman should also do so.

Lafayette, the ardent reader of Raynal, had an ongoing interest in American Indians—in particular the Oneida, several of whom had shared his triumph at Barren Hill. He thus accepted the invitation and promptly asked his new friend Madison to join them for the trip. For Madison both the trip and the prospects of spending more time with Lafayette were too alluring to decline: "It will," he wrote to his son, "carry me farther than I had proposed, but I shall be rewarded by the pleasure of his company and the further opportunity of gratifying my curiosity."

Soon leaving Philadelphia, Lafayette, Caraman, and Madison traveled to Trenton, New Jersey, and by September 11 were in New York City. From there the three traveled by barge to Albany, where, as planned, they met Barbé-Marbois. From Albany in late September the four men, joined by a fifth traveling companion identified only as Demanche, set off for Fort Schuyler.

Turning to a westward course and journeying up the Mohawk River valley by carriage, the party completed the trip's final miles on horseback. Knowing the region from his Continental army days, Lafayette savored the backcountry terrain. He reveled in impressing his travel companions who—as he put it to Adrienne—"were quite surprised to find that the country was as familiar to me as if I was entering the suburb of St. Germain." Moreover, in his travels he was also finding reminders of familiar interests: Notably—on Sunday September 26, during a stop at a Shaker community near Watervliet, New York—Lafayette, attending a religious service, saw in the congregants' namesake "shaking" a phenomenon he likened to Mesmer's "animal magnetism."

The party reached Fort Schuyler on September 29. Not until three days later, however, was the entire U.S. delegation—Arthur Lee, and fellow commission-members Richard Butler, and Oliver Wolcott—at the Oneida village treaty-signing site. There, Barbé-Marbois recalled, the travelers were greeted "with the hospitality that the savages show toward all those who are not their enemies." Barbé-Marbois was likewise pleased to learn that, in an area that had passed successively from French to British to American title, the Indians "still have great respect for the king of France . . . and speak of the French nation with reverence, even though their relations with us ended over twenty years ago."

At the Oneida village, after accepting casks of brandy brought by Lafayette, the tribesmen hosted a feast that included "a large salmon that had just been caught . . . milk, butter, fruit, and honey and in abundance." Following the meal, "We expressed the desire to see their dance." The Indians complied. But as Barbé-Marbois recalled:

> When the dance had gone on for two hours, we were so weary of it that we told the interpreters to ask the dancers to retire. But it was not so simple as that. They wanted to continue until daybreak, and as drunkenness had also become a part of it, the first two pleas that were made to them had no effect. Finally one of the dancers, who had once served under M. de Lafayette, took pity on us and spoke so eloquently that the dancers dispersed.

The actual treaty conference began on October 3. Lafayette enjoyed its rituals—the dances, formal gift giving, drinking, speeches, and finally the actual treaty signing. Often upstaging the official American delegation, he frequently made himself the center of attention. He delivered a well-received speech—the conference's opening oration—and over the coming days was heartened to learn of the stature he enjoyed among the tribesmen: "My personal credit with the savages—who are as much friends as enemies—has proved to be much greater that I had supposed." Once again he even found time to demonstrate, this time to the Indians, the wonders of "animal magnetism."

On October 4, Lafayette, Caraman, Madison, and Barbé-Marbois departed Fort Schuyler, this time by boat, hurrying down the Mohawk River toward Schenectady. Three days later a brief overland jaunt returned them to Albany.

———

By mid-October, Madison was back in Philadelphia. There, on the seventeenth, he wrote to Jefferson, by then in Paris, of his journey to Fort Schuyler. Knowing that Lafayette would soon be in Paris, Madison shared his own candid assessment of the marquis. While among the Oneida delegation, Madison wrote, the American negotiators had been taken aback by the alacrity with which Lafayette had dominated the proceedings: "The Commissioners were eclipsed." But all in all, Madison had been impressed: "The time I have lately passed with the M. has given me a pretty thorough insight into his character," he confided:

> With great natural frankness of temper he unites much address; with very considerable talents, a strong thirst of praise and popularity. . . . In his politics he says his three hobby-horses are the alliance between France and the United States, the Union of the latter and the manumission of the slaves. The two former are the dearer to him as they are connected with his personal glory.

For Lafayette, two priorities—the U.S.–France alliance and comity among the now independent American States—still outranked his concern for the liberation of enslaved peoples. Clearly, however, their fate increasingly weighed on his mind.

———

Over the weeks after their return to Albany, Lafayette and Caraman visited, among other cities, Hartford, Connecticut; Worcester, Massachusetts; Boston; Providence, Rhode Island; and Richmond and Yorktown, Virginia. Afterward, following another visit to Mt. Vernon, the two made their way to New York for their return voyage to France.[5]

In five months Lafayette had visited ten of the thirteen states—all except for the Carolinas and Georgia. At many stops, cities and states had bestowed upon him honorary citizenship. For the returning hero, however, such bonhomie could not mask a vexing truth: With the war over, a divisive regionalism now beset his adopted country. Exacerbating other woes, its central government was warring against the centripetal forces of state governments—the smaller polities seeking to increase their own powers at the Confederation Congress's expense. Indeed, in Trenton on December 11, when Lafayette addressed that body, it's prestige was approaching a nadir—demoralized to such a degree that members often skipped sessions, rendering it unable to obtain a quorum.

Aware of Congress's plight, Lafayette during his tour became a vigorous advocate for the central government—for "federalism." As he wrote to Adrienne: "In my present situation I like to think that my influence may not be useless to the domestic interests of the United States, to the union that should exist between them, in short, to the federal union."

In 1777 George Washington's grudging acceptance of Lafayette's services had rested on the young aristocrat's wealth and court connections. Only later did he win plaudits for his talents on the battlefield. By 1784, however, among leaders in both America and France, he was playing yet another role in the young republic—that of a rare symbol of unity in a nation otherwise riven by political and regional fractures. As Lafayette toured America that year, nothing exemplified that unifying role more than his repeated advocacy of "federalism."

Throughout the American Revolution, to Washington's consternation, regional and economic tensions had weakened national unity. By 1784, however, with the war concluded, those regional divisions had fully returned. Moreover, the hapless Confederation Congress lacked the powers to tax, to enact trade policies, and to otherwise provide effective national governance. Put another way, the Congress found itself in need of a unifying purpose and symbol.

French policy makers, meanwhile, were experiencing a similar frustration. To defeat an old enemy—and thereby, incidentally, to assist in the creation of a new American nation—the Bourbons had saddled their treasury with massive debt. By 1784, however, Versailles's ministers were watching helplessly as that new nation, reverting to old habits and bypassing France, quietly resumed its trade with France's eternal rival Britain.

As the Bourbons took note of the revival of American regionalism, a realization dawned on them: If they were ever to negotiate a relationship with the infant nation that would allow France to commercially exploit the military victory that its aid had made possible, the kingdom required a strong central-ized state with which to bargain. And through the promotion of Lafayette as a national American hero, French policy makers advanced precisely that end.

Within that fractured union, Lafayette, from the Bourbons' perspective, ap-peared the ideal intermediary—peerlessly Anglophobic, with equal loyalties to Philadelphia and Versailles. Moreover, observed Louis Gottschalk: "More than any other man who had a claim to the gratitude of Americans, he belonged equally to all Americans. Washington was a Virginian. Franklin, still abroad, was a Pennsylvanian. Adams was a New Englander. . . . But Lafayette belonged to no state or region."

As Lafayette concluded his American visit, Thomas Jefferson in Paris ap-provingly noted to Madison a growing willingness by Congress to regulate the nation's trade. And he attributed that trend in part to a visitor from France. Like-wise, Jefferson observed, European newspapers, in the wake of the 1783 peace treaty, seemed to be reevaluating their view of the new American republic. Until recently, he wrote, "they supposed every thing in America was anarchy, tumult, and civil war. The reception of the M. Fayette"—the image of the marquis pro-jected across Europe—"gave a check to these ideas."[6]

On December 21 Lafayette and Caraman, having returned to New York, boarded the French frigate *La Nymphe* for their return to France. Joining them were a twelve-year-old Oneida boy named Kayenlaha and fourteen-year-old John Edwards Caldwell, the orphaned son of an American army chaplain. The former he was bringing to be employed as a servant at Hôtel de Lafayette, at the behest of an Indian leader he met at Fort Schuyler; the latter, to complete his education, at the request of a group of his late father's friends. (The precise durations of the Paris residencies of Kayenlaha and Otsiquette, the other young Oneida who worked as a Lafayette family servant, remain unclear.)

A week before sailing, Lafayette wrote to Madison of his hopes to continue informal diplomacy on behalf of the United States. That expectation, he added, was made all the sweeter by a rumor that had found its way to him—that, soon replacing Benjamin Franklin in Paris, "M. Jefferson will certainly be The Minister to France."[7]

TWENTY-SEVEN

Diplomats

In autumn 1784 Jefferson, then passing an otherwise glum season in Paris, received a letter teeming with filial affection that seemed to herald better days. From Philadelphia—in a letter written on October 17—Lafayette expressed the joy he anticipated upon returning to Paris and personally welcoming Jefferson to France. In the meantime he extended an invitation: "My House, Dear Sir, my family, and Any thing that is mine are entirely at Your disposal and I Beg You will Come and See Mde. de Lafayette as You would act By Your Brother's wife."[1]

The coming weeks, however, brought no respite from Jefferson's travails; and when 1785 arrived, it found him still, for the most part, housebound with ailments. His diplomatic work, meanwhile, was hardly more gratifying; a lack of news from America likewise bedeviled him—prompting complaint on January 13 that even Congress's activities remained unknown to him: "Nothing can equal the dearth of American intelligence in which we live here. . . . We might as well be in the moon."

Deepening his frustrations were letters from American colleagues that arrived the next day. Upon opening them—causing, as Jefferson soon professed to Monroe, "mortification"—he realized that the cipher code he had been using was outdated. He corrected the lapse. But the error still left him unable to read recent incoming letters; moreover, dispatches he had sent over the past weeks had included passages cast in the out-of-date code: "Whether you have taken up a cypher established with some other person, or whether it is from my own stupidity that I am thus disappointed, I cannot tell."[2]

Jefferson sought solace that season in prodigious correspondence. Writing, for instance, to retired Virginia governor Benjamin Harrison, he answered a recent letter seeking help with a recently enacted commission from Virginia's legislature for a statue of George Washington. In Paris, for that legislature Jefferson was already overseeing commissions for two busts of Lafayette—one for Virginia's Capitol, another to be presented to the city of Paris. The commissions for both busts were eventually awarded to the Parisian sculptor Jean-Antoine Houdon.

Concerning the envisioned Washington statue, Jefferson took delight in informing Harrison that he and Franklin had persuaded Houdon to accept the additional commission. Moreover, the sculptor "without hesitating a moment" had "offered to abandon his business here, to leave the statues of kings unfinished, and to go to America to take the true figure by actual inspection." In view of Houdon's acceptance, Jefferson added, he personally agreed with those favoring life-size as opposed to monumental scale for the Washington statue: "We are agreed in one circumstance, that the size shall be precisely that of the life."[3]

He also invited friends to visit. To Madison he wrote in December 1784: "You can come in April, pass the months of May, June, July, August and most of September here, and still be back to the commencement of real business in the [Virginia] Assembly. . . . You shall find with me a room, bed and plate, if you will do me the favor to become of the family." Two days later, he extended the same invitation to James Monroe, "I have recommended the same measure to Mr. Madison," he wrote. "Perhaps you can make the voiage together."

To Madison, burrowing into nostalgia for Monticello, he imagined an idealized (albeit spouseless) future there with Madison, Monroe, and William Short—all bachelors then—owning neighboring estates. In fact, in Jefferson's December letter to Madison, he confided that he had already broached his idea to Monroe and Short: "Would you but make it a 'partie quarree' I should beleive that life had still some happiness in store for me," he wrote, ever haunted by Martha's death."[4]

Expecting Lafayette's return to Paris in January, with each passing day during the first weeks of 1785, Jefferson had reason to believe that he was on the eve of better days. The marquis, as it turned out, returned on January 26. Bearing mail for the American minister, by the day's end Lafayette had called on Jefferson.

But how well did the two men know each other that January 1785?

Well enough, obviously, in Lafayette's mind, for him to have extended his invitation to Jefferson the previous October: "My House, Dear Sir, my family, and Any thing that is mine are entirely at Your disposal."

But prior to Lafayette's January 1785 return to Paris, they had actually spent less time together than is often assumed—if only because opportunities for such interactions had been few: Jefferson had, after all, relinquished his Continental Congress seat in July 1776, twelve months before Lafayette's arrival in Philadelphia; and even after Washington ordered Lafayette to Virginia in early 1781, his time there was limited: Arriving on April 22, he left on November 1, seven weeks before sailing for France.

Further narrowing opportunities, the six months that Lafayette spent in Virginia were busy for both men. As each, shadowed by an enemy invasion, tended to his respective (often peripatetic) labors, both faced hectic days. Given those circumstances, the two interacted almost exclusively via letters and intermediaries—often at distances across the state's length and breadth. And even when Lafayette, in or near Richmond, wasn't actively engaging the enemy, the quotidian tasks of war—inspections, recruiting, drills, logistical duties, and the like—consumed most of his time.

Indeed, the date, setting, and duration of Jefferson's and Lafayette's first encounter remain unknown: When and where they first met, what was said, the impressions each made upon the other—all remain a mystery. Searches of diaries, letters, and other writings of both men and their associates yield no fleshed-out accounts of any encounters between the two that season—much less one described as a first meeting. Similarly unyielding are contemporary newspapers and memoirs by soldiers, state officials, and others positioned to witness that first handshake. In the end one searches in vain for a first-meeting account as specific as those chronicling the introduction of Lafayette and George Washington—on July 31, 1777, at Philadelphia's City Tavern.

In fact the May 8, 1781, meeting, in Richmond, of Virginia's Council of State, attended by both—and documented in that body's published records (albeit indicating only the presence of each man)—constitutes the only confirmed instance of the two men's paths crossing in Virginia—or, for that matter, anywhere else—prior to Jefferson's residency in Paris.

Even so, other available evidence, though without denoting precise dates, indicates that, beyond their May 8 encounter, their paths did likely cross on other occasions during those months. From Bowling Green, Virginia, fifty miles north of Richmond—on April 27, 1781, on the eve of Lafayette's initial arrival in the state capital—he wrote optimistically to Jefferson: "This Evening or to Morrow Morning I Hope to Be with Your Excellency." Lafayette, riding ahead of his army reached Richmond the following day; thus, if his hopes were realized, the two men's first meeting would have occurred, in Richmond on April 28.

Similarly, suggesting yet another encounter, on May 14—a week after the two men's confirmed joint attendance at the Council of State meeting—Jefferson ended a letter to Lafayette with the postscript: "Lest any Thing should suffer which it is in my power to prevent, I have concluded to stay here this Evening and to do myself the pleasure of calling on you at your Quarters tomorrow morning."

But whatever their mutual familiarity in 1781, it apparently provided sufficient basis for Lafayette to take Jefferson's measure: for, on August 14, from an encampment near Yorktown, writing to France's U.S. minister, the chevalier de la Luzerne, Lafayette assumed he knew Jefferson well enough to assess his character and predict his eventual acceptance of a (recently spurned) diplomatic post in Paris: For now, Lafayette wrote, "Mr. Jefferson declines" the appointment, "but if they permit him to go over later. I think he will accept. He is an intelligent man, a Southerner, and an eminent lawyer."

Moreover—indicating encounters of a more personal nature—Lafayette, in New York, on September 14, 1784, wrote to Adrienne: "I am very sorry my dear heart that I will not be able to welcome Mr. Jefferson to Paris. He is a charming man, talented and honest, and will have a little girl with him, who is said to be very friendly. I beg you to take both under your wing. Take them to Madame de Tessé and introduce them to your friends. Jefferson was Governor of Virginia in the early days when I commanded the army, and I am deeply indebted to him."[5]

Given the paucity of details concerning the two men's 1781 interactions in Virginia, one yearns for a vivid account of their reunion four years later in Paris. But, alas, that meeting's details are also lost. For whatever transpired between the two that day—January 26, 1785—in Paris, its details were eclipsed by heartbreaking news lurking among the letters that Lafayette brought to Jefferson: From a Virginia relative he learned of the death, from whooping cough, the previous October, of his youngest daughter, Lucy Elizabeth. In a cruel irony, it had been Lucy's birth two years earlier that had led to the death of Jefferson's wife, Martha.

The following evening Nabby Adams recorded in her diary that Jefferson missed a dinner at which he had been expected at the Adamses' home in Auteuil. Aware of the reason for their guest's absence—and knowing too of Jefferson's sadness after his spouse's death—Nabby observed: "Mr. J is a man of great sensibility and parental affection. His wife died when this child was born; and he was in an almost confirmed state of melancholy; [he] confined himself from the world, and even from his friends, for a long time; and this news has greatly affected him and his daughter." Indeed, so great was Jefferson's melancholy that it would be at least four months after learning of Lucy's death before he ventured out to dine.[6]

Following their thirty-day Atlantic crossing aboard *La Nymphe*, Lafayette and Caraman reached Brest on January 20. The marquis was eager to see his family. But knowing the Estates of Brittany was in session—in Rennes, while en route to Paris—he decided an appearance before that body was worth delaying his homecoming.

A representative body, the Estates of Brittany jealously defended the province's privileges. In that role it held distinct powers, including the right to consent to royal taxes and the power to levy local taxes for internal improvements—notably an extensive program of construction. The Estate's members included local nobles and high-ranking clergy. And because Lafayette had recently inherited properties in Brittany, he had concluded that a stop in Rennes, the province's inland capital, was worth his time.

When Lafayette arrived in Rennes on the twenty-third, the assembly's surprised members greeted him as a returning hero, insisting that he formally address the body the next morning. Lafayette's ties to Brittany derived more from maternal family ties and inherited lands than personal biography. So in his speech the following day, he strove to ingratiate. Saying that "he would always preserve a Breton heart," he asked to be invited to join its numbers in the near future.

Like his appearances before American legislative assemblies, Lafayette's interaction with the Estates of Brittany was mainly ceremonial. Even so, his appearance there marked his first in recent years, if ever, before an assembly in his own land. It also presaged other, more fateful, interactions in the coming months before other French assemblies. Before leaving the Breton capital, Lafayette arranged via an intermediary another appointment—a meeting with several royal ministers at Versailles—and on January 27, in Paris, after an overnight stop at Versailles, he reunited with his family.[7]

In Paris, Lafayette plunged into his usual socializing and diplomatic errands. Indeed, as they had during his 1782–84 visit, those two activities for the handsome, twenty-seven-year-old officer frequently merged into a single concentrated force—often accompanied by endearing understatement. In February, for instance, weeks after his return, nineteen-year-old Nabby Adams—numbering among a "large company" of dinner guests at Franklin's house at Passy—found herself charmed by the recently returned hero. "The Marquis de la Fayette I never saw before; he appears a little reserved, and very modest."[8]

Then and over the coming months, Lafayette continued to correspond with American officials, and, as he had promised Madison—at Versailles and among diplomats posted to Madrid—he worked to prod Spain toward a negotiated settlement over its claimed navigation rights to the Mississippi. Likewise, he also worked to win Versailles's intervention on behalf of the United States against the Barbary States for their ongoing depredations against American merchant ships in the Mediterranean. Mostly, however, after returning to France, Lafayette worked tirelessly, usually on his own, to promote U.S. trade with France—often at the expense of England. The sad news of Lucy Jefferson's death had colored the two men's January 1785 Paris reunion. But Lafayette soon impressed the American minister. Answering Madison's letter from the previous fall—the one noting Lafayette's "very considerable talents" and "a strong thirst of praise and popularity"—Jefferson, in March, offered his own emphatic, if similarly cautious, endorsement of the marquis. Writing partially in cipher (decoded and set in italics in the below quoted passage), he addressed Madison: "Your *character* of the *M. Fayette* is precisely agreeable to the idea I had formed of *him*. I take *him* to be of *unmeasured ambition* but that the *means he uses* are virtuous. *He* is *returned fraught* with *affection* to *America* and *disposed* to render every *possible service.*"

Knowing the unique products of the American Republic's regions, Lafayette, upon returning to France, promoted a range of their exports—from New England whale oil and furs to southern timber and tobacco. To open the French market to the South's tobacco, he argued for an end to a monopoly enforced by the country's own tobacco farmers through the Ferme générale—the Farmers-General. A state-sanctioned association of capitalists empowered to collect protective internal tariffs on select French goods, the Farmers-General pressed their influence at Versailles to maintain restrictions on the importation of potentially competing goods. Stymied in his own efforts to combat the Ferme générale's obstructions, Jefferson would lament: "I have struck at its root here, and spared no pains to have the farm itself demolished. But it has been in vain."

During those same months Lafayette also toured France's provinces—at each stop urging manufacturers to engage in trade with the United States. To bolster closer ties between the two countries, he likewise promoted educational exchanges. As he sought to arrange for his son George Washington to be educated in America, he offered to do the same in France for the sons of Nathanael Greene, Alexander Hamilton, and Henry Knox.

Inspired by his American experiences, Lafayette also took up a newfound interest in France's public affairs. Like many in Paris, he was soon reading *A Treatise on the Administration of the Finances in France*, a three-volume work published a year earlier by Jacques Necker, intermittently during those years the country's finance minister and associated with court efforts to modernize France's economy. To Madison, Lafayette reported that Necker's work "has Made [a] Great deal of Noise. It Has Raised a Party Spirit, where By Both Have to an Excess Hated or Adored Him. But I only Speak of the Book, which is a Very Sensible One, and Worth Your Reading."[9]

During those months Lafayette also embraced reformist movements—including, however fitfully, Irish nationalism and Dutch republicanism. More actively, he supported causes of greater relevance to French society—including campaigns to abolish slavery in France's overseas colonies and to win more rights for France's Protestant minority.

Although born into a Roman Catholic family and throughout his life a nominal adherent of that faith, Lafayette, like Jefferson, seems to have been a religious skeptic. He later recalled the occasional discomfort that those doubts caused Adrienne: "She only once or twice seemed in error about me, persuading herself that I was a fervent Christian." On one occassion an exasperated Adrienne affectionately concluded that he was probably better defined by a political faction that he eventually led: "'You are not a Christian?' she said one day, and as I did not answer: 'Oh, I know what you are. You are a Fayettiste!'"

Further distancing Lafayette from France's majority religion were his experiences in America, living among and fighting alongside Protestants. Those encounters had enhanced his sensitivity to the plight of Protestants in his native land. In 1598, King Henry IV, in his Edict of Nantes, had granted limited religious liberty to France's Huguenots—Calvinists and members of the Reformed Church of France, the country's largest Protestant population. In 1685, however, Louis XIV had revoked the edict.

Policies of religious intolerance propounded by Louis XIV and his successors led to the destruction of Huguenot churches, forced conversions to Catholicism, massacres of Protestants, religious civil wars, and—fatefully for France—a mass emigration of hundreds of thousands of Huguenots to destinations throughout the world, including North America. Moreover, as Lafayette wrote to Washington: "Marriages are not legal among [Protestants]. . . . Their wills Have no force of law. Their children are to be bastards."

Personalizing such injustices still more for Lafayette, in America he had befriended numerous Patriots with Huguenot ties—including John Laurens, Alexander Hamilton, John Jay, and Gouverneur Morris. Indeed, in June 1777 in South Carolina, it had been Benjamin Huger, grandson of a Huguenot exile, who had been the first American to welcome him to the New World.

In France in 1785 Lafayette focused his attentions on a traditional Huguenot bastion—*le Midi*—France's South, stretching east-to-west from the Mediterranean to the Atlantic. And by spring he was envisioning himself leading a revolt by Protestants, centered in Nîmes and other *Midi* locales. Lafayette's envisioned insurgency never materialized. Two years later, however, Versailles recognized non-Catholic marriages and permitted legally recognized Protestant burials—advances that nonetheless left Jefferson unimpressed: As a now unknown source paraphrased the Virginian's alleged reaction, "All this new law amounted to was the recognition that a Protestant was capable of begetting children, and there was always a risk that a corpse might become embarrassing."[10]

During that period Lafayette also joined efforts to moderate, if not end, slavery, in France's New World colonies and elsewhere. Earlier he had adopted the antislavery arguments of the Abbé Raynal; and soon after returning to Paris, Lafayette discovered another antislavery work—*Reflections on Negro Slavery*, by the philosopher the marquis de Condorcet, a work influenced by its author's associations with Franklin and Thomas Paine. Until the appearance of the ninety-nine-page work, Condorcet, by then in his early forties, had been known mainly for his works on mathematics. Soon thereafter, however, he would become famous as an advocate of human rights—including the rights of women.

Learning of Lafayette's praise, Condorcet soon contacted him: "No one," he wrote, "on our continent has helped more than you . . . to break those chains with which Europe endowed America. Perhaps the glory of overthrowing the slavery that we have imposed on the unfortunate Africans is also demanded of you."

Through Lafayette, Jefferson, in turn, also soon befriended Condorcet, a protégé of Voltaire. In fact, tellingly, Jefferson later began work on a translation of *Reflections on Negro Slavery*, but eventually abandoned the effort—possibly, speculates one scholar, because he did not share the philosopher's conviction that, in Jefferson's words, "the want of talents" observed in black slaves was "the effect of their degraded condition."

In spring 1785, meanwhile, shortly after hearing from Condorcet, Lafayette read in a New York newspaper of a new antislavery society whose organizational meeting had been attended by Alexander Hamilton. Writing to Hamilton, Lafayette asked to join the group—the New York Society for Promoting the Manumission of Slaves. Praising the society's mission—and apparently thinking of Washington and Jefferson—he added that its arguments seemed cast "in Such a Way as to Give no offence to the Moderate Men in the Southern States."[11]

More tangibly during that period, Lafayette began thinking concretely about a project he had pondered since at least 1783—and in which he had unsuccessfully attempted to enlist Washington as a partner. Seeking to implement—and demonstrate the practicality of—emancipationist doctrines he had contemplated, he began planning to purchase two plantations in France's colony of Cayenne, today's French Guiana.

On those two estates and a third he would purchase there in 1786 were planted clove and cinnamon trees and sugarcane. A 1789 list showed seventy slaves living on the estates. Following Lafayette's purchases of the plantations, a manager hired to operate them was instructed to pay the slaves a salary, to hold them to the same laws to which whites were subject, and to ban corporal punishment. Adrienne, meanwhile, corresponding with the manager's wife, arranged for religious education for the slaves and for an older enslaved woman to tend to their children's education.

In accord with that age's doctrine of gradual emancipation, Lafayette's plans called for the enslaved laborers' white overseers to instruct them in agricultural methods as they worked. Upon their gaining the expertise necessary to operate the plantations, as Lafayette soon explained to Washington, he planned to "free my Negroes in order to Make that Experiment which you know is My Hobby Horse." Months later Washington, long a slave-owner himself, offered his protégé his thoughts concerning the experiment: "The benevolence of your heart my Dr Marqs is so conspicuous upon all occasions, that I never wonder at any fresh proofs of it. . . . Would to God a like spirit would diffuse itself generally into the minds of the people of this country, but I despair of seeing it."

Lafayette's correspondence of that decade includes letters in which he discussed his Cayenne venture with Washington, Madison, and Hamilton—but not Jefferson. Indeed, few if any of Lafayette's extant letters to Jefferson from those years discussed the marquis's South American "Hobby Horse." Reciprocally, the venture goes conspicuously unraised in Jefferson's otherwise topically wide-ranging letters to Lafayette from those years. For the author of the Declaration of Independence—the owner of slaves in Virginia, who during those years, unbeknownst to the French government, shared a Paris household with an enslaved person—the topic of slavery was rapidly coming, literally, too close to home.[12]

TWENTY-EIGHT

Te Deum

After returning to Paris in January 1785, Lafayette saw little of Jefferson—likely to the surprise of both men—over the coming months. When the marquis wasn't traveling, his work in Paris, along with family and social obligations, consumed most of his time. Jefferson, for his part during that period, was similarly unavailable—dogged by ailments that kept him inside the Hôtel Tetebout.

By spring Lafayette and the Adamses were worried. In April, after visiting the Hôtel Tetebout, the marquis shared his concerns with James Madison—writing on the sixteenth: "Mr. Jefferson's Health is Recovering," he reported. "But He Keeps Himself too Closely Confined."

Days later, to coax him out, Adrienne and Lafayette asked Jefferson to join them and the Adamses for a *Te Deum*, the mass that takes its name from the singing of that praiseful hymn, at Notre Dame Cathedral. The ceremony was to celebrate the birth, days earlier, of Prince Louis-Charles. Upon his first breath, the prince—for whom the title Duke of Normandy, after a century of disuse, was revived—became, after his older brother, Louis-Joseph, second in line to the Bourbon throne.

Queen Marie Antoinette—Adrienne's friend—remained at Versailles with her newborn son. But the child's father, King Louis XVI, was expected to attend the *Te Deum*. And so on April 1, the appointed day of the service, Nabby Adams recalled, her family had an early meal and left for Paris. Having been asked by Madame Lafayette to meet at 2:00 at her family's residence, the Adamses took their carriage from Auteil to the rue de Bourbon. There, inside the Hôtel de Lafayette, after being welcomed by Lafayette and Adrienne, they found a clutch of other already arrived guests—including Thomas Jefferson.

An hour and a half later Jefferson joined the Adamses in their carriage for the final three miles of the day's trip, from the rue de Bourbon to the Île de la Cité, the snug bridge-hemmed island in the Seine from which the larger city grew and on whose southeastern corner the great cathedral sat. So crowded with celebrants were Paris's streets and sidewalks that afternoon that only the mass presence of soldiers kept traffic moving. As Nabby recalled: "Mr. Jefferson" speculated that "there were as many people in the streets as there were in the State of Massachusetts, or any other of the States."

Crossing the Pont Neuf to the Île de la Cité, the travelers eventually reached the cathedral—its marbled Gothic facade and two soaring towers agleam in the spring-afternoon sun. "It is the most beautiful building I have seen," Nabby recalled. Inside, the Lafayette entourage was soon seated, "in as good a place as any in the Church, which we owed to the Politeness of Mme. de la Fayette," Nabby's younger brother, John Quincy, wrote in his diary. "In the middle of the choir below us were several rows of benches, upon which the king's train sat when he came, while he and his two brothers were before all the benches, and directly opposite the altar."

However, before (or perhaps after) the Lafayette party took their seats, reported Nabby, one of its members quietly slipped away: "The marquis was with the king." Meanwhile other congregants continued to pour into the cathedral— its deep, otherwise shadowy recesses illuminated by its stained-glass windows and hundreds of flickering candles. Ministers, military officers, court officials, and other nobility, seated in chairs, filled the spaces closest to the altar; peasants stood distantly in the nave, closer to the edifice's three front entrances.

"Soon after we got there," John Quincy recorded, "the bishops arrived two by two. There were about twenty five of them. They had black Robes on, with a white muslin skirt which descended from the waste, down two thirds of the way to the ground; and a purple kind of a mantle over their shoulders." Then came the main event: Following the archbishop of Paris, Louis XVI entered the cathedral.

> The Archbishop of Paris had a mitre upon his head. When the king came, he went out to the Door of the Church to receive him: and as soon as his Majesty had got to his place and fallen upon his knees, they began to sing the Te Deum, which lasted about half an hour, and in which we heard some exceeding fine music. The voices were admirable. The Archbishop of Paris sung for about a Couple of Minutes, near the end, that it might be said, he had sung the Te Deum. His voice seems to be much broken. As soon as the singing was over the king and the Court immediately went away.

That evening fireworks exploded in Paris's sky. The Adams family, accustomed to New England Congregationalism's bare-bones austerity, found themselves taken aback by the day's pageantry—the pyrotechnics, unfamiliar Catholic rituals, Latin liturgy, exquisite stained-glass windows, ghostly white statues, tolling bells, clerical costumes, soaring organ cadences, incense, and opulently ornamental Gothic architecture—indeed the sheer *oldness* of the medieval cathedral. "What a charming sight," John Quincy exclaimed. "An absolutist king of one of the most powerful Empires on earth, and perhaps a thousand of the first personages in that Empire, adoring the divinity who created them, and acknowledging that he can in a moment reduce them to the Dust from which they sprung."

To Adrienne, meanwhile, according to her biographer, the Adamses' mere presence at the *Te Deum* marked for her a personal success: "It was nothing less than a triumph to have introduced so fanatically Protestant a family into Notre-Dame." Even to Adrienne's tastes, however, though she was accustomed to such pomp, the festivities erred on the side of excess: "It was too magnificent, and there was too much noise and bustle," she complained to Nabby.

Jefferson was similarly awestruck. Writing hours later to William Short—who, though invited, had failed to attend—Jefferson found himself at a loss to describe the event: "You lost much by not attending the Te-deum at Notre dame yesterday," he wrote:

It bids defiance to description. I will only observe to you in general that there were more judges, ecclesiastics and Grands seigneurs present, than Genl. Washington had of simple souldiers in his army, when he took the Hessians at Trenton, beat the British at Princeton, and hemmed up the British army at Brunswick a whole winter.

But what did Jefferson, the reliable republican, otherwise think—perhaps politically—of what he had witnessed? Unfortunately no other words describing his reaction survive. Perhaps, however, in their absence, the reaction of another articulate American republican—Nabby Adams—fairly approximates Jefferson's:

It was impossible not to make many reflections upon this august and superb ceremony, and upon the sentiments people discovered for their King. But in this government I should think it was right and necessary. If the man who has the whole kingdom at his disposal, is not respected, and thought of as next to their God, he will not long sustain his power. And however wrong it may be, it is unavoidable.[1]

TWENTY-NINE

The Patriarch of Passy

As spring returned to Paris in 1785, Lafayette and Adrienne had reason to be pleased with their efforts—beginning with the *Te Deum* at Notre Dame—to coax Thomas Jefferson out of his house into a more engaged life. Indeed—on May 24, seven weeks after the *Te Deum*—Jefferson, emulating his friends' initiative, collected Patsy at Panthémont; and the two set out to watch Marie Antoinette's ceremonial procession to Notre Dame in honor of the royal infant.

He also during those months returned to a long-deferred writing project. And in May, a Paris printer he hired produced two hundred copies of his *Notes on the State of Virginia*. Although appearing anonymously that spring and in a later American edition, Jefferson's authorship of the work was an open secret among his friends; and *Notes* would be the only book he published in his lifetime. Although encyclopedic in scope in describing its author's native state, the book's comments on race and slavery gained particular attention—especially its expressed view of the incompatibility of the black and white races. Absent other interventions, Jefferson wrote, the two were doomed to an inevitable race war: "Indeed I tremble for my country when I reflect that God is just: that his justice cannot sleep for ever."

With increasing frequency the Virginian also began hosting dinners at his residence. Better familiarizing himself with Paris, Jefferson likewise attended dinners and salons hosted by Lafayette's family (including Madame de Tessé) and Madame Helvétius (Anne-Catherine de Lignivile, comtesse d'Houdentot), widow of the philosopher Helvétius and a celebrated Paris doyenne. Jefferson also continued to call on the Adamses. On May 8 Abigail Adams noted to a friend: "We have as much company in a formal way as our Revenues will admit, and Mr. Jefferson with one or two Americans visits us in the Social friendly way."

For the Adams family, however, a sadness tinged the pleasures of that season's social calendar. Having arrived in Paris a year earlier, they now found themselves on the eve of yet another move. The previous fall, the war with England having formally ended, Congress had named John Adams to be the young nation's minister to the Court of St. James's. Although the family looked forward to living in London, there was much about Paris that they would miss— notably one particular individual: "I shall realy regreet to leave Mr. Jefferson, he is one of the choice ones of the Earth," Abigail lamented to her older sister, Mary. Reciprocating, Thomas and Patsy Jefferson were likewise saddened by the Adamses' imminent leave-taking: "The departure of your family has left me in the dumps," Jefferson soon wrote to John Adams. "My afternoons hang heavily on me."

For Jefferson their departure was doubly unwelcome—auguring yet another setback for his diplomatic work. He was still learning the emissary's profession, and with John Adams removed to London, Jefferson would be losing one of his two vastly more experienced American colleagues. More personally, he was losing companions who had helped make his first months in Paris bearable.[1]

———

Long before late May 1785, when the Adamses finally left France, Jefferson knew that he would soon become the only American emissary in Paris. That March, in a move that surprised no one, Benjamin Franklin had tendered his resignation as U.S. minister to France, and Congress, as expected, had appointed Jefferson as his replacement. Accordingly, on May 17, at Versailles, the Virginian presented his credentials to the king as the new *Ministre Plenipotentiare des Étas Unis d'Amerique.*

John Adams's long working relationship with Franklin had been fraught with intermittent tensions—and by 1785, those discords, exacerbated by Adams's resentments over what he saw as Franklin's ill-deserved glowing reputation, had descended into outright loathing. To the diplomat Arthur Lee, Adams that year wrote a letter dripping with disdain—pitying Franklin's kidney stones and his consequent immobility: "Dr F. is at present too much an Object of Compassion to be, one of Resentment," Adams wrote. "His Stone torments him, when he rides or walks to such a degree that he is wholly confined to his House, and of late is obliged to desist from his Walks in his Chamber." Moreover, Adams added, the profligate diplomat's growing dependence on bank loans "for Money, even to live on, have humbled him in Appearance."

Jefferson's more limited collaborations with Franklin, by contrast, had suffered no rifts. Even so, the two men's rapport had always been one of mere cordiality and mutual respect more than true affections. Central in Jefferson's mind, however, as Franklin prepared to leave Passy, was the octogenarian's celebrity in France.

Indeed, among the triumvirate of American heroes celebrated in France—Washington, Lafayette, and Franklin—Franklin reigned supreme: Washington, never having visited France, was too distant, and Lafayette's celebrity, though rising, could not yet match—in longevity or magnitude—that of Franklin. Indeed, since his first visit to Paris in 1767, Franklin had intermittently been a visitor to or resident of the city. Moreover, until recent years when ailments confined him to Passy, he had been a ubiquitous presence on Paris's boulevards and in its salons—a presence increased still more by countless items, from medallions to snuffboxes, decorated with pictures of him.

In fact, so ubiquitous were images of Franklin that, as he approached his Paris tenure's end, he had grown weary of sitting for portraits. To Parisians his image embodied what Dumas Malone called "ostentatious simplicity": They adored his spectacles, unpowdered hair, and his (however implausible to Americans) marten fur cap. Moreover, they admired Franklin's genuine achievements in politics, diplomacy, the sciences, and as an inventor. Indeed, that day's

Paris celebrated Franklin as both showman and polymath; as Malone also noted, upon the death of Franklin's friend Voltaire in 1778, the Pennsylvanian had become France's "recognized high priest of philosophy." (Tellingly, Jefferson recalled, it had fallen to Franklin to administer a "death's wound" to the speculations of "the Maniac, Mesmer.")

For his part, Jefferson entertained no illusions of matching Franklin's stature among the French. (Never mind snuffboxes; Jefferson then had yet to sit even for a portrait.) The Philadelphian's departure did, however, for Jefferson, mark a critical—and daunting—juncture: Indeed, during his decades in Paris, Franklin had accumulated broad associations in a wide range of circles— political, military, artistic, literary, and intellectual. And Jefferson, due to illness during his first months in Paris, had been unable to avail himself of the entrée to such circles that Franklin otherwise might have provided: Thus, with Franklin's departure from France, doors that the senior diplomat might otherwise have opened for his successor had irrevocably closed.

In July, Benjamin Franklin departed Passy. Five years later, upon the polymath's death, Jefferson, in a letter to a friend, recalled the eighty-year-old diplomat's exit from France: "When he left Passy, it seemed as if the village had lost its Patriarch." Jefferson concluded his letter with an anecdote that recalled the challenges that he knew he would soon face: "The succession to Dr. Franklin at the court of France, was an excellent school of humility," he remembered. "On being presented to any one as the Minister of America, the common-place question, used in such cases, was 'c'est vous, Monsieur, qui remplace le Docteur Franklin?' 'It is you, Sir, who replace Doctor Franklin?' I generally answered 'no one can replace him, Sir; I am only his successor.'"[2]

With the departures of Adams and Franklin, Jefferson—still new to Paris and with his limited command of the local tongue—suddenly faced the challenge of serving as U.S. minister without the support of seasoned senior diplomats. Now more than ever, he needed someone who knew his way around Versailles.

THIRTY

Holy Roman Empire

In summer 1785 Lafayette, with his zeal for all things American, might have seemed the obvious man to assist Jefferson as he wrestled with his expanded diplomatic duties. Reciprocally, because Lafayette had been Franklin's frequent partner in diplomatic pursuits, the marquis seemingly would have rushed to work with America's sole remaining senior diplomat in Paris.

But, alas, as Jefferson took up his new post that season, Lafayette was preoccupied with preparations for a long-contemplated three-month tour of Prussia. Prompted by his admiration of Prussia's military, Lafayette planned to observe army maneuvers scheduled for that summer's final weeks. He also hoped to promote American trade among Prussia's leaders.[1]

By the early eighteenth century, Prussia, along with its rival Austrian Hapsburg monarchy, had become the dominant state of the aging Holy Roman Empire, a fragile multiethnic assemblage of European polities ruling over much of Central Europe. Both states traced their common origin to A.D. 800 and Pope Leo III's crowning of the Frankish king, Charlemagne, to lead a vast state that the pontiff—aspirationally—named the "Holy Roman Empire."

By the decade when Lafayette set off on his tour, the Holy Roman Empire's reputation had waned. By contrast, that of Prussia—or more specifically, that of its army and ruler, Frederick II, popularly dubbed Frederick the Great—was surging. In the twenty-five years since he ascended Prussia's throne, Frederick, through military conquests, had transformed the once modest state into one of Europe's greatest powers. To burnish that reputation, he routinely invited foreign leaders to observe his famous army's drills. Indeed, capturing that army's centrality to Prussian life, one contemporary observed: "Other states possess an army; Prussia is an army which possesses a state."[2]

To serve as his assistant on the tour, Lafayette selected Jean-Baptiste Gouvion, a thirty-eight-year-old lieutenant colonel in the French army. An intermittent guest-resident at the Hôtel de Lafayette, Gouvion had served as an officer in the Continental army.

In mid-July the two commenced their journey, with Cassel—capital of the tiny state of Hesse-Cassel, as their first significant stop. By coincidence Hesse-Cassel was the source of the epithet "Hessians"—shorthand for all of the soldiers hired out by various Germanic states to the British army during the American Revolution. And while in Cassel, Lafayette met several Prussian officers who had fought in that war, among them Baron Wilhelm von Knyphausen—"Old Knip," who commanded the troops Lafayette had fought and been wounded by, in the Battle of Brandywine. To Washington the marquis described seeing "our Hessian friends, old Knip Among them": "I told them they were very fine Fellows—they Returned thanks and Compliments— Ancient foes ever meet with pleasure."

Lafayette and Gouvion reached Berlin, Prussia's capital, on August 5 and stayed there for three days before leaving for nearby Potsdam. There they witnessed a review of troops, a precursor to the grander maneuvers that they soon observed in Breslau—today's Wrocław, Poland—in Prussia's province of Silesia. In Potsdam by August 17, Lafayette was granted his first audience with the aged Frederick II—also known to his subjects *Der Alte Fritz,* "Old Fritz."[3]

Frederick II ranked among his age's most revered warriors. Raised by Huguenot governesses and tutors, the future monarch—encouraged by his mother, Queen Sophia Dorothea—during his early years had cultivated the habits of an aesthete. Likely homosexual, as a boy he learned French, read voraciously, and showed promise as a writer; he also became an accomplished flutist and composer—all to the abhorrence of his brutish father, King Frederick William I.

By 1740, however, when at age twenty-eight he ascended Prussia's throne, the new king had in many ways already become the man his father, who had reformed Prussia's army and bureaucracy, had long wanted him to be. In his first year on the throne, Frederick II, personally leading Prussia's army into battle, invaded Silesia. Other territorial conquests followed—all at the expense of Austria and other nearby states.

Beginning in 1743, Frederick began staging semiannual grand maneuvers involving thousands of soldiers. The war games—soon imitated but on a smaller scale by Austria—gave his army operational experience with new weapons, tactics, and formations. And by inviting foreign leaders to witness the games, he ensured that his army's abilities were known far and wide.

Lafayette shared his generation of European warriors' veneration of Frederick. And his experiences in the Continental army—fighting on American battlefields alongside baron von Steuben and other Prussian officers—had deepened his respect for the king and his military. But when—at Sans Souci, Frederick's summer palace in Potsdam in August 1785—the twenty-eight-year-old Lafayette was first presented to the seventy-three-year-old Prussian king, the monarch, a ghost of his former self, was in his life's final year.

"I went to Make my Bow to the King," Lafayette recalled, "and notwisdanding [sic] what I Had Heard of Him, could not Help Being struck By that dress and Appearance of an old, Broken, dirty Corporal, coverd all over with Spanish snuff, with His Head almost leaning on one shoulder, and fingers quite distorted By the Gout."

But Lafayette did find one lingering vestige of the king's glory years: "What surprised me much more is the fire and some times the softness of the most Beautifull Eyes I ever saw."

Lafayette, Gouvion, and others, traveling 220 miles southeastward from Potsdam to Breslau, soon joined Frederick outside the Silesian capital to observe thirty thousand soldiers, seven thousand of them on horseback, conduct eight days of mock battles. During the American Revolution, Lafayette had commanded no more than eight or nine thousand in any single engagement. At Breslau, he thus watched with awe as twenty thousand soldiers formed into a single line. Moreover, to his further amazement, the wizened king vigorously oversaw the maneuvers, barking orders and often plunging into the action on horseback—often to the detriment of his fragile health—on muddy, rain-lashed fields.

At each day's end Lafayette joined the king's entourage for three-hour meals. Those repasts, he recalled, "gave me the opportunity to Hear Him throughout, and to admire the Vivacity of His wit, the endearing charms of His adress and politness, so far that I did Conceive people could forget what a tyrannic, Hard Hearted, and selfish Man He is."

In conversations with Frederick, Lafayette enjoyed the advantage of being French, an aristocrat, and a young man—all traits that endeared him to the monarch. But tales of his deeds as a republican warrior proved less ingratiating to the absolutist ruler. One exchange darkly portended a later trip by Lafayette into Prussia: After listening for several minutes as Lafayette recalled his American experiences, the king suddenly fixed his eyes on the young officer.

"Sir," Frederick said slyly, "I know of a young man who, after visiting countries that embraced ideas of liberty and equality, took it upon himself to import those ideas into his own country."

Pausing, he asked if Lafayette knew the young man's fate?

"No, sire."

"Sir," the king responded, smiling. "He was hanged."

The anecdote's impression on the marquis remains unknown. But Frederick's nephew, Crown Prince Frederick William, was also present; and, after he ascended Prussia's throne, he remembered the story well enough to recall it to Lafayette during another encounter, under vastly different circumstances.

While in Breslau over those eight days, in a coincidence even more striking than his earlier encounter with "Old Knip," Lafayette watched the maneuvers and shared a dinner table each evening with the twenty-two-year-old Duke of York, King George III's second-oldest son, *and* Charles—now Lord—Cornwallis, the marquis's old nemesis. Now forty-six, Cornwallis was acting that month as a British envoy to the Prussian court, sounding out the possibilities of an Anglo-Prussian alliance.

At each meal Frederick made a point of seating Lafayette between Cornwallis and the Duke of York. Lafayette's accounts of the evenings' conversations—particularly with Cornwallis—are, however, frustratingly cursory. To Jefferson he wrote: "I fancy I may Have still More particular opportunities to know His opinions, and to introduce my ideas."

Whatever was said over those days, Cornwallis seems to have dominated their exchanges—the British general apparently peppering his former foe with queries concerning U.S. politics. To Washington, Lafayette recalled "having the British King's son on [one] side" and on the other, hearing the general "Make [a] thousand questions on American affairs." The sole question posed by Cornwallis that Lafayette *did* recall in his letter to Washington concerned a rumor circulating in London about Washington himself: "I Remember He Asked the duke of York if it was true you intended taking an House in London."

Of his Breslau exchanges with Lafayette, Cornwallis's own extant correspondence is only slightly more forthcoming—revealing if nothing else that he found the visit less than edifying. "My reception in Silesia was not flattering," he recalled. "There was a marked preference for La Fayette; whether it proceeded from the King's knowing more of France, and liking better to talk about it, I know not."

Moreover, Cornwallis, unlike Lafayette, was singularly unimpressed by the army he observed in Prussia. "The cavalry is very fine; the infantry exactly like the Hessian, only taller and better set up, but much slower in their movements," Cornwallis remembered. "Their maneuvers were such as the worst general would be hooted at for practicing; two lines coming up within six yards of one another, and firing in one another's faces till they had no ammunition left: nothing could be more ridiculous."

Throughout Prussia, Lafayette won an adulation among all classes similar to that he enjoyed in America and France—a gratification made all the happier by his "Highest satisfation" with Frederick's military: "Nothing Can Be Compared to the Beauty of the troops, the discipline that is diffused throughout, the simplicity of their Motions, the Uniformity of their Regiments."

One aspect of Prussia's military did trouble Lafayette, however—what seemed to him its cruel regimen. Twice, he reported, he witnessed Frederick berate three officers, eventually placing all under arrest: "Altho' I found much to admire, I had rather be the last farmer in America than the first general in Berlin."[4]

Because the next Prussian maneuvers would not be held until late September, Lafayette and Gouvion decided to make a quick trip to neighboring Austria, Prussia's archrival. Arriving in Vienna on September 2, they were soon presented to the forty-four-year-old Hapsburg emperor Joseph II—Marie Antoinette's older brother. As in Prussia, the two also received permission to observe military maneuvers. Traveling successively to Prague and Brandýs nad Labem (Brandeis on the Elbe), they were impressed by the demonstrations they witnessed—albeit involving far fewer soldiers than they had seen in Breslau. In Austria as in Prussia, Lafayette also missed no opportunity to promote American commerce.[5]

Returning to Prussia in early September, the two men spent several more weeks observing maneuvers and meeting with government leaders. Frederick, having fallen ill from the rigors and rains of the Breslau maneuvers, was not seeing guests that month. But his indisposition proved fortuitous for the marquis— creating an opportunity to spend two weeks with Frederick's younger brother, Prince Henry. To Washington the marquis reported, the question of whether the king or Henry was the better soldier was one "that divides the Military World."

But Lafayette had no doubt whom he personally preferred. Prince Henry was, he wrote to Washington, "By far the Best Acquaintance I Have Made." His abilities, wrote the marquis, were "first Rate, Both as a soldier and a politician," with "litterary knowledge, and all the Endowments of the Mind."[6]

By the month's end Lafayette and Gouvion were en route via Holland back to Paris. "The kind Reception I met with in Every part of my journey Has given me the Means to Hear, and to speak much, on the affairs of America," the marquis wrote to Jefferson.

Nonetheless Lafayette remained disturbed by what he viewed as falsehoods about America circulating in central Europe, distortions he attributed to British leaders and newspapers: "I find the Misrepresentations of Great Britain Have not Been fruitless," he reported to Washington. He particularly worried that "the want of powers in Congress, of Union Between the States" undermined the confidence of European governments to conduct business with the young nation.

In 1776 Jefferson's Declaration of Independence had introduced the world to a new independent republic. But, as he and Lafayette were learning, that republic's governing document, the Articles of Confederation—enacted in 1777 and which had come into force in 1781—had shortcomings that went beyond its fecklessness in the domestic sphere. It had also failed to inspire confidence in foreign climes.[7]

THIRTY-ONE

Hôtel de Langeac

In fall 1785—back from Prussia and resolved to work with America's chief diplomat in Paris—Lafayette arranged a meeting between Jefferson and several Frenchmen involved in commercial affairs. They in turn suggested that Jefferson ask Foreign Minister Vergennes to appoint a committee to study Franco-American trade. And by February 1786, Charles Alexandre de Colonne, France's controller general of finances, had, at Lafayette's initiative, established a committee comprising Lafayette, various Versailles ministers and bureaucrats, a merchant, members of the Ferme générale, and Pierre Samuel du Pont de Nemours, a noted economist and advocate of economic reforms.

Over the coming months, working through the committee and on their own, Lafayette, Jefferson, and the American consul general, Thomas Barclay, worked to find inroads for U.S. exports into the French market—to lower tariffs, open French ports, and remove monopoly obstructions for Virginia tobacco, New England whale oil, South Carolina rice, and Georgia timber. While producing mixed results at best, their efforts nonetheless brightened Jefferson's and Lafayette's hopes for expanded American commerce in France.[1]

By February 1786, meanwhile, Lafayette had only praise for his new partner in Paris: "Words Cannot Sufficiently Express to You How much I am pleased with Mr Jefferson's public Conduct," he wrote to Washington. To James Madison, Jefferson similarly praised *his* new partner: "The Marquis de Lafayette is a most valuable auxiliary to me," he wrote. "His zeal is unbounded, and his we[ight] with those in power great."

Jefferson was already overseeing the two commissions for busts of Lafayette by the sculptor Houdon—one for Virginia's Capitol, another for Paris's City Hall. But in February 1786—amid the surge of their mutual affections—Jefferson presciently anticipated a day when Lafayette would run afoul of Versailles. Pondering that possibility, he suggested another way that Virginia might demonstrate its appreciation of the marquis: "I am persuaded that a gift of lands by the state of Virginia to the Marquis de la fayette would give a good opinion here of our character," he wrote. "Nor am I sure that the day will not come when it might be an useful asylum to him."[2]

During those months American trade wasn't the only subject weighing on Jefferson. Since learning in 1785 that he would be replacing Franklin as U.S. minister to France, he had concluded that his current residence, the Hôtel Tetebout, failed to project a suitable aura for the republic he represented.

Moreover, since arriving in Paris, Jefferson had been irked that Congress—in contrast to the largesse shown Adams and Franklin—required him to pay from his salary rent and other costs associated with furnishing and running his residence. Indeed, by spring 1785, when Jefferson learned of his new appointment, the Hôtel Tetebout was already straining his purse. Thus, during those months, as he pondered a new, more expensive residence, he grew ever more anxious about his finances. Congress eventually declined Jefferson's request. Nevertheless, the following October, he leased a new pricier residence. The house sat snugly on Paris's then-verdant western edge, on the rue Neuve de Berri (today's rue de Berri), at its intersection with the Champs-Élysées. Called the Hôtel de Langeac, the town house's construction had commenced in 1768 as the intended home of a mistress of a minister in the court of Louis XV.

Like Jefferson's former Paris residence, the Hôtel de Langeac served as his office and home. Fittingly, its interior contained no fewer than twenty-four rooms, two of them oval-shaped, as well as a water closet, an unusual amenity for that era. The walled estate's grounds offered a stable, servants' quarters, a kitchen garden, and an English garden. A dry moat provided a buffer between the estate and the busy Champs-Élysées.

Rent on the town house came to 7,500 livres per year—3,000 more than the Hôtel Tetebout; with its twenty-four rooms, the Hôtel de Langeac was still smaller than the Paris missions of other, older, countries. Even so, the freestanding two-story mansion, with its neoclassical facade, projected, as Jefferson intended, aristocratic elegance.

Like Tetebout, however, the Hôtel de Langeac came with no furniture. Thus, prior to moving in on October 17, Jefferson decided that the larger house required the purchase of more furniture and objets d'art, as well as the hiring of a larger household staff. Furthermore, because the Hôtel de Langeac came with its own stables and gardens, its new master also deemed it fitting to acquire horses and carriages and to hire his own coachman and a full-time gardener. After moving into the Hôtel de Langeac, as Jefferson's financial woes deepened, so too did his resentments over what he perceived as Congress's parsimony.

The Hôtel de Langeac sat in the newly built Faubourg du Roule, one of eleven new faubourgs—suburbs—that in recent years had expanded Paris's area. As scaffolds and workmen transformed the city into one large construction site, its cobblestone streets resonated in a symphony of clanging hammers, the sawing of lumber, and the scraping of trowels.

To be sure, even as Versailles's ministers were fretting over their increasingly depleted treasury, in Paris state-funded construction—along with projects underwritten by nobles such as the duc de Orléans and merchant princes of the city's rising bourgeoisie—were keeping legions of carpenters, masons, and plasterers in work: "The building mania gives an air of grandeur and majesty to the city," noted one observer. "The speculators cry out for the contractors who, with plan in one hand and a contract in the other, bring balm to the hearts of the capitalist."[3]

Financial strains aside, by the season of his move to the Hôtel de Langeac, Jefferson had regained his health. And with Lafayette's help, he had found his footing as a diplomat. Consequently he felt increasingly free to enjoy Paris. From the Hôtel de Langeac, he took daily walks in the nearby Bois de Boulogne—in good weather, four or five miles each day. He also established relationships with Parisian wine merchants and, in his new gardens, experimented with the cultivation of various grape species—often with seeds sent from Virginia. He likewise instructed servants to grow other produce familiar to him—including watermelons, cantaloupes, sweet potatoes, and maize. "I cultivate in my own garden here Indian corn for the use of my own table, to eat green in our manner," he exulted.[4]

In late 1785, however, even as Jefferson warmed to Paris, he remained very much the Piedmont Virginian who had arrived in France a year earlier. In September, to Charles Bellini, an Italian-born teacher of modern languages at the College of William and Mary, he playfully referred to himself as a "savage of the mountains of America"—and offered his views "on the vaunted scene of Europe!"

To the extent that Jefferson's letter drew on firsthand experience, his reference to "Europe" actually referred solely to France. Aside from brief stopovers on British soil en route from Boston, France was the European country he had then visited, and indeed, even within France his travels, as he wrote that day, were limited. Even so—if nothing else—his September 1785 letter to Bellini, commencing with matters of class, did offer a wide-ranging tour of the geography of his evolved opinions up to that day on the New and Old Worlds' respective merits:

> I find the general fate of humanity here most deplorable. The truth of Voltaire's observation offers itself perpetually, that every man here must be either the hammer or the anvil. It is a true picture of that country to which they say we shall pass hereafter, and where we are to see god and his angels in splendor, and crouds of the damned trampled under their feet.

"The great mass of the people are thus suffering under physical and moral oppression," he wrote—especially when compared with "that degree of happiness which is enjoyed in America by every class of people."

While Jefferson subscribed to no particular organized religion, steeped in his native Virginia Piedmont's cultural conservatism, he condemned what he saw as unashamed and routine violations of marital fidelity within Paris's elite circles. "Conjugal love," he complained, "having no existence among them, domestic happiness, of which that is the basis, is utterly unknown. In lieu of this are substituted pursuits which nourish and invigorate all our bad passions."

In matters scientific, Jefferson, taking a more mixed view, saw France's "mass of people" as "two centuries behind ours"—but "their literati half a dozen years before us." Concerning social manners, however, his view of France approached full-throated admiration:

Without sacrificing too much the sincerity of language, I would wish [my] countrymen to adopt just so much of European politeness as to be ready [to] make all those little sacrifices of self which really render European manners amiable, and relieve society from the disagreeable scenes to which rudeness often exposes it.

Jefferson particularly admired French dining etiquette. "In the pleasures of the table they are far before us, because with good taste they unite temperance. . . . I have never yet seen a man drunk in France, even among the lowest of the people."

There was yet one other realm in which the diplomat ranked French achievements superior to those of his native land, but that, he lamented to Bellini, would have to await a fuller exposition: "Were I to proceed to tell you how much I enjoy their architecture, sculpture, painting, music, I should want words. It is in these arts they shine. The last of them particularly is an enjoiment, the deprivation of which with us cannot be calculated."

Having shared a year's worth of first impressions, Jefferson closed his dispatch to Bellini on a humble note—the note of an innocent abroad, one aware of his biases and that many of them would likely be transformed by coming days: "I am running on in an estimate of things infinitely better known to you than to me, and which will only serve to convince you that I have brought with me all the prejudices of country, habit and age."[5]

In the meantime, with his larger house and improved health, Jefferson, during that same fall of 1785, played host to a stream of guests—including American sailors stranded abroad, French and American veterans of the American Revolution, and assorted American writers, inventors, and artists.

Typically, dinners at the Hôtel de Langeac and the households of other American diplomats in Paris commingled American and French sensibilities. "There is no such thing here as preserving our taste in anything," Nabby Adams noted after a gathering in the home of U.S. consul general Barclay. "We must all sacrifice to custom and fashion."

Under Jefferson's roof, dinners were prepared by a succession of caterers and increasingly, as he evolved into a skilled chef, by James Hemings. According to an early Jefferson biographer, in Paris the Virginian's "manners had the grace, finish, suavity and unpresumingness . . . of a well-bred Frenchman." At table "he ate delicately and sparingly of light materials, and chose the lightest wines of French vintage." Even so, according to William Short, in Paris the diplomat retained a "fastidious adherence to American ideas of decorum" when "American and French standards differ[ed]." Conversational forays into the realm of the "broad . . . in his presence, always made him literally, 'blush like a boy.'"

One fashion of that age's elite Paris society that Jefferson did embrace—and later adopted in Monticello and Washington—was the use of individual tables in dining rooms. The practice deepened conversational intimacy, reduced the necessity of interruptions by servants during dinners, and, finally, according to Jefferson, reduced the chances of servants repeating often false versions of overheard exchanges. The dissemination of such distortions, Jefferson believed, owed to the fact "that much of the domestic and even public discord was produced by the mutilated and misconstrued repetition of free conversations at dinner tables by these mute but not inattentive listeners."

In many ways Jefferson, in late 1785, stubbornly remained the Virginia highlander, fundamentally skeptical of French culture, who had arrived in Paris a year earlier. But slowly—if only concerning customs that reinforced prior dispositions—he was finding aspects of France worthy of adoption.[6]

THIRTY-TWO

England

The reason for my importing harness from England is a very obvious one. They are plated, and plated harness is not made at all in France as far as I have learnt. It is not from a love of the English but a love of myself that I sometimes find myself obliged to buy their manufactures.

THOMAS JEFFERSON TO LAFAYETTE, NOVEMBER 3, 1786

I t was always in the cards that Jefferson, while living in France, would make a proper visit to England. En route to France in July 1784, he, daughter Patsy, and James Hemings had touched briefly on British soil—on the Isle of Wight and at Portsmouth. But those had been layovers by weary travelers at busy ports, hardly real visits. As it turned out, when Jefferson finally did make a sustained visit to England—for five weeks in spring 1786—diplomatic matters nominally occasioned the outing. More saliently, his friends John and Abigail Adams were living in London, and he had long desired to visit his forebears' country.

The commission created by Congress that had brought Jefferson to Paris was scheduled to expire in May 1786. Given that, its two remaining members decided to meet in London and tie up its final business. They particularly hoped to conclude a trade agreement with Portugal, and also to meet with emissaries of the Barbary States in a final effort to end those polities' depredations against American merchant ships in the Mediterranean. In the end Adams and Jefferson did conclude a trade treaty with Portugal's emissary in London, but it was eventually rejected by Lisbon. The meetings with the Barbary emissaries similarly came to naught.

Although Jefferson's London visit produced no lasting diplomatic successes, it did provide five weeks for him to give free rein to the pent-up curiosities of a lifetime concerning English places, history, and culture. Since her family's move to London, Abigail had maintained a lively correspondence with Jefferson and had repeatedly invited him to visit. A measure of their continuing affections, each regularly shopped for the other in their respective cities of residence— afterward dutifully sending the other the requested purchases.

Typifying those exchanges, in September 1785 Jefferson wrote to Abigail, "I immediately ordered the shoes you desired . . . I have also procured for you three plateaux de dessert with a silvered ballustrade round them, and four figures of Biscuit [unglazed pottery]. . . . With respect to the figures I could only find three of those you named, matched in size. These were Minerva, Diana, and Apollo." Jefferson later purchased a figurine of Mars to round out the set. But, alas, when the figurines arrived in London, all the gods and goddesses had lost their heads in transit.[1]

Jefferson left Paris on March 6, 1786. Via a mutual friend Abigail had suggested that he bring his daughter Patsy "and let her tarry with me" as he and her husband tended to their diplomatic errands. Instead, accompanying Jefferson to London was twenty-nine-year-old Col. William Stephens Smith. An aide to Lafayette during the war in America, Smith was Adams's legation secretary in London, and that summer he would marry Nabby Adams. Traveling to Calais by carriage and from there crossing to Dover, the two men reached London on March 11. After securing lodging, Jefferson found his way to the Adams's brick house at the northeast corner of Grosvenor Square. There, over the coming weeks, as Nabby recalled, their guest "dined with us whenever he has not been otherwise engaged, and made this House a kind of Home," an arrangement "very agreeable to us all."[2]

Intermittently throughout Jefferson's London stay, diplomatic matters occupied his and John Adams's time. But the sojourn's highlight was a six-day carriage trip that the two men took through the English countryside. Setting off from London on April 2, their excursion focused on English country estates, including Hampton Court, Stowe, Woburn Farm, and Blenheim.

Both men took copious notes during the trip—reflections as revelatory of their respective interests as of the depicted places. Adams, for instance, more than Jefferson, indulged the role of public moralist. In the town of Worcester, site of the English Civil War's final battle in 1651, he complained of towns-people who appeared "so ignorant" of local history: "Provoked," Adams scolded several, asking: "Do Englishmen so soon forget the ground where liberty was fought for? Tell your neighbors and your children that this is holy ground; much holier than that on which your churches stand."

The New England Congregationalist likewise found fault with encountered statuary and architecture that, by Adams's lights, reflected sybaritic tastes: "The temples to Bacehus [*sic*] and Venus are quite unnecessary, as mankind have no need of artificial incitement to such amusements." But if Adams played the public moralist during the tour, Jefferson was the detached aesthete. Less the conventional tourist disposed to being impressed with each stop's bounties, he traveled more as the touring envoy for his own estate—scouting for ideas to improve Monticello.

In fact the tour's itinerary had been derived largely from places depicted in a favorite Jefferson book—Thomas Whately's *Observations on Modern Gardening*: "I always walked over the gardens with his book in my hand," he recalled. "My enquiries were directed chiefly to such practical things as might enable me to estimate the expence of making and maintaining a garden in that style."

Jefferson's notes on Blenheim typify that practical approach. Adams's notes summarized the estate—and for that matter two others in the same sentence—with one word: "superb"; Jefferson's notes, by contrast, take a more nuanced measure of the scene:

> The water here is very beautiful, and very grand. The cascade from the lake
> a fine one. Except this the garden has no great beauties. It is not laid out in
> fine lawns and woods, but the trees are scattered thinly over the ground. . . .

The gravelled walks are broad. Art appears too much. There are but a few seats in it, and nothing of architecture more dignified. There is no one striking position in it.

At Stratford-upon-Avon, the two visited the half-timbered house believed to be Shakespeare's birthplace. There, recorded Adams, they were shown "an old Wooden Chair in the Chimney Corner, where He sat." Afterward, approaching the chair, they engaged in a tourist ritual of that day that to modern ears would seem calculated to inflict heart attacks among museum staffs and conservators: "We cutt off a Chip [of the chair] according to the Custom," Jefferson recalled. Now in the custody of the Thomas Jefferson Foundation, in Charlottesvillle, Virginia, the chip has thus far generated no cultural artifacts repatriation lawsuits by British plaintiffs.[3]

In London on Sunday evening, March 30, in a private residence, Jefferson joined for dinner the Adamses and other guests, including diplomats from Venice and Prussia. Beyond the men, Abigail noted, "Many very Brilliant Ladies of the first distinction were present." Their hosts' home —"a most superb Building," she also recalled, was "beautifully situated, fronting St James park, one end of the House standing upon Hyde park."

The evening's hosts, John and Lucy Ludwell Paradise, were middle-aged American expatriates: Lucy came from a prominent Virginia family—hence her interest in meeting Jefferson. Her Greece-born husband, John, whom Jefferson had known in Virginia, was a fellow of the Royal Society, comprising Britain's leading scientists.

Jefferson enjoyed the company of both Paradises, but he was more drawn to John, in whom he saw an opportunity to unravel a mystery that had long intrigued him: In that age before recorded sound, Jefferson hoped, through John, fluent in modern Greek, to gain insight into how the ancient Greek language sounded as a living tongue.

At least twice while in London, Jefferson attended the theater with the Adamses. But the fact that he left behind few words about those evenings likely attests more to his relative indifference to the dramatic arts than to the merits of what he saw. For that matter—little interested in socializing as an end unto itself—Jefferson left no accounts of most of his London outings with the Adamses—including the annual ball hosted by the French Embassy, which he, the Paradises, and the Adamses attended.

In stark contrast were Jefferson's notes on technological advances he observed. Exploring the early stirrings of Britain's Industrial Revolution, he was often beside himself in wonderment; celebrating what that age still called "the mechanical arts," he reveled in inspecting—sometimes purchasing—inventions and gadgets.

The use of steam power in British gristmills particularly impressed Jefferson—reinforcing his conviction that the same energy would soon propel ships on America's rivers. More so than France, England was already being transformed by the Industrial Revolution: "I could write you volumes on the improvements which I find made and making here in the arts," he reported to a friend.

In England, Jefferson purchased and sent to America a trunk of clothes for the wife and sister-in-law of a friend in Virginia. For others he bought numerous books. But most of his purchases were for himself—books and instruments for scientific observation or surveying, including a thermometer, solar microscope, theodolite, hydrometer, and protractor. For later delivery to himself in Paris, he also ordered a new carriage, a portable copying press, and a plated harness for riding.[4]

By the late 1780s Lafayette had been the subject of paintings or engravings by numerous artists, including Jean-Baptiste-Louis Le Paon, Adrien Carpentiers, William Angus, and Charles Willson Peale. In London—making a late start in his own pictorial bid for posterity—Jefferson sat for his first portrait. The resultant work, by the young American-born artist Mather Brown—soon hung in the Adams household. Later, at the subject's request, Brown completed and sent to Paris a second rendering of Jefferson.[5]

In London, Jefferson and John Adams also visited the studio of Mather Brown's teacher, the Anglo-American painter Benjamin West. To West and three other American painters that Jefferson met in London—Mather Brown,

John Singleton Copley, and John Trumbull—he posed a question about the commissioned statue of Washington by Houdon that he was overseeing.

All four, Jefferson soon reported to Washington, shared his dissent from the neoclassical convention that even contemporary warriors be depicted wearing the togas of classical Greece and Rome: "I think a modern in an antique dress as just an object of ridicule as an Hercules or Marius with a periwig and chapeau bras [three-cornered hat]."[6]

In England, Jefferson also had his only two encounters with King George III, the man who had been the object of much of the Declaration of Independence's scorn ("The history of the present King of Great Britain is a history of repeated injuries and usurpations. . . ."). In the king's court and government most resentments over the late rebellion in the thirteen colonies had faded into a grudging acceptance of the new order. Vestigial antipathies persisted less as dreams of reconquest, and more as hopes that the fragile federation of former colonies—bound by its weak Articles of Confederation—would unravel of its own accord.

At forty-seven, the bewigged king whom Jefferson met in 1786 was no longer the slim, athletic young man who had ascended the throne almost three decades earlier. Even so, still vigorous and relatively fit, neither was he the corpulent and befuddled monarch to which later caricatures reduced him. Furthermore, contrary to widespread perceptions in America then and later, the policies that, as early as 1765, had sparked American discontents against Britain had originated not with George III but among his ministers. Furthermore, not until 1773, after the Boston Tea Party, did his own opposition harden against the colonists. Also contrary to widespread misconception, George III, relative to other European monarchs, possessed relatively few powers— Britain's throne having since 1689 become largely subordinate to Parliament.

John Adams had broached the idea of presenting Jefferson to the king during a meeting he and Jefferson had with Britain's foreign secretary Lord Carmarthen. And based upon Adams's own first meeting with the king nine months earlier, the two Americans had every reason to expect that Jefferson's presentation would go equally well. Indeed, shortly before Jefferson's visit, Abigail, writing to Jefferson, had described the king's welcoming of her husband as having "been as gracious and as agreeable as the reception given to the Ministers of any other foreign powers."

Presumably—and no records suggest otherwise—Jefferson's own first presentation to the king, on March 14 at St. James's Palace, proceeded uneventfully. The following day, however, Jefferson, along with Adams, returned to the palace—this time for a levee in the King's Presentation Room—a space used for large gatherings. King George and his consort, Charlotte, were present, but beyond those details, the gathering is recalled mainly for how badly it went for the Americans.

Jefferson never spoke publicly of the encounter, and his single extant written comment about it is both brief and vague: "On my presentation as usual to the King and Queen at their levees, it was impossible for anything to be more ungracious than their notice of Mr. Adams & myself." Seven decades later it fell to Charles Francis Adams, while editing the autobiography of his grandfather John Adams and drawing on family lore, to specify the precise form of George III's affront: "The king turned his back upon the American commissioners, a hint which, of course, was not lost upon the circle of his subjects in attendance."[7]

On April 26 Jefferson departed London. By the twenty-eighth he was back under the Hôtel de Langeac's welcoming roof—returned from what would be his only sustained stay on English soil.[8]

THIRTY-THREE

Historical Scenes

On May 1, 1786, soon after Jefferson's return to Paris, he began reviewing the Hôtel de Langeac's account books for the days he was away. Over the coming weeks suspicions of "embezzlements and depredations" hardened into certainty, and on June 26 he dismissed Marc—no other name survives—his maître d'hôtel. To the post he promoted his valet de chambre (butler), Adrien Petit, formerly of the Adamses' Auteil residence and under whom daily costs for the house's daily main meal soon fell by 20 percent.

Otherwise, upon returning to Paris, Jefferson resumed his usual diplomatic appointments and correspondence. As always, he also found time for other enterprises—including monitoring progress on Houdon's marble sculptures of Lafayette and Washington.

And on May 22, on behalf of the state of Virginia, Jefferson paid for a plaster-of-Paris model for a proposed new capitol in Richmond. Becolumned with a recessed portico, the envisioned capitol was modeled after Maison Carrée, a surviving ancient Roman temple in Nîmes. Jefferson had contemplated the proposed building since 1785, when he was asked by the state to develop its design. To construct the edifice's 1:60 scale model, he hired Jean-Pierre Fouquet, a prominent local practitioner in the architectural-model-making métier.

Fouquet was to work from a design rendered by Parisian architect Charles-Louis Clerisseau, based on sketches by Jefferson. Virginia's new Capitol was completed three years later. Rising from Richmond's Shockoe Hill, on which Jefferson lived while governor, the edifice—even today as I-95 traffic hastens by in noisy proximity—remains a jewel of American neoclassical public architecture.

Visitors, meanwhile, in 1786, continued to find their way to the Hôtel de Langeac—among them the American adventurer John Ledyard. Then in his midthirties, Ledyard was of average height, broad shouldered, with an aquiline nose. "His flowing blond hair was so light it was almost white," recalled a contemporary. "His cornflower blue eyes gave a faraway look to his appearance." The son of a prosperous Connecticut merchant sea captain, Ledyard as a young man had abandoned in succession contemplated careers as a Christian missionary to American Indians and as a lawyer. After dropping out of Dartmouth College, he became a seaman in the transatlantic trade.

In early 1776, while in England, after being arrested—likely for vagrancy—Ledyard was ordered by a court to join the military, and he enlisted in the British marine. Soon thereafter, with his knowledge of American Indian languages, he was recruited to sail on James Cook's third and final voyage of exploration. Thus, in July 1776—as Jefferson was drafting the Declaration of Independence—Ledyard sailed from England with Cook's expedition.

By 1783 Ledyard had returned to the now-independent United States and published a book on his voyage. Later that year he joined a venture, funded by the politician and financier Robert Morris, to participate in the newly opened American trade with China. Its costs, however, proved excessive for Morris, and by late 1784 Ledyard was back in Europe, seeking new backers for another China-trade enterprise.

In Paris in 1785 Ledyard became a fixture at the Hôtel de Langeac. There, he enjoyed lively dinners with Jefferson, Lafayette, David Humphreys, Thomas Barclay, William Short, and others. Indeed, Ledyard became such a fixture and object of interest in the households of Jefferson *and* Lafayette that, after Ledyard's departure from Paris, Jefferson found himself having to apologize for being unable to retrieve from Ledyard's circle of local admirers his book *A Journal of Captain Cook's Last Voyage to the Pacific Ocean*, published in 1783: "I am sorry it is not in my power to send you your book," Jefferson wrote. "Very soon after I received it from you I lent it to Madame de la fayette, who has been obliged to lend it from hand to hand and has never returned it."

Inexorably, during Ledyard's Paris visit—principally, apparently, under Jefferson's sway—Ledyard's commercial aspirations gave way to a different travel resolve—to become the first man to walk around the world. For Jefferson the contemplated venture no doubt rekindled tales that enthralled him as a boy of his father's wilderness adventures, surveying the Virginia–North Carolina border. And in early 1786 Jefferson and Lafayette commenced efforts to gain financial support for Ledyard's project from Russia's government, as well as to secure permission for him to walk west-to-east across Russia and, from its east coast, to sail to North America.

To place their request before Russia's Prussian-born czarina—Catherine the Great—Lafayette wrote to his friend the comte de Ségur, France's ambassador in Saint Petersburg. He also approached the baron de Grimm, the czarina's unofficial emissary in Paris. The marquis likewise sought to win French government support for his friend's venture.

In Paris, meanwhile, during his entire stay Ledyard remained dependent, financially and otherwise, on Jefferson and Lafayette. And in late 1786, so that Ledyard might begin his expedition, Grimm—expecting any day to receive a letter containing the czarina's endorsement of the project—advanced him funds for his travels. Shortly afterward, Lafayette, drawing on his personal funds, supplemented Grimm's largesse.

Ledyard soon departed Paris. En route to Russia, he stopped in London in hopes of finding other financial backers. While there, feeling nostalgic, he wrote to Jefferson: "I shall never wish to die while you the Marquis and Mr. Barclay are alive." To another correspondent—revealing his still greater affections for Lafayette—he vowed: "If I find in my travels a mountain as much elevated above other mountains as he is above ordinary men, I will name it *La Fayette*."

In August, meanwhile, Jefferson received word of Catherine's denial of his request on Ledyard's behalf; "She thinks it chimærical," he informed his friend.

Undaunted, however, Ledyard set out on his trip: Indeed, before being arrested by the czarina's agents and expelled from the country, he got all the way, in September 1787, to the Siberian town of Yakutsk in Russia's Far East.

Two years later, in January 1789, Ledyard died—in Cairo, of unknown but apparently natural causes—while preparing for an expedition to explore the sources of the Nile. Ledyard's contemplated explorations had largely come to naught. For Lafayette and Jefferson, however their association with him, even after his death, proved consequential.

During the mid-1780s, through Catherine's communications with Lafayette concerning Ledyard, the czarina became aware of their shared interest in North American Indian languages. And that shared interest—and Lafayette's promise to assist with an Indian lexicon she was preparing—soon led to an invitation, which he accepted, to visit her during a royal visit to Crimea planned for spring 1787.

As for Jefferson, before and after Catherine denied Ledyard permission to walk across Russia, the Virginian remained captivated by his project. Moreover, repeatedly, before Ledyard settled on walking across Russia, Jefferson had tried to persuade him to organize an east-to-west overland transit of North America. It was the same transcontinental journey that, decades later, as president—in the wake of his transformative Louisiana Purchase, which doubled the size of the United States—he would assign to the explorers Lewis and Clark.

As spring 1786 gave way to summer, Jefferson more than any time since arriving in Paris, also immersed himself in the city's public life: He attended concerts and plays, and, on the afternoon of June 18, after purchasing a ticket, he watched a balloon piloted by Pierre Testu-Brissy ascend from Luxembourg Gardens into a Paris sky pregnant with thunderclouds—bound, as it turned out, for a landing seventy-five miles north of the city eleven hours later. While amid the storm clouds—testimony to Benjamin Franklin's enduring impression on Paris—Testu-Brissy conducted electrical charges through an iron bar he had brought along to corroborate the Philadelphian's experiments with electricity.[1]

Jefferson likewise better acquainted himself with Paris's arts milieu. Since visiting London, he had corresponded with John Trumbull, the young painter from Connecticut he had met in the English capital. The artist was then garnering praise for a project he had commenced—to memorialize, in a series of paintings, the recent war in America. Decades later Trumbull recalled: "Jefferson had a taste for the fine arts, and highly approved my intention of preparing myself for a national work. He encouraged me to persevere in this pursuit, and kindly invited me to come to Paris, to see and study the fine works there, and to make his house my home, during my stay."

In early August 1786, taking up Jefferson's invitation, the thirty-year-old artist arrived in Paris and settled into the Hôtel de Langeac for an extended stay. Born into a prosperous New England family, the Harvard-educated Trumbull was the son of a former Connecticut governor. In 1777, following a dispute over a promotion during a brief stint in the Continental army as an aide to Washington, Trumbull had moved to England. There he began his studies with Benjamin West. Trumbull's teacher was renowned for canvases depicting biblical, mythological, and historical subjects—among the latter, scenes from the Seven Years' War. West eventually suggested that he paint scenes from the American Revolution. But because a childhood accident had impaired Trumbull's vision in his left eye, rendering the painting of large works difficult, West suggested that he work on small canvases.

By spring 1786, when, through West and John Adams, Trumbull met Jefferson, he had completed canvases depicting the June 1775 Battle of Bunker Hill and the death, six months later, of the Patriot general Richard Montgomery during the ill-fated American siege of Quebec. The paintings won enthusiastic reviews. But Trumbull, seeking a broader audience, found himself unable to find a suitable engraver in England to reproduce the images. Therefore, carefully packing the two canvases, he took both to Paris, where he hoped to find an engraver to bring his scenes to the wider world.

When he was leaving for Paris, another task weighed on Trumbull. By longstanding tradition, his chosen genre, history painting, usually placed notable individuals in the foreground of depicted scenes. In re-creating those events the genre's practitioners assumed a certain license. To heighten drama and to get all the essential dramatis personae on their canvases, painters tended to present pivotal moments—a key officer's death, perhaps, or a surrender ceremony—from depicted events. In the process it was not unusual for artists to wildly or slightly fictionalize details of historical events—altering the setting or including notable individuals who had played a role in the depicted episode but had not been present at the moment the canvas memorialized. Put another way, in depictions of actions, history painting prioritized plausibility over accuracy.

However, when works presented recent events—with personages familiar to contemporary audiences—painters often went to great lengths to re-create faithfully the appearances of depicted individuals and to render accurately the event's setting. Therefore, before placing the first brushstrokes on such works, painters often conducted exhaustive research. When possible, they attempted to locate—and arrange sittings for preliminary studies of—individuals to be depicted. Failing in the latter—when, for instance, a subject was deceased—painters would sometimes seek out an offspring who resembled the individual.

In executing his first two American Revolution paintings, Trumbull had based his depictions of prominent individuals on extant portraits that he located. He hoped, however, that future works in his series would be based on his own encounters with their subjects. While in Paris, he thus hoped to conduct sittings with Rochambeau, Lafayette, and other French officers who had played a role in the American victory. To facilitate those appointments, he carried with him to France letters from John Adams to Lafayette and other French officers—introducing himself, in Adams's words, as "a Painter who has given Proofs of uncommon Genius & Talents for his Art, and is disposed to consecrate both to the Glory of his Country."

Days after arriving in Paris, often accompanied by Jefferson, Trumbull began calling on painters he admired and inspecting local art collections—visits that left him overjoyed. As Jefferson confided to a friend, "He was yesterday to see the king's collection of paintings at Versailles, and confesses it surpassed every thing of which he even had an idea. I persuade[d] him to stay and study here, and then proceed to Rome."

Compared with his knowledge of architecture and music, Jefferson, when he arrived in Paris, knew relatively little about painting; and as Trumbull guided him through that world, the thirty-year-old painter became a sort of aesthetic mentor for the forty-six-year-old diplomat. Prior to Trumbull's arrival, Jefferson knew the sculptor Jean-Antoine Houdon and a few other artists. But through Trumbull he soon met the history painter Jacques-Louis David and other denizens of Paris's art world. More generally, through Trumbull—and other friends, such as Madame de Tessé, Maria Cosway, Madame de Staël, and Madame de Corny—Jefferson, deepening his knowledge of the visual arts, gained entrée into a broad milieu of artists, French and expatriates, previously outside his usual circles.

In the coming years Trumbull, eventually working on large canvases, found an ironic advantage in his optical handicap. Forced to rely on his single working eye—and overcompensating for his monocular tendencies—he imparted to his canvases an extraordinary level of detail, a vividness that placed him beyond most history painters of his generation: "His natural talents for this art seem almost unparalleled," Jefferson marveled.

Meanwhile, at the Hôtel de Langeac, during the late 1780s as the Jefferson-Trumbull friendship ripened, the painter conceived of yet another canvas for his American Revolution series, a work not on his original list for the series. But, unlike others on that list, this work involved no muskets, cannons, swords, or Lafayette—nor, for that matter, any French officers. Furthermore, because Trumbull was staying under the roof of a man intimately familiar with the envisioned painting's subject, he did not have to go far to commence his research: "I began," Trumbull recalled, "the composition of the Declaration of Independence, with the assistance of his [Jefferson's] information and advice."

———

That project's culmination years later would be telling of Jefferson's approach to shaping his image for posterity. More saliently, he was aware by then that his nonmilitary, often noncentral, role in the American Revolution and his later partisanship during the Republic's early years guaranteed that he would never become, as did Lafayette, a heroic, unifying symbol for his country's painters. Beyond that, Jefferson, for all his personal shortcomings, never had a taste for the sort of aesthetic self-aggrandizement that so enthralled Lafayette.

When opportunities did arise for Jefferson to direct the shaping of his image for posterity, he tended to err on modesty's side. Trumbull's painting commemorating the Declaration of Independence typifies such understatement: Another historical actor, for instance, might have encouraged that episode's depiction as a grandly heroic solo feat—replete, perhaps, with stage-managed lightning, stone tablets, and the protagonist cast as some (albeit beardless) latter-day Moses. Instead, with Jefferson's encouragement, Trumbull, conjuring a scene that never actually occurred, memorialized the moment as five men humbly submitting their work to their Second Continental Congress colleagues.

Indeed, from the painting's inception, in Paris in 1787, the Declaration's (then unacknowledged) author had urged Trumbull to present in his composition all five members of the committee named to draft the document. Decades later Trumbull was commissioned to execute the scene on a larger canvas. As he was deciding which other delegates to depict (in addition to the five presenting the Declaration), Jefferson, along with Adams, advised—democratically— that a member's signature on the Declaration "ought to be the general guide" in determining his inclusion.[2]

THIRTY-FOUR

"No Rose without Its Thorn"

My glass shall not persuade me I am old,
So long as youth and thou are of one date
—WILLIAM SHAKESPEARE, *Sonnets* [22]

Decades later, Jefferson, recalling their shared pleasures of the mid 1780s, wrote wistfully to John Trumbull of "our charming Coterie of Paris, now scattered & estranged but not so in either my memory or affections." Among that circle of artists and bon vivants to which Trumbull initiated Jefferson, no individual left a more indelible mark on the widower-diplomat than the painter Maria Luisa Caterina Cecilia Hadfield Cosway.

Trumbull had met Maria and her husband, Richard Cosway, also a painter, in August 1786, while visiting Jacques-Louis David's Paris studio. Maria, twenty-six years old, and Richard, forty-three, lived in England. A commission attained by Richard that summer had brought the Cosways to Paris for an extended stay.

Trumbull instantly liked the couple and soon joined them for outings throughout Paris and, given Trumbull's affections for the Cosways, it was inevitable that Jefferson would eventually meet them. The occasion was a visit, on September 3, by Jefferson and Trumbull to Paris's Halle au Blé, a large circular, limestone building that housed the city's grain market.

A wooden dome capped the building. Jefferson, always infatuated with domes, knew of the Halle au Blé by reputation; indeed, before seeing it— ever alert to inspirations for future public buildings in Richmond—he suspected that it might serve as a model for a new public market in Virginia's capital.

Thus, when, with Trumbull, he finally visited the Halle au Blé, Jefferson was not disappointed: The market's interior, illuminated by skylights set into its domed roof, dazzled him. But what Jefferson was not prepared for was the young woman he met that day. Seeking an opportunity to introduce Jefferson to his new friends, Trumbull had asked the Cosways to join them at the market.

Maria Cosway was intelligent, pretty, and slim, with blue eyes and a mass of curly golden hair. Adding to her allure for Jefferson, she was also a painter, composer, and musician. Smitten, he later recalled that, seconds before meeting Maria Cosway, the Halle au Blé had dazzled him; in an instant, however, the building, in his mind, collapsed into a "parcel of sticks and chips." More to the point, Maria possessed "qualities and accomplishments, belonging to her sex, which might form a chapter apart for her: such as music, modesty, beauty, and that softness of disposition which is the ornament of her sex and charm of ours."[1]

Maria's husband, Richard Cosway, born and raised in England, was a frequent recipient of commissions to paint miniatures of Britain's aristocracy, including the royal family. Consequently—if only for the social connections generated through such opportunities—of the two Cosway artists, Richard in 1786, was the more prominent.

Born in Italy to English parents, Maria nonetheless ranked as a gifted and accomplished painter in her own right. Her father had been the owner of inns patronized by wealthy travelers—particularly Englishmen on their "grand tour." As a girl, Maria studied music, languages, and the arts. In Florence and Rome she continued her studies in drawing and painting, winning election at nineteen to Florence's Academy of Fine Arts. Relocating after her father's death to his native England, she gathered around her a circle of artist friends who included her prosperous, well-connected future husband.

In what was likely a marriage of convenience, Richard soon wed Maria, seventeen years his junior. Their home—at Schomberg House, on fashionable Pall Mall in London's Borough of Westminster—eventually housed Richard's eclectic collections of art. Moreover, the couple became renowned for the frequent evenings of music that they hosted, as well as a salon attended by luminaries of London's artistic and literary societies. During those same years, meanwhile, Richard, envious of his wife's talents, discouraged her from showing her works in juried exhibitions, and also made no secret of his frequent extramarital affairs.

John Trumbull later recalled that, in the weeks after visiting the Halle au Blé, what had been his social trio with the Cosways became a quartet: "Mr. Jefferson joined our party almost daily." From Versailles to the Louvre, the Palais Royal to Saint-Germain, Trumbull recalled, the expanded entourage "was occupied with the same industry in examining whatever relates to the arts."

During their 1786 Paris sojourn the Cosways lived on the Right Bank, on the rue Coq-Héron, a half mile north of the Louvre. And over the coming weeks, Jefferson and Maria were increasingly drawn to each other. Extant records render it impossible to determine on which of their approximately ten or twelve outings over a two-week period the two were alone together, but those occasions were apparently frequent: The ambitious Trumbull was often busy with his own pursuits, and on September 9 he left Paris for extended travels in Europe. As for Richard Cosway—busy with his painting commissions and otherwise seemingly indifferent to his marriage—he apparently had better uses for his time in Paris than sightseeing.

Jefferson, for his part during those weeks, seems to have seized upon every opportunity to see Maria—eventually even inventing pretexts for canceling appointments to be with her. "Lying messengers were to be dispatched into every quarter of the city," he recalled of one particular day's pretexts.[2]

Jefferson's recollections of their outings, in a letter to Maria, read like a guidebook to the public gardens, parks, picturesque estates, and architectural follies in and around that day's Paris: "the Port de Neuilly, the hills along the Seine, the rainbows of the machine [the waterworks at the Château] of Marly, the terras [terrace] of St. Germains, the chateaux, the gardens, the [statues] of Marly, the pavillon of Lucienne [Louveciennes]."

At the Bois de Boulogne's edge, they visited the Renaissance-style Château de Madrid, and inside the Bois they strolled amid the Chinese-styled gardens of the Parc de Bagatelle; northwest of Paris, they visited the gardens of the Désert de Retz, a park—created by François Racine de Monville, an eccentric aristocrat, that spread over more than ninety acres of his estate. Its architectural curiosities included—still include—a house disguised as an ancient column ascended via an interior winding staircase. ("How grand the idea excited by the remains of such a column!" recalled a delighted Jefferson.) On still other outings in Paris, they attended a concert of Haydn symphonies, a play, and (with Patsy) a light-opera performance.

Whether platonic or intimate, the precise nature of Jefferson's and Maria Cosway's relationship remains unclear. If the latter, it contradicted his professed abhorrence of the sort of disregard for marital fidelity practiced by Lafayette and others among Paris's *gratin*, its upper crust. But then again, such license would also perhaps have accorded with Jefferson's youthful—1764—seeming assertion of the sexual consolations accorded the unmarried man: "Many and great are the comforts of a single state." Indeed, even Dumas Malone—among modern Jefferson biographers, the most exhaustive and one of the most admiring—concedes the possibility of physical intimacies between the two: "Illicit love-making was generally condoned in that society, as he [Jefferson] himself had noted," observed Malone. "If he as a widower ever engaged in it, this was the time."

The Jefferson-Cosway letters—while offering evidence for both possibilities—in the end support no firm conclusions. Indeed, the veil their correspondence casts over such matters is rendered all the more opaque by the florid language of late eighteenth-century correspondence: To be sure, usages that to modern readers may suggest intimate familiarities in that age often connoted mere politeness.

The beginning of the end of Jefferson and Maria's dalliance commenced on September 18, 1786. On that sunny autumn afternoon, as the two were strolling in the Cours-la-Reine—a public park along the Seine, between today's Place de la Concorde and the Place du Canada—the-forty-three-year-old diplomat, unmindful of his age, impulsively attempted to vault a fence and injured his right wrist.

After the mishap two surgeons were successively summoned but to little avail; for the next few months the right-handed diplomat was, for all practical purposes, deprived of the hand's full use for writing—and, indeed, for his remaining years, the injury's effects never fully disappeared.

Whatever subsequently transpired between Jefferson and Maria seems to have hastened the conclusion of their dalliance. Beyond that, with Richard by late September having completed his commissions, the Cosways were by then already preparing to leave Paris. Indeed, during those weeks they seem to have moved up the date of their planned departure. If so—and, indeed, if Jefferson and Maria's friendship had included sexual intimacies—the married couple's earlier-than-planned-departure, one speculates, was possibly because Richard, an English gentleman mindful of social appearances, had learned of his wife's activities.

Two days after Jefferson's accident Maria sent him a note. "I have appeard a Monster," she wrote, "for not having sent to know how you was, the *whole day*. I have been More uneasy, Than I can express." She promised to try to visit the next morning; and then—mindful that her Paris sojourn was drawing to a close—added wistfully: "Oh I wish you was well enough to come to us tomorrow to dinner and stay the Evening."

A week later—still housebound on October 5—Jefferson awkwardly grasped a pen in his left hand and slowly wrote a note to Maria: "I have passed the night in so much pain that I have not closed my eyes," he scrawled. Over the past few days Jefferson—inexplicably in increasing pain and denied the use of his writing hand—had grown dependent on William Short. He dictated official correspondence to Short and, in some cases, relied on him as a proxy—with Short substituting for him at public events such as the late September unveiling, at Paris's Hôtel de Ville, of Houdon's bust of Lafayette.

The marquis, away in Auvergne, as it turned out, was also unable to attend the ceremony but sent Adrienne in his stead—and she thoroughly enjoyed the ceremony, during which Short read a statement Jefferson had prepared. "I am pursuaded," Short later reported, "that she did not receive more pleasure on the night of her marriage."

Before his accident Jefferson had planned to accompany Louis XVI's court on its annual late fall visit to the royal château at Fontainebleau, outside Paris. Afterward he had planned to depart on a long-contemplated six-week tour of the South of France. In the end, however, his infirmity led him to cancel both outings.

More immediately, as Jefferson lamented in his October 5 letter to Maria, he would have to miss seeing her and her husband later that same day, the day they were scheduled to leave Paris: "It is with infinite regret therefore that I must relinquish your charming company for that of the Surgeon whom I have sent for to examine into the cause of this change," he wrote.

That same day Maria sent a note to Jefferson: "I am very, very sorry indeed, and [. . .] or having been the Cause of your pains in the [Night]," she wrote. "We shall go I believe this Morning, Nothing seems redy, but Mr. Cosway seems More dispos'd then I have seen him all this time. I shall write to you from England. . . . I shall remember the charming days we have past together, and shall long for next spring."

By the next sunrise, October 6, Jefferson had learned that the Cosways' departure had been delayed but that they were leaving that day. He decided he could not wait for the spring to see her again. Soon leaving his house, he accompanied the Cosways to the Saint Denis post house, north of Paris's center, to see them off on a carriage bound for Antwerp—the first leg of their journey back to London. In Saint Denis, feigning gaiety, he shared refreshments with the couple and bade them farewell.

In the weeks ahead, Jefferson, again taking his quill into his left hand, slowly, awkwardly, wrote—and, at least once, rewrote—to Maria a twelve-page letter.

Striking in its candor, the missive, dated October 12, 1786, and known to Jefferson scholars as the "Head and Heart letter," commences with an account of their parting at Saint Denis: "Having performed the last sad office of handing you into your carriage at the Pavillon de St. Denis, and seen the wheels get actually into motion, I turned on my heel and walked, more dead than alive, to the opposite door, where my own was awaiting me."

Most of the letter, however, as the below sample attests, consists of a sustained meditation, comparing the virtues of the cerebral life with those of a more passionate existence. In the style of novelist Laurence Sterne, a mutual favorite of his and Cosway, Jefferson cast his ruminations as a debate between "Head" and "Heart."

> Head: I wished to make you sensible how imprudent it is to place your affections, without reserve, on objects you must so soon lose, and whose loss when it comes must cost you such severe pangs.
>
> . . .
>
> Heart: We are not immortal ourselves, my friend; how can we expect our enjoiments to be so? We have no rose without it's thorn; no pleasure without alloy.[3]

By the following January, even as Jefferson longed for Maria Cosway, he had grown infatuated with another bright young, married woman who lived in London. In fact, Angelica Church and Maria Cosway were friends.

Thirty years old when she and Jefferson met in Paris, Church—like Cosway—was witty, well read, and beautiful. Unlike Cosway, however, Church had been born in America, and to a wealthy family at that; moreover, in contrast to Maria Cosway's loveless marriage to Richard Cosway, Church—the wife of the English politician and merchant, John Barker Church—seems to have been happily married.

Indeed, in London, Paris, and New York, the Churches were admired members of elite society. And though Jefferson first met Angelica Church in early 1788, by then he already knew many people in her life—including, in Paris, Lafayette, for whom she would in due time have a singular opportunity to demonstrate her affections.

Moreover, Angelica Schuyler Church was a daughter of Continental army general Philip Schuyler—and thereby sister-in-law of Alexander Hamilton. (Jefferson and Angelica's brother-in-law then barely knew each other—possibly having met in Philadelphia in 1783.) Angelica had been married to John Barker Church since their 1777 elopement. In America during the American Revolution, the wealthy British-born merchant had run various businesses and held various civilian posts in the Continental army. Since 1785, after a two-year residence in Paris, the couple had lived in London.

Jefferson met Church in Paris while she was visiting, for two months, her friend the painter Madame de Corny, also a Jefferson friend. Escorted from London by John Trumbull, Church arrived in Paris in December 1787. And just as Jefferson had met Maria Cosway through Trumbull, so through the painter he also met Church. Likewise, as Jefferson had been instantly smitten with Cosway, so he was immediately captivated by Church.

Over the next two months, with others and on their own, Jefferson, with Maria Cosway's blessings, enjoyed Church's company. But when Church, in winter 1788, concluded her visit, he was again bereft. Over the coming months, as he had after Cosway left Paris, he contemplated plans—fantasies—of other outings with Church: He begged her to return to Paris, even proposed they make a trip to America. In the end, however, because their relationship lacked the intensity of that he had shared with Cosway, so their parting, while sad for Jefferson, lacked the heartbreak of his farewell to Cosway; the two remained lifelong correspondents.[4]

Traveling alone, Maria Cosway, in August 1787, did return to Paris, and stayed until December. But, disappointing Jefferson, she made little effort to see him. In London in May 1790, Maria gave birth to her and Richard's first child, Louisa. In 1790, ostensibly for her health, sans husband and daughter, Maria left London for Italy, for what became a four-year absence. In 1796, however, having by then returned to England, she and Richard were thrown into grief that July by Louisa's death. In 1801, increasingly drawn to Roman Catholicism, Maria again left London and Richard; over the coming years she founded religious schools for girls in Lyon, and, in 1812, in Lodi, Italy. Her marriage to Richard ended with his death in 1821.

Intermittently for the rest of her life Maria corresponded with Jefferson; closing a 1790 letter, he vowed: "*je vous aimerai toujours*"—"I will always love you." Even so, their farewell, four years earlier, at the Saint Denis post house, had marked the denouement of their star-crossed dalliance. She died in Lodi in 1838.[5]

PART FIVE

Revolutionary Tide,
1786–1789

THIRTY-FIVE

Assembly of Not Ables

In fall 1786, as Jefferson, holed up at the Hôtel de Langeac, nursed his broken wrist and heart, he and Lafayette were following events on both sides of the Atlantic—including reports of a revolt in western Massachusetts staged by Continental army veterans and state militias. Led by Capt. Daniel Shays, the rebellion had been sparked by merchants' efforts to collect debts from already cash-strapped war veterans. Most observers agreed that the localized outbreak signaled a broader financial crisis shadowing the fragile federal government.

Even so, writing to Washington, Jefferson took a sanguine view of "Shay's Rebellion," dismissing it as a transient episode—possibly even a purgative for the fledgling Republic. "I hold it that a little rebellion now and then is a good thing, & as necessary in the political world as storms in the physical."[1]

Lafayette, by contrast, found the uprising troubling and worried over reports that Congress was considering remobilizing elements of the Continental army to suppress the revolt. Fearing that such a response would aggravate resentments against the federal government, he hoped instead that Congress would try to tamp down such discontents: "I trust more to the exertions of each [state] government, and the good sense of the people, than to any Continental measure in this business."[2]

During the same period, however, another crisis was weighing on Lafayette's mind. But unlike the distant rebellion in Massachusetts, this other difficulty, concerning France's national treasury, lay in close enough proximity for him to contemplate playing a role in its resolution.

During that age European governments facing financial crises had often repudiated all or part of their debts. In late 1786, however, as Louis XVI's court faced alarming indebtedness, for reasons that remain a mystery it elected to not avail itself of that remedy. Instead it embarked on policies intended to increase revenues.

Toward that end, Finance Minister Charles-Alexandre de Calonne persuaded the king that mere tax increases would not solve France's woes. "I shall easily show," he argued, "that it is impossible to tax further, [that it is] ruinous to be always borrowing and not enough to confine ourselves to economic reforms." By Calonne's lights, only a cession of privileges by the country's nobility and clergy—notably their exemption from most of France's taxes—could right the treasury.

The Bourbon court knew that winning the reforms would require support from all parts of French society—support made more difficult to attain given the ministers' and royal family's growing reputation for personal profligacy. Marie Antoinette, in particular, had gained notoriety for spendthrift habits—including her high-stakes gambling, expensive wardrobe, and other indulgences. To reduce such perceptions, the Bourbon court soon began pondering how it might win—and conspicuously demonstrate—broad public support for Calonne's measures.

In another day Louis and his ministers might have called on France's *parlements* to enact their reforms: A king's decrees, after all, only became official after ratification by the *parlements*. Their history stretching back to the thirteenth century, France's *parlements*—unlike Britain's Parliament—were provincial appellate courts, not legislative bodies. Thirteen *parlements*, spread across France, existed in 1787. The most powerful of them, that of Paris, was composed of 240 magistrates.

Traditionally magistrates serving in France's *parlements* belonged to the *noblesse de robe* (nobility of the robe). Unlike members of the *noblesse d'épée* (nobility of the sword), whose prestige was attached to the knightly class and a particular region, nobles of the robe derived their status from the particular office that each had either inherited or purchased. By the late eighteenth century, however, robe-sword distinctions among the nobility were breaking down.

Parlement members, thus unbeholden to the king for their offices, enjoyed a distinct independence. Moreover, by the 1780s, as noblemen, they increasingly viewed their interests as divergent from those of Versailles's court. Consequently, Louis and Calonne, in 1787, reasonably assumed that the *parlements* would likely oppose the reforms they sought.

Thus—in December, at Calonne's urging—Louis summoned a meeting, to convene the following January, of yet another body—the Assembly of Notables. Established two centuries earlier, that assembly by tradition was composed of high-ranking members of the three categories—"estates"—into which the king's subjects were traditionally grouped: the "First Estate" (clergy), the "Second Estate" (noblemen), and the "Third Estate" (peasants and all other subjects). By 1787, however, the Third Estate's numbers included such powerful corporate bodies as Paris's formidable merchant guild.

Unlike members of *parlements*, however, those of the Assembly of Notables members traditionally were appointed by the king. It had been 160 years since the Notables last met. And because its members served by royal appointment, the assembly in no sense constituted a representative body. By tradition it could only advise and ratify—not veto—royal prerogatives.

After his name appeared on a preliminary list of nobles expected to be called to the Assembly of Notables, Lafayette canceled his planned journey to Crimea to visit Czarina Catherine. A signal moment, after all, seemed close at hand: For the past decade, most of his political activities had focused on America, not France. Recently, however—with Foreign Minister Vergennes as his mentor—Lafayette was edging into his native land's domestic politics.

The financial crisis France faced in the late 1780s had its roots in centuries of accumulated arrangements struck among the country's monarchy, nobility, and clergy. The inequitable tangle of privileges and concessions had resulted from successive civil wars and competing rivalries among interests, groups, classes, and places. Certain provinces (notably Brittany), nobles, and the Catholic Church, for instance, were largely exempt from France's taxes, whose burdens fell mainly on peasants. Moreover, all able-bodied and untitled men and women who could not afford a fee to exempt them were subject to the hated *corvée* that mandated periodic work on the country's roads and bridges. Exacerbating these inequities was an unfair and illogical schedule of duties on goods and services exchanged in the country's internal commerce.

By 1785, however, Louis and Calonne, and other ministers at Versailles had come to blame France's financial crisis on a single event—the decision to assist the American war against Britain, a commitment that left the treasury with massive debts. To the kingdom's debt that, in 1776, had stood at 37 million livres, Versailles—for the pleasure of watching its old enemy Britain defeated on foreign shores—had, by the war's end, according to one account, borrowed another 1,250 million.[3]

In February 1787, reacting to recent developments—and the ironies of an absolutist king summoning a deliberative assembly—Jefferson, writing to a friend, commented: "We talk and think of nothing here but the Assemblée des Notables. Were all the puns collected to which this assembly has given rise, I think they would make a larger volume than the Encyclopedie." With Washington, meanwhile, Lafayette shared one of the more popular of those puns: Of "the Assembly of Notables," he wrote: "Wicked People say not able."[4]

Puns aside, however, many were pondering exactly what role the republican-monarchist Lafayette might play in such an assembly: Would he bring to it the same unbridled—if often merely rhetorical—republicanism that he had brought to the American war? Or would he, deferring to the Versailles court, embrace the reforms Calonne was seeking? Whatever path he chose, he was bound to capture attention.

———

Certainly the hold that America and Lafayette held on Paris showed no signs of waning. Books and plays trumpeted both: In the city's vaudeville theaters, two similarly titled plays—*L'Héroine américaine* and *Le Héro américain*—

numbered among the most popular productions of 1786. Amid the enthusiasm for things related to America, Parisians were all the more perplexed
when, in late 1786, Calonne's list of the 144 Assembly of Notables appointees
circulated and Lafayette's name was conspicuously absent among its 39 appointees from the nobility of the sword. Rumors soon circulated purporting
to explain the omission—deeming the marquis variously too young, too radical, or too obscure in noble ranking.

In the wake of the snub, meanwhile, Lafayette's "ardour did not permitt him
to be quiet." In short order, however, Calonne—apparently recalculating the
young man's value to his cause—removed Adrienne's uncle, the marquis de Noailles, from his list and replaced him with Lafayette. Eventually Lafayette even
numbered among twenty-two Notables invited by the king to reside at the royal
château during the sessions.

Why the reevaluation? No doubt, Lafayette's own lobbying played a role;
moreover, Calonne's omission of Lafayette on the initial list certainly underestimated the young officer's popularity. Of equal or perhaps greater importance,
the omission also underestimated the king's personal affection for Lafayette.
Beginning in fall 1786, after all, Louis had played cards with the marquis at least
four times over a ten-week period. Truth be known, the marquis's popularity
that season stretched from theatergoers to readers to the royal court. As the
Lafayette biographer James R. Gaines observed: "Actually, it [took in] four
worlds" by that season—America, France, the philosophes, and Versailles."[5]

By January 1787 Lafayette was looking forward to playing a role in solving
France's financial problems. Ironically downplaying the assembly's elitist bent,
in a letter to William Smith, he imagined the surprise of John Adams (by then
Smith's father-in-law) at the news "that we should turn out such republicans as
to have Assemblies." But while not blind to the body's political weakness—
and its dependence on monarchical largesse—Lafayette also considered its con-
vening a measure of progress for representative government in France: "Such
as it is, I confess I would not have fore told it twelve months ago."

To Washington, Lafayette took a measured view of the challenges that
would face the Notables. "There is at Bottom a desire to Make Monney Some

How or other, in order to put the Receipt on a level With the Expenses," he wrote. "Enormous . . . Sums [have been] Squandered on Courtiers and Superfluities."6

To a friend in mid-January 1787, Jefferson hailed Lafayette's securing of a seat in the assembly as a sign of Versailles's recognition of his nonmilitary talents: "This shews that his character here is not considered as an indifferent one; and that it excites agitation." To Madison that same month Jefferson elaborated on his view of Lafayette's new role. For months Jefferson had assumed the marquis was destined to play an important role in France's government—but that task, he confided to Madison, came with peril: "His education in our school has drawn on him a very jealous eye from a court whose principles are the most absolute despotism."

But, then again, Louis, by Jefferson's lights, seemed to have embarked on a moderating course—and that course, he believed was, with each passing day, placing his friend on increasingly safer ground. "I hope he has nearly passed his crisis," wrote Jefferson. "The king, who is a good man, is favorably disposed towards him: and he is supported by powerful family connections, and by the public good will. He is the youngest man of the Notables, except one whose office placed him on the list."

Before his letter's end, however, Jefferson—resorting to cipher—deployed both praise and criticism regarding his friend. "The Marquis de Lafayette is a most valuable auxiliary to me," he allowed.

> His zeal is unbounded, and his we[ight]with those in power great. His education having been merely military, commerce was an unknown feild to him. But his good sense enabling him to comprehend perfectly whatever is explained to him, his agency has been very efficacious. He has a great deal of sound genius, is well remarked by the king and rising in popularity. He has nothing against him but the suspicion of republican principles. I think he will one day be of the ministry. His foible is a canine appetite for popularity and fame.

Earlier Madison-Jefferson exchanges had highlighted what both men viewed as Lafayette's hunger for fame and for often acting without adequate forethought—an opinion, incidentally, also held by John Adams. Indeed, years later a letter from Adams to Jefferson, recalling a conversation during the latter's first months in Paris, would attest to a view both held as to what they regarded as Lafayette's lack of intellectual rigor. Adams recalled:

> . . . when LaFayette harrangued you and me, and John Quincy Adams, through a whole evening in your Hotel in the Cul de Sac, at Paris; and developed the plans then in operation to reform France: though I was as silent as you was, I then thought I could Say Something new to him: In plain Truth I was astonished at the Grossness of his Ignorance of Goverment and History, as I had been for years before at that of Turgot, Rochefaucault, Condorcet and Franklin.[7]

The Assembly of Notables was scheduled to convene on January 29. But as its opening approached, illnesses among three Versailles ministers prompted a postponement. Among the bedridden ministers, none was of greater importance and closer to the king than the comte de Vergennes, foreign minister since 1774.

On February 13, Vergennes breathed his last. Besides having been the king's closest adviser among all his ministers, observers believed Vergennes had the best chance of wrangling from the nobles the reforms necessary to head off impending insolvency. Moreover—rendering his death of still more note for Lafayette and Jefferson—Vergennes, while in no sense a republican, had been among the staunchest advocates among Versailles' ministers for French support of the American rebellion. Beyond that, he was a stabilizing figure in European politics; observed Jefferson in mid-January as Vergennes lay dying: "He is a great and good minister, and an accident to him might endanger the peace of Europe."

Moreover, for Lafayette, in matters concerning France's politics, Vergennes had become a mentor of sorts; and, as the Lafayette biographer Louis Gottschalk observed, for Lafayette—and indeed for France—the minister's death thus possibly created a fatal vacuum: "Perhaps, if he lived, reform might have been achieved by timely concessions rather than by revolutionary compulsion," wrote Gottschalk. "His exit left Jefferson as Lafayette's chief political adviser in France, and Jefferson was neither so oblique nor so cautious as Vergennes would have been."[8]

Tellingly, the government complex built at Versailles, in the late seventeenth century by the absolutist Louis XIV, offered no legislative assembly hall. It did, however, host an entire bureaucracy devoted to the staging of ceremonies designed to project royal authority. And plans soon emerged for the Notables to meet in the adjacent town of Versailles in the Hôtel des Menus-Plaisirs du Roi, the headquarters of the government bureaucracy that staged those royal ceremonies.

More specifically the Notables were to convene in a building that stood in the Hôtel des Menus-Plaisirs' courtyard. The room inside the building where the assembly was to gather measured 120 feet in length and 100 feet in width. The austere high-ceilinged space was normally used as a warehouse for furniture and other items, and in the weeks before the assembly convened, Louis's ministers spared no expense in transforming it into an assembly hall intended to convey the Notables' political legitimacy as well as the body's ties to the Bourbon crown. Indignant over the remodeling costs and suggesting that other spaces at Versailles might have been used for the meeting, *Mémoires secrets*, an underground newspaper of that era, accused the king and his ministers of "tossing several millions out the window for a vain and ephemeral ceremony." Louis did, however, draw the line at the gilded spectator boxes installed in the hall. Visiting the site during its construction and finding the boxes inappropriately theatrical, he ordered them removed and replaced with less ornate visitors' seating.

At 10:00 a.m. on February 22 the Notables filed into their freshly painted Hôtel des Menus-Plaisirs venue. An hour later Louis—speaking from his throne beneath a purple canopy—addressed the body: "Gentlemen," he announced. "I have chosen you among the various orders of the state, and have gathered you around me to inform you of my plans."

As the thirty-two-year-old king outlined his plans, Lafayette concluded that they comported with many of the reforms that both he and Jefferson had sought over the past few years—changes that would enshrine free trade as the country's guiding philosophy and, in the process, "improve the nation's revenue." Louis also spoke of his desire, through free trade and a more equitable tax system, to "bring relief . . . to the most indigent of my subjects."

After speaking for less than twenty minutes, however, Louis departed, ceding the floor to other speakers—including, eventually, Finance Minister Calonne. For much of that day and the next, Calonne detailed the reforms he sought—including a uniformly applied "land tax," whose burden would fall equally on all parts of French society, even the Church. He also called for a drastic overhaul of the *corvée* and enactment of a single tariff for all goods to replace the country's confusing array of fees then in effect. To win the Notables' goodwill, Calonne also called for the creation of local assemblies across France—bodies vested with limited actual powers but that would nonetheless give voice to local concerns.[9]

Seated in the assembly hall's observers section, Jefferson attended the Notables' opening-day session. Soon writing to Abigail Adams he pronounced himself heartened by what he considered a milestone, however symbolic, on France's journey toward representative government. But he was troubled that it had been the king—not his subjects—who summoned the assembly: "This occasion, more than any thing I have seen, convinces me that this nation is incapable of any serious effort but under the word of command."

The deliberations had commenced cordially, but the king and his ministers soon found themselves frustrated. Before the end of the second day's session, the body's members were informed that henceforth they would gather in most of their daily sessions not as a single body, but in seven individual "bureaus"—committees—each headed by a high-ranking nobleman, a "prince of the blood," selected by the king. In Lafayette's case, he was placed in the Second Bureau.

Over the next two months, meeting together and in the seven bureaus, the Notables discussed Calonne's proposals but, in the end, failed to endorse the reforms sought by the king. The sessions did, however, furnish the occasion for Lafayette's first conspicuous foray into France's political life. The moment came during an April 24 debate within Lafayette's bureau over a proposed reorganization of royal lands in a manner intended to yield greater revenues for the treasury.

While supportive of most of Calonne's proposals, Lafayette never accepted the proposition that spending on the American war effort had caused France's financial quandary. In his view the deficit arose from mismanagement and cronyism, not war expenditures. Of particular concern to Lafayette was the mismanagement of royal lands—notably recent episodes in which agents acting in the king's name had purchased, at inflatcd prices, properties from nobles with close ties to the court.

Before speaking, Lafayette requested permission to read from a text he had prepared, and exacted a promise that it would later be presented to Louis with a notice that its words originated with him and him alone. Like Jefferson, Lafayette never became a great orator. A contemporary recalled that he spoke "without metaphor or colored images but with the precise word to express the precise idea, without passionate verve but with a flow of words that stirred because of their apparent conviction."

Soon after he began reading, however, Lafayette delivered a provocative line: "The monster of speculation must be attacked instead of fed." Rising to his feet, the king's brother, the comte d'Artois—accusing Lafayette of making an ad hominem attack—demanded that he cease speaking.

As Lafayette and his supporters remonstrated, the comte d'Artois, the head of Lafayette's bureau, stood his ground. But so too did the marquis's defenders. One, speaking directly to Lafayette, noted that his actions in America had already made him one of France's heroes; "Now you especially deserve that title," the admirer exclaimed, lamenting that no sculptor was present to capture "this moment when your patriotic zeal puts you in the ranks of His Majesty's most faithful servants."

Moments later Lafayette, resuming his speech, called for an investigation into the administration of royal lands—and, more specifically, the purchases he had described. He acknowledged that the specifics of his charges might be in error: "But my patriotism is roused and requests a serious investigation. . . . [T]he dissipated millions have been raised by taxation and that taxation can be justified only by the genuine need of the state; that the many millions granted to corruption or selfishness are the fruit of the sweat, the tears, and perhaps the blood of the people."

If Lafayette's rhetoric that day anticipated Churchill's, his speech—read from a text in his usual unadorned style—set no record for histrionics. Nevertheless, a prominent national hero and member of the nobility, otherwise revered for achievements in a foreign war, had openly challenged a royal minister—and by that act, Lafayette had added another dimension to his claim on France's popular imagination.

The Notables' sessions were officially nonpublic, but newspaper accounts of Lafayette's speech soon appeared on both sides of the Atlantic—one of which he sent to George Washington. In an accompanying letter, Lafayette proudly recalled both the speech and the comte d'Artois's futile objection to it: "It was thought proper to intimidate Us, and the King's Brother told in His Majesty's name that such motions ought to Be signed—upon which I signed the inclosed."

Two days later the assembly, having produced inconclusive results, adjourned for the Easter holidays. For the time being the body, unwilling to endorse the reforms sought by Louis but prevented by law from asserting its own will, had lived up to its punned name: Not Able. Even so, Lafayette, now twenty-nine years old, had emerged from the episode with an enhanced reputation: Once again, tongues in Paris were wagging about him—only this time, in praise of actions taken on French soil.[10]

THIRTY-SIX

"To See What I Have Never
Seen Before"

Amid the late-January chill of 1787, as the upcoming reconvening of the Assembly of Notables had dominated Parisian conversations, Thomas Jefferson was dreaming of a place in the sun. To Madison he confided: "I am now about setting out on a journey to the South of France, one object of which is to try the mineral waters there for the restoration of my hand, but another is to visit all the seaports where we have trade, and to hunt up all the inconveniencies under which it labours, in order to get them rectified. I shall visit and carefully examine too the Canal of Languedoc."[1]

Jefferson had contemplated this trip for months. And on February 28, 1787, he finally left Paris. Hours before leaving, however, he found time to write to Lafayette; concerning his friend's work with the Notables and their pondering of reformed governance for France, Jefferson, departing from his usual Anglophobia, counseled a moderate course, urging him to keep "the good model of your neighboring country before your eyes [so that] you may get on step by step towards a good constitution. Tho' that model is not perfect, yet as it would unite more suffrages than any new one which could be proposed, it is better to make that the object. If every advance is to be purchased by filling the royal coffers with gold, it will be gold well employed."

Jefferson's letter also included a wistful request: "I flatter myself I shall hear from you sometimes," he wrote. "Send your letters to my hotel as usual and they will be forwarded to me." In asking Lafayette to write, Jefferson knew there would be many more lodgings to which letters would need to be forwarded than when he first conceived his trip. For, in the end, an itinerary originally confined to a few places over mere weeks had swollen into "a journey of three months." Moreover, in planning the trip, he had tried as much as possible to create opportunities to travel *and* be alone—or at least without an entourage.

Such touring was unusual for a diplomat of Jefferson's stature—and he had not arrived at his preferences causally: He savored the company of friends; he likewise cherished solitude; it was the region between the two that ill-suited him: "Between the society of real friends and the tranquility of solitude, the mind finds no middle ground." To safeguard both solitude and privacy, Jefferson, paying all the trip's costs himself, designated it a personal rather than an official excursion—in part to avoid the obligation of bringing along a servant and rider from the Hôtel de Langeac.

Rather than travel with a servant from his residence—one likely to fill idle moments with chitchat, and later gossip about the journey at the Hôtel de Langeac—he had decided to depart Paris alone. "I was quite determined to be master of my own secret, and therefore to take a servant who should not know me." Upon reaching the first major city on his sojourn, he would hire a servant, retain his services until the next city, and thereafter and at other major subsequent junctures replace each servant with another. Likewise, at post stations along the way, he would hire a fresh postilion and horses.[2]

After leaving the Hôtel de Langeac on February 28, he stopped that night at Fontainebleau, fifty miles southeast of Paris. There, without success, he tried to find a servant to accompany him to his next stop. Days later, however, at Dijon, he met and hired a servant, "a very excellent one" whom he called "Petit Jean"— his full name is now lost—who proved so compatible that Jefferson retained him for the tour's duration. Similarly over the coming months, during stays of a day or longer in the same place, he would also hire a *valet de place* for additional help and as a local guide.[3]

In early March, striking due south from Dijon, Jefferson passed through Châlons, Macon, Lyon, and Orange. From Paris to Dijon three horses pulled his carriage, and afterward always four or five. On March 19 he stopped in Nîmes, locus of Lafayette's unrealized 1785 Protestant revolt, where he lingered for several days. There and in the area, Jefferson inspected architectural treasures of Nîmes's past as the capital of a Gallic tribe and later as an outpost of classical Rome's territories of Gaul. Among those vestiges of past eras were the Pont du Gard aqueduct over the Gardon River ("a sublime antiquity"), the Nîmes amphitheater, Roman baths, and the Maison Carrée—the ancient temple on which he had based his design for Virginia's Capitol in Richmond. To Madame de Tessé he exulted: "Here I am, Madam, gazing whole hours at the Maison quarrée, like a lover at his mistress. The stocking-weavers and silk spinners around it consider me as an hypochondriac Englishman, about to write with a pistol the last chapter of his history."

Jefferson's passion for antiquities was genuine. But as he confided to John Jay, his Nîmes stay also provided a cover for a prearranged meeting in the area with a shadowy Brazilian named José da Maia, with whom he had recently corresponded. Traveling under the pseudonym Vendek, da Mais was seeking U.S. support for a revolt in Brazil against its Portuguese rulers. "I took care to impress on him," Jefferson recalled to Jay, "that I had neither instructions nor authority to say a word to any body on this subject, and that I could only give him my own ideas as a single individual: which were that we were not in a condition at present to meddle nationally in any war."

From Nîmes, passing through Arles, Jefferson reached Marseille on April 4. "My journey from Paris to this place has been a continued feast of new objects, and new ideas," he wrote to Chastellux. "To make the most of the little time I have for so long a circuit, I have been obliged to keep myself rather out of the way of good dinners and good company. Had they been my objects, I should not have quitted Paris. I have courted the society of gardeners, vignerons, coopers, farmers &c. and have devoted every moment of every day almost, to the business of enquiry."

Anticipating a passage through the city of Tours and a scientific matter he hoped to investigate near there—a theory of Voltaire's drawn from observations at a local habitat, alleging the spontaneous growth of shells—Jefferson asked if Chastellux knew of a local abbot to whom he could provide a letter of introduction. "I have found the Abbés in general most useful acquaintances," Jefferson explained. "They are unembarrassed with families, uninvolved in form and etiquette, frequently learned, and always obliging." If the favor was granted,

> I will only beg to be announced but as a voyageur etranger simplement, and that it be addressed à Monsr. Jefferson à Tours, poste restante [general delivery]. This deception keeps me clear of those polite obligations to which I might otherwise be engaged, and leaves me the whole of the little time I have to pursue the objects that always delight me.[4]

From Marseille, Jefferson bent northwesterly for the twenty-five-mile inland journey to Aix-en-Provence. Arriving there on March 26 and taking a room at the Hôtel Saint-Jacques, he remained in Aix for four days. During his stay he repeatedly soaked in the Provençal capital's heated mineral waters, but to no avail: "Having taken 40. douches, without any sensible benefit, I thought it useless to continue them," he reported to William Short. "My wrist strengthens slowly: it is to time I look as the surest remedy, and that I believe will restore it at length."[5]

In Jefferson's absence Short regularly called on or inquired about Patsy Jefferson at Panthémont; and while at Aix, a letter from her—written in early March—caught up with the traveler. In her letter and one that he soon wrote in response, the two discussed Patsy's studies, her father's hopes for her, and his unhealed wrist. Beyond his injury, Jefferson, while in Aix, agonized over another, less tangible source of vexation. It had been six months since he bade farewell, at the Saint-Denis post house, to Maria Cosway—the inspiration for the folly that had left him with the injured wrist; as he imagined her reaction to the places through which he had recently passed, she remained much on his mind. "I have not thought of you the less," he wrote to her—relegating his tour, measured against her absence, to a "peep only into Elysium": "I am born to lose every thing I love," he lamented. "Why were you not with me? So many enchanting scenes which only wanted your pencil to consecrate them to fame."[6]

Even so, Aix did, in the end, lift Jefferson's spirits: "I am now in the land of corn, wine, oil, and sunshine," he rhapsodized to Short.

> What more can man ask of heaven? If I should happen to die at Paris I will beg of you to send me here, and have me exposed to the sun. I am sure it will bring me to life again. It is wonderful to me that every free being who possesses cent ecus de rente [annual revenue of one hundred *écus*, a silver coin then circulating], does not remove to the Southward of the Loire. It is true that money will carry to Paris most of the good things of this canton. But it cannot carry thither it's sunshine, nor procure any equivalent for it. This city is one of the cleanest and neatest I have ever seen in any country.[7]

The local variation of the south of France's Occitan tongue (also known as the langue d'oc) likewise enchanted Jefferson. "The Provençale stands nearer to the Tuscan than it does to the French," he wrote to Short, "and it is my Italian which enables me to understand the people here, more than my French. . . . [O]n the whole it stands close to the Italian and Spanish in point of beauty. I think it a general misfortune that historical circumstances gave a final prevalence to the French instead of the Provençale language." Indeed, a measure of France's linguistic diversity during that age and later—and the challenges facing reformers in Paris seeking support across the kingdom for their work—as late as 1863, by one account, a quarter of all recruits to France's army spoke a "patois" and no other tongue.[8]

―――――――――

By then, Jefferson was inhaling the powerful elixir of the open road. His spirits were raised still higher by the dawning realization that he was now free to indulge a lifetime of curiosities—truly free, as he soon put it to Lafayette, "to see what I have never seen before." Now—unencumbered by social obligations and determined to document his travels copiously—he approached his days with a discipline more befitting an observant journalist than a casually curious tourist.

Along the way Jefferson deepened his growing conviction that unlike England, the United States was ill suited for industrial manufacturing in its immediate future. Accordingly, while visiting Lyons from March 11 to 15, he avoided the city's famous silk and printing industries; to William Short he reported: "I have not visited at all the manufactures of this place: because a knowlege of them would be useless, and would extrude from the memory other things more worth retaining. Architecture, painting, sculpture, antiquities, agriculture, the condition of the labouring poor fill all my moments."

During the tour, perpetually observing and inquiring about such matters as local diets, rates for hourly labor, and the use of fertilizers, Jefferson also adjusted his view of the lives of France's common people—acknowledging variances from his earlier, harsher view. Before his 1787 tour his only other exposure to such lives outside of Paris had been on his October 1785 trip to Fontainebleau—an outing that sealed for him a conviction that "numberless instances of wretchedness" characterized daily life for that class.

Even so—ever the republican—Jefferson, while acknowledging regional variances during the tour, never budged from his view of France's government and nobility as malevolent forces hindering a more equitable distribution of land and wealth. France's peasantry, he believed, experienced "all the oppressions which result from the nature of the general government, and from that of their particular tenures, and of the Seignorial government to which they are subject. What a cruel reflection that a rich country cannot long be a free one."

Notably, however, his reference to a country that is "free" implicitly compared conditions under France's absolutist monarchy to those in the ostensibly "free" republic that Jefferson, as a diplomat, represented. In that, he ignored the continued existence in the United States of a human chattel slavery by then largely unfounded on European soil.

From Toulon on April 7 Jefferson wrote to William Short: "Hitherto my journey has been a continued feast on objects of agriculture, new to me, and, some of them at least, susceptible of adoption in America." Moreover, Jefferson added, that fixation suddenly required additional travel: "Information received at Marseilles—a letter from South Carolina rice planter and jurist William Drayton Sr.—encourages me in my researches on the subject of rice . . . just beyond the Alps." Truth be known, however, this student of Latin—and, more generally, an admirer of Italian culture from Cicero to Palladio—required little prodding to cross into Italy; and Jefferson was soon contemplating straying as far as Rome.[9]

As he toured, Jefferson refined an approach to travel that he later shared with friends. "On arriving at a town, the first thing is to buy the plan of the town, and the book noting it's curiosities. . . . Walk round the ramparts when there are any. Go to the top of a steeple to have a view of the town and it's environs." He likewise had thoughts on how to assess the merits of competing places and vistas.

> When you are doubting whether a thing is worth the trouble of going to see, recollect that you will never again be so near it, that you may repent the not having seen it, but can never repent having seen it. But there is an opposite extreme too. That is, the seeing [of] too much. A judicious selection is to be aimed at, taking care that the indolence of the moment have no influence on the decision.

Although Jefferson tried to preserve stretches for solitude, he was rarely without company at each visited place. Each stop posed the same question: With whom would his limited time there be best expended? "Take care particularly not to let the porters of churches, cabinets &c. lead you thro' all the little details in their possession, which will load the memory with trifles, fatigue the attention and waste that and your time," he advised. "It is difficult to confine these people to the few objects worth seeing and remembering. They wish for your money, and suppose you give it more willingly the more they detail to you."[10]

For Jefferson, his journey—like all the best travel combining caprice and discipline—increasingly put him in a reflective mood. To another correspondent he marveled at how "The plan of my journey, as well as of my life" had always been "to take things by the smooth handle"—and that among the events in his life, "few occur which have not something tolerable to offer me."[11]

From Aix, Jefferson returned to Marseille. From there, traveling westwardly over the coming days, he passed through Aubagne, Le Beausset, Toulon, Hyères, Cuers, Pignans, Luc, Vidauban, Napoule, and Antibes. On April 10 he arrived in Nice, then part of the independent kingdom of Piedmont-Sardinia. Now five weeks into his tour, Jefferson turned his thoughts to his friend Lafayette and his work with the Assembly of Notables. The next day he sat down and wrote him a letter; the missive—worth quoting at length—commenced in a casual tone: "Your head, my dear friend, is full of Notable things; and being better employed, therefore, I do not expect letters from you. I am constantly roving about, to see what I have never seen before and shall never see again."

> In the great cities, I go to see what travellers think alone worthy of being seen; but I make a job of it, and generally gulp it all down in a day. On the other hand, I am never satiated with rambling through the fields and farms, examining the culture and cultivators, with a degree of curiosity which makes some take me to be a fool, and others to be much wiser than I am. I have been pleased to find among the people a less degree of physical misery than I had expected. They are generally well clothed, and have a plenty of food, not animal indeed, but vegetable, which is as wholesome.

Eventually, however, the letter departed in tone and substance from any Jefferson had written the marquis before. To other correspondents, Jefferson had occasionally expressed his expectation that Lafayette might someday become a leader of France.

Rarely if ever in letters *to* Lafayette had Jefferson shared such expectations, but on April 11, 1787, he did just that. Indeed—raising the possibility that Jefferson's encouragement actually inspired Lafayette—when Jefferson, in Nice, finally wrote such a letter to Lafayette, the oration that would herald the marquis's arrival as a leader of France was only thirteen days away.

Jefferson's confidence in his absent friend—commingling, no doubt, with the exhilarations and loneliness of the open road—produced a concluding passage that was startling in both its professed admiration and intimacy: "I have often wished for you," it began. "I think you have not made this journey." Jefferson then plunged into a peroration as to why the marquis—as the future leader of his country—should, however temporarily, shed the trappings of his life as a nobleman, and, following Jefferson's example, tour France without the ostentations of his class:

It is a pleasure you have to come, and an improvement to be added to the many you have already made. It will be a great comfort to you to know, from your own inspection, the condition of all the provinces of your own country, and it will be interesting to them at some future day to be known to you. This is perhaps the only moment of your life in which you can acquire that knolege [*sic*]. And to do it most effectually you must be absolutely incognito, you must ferret the people out of their hovels as I have done, look into their kettles, eat their bread, loll on their beds under pretence of resting yourself, but in fact to find if they are soft. You will feel a sublime pleasure in the course of this investigation, and a sublimer one hereafter when you shall be able to apply your knolege [*sic*] to the softening of their beds, or the throwing [of] a morsel of meat into the kettle of vegetables. You will not wonder at the subjects of my letter: they are the only ones which have been present to my mind for some time past, and the waters must always be what are the fountain from which they flow. According to this indeed I should have intermixed from beginning to end warm expressions of friendship to you: but according to the ideas of our country we do not permit ourselves to speak even truths when they may have the air of flattery. I content myself therefore with saying once for all that I love you, your wife and children. Tell them so and Adieu. Your's affectionately,

TH: JEFFERSON [12]

No highway along the Mediterranean then linked Nice to northern Italy's coastal city of Genoa. The best land route into Italy from Nice, Jefferson was told, ran across the Alps to the town of Coni—today's Cuneo—127 miles from Nice. Moreover, because snow remained too dense for a carriage to pass through the road's higher elevations, he and his baggage would cross the Alps with pack mules. Before departing from Nice, he wrote to William Short: "Let my daughter know I am well and that I shall not be heard of again in three weeks."

On April 13, Jefferson's forty-fourth birthday, his mule caravan began its winding ascent toward the Col de Tende—elevation 6,135 feet—the pass through the Alps nearest to Nice. As the travelers ascended into the mountains, Jefferson found the road visually sublime and a marvel of engineering prowess; while passing over three successive mountains, he also observed that olive trees spotted at lower elevations disappeared as the road climbed, only to reappear in lower regions. In time he formulated a continuum of plants—from tenderest to hardiest, based on their vulnerability to cold: caper, orange, palm, aloe, olive, pomegranate. walnut, fig, and almond.

Scientific speculations, however—as a letter to Maria Cosway (who remained ever in his thoughts) soon made clear—had not crowded out aesthetic meditations: "Imagine to yourself, madam, a castle and village hanging to a cloud in front . . . ," he wrote to her.[13]

Rice had been Jefferson's ostensible reason for crossing the Alps—he wanted to inspect a local husking mill to determine whether its machines might prove useful in South Carolina. Likewise, he wanted to investigate strains grown in Italy's Piedmont that might prove suitable for cultivation in that state.

After crossing the Alps, he pursued both inquiries in several places. After investigating the husking machines, he soon wrote to William Drayton that the hullers were similar to those already in use in South Carolina. The research for the other topic, by contrast, proved both more promising and logistically complicated. Under penalty of death—defying local law that banned the export of the local strain of rice in its raw form—Jefferson hired a muleteer to smuggle a sack of the crop to Genoa, and lest that shipment failed to reach him, he placed a few scoops in his own pockets.

South of Milan, at a dairy in the village of Rozzano, Jefferson observed the production of the local cheese—recording in his Memorandum book a 645-word account of the process. ("In 3. hours the whole mass is scummed a second time, the milk remaining in a kettle for cheese, and the cream being put into a cylindrical churn, shaped like a grindstone, 18.I. radius and 14.I. thick. . . .") And, close to Turin, he investigated the local viticulture: "There is a red wine of Nebiule [Nebbiolo] made in this neighborhood which is very singular . . . about as sweet as the silky Madeira, as astringent as Bordeaux, and as brisk as Champagne."

Jefferson left no further details, but he also made "a fine excursion" to Lake Como and likewise visited Turin and Milan. In the latter he visited the Duomo (cathedral). While he praised the Gothic edifice as "a worthy object of philosophical contemplation," he also "placed [it] among the rarest instances of the misuse of money."[14]

In Italy, Jefferson had visited Genoa, Milan, and Turin. And while, as he explained to Maria Cosway, he had longed to visit the Eternal City, "I calculated the hours it would have taken to carry me on to Rome. But they were exactly so many more than I had to spare." In the end, as he lamented to another friend—caught in "a conflict between duty . . . and inclination, . . . Milan was the spot at which I turned my back on Rome and Naples."[15]

To hasten his return to France by sea, Jefferson, on April 28 in Genoa, boarded a Marseille-bound *felucca*, a small, open sailboat with a limited crew. Soon after the vessel weighed anchor, however, as he recalled in one of several letters to Patsy from the tour, he became "mortally sick." A shift in winds, meanwhile, after two days hugging the Mediterranean coast, forced the craft to anchor at Italy's port of Noli. Eager to return to France, he spent the next two days "clambering the cliffs of the Appennine, sometimes on foot, sometimes on a mule according as the path was more or less difficult, and two others travelling thro' the night as well as day, without sleep."[16]

On May 2 Jefferson reached Antibes. Three days later he was back in Marseille. There, as he caught up on correspondence, daughter Patsy numbered among those to whom he wrote; and to her he provided a résumé of his travels up to that date:

> In order to exercise your geography I will give you a detail of my journey. You must therefore take your map and trace out the following places. Dijon, Lyons, Pont St. Esprit, Nismes, Arles, St. Remis, Aix, Marseilles, Toulon, Hieres, Frejus, Antibes, Nice, Col de Tende, Coni, Turin, Vercelli, Milan, Pavia, Tortona, Novi, Genoa, by sea to Albenga, by land to Monaco, Nice, Antibes, Frejus, Brignolles, Aix, and Marseille.

By May 8 Jefferson was in Avignon. There—apparently bypassing the Papal Palace (or finding it unworthy of mention)—his mind was already straying down the road to the manmade wonder that ranked among the principal attractions that prompted his journey.[17]

THIRTY-SEVEN

Canal Royal en Languedoc

On May 12, 1787, at the Mediterranean port of Cette—today's Séte— Jefferson's course turned to the heart of that spring's tour, the Languedoc Canal's 150-mile passage to Toulouse—a three-page map of which he had purchased in Marseille. As he recounted to William Short: "I dismounted my carriage from it's wheels, placed it on the deck of a light bark, and was thus towed on the canal instead of the post road. That I might be perfectly master of all the delays necessary, I hired a bark to myself by the day, and have made from 20. to 35 miles a day . . . always sleeping ashore.

"Of all the methods of travelling I have ever tried this is the pleasantest," he wrote to Short: "I walk the greater part of the way along the banks of the canal, level, and lined with a double row of trees which furnish shade. When fatigued I take seat in my carriage where, as much at ease as if in my study, I read, write, or observe . . . the varying scenes thro' which I am shifted, olives, figs, mulberries, vines, corn and pasture, villages and farms."

With ropes and a single horse, two people pulled the barge along the plane-tree-shaded path that paralleled the waterway. Opened in 1681, the 150-mile-long Canal royal en Languedoc—the eastern half of today's Canal du Midi—linked a series of navigable waterways between France's Mediterranean and Atlantic coasts. The canal ran east-to-west from Séte to Toulouse, where a lock connected it to the Garonne River, which, descending from the Pyrenees, flowed northeasterly to Bordeaux and the Atlantic Ocean. The canal was constructed to spare French traders the time and costs—and exposure to Barbary piracy—associated with sailing around the Iberian Peninsula. Everything about the waterway fascinated Jefferson—the mechanics of its operation as well as the various watersheds along its course from which it drew its waters—passions later manifest in his preoccupations as U.S. president with rivers and western expansion.

Indeed, Jefferson became so captivated by the canal's hydrology and watersheds that, interrupting his passage along its length, he spent an entire day riding forty miles on horseback, north into the Montagnes Noires, inspecting the basins and channels by which that mountain range's watershed supplied (still supplies) much of the canal's water.

The shallow-draft boat transporting Jefferson to Toulouse stretched to seventy feet in length with a seventeen-foot berth. Of the two persons at any given moment on the canal path pulling the craft, he noticed, one was invariably female. Beyond that, "The locks are mostly kept by women, but the necessary operations are much too laborious for them." That and similar labor patterns he had noticed during his travels in France prompted a more general complaint:

> The encroachments by the men on the offices proper for the women is a great derangement in the order of things. Men are shoemakers, tailors, upholsterers, staymakers, . . . [dress]makers, cooks, door-keepers, housekeepers, housecleaners, bedmakers. They coëffe the ladies, and bring them to bed [possibly a reference to *accoucheurs,* male midwives]. The women therefore, to live are obliged to undertake the offices which they abandon. They become porters, carters, reapers, wood cutters, sailors, lock keepers, smiters on the anvil, cultivators of the earth &c.[1]

At Toulouse on May 22, Jefferson's carriage was rolled off the barge. By the twenty-fourth, having taken a northwesterly course, he was in Bordeaux, and, by June 1, having passed through Blaye, Rochefort, and La Roche-sur-Yon, he reached the port of Nantes. From there, striking out for Brittany, he briefly visited Lorient and Rennes. On June 6 he was back in Nantes, and after traveling up the Loire—in haste, not dallying in Tours to investigate Voltaire's alleged spontaneously growing shells—he stopped in Orléans on June 9 and the following day returned to Paris.

Petit Jean—the servant whom he had hired in Dijon and who worked for him during the entire tour—stayed at the Hôtel de Langeac in Jefferson's employ for another nine days; "Pd. & gave Petit Jean in full on his leaving me 72f," recorded Jefferson in his Memorandum book's July 10 entry. But who was Petit Jean? How old was he, and did "Petit" refer to his age or physical stature?

Moreover, what qualities did Jean possess that led Jefferson, who had vowed to switch servants at each stop, to retain his services for the entire four-month tour, and, for another nine days at the Hôtel de Langeac?

Aside from a handful of fleeting references to payments to Petit Jean in his Memorandum book—Jefferson's writings from the tour, his notes and correspondence, yield no further clues. One speculates that the American minister's frequent aloofness, reinforced by that age's habits of class deference, minimized conversations between the two men. Moreover, like most of Jefferson's servants, free or enslaved, Petit Jean likely remained in fundamental ways for Jefferson an invisible person.

Between Petit Jean and the various postilions who drove his carriage and each *valet de place* he hired at major stops, minimally two and often three persons attended to Jefferson's needs at any given moment during his trip. Even so, a week after returning to Paris, writing to a friend, he reflected: "I was alone thro the whole [tour], and think one travels more usefully when they travel alone, because they reflect more."

Upon returning to Paris, Jefferson had concluded his four-month, twelve-hundred-mile tour—his first and only foray into what Charles de Gaulle later called *la France profonde*, the country away from France's cities in its villages and rural spheres. "He now knew," Dumas Malone wrote, "the French land and people in a way that Franklin never did and that no other leading American of the day even approached." Two months later, writing to his nephew Peter Carr, Jefferson, by then reimmersed in Paris's swirl of life, reflected on the intangible costs of such excursions: "Travelling," he wrote, "makes men wiser, but less happy."

That spring, on his forty-fourth birthday, Jefferson had inhaled the bracing air of the Col de Tende; seven months before that he had injured his wrist in a vainglorious attempt to impress a younger woman. And now—though he was still middle-aged—writing to his nephew, the world-weariness of an older soul weighed on him: "When men of sober age travel, they gather knowlege which they may apply usefully for their country, but they are subject ever after to recollections mixed with regret, their affections are weakened by being extended over more objects, and they learn new habits which cannot be gratified when they return home." Apparently, in his own pursuit of happiness, even the author of the Declaration of Independence was not immune to the coveting of roads untaken, lives unlived.[2]

THIRTY-EIGHT

Bed of Justice

As Jefferson, approaching his tour's end on May 25, 1787, reached the port of Bordeaux, the Assembly of Notables, in Versailles that same day, was concluding its final session. King Louis XVI—exasperated by what he viewed as the body's three months of recalcitrance in addressing his proposed revenue measures—had grown so distraught that he ordered its dismissal.

But while the assembly disappointed the king, it did pass measures that, while lacking the force of law, gave impetus to reformist currents circulating in France—particularly among the nobility. In addition to authorizing provincial assemblies—again, without clearly defined powers—the assembly had made progress on opening France to free trade; beyond that, by reducing internal tariffs and the reviled salt tax called the *gabelle*—both of which hit the poor disproportionately hard—it had also advanced a fairer tax system.

Particularly gratifying for Lafayette, the Notables had likewise issued measures calling for reduced spending at Versailles: "We Have got the King to make Reductions and improvements to the Amount of forty millions of livres a year," he gloated to Washington. Additionally: "We are proposing the means to insure a Better, and more public method of Administration."[1]

Their reforms notwithstanding, however, the Notables had, in the end, refused to grant the king authorization for any new taxes or loans. In the wake of that setback, Louis and his new finance minister, Étienne-Charles Loménie de Brienne, the archbishop of Toulouse—replacing the increasingly unpopular Calonne—might have won their desired revenue measures by turning to the Parlement of Paris. Instead, they procrastinated—creating time and opportunity for popular opinion to expand the scope of the original, limited measures presented to the Notables. Among those new demands, noted Jefferson, came calls "for a fixed constitution, not subject to changes at the will of the king."

A clash—specifically concerning a stamp tax sought by the king—eventually erupted between Versailles and the *parlement* of Paris. To compel the court's registration of the measure, the king and Brienne turned to a venerable legal ploy—a special session of the parlement called a *lit de justice* ("bed of justice"). Its name derived from the canopied and multicushioned throne—*le lit*—on which the king sat as he oversaw the sessions. Its rituals were elaborate, but the *lit de justice*'s purposes were straightforward: The king and his ministers read aloud the measures they sought to enact and then declared them registered.

Tensions in 1787 between Louis and the *parlement* of Paris were already fraught that summer when he had summoned them to Versailles for a *lit de justice*. And on August 7 the *parlement* declared the king's stamp tax invalid—ruling that only the country's ancient Estates-General possessed authority to approve new taxes. The *parlement* further declared that although the Estates-General—an assembly representing the country's three estates—had not convened since 1614, if Louis wanted to enact new taxes, he would have to reconvene that body. Reacting to the ruling, Louis banished the Paris *parlement*'s members to Troyes, ninety miles from Paris.[2]

Facing public outrage, Louis soon capitulated, and in September the *parlement*'s members returned to Paris. Two months later, however, as Versailles's treasury dwindled closer to insolvency, Louis again summoned the *parlement* to Versailles for yet another *lit de justice*—this time to register an edict to authorize a large loan.

This time, the *parlement* obliged him. But in exchange for registering the edict, it exacted a promise—that Louis convene the Estates-General by 1792. Attending the latest *lit de justice* and outraged by the deal, the duc d' Orléans— a cousin of the king, already harboring aspirations to usurp as a regent Louis's royal authority—objected: The king, he inveighed, had no legal right to enter into such a bargain. Louis, for his part, was in no mood to brook interference. "The registration," he answered his cousin, "is legal because I have listened to everyone's opinion."[3]

THIRTY-NINE

A Parade in Aurillac

At seven o'clock on Saturday, September 1, 1787, breaking the silence of a cool autumn morning in south-central France, a cascade of drums summoned Aurillac's craftsmen to the town's edge. There, in a clearing alongside the town's main road, each man gathered under his respective guild's flag. Arriving too was the town's band, whose members soon unpacked their instruments and began warming up. In Lafayette's native Auvergne, Aurillac sat in a valley amid the Cantal Mountains, a range of extinct volcanoes worn by millennia into soft rolling hills. The town itself, with its broad avenues and gray buildings of locally quarried basalt, rose alongside the Jordanne River's west bank.

Aurillac had welcomed important visitors before. But few if any of its ten thousand inhabitants could remember one of the stature of that morning's arrival. Indeed, one who was there would recall it as the first time he ever gazed upon a hero: "One could not tire of looking at him," he remembered.

Later that morning the band began playing, and cheering commenced before most could see the marquis de Lafayette. Behind his carriage the band, along with the guildsmen and the town's highest-ranking clergy and nobility, formed a retinue, and to the blare of cheers and music, they followed Lafayette into Aurillac.

Moving along the river, up the Cours Monthyon, the procession soon arrived on the rue de la Bride, in the heart of the town. Through streets swept and cleared of traffic for the occasion, the noisy retinue passed shops and businesses closed for the day by order of the police. Several times during the parade the lanky-framed Lafayette, dismounting from his carriage, stood and listened to speeches in his honor. Still other welcoming orations greeted him as he arrived at his lodging.

That evening the town's leaders staged a fireworks show and a ball—though ladies attending the latter were disappointed that, instead of dancing, the gala's honoree spent the evening conversing with a prominent nobleman. The following morning Lafayette attended mass at the Church of Notre-Dame-aux-Neiges, where he sat in a special seat reserved for him by the parish priest. Afterward he spent the remainder of the day visiting the homes of prominent residents, and on Monday, he departed Aurillac with no less fanfare than he had entered.

It had been three months since the Assembly of Notables had met in its final session, and Lafayette's actions during that body's brief life—particularly his April 24 speech, castigating corruption and waste at Versailles—had brought a renewed luster to his heroic stature. And his welcome at Aurillac—like a similarly robust reception days earlier in his native Chavaniac—had provided reassuring confirmation that his status as a national hero now reached beyond Paris and Versailles, deep into all classes across the kingdom.

Indeed, on September 4, the day after he left Aurillac, forty miles to the west in the Auvergnois town of Saint-Flour, Lafayette received another boisterous welcome—capped by a banquet during which a local poet praised the honoree who, through "his noble exploits, unendingly narrated in two hemisphere, had learned to regard without discrimination all humans as his brothers."[1]

Soon after the Assembly of Notable's adjournment, Lafayette had been laid up with a recurring chest ailment that had bedeviled him since the assembly's original session. His spirits, however, were soon brightened by the news, in a letter from Washington, that Congress, with broad endorsements from

America's state legislatures, had, on February 27, authorized a meeting in Philadelphia—a "Convention of the States to revise, and correct the defects of the federal System."[2]

Once recuperated and caught up on matters neglected during his residency at Versailles, Lafayette departed Paris to turn to acting on the most tangible of all the assembly's achievements—its establishment of provincial assemblies across the country. In his case he traveled to the town of Clermont and there assisted in making arrangements for the Auvergne's assembly. The body's organizational session opened on August 14 and adjourned on August 21. Afterward he set out on a tour of the province.

In Jefferson's April letter from Nice—which reached Lafayette as the Notables were concluding their work—he had advised his friend to make a tour of France "absolutely incognito," focused on learning about the lives of the kingdom's humbler souls. In the end, however, Lafayette confined his version of the tour prescribed by Jefferson to his native Auvergne—and conducted it in a manner anything but incognito.

Socially and geographically Lafayette's tour thus lacked the breadth that Jefferson had advised. The circuit did, however, as Jefferson had also counseled ("I think you have not made this journey . . .") take the marquis to places he had heretofore rarely or never visited—albeit all in his native province. After all, in addition to the welcome Lafayette received in his native Chavaniac, the tour provided opportunities for welcoming receptions in other towns of the Auvergne—places where he was hardly a familiar presence.

Similarly, while Lafayette's tour did not, as Jefferson had hoped, focus on France's poor, it did consolidate support among the Auvergne's nobility and bourgeoisie. Indeed, one wary colleague in the Auvergnois assembly even saw in Lafayette's tour a deliberate effort to build political support among those ranks—albeit through an itinerary that left little to serendipitous chance: "He would announce in advance his arrival in cities where he was likely to receive an honorable reception."[3]

By that fall Lafayette had returned from the Auvergne to Paris and the familiar comforts of the Hôtel de Lafayette. To Washington he proudly reported: "I Made a tour through the province, wherein I was Received By all Classes of the inhabitants with the Most Affecting Marks of love and Confidence."

In later years, idealizing his youth and first forays into France's domestic politics, Lafayette would claim to have already acquired by then a robust disdain for monarchies. But in fact, as late as 1787 he still rarely used the words "republican" and "republicanism," except when referring to other countries—often ancient states, safely consigned to the distant past.

When Lafayette did speak of republics among contemporary nation-states, he referred principally to the United States and the Dutch Republic. And during those years, when he discussed France's future in such terms, he allowed that for him the term "republican" conveyed support for a constitutional monarchy—not wholesale antimonarchicalism. As Louis Gottschalk observed: "The fact was that Lafayette, like nearly every other political writer and thinker of his day, did not believe that a country as large as France could dispense with a monarchy."

That view notwithstanding, by 1787 the respective fortunes of Lafayette and Louis XVI were moving in opposite directions—the former ascendant, the latter waning. And for this son of the Auvergne, those vagaries were creating both new opportunities and new dangers. In the meantime, any expectations of his being offered a ministry at Versailles had long vanished, as had his invitations to play cards with the king. As Lafayette reported to Washington: "The Great Men about Court, some friends excepted, don't forgive me for the liberties I Have taken, and the success it Had Among the other Classes of the people."[4]

FORTY

Polly and Sally

S oon after Jefferson's return to Paris on July 1, 1787, a celebrated British-born American patriot passed through the Hôtel de Langeac. Thomas Paine "is here on his way to England," Jefferson reported. By any measure Jefferson—as evidenced by his request to the painter Mather Brown for a portrait of Paine—admired the radical author, and among American Patriots, he was hardly alone in that veneration: Paine's pamphlet *Common Sense*—published in Philadelphia in January 1776 under the anonymous name "an Englishman"—had in a sense conjured the movement for American independence.

More specifically Paine had argued that the long-range welfare of the inhabitants of Britain's thirteen colonies lay not in incremental reforms, but in severing ties with the mother country and establishing their own republic.

The fifty-year-old Paine's once full head of dark hair had thinned. But with his intense blue eyes and at a height of five feet ten inches, he remained a striking presence. The son of a corset maker, Paine had emigrated to America in 1774, and only then did he gravitate toward radical republicanism. As his biographer Harvey J. Kaye noted, Paine was "a workingman before an intellectual." But although his ideas were widely admired among Patriot leaders, Paine could be personally cantankerous, and many—including John Adams—came to despise him.

When Paine arrived in Paris, however, it was, as Jefferson noted, engineering rather than politics that brought him to the Hôtel de Langeac. "He has brought the model of an iron bridge, with which he supposes a single arch of 400 feet may be made." Paine's notion of using iron to construct bridges, a novel idea in that age, fascinated Jefferson, and he and the author of *Common Sense* later exchanged letters dense with technical details concerning what Jefferson called the "beauty and strength" of Paine's contemplated bridge.

During his later years Paine designed and—in a few instances—built several such bridges; the particular one that he was planning during his Paris visit, though never built, would have crossed the Schuylkill River at Philadelphia. But as much as Jefferson might otherwise have preferred that July to lose the summer's days in sustained conversations with Paine, he had scarce time to dawdle.

The forty-four-year-old diplomat had, after all, been away for four months, and there was unattended business to take care of, accumulated mail to read. Among the latter were two letters, both written days earlier by Abigail Adams, that stood out like comets in a clear night sky: "I have to congratulate you upon the safe arrival of your Little daughter, whom I have only a few moments ago received," she had written on June 26, announcing the arrival in London of his eight-year-old daughter Polly.[1]

But if news of Polly's presence in England delighted Jefferson, it was also expected. In fact, her arrival culminated two years of his efforts to bring her to Europe. Five years earlier, in 1782, in the wake of Martha's death, he had sent Polly, then five years old, and her younger sister, Lucy, born that same year, to live with Francis and Elizabeth Eppes. Two years later, intending to send for Polly and Lucy when they were older, Jefferson—with their older sister, Patsy, and his enslaved servant James Hemings—had departed for Paris.

In January 1785, however, upon learning of Lucy's death the previous spring, Jefferson, plunged into mourning, grew obsessed with a new resolve: "I must have Polly," he pleaded to Francis Eppes in early May. But concerned for her safety, he also specified that he "would not have her at sea but between 1st. of Apr. and Sep." Additionally, he stipulated that she be accompanied by a proper chaperone "Is there any woman in Virga. could be hired to come," he inquired.

Confounding Jefferson's reasonable fatherly wishes was an equally understandable impediment: Since being left with the Eppeses, Polly had grown attached to them and their household. For all practical purposes the Eppeses and their James River plantation represented the only family and home she truly knew. Jefferson, by contrast, loomed in her life less as a flesh-and-blood presence than a spectral father figure—a circumstance undiminished by the Eppeses' oft-expressed admiration, in Polly's presence, of her father in Paris.

In subsequent correspondence the Eppeses—aware of Polly's attachment to their family but also respectful of Jefferson's legal rights and paternal longings—tried gently to dissuade him from his resolve. Illustrative of the Eppeses' quandary was Francis's plea to Jefferson in a May 23, 1786, letter:

> I am sorry you are so desirous of having Polly sent to you as I am certain nothing but force will now bring it about. We have try'd every argument we are capable of in order to enduce [her] to agree to it. I have told her you wou'd meet her in Philadelphia and that I wou'd accompany her to that place. This however had no affect except distressing her. She is in tears when ever its mentiond.[2]

Francis's letter echoed sentiments Polly herself expressed to her father: "I want to see you and sister Patsy, but you must come to Uncle Eppes's house," she wrote in 1785. "I should be very happy to see you, but I can not go to France," she pleaded two years later.

But Jefferson remained unswayed. And by spring 1787, the Eppeses were resigned to finding a stratagem to entice her to sail, a suitable departure date, and a chaperone to accompany her. In the end they decided that Polly would sail on a London-bound ship captained by Andrew Ramsay, a family friend. Because no older chaperone could be engaged, Ramsay (also spelled "Ramsey") agreed to keep an eye out for the girl during the crossing. Otherwise Polly's day-to-day supervision would fall to Sally Hemings, the young enslaved girl owned by Jefferson. Then in her early teens, Sally was the younger sister of Jefferson's servant James. Beyond that, Sally—having been fathered by the planter John

Wayles, Martha Jefferson's father—was thus the half sister of Jefferson's late wife—rendering James and Sally Hemings an uncle and aunt to Polly and her sister, Patsy.

Captain Ramsay agreed to, upon reaching London, bring Polly and Sally to the Adams residence, where they would stay until Jefferson could be summoned from Paris. Failing, however, to entice Polly aboard the ship, the Eppeses eventually settled instead for a ruse: They arranged for Ramsay to dock his ship, the *Robert*, in May on the James River near the Eppeses' plantation. Over the next few days, Polly and her cousins were encouraged to play hide-and-seek aboard the ship. On what would be their games' final day, the children were allowed to play longer than usual, and Polly fell asleep aboard the ship. As she slumbered, the *Robert* weighed anchor; when she awoke, she and Sally were at sea—London-bound.[3]

Abigail Adams's June 26, 1787, letter to Jefferson described Polly, after her voyage, as disoriented and discomfited. "At present every thing is strange to her," Abigail wrote, "& She was very loth to try New Friends for old. She was so much attachd to the Captain & he to her, that it was with no Small regreet that I Seperated her from him, but I dare say I shall reconcile her in a day or two."

Eventually Abigail tried appealing to Polly's sense of sisterly rivalry—telling her that during the Adamses' entire time in Paris, she had never seen her sister Patsy cry—a dubious strategy since Polly likely had no memories of her sister. Whether she did or not, Polly had a ready reply to Abigail's taunt: Her sister "was older," Polly retorted, "& ought to do better, besides she had her pappa with her."

Persisting, Abigail showed the girl Mather Brown's portrait of her father—but also to no avail: "She says she cannot know it, how should she when she should not know you." But Abigail remained undaunted; anticipating the rapport that soon grew between them, she predicted that, after a "few hours acquaintance . . . we shall be quite Friends I dare say."[4]

In her June 26 letter Abigail said little about Polly's traveling companion, Sally Hemings: "She has a Girl of about 15 or 16 with her, the sister of the servant you have with you." By the following day, however, when Abigail again wrote to Jefferson, she elaborated: "The Girl who is with her is quite a child, and captain Ramsey is of opinion will be of so little service that he had better carry her back with him, but of this you will be a judge. she seems fond of the child and appears good Naturd."[5]

In her June 26 letter Abigail expressed her hopes that he might bring Patsy along to London when he came to pick up Polly. "It would reconcile her little Sister to the thoughts of taking a journey." Her urgency expressed, Abigail graciously—if disingenuously—added: "As I presume you have but just returnd from your late excursion, you will not put yourself to any inconvenience or Hurry in comeing or Sending for her."[6]

Jefferson, elated to learn of Polly's arrival, answered Abigail's letters hours after reading them on July 1—the day he returned to Paris. "A thousand thanks to you, my dear Madam, for your kind attention to my little daughter. Her distresses I am sure must have been troublesome to you: but I know your goodness will forgive her, and forgive me too for having brought them on you."

Jefferson's next sentence, however, left Abigail nonplussed: "Petit," he wrote, "now comes for her." Instead of coming himself for Polly—with Patsy in tow, as Abigail had suggested—Jefferson was instead dispatching to London Adrien Petit, his valet de chambre at the Hôtel de Langeac. "The pleasure of a visit to yourself and Mr. Adams would have been a great additional inducement" for making the trip himself, he wrote. But the demands of work, he pleaded, required his presence in Paris. Having "just returned from my journey, I have the arrearages of 3. or 4. months all crouded on me at once."

Jefferson's claim that a backlog of work prevented his coming to London is not without plausibility. But his biographer Fawn M. Brodie suspected another motive: "A better reason was that he was daily expecting the arrival of Maria Cosway." During that period Jefferson, with each passing day, was awaiting Cosway's promised return to Paris—the trip she eventually did make two months later, in August 1787.

Having decided to dispatch Adrien Petit to London, Jefferson had arranged for Petit Jean—his erstwhile Dijonnais traveling companion—to remain and work at the Hôtel de Langeac for most of his valet de chambre's absence. The following day, July 2, Adrien Petit departed for London. In his baggage he carried letters from Jefferson for the Adamses, Maria Cosway, and other London correspondents. He also brought cash, with instructions from Jefferson to pay any expenses incurred by Abigail on Polly's and Sally's behalf.[7]

After arranging Polly's and Sally's passage from London to Paris, Jefferson also plunged into the backlog of diplomatic work that awaited his return from the South of France—matters concerning U.S. commerce as well as foreign policy toward France and Europe.

He also caught up with the latest reports on a recently convened gathering in Philadelphia charged with reforming the country's governance. Upon his return to Paris—having only sketchy information concerning that assembly—Jefferson assumed that the body was modifying the Articles of Confederation, not replacing it with another governing document. He also assumed any alterations to the Articles would be minimal: "Amendments . . . relative to our commerce will probably be adopted immediately," he predicted to a correspondent. "Others must await to be adopted one after another in proportion as the minds of the states ripen for them." By mid-August, however, Jefferson had learned of the assembly's intention to draft a brand-new governing document. "I remain in hopes of great and good effects from the decisions of the assembly over which you are presiding," he wrote in mid-August to the body's president, George Washington.[8]

Jefferson likewise was following developments in Paris and Versailles—particularly the clash between the king and the *parlement* of Paris. Indeed, as Lafayette that summer—at Versailles, in his native Auvergne, and in Paris—basked in growing public adulation, so Jefferson delighted in what seemed to be a new order emerging across France. Writing to Crèvecoeur, on August 16—the day Louis summoned the *parlement* to Versailles for a *lit de justice*—he saw hubris in the king's arrogance toward the *parlement*. Commensurately, however, in the *parlement*'s refusal to register Louis's decree for new taxes and his subsequent attempt to nullify that refusal with a *lit de justice*, Jefferson saw an inexorable march by France toward a brighter day. "Your nation is advancing to a change of constitution," he wrote. "The young desire it, the middle aged are not averse, the old alone are opposed to it."[9]

Two weeks later, as Louis's actions reverberated in Paris's streets, Jefferson welcomed the upheaval, believing it had stimulated a lively exchange equal to that of Britain's vaunted free speech: "All tongues in Paris (and in France as it is said) have been let loose, and never was a license of speaking against the government exercised in London more freely or more universally," he wrote to John Adams on August 30. "Caracatures, placards, bon mots, have been indulged in by all ranks of people, and I know of no well attested instance of a single punishment."

Recounting public reaction to the king's *lit de justice*, Jefferson described "mobs of 10; 20; 30,000 people collected daily" around the *parlement*'s Paris assembly hall, and after Louis exiled the members from Paris to the town of Troyes, he reported, the government at Versailles had added still more national guards to the soldiers already patrolling Paris's streets; beyond that the king "suspended privileged places, forbad all clubs." In the meantime, Jefferson added, "The king, long in the habit of drowning his cares in wine, plunges deeper and deeper; the queen cries but sins on."[10]

On July 15 that summer, Polly Jefferson—two weeks shy of her ninth birthday—arrived in Paris. Disoriented and unhappy, in her young life she had already been pounded by traumas: Her mother had died four years after her birth; soon thereafter she was placed with relatives; more recently she had been tricked into leaving those relatives and sailing to England; and, weeks later—for her journey from London to Paris with Adrien Petit and Sally Hemings—she had been forcibly torn away from both Abigail Adams and Captain Ramsay. "She had got so attached to Captn. Ramsay that they were obliged to decoy her from him," reported Jefferson, betraying no emotion, in a letter to his own sister Mary. "She refused to come with the person I sent for her."

Recounting Polly's reunion in Paris with himself and Patsy, Jefferson wrote: "She did not know either her sister or myself, but soon renewed her acquaintance and attachment." Describing another development that—contrary to his apparent wishes—seems unlikely to have reassured his Protestant relatives in Virginia, he added: "She is now in the same convent with her sister, and will come to see me once or twice a week."

Abigail Adams, for her part, was gladdened to learn of Polly's safe arrival in Paris. But to Jefferson she confessed to worrying over the girl's fate in her new school: "I never felt so attached to a child in my Life on so short an acquaintance," Abigail wrote. "Tis rare to find one possessd of so strong and lively a sensibility. I hope she will not lose her fine spirits within the walls of a convent, to which I own I have many, perhaps false prejudices."[11]

In July 1787 Polly, arriving at the Hôtel de Langeac, reunited with her sister, Patsy, after almost four years apart. At the age of eight, Polly was dark haired, pretty, and—like her mother—possessed of delicate features. Patsy, at fifteen, while not pretty, was attractive, and, like her father, tall with red hair. Beyond that, Patsy—gregarious, self-possessed, fluent in French, and six years older than Polly—assumed the role of big-sister/protector. After arriving in Paris, Polly, soon joined Patsy at the Abbaye Royale de Panthémont.

Adrien Petit, however, did bring from London one new permanent resident to the Hôtel de Langeac. Sally Hemings, after arriving in Paris, eventually joined her brother James as a household servant in the American minister's residence. Whether Sally and her brother lived in the servants' quarters adjacent to the town house or in a space designed for servants in its mezzanine remains unclear. One circumstance, however, does seem clear: Providing Sally fraternal companionship and a role model for her own aspirations in Paris was her brother. Indeed, when Sally arrived in Paris, James—working under Adrien Petit and soon to supervise others—was close to finishing his apprenticeship as a chef and about to (with a raise in salary from Jefferson) become manager of the Hôtel de Langeac's kitchen.

Jefferson, as he had done with James, failed to alert French officials of Sally's arrival. But—as he had also done with James to discourage him from seeking the legal freedom to which he was eligible on French soil—Jefferson did pay Sally a monthly salary—in her case, twelve livres—for her work. Again, as he had done for James, he also purchased clothes for Sally.

There was also a medical component to Sally Hemings's move to Paris. Jefferson was an early believer in smallpox inoculation; before coming to Paris he and both of his daughters had already undergone the treatment; and prior to Sally's arrival, he had arranged for her to have the procedure at a cost to him of 240 livres. Because Paris law banned administration of the treatment inside the city, Sally was sent to a family of English doctors—led by its patriarch, Robert Sutton, Sr.—just outside the city limits. There—assuming the doctor adhered to his usual protocol—in a house established for such treatments, Sally, after receiving the inoculation, would have remained in quarantine for the next forty days.

———

Like Polly Jefferson's, Sally Hemings's life had been punctuated by familial alienation and losses. Sally's father—the planter John Wayles (Thomas Jefferson's late father-in-law)—had never acknowledged paternity of her and her siblings. And after Wayles's death in 1774, Sally and her mother and siblings became the property of Thomas Jefferson. And though Sally's move to Paris reunited her with her by then twenty-seven-year-old brother James, it also separated her from her mother and siblings in Virginia. Moreover, like Polly, Sally also had suffered the loss of a sister the previous year.

Despite similar familial misfortunes, however, Sally's plight was obviously worse than Polly's. There were the stark differences in their legal and material circumstances, and the reception Sally received in London and Paris certainly fell short, in warmth and attention, of that accorded Polly. Beyond that, in France, Sally, though legally free—like her brother James—remained, in ways both obvious and ambiguous, dependent on her Virginia master, Thomas Jefferson. Compounding her disorientation, Sally had, in the summer of 1787, suddenly become a resident of Europe's largest city, a metropolis whose population of seven hundred thousand exceeded that of all of Virginia; it was a city at once more opulent, more dangerous, more ethnically and class diverse, dirtier—and more interesting—than any place she had been before.

Moreover—though still in her early teens and with no prospects for formal instruction—she found herself cast into a world that spoke a tongue she had yet to learn; adding to her bewilderment, that milieu was dominated by the—to her unfamiliar—rites, festivals, and holidays of Roman Catholicism. Equally daunting, behind the Hôtel de Langeac's walls, Sally faced the challenge of finding her way in an enclave populated almost exclusively by men—and, with the exception of her brother, men of lighter skin hue than her own.[12]

A circa 1700 map of France with pre-Revolution borders. *(Engraving by Claude-Auguste Berey; courtesy of the Bibliothèque Nationale de France)*

An 1887 *Century Magazine* engraving of Monticello, the estate of Thomas Jefferson. The estate sits atop an 867-foot mountain in Albemarle County, Virginia, in the state's Piedmont region, three miles west of Shadwell, Jefferson's boyhood home. *(Courtesy of the Library of Congress)*

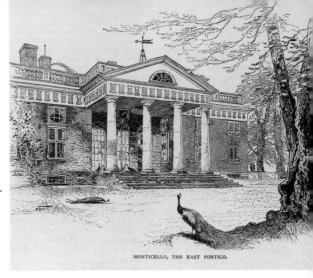

MONTICELLO, THE EAST PORTICO.

A lithograph depicting Château de la Grange-Bléneau, Lafayette's 700-acre estate, forty miles southeast of Paris. Lafayette's properties were confiscated during France's Revolution. However, by 1800, following their release from prison in northern Europe, Gilbert and Adrienne had moved to and gained title to La Grange, formerly owned by her family and which survives today. *(Courtesy of the David Bishop Skillman Library, Lafayette College)*

A hand-bell reportedly given by Jefferson's wife Martha Jefferson on her deathbed to Sally Hemings. The bell would have been used by Martha to summon Sally and other enslaved attendants. Except for a silhouette of Martha Jefferson, no contemporary images of either her or Hemings are known to exist. *(Courtesy of the Moorland-Spingarn Research Center, Manuscript Division, Howard University, Washington, DC)*

Boston-born painter Mather Brown's 1786 portrait of forty-two-year-old Jefferson, the first portrait for which he ever sat. Executed in London during Jefferson's England visit that year, the work renders him more dandyish in appearance than in later images. *(Courtesy of the National Portrait Gallery)*

A legendary predator, the Beast of the Gévaudan, depicted in an eighteenth-century engraving, reputedly roamed the mountainous Auvergne wildernesses that Lafayette explored as a boy. The "beast" was likely a large lynx, some other known species of forest mammal, or even a human being. Whatever the legend's origins, the chimerical creature whetted Lafayette's early appetite for romantic adventure. *(Courtesy of the Bibliothèque Nationale de France)*

A lithograph from an image by artist Clara Greenleaf Perry of Chateau de Chavaniac, the eighteen-room childhood home of Marie-Joseph-Paul-Yves-Roch-Gilbert du Motier, marquis de Lafayette, in central France's highland province of Auvergne. Like Jefferson, Lafayette came from a privileged background in a hinterland, upland region. Though altered since Lafayette's days, the estate survives today. *(Courtesy of the David Bishop Skillman Library, Lafayette College)*

An 1894 engraving from a miniature of unknown origin of Marie-Adrienne-Françoise de Noailles, marquise de Lafayette. Like her husband, she came from a noble family. Unlike her spouse's, however, Adrienne's family in Paris, the Noailles, enjoyed close ties to Versailles's royal court. *(Courtesy of the David Bishop Skillman Library, Lafayette College)*

Le départ de la Victoire à Los Pasajes, an 1845 painting by Hélène Feillet, imagines Lafayette's April 20, 1777, departure from Spain's Atlantic port of Los Pasajes aboard *La Victoire* for his first trip to America. Identified figures ashore include (far left and immediate right) Lafayette and Johann Kalb, one of several other European officers recruited to assist the American Patriots and who sailed aboard *La Victoire*. *(Courtesy of the Collections de la Fondation Josée et René de Chambrun)*

Lafayette at Yorktown, Jean Baptiste Le Paon's circa 1783 portrait, depicts the twenty-four-year-old marquis among the heroes of the October 1781 Virginia battle that concluded the American Revolution's major fighting. While the exotically dressed figure to Lafayette's right—ostensibly a groom for the depicted horse—is often assumed to be the spy later known as James Lafayette, recent scholarship casts doubt on that assumption. *(Courtesy of the Lafayette College Art Collection, Easton, Pennsylvania. Gift of Helen Fahnstock Hubbard in memory of her husband, John)*

A 1784 broadside featuring a portrait by John Blennerhassett Martin of the enslaved man, later known as James Lafayette, whose anti-British espionage assisted Lafayette in helping to secure the Patriots' 1781 Yorktown victory. A facsimile of a testimonial written by Lafayette during a 1784 visit to Richmond, Virginia, on James's behalf appears beneath the portrait. The portrait's subject won his freedom in 1787. *(Courtesy of the New York Public Library)*

Jefferson's twenty-four-room Paris residence, Hôtel de Langeac (above, in image's far left foreground) sat on what was then Paris's leafy western edge, at the northeastern intersection of the Champs Elysées and what is now rue de Berri. The above view looks east, down the Champs Elysées, toward Paris's center. The building was demolished in 1842. *(Engraving by F. N. Martinet, in* Histoire de Paris, et Description de Paris, et de ses plus beaux monuments, *1779; courtesy of the Thomas Jefferson Foundation)*

Watercolorist and Jefferson friend Maria Hadfield Cosway, in a 1785 engraving after her husband, the English artist Richard Cosway. She was twenty-six when, in Paris, she met the forty-three-year-old Jefferson. The two became close and were possibly intimate. *(Courtesy of the Thomas Jefferson Foundation)*

Alexander Hamilton as depicted in an 1806 portrait by John Trumbull after Giuseppe Ceracchi. Hamilton spoke French, came from foreign shores, and was close in age to Lafayette; the two established an easy rapport. Hamilton and Jefferson, by contrast, were never close. In Paris, however, Jefferson did grow close to Hamilton's sister-in-law, Angelica Schuyler Church. *(Courtesy of the National Portrait Gallery)*

The opening, at Versailles, of France's Estates-General, May 5, 1789, attended by Lafayette as a delegate and Jefferson as an observer. The body, whose numbers included 1,200 deputies, was summoned by Louis XVI to address France's financial woes. But as its members, soon styling themselves the National Assembly, embraced broader purposes, the king soon confronted greater challenges. *(1790 engraving by Isidore-Stanislas Helman, after a drawing by Charles Monnet; courtesy of the Bibliothèque Nationale de France)*

Benjamin Blyth's circa-1766 pastel of Abigail Smith Adams. During her husband John Adams's diplomatic stint in Paris, Abigail befriended both Jefferson and Lafayette, but grew particularly close to Jefferson. *(Photograph courtesy of the Library of Congress; portrait owned by the Massachusetts Historical Society)*

Reflecting the acclaim enjoyed by Benjamin Franklin in late-eighteenth-century Paris, a contemporary snuffbox features a print portrait of him to the right of (left to right) Voltaire and Jean Jacques Rousseau, underscored by a praiseful epithet: *Le Flambeau de l'univers* (the light of the universe). Jefferson's relations in Paris with fellow diplomat Franklin were mutually respectful but never close. Lafayette, by contrast, established a close rapport with the diplomat, five decades his senior. *(Photograph by Dennis P. Buttleman, Jr.; snuffbox owned by the Masonic Library and Museum of Pennsylvania, Philadelphia)*

John Trumbull's masterpiece (shown above) *The Declaration of Independence, July 4, 1776.* In the fictional scene—the depicted ceremony never occurred—Jefferson, the document's principal author, presents the Declaration to the Second Continental Congress. Standing alongside Jefferson are his fellow members of the committee tasked with drafting the document—to the left of Jefferson, John Adams, Roger Sherman, and Robert Livingston; to the right of him, Benjamin Franklin. Trumbull first conceived of the painting while living in Paris with Jefferson and executed a portrait of him in 1788 (right). The eventual tableau—a small version and a larger canvas—was completed decades later. The larger canvas, commissioned by the federal government, was installed in the U.S. Capitol rotunda in 1826. *(Declaration of Independence, July 4, 1776 courtesy of the Architect of the Capitol; Jefferson portrait courtesy of the Thomas Jefferson Foundation)*

Declaration of Rights of Man, an allegorical engraving from 1791, depicts Lafayette and his ally Honoré-Gabriel Riqueti, comte de Mirabeau, who, with Jefferson, numbered among those who assisted Lafayette in drafting the founding document he wrote for the constitutional monarchy he envisioned. Unlike Jefferson, whose authorship of his 1776 document was not widely known for decades, Lafayette's authorship of his declaration immediately won wide acclaim. *(Courtesy of the David Bishop Skillman Library, Lafayette College)*

During France's Revolution, yet another gesture—captured in this engraving of an image by François-Joseph-Aimé de Lemud—demonstrated Lafayette's knack for creating national icons. For the newly created National Guard, he proposed to Paris's city government that on each soldier's hat—his *tricorne*—there be attached a cockade of three colors: white, the official color of Versailles' House of Bourbon; and the blue and red of the City of Paris's rival government. The cockade served as inspiration for the Republic of France's *tricolore* flag, adopted in 1794. *(Courtesy of the David Bishop Skillman Library, Lafayette College)*

A passport signed by Lafayette preparatory to Jefferson's September 1789 departure from France. That era's passports, not required for foreign travel, were issued mainly to assist bearers in proving their identity in foreign climes. Reflecting that season's tensions between France's rival governments in Versailles and Paris, Jefferson, covering his bets, carried two passports—one signed by Lafayette, another by Louis XVI. *(Courtesy of the Thomas Jefferson Papers, Manuscript Division, Library of Congress)*

Lafayette with his wife, Adrienne, and two daughters in Olmütz prison, Austria (today's Olomouc, Czech Republic). After being detained in August 1792, as he was leading French troops in northern France, Lafayette spent the next five years in a succession of Austrian and Prussian prisons. Adrienne and their two daughters voluntarily joined him in October 1795, and the family's plight soon became an international cause célèbre. *(Circa 1830 engraving by Philbert Langlois after Ary Scheffer; courtesy of the David Bishop Skillman Library, Lafayette College)*

Etching of unknown origin of Lafayette's August 15, 1824, arrival at Castle Garden, then on an island in New York harbor (known today as Castle Clinton, in the city's Battery Park). The arrival commenced Lafayette's 1824–25 American tour, a thirteen-month journey that took him to 182 towns and all twenty-four states. *(Courtesy of the David Bishop Skillman Library, Lafayette College)*

FORTY-ONE

The Perpetual Union's
Final Days

On any occasion Lafayette relished mail from America. But it was with a distinct joy on Christmas Day 1787, while passing through central France's town of Nemours, that he opened a letter that caught up with him as he was returning to Paris from Clermont, after attending the Auvergne's provincial assembly.

The letter, written in Philadelphia, came from George Washington—penned, he apologized, "in the midst of hurry, and in the moment of my departure from this City": "The principal, indeed the only design of it, is to fulfil the promise I made, that I would send to you the proceedings of the Federal convention, as soon as the business was closed."

Enclosed was a copy of the proposed new governing document for the republic. Intended to replace the Articles of Confederation, the "Constitution" had been endorsed the previous day by Washington and his colleagues in Philadelphia. "It is the production of four months deliberation," explained Washington, who was exhausted and eager to return to Mt. Vernon to resume his by now increasingly nominal retirement. As for the enclosed Constitution,

"It is now a child of fortune," he wrote. "To be fostered by some and buffeted by others, what will be the General opinion on, or the reception of it, is not for me to decide, nor shall I say any thing for or against it: if it be good I suppose it will work its way good. If bad, it will recoil on the Framers."[1]

Although passed that fall of 1787 by the Philadelphia assembly, the new Constitution still required ratification by nine of the thirteen states to finalize its official status. In the meantime, the outgoing Confederation Congress had selected March 4, 1789, as the date for the new document to become operational.

As Lafayette expected, the Constitution called for the creation of an elected bicameral congress (with upper and lower houses) empowered to tax, assume national debts, and enter into foreign treaties. It also created a system of federal courts coequal in powers to the new government's other two (legislative and executive) branches. More generally, the compact strengthened the republic's central government, giving it new powers over the individual states.

To exercise Congress's will—and to otherwise provide firm and ready leadership—the executive branch was to be headed by an elected president. Otherwise extant institutions of the individual states—legislatures, offices, and courts, albeit now subordinated in powers to the federal government—were to remain in place.

Washington, as it turned out, had—on September 18, the day after the Philadelphia convention adjourned—also sent Jefferson a copy of the Constitution. In an accompanying letter, Washington noted that he had no doubt that "you have participated in the general anxiety which has agitated the minds of your Countrymen on this interesting occasion." As a consequence, weeks before Lafayette's copy reached its addressee, Jefferson had read the document.[2]

By December 20, having had several weeks to ponder the Constitution—and accept the Articles of Confederation's demise—Jefferson wrote a long letter to James Madison—fifteen hundred words of which were devoted to his thoughts on the new governing document. Madison was the Constitution's principal architect, and after praising most of the document's features, Jefferson arrived at the heart of his letter: "I will now add what I do not like."

First the omission of a bill of rights providing clearly & without the aid of sophisms for freedom of religion, freedom of the press, protection against standing armies, restriction against monopolies, the eternal & unremitting force of the habeas corpus laws, and trials by jury in all matters of fact triable by the laws of the land & not by the law of Nations.

In due course Jefferson turned to an aspect of the Constitution that had troubled Lafayette—the office of the president and, more specifically, the lack of limits on the number of terms the president could serve in the envisioned federal government: "I dislike," he wrote,

the abandonment . . . of the necessity of rotation in office, and most particularly in the case of the President. Experience concurs with reason in concluding that the first magistrate will always be re-elected if the constitution permits it. He is then an officer for life.

Moreover, Jefferson feared, longevity in office renders officeholders susceptible to dominance by foreign intriguers who "will interfere with money & with arms."

Nearing his letter's end, Jefferson struck a conciliatory note: "I have thus told you freely what I like & dislike." But, he added, "it is my principle that the will of the Majority should always prevail. If they approve the proposed Convention in all it's parts, I shall concur in it chearfully, in hopes that they will amend it whenever they shall find it work[s] wrong."[3]

FORTY-TWO

"Our Affairs at Amsterdam Press on My Mind Like a Mountain"

In the waring weeks of 1787 Jefferson and Lafayette, frequently joined by Thomas Paine—still in Paris seeking funding for his bridge—met often to discuss the new United States Constitution. A measure of the rapport that grew between Jefferson's two friends, Lafayette tried, without success, to persuade France's Royal Botanical Garden to fund Paine's bridge project; and indeed well into the first weeks of 1788, the three men continued their colloquy on America's new governing document. To Henry Knox, Lafayette reported in February: "Mr. Jefferson, Common Sense, and myself are debating [the Constitution] in a convention of our own as earnestly as if we were to decide upon it."[1]

Alas, however, a more immediate urgency soon intruded upon those exchanges. Recalled Jefferson:

> I was daily dunned by a company who had formerly made a small loan to the US. the principal of which was now become due; and our bankers in Amsterdam had notified me that the interest on our general debt would be expected in June; that if we failed to pay it, it would be deemed an act of

bankruptcy and would effectually destroy the credit of the US. and all future prospect of obtaining money there.

The lame-duck Confederation government would soon exhaust its funds, and no further outlays could be issued until the new Congress, created by the Constitution, convened. Deepening the crisis, the latest round of interest owed on American loans from Dutch banks was due in June. Paris banks, meanwhile, were refusing to advance any more funds to the American government—jeopardizing even Jefferson's salary.

For Jefferson his lack of authority to address the crisis was compounded by his limited expertise in such matters. Those two impediments, he later wistfully recalled, had not burdened his friend John Adams during an earlier diplomatic posting: "Mr. Adams, while residing at the Hague, had a general authority to borrow what sums might be requisite for ordinary & necessary expences. interest on the public debt, and the maintenance of the diplomatic establishment in Europe, had been habitually provided in this way."

An action mandated by the new Constitution complicated Jefferson's plight: Weeks earlier—in an election spread over three weeks in late December 1788 and early January 1789—Washington had, as expected, been elected as the country's first president. Moreover, in a less-foreordained event, John Adams was elected the republic's first vice president. Ironically, a desire to secure more stable foreign credit had been a major driving force behind the new Constitution's creation. In the meantime, as Adams prepared to return to America, the vice president–elect, Jefferson lamented, "had referred our bankers to me for future council on our affairs in their hands. but I had no powers, no instructions, no means, and no familiarity with the subject."

In late February, however, Jefferson learned that Adams—because he had served as U.S. minister at The Hague—was planning, before leaving London with his family, a quick trip to the seat of the Dutch government for an official farewell. For Jefferson his friend's planned trip seemed a fortuitous coincidence: Wasting no time, on March 2 he wrote to Adams: "I received this day a letter from Mrs. Adams of the 26th. ult. informing me you would set out on the 29th. for the Hague. Our affairs at Amsterdam press on my mind like a mountain."

Jefferson's tour of southern France and Italy—its planning and execution—
had ranged over months. But this trip, assuming he could catch up with Adams, would be planned *and* conducted in extreme haste. "I am so anxious to
confer with you. . . . I will set out the moment some repairs are made to my
carriage," Jefferson assured Adams in his March 2 letter. "It is promised me
at 3. oclock tomorrow; but probably they will make it night, and that I may
not set out till Tuesday morning. In that case I shall be at the Hague Friday
night."[2]

But Jefferson's carriage, as it turned out, was ready the next day, and so that
afternoon, March 3, accompanied by a Hôtel de Langeac servant named
Espagnol, he set off over post roads for Holland. "I went," he recalled, "the
direct road by Louvres, Senlis, Roye, Pont St Maxence, Bois le duc, Gournay
Perronne, Cambray, Bouchain, Valenciennes, Mons, Bruxelles, Malines, Antwerp, Mordick [Moerdijk] and Rotterdam, to the Hague." Arriving at The
Hague on March 10, "I happily found mr Adams," whom Jefferson had not
seen since his 1786 visit to England.

By the next day, March 11, the two Americans were in Amsterdam, meeting with the bankers who held their country's loans; with Adams making the
American case, the financial crisis was soon resolved. "Mr Adams accordingly
executed 1000. bonds for 1000. florins each, and deposited them in the hands
of our bankers, with instructions however not to issue them until Congress
should ratify the measure," Jefferson remembered.

> I had the satisfaction to reflect that by this journey, our credit was secured,
> the new government was placed at ease for two years to come, and that as
> well as myself were relieved from the torment of incessant duns, whose just
> complaints could not be silenced by any means within our power.
>
> This done, he [Adams] returned to London, and I set out for Paris; and
> as nothing urgent forbade it, I determined to return along the banks of the
> Rhine to Strasburg, and thence strike off to Paris.

With the financial crisis behind him, Jefferson took a leisurely pace on
his return trip. "I accordingly left Amsterdam on the 30th of March, and

proceeded by Utrecht, Nimeguen, Cleves, Duysberg, Duseldorff, Cologne, Bonne, Coblentz, Nassau, Hocheim, Frankfort & an excursion to Hanau."

As he had during his tour of France and Italy, Jefferson, while returning to Paris, though hampered by his lack of fluency in German, found time for sightseeing and indulging his interests in architecture, art, agriculture, history, commerce—and politics. "The transition from ease and opulence to extreme poverty is remarkeable on crossing the line between the Dutch and Prussian territory," he noted on April 1, airing his republican biases. "The soil and climate are the same. The governments alone differ. With the poverty, the fear also of slaves is visible in the faces of the Prussian subjects."

A day later in Düsseldorf, he noted, "The gallery of paintings is sublime, particularly the room of [Adriaen van der] Werff." He also gave free rein to his interest in southwestern Germany's Riesling viticulture. Near Cologne he noted: "Here the vines begin, and it is the most Northern spot on the earth on which wine is made. Their first grapes came from Orleans, since that from Alsace, Champagne &c. It is 32. years only since the first vines were sent from Cassel, near Mayence, to the Cape of good hope, of which the Cape wine is now made."

Writing from Frankfurt on April 9 to William Short, he also recalled seeing, in Prussia, familiar faces: "I met at Hanau with many acquaintants, the officers who had been stationed in Albemarle while in captivity." Indeed, numbering among those familar faces was Jefferson's former violin partner at Monticello, Friedrich Wilhelm von Geismar.

Mainly, however, what struck Jefferson as he rambled through the Rhineland and its environs was a culture that seemed unexpectedly familiar:

> The neighborhood of this place is that which has been to us a second mother country. It is from the palatinate on this part of the Rhine that those swarms of Germans have gone, who, next to the descendants of the English, form the greatest body of our people. I have been continually amused by seeing here the origin of whatever is not English among us. I have fancied myself often in the upper parts of Maryland and Pennsylvania.

Jefferson had reached Frankfurt on April 6 and lingered there for four days. From there, passing through Mainz, Rüdesheim, Johannisberg, Oppenheim, Worms, Mannheim, and Heidelberg, he reached Strasbourg on April 16. Seven days later, after passing through Champagne, the American minister was back in Paris.[3]

FORTY-THREE

"The Devil, More Cunning"

To placate popular opinion, Louis XIV, in his quest for new revenues, had in 1787 promised to reconvene France's Estates-General by 1792. But across France, by the following January, calls had risen for reforms broader than those that originally prompted the summoning of the Estates-General. Driving the urgency was the country's worsening financial plight and the Bourbons' growing unpopularity—the latter in part due to outrage over Louis and Marie Antoinette's increasingly satirized lavish personal spending. Even so, while no significant voice was calling for the monarchy's outright abolition, calls were rising for guarantees of rights similar to those enshrined by the American Revolution.

Increasingly, meanwhile, critics of the high-born, wealthy Lafayette—including many friends—were wondering whether, at twenty-nine, he remained willing to endure personal sacrifices to advance the causes he publicly favored. During the American Revolution, Lafayette had repeatedly placed himself in harm's way, and in 1787, in the Assembly of Notables, he had thrilled the French public by attacking the Bourbon court's profligate spending. By spring 1788, however, much of Lafayette's opposition to the court, while often dramatic, nonetheless seemed limited to symbolic gestures unlikely to result in serious personal repercussions.

In May, for instance, he agreed to affix his name to a petition to Louis, drafted by his fellow Breton nobles. The appeal, based on the region's unique history, argued for a continuation in Brittany of historical—but recently trimmed—exemptions from royal decrees. Lafayette had numbered among the petition's three hundred signatories. A month later the twelve nobles who delivered the petition to Versailles were incarcerated in Paris's Bastille prison. Lafayette, however, suffered conspicuously less severe consequences. Officially "disgraced" at court, he also lost a military command he had expected to assume that summer.

In standing with Brittany's nobles, Lafayette had vowed to "associate myself with every opposition to arbitrary acts, present or future, which threaten or may threaten the rights of the nation." But to critics his actions seemed less about the "rights of the nation" and calculated more for show than active sedition.[1]

Months later Jefferson, recounting the episode to Madison, went out of his way to assure his fellow Virginian of their mutual friend's safety—noting that the token punishment meted out had done "nothing more than to take from him a temporary service on which he had been ordered." To Jefferson, Versailles's reaction to the episode seemed a token gesture—intended "more to save appearances for their own authority than any thing else." Jefferson nonetheless took heart that Lafayette had emerged with his rebel credentials newly polished. "Since this he has stood on safe ground, and is viewed as among the foremost of the patriots."[2]

Other observers, however, including many allies, saw in Lafayette's signing of the petition a missed opportunity to go on record as favoring a curb on noble privileges.

To Condorcet he seemed to be clinging to outdated notions of aristocratic privilege. "If you go to Lafayette's house," the philospher playfully advised the Italian-born physician and American Patriot Philip Mazzei, "try to exorcise the devil of aristocracy that will be there to tempt him in the guise of a councilor of parlement or a Breton noble. For that purpose take along in your pocket a little vial of Potomac water and a sprinkler made from the wood of a Continental Army rifle and make your prayers in the name of Liberty, Equality and Reason."

For his part, Mazzei, then living in Paris, after soon visiting the Hôtel de Lafayette, assured Condorcet that the marquis remained every bit the Hero of Two Worlds. If appearances seemed to the contrary, he reminded the philosopher: "When it is not possible to do all the good that is desired, one must not fail to do what one can." Such openness to compromise, after all, Mazzei added, had secured the Patriots their victory in the American war.

To Mazzei's riposte, Condorcet soon answered that while compromise had served its purpose in the American Revolution, it could not—at least on the issue of noble privileges—play a similar role in resolving France's difficulties. Even before its revolution, America, after all, had been a country with no formalized noble class. Moreover, as Jefferson had observed, even the poorest among America's white population generally toiled in material conditions superior to those of their French peasant counterparts.

Put another way, by early 1789, as Condorcet understood and Lafayette was yet to concede, any solution to the challenges facing France would require the abolition of noble privileges. To Mazzei, Condorcet soon offered a mischievous explanation for how Lafayette had been deluded into believing that France's season of reform might unfold—as had America's—with scant attentions to matters of class: "The devil, more cunning than he, had slipped behind him and whispered to him that comparison with America."[3]

FORTY-FOUR

"To Navigate in Such a Whirling"

In February 1789 Lafayette welcomed to Paris his old friend Gouverneur Morris—the former Continental Congress delegate with whom he had allied in the late 1770s to oppose the Conway Cabal's challenge to George Washington. More recently, as a delegate in Philadelphia, Morris had written most of the U.S. Constitution's final draft, including its stirring ("We the People . . .") preamble.

Now thirty-six, Morris had moved to Paris to represent the European business interests of his mentor, the politician and financier Robert Morris (no relation). But Gouverneur Morris's own interest in politics remained acute, and in March 1789 he could not help but notice what he viewed as a fascination with Britain's constitution then sweeping Paris. "Every Thing," he reported to George Washington, "is a l'Anglois and a Desire to imitate the English prevails alike in the Cut of a Coat and the form of a Constitution." Jefferson, for his part, took a broader view of the trend—implicitly acknowledging its additional origins in American and, for that matter, Dutch constitutions: To Madison he wrote, "Every body here is trying their hands at forming declarations of rights" or, as they were alternately called, "Charters."

To posterity's good fortune, Gouverneur Morris, beyond tending to Robert Morris's business in Paris, also delighted in immersing himself in, following, and privately chronicling (in a notebook purchased shortly after his arrival) all aspects of the city's upper-class social and political milieus—including the respective tribulations of his friends Lafayette and Jefferson.

Inevitably Paris's fascination with constitutions—including America's new federal Constitution and those of individual states—dovetailed with a public desire to adopt a similar governing document for France. Indeed, those preoccupations had already captured Paris when on June 23, 1789, Louis XVI took an action that, at first blush, seemed to dash hopes for major reform of France's governance—instructing the Estates-General that their votes must continue to be counted by estates rather than heads. Paradoxically, however, his action only deepened Paris's ardor for written constitutions.[1]

Lafayette learned of Jefferson's work on a "Charter of Rights for the King and Nation" during a conversation at Versailles, on June 2 with Jefferson, William Short, and Jean-Paul Rabaut de Saint-Étienne, a French Protestant politician representing a Third Estate bailiwick in Nîmes. Jefferson's project intrigued Lafayette, and concealing any resentments he might have felt, the marquis encouraged his friend's work on the document.

Jefferson had written a draft—albeit not adopted—for Virginia's 1776 Constitution. And in 1789, after pondering a similar document for France and refining his ideas through interactions with both French and American associates, he sent Lafayette a "sketch of my idea" for a "charter of rights." In Jeffersonian fashion, the charter's workings—its envisaged government—were as simple, and as complex, as any of his other political and legal handiwork—or, for that matter, any of the clocks, pedometers, and other mechanical inventions that won his attentions over his lifetime.

Even so, Jefferson's charter for France was anything but revolutionary: The king, in exchange for relinquishing most of his powers, would be paid eighty million livres and all of his debts assumed by the nation. Noble privileges would be abolished, judicial due ("regular") process established, and the country's press protected. The enactment of new laws would still require the king's consent; otherwise all lawmaking powers would be vested in the Estates-General. All powers to levy taxes would rest solely in the Estates-General and not require the king's consent.[2]

On June 3, Jefferson sent copies of his charter to two members of the Estates-General who, if they approved it, were positioned to ease its passage through that body: Lafayette and Rabaut de Saint-Étienne.

Adding urgency to Jefferson's actions, he assumed that summer that he would soon be departing France on a leave of absence requested the previous November—and that by the time he returned to Paris, the season for such accommodations would have passed. Even so, as a foreigner—and diplomat—Jefferson suspected that some in France would resent his initiative as the intrusion of an interloper. Thus, in his June 3 letter to Rabaut in which he enclosed a rough draft of his charter, intellectual humility—or a pose designed to convey such modesty—replaced his usual steely confidence: "I have ventured to send to yourself and Monsieur de la Fayette a sketch of my ideas of what this act might contain without endangering any dispute," Jefferson wrote. "But it is offered merely as a canvas for you to work on, if it be fit to work on at all. I know too little of the subject, and you know too much of it to justify me in offering any thing but a hint." In a briefer letter to Lafayette written that same day, Jefferson—alluding to Rabaut—similarly offered an "apology for my meddling in a business where I know so little and you and he so much."

Entanglements of vanity no doubt played a role in Jefferson's work on his charter for France. But as he made clear to Rabaut, his charter also issued from genuine affection for the only foreign land in which he would ever live: "What excuse can I make, Sir, for this presumption. I have none but an unmeasurable love for your nation and a painful anxiety lest Despotism, after an unaccepted offer to bind it's own hands, should seize you again with tenfold fury."

Jefferson's planned return to America was postponed. Moreover, by the following summer, a quickening pace of events rendered it clear that Versailles's halls no longer—if they ever had—offered quarter for a document that envisioned a supplicant Third Estate and a benign king blessing a new political order. Writing to Jefferson, Lafayette soon thanked his friend for the charter. But he also made clear that whatever chances for adoption the document once possessed had receded into the past: Lamented Lafayette, "It is very Hard to Navigate in such a Whirling."[3]

FORTY-FIVE

Vive le Tiers État!

On July 13, 1788, culminating a freakish cold streak, violent hailstorms pounded much of central France. Across a swath that stretched from Normandy's capital of Rouen in the north and Toulouse in the south, the storms' icy pellets destroyed apples in Normandy, grapevines in Alsace, Burgundy, and the Loire, and wheat in the vast plain around Orléans.

In the Midi they even damaged the orange and olive crops that had so enchanted Jefferson. Typifying the reports that soon found their way to Versailles came one from the province of Île-de-France, but south of Versailles and Paris: "The once beautiful countryside has been reduced to an arid desert."

Dealing more destruction, a drought across much of the same storm-hit swath followed the summer's cold. And after the drought came, in late 1788 and early 1789, a winter of such bone-chilling cold that rivers froze and watermills ceased turning—rendering it impossible to grind into flour the scarce wheat that had survived the summer.

Increasing the misery, the frozen rivers and heavy snow hampered efforts to move emergency food shipments into the most devastated provinces. Across the kingdom many of Louis's humbler subjects—already reeling from the previous fall's poor harvest—found themselves reduced to begging, scavenging (including the boiling of tree bark into a makeshift gruel), and otherwise facing death from exposure and starvation. "Every scourge has been unloosed," recorded a traveler passing through Provence. "Everywhere I have found men dead of cold and hunger, and that in the midst of wheat for lack of flour, all the mills being frozen."

Compounding the Job-like cycle, the winter freeze begat a ruinous spring thaw. Along the Loire, floodwaters, breaking crudely built dikes, drowned fields, pastures, and orchards, as well as the streets of Blois and Tours. Across France prices for bread and firewood soared—the former by almost 100 percent between summer 1787 and February 1789. In Paris, by the of winter 1788–89, by one estimate, as much as one-fifth of the city's population—about one hundred thousand residents—were beneficiaries of some sort of relief.

Among Parisians, particularly the poor, the disaster exacerbated already growing discontents—discords in which at least one well-off observer, Gouverneur Morris, viewing the turmoil through the prism of his own class bias, saw the pernicious hand of opportunist priests: "The great Mass of the common People have no Religion but their Priests, no Law but their Superiors, no Moral but their Interest."[1]

Paris was indeed hungry that season, and responding to the disaster, Finance Minister Necker forbade the export of French grain; the government also instituted policies intended to hasten and increase imports of rice and cereals into the country. But those efforts soon proved disappointing. In France's Mediterranean ports, an ongoing Russo-Turkish war disrupted grain shipments; similarly, conflicts in the Baltic disrupted imports from Poland and East Prussia. Moreover, during that winter, ice blocked the Seine Estuary, impeding the unloading of arriving cargoes at Le Havre and other nearby ports.

Those worsening difficulties widened the gap between France's rich and poor, and by early 1789 it was difficult to imagine any solution to the kingdom's crisis that would leave noble privileges intact.[2]

Lafayette thus cautiously joined the Second Estate's members favoring curtailment of noble privileges. Though hardly the first of France's reformers to champion such restrictions, he numbered among the first prominent individuals of the country's nobility and military to endorse them. He even helped to found a society that advocated liberal reforms. Soon known as "the Thirty," its members—also calling themselves "the patriots" and still later "the Constitutionalist club"—included Condorcet; the lawyers Gui-Jean-Baptiste Target and Henri Bergasse; the clergyman and writer the Abbé Sieyès; Lafayette's brother-in-law, the vicomte de Noailles; and the journalist, politician, and orator the comte de Mirabeau.[3]

By the late 1780s a consensus had emerged that meaningful reforms required a national legislature—one more democratically elected and responsive to the country's entire population than past assemblies.

In late 1787 Louis had agreed to reconvene the Estates-General, the assembly that nominally represented the country's three estates. Over the coming months, however, deepening troubles prompted him to move up the body's scheduled convocation. The crisis came to a head in August 1788 after Finance Minister Brienne declared the royal treasury empty and the *parlement* of Paris again refused to register royal decrees authorizing the borrowing of more money and reforms to the country's tax system. Capitulating on August 8, Louis and Brienne set May 5 of the following year as the date for the Estates-General to reconvene. Two weeks later, on August 25, Brienne—facing widespread criticism and having persuaded Jacques Necker to again become finance minister—resigned from the office.

In France's past the Estates-General had played a role more symbolic than substantive in the country's life. Authorized to advise but not govern, the body had routinely engaged in rigorous debates only to have its advice ignored. Even so, by 1789, French reformers found reason for cautious optimism that the upcoming Estates-General would enjoy real powers.

In the meantime questions dogged the Bourbon court and the country's putative reformers: How, for instance, would the Estates-General's deputies be elected? What would be their total numbers? How would its members be distributed among the country's three estates, and how would their votes be counted? Much turned on both components of that latter question: To wit, in past convocations, each of the three orders had been accorded a roughly equal number of members—an equation that enabled the First and Second Estates (respectively, clergy and nobles) to prevail over the Third Estate (peasants and all other subjects of the kingdom).

A January 1789 royal decree answered that latter question, but simultaneously created another mystery. Finance Minister Necker stipulated that in the forthcoming Estates-General the Third Estate's numbers were to be doubled: The first two estates would each be accorded three hundred deputies and the third six hundred, creating a counterbalance against France's otherwise privileged estates.

More pointedly, in Europe's most populous country—with twenty-eight million inhabitants—the clergy and nobles represented but 4 percent of its total population. Who could truly assess the dangers of sustaining such inequities?

To Lafayette and his fellow self-styled "patriots"—later also known as "Fayettists"—Necker's decree seemed at first glance to suggest that the assembly—ostensibly giving the Third Estate actual powers—might produce meaningful reforms. But then again, the decree failed to indicate how the assembly's votes would be counted. If, as in the past, after the three estates met and voted in separate sessions, the doubling of the Third Estate's numbers would in the end replicate the same two-to-one dominance of the first two estates—thus proving a meaningless reform.

The issue of the Third Estate's powers transcended mere mathematics. No prominent politicians, Lafayette included, envisioned a France without a hereditary monarch. Even so, embedded in the mystery of how the Estates-General's votes would be counted was a broader question: of whether France would remain wedded to its history as a monarchy but with special privileges for nobles and clergy, or whether, as Lafayette and his ilk hoped, it became a modern nation—a constitutional monarchy whose sovereignty resided in France's people—with laws derived not from absolutist traditions but a written constitution.[4]

A measure of Louis's professed newfound interest in conditions across France, in the same December 1788 decree in which he outlined election procedures, he also had instructed each of the country's electoral assemblies to produce a *cahier de doléances* ("memorandum of grievances")—a recitation to be considered by the royal court of specific needs and complaints. The resultant *cahiers*—25,000 were soon produced—were necessarily penned by the country's literate class. In many cases they thus glossed over the problems of France's peasantry or resulted in depictions steeped in ideology. Even so, in the breadth of their reach, the *cahiers* represented an unprecedented effort by a ruler to fathom the conditions of his entire population.[5]

Louis's doubling of the Third Estate heartened Lafayette and his fellow members of the Thirty. But they differed over how best to take advantage of his concession. To maximize the Third Estate's strength, Lafayette wanted nobles to seek seats in that order's assembly. Thereby, he argued, liberals should be able to dilute expected conservative forces among the Third Estate's representatives. Mirabeau, by contrast, favored reform-minded nobles seeking seats in their own Second Estate assembly, thereby diluting the strength in that order of predictable efforts to preserve noble privileges.

In the end Mirabeau's strategy was adopted, and by February 1789, Lafayette had left for the Auvergne. Although he owned property in several provinces, he concluded that his native Auvergne afforded him the best chance of electoral victory.[6]

On March 29, following a week of debates, Lafayette won the race for the second of five deputies elected in the Auvergne's administrative district of Riom. A month later—on April 29, the day before George Washington took the oath of office as the United States' first president (in its new capital of New York)— Gouverneur Morris wrote to the president-elect of Lafayette's own recent electoral victory: "Monsieur de la fayette is since returned from his political Campaign in Auvergne, crowned with Success," Morris wrote. "He had to contend with the Prejudices and the Interests of his order, and with the Influence of the Queen and Princes (except the Duke of Orleans) but he was too able for his Opponents. He played the Orator with as much Eclat as he ever acted the Soldier."

But Lafayette's triumph had not come easily: Despite his popularity in the Auvergne, the conservative province, seeking to preserve noble privileges, overwhelmingly favored that the Estates-General vote by orders, not heads. It thus gave Lafayette a slight victory margin—198 out of 393 votes. But even that narrow win had come with a price: Expecting that Louis would ultimately rule that the estates would vote by head, not orders, Lafayette had been required to agree, in instances when that issue arose, to join with his fellow nobles in opposing voting by head.[7]

On the morning of Tuesday, May 4, Estates-General deputies from across France, each representing his particular order, converged at Versailles. Forming into those separate orders, they commenced a "grand procession" through Versailles's streets toward the Church of St. Louis. Gouverneur Morris, who, with Jefferson, witnessed the mile-long procession, called it "the last gala day of the old monarchy." Each of the orders, Morris recalled, was attired in the same style of costume worn at the last Estates-General assembly over almost two centuries earlier: "The nobles glittered in gorgeous dresses and orders. The bishops, superb in violet robes, were followed by their humble curés in modest garb. The Commons were in black mantles, very plain, and hats without feathers."

In theory the Third Estate's delegation represented the vast majority of France's population of 28 million. But although elected by the broadest franchise in European history, its delegates were unlike most of the voters who elected them. More specifically, the delegates were overwhelmingly "bourgeois in character"—literate and educated. No peasants or artisans, for instance, numbered among the Third Estate's 610 representatives at Versailles; 25 percent were lawyers, 13 percent came from business (seventy-six merchants, eight manufacturers, and one banker); 11 percent were landowners; and at least 43 percent held other public offices.[8]

The following day, May 5, the three estates gathered in an assembly hall constructed for the occasion in a courtyard at the Hôtel des Menus-Plaisirs. The new hall sat on the same spot on which had stood the building, by then demolished, that had housed the Assembly of Notables. In fact, the new building—accommodating the Estates-General's twelve hundred members—had been designed by Pierre-Adrien Pâris, the same architect responsible for its predecessor's conversion into an assembly hall. Recalled Jefferson: "Had it been enlightened with lamps and chandeliers, it would have been almost as brilliant as the opera." Jefferson, in fact, that season, became a regular observer of the sessions: "I went therefore daily from Paris to Versailles, and attended their debates, generally till the hour of adjournment."

In that first session, on May 5, Louis, surrounded by his ministers, sat atop a raised platform beneath a ceremonial canopy at the front of the hall. The nobles and clergy sat in tiered seating to the monarch's left and right. Facing the king, stretching to the hall's far end, sat the Third Estate—its numbers twice those of the other two estates.

The session began with brief words from the king—pleas for fiscal reforms, condemnations of what he viewed as radical ideas undermining his rule, and wishes for his subjects' welfare. Necker soon took the floor—launching into a lengthy oration, mainly on finances, that eventually exhausted his voice. A clerk was eventually summoned to complete the speech.[9]

Necker's lack of clarity on the single issue that consumed all the deputies—whether the three estates would be voting by orders or by head—exasperated Lafayette and his colleagues. Before Necker concluded, however, the hall did hear some guidance on the matter: Warning against divisions that would jeopardize the country's regeneration, the finance minister advised the estates, for the time being, to meet separately—thereby giving the upper orders a chance to win "merit for a generous sacrifice."

In Necker's view, the clergy and noble orders, by meeting on their own, might each find a manner to renounce magnanimously their respective privileges—thereby earning the Third Estate's goodwill and presumably mitigating its pent-up resentments.

Those like Lafayette who had hoped that the Estates-General would be empowered to create fundamental change for France were perplexed: If Louis intended, as seemed to be the case, to impede such actions, how then to explain the king's recent expressions of support for Third Estate? And why did he go to such lengths to learn of its views? And finally, if Louis, as he also indicated, truly intended to preserve inherited privileges for nobility and clergy, what did that portend about prospects for a "new constitution"—a subject that had gone conspicuously unmentioned in Necker's speech?[10]

The next day, May 6, each of the three orders gathered in separate areas of their shared venue. However, before their deliberations could commence, each estate was required to review its members' credentials and thus confirm its legal credentials as an estate. While the Second Estate, the nobility, completed that entire process quickly, the First Estate, the clergy, seeking a compromise with the Third Estate, hesitated in formally confirming itself as an estate. And beginning in June—during the delay caused by that hesitation—members of both the First and Second Estates began defecting into the Third.

Lafayette, meanwhile, was growing increasingly ill at ease. In accord with Mirabeau's proposal to the Thirty—a proposal supported by the club's majority—Lafayette had agreed to seek a deputy's seat from Auvergne's Second, as opposed to its Third, Estate. But to win the seat he had been compelled to promise to vote with the province's conservatives on vote-count-related issues.

Over the spring of 1789 Lafayette's discomfort deepened. As early as May 6, however—mere hours after Necker had informed the deputies that they were to meet and vote separately—Thomas Jefferson, aware of his friend's dilemma, had written a letter to him that clarified Lafayette's quandary and suggested an obvious resolution: "As it becomes more and more possible that the Noblesse will go wrong, I become uneasy for you," Jefferson wrote. "Your principles are decidedly with the tiers etat [Third Estate], and your instructions against them. A complaisance to the latter on some occasions and an adherence to the former on others, may give an appearance of trimming between the two parties which may lose you both."

Jefferson's frankness violated the unwritten rule that diplomats avoid involvement in their host country's political life. But then again—devoted to Lafayette's welfare as well as the spread of democratic government—he found it impossible to stay silent as his friend seemed poised for a headlong dive into what, to Jefferson, seemed political disaster.

If Lafayette persisted in aligning with the nobles, Jefferson warned, future attempts to join with the Third Estate would be received "coldly and without confidence." He thus counseled: "Take at once that honest and manly stand with them which your own principles dictate," adding: "The Noblesse, and especially the Noblesse of Auvergne will always prefer men who will do their dirty work for them. You are not made for that."[11]

Four days later, writing to George Washington—by then, unbeknownst to most Parisians, president of the United States—Jefferson unapologetically acknowledged that his efforts to save his friend had breached diplomatic protocol: "I have not hesitated to press on him to burn his instructions and follow his conscience." But, Jefferson added, he also believed that Lafayette possessed a popularity capable of transcending factionalism: "I am in hopes that base is now too solid to render it dangerous to be mounted on it."[12]

FORTY-SIX

"The Mephitic Atmosphere
of Prejudices"

Weighing Jefferson's advice in spring 1789, Lafayette considered re-
signing his place among the nobles and seeking a seat in the Third Estate. But as in the past, when facing such dilemmas he vacillated—assuming that
his best course would eventually become apparent.

Meanwhile, public exasperation with Louis continued to wax. Pamphle-
teers, orators, and habitués of coffeehouses and boutiques agitated for a national assembly vested with real powers to address the country's woes. Reflecting
and increasing that agitation was a pamphlet, *What Is the Third Estate?*, published the previous January by the clergyman Abbé Sieyès. His pamphlet
argued that while the Third Estate's moral legitimacy had long gone unrecog-
nized, its recognition was inevitable and the days of its suppression were drawing to an end: "What is the Third Estate? Everything. What has it been until
now in the political order? Nothing. What does it want to be? Something."[1]

The Third Estate's growing strength and indictments of France's social inequities heightened Lafayette's dilemma. As a delegate, after all, he remained

pledged to assembling with the First Estate, a predicament that, in at least one session, he found overwhelming: "I went away in the middle of the deliberations, because our room was suffocating, and the mephitic atmosphere of predudices ill agrees with my chest."

Jefferson's unease over his friend's path, meanwhile, deepened: "As it becomes more and more evident that the Nobles are wrong, I begin to worry about you," he wrote to Lafayette in May. "Your principles are with the Third Estate, but your instructions are against them."

On June 17 at Versailles, led by Sieyès and Mirabeau, the Third Estate's delegates, reaching the limits of their patience, declared themselves an independent National Assembly. They also pledged to adhere to a principle of one man, one vote—and reiterated their past invitations for deputies from the other two orders to join their numbers.

Initially their entreaty produced only a trickle of acceptances. Its more dramatic impact came a week later: On Saturday morning, June 20, the deputies of the nascent National Assembly arrived for a scheduled session at the Hôtel des Menus-Plaisirs to find its doors locked, with armed guards barring their way. The hall, they learned, was closed that day as workers reconfigured its interior for a *séance royale* (royal session) scheduled for the following Monday; reacting to recent turmoil, Louis would be addressing all three estates.

Weeks earlier the delegates would likely have viewed being shut out of their venue as a mere inconvenience. But by then, deepening distrust of court motives magnified the perceived slight. More to the point, since June 17, when the Third Estate's delegates declared themselves a National Assembly, their usual venue had acquired a symbolic importance. To the delegates, as the historian Simon Schama has observed, the chamber where they gathered "was no longer simply a piece of royal property to design at the King's pleasure. It had become, in effect, the first territory staked out by the Nation."

The deputies immediately began hunting for another venue—soon finding, on Versailles's rue Saint-François, an unlocked door that led to an indoor tennis court. It was inside that sunny interior, with its ample windows—a scene later immortalized in an engraving based on a pen-and-ink drawing by Jacques-Louis David—that the deputies swore their "Oath of the Tennis Court."

The deputies pledged to remain united until France gained a written constitution. Moreover, asserting a transcendent inviolability, the body's members swore: "Nothing can prevent it from continuing its deliberations, in whatever locale it may be forced to establish itself; . . . wherever its members are gathered there is the National Assembly."[2]

However improbable, it was the king who eventually recruited a full complement of deputies for the new National Assembly. On June 23 Louis had decreed that votes in the body must continue to be counted by estates rather than heads. But four days later, determined to replenish the royal court's coffers and seeking to end the stalemate that had settled over Versailles he ordered all members of the First and Second Estates still in their original assemblies to go over to the Third.

Louis hoped his order would provide an increasingly restless public evidence of his determination to address the country's problems. His action, however, also had the effect of legitimizing the National Assembly. As Gouverneur Morris aptly summarized, the Third Estate's members "have succeeded, but the nobles deeply feel their situation. The King, after siding with them, was frightened into an abandonment of them. He acts from terror only."[3]

One did not have to look far for the sources of the fears driving the king's concession to the Third Estate. In and around Paris and Versailles, riots and other harbingers of discord were growing. Since May an army composed of royal and foreign (primarily German and Swiss) mercenaries had been ringing the outskirts of both places. The presence of the forces—reputedly arranged by Marie Antoinette and the comte d'Artois—was intended to shore up absolutist contingents at Versailles. And by early July the number of troops encircling Paris and Versailles had swollen to 25,000.[4]

Increasingly Louis worried over the loyalty of the Gardes Françaises—the French Guard—an infantry regiment by tradition attached to the country's reigning monarch. Most of the Guard's 3,600 soldiers, drawn from Paris's poorer districts, identified with the Third Estate; moreover, within the Guard's ranks, resentments were growing over the harsh Prussian-style discipline imposed on them by the duc du Châtelet, the regiment's newly appointed commander.

By late June 1789, Louis's worries over the French Guards' loyalty issued from events occurring in and around the Palais-Royal, a Parisian complex of covered arcades owned by his cousin, the duke of Orléans. Built in the seventeenth century as the personal residence of the royal minister Cardinal Richelieu, the estate by 1780 had passed to Orléans, who lived there but had also developed the vast space into a complex of shops, cafés, gardens, and a theater.

By early June 1789, as its owner's political ambitions became more overt, the complex had also grown into the city's "liberty pole"—a center for popular opposition to the throne. Inside its coffeehouses, recalled the English writer Arthur Young, orators, standing on chairs and tables, openly vented their distaste for Louis. "The eagerness with which they are heard and the thunder of applause they receive for every sentiment of . . . violence against the present government cannot be easily imagined." In the arcade's shops, Parisians could buy seditious pamphlets, underground newspapers—and even fireworks.

Indeed, on the night of June 27, Paris's sky near the Palais-Royal was lit up in celebration of the decree issued that day by which Louis, capitulating to popular demand, summoned the three estates to meet together in one assembly.

The next day mutinous companies of French Guard troops arrived at the complex to noisily avow their intention to refuse any order to fire on antigovernment protesters. Two days later two members of the mutinous Guard companies, in civilian clothes, repeated their vow before the National Assembly. Over the next twenty-four hours, as Louis sought to quell the growing defiance, both soldiers, along with twelve other mutineers, were arrested and dispatched to Paris's Abbaye prison. Hours later that night, the evening of June 30, as word of their imprisonment spread, a mob went to Abbaye and easily won their release.[5]

Four days later Lafayette and Adrienne, along with Gouverneur Morris and other Americans, attended a dinner hosted by Jefferson to celebrate the thirteenth anniversary of the Declaration of Independence. After the meal Morris—still shaken by events around the Palais-Royal—had a conversation with Lafayette in which he urged him to "preserve, if possible, some constitutional authority to the Body of Nobles, as the only means of preserving any Liberty for the people."[6]

Whatever the contents of Lafayette's envisioned constitution, Thomas Paine observed during those days, the time for its completion was drawing to a close: "If the National Assembly should fail in the threatened destruction that then surrounded it, some trace of its principles might have a chance of surviving the wreck. Everything was drawing to a crisis."[7]

Over those weeks, meanwhile, the former Third Estate's deputies—newly energized as the self-anointed "National Assembly" but still lacking a royally designated meeting hall—gathered regularly for sessions in the town of Versailles's Church of Saint Louis.

During that period Jefferson went to Versailles for "Ambassadors' Day," an annual court event. Accompanying him was Philip Mazzei. "After the levee," Mazzei recalled, "Jefferson and I"—curious about the National Assembly, meeting in the nearby Saint-Louis—ventured to the church to hear their discussions. "Stepping on the threshold, [Jefferson] cast a glance inside and said: This is the first time that churches have been made some good use of."

In its ad hoc meeting hall the Third Estate—the self-reconstituted National Assembly—had found a unified voice. But, Jefferson's optimism aside, it remained unclear as to whether the rest of the country would hear that voice and whether the body's work would truly come to "good use."[8]

FORTY-SEVEN

"Paid at Panthémont in Full"

Paris's brutal weather of 1788–79 froze the Seine. During daylight hours, carriages crossed the river's ice, as skaters and sledders frolicked on its hardened surface. But for Jefferson the cold aggravated a deepening homesickness for Virginia. "We are at present experiencing a degree of cold more like that of Siberia than of Paris," he complained in December 1788. "The thermometer was down at 8°. about the end of the last month, and it has been this month at 6°."

Across the city, he later recalled, "all out-door labor was suspended." Without wages, Paris's poor could purchase neither the bread nor firewood needed for cooking and heat. Stepping into that breach and purchasing "immense quantities of fire-wood," the government kept "great fires" burning "at all the cross-streets, around which the people gathered in crouds to avoid perishing with cold." Bread, meanwhile, was purchased "and distributed daily gratis, until a relaxation of the season should enable the people to work." Indeed, such "was the scarcity of bread that from the highest to the lowest citizen, the bakers were permitted to deal but a scanty allowance per head, even to those who paid for it." Beyond that, "In cards of invitation to dine in the richest houses, the guest was notified to bring his own bread." Moreover, "Every person who had the means, was called on for a weekly subscription, which the Curés collected and employed in providing masses for the nourishment of the poor."[1]

William Short's absence while touring Italy compounded Jefferson's melancholy. "The long continuance of this severity, and the snow now on the ground give physical prognostications of a hard winter," he wrote that December to his young assistant. "You will be in a privileged climate and will have had an enviable escape from this."[2]

In November 1788, amid the Paris cold, Jefferson had decided that it was time to go home—if only for a few months' leave of absence. With the Confederation Congress that had dispatched him to France having completed its final session and soon to be superseded by a new Congress, there was little left for him to do in the interim. Moreover, having been absent from Monticello for four years, business matters there required his attention. And, by the following year, yet another concern provided further incentive to return to Virginia—Patsy's growing interest in Roman Catholicism.[3]

His surviving writings betray no reference to the matter—it was not the sort of problem he would have wished to memorialize—but according to family lore, Jefferson, in April, was "startled" by a letter he received from Patsy. By then sixteen years old, she was "requesting permission to enter the convent and spend the rest of her days in the discharge of the duties of a religious life." According to the author of those words, his great-granddaughter Sarah N. Randolph, Jefferson "acted on this occasion with his usual tact." According to her account:

> He did not reply to the note, but after a day or two drove to the Abbaye, had a private interview with the Abbess, and then asked for his daughters. He received them with more than usual affectionate warmth of manner, and, without making the least allusion to . . . [Patsy's] note or its contents, told his daughters that he had called to take them from school, and accordingly he drove back home accompanied by them.

Notwithstanding his silence otherwise concerning the alleged incident, on April 20, 1789, Jefferson did record in his Memorandum book: "Paid at Panthemont [sic] in full 625" livres, and two days later another outlay of 66 livres for farewell gifts for the girls' teachers. By then Patsy and Polly were living at the Hôtel de Langeac—albeit with their education not entirely suspended. With private tutors Polly continued to study Spanish, and both daughters' harpsichord instruction went on as well.

Indeed, even before removing the girls from Panthémont, Jefferson had grown intent on preempting Patsy's interests in Roman Catholicism and, in their place, inculcate in her the social skills necessary to ease her transition into adult society.

To advance the latter he had encouraged her to take her meals at Panthémont not with other students but with the school's abbess, Madame Béthisy de Mézières, a member of a noble family at whose table other prominent nobles often dined. During that period, he also invited Patsy regularly to join Gouverneur Morris and other guests for dinners at the Hôtel de Langeac and to "make it a rule hereafter to come dressed otherwise than in your uniform." Jefferson also began spending more on Patsy's wardrobe and instructed Sally Hemings to devote increasing time to assisting his oldest daughter as a lady's maid. But while Jefferson encouraged Patsy's participation in Paris's social life, he tellingly declined to introduce her to its salons.

Spring 1789, meanwhile, had arrived with no response to Jefferson's requested leave of absence. Thus, on April 14, as the lease on the Hôtel de Langeac approached its end, he had no recourse but to renew the contract. In the meantime, though the diplomat remained eager to go home, increasingly interesting activities at Versailles were providing ample distractions from his other concerns.[4]

FORTY-EIGHT

"A Catechism of France"

In Paris amid the New Year's Day celebrations of 1788, Lafayette had found time to write to George Washington: "I am Returned from the provincial Assembly of Auvergne." There "I Had the Happiness to please the people and the Misfortune to displease Government to a very Great degree—the Ministry Asked for an Encrease of Revenue—our province was Among the few who Gave Nothing, and she Expressed Herself in a Manner which Has Been taken Very Much Amiss."

If anything, however, as Lafayette made clear, he wore Versailles's umbrage toward the Auvergne assembly as a badge of honor—and as a harbinger of greater challenges to the Bourbon court. "The internal Situation of france is Very Extraordinary . . . "[T]he parliaments are every day passing the boundaries of their Constitution . . ."[1]

In that age's transatlantic milieu the word "constitution" had two distinct meanings—one older than the other. In alluding to "the boundaries of *their*" [emphasis added] "Constitution," Lafayette was invoking the older meaning, not any specific written document. As he, Jefferson, and Washington were aware, the word generally held a different meaning for European reformers than in its American usage.

Among Europeans the word—generally associated with Britain's governance since 1688—tended to refer to a broad understanding, embodied in an accumulation of laws and customs, written and unwritten—of what *constituted* a kingdom; the arrangement, by which monarch and subjects were bound into a single polity. In the end, then, it was Jefferson's view of France's unique needs—not Anglophilia—that animated his 1787 advice to Lafayette to keep "the good model of your neighboring country before your eyes [so that] you may get on step by step towards a good constitution. . . . Tho' that model is not perfect, yet as it would unite more suffrages than any new one which could be proposed." Put another way, to Jefferson Britain's "constitutional monarchy" was preferable to the Bourbon throne's "absolutism."

But even as Lafayette, in his 1788 New Year's Day letter to Washington, alluded to the word's older meaning—a body of precedents—he devoted most of his thoughts to the concept's newer usage—denoting a written document—and, more specifically, the Constitution recently adopted in Philadelphia. By January 1788, after all, a consensus prevailed that France would eventually adopt a written constitution—and at that, one that Lafayette would likely play a role in drafting. But would the political arrangement embodied in that document more resemble Britain's constitution of 1688, or America's of 1787?

———

So far as is known, no one ever accused the marquis de Lafayette of lacking a sense of personal destiny; and that self-confidence burned as brightly in his foray into constitution writing as on any battlefield. A letter to Madame Simiane found him boasting of his authorship of a document that he hoped would be adopted as a "declaration of rights" for the people of France. Indeed: "Mr. Jefferson was so well pleased that he insisted on my sending it to General Washington." Until then he could only await that blessed day when "that declaration, or something very like it, will be the catechism of France." In fact—along with Jefferson and Gouverneur Morris—Lafayette by then numbered among several writers vying to draft a governing document for the kingdom of France.[2]

Lafayette's advocacy of written constitutions in France had actually begun in the Assembly of Notables, when he proposed the adoption of such a document by each of the country's provincial assemblies. By 1788 he was advocating a constitution for the entire kingdom—one permanently binding the king and his subjects into a new relationship. That same constitution, Lafayette also assumed, would enshrine individual liberties, as well as limit and regulate the powers of the new government's legislative, executive, and judicial branches.

Lafayette's work in earnest on a French constitution—what eventually became the Declaration of the Rights of Man and the Citizen—began at least six months before the Third Estate's Tennis Court Oath of June 20, 1789. By early July, when he, along with Gouverneur Morris and others, attended a celebratory July 4 dinner at the Hôtel de Langeac, Lafayette had settled into marathon writing sessions. On July 6—having already provided Jefferson with two successive drafts of his Declaration—he wrote to his friend: "Will you send me the Bill of Rights with Your Notes? I hope to see You to Morrow. Where do You dine?"

Jefferson answered that same day: "I will bring you the paper you desire tomorrow, and shall dine at the Duchess Danville's"—Madame d'Enville, a noblewoman and friend of both men—"where I shall be happy to meet you."

In all likelihood most of the two men's conversation the next day—July 7—concerned a contretemps between Finance Minister Necker and National Assembly delegate Mirabeau—rivals in the National Assembly and both popular figures among Lafayette's faction in that body. Even so, the two likely also found time to discuss the latest draft of Lafayette's Declaration.

Two days later, however, Lafayette again wrote to Jefferson. "To Morrow I present my bill of rights about the middle of the sitting." He would, Lafayette wrote, be "pleased" if Jefferson would "Consider it Again, and Make Your observations."

Heightening Lafayette's urgency was a preliminary report that the National Assembly received on July 9—the same day that he solicited Jefferson's final "observations." The report came from a committee created to advise the assembly on the desired elements for a written constitution. It recommended that the document begin with a brief "declaration of rights"—a preamble, enumerating the rights to be guaranteed in the document's subsequent text. Otherwise the report offered scant guidance—not even a timetable for the document's completion, only a suggestion that it be prepared carefully and in no rush.[3]

The document Lafayette referred to in his July 9 letter to Jefferson was the third version of his Declaration that he had asked the American minister to review. Between January and July 1789, the marquis produced three known drafts of the document. During those months, meanwhile, the winds buffeting France's politics—accelerating from gale to hurricane force—heightened public expectations for reform. And the three extant drafts of Lafayette's Declaration, in succession, reflected those changing expectations, as well as shifting alliances in the National Assembly.

Through all its drafts, however, Lafayette never intended for his document to convey, as had America's Constitution, a comprehensive governmental system. Instead, he sought to produce a statement of rights and principles to precede a longer, more detailed governing document that the National Assembly would later draft and adopt.

In a broader sense, however, Lafayette envisioned his Declaration playing for France the roles played by two documents in U.S. history—the Declaration of Independence *and* (albeit in a limited sense) the U.S. Constitution. Lafayette clearly venerated both documents: He had recently praised the latter, and, as early as 1782, in the Hôtel de Lafayette—"in the Most Conspicuous part of my Cabinet"—he had installed a framed copy of the Declaration of Independence. Alongside that replica, in an empty space within the same frame, as he had avowed his longing for the day when he would install in it a "declaration of the rights of France." And who could say that—even in 1782—the marquis was not already envisioning himself as that document's author?

Indeed, as Jefferson's Declaration of Independence had presented Britain's former North American colonists to the world as a brand-new polity, so Lafayette aspired through his document to reintroduce his native land's Third Estate—now christened *la nation*.

In retrospect, it was logical that Lafayette, while writing his Declaration, should have sought Jefferson's counsel. Inevitably, however, a question arises: What role did Jefferson play in drafting Lafayette's Declaration? And was it of a degree that warrants calling him a collaborator in the document's formulation?

Lafayette's personal copies of his Declaration's first and second drafts have not survived. The only extant two copies of those drafts were found among Jefferson's papers—a circumstance that would seem to open a window into the extent of his involvement in the document's drafting. Alas, however, that window closes even as it opens: No comments by Jefferson appear on the first draft, and while the second does include at least two brief marginal comments in his hand, they are minor quibbles: one a query concerning Lafayette's use of the words "property" and "honor"; the other an equally minor—though apt—suggestion for improving a passage's clarity.

Of course, other—now lost or destroyed—drafts of the Declaration might have yielded further evidence of Jefferson's role in its creation. Beyond that—though we can never know what was said—much, perhaps most, of Jefferson's influence on Lafayette's Declaration probably came through ongoing conversations between the two men.

In addition to calling on Jefferson, however, Lafayette, while writing his Declaration, likely also availed himself of the published works of Montesquieu, Locke, Rousseau, and other writers associated with constitutionalism. For that matter, his amply documented socializing during that period, with friends such as Condorcet and Gouverneur Morris—well-versed in constitutional matters—likely included prolonged discussions of his writing project.[4]

As it turned out, however, other matters besides his Declaration weighed on Lafayette on July 9, when he wrote to Jefferson to inform him that "to Morrow I present my bill of rights about the middle of the sitting" and that he would be "pleased" to again hear his friend's "observations" on his latest draft.

In recent days Lafayette had won the Versailles court's displeasure for his association with a protest by National Assembly delegate Mirabeau against the presence of Louis's troops in and around Paris and Versailles, and now he feared imminent arrest: "They are very Angry with me for Having supported the Motion Against the Coming of the troops," he wrote to Jefferson. "If they take me up You Must Claim me as an American Citizen." Poignantly he closed his missive: "Bonjour, My dear friend, I Beg You to Answer as soon as you get up, and wish to Hear from You about eight or Nine at last."[5]

But Lafayette was not arrested that day or the next; and "to Morrow" came and went without his presenting his Declaration to the National Assembly. The delay gave him time to produce a third draft—the one that he delivered the next day, July 11, to the legislature's delegates.

Lafayette's Declaration, however, was not the assembly's first order of business that day at the Hôtel des Menus-Plaisirs. Another matter demanded immediate attention—the controversy over the king's troops (the French Guards) in Paris and Versailles. With growing regularity the troops—those who had not defected—had been battling proassembly mobs in the streets of both Paris and Versailles. Days earlier the assembly had formally requested that the king remove his forces, and that day—just before they gathered for their January 11 session—the delegates received the king's answer to their request: The troops, he responded, were needed to preserve civil order and would not be withdrawn. To reduce tensions, however, he was willing to move with the National Assembly from Versailles to another, more tranquil locale.

The delegates debated possible responses to the king's latest move—including accepting his offer and possibly weakening themselves, or defying him and thus risking arrest and the assembly's survival. But ultimately they reached no decision that day; afterward Lafayette took the floor.

A French observer later recalled Lafayette's remarks before presenting his Declaration as possessing "the noble simplicity of a hero-philosopher." To another "it seemed as if we were listening to Wazington [*sic*] speak to the people on a square in Philadelphia"—the city where both the Declaration of Independence and the American Constitution had been drafted.

Not surprisingly Lafayette's final draft of his 1789 Declaration—the one he delivered that July 11 to the National Assembly—opened with an affirmation of natural rights similar to the one that commenced Jefferson's 1776 Declaration:

> Everyman is born with inalienable and imprescriptible rights. Such are the liberty of all his opinions, concern for his honor and his life, the right of property, the full disposal of his labor, [and] of all his talents, the communication of his thoughts by all possible means, the pursuit of his well-being, and resistance to oppression.

The rest of the Declaration's third draft repeated, with slight organizational and sentence changes, the second draft's contents. Several alterations—some of omission—were seemingly designed to mollify entrenched interests: Gone was the second draft's affirmation of religious liberty ("No man may be disquieted on account of his religion"). Similarly the new draft affirmed an ongoing need to preserve "distinctions necessary to the social order." And perhaps in deference to the clergy, a reference included in the second draft to furthering "the progress of enlightenment"—heresy to most clerics—was nowhere to be found.

Years later Lafayette recalled his Declaration as a "profession of faith, fruit of my past, pledge of my future," yet also "at the same time a manifesto and an ultimatum." But if the Declaration that he presented that day retreated from its second draft's bolder liberalism, its delivery came at a fraught moment in France's history.

Even as the National Assembly faced growing factionalism, external forces were threatening the body's very existence. And amid that troubled milieu, Lafayette faced the task of crafting a statement of rights that—to advance the reforms that he championed—first needed to win a majority in the fractious assembly. In 1776, after all, his friend Jefferson, to win passage of his Declaration, had been compelled to accept the removal of that document's antislavery passage. And so Lafayette, in 1789, felt similarly induced to craft a document that retreated from the more liberal expressions included in its earlier iterations.[6]

As Lafayette concluded the reading of his document, the Hôtel des Menus-Plaisirs erupted in applause. Taking the floor to second the Declaration, the marquis de Lally-Tollendal praised the document and its author: "He speaks of liberty as he has defended it." But as Lafayette had expected, Lally also proposed that the Declaration's formal adoption be postponed until a longer, more detailed, constitution could be appended to it.

More troubling for Lafayette were Lally's other comments: He openly speculated as to whether the marquis's handiwork—with its obvious debt to America's historical experience—provided an apt model for France. As Lally concluded, the assembly referred the document to its bureaus for further evaluation.

Over the coming days, Lafayette's Declaration won wide acclaim, as its text, printed in mass quantities, circulated through Paris's streets. The document's author, for his part, knew well that France faced dire challenges—but had no misgivings about the words he had presented to the assembly. There had been compromises, and Lafayette knew that a "knowledge of liberty" hardly ensures its practice. But he took pride in having drafted what he later called the "First European Declaration of the Rights of Man and of Citizens."

Moreover, he knew that he had not completed the mansion of liberty that he envisioned for France. But, as Lafayette's biographers Louis Gottschalk and Margaret Maddox observed, he had provided his compatriots "some usable building materials."[7]

FORTY-NINE

"Aux Armes!"

On Sunday, July 12, 1789, as Gouverneur Morris and his carriage driver headed toward the Hôtel de Langeac, he looked forward to dinner and discussing with Jefferson the quickening events reshaping France's politics. In the city's northwest, close to chez Jefferson, however, as Morris's carriage clanked toward the Place Louis XV—today's Place de la Concorde—an unexpected sight snared his and his driver's attention. Behind their carriage, soon overtaking it, came a rush of traffic—on foot, on horseback, and in carriages.

By rights, Paris's attentions that Sunday should have belonged to the Declaration of the Rights of Man that Lafayette delivered to the National Assembly the day before. That morning, copies of it circulated through the city; its text had been read at the Hôtel de Ville, before Paris's Assembly of Electors—the 180-man body originally elected to select the local delegation to the Estates-General but now struggling to organize a de facto government for their troubled city.

But eclipsing Lafayette's declaration that morning was other news: The previous day, according to reputable sources, Louis had dismissed Finance Minister Jacques Necker and his moderate allies in the Versailles court, replacing them with conservative royalists. For reformers in Paris, Necker's dismissal seemed a signal that Louis, weary of the city's challenges to his authority, was preparing a military crackdown.

Moments after the civilian traffic another surge of movement rumbled behind Morris's carriage. Soon overtaking his conveyance came "a body of cavalry," with "sabres drawn" in pursuit of the civilians. The pursuers belonged to the Royal-Allemand, a cavalry regiment commanded by the prince de Lambesc and recruited among German-speaking soldiers of northeastern France's regions of Alsace and Lorraine.

Typifying the cat-and-mouse encounters between mobs and military units on Paris's streets during those weeks, Lambesc's dragoons, having just chased the mob out of the nearby Place Vendôme, were now attempting to disperse them from the Place Louis XV.

His curiosity piqued, Morris ordered the driver to proceed to the Place Louis XV. There, from a safe distance, Morris gazed upon the regiment that moments earlier had overtaken his carriage. By then, however, the regiment's soldiers and their horses were in full retreat, and the civilian mob that had been the object of their pursuit was now hurling rocks at the Royal-Allemand cavalry.

Forced out of the Place Louis XV by the dragoons, the mob had filled the adjacent Tuileries Gardens. There, amid a pile of freshly hewed stones, building materials for a new bridge across the Seine (today's Pont de la Concorde), the insurgents found both a redoubt and an arsenal. Shielded by the pile, as Morris watched, "perhaps an hundred" civilians were hurling stones at the regiment.

The Officer at the Head of the party is saluted by a stone, and immediately turns his horse in a menacing manner toward the assailant. But his adversaries are posted in ground where the cavalry cannot act. He pursues his route, and the pace is soon increased to a gallop, amid a shower of stones. One of the soldiers is either knocked from his horse or the horse falls under him. He is taken prisoner, and at first ill-treated. They fired several Pistols, but without effect; probably they were not even charged with ball.

At the Hôtel de Langeac, Morris learned that Jefferson had just returned in his own carriage from the Place Louis XV where he too had witnessed the skirmish. Indeed, throughout those weeks Jefferson remained insatiably curious about the turmoil roiling Paris. Recently and over the coming weeks, he and William Short roamed the city, observing the disturbances.

Perhaps steeled by his experiences as Virginia's wartime governor, Jefferson seemed almost sanguine concerning the discord he witnessed. Typifying that attitude, he believed the confrontation at the Place Louis XV belonged to a gathering inevitability: "The progress of things here will be subject to checks from time to time of course," he wrote to Thomas Paine of the melee. "Whether they will be great or small will depend on the army. But they will be only checks."[1]

In fact—unbeknownst to Jefferson and Morris as they met that night at the Hôtel de Langeac—earlier that evening, during the Place Louis XV confrontation, mutinous companies of the royal guards, arriving to assist the beleaguered Parisians, had chased the Royal-Allemand away from the area.

Although only one civilian died during the Place Louis XV skirmish, the fact that Parisians had battled German-speaking troops had the effect of lending credence to rumors, already circulating, concerning plans by Louis to order massacres of Parisians and to deploy foreign armies to enforce his will.

———

Culminating weeks of frustration for the king, Necker's dismissal had been prodded by Marie Antoinette, the duke of Artois, and other court conservatives. Moreover—not content with merely dismissing the favorite minister of National Assembly liberals—Louis also had ordered the Swiss-born Necker to leave the country and to keep both his dismissal and exile a secret. Word of Louis's wishes—via an emissary bearing a letter from the king—had reached Necker at 3:00 p.m. on Saturday, July 11, the day before the skirmish at the Place de Louis XV.

By the next morning, as word of Necker's exit spread through Paris's streets, that news metastasized into darker rumors. According to one, Louis—having resolved to vanquish rather than negotiate with his enemies—had ordered his troops to make an all-out assault on Paris. Mobs—such as those at the Place

Louis XV—quickly materialized in Paris's streets. One gathered that same Sunday before a Palais-Royal waxworks gallery, robbed it of facsimiles of the heads of Necker and the duke of Orléans—both of which, held aloft on poles, were soon paraded through Paris's streets.

Morris, for his part, had learned of Necker's dismissal earlier that Sunday, during a visit with his friend Marshal de Castries. "He is much affected at this Intelligence, and, indeed, so am I," Morris recorded in his notebook; later that day, at the Palais-Royal, he added: "The news of Necker's dismissal came, and was greeted with a cry of rage."

Indeed, in the Palais-Royal's Café Foy, the journalist Camille Desmoulins had climbed upon a table and urged preparations for battle: *"Aux armes!"* he shouted, accusing the king of planning carnage on a scale similar to that of the infamous St. Bartholomew's Day Massacre perpetrated against Protestants in 1572 by King Charles IX. In that outrage, conducted over several weeks, tens of thousands of Protestant subjects perished in targeted killings orchestrated by the court. Only now, Desmoulins warned, France's sovereign was planning a "St. Bartholomew of patriots."

Although Morris was a deist, his notes for that day—July 12—swelled with Old Testament-worthy augury: "Daily this great necessity grew more terrible— the great army of the unemployed increased and clamored for bread," he wrote: "Rumor announced the approach of a large army from Versailles to the capital." Indeed, by late afternoon Morris was repeating the day's most incendiary rumor—a vow attributed to the baron de Breteuil, a key minister to the king: "If it is necessary to burn Paris, burn Paris."

As Morris and Jefferson soon learned on July 12, others in Paris used Breteuil's alleged vow to torch Paris as an invitation to attack the Ferme générale's detested wall that ringed the city. Unlike the older enclosures that had encircled Paris, the Ferme générale wall—whose construction had commenced five years earlier—was built not to protect the city from invasion but to further private pecuniary interests. More specifically, the Ferme générale had built the wall to enforce its monopoly on the collection of internal customs duties on goods entering Paris.

At regular intervals metal gates interrupted the wall's fifteen-mile length; adjacent to and rising over each gate were fifty-four *barrières*—neoclassical-style buildings in which agents collected customs duties and otherwise regulated traffic in and out of Paris. To Jefferson—who regularly when going to Versailles passed through the Ferme générale *barrière* nearest his residence—the ornate edifices were "the palaces by which we are to be let in and out." Indeed, Jefferson's friend Philip Mazzei described the Hôtel de Langeac as "a beautiful villeta . . . within gunshot distance of the city wall." And on the evening of July 12—as mobs destroyed sections of the wall and set fire to forty *barrières*— five years of accumulated resentments burst into view.

Curiously, however, across much of the city, even as Parisians vented their resentments and braced for a military attack, an atmosphere of carnival nonetheless prevailed. Recounted Morris: "Fêtes and dinners enlivened the frequenters of the Palais Royal Gardens, and a ball in the Champs Élysées kept up the spirits of the fishwomen and the dwellers in the Faubourg Saint Antoine. Everything and everybody in Paris seemed ready for civil war."[2]

Tellingly, Morris and others that season still often eschewed the term "revolution" in describing the tumult. To be sure, by the late eighteenth century, "revolution" in most quarters had already acquired its modern usage—connoting a dramatic overthrow of entrenched authority. Many, however (including Jefferson), as late as the 1780s—while sometimes using the word to refer to political rebellion—also employed it in its earlier usage—as a noun, derived from the astronomical sciences, referring to the motions of heavenly bodies.

To describe violent challenges to governments, Jefferson (then) often preferred the term "civil war." Indeed, with the exception of upheavals associated with Britain in 1688 and America in 1776–83, he still rarely used the term when discussing political matters. "The parties are so irreconcileable that it is impossible to foresee what issue it will have," he thus lamented to John Jay in spring 1789. If the impasse paralyzing the Estates-General continued, he predicted, "This would bring on a civil war."[3]

FIFTY

Hôtel de Ville

By the morning of July 13, 1789, after the previous evening's disturbances, Paris's attention was focused on the Hôtel de Ville, administrative headquarters for the city's government—effectively City Hall. Inside the Renaissance-style edifice and the plaza in front of it—the Place de Grève, today's Place de l'Hôtel de Ville—nervous Parisians gathered, clamoring for action. Some called for arresting the mobs roaming in the city, attacking the king's soldiers; others roared antiroyalist sentiments.

For weeks Paris's de facto mayor, its provost of merchants, and the electors who assisted him in governing the city had pondered asking the king and the National Assembly to revive a citizens' militia to protect Paris. But the request had never found its way to Versailles.

Now, however, facing growing crowds in and outside the Hôtel de Ville, the city's leaders understood that, with procrastination no longer an option, calm must be restored to the city. In the building's main assembly room they eventually reached a decision: Around eight o'clock that morning the provost of merchants and the electors announced to the crowds in the Place de Grève the authorization of a citizens' militia, asking that all males fit for service repair to their respective neighborhoods and report for duty. Some in the plaza began dispersing; those who remained appeared to be calmed by the announcement.

So far, so good.

For the time being the crisis seemed tamped down. As the officials returned inside to resume deliberations, several carried "trophies"—city flags that had been flying outside, each a solid vertical field of blue and red. In their meeting room the city officers, finding a prominent place to display the standards, mounted them above a fireplace. Coincidentally close by, and just beneath the flags, sat Jean-Antoine Houdon's marble bust of Lafayette—the same bust whose dedication William Short had attended three years earlier in Jefferson's stead.

According to the meeting's recorded minutes, at that moment several electors became "empowered by a sudden inspiration." The juxtaposition of the flags and the bust seemed a sign too obvious to ignore: As the room resounded with endorsements of the idea, it became clear that, in searching for a militia leader, their best option would be to "defer to the command of M. de la Fayette." In Condorcet's words, the electors would call upon a "storybook hero who, thanks to the éclat of his adventures, his youth, his bearing, and his renown could enchant . . . the imagination and rally all of the popular interests to his side."[1]

As Paris's electors were contemplating Lafayette's bust, the flesh-and-blood marquis, meanwhile, was at Versailles—deep in deliberations with his fellow National Assembly delegates. By then again meeting in the Hôtel des Menus-Plaisirs, they were seeking to avert the crisis stoked by the king's forces. Minimally the delegates hoped to persuade Louis to remove his troops from Paris. That afternoon, however, those hopes grew even dimmer when a delegation they dispatched returned with word that the king had no plans to withdraw the soldiers.

The latest rebuke coincided with new rumors circulating that Louis planned, later that night, to order royal troops to arrest specific delegates, seize the Hôtel des Menus-Plaisirs, and declare the assembly dissolved. Most delegates were uncertain of their best course. But for individual delegates like Lafayette who had reason to fear arrest, remaining in the assembly hall seemed the safest option.

Beyond that, most delegates believed that any remaining chance of resolving the crisis required their uninterrupted work; thus they soon passed a motion to remain in constant session for the time being. Realizing that the assembly's president, the elderly archbishop of Vienne, was too frail to preside over late-evening sessions, the delegates voted 711 to 589 to make Lafayette the body's vice president.

Responding to their vote, Lafayette reminded the delegates of his earlier promise to Auvergne's Second Estate constituents to oppose all efforts to combine the three estates: "On another occasion I would have reminded you of my inadequacy and the peculiar situation of myself." But new circumstances, he added, compelled new priorities: "My chief sentiment is to accept with enthusiasm the honor which you have done me and . . . and never to separate myself from your efforts to maintain peace and confirm public liberty."

After the body ended formal debates at 11:30 p.m., more than a hundred delegates remained in the hall—some sleeping in their seats, others on the floor. Still others milled about the chamber, chatting with other delegates. Lafayette, for his part, soon stretched out on a bench for the night. Over the next restless hours he found time to pen a letter to Madame Simiane: "There is nothing more singular than the situation in which we find ourselves," he wrote. Indeed, anticipating the coming hours—July 14, 1789, a day soon immortalized in world history—he predicted, "The day will be interesting. The national party and the ministerial party are going to become quite distinctly separate now."[2]

———

Meanwhile, back at the Hôtel de Ville on that same evening of July 13, Paris's electors had also remained in session. In fact, deep into the wee hours of the fourteenth, well after Versailles's delegates had suspended their debates, several electors, still in the Hôtel de Ville, were trying to cobble together a provisional city government capable of restoring calm to Paris. Working with royal officials, the electors were also searching for a way agreeable both to them and Louis's court to authorize their promised citizens' militia.

At 2:00 a.m. on July 14 the electors' task became still more urgent with the arrival in their midst of a group of Parisians with an alarming report. As described by accounts written by the electors, the group wore "on their faces every sign of fright and alarm . . . crying that all had been lost, the City taken, and the Rue de Saint-Antoine inundated with 15,000 soldiers who might seize the Hôtel de Ville at any moment."

Like so many rumors then in circulation, the stories of the gathering troops were unfounded. Even so, for already nervous citizens and electors, the reports sounded sufficiently plausible to spark alarm. And by six o'clock that morning, the Place de Grève teemed with "multitudes" bearing "arms of every variety." Moreover, many among those gathered, fearing imminent war, had resolved to settle in for a longer duration; thus, even as newly arriving Parisians reached the plaza, those already there—intent on acquiring provisions for a sustained stay—soon rushed westward to nearby Les Halles, the city's main farmer's market. As a result "carts of flour, wheat, wine, and other comestibles, guns, ammunition"—all heading toward the Hôtel de Ville—soon filled nearby streets.

At around seven o'clock, when fresh reports of troop movements reached the Hôtel de Ville, tensions in the plaza reached a dangerous level. The provost of merchants and the electors ordered all citizens with weapons to report to their local district headquarters of Paris's militia (there were sixty military districts spread across the city). Militia members were also instructed to show their loyalty to Paris by wearing cockades displaying the city's colors of blue and red. They were further ordered to commence construction of the city's defenses—to begin removing paving stones from streets, digging trenches, and building barricades.

To acquire armaments for the nascent army, details were dispatched to two royal military installations reputedly being used as depots for weapons and gunpowder—one a complex otherwise used as a residence for old and disabled soldiers called the Hôtel des Invalides; the other, the medieval fortress more recently used as a prison called the Bastille Saint-Antoine.[3]

FIFTY-ONE

Commandant de la Garde Nationale

Between Charles-François de Broglie, Louis's newly appointed minister of war, and Pierre-Victor, baron de Besenval, the head of Swiss Guard troops in France, the two officers commanded close to twenty thousand soldiers in and near Paris. So why did they do so little to impede the simmering insurrections around the city that July?

To the historian Munro Price that question remains "the most perplexing riddle of the revolution in Paris." No doubt the size of the growing mobs around Paris instilled caution in the two commanders; beyond that, the growing frequency of mutinies within their forces could hardly have been reassuring.

Whatever the reasons behind their inaction, this much is clear: The detail the Hôtel de Ville's electors dispatched to the Invalides was initially met by its governor with stalling—though a mob of eighty thousand Parisians did eventually break into the complex and seize thirty thousand muskets and several cannons. The second detail—the one sent to the Bastille Saint-Antoine—achieved a more mixed outcome. Before the day's end, however, events did confirm Lafayette's prediction that July 14 would be an "interesting" day.

On Paris's eastern edge, in the crowded working-class neighborhood of the Faubourg Saint-Antoine, the Bastille—a corruption of the word *bastide* ("fortified town")—had been constructed as a fortress in the fourteenth century. Contiguous on two sides with a medieval wall that once surrounded the city, the edifice was built to guard Paris against an attack along its eastern edge. In that role, the Bastille also had protected the Porte St. Antoine, a gate in the city wall. By the fifteenth century, however, the fortress, with its eight looming towers and crenellated turrets, served mainly as a state prison.

The edifice's past notwithstanding, however, even casual observers by early July 1789 recognized that the Bastille's days as an important prison were well behind it. Only a handful of inmates remained behind its walls, and its defenses were commensurately weak. Moreover, in past weeks, a growing array of cannons, most trained on the rue Saint-Antoine below, had appeared on its towers' roofs. Moreover, Louis's army was storing weapons and hundreds of pounds of gunpowder in the fortress. Given that, when the three-man detail dispatched by Paris's electors approached the Bastille on July 14, it was widely viewed as a threat to the city, or, opportunistically—if the electors' hopes could be realized—a rich source of munitions.[1]

By the time the Hôtel de Ville's emissaries reached the Bastille, a noisy crowd was gathered before its eastern facade. Making their way through the crowd, the three men soon spoke with Bernard-René Launay, governor of the moat-encircled fortress. In his late twenties Launay's father had also served as the Bastille's chief royal officer. Indeed, Launay fils had been born behind its walls. After several minutes Launay—having invited the three inside for a meal and further talks—ordered the fort's large iron gate raised and the drawbridge spanning its moat lowered.

Although the men conversed for several hours, in the end the emissaries returned to the Hôtel de Ville with mixed news. Launay had refused to surrender the Bastille. He did promise, however, that if the electors accepted his refusal, he would forbid his soldiers from firing on insurgent Parisians. The winning of such a promise had numbered among the instructions given the detail. Thus, after hearing their account of the exchange with Launay, the electors were inclined to accept his offer. Before they could announce their decision, however, cries of "Perfidy!" and "Treason!" rose from the crowds in the Place de Grève. In developments of which the electors were initially unaware, two injured men had arrived in the plaza—one with an arm wound, one more gravely hurt. Also arriving—like the other two, transported by wagon—were as many as twenty other casualties.

The arrivals soon shared the same story: After the departure from the Bastille that day of the detail sent from the Hôtel de Ville, the fortress's gate had again been opened and its drawbridge lowered. And among the crowds gathered outside, numerous Parisians, most bearing arms, had interpreted those actions as an invitation to enter the redoubt. As the citizens streamed over the drawbridge, however, the prison's guards opened fire on them.

Upon learning of the attack on the civilians, the electors dispatched a second detail to the Bastille to remonstrate with Launay over his broken promise. But as the new detail approached the fortress, the garrison inside was already exchanging fire with armed Parisians. The die was cast; recalled a member of the detail: "A deputation is no longer what they want; it is the siege of the Bastille, the destruction of this horrible prison, it is the death of [Launay] that they demand in great cries."

By the day's end the Bastille had fallen to Paris's insurgents, whose numbers soon removed the citadel's weaponry and ammunition. Simultaneously the edifice's seven prisoners—all aging men—were freed. The battle had cost eighty-three civilians their lives. Among the Bastille's defenders, one died during the battle; two others were captured and later hanged. Launay, after fighting defiantly, was captured; soon thereafter, however, while attempting to escape, he kicked one of his citizen-guards. Seconds later he fell amid a blur of blades and gunfire. Afterward the guard whom he had kicked—a cook by vocation—methodically decapitated the royal officer's lifeless body; Launay's head, hoisted on a pike, could soon be seen being paraded through Paris's streets.

A similar fate soon befell another Parisian leader. Throughout the day Jacques de Flesselles, the city's provost of merchants, had supported the electors. But seeking a middle course, he had refused to provide weapons to the insurgent citizens. For his alleged apostasy he was executed by gunfire on the steps of the Hôtel de Ville. Minutes later, after angry citizens decapitated his body, his head joined that of Launay; mounted atop a pike, it too was carried through Paris's streets.[2]

Hours later, on the evening of the fourteenth, when word of the day's events in Paris reached Lafayette, he was presiding over the National Assembly, again standing in for the archbishop of Vienne. As the delegates interrupted their work to be briefed by two emissaries from the Hôtel de Ville, the delegate François-Alexandre-Frédéric, duc de la Rochefoucauld-Liancourt, a confidant of the king, left the assembly hall to go to the royal apartments and inform Louis of the latest news: according to an oft-repeated story, when told of the day's events, the monarch asked, "It's a revolt?"

"No, sire," answered the duke. "It's a revolution."

Around eleven o'clock the following morning, Louis, having concluded his position was untenable, appeared with his two brothers in the Menus-Plaisirs. There he told the National Assembly—the first time he had publicly called it that—of his intention to withdraw his troops from Paris. "The cause of the people triumphed," Lafayette later recalled.

In Paris that same morning, Pierre-François Palloy, a thirty-four-year-old building contractor who had participated in the previous day's storming of the Bastille showed up, unbidden, at the vanquished building with an eight-hundred-man-strong demolition crew. Some Parisians by then already favored preserving the edifice as a monument to the struggle against absolutism. Others, however, feared its recapture by the king's forces. One rumor even posited the existence of a secret tunnel linking the Bastille with the Château de Vincennes, a royal fortress, just outside Paris, five miles to the east; via the tunnel, the rumor suggested, royal soldiers might try to recapture the edifice. Enflamed by such fears, many Parisians called for the Bastille's immediate demolition.

Lafayette and Paris's electors, after balking for several hours, eventually granted Palloy permission to raze the fortress. He was paid handsomely for the job, and by the following November his work was complete. During and after the demolition Palloy also profited from the sale of souvenirs—including small models of the fortress fashioned from masonry scavenged from its remains. And even as the edifice's honeycomb of chambers successively fell to Palloy's wrecking crew—comprising, at its height, a thousand men—he continued to sell guided tours of its dwindling interior. Indeed, Jefferson's Memorandum book, in its July 20 entry, records: "Pd. seeing Bastille"—admission six livres.

———

For Lafayette, meanwhile, questions over the Bastille's fate were the least of the problems he was facing. On July 15—the same morning that Palloy had showed up at the site of the defeated fortress—the marquis de La Salles, the citizens' militia's interim commander, decided that the moment had come to find a permanent leader for the force. At the Hôtel de Ville, he resigned his post. With that, according to the official report of the session, Médéric-Louis-Élie Moreau de Saint-Méry, the electors' president—gesturing toward the meeting room's fireplace and the bust of Lafayette on its mantel—declared that the time had arrived to entrust the "defense of French liberty . . . to the illustrious defender of the liberty of the New World."

As the electors ratified Saint-Méry's nomination of the marquis to lead the Paris Guard, the army's putative commander remained unaware of their action. Along with a hundred other National Assembly delegates, Lafayette was still in Versailles, preparing to leave for Paris. Around two o'clock that afternoon—with the marquis, as the assembly's vice president, traveling in the lead carriage—the delegates' forty-carriage retinue set out on their twenty-mile journey.

Hours later the carriages rolled up to the Hôtel de Ville, and the delegates streamed inside. In the electors' now-crowded meeting room, Lafayette took the floor. With words remembered as "filled with that eloquence which he possesses," he addressed the assemblage; the marquis "congratulated the Assembly of Electors and all the citizens of Paris on the liberty they had won by their courage"—triumphs, he noted, for which they also owed the "justice of a beneficent and disabused monarch."

Applause and cheers greeted Lafayette's remarks and his reading of the king's promise to the National Assembly to remove his troops from Paris. After several other speeches, the session seemed to be approaching its end when "all the voices joined together to proclaim Monsieur the Marquis de Lafayette Commander-General of the Parisian Militia."

"Accepting his honor with every sign of respect and gratitude," Lafayette "drew his sword; and swore to sacrifice his life for the preservation of this precious liberty that he was entrusted with defending." Renewed cheers filled the room, but even as they waned, still more huzzahs erupted for another hero present—fifty-two-year-old Jean-Sylvain Bailly, the National Assembly delegate who, as a Third Estate delegate from Paris, had administered the Tennis Court Oath.

Bailly was a famous astronomer; among his other achievements, he had calculated an orbit of Halley's comet. His name arose that day at the Hôtel de Ville as he was nominated—and elected by acclamation—as Paris's new civilian leader. With that vote the title provost of merchants was abandoned for one that seemed more fittingly republican: "mayor of Paris." Afterward the attendees crossed the Seine to Notre Dame to mark the occasion with a *Te Deum*.

By the following day—July 16—reports were reaching the Hôtel de Ville of challenges to royal authority elsewhere in France. From Lille, Rouen, Dijon, Rennes, and other locales came word of rebellions in which other French subjects of Louis were burning prisons, freeing prisoners, and demanding lower bread prices. In a broader sense, however, Versailles's authority—however often illusory—over France seemed to be waning; and that of Paris waxing. Reflecting those altered circumstances, Lafayette soon requested a change in his title and that of the troops he commanded: Henceforth the former leader of the Parisian guard became commander of the National Guard.

Reflecting the deepening insurrection, on the fifteenth, when Lafayette left Versailles for the Hôtel de Ville, he had not anticipated an extended stay in Paris. But within twenty-four hours of his arrival—with no signs of an abatement of tensions in the city—he knew he was in for a longer stay.

Still more foreboding, Paris's rumor-besotted crowds, whose numbers seemed to increase with each passing day, were being manipulated by leaders with disparate goals and motives. "I reign in Paris," Lafayette lamented to Madame Simiane on the sixteenth, "and it is over an infuriated people driven by abominable cabals."[3]

FIFTY-TWO

"Vive la Nation!"

The disturbances that roiled Paris in July 1789 erupted, for the most part, south and east of Thomas Jefferson's verdant Faubourg du Roule, in the city's west. In early August the diplomat wrote to John Trumbull that the disorders had never been "what the Londoners beleived in their hopes. I never was more tranquil in my house than thro the whole of it. I went much too into the city, and saw there was no danger but for a very few characters. Property was sacred thro' the whole."

Notwithstanding Jefferson's reflexive desire to suppress British schadenfreude, July's heat and turmoil did in fact bring lawlessness (if not mortal dangers) to his neighborhood. Repeated break-ins by "common robbers"—one costing him a prized set of candleholders—prompted him to have bars and bells installed on the Hôtel de Langeac's windows. On July 8, six days before the Bastille's fall, writing to Foreign Minister Armand-Marc, comte de Montmorin (Vergenne's successor), he requested that a police *corps de garde* be established and housed in the nearby—and by then unused—Grille de Chaillot. (Replacing the Grille de Chaillot but accorded the same name, a new customs house had been erected at the site of today's Arc de Triomphe, a half mile west of Jefferson's residence—like its predecessor, on the Champs-Élysées.) To Jefferson it seemed the ideal site for a new police station.

"My hotel," he wrote, "having been lately robbed, for the third time, I take the liberty of uniting my wish with that of the inhabitants of this quarter, that it might coincide with the arrangements of the Police to extend to us the protection of a guard." The additional oversight, he suggested, would likewise safeguard the thoroughfare that ran alongside his residence's southern edge. "The Champs elyseés where accidents are said to happen very frequently," he noted, is "very distant from any corps de garde."

Even so, throughout those weeks, even after the violence associated with the Bastille's fall, Jefferson—no doubt recalling Richmond's dark days of 1781—continued to roam the city with his legation secretary. "Mr. Short and myself have been every day among them in order to be sure of what was passing," he wrote to John Jay on July 19. "I went yesterday to Versailles to satisfy myself what had passed there; for nothing can be believed but what one sees, or has from an eye witness. They believe there still that 3000 people have fallen victims to the tumults of Paris."[1]

Throughout Paris after the Bastille's fall, the persisting presence of royal troops—Louis's promise to withdraw them notwithstanding—continued to stoke fears and inspire mobs. Hunger also fueled discontents, as bread shortages and high prices continued to bedevil Parisians—both of which, in turn, sparked rumors of food hoarding by royal officials and bakers—concerns that in turn led to food riots and even attacks on individual bakers.

Compounding woes, in Paris and throughout France, rumors of impending foreign invasion forces strained already tense nerves. Troops from Marie Antoinette's native Austria were said to have invaded from the Netherlands; still other European monarchies—alarmed at the prospects of a challenge from below to the rule of their Versailles counterparts—were said to be conducting, or planning, similar assaults: By various accounts British troops had arrived in Brest and Saint-Malo; Swedish forces were headed toward France's northeast border, and Spanish forces were preparing to attack Bordeaux.

The wildly inaccurate reports contributed to a national frenzy of rumor-driven panic soon known as *la Grande Peur*—"the great fear." In the heated imagination of that season's France, accounts of foreign invasions coincided with and often blurred into reports of other malevolent acts allegedly committed by "brigands." Nominally the term referred to highway robbers, but by July it became associated with purported hireling gangs roaming across France and dedicated to administering revenge against the Third Estate for its triumphs over the country's nobility.

Brigands, it was said, had burned crops, barns, and houses, as well as committed acts of murder, rape, and dismemberment. In reaction to the alleged attacks, or in preparations for them, peasants armed themselves. In many cases they violated feudal contracts or torched the châteaux of noble families. Indeed, such burnings became conspicuously common in several regions—including Alsace, Burgundy, Normandy, Picardy, and the Franche-Comté. Beyond the lawlessness arising from *la Grande Peur*, it also resulted, throughout France, in a hollowing of Bourbon authority—as local insurgencies rose to fill power vacuums created by faltering outposts of royal officialdom.[2]

In Paris, meanwhile, forty-eight hours after the Bastille's capture, the crowds around the Hôtel de Ville showed no signs of thinning. Lafayette, for his part, was eager to return to Versailles to tend to responsibilities in the National Constituent Assembly, the recently declared successor body to the National Assembly. Even so, he dared not leave Paris. His letter of July 16 to Madame Simiane, gave voice to his frustrations: "Forty thousand souls gather, the fermentation is at its height, I appear, and one word from me disperses them. I have already saved the lives of six people who would have been hanged in various quarters. . . . The well-being of Paris demands that I not remove myself for a moment."

In the end the same geographical shift in France's political center of gravity that had prompted him to rename his army (from the Paris to the National Guard) now rendered him effectively a hostage to Paris. For the time being any return to Versailles would have to wait.

Indeed, Lafayette noted, the crowds swelling the Place de Grève had doubled in a single day. And calls were growing for the king himself to come to Paris and publicly avow his intention to remove his troops—and his fealty to the new, self-proclaimed nation: "As I write," Lafayette reported to Simiane, "eighty-thousand people surround the Hôtel de Ville and say that they are deceived, that the troops are not withdrawn, that the king must come. Even at this moment, they issue terrible cries. If I were to appear, they would calm them themselves; but others will replace them."[3]

At Versailles that same night, still other actions were scrambling the country's already confusing politics. Hours earlier Louis had ordered the foreign troops massed in Paris to leave the country. And in those instructions, the king's brother the comte d'Artois and other die-hard royalists allied with Marie Antoinette spotted an opportunity. Taking advantage of the foreign troops' exit, using it as a cover for their own departure, they had quietly slipped out of France. Even Marie Antoinette began packing for a—soon-canceled—departure from Versailles by herself and her husband.

That same evening, meanwhile—according to a memoir by Madame Campan, Marie-Antoinette's lady-in-waiting—"a committee was held in the King's apartments, at which a most important question was discussed: whether his Majesty should quit Versailles and set off with the troops whom he had recently ordered to withdraw, or go to Paris to tranquillise the minds of the people."

As recalled by Campan, on the morning of the seventeenth the queen revealed to her the plans produced by the meeting: "The King will go to the Hotel de Ville to-morrow. . . . [H]e did not choose this course for himself; there were long debates on the question."[4]

Weighing options, Louis concluded that his best chance of preserving his reign lay in complying with growing calls to appear in Paris and—symbolically, at least—submitting to the nascent government there. Decision made, he updated his will and delegated his brother the comte de Provence to act in his stead while he was away—and, should Louis fail to return, to reign as his successor. (Alone among the royal princes, the comte de Provence had decided to remain in France.)

After praying with his family in the royal chapel, Louis, dressed in a plain frock morning coat, set off for Paris. Instead of his usual complement of royal allies and retainers—considerably reduced over the past few days—the king's retinue was joined for the twenty-mile trip by hundreds of his subjects, many of them wearing Paris's blue-and-red cockade. Members of the newly organized—and hastily, if un-uniformly, uniformed—citizen's militia of Versailles comprised the core of the king's official escort. Also in the procession, however, were hundreds of National Constituent Assembly delegates and, at its rear, a multitude of Versailles townspeople—many shouting,*"Vive le roi!"* and *"Vive la nation!"* and brandishing flintlocks, pikes, and pruning hooks.[5]

At close to three o'clock that afternoon—near Sèvres, on Paris's southwestern edge—Paris's newly appointed mayor, Jean-Sylvain Bailly, and other city officials greeted the king: "I bring your Majesty the keys to the good city of Paris," said Bailly, the astronomer-cum-politician.

The mayor's words spoken and the key presented, the Versailles militia departed. The National Guard, led by Lafayette on a white horse, escorted the entourage along the four remaining miles of the journey. Over the next one and a half hours, it passed through streets lined with tens of thousands of Parisians, many wearing the city's—and now the Revolution's—ubiquitous blue-and-red cockade.

Crowd estimates varied widely. Gouverneur Morris, who was there, speculated that "at least eighty thousand Men" were in Paris's streets that day, all prepared to follow Lafayette. But Jefferson, who also witnessed the scene, recalled "about 60,000 citizens of all forms and colours, armed with the muskets of the Bastille and Invalids as far as they would go, the rest with pistols, swords, pikes, pruning hooks, scythes &c. lined all the streets thro' which the procession passed." Moreover, along the parade route, he recalled, "in the streets, doors and windows, [spectators] saluted them every where with cries of 'vive la nation.'" By Jefferson's account, in contrast to the crowds who had escorted the royal entourage from Versailles, among those who ushered the procession on its final Paris miles, "Not a single 'vive le roy' was heard."

Indeed, what caught Morris's attention that day was that the marquis seemed to eclipse the king in the public eye. Observed the New Yorker to his diary, "Our friend Lafayette, elected general of the militia of Paris, precedes his sovereign. They move slowly, amid the acclamations of 'Vive la nation!' Each line composed of three ranks; consequently it is a body six deep extending that distance. The Assemblée Nationale walk promiscuously together in the procession. The King's Horse Guards, some of the Gardes du Corps, and all those who attend him, have the cockades of the city, viz., red and blue. It is a magnificent procession in every respect."[6]

By 4:00 p.m., the entourage reached the Hôtel de Ville. Amid cheering thousands, Lafayette and the king climbed the building's steps as an honor guard, with swords unsheathed, awaited them at its entrance. As the two entered, Louis seemed taken aback by the clang of metal as the guards raised their swords over him to form a ceremonial welcoming arch.

Inside, now even more visibly uncomfortable, the king was escorted to a throne that had been placed in the electors' assembly hall. After he was seated the room grew quiet, and Mayor Bailly approached the king, carrying a blue-and-red cockade—the same colors of Paris that, worn by thousands that day, had been ubiquitous on Louis's journey from Versailles. Addressing the king, Bailly expressed his hope that Louis would join his subjects in wearing the cockade.

Without uttering a word, Louis, reached out, accepted the cockade, and pinned it to his hat.

The room erupted with cries of *"Vive le roi!"*

The king was momentarily speechless, but gently prodded by Bailly, he soon spoke. In faint words audible only to Bailly but that Bailly, in a louder voice, repeated to the room—Louis said that he loved his subjects and longed for a restoration of peace.[7]

By that evening Louis was back at Versailles—reunited with his family, his court, and his updated will. His gamble—in choosing to spend a day in Paris over permanent exile from France—had, for the time being, triumphed. Simultaneously, however, his appearance in Paris also seemed to most observers a boon to the prestige of Lafayette, Bailly, and other officials at the Hôtel de Ville. As for the king, if nothing else he had won time to contemplate his next move. Indeed, Gouverneur Morris recalled hearing—as Louis departed the Hôtel de Ville—from the crowds surrounding him, for the first time that day, the once-familiar exultation: *"Vive le Roi."*[8]

In the end, however, the day had belonged to Lafayette. Indeed, as an admiring Morris soon recalled in a letter to George Washington: "He had his Sovereign, during the late Procession to Paris, completely within his Power. He had marched him where he pleased; measured out the Degree of Applause he should receive as he pleased; and if he pleased could have detained him Prisoner." Morris likewise detailed Lafayette's rejection of a royal post—governorship of the region around Paris—dangled before him: "The Command of the military in that City was the utmost of his Wishes," recalled Morris. "He declared that he was satiated with Power."

Moreover, in Lafayette's view Louis had effectively "turned himself over as my prisoner." Through his public display of humility, the king, Lafayette wrote, had "attached me to his service more fully than if he had promised me half of his kingdom." Even so, mere displays of deference would never appease Lafayette: "If the king refuses the constitution," he vowed, "I will fight him. If he accepts it, I will defend him."[9]

FIFTY-THREE

The Sea Running High

A revolt is a sort of whirlwind in the social atmosphere which swiftly
forms in certain temperatures and, rising and travelling as it spins,
uproots, crushes, and demolishes, bearing with it great and sickly
spirits alike, strong men and weaklings, the tree-trunk and the wisp
of straw. Woe to those it carries away no less than to those it seeks to
destroy; it smashes one against the other.

VICTOR HUGO, *LES MISÉRABLES*

Louis XVI, on July 17, had deferred to Lafayette, newly appointed as commander of France's National Guard. But over the coming days, the people
of Paris proved less malleable. As the thirty-one-year old officer struggled to
manage a city beset by fear, factionalism, rumors, and hunger—a single gruesome
episode soon underscored his challenge.

During Jacques Necker's brief exile, the seventy-three-year-old Joseph-
François Foullon de Doué had served as Louis's finance minister. Before, during, and following his brief tenure in that post, Foullon—often vilified in Paris's
prorevolutionary press—garnered opprobrium as a callous speculator in the
grain market. Through "odious speculation," it was said, he had won "a stunning fortune" at the expense of Paris's hungry and, in many instances, starving citizens. Indeed, the likely apocryphal quotation "Let them eat cake,"
attributed to Marie Antoinette, may have originated with an anecdote concerning Foullon.

Whatever Foullon's role in the let-them-eat-cake anecdote, this much is certain: On July 22 at five o'clock in the morning he arrived at the Hôtel de Ville, captive of an angry mob vowing to execute him. Neither Bailly nor Lafayette were in the building. A group of electors present, however, noting that Foullon had not been formally accused of any crime, urged his captors to take him to the Abbey of Saint-Germain-des-Prés prison, about a mile distant on the Left Bank.

Disobeying the electors, the growing mob soon called for the prisoner's summary execution. "Hang him!" it called to Bailly. Hours later, when Lafayette arrived, the mob had forced its way into the electors' assembly room. There the National Guard's commander confronted the rowdy lynch mob.

Eventually, however, its voices quieted as Lafayette, appealing for the rule of law, explained that the moment "obliges me to speak to you with the liberty and frankness that form the basis of my character. You want to execute without trial this man before you: it is an injustice that would dishonor you, that would dishonor me. . . . I will not permit it."

Lafayette urged that Foullon be taken to the Abbey of Saint-Germain-des-Prés. Fatefully however, his eloquence, though well received in the assembly room, went unheard by the still-growing crowds on the Place de Grève—for centuries a venue for public executions. And soon after Foullon was taken into the plaza, he was seized by the mob and hanged from a lamppost. Moments later, when the rope attaching him to the post broke, sending him to the ground, a flurry of attackers besieged him with knives and other bladed instruments. Soon thereafter Foullon's severed head, mounted on a pike—its mouth stuffed with hay, an expression of the mob's contempt—was being triumphantly paraded through the Place de Grève. Amid the celebration, members of the mob spotted a cabriolet, a small open carriage, bearing Foullon's son-in-law Louis-Bénigne-François Berthier de Savigny. A royal official, Berthier was in custody and being transferred for trial after being accused of driving up grain prices. Minutes later, in a grisly family reunion, Berthier's head, mounted on its own pike, joined that of his father-in-law.[1]

Fourteen months earlier Lafayette had lamented what he saw as a political lethargy afflicting his countrymen. "The people in General Have no inclination to Go to Extremities," he wrote to Washington. "Liberty or death is Not the Motto on this Side of the Atlantic." By Lafayette's lights, enlightened reformers had scarce options: Faced with "Want and ignorance," he added, "the only Way is to Reason or persuade the Nation into a Kind of Passive discontent or Non obedience which May tire out the Levity and Undo the Plans of Governement."

Now, however, with the murders of Foullon and Berthier, Lafayette faced a citizenry thoroughly shed of its alleged passivity. On July 23—a day after the two men's deaths—he submitted to Bailly his resignation as commander of the National Guard: "The people did not heed my advice; and the day I lack the confidence they promised me I must, as I said in advance, leave a position in which I can no longer be useful."

After representatives from all sixty of Paris's districts gathered, however, Lafayette's resignation was refused. Indeed, the district leaders unanimously reaffirmed his command. Ambivalently he agreed to remain in the post: "What to do? I am in despair," he wrote to a friend on the twenty-fourth. "I cannot abandon the citizens who place all of their confidence in me, and if I remain, I am in the terrible situation of witnessing evil without remedying it."

———

Writing on July 25, Thomas Jefferson could not resist a turn at gallows humor. "The cutting off heads," he wrote to Maria Cosway, "is become so much à la mode, that one is apt to feel of a morning whether their own is on their shoulders." More soberly, he ventured that the attempts by royal officials to flee France had disposed the public to believe the worst concerning their deeds. Commensurately, when such officials were caught and returned to the city, their reentry as prisoners had the effect of inflaming retributive passions.

Thus, Jefferson reasoned, so long as France's roads teemed with fleeing officials who could be nabbed and returned to Paris, executions were bound to continue. "Whether this work is yet over, depends on their catching more of the fugitives. If no new capture re-excites the spirit of vengeance, we may hope it will soon be at rest, and that order and safety will be reestablished except for a few of the most obnoxious characters."

Jefferson, however, using the nonastronomical meaning of "revolution," concluded his missive on a wistful note: "My fortune has been singular, to see in the course of fourteen years two such revolutions as were never before seen. But why should I talk of wars and revolutions to you who are all peace and goodness."[2]

The center of France's political life during those July weeks was increasingly shifting to Paris. But Versailles still played a critical role in the country's life—if less now as the home of the royal court and more that of the National Constituent Assembly. Notably on August 4—though Lafayette was not present—it met in an extended session that, of enormous consequence to him and the entire nation, soon became enshrined as "the night the Old Regime ended."

Meeting from six o'clock in the evening until two in the morning, the assembly repealed multiple privileges of the nobility and clergy. Driving the action were more than a dozen delegates drawn from all three estates. Days later the conservative delegate the marquis de Ferrières explained his support for measures that, under other circumstances, he would certainly have opposed: "It would have been useless, even dangerous," he wrote, "to oppose the general will of the nation. It would have designated you, you and your possessions, as victims of the furor of the multitudes."

Credit for the August 4 renunciations was widely shared, but though he had been absent for the session, one delegate came in for particular praise. Typical of the plaudits was a print depicting its subject in a heroic pose accompanied by a caption: "The French Nation aided by Lafayette defeats the despotism and feudal abuses that oppressed the people."[3]

During those busy weeks Lafayette also led a committee assigned to recommend policies to transform the ragtag National Guard into a formidable army. The committee met daily at the Hôtel de Ville, often in extended sessions. Attesting to the importance that he attached to the panel's work, Lafayette made time in his schedule to sit in on at least part of each day's meeting.

After consulting with French army veterans—including many who had fought in the American war—the committee eventually produced suggestions that eased the guard's transition into a more polished army. Most visible to the public was its adoption of a uniform: rank and file soldiers were to have royal blue coats set off by white lapels and facings and a scarlet collar and yellow buttons; to be worn with a white vest and white breeches—plus black leggings in winter, white in summer. Officers' uniforms—though adorned with epaulets, swords, trimmings, and other accoutrements—were to replicate the same colors and style. During the American Revolution Lafayette had purchased uniforms for men under his command. By contrast, the National Guard's envisioned final troop numbers—31,058 men—precluded such personal largesse. These soldiers would be required to purchase their own uniforms, an expenditure that effectively meant their ranks would be filled by recruits exclusively from the propertied classes.

Other recommended reforms concerned pay and the organization of each of the units that were to comprise the army's total of six divisions. Most were ideas that any reasonable panel led by a talented officer could have promoted, with the exception of a small but conspicuous detail, one personally suggested by Lafayette—and through which his committee left its most enduring mark.

Two days before the Bastille's fall, Camille Desmoulins had suggested that Paris's civilian antiroyalists signify their fraternity by wearing green cockades. Shortly thereafter, adopting the colors of Paris as their own, the National Guard and their civilian supporters began wearing red-and-blue cockades. But even as those cockades soared in popularity, officials at the Hôtel de Ville had grown concerned that blue and red were also the colors of the Orléans family. More saliently, that family's most prominent member, the duke of Orléans, had long since emerged as a rival to Louis and—more ominously for Lafayette and his allies—a leader of a competing faction within Paris's antiroyalist agitation.

Changes would have to be made to prevent any mistaking of the National Guard's loyalties. Beyond that, Lafayette sensed an opportunity to secure the support of Louis and his adherents. Toward that end, he suggested that attached to each soldier's hat, his *tricorne*, there be a cockade of three colors—the blue and red of Paris, as well as white, the color of the house of Bourbon.

Lafayette's cockade soon appeared on the National Guard's new uniforms; and, as its popularity exploded, the cockade appeared on myriad other items—including sashes, women's shifts, shoes, and watch fobs. To be sure, just as the marquis later called his blueprint for France's government the "First European Declaration of the Rights of Man and of Citizens" his tricolor cockade—the inspiration for France's tricolor flag adopted in 1794—was more than a trio of unifying colors. Indeed, it became a powerful symbol of something new under the European sun—the emblem of the continent's first citizen's army: "I place before you a cockade," he declaimed shortly after its unveiling, "which will go around the world." The forces the cockade represented, "civil and military," he predicted, are "bound to triumph over the old tactics of Europe" and "reduce arbitrary governments to the alternative of being conquered unless they imitate it."[4]

By August the marquis—extolled in poems, engravings, and songs—found himself celebrated as the French Revolution's paterfamilias. But he also knew from experience the speed with which clear skies can give way to heavier weather. Indeed, intuiting the coming turbulence, Gouverneur Morris puzzled over how his friend would fare in stiffer winds: "If the clouds which now lower should be dissipated without a storm, he will be infinitely indebted to fortune; but if it happen otherwise, the world must pardon much on the score of intention. He means ill to no one, but he has the *besoin de briller*"—the need to shine. "He is very much below the business he has undertaken, and if the sea runs high he will be unable to hold the helm."[5]

FIFTY-FOUR

Duties Owed the King

Thus it is that if, as Lafayette said, insurrection is the most sacred of
duties, sporadic revolt may be the most disastrous of blunders.
—VICTOR HUGO, *LES MISÉRABLES*

At just before three o'clock on August 26, 1789, the parquet floor of the
Hôtel de Langeac's salon gleamed with its usual polish. The circular
room's two outsized wall mirrors and the rising sun emblazoned on its domed
ceiling only brightened the shimmer. Like the salon's shape, the mural, by
the fashionable Parisian painter Jean-Simon Berthélemy, belonged to a remodeling project Jefferson commissioned shortly after moving into the town
house four years earlier.

Of the Hôtel de Langeac's twenty-four rooms—particularly on days like
that one when he had grave matters to ponder—the salon ranked among
Jefferson's favorites. Indifferent to the surrounding opulence, he would
sit by the mezzanine-level room's tall windows and gaze on the gardens
below.[1]

At forty-six, Jefferson remained tall with pale skin. Only a few added
pounds and his thinning red hair—concealed that afternoon under the powdered wig that he reluctantly donned for such occasions—attested to the passage
of the thirteen years since he had drafted the Declaration of Independence.

That August, Jefferson was still checking each day's mail for the leave of absence he had requested nine months earlier. In the meantime the diplomatic projects he had initiated on instructions from the now-defunct Confederation Congress were completed, approaching completion, or abandoned. Recent weeks had left him with time to closely follow, often as a firsthand observer, the political turmoil transforming France. During those summer days he even found time, as he informed John Trumbull, to "have searched every shop in Paris" on an ultimately failed quest to replace the prized candlesticks he had lost to burglars in July.

However, by that afternoon—August 26—those carefree days seemed behind him. A day earlier Lafayette had written, asking that he host a secret dinner for Lafayette and other National Constituent Assembly delegates. Jefferson had immediately agreed to the request. But as he gazed out of the Hôtel de Langeac's windows that day and awaited his soon-to-arrive guests, he worried about the gathering's possible repercussions.[2]

Now in his fifth year as a diplomat, Jefferson knew that by hosting the gathering, he risked potential embarrassment. But then again, there was no gainsaying the debt of gratitude, stretching back to 1781, that he owed Lafayette. In recent months Jefferson, reciprocating Lafayette's many kindnesses, had undertaken myriad tasks that, breaching diplomatic protocols, involved venturing into his host country's politics. But his friend's latest request gave Jefferson particular pause: This time, he wondered, might his friend have asked him to stray too far from diplomatic propriety?

Indicating Jefferson's growing caution, weeks earlier he declined an invitation to a conference devoted to formulating ideas for France's constitution. The entreaty came from a National Constituent Assembly delegate, the archbishop of Bordeaux. The cleric believed that Jefferson—though an emissary of a foreign state—might nonetheless offer valuable advice to a panel seeking to enshrine universal rights in a governing document for France. "There are no foreigners any more in our opinion when the happiness of man is at stake," the archbishop had implored.

Jefferson had turned down the invitation, but rather than ask William Short to draft his response, he did so himself—"the only document of importance written entirely in French by Jefferson himself," according to the historian Gilbert Chinard. While vaguely alluding to diplomatic protocols that might render his presence inappropriate, Jefferson's missive claimed that pressing work precluded his attendance.

But his excuse was a dodge. In recent months, he had found ample time for pondering constitutions for France—both the one he had written and the one drafted by Lafayette. Moreover, Jefferson's calendar, winding down during those weeks, was anything but crowded. In truth, growing misgivings over those earlier activities weighed on his mind; as Jefferson later admitted, he declined the invitation due to "obvious considerations that my mission was to the king as Chief magistrate of the nation, that my duties were limited to the concerns of my own country, and forbade me to intermeddle with . . . internal transactions."[3]

Since July 11, when Lafayette presented his declaration of rights to the National Assembly, two successive committees of the national legislature had pondered modifications to the document. To varying degrees most of the panels' suggestions advised dispersing the National Constituent Assembly's powers through the creation of an upper house and assigning the king some sort of veto over both houses' actions.

The declaration eventually adopted by the assembly—longer than Lafayette's text and organized into seventeen articles—retained language similar to his version. His version, for instance, had opened with the statement, "Men are born and remain free and equal in rights." And Article 1 of the version eventually adopted by the assembly—albeit now preceded by a preamble—began with those same words.

The adopted document omitted a provision in Lafayette's version that described a convention process by which the constitution might be altered. But otherwise the changes in the adopted version were, in the main, additions that brought more specificity to rights and processes described in Lafayette's document. Alternately perhaps—the devil lurking in the details—the revision subtly reduced rights that Lafayette's document had guaranteed to citizens.

Whatever its effect, the assembly's overhaul of the document Lafayette had presented on July 11 was undertaken in part to accommodate recent events.

Even so, the version it adopted in late August failed to address several vexing questions, including Louis's ongoing refusal to accept a constitution in general as well as the assembly's August 4 reduction of noble privileges.

Moreover, the delegates, in debates among themselves, had been unable to agree on the degree to which, if at all, the king should enjoy a veto over the government's legislative branch. One faction of delegates—the "Anglophiles"—favored awarding Louis an absolute veto over all legislative acts. The other main faction—the "Patriots," whose numbers included Lafayette—preferred giving him no veto at all, or merely one similar to that possessed by the U.S. president, one that could be overridden by the legislators.

———————————

By late August, Lafayette feared that divisions among his Patriot faction were threatening the united front he deemed essential to defeating the Anglophiles. Moreover he worried that, left to themselves, the Anglophiles would enact a declaration that gave the king powers to thwart the assembly's will. Such a declaration, Lafayette feared, would be ill-suited to meet growing challenges to France's governance. Accordingly, on August 25, he had written to Jefferson asking him to host a dinner.[4]

To Jefferson, Lafayette described the gathering as a final chance to prevent a total collapse of civil order:

> We shall be some members of the National Assembly—eight of us whom I want to coalize as being the only means to prevent a dissolution and a civil war.
>
> The difficulty between us is the King's veto—some want it absolute, others will have no veto—and the only way to unite them is to find some means for a suspensive veto so strong and so complicated as to give the King a due influence. If they don't agree in a few days, we shall have no great majority in a favor of any plan, and it must end in a war.[5]

In his own efforts to heal Patriot divisions, Lafayette had already hosted one or two meetings in his home. But after they failed to break the impasse, it occurred to him that Jefferson's presence, and prestige, might inspire more fruitful conversations. Indeed, Lafayette later reflected, he became so fixated on healing that breach, he was even prepared to sacrifice his own governmental preferences: "Whatever they should now agree on, he, at the head of the National force, would maintain."

In his August 25 letter to Jefferson, Lafayette thus emphasized the moment's urgency. "These gentlemen," he wrote, "wish to Consult You and me, they will dine to morrow at your House as Mine is alwais full. I depend on you to receive us. Perhaps will they Be late but I shall Be precisely at three with you and I think this dinner of an immediate and Great importance."[6]

The guests arrived as scheduled on the afternoon of August 26. Like Jefferson, the marquis still had red hair—though that day, like Jefferson's, it was concealed under the powdered wig that he donned on formal occasions. At thirty-two Lafayette was also, like his American friend, still tall and thin. In sartorial aplomb, however, there was no contest between the two men: In his National Guard uniform, with its white-braided, red-collared blue coat with gold epaulets, Lafayette personified martial elegance.

As he and his fellow attendees—seated on decoratively carved chairs upholstered in blue silk—gathered at a fifteen-foot table, the room soon filled with conversation. Typifying Jefferson's hospitality, superb wines, various meats and fishes, as well as vegetables from the estate's garden, soon appeared. Presumably, to encourage candor—and adhering to the current Paris fashion—he had arranged for small serving tables to be placed between each of the guests, thus eliminating the need for the constant coming and going of possibly indiscreet servants—a growing concern at such gatherings in that revolutionary season.[7]

The dinner lasted until ten o'clock; its conversation, by Jefferson's own account, was riveting. Later, doubtless romanticizing the evening, he recalled a "coolness and candor of argument unusual in the conflicts of political opinion . . . truly worthy of being placed in parallel with the finest dialogues of antiquity, as handed to us by Xenophon, by Plato and Cicero." Even so, throughout the evening, Jefferson seldom spoke, later recalling himself as "a silent witness" to the exchanges—a reticence born in part from the continuing limits of his facility with the French language.[8]

Less than thirty-six hours after the gathering—Jefferson's understanding of its exchanges clarified through postdinner conversations with Lafayette—he assumed that he grasped enough of what had transpired to speculate about the evening's consequences. Writing to Madison, he noted that the most enlightened numbers among the Patriots faction had prevailed, and expressed satisfaction that the delegates seemed launched on a sound path—with America's system of governance as "professedly their model." Jefferson was likewise heartened that most of the delegates seemed bent on reducing monarchical, noble, and clerical privileges. More particularly, they favored vesting most powers in a bicameral legislature—the existing assembly coupled with "a senate also, chosen on the plan of our federal senate by the provincial assemblies."

Anticipating deviations by the envisioned government from its American antecedents, Jefferson expected France's reformers to make "such changes" necessary to accommodate "difference[s] of circumstance." In short, after a year of turmoil, he perceived France as close to establishing the form of government that he had long believed, historically and culturally, best suited to the country's unique needs—a constitutional monarchy.

Indeed, decades later—attaching exaggerated significance to the August 26 dinner—Jefferson would memorialize it as marking a milestone in French history: "This Concordate decided the fate of the consti[t]ution," he wrote. "The Patriots all rallied to the principles thus settled, carried every question agreeable to them, and reduced the Aristocracy to insignificance and impotence."

In fact, however, Jefferson's own writings reveal that he initially had a less sanguine, more ambivalent reaction to the evening's discussions. Contrary, for instance, to his later assertion that the dinner "decided the fate of the consti[t]ution," at the time he concluded—correctly—that disagreements over the constitution and other pressing matters would persist among the delegates. And while a consensus among the guests seemed to have expressed support for an approach to self-governance similar to that of America's Patriots, Jefferson worried that some delegates would favor departures from that model "nei-ther necessary nor advantageous."

Pointedly, he suspected that some of those departures would be initiated by delegates "versed in theory and new in the practice of government." Likewise, he worried that the body's members included more *philosophes* than experi-enced lawmakers, and that some delegates seemed "acquainted with man only as they see him in their books & not in the world." Beyond that, he believed the assembly's members included scoundrels "of wicked principles & desperate fortunes, hoping to pillage something in the wreck of their country."

Like Lafayette, Jefferson feared yet another looming danger: the imminent demise of unifying foils. Over the past months Louis and Marie Antoinette had provided reformers—clergy, nobles, and Third Estate alike—a common enemy. But now, as the monarchy faltered before an ascendant national legisla-ture, old divisions were resurfacing; allies, Jefferson noted, "hooped together heretofore by a common enemy, are less compact since their victory." Given that, he believed, prolonged delays in completing France's constitution increased the perils facing the country. Moreover, in the growing popularity of the duc d'Orléans, Jefferson saw a force capable of scuttling all that had been won. The king's cousin—the Palais-Royal's resident-owner—Jefferson inveighed, was "a man of moderate understanding, of no principle, absorbed in low vice."

When the sun rose on August 27—the morning after the dinner—Vendome, Jef-ferson's coachman, hitched up the two horses of the Hôtel de Langeac's car-riage for the twenty-mile ride to Versailles. There Jefferson attended a scheduled meeting with the foreign minister, the count of Montmorin. The tête-à-tête had been arranged to discuss a handful of remaining Franco-American diplomatic matters.

But as they talked, Jefferson grew anxious about his violation of diplomatic protocol the night before. "The duties of exculpation weighed on me." More-over, after five years he knew how the city's diplomatic grapevine worked. Thus, wary that word, likely embellished, of the dinner might find its way back to the court, Jefferson decided to give the foreign minister his own firsthand account of the evening.

With "truth and candor" he recounted the gathering and "how it had happened that my house had been made the scene of conferences of such a character." But after Jefferson completed his mea culpa, France's foreign minister responded with his own surprise: "He told me he already knew everything which had passed." As Jefferson later recalled,

> Far from taking umbrage at the use made of my house on that occasion, he earnestly wished I would habitually assist at such conferences, being sure I should be useful in moderating the warmer spirits, and promoting a wholesome and practicable reformation only.

Montmorin's sources, Jefferson realized, had been even better than he had suspected: "I have no doubt indeed that this conference was previously known and approved by this honest minister, who was in confidence and communication with the patriots, and wished for a reasonable reform of the Constitution."

Jefferson had entered the meeting with a heavy heart. Now he felt unburdened; suddenly it seemed that the advice he had been offering sotto voce to the country's reformers also enjoyed the blessings of the Versailles court—even extending to the foreign minister and the king himself.

Bolstered by the vote of confidence, before leaving, Jefferson reassured Montmorin. "I told him I knew too well the duties I owed to the king, to the nation, and to my own country." Moreover, to the degree that Jefferson played "any part in councils concerning their internal government" in the future, he promised to "persevere with care in the character of a neutral and passive spectator, with wishes only and very sincere ones, that those measures might prevail which would be for the greatest good of the nation."[9]

The two men parted company that morning, each professing confidence that, assisted by the American minister's steadying influence, the coming months would produce a new political order for France—one that would provide greater democracy and also leave Louis XVI securely on the kingdom's throne.

From Versailles, Jefferson hastened back to the Hôtel de Langeac. There he had an important letter to answer—a recently arrived missive whose delay in reaching him only enhanced its significance. To John Jay, Jefferson wrote that day: "I am honoured with your favor of June 19 informing me that permission is given me to make a short visit to my native country, for which indulgence I beg leave to return my thanks to the President, and to yourself."

Ostensibly Jefferson intended, after a stay in Virginia, to return to Paris. But in his bones he assumed that by the time he returned, France's future would belong to a new government, one possibly led by his friend Lafayette. Given that, perhaps Jefferson—facing the end of his own personal connection to the turmoil—felt a need to conflate his own personal history with that of France; if so, he likely had a commensurate need to believe that his August 26 dinner for the delegates had marked a critical juncture in the country's history. Whatever the case, the gathering, for all practical purposes, did bring down the curtain on Thomas Jefferson's French Revolution.[10]

FIFTY-FIVE

Adieus

Days after his August dinner for Lafayette's allies, an illness befell Jefferson, otherwise undetailed amid his papers, that "confined me to my chamber [for] six days." In all probability his indisposition's cause was a migraine—possibly triggered by a family crisis. Indeed, during those days—before and after reassuring France's foreign minister of his desire to keep Louis XVI on his throne—the sovereign of the Hôtel de Langeac was apparently facing his own domestic rebellion.

Jefferson's daughters Patsy, on the eve of her seventeenth birthday, and Polly, now eleven, were both by then comfortable in French and relishing their post-Panthémont Paris life. They thus had no wish to return to Monticello. Adding to Jefferson's discontents, Patsy during those months had developed an infatuation with his twenty-nine-year-old assistant, William Short—affections soon reciprocated by Short.

Under other circumstances Jefferson might have welcomed the prospects of a romance between his sixteen-year-old daughter and his young protégé. But complications provoked his wariness. When Short arrived in Paris in 1784, he was twenty-five years old, handsome, of slight build, and with sandy hair. Shortly thereafter, to improve his language skills, he had left Jefferson's household to live with the Royer family in Saint-Germain-en-Laye, fifteen miles outside of Paris. By April 1785, however, word had reached Jefferson of Short's infatuation with the family's teenage daughter, known familiarly as Lilite.

The details remain murky. But by April 1786, after Congress had formally appointed Short as his private secretary, Jefferson, aware of the relationship— by his lights an impropriety—was beseeching his errant protégé to "come home." In a letter to Short, he made explicit his concerns: "A young man indeed may do without marriage in a great city. In the beginning it is pleasant enough; but take what course he will whether that of rambling, or of a fixed attachment, he will become miserable as he advances in years."

Jefferson's admonitions notwithstanding, in late 1789 Short was probably still conducting his affair with Lilite. Moreover, as Jefferson was aware, the young man was also loath to leave Europe—a circumstance unlikely to have rendered him a desirable husband for his older daughter. As for Patsy, while she by then clearly enjoyed living in Paris, her thoughts during that period—based on her own writings—about returning to Virginia remain unclear.

Sally Hemings, meanwhile, increasingly savoring the relative freedom of movement she enjoyed in Paris, seems by then to have been resisting a return to Virginia. As she was likely aware—the legal process's trouble and costs notwithstanding—France routinely granted petitions for freedom to enslaved persons brought onto its soil. According to the historian Annette Gordon-Reed, in the city of Paris, during the entire eighteenth century, not one such entreaty was rejected. Further complicating matters for Jefferson, Sally Hemings was possibly pregnant with his child. According to Madison Hemings, a son later born to her, soon after arriving in Paris, Sally Hemings became "Mr. Jefferson's concubine," and by the time he was preparing for his return to Virginia, was "'enciente'"—pregnant—"by him."

Sally Hemings was about sixteen as Jefferson prepared to leave Paris, Jefferson forty-six, and whether or not the two had sexual relations in Paris remains unclear. (If not, there is little doubt they did later.) Whether in Paris or Virginia, however, in engaging in such intimacies, Jefferson would have been acting with a license common among slave-owning planters of his milieu.

But while the arrogation of such liberties enjoyed ample precedent within that milieu, their public acknowledgment remained taboo. In Virginia such relations violated publicly affirmed (but privately often breached) strictures against the mixing of races.

In Paris, Jefferson had routinely socialized with Lafayette, Condorcet, the Adamses, and others more liberal than he on matters of race and slavery (if not class). Regardless of how he had broadened his horizons in the arts, he remained, politically and socially, the Virginia slaveholder and planter who had arrived in Paris five years earlier.

Moreover, in Paris, which venerated America for its devotion to *la liberté*, any scrutiny drawing public attention to the presence of enslaved persons in the household of that nation's emissary to France would have exposed Jefferson to embarrassing charges of hypocrisy—still more so if it became known that one of those persons was carrying his child.

Thus, if Jefferson did, while in Paris, have sexual relations with Hemings, he would have done his best to keep it a secret. Patsy Jefferson's biographer Cynthia Kierner speculated that Patsy simply accepted "the extramarital exertions of her widowed father"—or perhaps "was simply unaware of what Jefferson and Hemings did together in some corner of his big Parisian house." None of Patsy's surviving letters, according to Kierner, cast conclusive light on the mystery.

Beyond that, Jefferson's friends in Paris—including Lafayette, Morris, and Trumbull, even without a request from him—would have been disinclined to reveal a Jefferson-Hemings relationship. Minimally they would have exercised discretion when discussing it—if indeed they knew of the alleged relationship. And none mention it in their writings. (Then again—to be fair—such evidential silence might just as easily be deployed to argue that the alleged encounters never occurred.)

Beyond, however, questions of who did or didn't know about the alleged Jefferson-Hemings relationship, Sally in 1789—pregnant or not—surely would have known that, if she returned to Virginia, she faced a bleak future. According to Madison Hemings:

He desired to bring my mother back to Virginia with him but she demurred. She was just beginning to understand the French language well, and in France she was free, while if she returned to Virginia she would be re-enslaved. So she refused to return with him. To induce her to do so he promised her extraordinary privileges, and made a solemn pledge that her children should be freed at the age of twenty-one years. In consequence of his promise, on which she implicitly relied, she returned with him to Virginia.[1]

Sally Hemings left behind no writings, and it remains unclear whether she ever learned to read and write. Reinforcing the silence, no reference to the relationship has been located among Jefferson's surviving writings. Not until the late twentieth century did scholarship, drawing on DNA testing and textual research, by the historian Annette Gordon-Reed confirm as a virtual certainty the persistent reports—first raised publicly by Jefferson's political enemies but long denied by most scholars—of sexual relations between the two.[2]

By August 30 Jefferson had arranged for William Short to serve during his absence as U.S. chargé d'affaires. On Sept. 17 a farewell dinner for Jefferson at the Hôtel de Langeac gathered Lafayette, Gouverneur Morris, the Marquis de Condorcet, and Louis XVI's confidant the duc de la Rochefoucauld-Liancourt. During that evening a skeptical Morris queried Lafayette about the resolve of the National Guard troops under his command.

"He says they will not mount guard when it rains," the American later recorded. "But he thinks they will readily follow him into action. I incline to think that he will have an opportunity of making the experiment."[3]

On September 26 Thomas, Patsy, and Polly Jefferson, along with James and Sally Hemings, departed Paris. Traveling by carriage—with valet de chambre Adrien Petit to assist their overland journey—the party reached Le Havre two days later. From Le Havre, Petit soon returned to Paris. Gales, however, delayed the other travelers for ten days at the Normandy port. At 1:00 a.m, on

October 8, they finally departed Le Havre. Sailing aboard the packet *Anna*, they reached Cowes on the Isle of Wight twenty-six hours later. There they were to meet another ship for their Atlantic crossing. Storms, however, again delayed their departure—giving Jefferson time to read the latest newspaper accounts of events in France. At noon on October 22, after a rainy delay of two weeks, the *Clermont*, an American ship that Trumbull had booked for them, weighed anchor. Days later, as the passengers plunged into the gray heart of their autumnal Atlantic crossing, their last glimpse of the Old World's coast faded like a spent dream behind the stern of their westbound craft.[4]

PART SIX

———

Diverging Paths
1790–1824

FIFTY-SIX

"Despotism to Liberty, in a Feather-Bed"

On April 2, 1790, four months after Jefferson's arrival at Norfolk, Virginia, he finally wrote to Lafayette. Lightheartedly he wrote of his new post ("Behold me, my dear friend, dubbed Secretary of state. . . .") but soon struck a sober tone. The United States—its powers and self-confidence bolstered by its new Constitution—was grappling to find its place among the world's nations; and with powerful administration interests seeking closer ties to England, Jefferson realized that past Franco-American reciprocities likely would soon give way to divergent paths. He thus felt obliged to reassure his Paris friend that "wherever I am, or ever shall be, I shall be sincere in my friendship to you and to your nation."

Writing from the nation's recently established New York capital—after "ten days harnessed in new gear"—Jefferson soon turned to events in France. Since he left Paris, the news from France had only worsened—with riots continuing to flare across the country's entire breadth. Even so, writing to Lafayette, Jefferson sought to put a bright face on the latest news; one cannot know what was in his heart: Possibly recalling his own anguish during his days as Virginia's governor, perhaps he sought to provide moral encouragement to his friend. Or perhaps—amid the challenges facing him in New York—Jefferson's past preoccupations with matters in France, as he had put it to Madame de Corny—were becoming in his mind less flesh-and-blood reality than "those of a romance."

Whatever his inner thoughts, Jefferson, writing to Lafayette, now, once again, eschewed his past term of choice—"civil war"—to describe the tumult into which France was slipping. In its place he again deployed the word "revolution" in its political usage with its more (to Jefferson) hopeful connotations: "So far it seemed that your revolution had got along with a steady pace: meeting indeed occasional difficulties and dangers, but we are not to expect to be translated from despotism to liberty, in a feather-bed." But even as Jefferson expressed his blithe hopes concerning what he now called France's "revolution," he could not conceal concerns for his friend's safety: "I have never feared for the ultimate result, tho' I have feared for you personally."

Unbeknownst to Jefferson as he wrote to Lafayette that April of 1790, the challenges his friends in France were facing were escalating at a pace beyond his imagination. Indeed, the chances of France being "translated from despotism to liberty, in a feather-bed" were daily withering. Not that such hopes did not persist in France. Indeed, even as political divisions continued to beset the country's fragile constitutional monarchy, the Revolution's defenders, in cities and villages, had taken to staging "festivals of federation" to shore up support for the new government. The elaborately staged events involved specially designed costumes, sets, and music composed for the occasion.

On February 4, 1790, Louis—belatedly, by many lights—had appeared before the National Constituent Assembly and sworn to "defend and maintain constitutional liberty, whose principles the general will, in accord with my own, has sanctioned."

In that same spirit—and in accord with decrees, passed in August 1789, abolishing feudalism—the National Assembly, on June 19, 1790, officially abolished all noble ranks and titles. The Revolution had already abolished the collection of tithes by the country's Catholic Church, confiscated the Church's lands and banned monastic vows; and on July 12, completing the church-to-state subordination, the assembly formally dissolved all religious orders. For better or worse, a new day was dawning.[1]

FIFTY-SEVEN

"Cromwell Would Not Have
Entered Alone"

A mong the other news that Jefferson had learned from the newspapers he read in fall 1789 during his layover at the Isle of Wight's port of Cowes was that, on the morning of October 5—nine days after he departed Paris—a mob there, dominated by market women angered by high bread prices, had gathered on the Place de Grève. The assemblage brandished pitchforks and pikes; more ominously they rolled cannons over the plaza's cobblestones; equally troubling, some among their numbers had just been ejected by National Guardsmen from the Hôtel de Ville when Lafayette arrived on the scene later that morning.

Convinced that an aristocratic plot promulgated by the king had caused the high prices, and that an attack on Paris was imminent, the mob's leaders were soon calling for a march to Versailles. Lafayette opposed such a display; and from nine o'clock that morning to four that afternoon, in closed meetings and public debates in the Place de Grève, he tried to dissuade the mob from that course.

Around five o'clock, however, upon learning that part of the mob had already set out for Versailles, Lafayette decided to try to control what he could not defeat:

In a by-then-pounding rain—mounting his white horse and leading several thousand National Guard soldiers—he rode off to catch up with the marchers.

Louis and Marie Antoinette were both away from the palace when Lafayette, his National Guard troops, and the thirty thousand Parisian marchers arrived at Versailles that afternoon. By that evening, after both had returned, a stalemate had set in: The protesters—their march blocked by a fence with a locked gate that surrounded the château—stood face-to-face with royal forces protecting those inside.

Upon reaching Versailles just before midnight, Lafayette had called on the National Constituent Assembly, meeting in a special evening session at the Hôtel des Menus-Plaisirs. There—amid rising confusion over the motives of the king as well as those of the citizens outside—the delegates debated how best to avert the looming disaster. Toward that end, they eventually agreed to dispatch Lafayette to meet with Louis.

After midnight, accompanied by two members of Paris's civilian government, Lafayette made his way on foot through the crowds already filling the Place d'Armes, the fan-shaped plaza on the château's eastern side. When they reached its locked gates, the Swiss Guard detail posted there initially balked at admitting them. But after receiving word that Lafayette was expected, they cautiously admitted the three into the château's inner courtyard. Once inside the palace, they were escorted upstairs and entered the royal apartments.

There the men were soon escorted into the Salon de l'Oeil de Boeuf (Bull's-Eye Room), one of the king's antechambers. As they entered a member of the royal court—invoking the name of the British general responsible for the execution of Charles I—shouted: "There's Cromwell!"

"Cromwell would not have entered alone," Lafayette answered. But his nimble riposte notwithstanding, he knew he faced a perilous situation. One abrupt move and, as he later recalled, "instead of being a guardian, he would have been a usurper."

To Louis, in a trembling voice, Lafayette explained the circumstances that had brought him to the royal chamber: "Sire, I thought it better to come here, to die at the feet of Your Majesty, than to die uselessly on the Place de Grève."

Present with the king were his brother the duc de Provence, Necker, and other advisers. Asked to specify the demands they carried, the three answered as the king listened intently. As they heard out their visitors, Louis and his advisers realized that they had already provisionally or even publicly granted several of their demands—including Louis's acceptance of the Declaration of Rights, his recognition of the National Constituent Assembly, and royal assistance in addressing Paris's shortage of bread.

Two of Lafayette's demands, however, stood out as new to their interlocutors—that Louis entrust the National Guard troops in Paris and Versailles to serve as his sole bodyguards, and that he and the court accompany Lafayette back to Paris and take up permanent residence there in the Tuileries, the royal palace abandoned by Louis XIV in 1672, when he decamped for Versailles, and since then used as a public theater and gardens.

To the demand regarding his personal bodyguard, Louis eventually indicated his acceptance; as for the suggestion that he move to Paris, he gave no answer. In the meantime he accepted Lafayette's offer to attempt to placate the crowds gathered outside the château, and thus defuse a standoff growing more fraught with each passing hour. Indeed, later that morning, a handful of armed protesters slipped into the royal apartments and briefly confronted the palace guards. Though the intruders were quickly repelled, one guard was killed by gunfire.

Moreover, by daybreak on October 6 the demonstrators gathered outside, finding allies among the king's forces, were amiably conversing with the same soldiers with whom, hours earlier, they had almost clashed. But as the morning sun renewed the crowd's rage, calls rose among its numbers for the king and queen to appear before them. By then, the Parisians were focused on a singular demand—that both the royal court and the national assembly relocate to Paris, capital of *la nation*.

Amid Versailles's disarray, noisy demonstrators now filled the *cour de marbre*, the marble courtyard, an ornate space just outside the royal apartments, normally accessible only to the king and his family. And when the din showed no sign of waning, Lafayette, though weary from a sleepless night, decided to address the demonstrators. Stepping from the royal apartments onto a second-floor balcony overlooking the courtyard, he tried with little success to tamp down their calls.

Eventually giving up, he stepped inside to where Louis and Marie Antoinette had been discreetly observing his efforts and made them an offer: If the royal couple were to accompany him back to Paris, he would guarantee their safety.

Barely hesitating, the two accepted his offer.

Moments later, at Lafayette's suggestion, Louis stepped onto the balcony and announced his intention of going to Paris, of trusting his welfare "to the love of my good and faithful subjects."

As the applause that greeted Louis's decision faded, he and Lafayette returned inside. Both the king and the queen, however, were taken aback by Lafayette's next proposal. "Come with me," he said, looking at Marie Antoinette.

Cautiously she agreed to greet her subjects. Leaving Lafayette and Louis inside, but taking her two children with her, she stepped onto the balcony. The crowd below, however, objected noisily: "No children."

After taking her children inside, the queen returned to the balcony and—standing alone and vulnerable—nervously faced her subjects.

Moments later, to the surprise of all, Lafayette joined Marie-Antoinette on the balcony. And in a gesture that he later recalled as entirely improvised, the Hero of Two Worlds, bowing low, kissed his queen's hand.

Lafayette's enemies later saw his gesture as emblematic of his duplicity—of an alleged tendency to toggle between Patriot and Royalist causes; whatever his motivations that day, his gesture certainly risked alienating Patriot partisans. But, then again, Lafayette deemed the king and queen essential for the creation of the constitutional monarchy that he envisioned for France. Beyond that, he genuinely liked the royal couple. After all, while he, like other Patriots, had been given cause in recent months to resent the two, they remained, in his mind, flesh-and-blood personages—rather than mere symbols of Royalist excess. To be sure, as recently as the fall of 1786, Lafayette had regularly socialized with the king. Similarly, his association with Marie Antoinette stretched back to his adolescence when, at a court function, he had awkwardly danced with her. Moreover, his ties to the queen were deepened by his spouse's close friendship with her.[1]

But if Lafayette gambled that day, he won mightily.

As he kissed Marie Antoinette's hand and rose from his bow, cries of *"Vive la reine!"*—a phrase unheard for many years—rose from the courtyard below.

That afternoon—October 6, 1789, at six o'clock, the royal family—riding in a carriage flanked by Lafayette mounted on his white horse—left Versailles for Paris. A hundred carriages, carrying National Constituent Assembly delegates, trailed behind them. Thousands of others marched on foot—among them the Parisian market women who had prompted the original march from Paris to Versailles. Hours later, after nightfall, the royal family moved into a complex of apartments inside the Tuileries Palace, just west of the Louvre, on the Seine's Right Bank.

The following November, the National Constituent Assembly, leaving Versailles's Hôtel des Menus-Plaisirs, followed Louis to the Tuileries. There, the delegates converted into an assembly hall a high-ceilinged cavernous building, the Salle du Manège, formerly a royal riding academy on the palace grounds.

Thanks to Lafayette's deft, often improvised leadership, a calamitous two-day episode had ended with minimal violence—two royal guards had died at Versailles—and a restoration of order. Even so, the coming months would bring no cessation of discord: Indeed, ominously, five days after moving into his gilded cage at the Tuileries Palace, Louis XVI would secretly write to King Charles IV of Spain, alleging mistreatment. Louis's younger brother the comte d'Artois, meanwhile, was writing to Austria's emperor Joseph II (whom Lafayette had met four years earlier in Vienna), asking that Joseph launch an invasion of France to rescue his sister Marie Antoinette.

On July 14, 1780, eleven months after Jefferson had sailed from France, a crowd estimated at 350,000 gathered in a specially constructed amphitheater on Paris's west to commemorate the one-year anniversary of the Bastille's fall. Present for the Paris festivities—on the Champ de Mars, site of today's Eiffel Tower—was the entire National Constituent Assembly and court officials, including the king himself. The Revolution that summer remained in the path of political crosswinds. Even so, Lafayette, as commander of the National Guard, remained the Revolution's dominant leader.

As it turned out, hard rains gusted by high winds of the literal sort intermittently pounded the field much of the day. But the festival—the Fête de la Fédération—reached its emotional apogee late in the afternoon as the showers abated. Following a Latin Mass, as sunlight pierced the day's clouds, Lafayette—accompanied by the rumble of five hundred drums—solemnly climbed the high altar's steps. Gouverneur Morris, present for the pageant, recalled the moment when the nation's hero reached the platform's top: "Lafayette placed his sword on the altar, and gave the signal for taking the oath. One moment of intense silence, while he swore to be faithful to nation and king; then all swords drawn, all arms raised, and from all lips came the oath, 'I swear.'" Moments later, Louis XVI, rising from his seat, dutifully reciprocated the oath: "I, King of the French, swear to protect the constitution I have accepted," he vowed—his words immediately followed by those of Marie Antoinette: "The king's sentiments are mine," she said.

"Frantic enthusiasm," Morris reported, greeted the vows, and Lafayette did not disappoint his admirers that day. Others, however, found their affections waning for what many saw as Lafayette's growing penchant for theatrical preening. Typifying such wariness, the weekly *Révolutions de Paris* mocked his presentation that day and its over-the-top acclamation by the event's nominal sponsors—the *fédérés*, representing National Constituent Assembly members from across the country; following Lafayette's oath, the journal reported, crowds rushed him to kiss "his hands, his thighs, and boots." Even his white horse became an object of adulation. Mindful of a horse elevated by the Roman emperor Caligula to his government's senate, the correspondent noted: "Had there been any election at that time, the popular madness might have bestowed upon Lafayette's mount similar honors."[2]

Over the coming months Parisians debated the degree of Louis's fealty to the country's still-fragile constitutional monarchy. Even so, most observers were convinced that—however grudgingly or in his own self-interest—he supported the arrangement. In late June 1791, however, the city awoke to disturbing news: In a scheme concocted by the queen days earlier, Louis and Marie Antoinette, on the evening of June 20–21, 1791, had fled the Tuileries Palace. Traveling in two carriages, the couple and a royal entourage—disguised as the party of a

Russian baroness—had set off for Montmédy, a French military citadel on the kingdom's northeastern frontier.

To this day, murkiness surrounds the purpose of the royal couple's trip and its destination. Louis later claimed that he had desired only, at a safe distance from Paris, to renegotiate the constitution. His critics countered that, bent on fomenting a counterrevolution, he intended to return to France with an army of Royalist soldiers from Marie Antoinette's native Austria. Whatever the couple's intentions, fifty miles southwest of Montmédy, their entourage, having been recognized at an earlier stop, was detained in the village of Varennes. There, the couple was eventually arrested and—pending other arrangements— returned to their Paris palace.

The foiled escape, undermining the constitutional monarchy's fragile popular support, energized radicals who favored an outright republic, a polity shorn of even figurehead monarchs. Likewise, the royal couple's alleged duplicity— supposedly scheming with Austria's royal court—seemed to confirm rumors of foreign meddling in France's politics. Lafayette and other reformers of aristocratic origins, meanwhile, quickly found themselves uncomfortably cast as defenders of the old order.

Increasingly, even as Lafayette's conservative critics suspected him of being an "Auvergnac Cromwell," reformers accused him of Royalist sympathies. Indeed, by then suspicions of the latter were so widespread that rumors were linking him romantically with Marie Antoinette. Though ill founded, the allegations even found their way into a series of underground pornographic books funded by political opponents, that depicted Marie Antoinette—the subject of other such slanders—and Lafayette in flagrante delicto.

In late June, 1791, when Parisians learned of Louis and Marie-Antoinette's arrested flight toward exile, turmoil was already roiling their city. That same month, the termination of a public-relief work project had left thousands of men jobless. By the middle of the next month, public indignation over both—the royal couple's attempted escape and the labor unrest—was stirring mass protests.

Sparking more agitation, the National Constituent Assembly, on July 15, voted to clear Louis of all criminal charges for his attempted flight. The vote followed the king's promise to accept a new constitution the assembly intended to promulgate. More saliently, particularly for Lafayette, the body's exoneration of Louis came after it decided to prosecute the Marquis de Bouillé for the royal couple's foiled escape. Fueling more public ire, the delegates also voted to restore Louis's former centrality in France's government.

Outraged, Paris's radicals began planning a protest: on the morning of July 17, they would assemble at the site of the Bastille; and, from there, march to the Champ de Mars, site of the previous year's Fête de la Fédération. There, on the altar platform constructed for the 1790 fete, they would conduct an en masse signing of a petition demanding that Louis be held accountable for his attempted flight.

Before noon on the 17th, crowds of Parisians, "perhaps 50,000" by one estimate, were already at the Champ de Mars's altar when two men were discovered, for reasons still unclear, to be hiding under the platform. Accused of being royalist sympathizers with plans to detonate an explosive, both were set upon and lynched by the crowd. Their heads *de rigueur* were soon removed, mounted on pikes, and paraded around the field.

Earlier that morning, as the demonstrators had marched to the Champ de Mars, they had intermittently fought with Lafayette and the National Guard. One demonstrator, without success, even attempted to assassinate him. That afternoon, after word of the lynchings reached the Hôtel de Ville, Mayor Bailly declared martial law and set off with a National Guard battalion for the crime scene; once there, he intended to join forces with Guardsmen under Lafayette's command. That evening, however, when the two leaders met, they were greeted with a hail of rocks hurled by demonstrators.

Lafayette later claimed that National Guardsmen answered the provocations with musket-discharges, warning shots, fired into the air. Whatever actually happened that day, the gunfire escalated into a lethal fusillade that left many demonstrators dead or wounded. Accounts of casualties vary widely—from about fifty to hundreds killed. But the demonstrators sustained the heaviest losses. More saliently for Lafayette, the incident—soon known as the Champ de Mars massacre—destroyed his revolutionary credentials.

By late 1791 the omens were clear: For the Hero of Two Worlds, an avalanche loomed; on June 2, anticipating catastrophe, he wrote to Jefferson: "Altho Every Motive of Regard and Affection Conspire to Make me Lament our separation. I Lament it still more on Account of our Revolution wherein Your Advices would Have Greatly Helped us, and Could Not fail to Have Had a Great Weight Among our Constitution Makers."[3]

Through the summer of 1791 Lafayette—though linked in the public mind with Louis's failed escape and the civilian deaths on the Champ de Mars—had remained determined to cling to public office. By fall, however, bowing to inevitability, he resigned his National Guard command. Declaring himself retired, he returned to Chavaniac, in his native Auvergne, vowing to reside—for the first time in his adult life—at his boyhood home, the Château de Chavaniac.

That same fall, meanwhile, Louis XVI finally accepted France's first constitution, and moderates urged a declaration that the Revolution had reached its end. Radicals, however—quickly dominating the country's latest representative body, the newly created Legislative Assembly—rejected the suggestion.

Simultaneously, fears were growing across France of a counterrevolution sponsored by forces abroad—exiled conservative émigrés in league with absolutist monarchs. Both had threatened actions to restore the unfettered powers of France's Bourbons. In December 1791, France's minister of war summoned Lafayette from his barely begun "retirement" to lead the Army of the North, one of three forces deployed to thwart any such incursions. Departing Chavaniac, he hastened to Metz, in northeastern France, and took up his new command.

By spring 1792, as the Revolution grew ever more anti-Royalist in tone, the kingdoms of Austria and Prussia began actively planning an invasion of France. In response Louis, on April 20—under duress and by then reduced to figurehead status—declared war on both countries. In Metz, meanwhile, Lafayette—drilling his troops and drawing on his American experiences from a decade earlier—was attempting to overcome dire shortages in manpower and matériel.

There he also corresponded with both Washington and Jefferson. To Lafayette, Washington confessed of feeling "not a little anxious for your personal safety, and I have yet no grounds for removing that anxiety." For his part, Jefferson—still secretary of state and increasingly embroiled in American foreign policy disputes—congratulated his friend for commanding an army dedicated to fighting "the monster Aristocracy, and . . . its associate Monarchy."

Turning to U.S. politics, Jefferson commented on what he saw as his own battle against royalist forces. Specifically he chastised Philadelphia colleagues who seemed to effectively favor the implementation of "an English constitution" for the United States—ironically the same form of government that Jefferson, while in Paris, had prescribed for France.[4]

In Metz, meanwhile, Lafayette, following events in Paris, anguished over the growing factionalism in France's politics. On June 16, writing to the Legislative Assembly, he lambasted growing discords that were, by his lights, endangering France's constitution and its liberties. His principal target was Paris's radicals—particularly those of the city's Jacobin Club. In Lafayette's view, the increasingly powerful club was "organized like a separate empire" and "blindly controlled by a few ambitious leaders." Moreover, he warned that the Jacobins constituted "a sect," a "distinct corporation in the middle of the French people, whose powers they usurp by subjugating their representatives."

Over the coming days Lafayette's letter, widely published in newspapers, earned its author the enmity of the radical leader Maximilien Robespierre. A former legislative colleague of Lafayette's, Robespierre had by then become an influential member of the Legislative Assembly. Fatefully for Lafayette, the thirty-four-year-old Artois-born lawyer was also a leader of the Jacobin Club, and on June 18 Robespierre opened the club's discussion of his former colleague's letter with a stark admonition: "Strike down Lafayette and the nation is saved."

Two days later, as antiroyalist sentiments surged, thousands of armed radicals invaded the Tuileries Palace and threatened the king. The confrontation, however, ended peacefully: Louis—ever willing to adopt the Revolution's symbols to defuse immediate perils—even donned a red "liberty cap." For good measure, sharing wine with the insurgents, he offered them a royal toast.

Upon learning of the Tuileries attack, Lafayette—without seeking permission from anyone in Paris or notifying any of his aides in Metz—immediately left for the capital. Appearing on June 28 before the Legislative Assembly, he condemned the attack on the palace and demanded that its perpetrators be "pursued and punished as traitors."

From Robespierre's perspective, Lafayette's appearance before the assembly not only confirmed his Royalist sympathies; it also reaffirmed the necessity of permanently removing him from France's public life. Indeed, from the perspective of Paris's radicals, Lafayette's very presence in the city—when he was supposed to be commanding an army in Metz—in itself constituted dereliction of duty. A measure of the radicals' ire, a fifteen-page pamphlet entitled *Crimes of Lafayette in France*, soon appeared.

Pressing an accusation briefly mentioned in the pamphlet but developed at length over the coming weeks, the radicals accused Lafayette of joining Royalist intrigues sponsored by the German-born general Nicolas Luckner, then commanding France's Army of the Rhine. The evidence for such activity was dubious—mainly words from the two officers' correspondence parsed for improbable meanings. Even so, the Royalist stain on Lafayette's reputation was now indelible.

That June, in 1792, Lafayette had returned to Metz after speaking before the Legislative Assembly. But even in his absence, events in Paris continued to erode his prestige. In July thousands of *fédérés*—National Guardsmen from France's provinces—streamed into the city to attend the annual July 14 celebration. But some of the arriving soldiers had plans beyond the festivities; from Paris, they intended to continue northward and reinforce France's armies deployed on its northern frontiers.

Indeed, even after the July 14 fete—as fears waxed of imminent invasion by Austrian forces—guardsmen were still arriving in Paris. Over those weeks bonds hardened between the newly arrived *fédérés* and radicals in Paris's government, military, and citizenry. And, on the morning of August 10—in a coordinated assault resulting from those ties—forces representing Paris's city government, newly styling itself a revolutionary commune, seized the Tuileries Palace. The king and queen managed to escape and find refuge in the Legislative Assembly. Others, however, were less fortunate. Before mid-day, nine hundred souls lay dead in and around the palace—two-thirds of them Swiss Guards.

On August 13 Paris's revolutionary commune arrested Louis and Marie Antoinette and moved them to Paris's Temple Prison. A week later the body decreed that all persons be addressed as "Citizen"—*Citoyen* or *Citoyenne*—rather than "Monsieur" or "Madame." Three weeks later, between September 2 and 6, in a horrifying glimpse of future violence, some twelve hundred inmates of Paris's prisons were summarily executed by mobs or by mob-inspired extralegal revolutionary "tribunals." Rumors of the prisoners rising up to assist foreign invaders and royalist forces inspired the killings, soon known as the September massacres. Their numbers included more than two hundred priests who had refused to submit to restrictions imposed on clergy by the Revolution.

On September 22 France's national legislature officially declared the country a republic. Even so—weeks earlier, on the evening of August 10—the world of Louis, Marie-Antoinette, and thousands of other aristocrats and liberals, including Lafayette and his family, was already being turned upside down. That evening and in the days after the mob invasion of the Tuileries Palace, France's weakened Legislative Assembly effectively abdicated all its powers to the insurgent Commune of Paris and a hurriedly gathered Provisional Executive Council—both soon replaced by a self-declared National Convention.

Underscoring its ambitions, the convention decreed a new calendar for France—designating September 22, 1792, the day after the monarchy had been abolished—as the start of a new Republican era. The new calendar likewise decreed a new ten-day week and new names—all purged of mythical or religious associations—for all days and months.

Worsening Lafayette's plight, even as Paris's radicals were branding him a traitor, monarchical governments across Europe, fearful for their survival, were castigating him as an agent of France's Revolution. Further inflaming the crisis, to suppress those forces Austrian and Prussian were soon massing troops along France's northern border. More ominously, an invasion ostensibly intent on merely restoring France's Bourbon dynasty was also secretly bent on territorial conquest.

On August 17 the Provisional Executive Council promulgated an order ending Lafayette's army command and summoning him to Paris. Two days later the Legislative Assembly—weakened but now dominated by radicals— adopted a resolution accusing him of "plotting against the nation and of trea- son against the nation."

When word of his removal from his command and the summons to go to Paris reached Lafayette, hc was encamped at Sedan, in northern France, with troops of his Army of the North. But knowing a death sentence when he read one, he decided that the time had come to flee his native land. He would, he decided, go to a neutral—Dutch—port and embark for England. There he would gather his family and sail to permanent exile in America.[5]

FIFTY-EIGHT

A Clomping of
Approaching Horses

On August 19, 1792, in the Austrian-ruled Netherlands (today's Belgium), just outside the northeastern gate of the town of Rochefort, a steady drizzle dampened the unseasonably cold evening. Fifteen soldiers of the Austrian Hapsburg Empire's army, standing guard, were warming themselves at campfires. The cadre belonged to a vast mobilization of Prussian and Austrian forces—later known as the First Coalition—gathered along France's northern border, poised for invasion. Indeed, even as the guards hovered over their fires, some of their cohorts were already crossing into France. Ostensibly the invading forces intended merely to restore France's Bourbon king and queen to their throne, but they also carried secret orders to retain conquered territory.

Shortly after nine that night, a clomping of approaching horses interrupted the soldiers' reverie. Reaching for loaded muskets, they aimed in the sound's direction. Amid the bustle, a stranger on horseback, wearing a French army officer's uniform, rode into their midst. Though French, he spoke German. Introducing himself as Jean-Xavier Bureau de Pusy, until recently a captain of engineers in the French Army, he told them that, disenchanted by a recent coup by Paris's radicals—he had decided to flee his homeland.

Speaking to the sentries' commander, Pusy elaborated that, as a noncombatant bound for nearby neutral Holland, he was requesting right of transit through Coalition-held territory. Pusy then added that he was not alone: Some forty men—several other officers and their servants—were waiting for him farther back on the road. After pondering the request, Capt. Comte Philippe d'Harnoncourt agreed to authorize the safe passage. He and his cadre would even escort the Frenchmen into Rochefort and arrange lodging for them for the night. His request granted, Pusy backtracked down the road to gather his fellow émigrés.

In total the entourage that Pusy soon returned with included twenty-one officers, twenty-three servants, and fifty-nine horses. Plans called for the train to pass through the Rochefort gate and its men to be escorted to an inn. However, as the entourage passed through the gate—with still more soldiers and onlookers lining the town's single road—someone in the crowd recognized one of the passing officers.

The consequences of the officer's "canine appetite for popularity and fame," decried years earlier by a friend, now imperiled his passage. Assuming that his best hope lay in candor, General Lafayette—until recently commander of France's Army of the North—ordered Pusy to introduce him to Harnoncourt. In the ensuing conversation Lafayette reiterated his plans to go to Holland.

Harnoncourt, however, answered that he felt obliged to alert his commanding officer of the presence of such a prominent French officer. For the evening, he explained, Lafayette and his men would be lodged at the local Auberge du Pelican. But first the soldiers would have to be searched, and guards posted to prevent their leaving. More ominously, Harnoncourt also added, the Frenchmen, before leaving Rochefort, would be required to obtain passports signed by the Coalition's regional commander, Maj. Gen. Johann von Moitelle, in Namur, forty miles to the north.

Lafayette protested, rebuking Harnoncourt for breaking his word. Moreover, he and the other French officers soon drafted a statement asserting that, having renounced their country and commissions, they were officially noncombatants—and therefore entitled to safe passage under international law.

The next day Moitelle, learning of Lafayette's detention, reacted with glee. Moreover, as word of his capture rose up the First Coalition's chain of command, it became clear that, for the time being, no passports would be issued for the captured men. For all practical purposes they had become prisoners of the Austrian forces.

When news of Lafayette's capture reached Paris, his Jacobin adversaries erupted in joy: "Lafayette has just escaped the law, but he cannot escape the hatred of the nation and the horror of posterity," crowed one Legislative Assembly delegate. Still another deputy proposed the razing of the Hôtel de Lafayette and in its place the erection of a pillar marking Lafayette's perfidy. The town house was not immediately demolished but instead confiscated and eventually sold. A mob, however, did burst into the Hôtel de Ville and destroy Houdon's bust of Lafayette. To a confidant, the Paris writer, salonnière, and only daughter of Jacques Necker, Madame de Staël (a friend of both Jefferson and Lafayette), soon pronounced the captured officer "the most hated man of France."

That August, meanwhile, Adrienne was still living at the Château de Chavaniac, where she and her husband had moved a year earlier. There, as France's Revolution acquired an increasingly anti-aristocratic cast, her worries over the welfare of her absent husband increasingly mingled with those for herself and their children. Even so, Lafayette had remained characteristically sanguine about their future—and ever determined to get to Holland. There at The Hague, if all went as planned, he would be assisted by William Short.

Jefferson's former assistant remained a diplomat. Having failed to obtain his mentor's former post as U.S. minister to France, Short that year had secured a position as minister to the Dutch Republic; and Lafayette had already written to Short. In a letter from Rochefort claiming American citizenship, he requested Short's intervention with Austrian officials to win his release. And in another letter from Rochefort—to Adrienne, written on August 21—he repeated his determination to reach Holland and England, both still neutrals in the war against France:

> I am making no apology at all, either to my children or to you, for having ruined my family. Not a single one of you would have wanted to benefit from

my having acted against my conscience. Come join me in England; let us establish ourselves in America; we will find there the liberty that no longer exists in France, and my love will try to compensate you for all the joys you have lost.[1]

The following day, however, August 22, his petition to Short came to naught, and Lafayette was transferred from Rochefort to Namur. There, he and the other detainees were received hospitably by Austrian officials; during a brief stay at a former Franciscan monastery, a succession of officers, flattering Lafayette and stressing his heroism in America, praised him as a defender of liberty and George Washington. But when one officer addressed him as "Marquis," Lafayette corrected him, noting his support for the National Assembly's 1790 abolition of France's noble titles.

Yet another officer, Gen. Prince Charles-Eugéne de Lorraine (formerly of Lambesc) praised Lafayette's devotion to constitutionalism. He added that Austria's court did not necessarily consider Lafayette an enemy—and would treat him according to international law, and ultimately provide him a passport to a neutral country.

However, when Lorraine intimated that that same court would be even more disposed to extend those courtesies were the distinguished prisoner to share his knowledge of French military plans, Lafayette reacted indignantly—vowing that he would never betray his principles or country. Eventually Austrian officials at Namur, after failing to entice Lafayette's cooperation, seized the captives' personal effects, formally declared them prisoners of war, and dispatched them to Antwerp.

The following morning the prisoners were moved forty miles southeast, from Namur to the town of Nivelles, also in present-day Belgium. By then, unbeknownst to Lafayette, Prussia's ruler, Frederick William II, was already taking a keen interest in his case. As crown prince, Frederick William had met Lafayette during his Prussian tour, and silently witnessed the exchange in which his uncle Frederick the Great coyly asked if Lafayette knew the fate of "a young man who, after visiting countries that embraced ideas of liberty and equality, took it upon himself to import those ideas into his own country." Frederick William had likewise heard his uncle's answer to his own question: "He was hanged."

Given his memories of Lafayette's 1785 visit to Prussia, Frederick William had not forgotten the captive officer appearing before him. Moreover, since those years, among Europe's courts Lafayette had come to be associated with the Revolution that had upended France's Bourbon throne. His name had also become attached to the increasingly popular cause of constitutional government—a proposition equally anathema to Europe's despots.

Therefore viewing Lafayette as a danger to all of Europe's thrones, Frederick William had reacted with delight upon learning of his capture. Indeed, from the monarch's perspective, Lafayette's mission was "to foment insurrection everywhere he believes it his duty to preach." Thus, Frederick William concluded, the French officer should be held captive until Louis XVI could be restored to France's throne—and only then should his ultimate fate be decided.

By then Frederick William had notified Austrian officials that, by the laws of both Prussia and Austria, Lafayette, and possibly the other captured officers, warranted classification as prisoners of state, not prisoners of war. The former category was assigned to inmates deemed, for ideological reasons, an ongoing threat to the state. Frederick William also asked Austria's emperor Francis II to permit the prisoners to be transferred to Prussian soil and into Prussian custody—more distant from Paris than the Austrian Netherlands.

———

By August 23, when the prisoners reached Nivelles, Austrian officials there had their orders: Acting on instructions from Frederick William, the prisoners were informed of their respective immediate fates. Twelve of the officers—those whose only military service in the French Revolution had been with the National Guard—were released and ordered to leave Austrian Hapsburg territories immediately.

Lafayette, three other officers, and their servants, however, were assigned a less certain fate. They were to be transferred to Luxembourg, Austria's headquarters for its invasion of France. There a military tribunal would formally hear their case. Like Lafayette, the three other officers singled out for the Luxembourg tribunal were formerly politically prominent in France's Revolution as members of the national legislature: Alexandre-Théodore-Victor, comte de Lameth; Marie-Charles-César de Faÿ, comte de La Tour-Maubourg; and Jean-Xavier Bureau de Pusy. Indeed Maubourg and Lameth had numbered among Lafayette's allies who had secretly gathered under Thomas Jefferson's roof in August 1789.

Upon learning of his continued detention, Lafayette—recalling Frederick the Great's he-was-hanged anecdote—became convinced that imminent execution awaited. Indeed, during that period, even as Lafayette continued to refuse to cooperate with his captors, he wrote to Frederick William demanding his release. The monarch never replied. Thus, by September, when Lafayette appeared before the Luxembourg tribunal, his conviction seemed a foregone conclusion. The panel was, after all, dominated by men of a royalist bent—including a Prussian minister and a nobleman designated to represent the imprisoned Louis XVI. The trial, as its most famous defendant recalled, produced predictable results: "After each member had sung my praises in the name of his government, it was decided that the existence of M. de Lafayette . . . was incompatible with the security of the governments of Europe."

In the end the tribunal, ordering the four officers' indefinite detention, officially declared them prisoners of state. Singling out Lafayette, the Prussian minister called him "not only the man of the French Revolution, but of universal liberty"—a devotion, he added, that Lafayette had proved in both America and Europe. Although Prussia five years earlier had managed to tamp down a Dutch rebellion, the Prussian minister warned that Lafayette's "mere presence"—were he free—"would electrify all of Holland." For Lafayette the verdict offered cold comfort. He would live another day—or weeks, months, perhaps years. But the pronouncement offered no certainty of his eventual release. Nor, for that matter, did it preclude a later appointment with the executioner.

In short order the monarchs of Austria and Prussia decided that the four officers, for their continued incarceration, would be held in a citadel in Wesel in Prussia's Rhineland—more distant from the war front than the Austrian Netherlands and therefore less vulnerable to French supporters who might seek to rescue the prisoners.

Befitting high officers of that day, the prisoners would be permitted to be joined by their servants during their imprisonment. Thus, after being brought to Wesel, Lafayette and the three other officers, handed over by Austrian soldiers to their Prussian allies, began their new life as prisoners of state on September 12, 1792. The presence of their servants notwithstanding, their captivity did not begin auspiciously: Not allowed to communicate with one another, each of the four officers was confined to his own cramped, vermin-infested cell. In Lafayette's case, however, prohibitions banning the sending or receiving of mail isolated him still more from the outside world.[2]

On September 20, 1792, France's National Convention, having replaced the Legislative Assembly as the nation's governing body, met in its first session. In the next session, by unanimous vote, it abolished the monarchy. Soon thereafter, further emboldening the Convention's deputies, stunning news reached Paris: On September 20 French forces had defeated Prussian invaders at the Battle of Valmy in northern France.

On December 3 the Convention voted to place Louis on trial for "conspiring against liberty" and attempting to injure "the safety of the state." Indeed, in retrospect, the monarchy's abolition had ratified an ongoing campaign of persecution against the Revolution's perceived domestic enemies. And in what soon grew into an orgy of violence, on January 21, 1793, the thirty-eight-year-old Louis XVI was guillotined in a Paris plaza recently renamed the Place de la Révolution—the same expanse (not far from Jefferson's Hôtel de Langeac) formerly called the Place Louis XV and today called the Place de la Concorde. There also, nine months later—on October 16, two weeks shy of her thirty-eighth birthday—Marie Antoinette followed her late husband to the guillotine.[3]

FIFTY-NINE

Reign of Terror

The Greeks thought they had as many gods as fountains, and the Persians as many as they could see stars, so the French reckon up as many kings as they see gallows.

—Victor Hugo, *Notre-Dame de Paris*

On September 10, 1792, three weeks after her husband was detained in the Austrian-ruled Netherlands, Adrienne Lafayette was placed under house arrest at the Château de Chavaniac. The following month in Paris, her sister, mother, and grandmother were placed under similar surveillance. A year later, in November 1793, Adrienne was taken to a makeshift jail in the village of Brioude, a few miles from Chavaniac. Anticipating the worst, she already had placed her daughters in the care of an elderly aunt of her husband and sent her son, George Washington, into hiding in the mountains with his tutor, Félix Frestel. By June 1794, however, Adrienne, her sister, mother, and grandmother had all been transferred into even more stringent custody. Adrienne that month was moved to Paris's La Petite Force, a three-story women's prison in the city's Marais district.

By then the Revolution's zealots, deploying their execution instrument of choice, the recently invented guillotine, were sending thousands of souls to their death. Indeed, by spring April 1794, when Adrienne arrived in Paris—during the bloodiest days of the Revolution's infamous Reign of Terror—some sixty people each day were being fed to the grim contraption's razor maw. During the Revolution scores of Lafayette's associates, friends and foes alike, faced the guillotine—among them the Paris mayor Jean-Sylvain Bailly, the radical assembly member Georges Danton, the chemist Antoine Lavoisier (prime mover behind the Ferme générale's tariff wall), and Lafayette's rival the duke of Orléans (unspared, despite his newly adopted republican moniker—Philippe Égalité).

Jefferson's and Lafayette's friend Nicolas de Condorcet, for his part, avoided the guillotine only because in March 1794 he died in a prison cell—whether by murder or suicide remains unclear. Likewise, Lafayette's cousin François-Claude-Amour, marquis de Bouillé, also avoided execution—managing to flee France in late 1791, eventually making his way to England.

During the 1790s Thomas Paine, through his deepening involvement in France's politics and pro-Revolution published writings, alienated former admirers in America (notably George Washington) as well as key leaders of France's government (including Maximilien Robespierre). In November 1793 he was arrested and placed in a Paris prison.

Following what Paine later called deliberately ineffectual efforts by Gouverneur Morris—by then U.S. minister to France—to secure his release, he was eventually sentenced to death. On July 24, 1794, however, due to a prison guard's error, Paine was not guillotined on schedule. Moreover, thanks to Robespierre's own execution four days later and sustained lobbying by James Madison—Morris's successor as U.S. minister to France—Paine won his freedom the following November.

Jefferson's friend and Adrienne Lafayette's aunt, Madame de Tessé, and her husband, the comte de Tessé, likewise survived the Revolution. Fleeing France after having deposited money in a Swiss bank, they eventually purchased an estate in Prussian Holstein; she and Jefferson corresponded until her death in 1813.

Other relatives of Adrienne fared less well: One of her sisters, her mother, and her grandmother all met their deaths on July 22, 1794, on a guillotine in eastern Paris's Place du Trône (then recently renamed Place du Trône-Renversé—Place of the Toppled Throne—and today Place de la Nation). Indeed, between June 13 and July 28, a total of 1,306 Parisians met their deaths in that plaza.

Over those same months France's government also confiscated Lafayette's estates in France and plantations in Cayenne. Although he had intended to free the plantations' enslaved laborers, he had yet to do so—and they were re-sold as slaves. In 1794, however, France's National Convention outlawed slav-ery in all of the country's colonies—though not until 1817 would a similar ban be issued on French participation in the slave trade.

Adrienne, meanwhile, had been held in Paris's La Petite Force prison since June 1794. During her captivity Jefferson's successors as U.S. minister to France—Gouverneur Morris and James Monroe—each lobbied for Adrienne's release. In the end she languished in La Petite Force until February 1795. Her reprieve, however, likely owed less to efforts by the American envoys than to Robespierre's own appointment with the guillotine—on July 28, 1794—a de-mise often regarded as ending the Reign of Terror.[1]

After her release from prison, Adrienne, fearing for the safety of fifteen-year-old George Washington Lafayette, resolved that he leave France. By then, President Washington, the boy's namesake, was already arranging secret pay-ments from the federal treasury to support Adrienne and her family. Assum-ing Washington's ongoing sympathy for her family's plight, Adrienne wrote in mid-April 1795 to inform him that her son had recently sailed for Ameri-can shores. There, she hoped, he would be placed "under the protection of the United States." Washington—advised by aides that Lafayette's son's pres-ence on U.S. soil could exacerbate already troubled Franco-American diplo-matic relations—reacted cautiously to the fait accompli presented him.[2]

In late August Lafayette's son and his tutor, Félix Frestel, arrived in Bos-ton. Communicating with President Washington through Treasury Secretary Alexander Hamilton, the two soon took up residence incognito in a New Jer-sey farmhouse across the Hudson from Manhattan.

In early 1796, however, Washington, relenting from his earlier hesitation, invited both to his official home in Philadelphia. Living there with the presi-dent, were his wife, Martha, two grandchildren from her earlier marriage, and a handful of aides. The mansion's staff also included up to seven slaves from Mt. Vernon. Although Pennsylvania in 1780 had abolished slavery, the state permitted slaves to remain there for up to six months. Thus, before each enslaved person could reach his or her sixth month in the state, Washington periodically rotated them between Philadelphia and Mt. Vernon.

By all accounts the two Frenchmen meshed seamlessly into the president's ménage. Indeed, their presence—stoking Washington's paternal instincts—deepened his sympathies for the plight of the entire Lafayette family. To a colleague he confessed that "the visible distress of his Son, who is now with me, & grieving for the unhappy fate of his parents . . ." was "giving a poignancy to my own feelings."

———

Washington welcomed the two young men successively into his Philadelphia and Mt. Vernon households. In the latter—joining Washington for the first months of his presidential retirement—Lafayette and Frestel lived until October 1797. Moreover, soon after their spring 1796 arrival in Philadelphia, the president—brushing aside earlier hesitations—had quietly initiated a diplomatic overture to secure the release of Lafayette père.[3]

SIXTY

"The Unhappy Fortunes of
M. de la Fayette"

Scarce half I seem to live, dead more than half.
O dark, dark, dark, amid the blaze of noon,
Irrecoverably dark, total eclipse
Without all hope of day!

—John Milton, "Samson Agonistes"

Inexorably, after Thomas Jefferson, in March 1790, assumed his duties as U.S. secretary of state, he grew enmeshed in debates with colleagues. With Washington, Vice President John Adams, Treasury Secretary Alexander Hamilton, and others he clashed over what he saw as domestic policies that unfairly favored northern over southern interests, and foreign policies that preferred Britain to France. In December 1793, exasperated, he resigned from the office and returned to Monticello.

Thus removed from federal politics, Jefferson did not learn of George Washington Lafayette's presence in America until ten months after his arrival in Boston. In June 1796—having read in a newspaper that the boy was in Philadelphia—Jefferson wrote to President Washington, enclosing a letter for Lafayette fils.

Writing in English, Jefferson expressed "the satisfaction with which I learn that you are in a land of safety where you will meet in every person the friend of your worthy father and family," soon adding: "You were perhaps too young to remember me personally when in Paris." He nonetheless asked that the young man feel free to call on him on any "occasion . . . wherein I can be useful" and expressed hopes that he might someday visit Monticello.

Soon answering the letter, writing in French, Lafayette fils reciprocated his and his family's affection for Jefferson. Noting that his father often mentioned Jefferson in his letters, he assured him: "Although quite young myself, when you were in France, I recall perfectly well having often had the honor of seeing you there."

In truth, of course, the hardships faced by George Washington Lafayette during the French Revolution paled beside those of many of his compatriots— thousands of whom died violently during those years. Then and later the Revolution's defenders have cast its executions as understandable, if not justifiable, measures by a government and country facing grave external and internal threats: According to such arguments, France during those years endured invasions by multiple foreign armies; internally, armed open rebellion erupted in several provinces—notably the Vendée on central France's Atlantic coast. Further discomfiting leaders in Paris, the country faced continuing urban and rural social unrest—much of it fueled by hyperinflation and the economy's collapse. Moreover, the entire Catholic Church and its adherents detested, and often sought to undermine, the Revolution. Finally, throughout the entire course of the upheaval, deadly factional rivalries afflicted the government.

But while debates persist over the French Revolution's methods, its trajectory of violence is settled history: To wit, after the upheaval commenced in 1789, its perceived enemies were—in increasing numbers—routinely dispatched by lynchings, beheadings, shootings, and other violent, often extralegal, acts. Escalating the brutality, the radical Jacobin coup of August 1792 began with a mass slaughter of Swiss Guards by a mob at the Tuileries Palace. Those killings, which influenced Lafayette's decision to flee France, inaugurated a deluge of officially and unofficially sanctioned murder—including, in Paris and other French cities, the notorious September Massacres of September 2–7, 1792. Thereafter officially sanctioned persecution of aristocrats and the Revolution's other perceived enemies expanded.

Typifying such brutality, in September 1792 Louis-Alexandre de La Rochefoucauld—a close friend of Jefferson and Franklin, and a leading liberal of the day—after being identified as an "aristocrat" by a mob in Normandy, was dragged from his carriage and hacked to death in front of his horrified wife and daughters. That same month a mob took off the head of Philippe Égalité's sister-in-law, the princesse de Lamballe, and waved it on a pike in front of the windows of her close friend Marie Antoinette.

Reacting to such killings, Thomas Jefferson wrote to William Short from New York in January 1793: "My own affections have been deeply wounded by some of the martyrs to this cause," Jefferson allowed, "but rather than it should have failed, I would have seen half the earth desolated. Were there but an Adam and an Eve left in every country, and left free, it would be better than as it now is."

But how to explain Jefferson's callousness—or naïveté—over the outrages whose victims even included friends of his? Short later speculated that his mentor's "greatest illusions in politics have proceeded from a most amiable error on his part; having too favorable [an] opinion of the animal called Man." But domestic U.S. politics also explains Jefferson's attitude: During the 1790s, for Jefferson and other American leaders, political differences often manifested themselves as opinions—pro or con—on France's Revolution. John Adams and Alexander Hamilton, members of the Federalist Party—antecedent successively to the later Whig and Republican Parties—opposed the Revolution. Jefferson, Madison, and other members of the Democratic-Republican Party founded by the two men—antecedent of today's Democratic Party—supported it.[1]

Lafayette's jailers, meanwhile, continued to detain him and his three fellow French officers—often incommunicado—at a succession of (secret until located by his supporters) prisons under often grim conditions. The first three were in

Prussia: in Wesel, Magdeburg, and Neisse. The fourth, to which they were moved in May 1794, was in Austria.

All the while—his apparent indifference to other suffering notwithstanding—Secretary of State Jefferson, until his December 1793 departure from that office, had continued to work for his friend's release. From Philadelphia—to which the U.S. capital had been relocated before Lafayette's imprisonment—and through State Department envoys in Europe, he explored gambits to free Lafayette. Writing in 1793 to a member of Britain's Parliament who had relayed news of the prisoner's condition, Jefferson assured him of his and President Washington's continuing concerns: "It was with deep concern that [Washington] learnt the unhappy fortunes of M. de la Fayette," Jefferson wrote. "His friendship for him could not fail to inspire him with the desire of relieving him."

The fact, however, that the U.S. had no diplomatic relations with Prussia or Austria complicated efforts by federal officials to end Lafayette's imprisonment. Moreover, their desire to preserve U.S. neutrality in Europe's war required Washington, Jefferson, and others seeking Lafayette's release to work discreetly—and to make clear that they were acting as private citizens, not agents of the federal government.

In London, meanwhile, Jefferson's friend Angelica Church and others—including her husband, House of Commons member John Barker Church—were likewise seeking to secure Lafayette's release. Eventually, after developing a plan, they enlisted Justus Erich Bollmann, a young German surgeon and adventurer, to execute it.

Traveling to the Continent, Bollmann learned the location of Lafayette's latest prison—Olmütz, in the Austrian Hapsburg principality of Moravia. Arriving on July 24 in Olmütz (today's Olomouc, in the Czech Republic), Bollmann began gathering information on the prison, cultivating officials associated with it, and planning the breakout. In late September, while in Vienna obtaining equipment for the plan's execution, he met, in a coffeehouse—by a remarkable coincidence—a young man whose personal association with (and affections for) Lafayette stretched back to his childhood.

The twenty-one-year-old American medical student Francis Kinloch Huger, then touring Europe, was the son of Benjamin Huger, who had hosted Lafayette on South Carolina's Winyah Bay in 1777. Upon learning of Bollmann's plot, Huger volunteered to assist.

By mid-October the two were in Olmütz. There, through Karl Haberlein, a surgeon employed by the prison, who made regular medical calls on Lafayette, the two men established communications with the object of their mission. (In that day's Prussia, the term surgeon generally connoted a general doctor rather than one who operates on patients.) The kindly if unsuspecting Haberlein agreed to deliver letters between the two young men and the famous inmate—the man his jailers called "State Prisoner #2." Hidden, however, in the missives between the two parties were details—some written in lemon juice, invisible until heated over a candle—of their evolving plans.[2]

As their plot evolved, the conspirators decided to take advantage of a perquisite accorded Lafayette. Concerned for the famous inmate's welfare, the prison's commander had—since early October, on orders from Emperor Francis II—been allowing him regular weekly outings beyond the prison's walls in a light open carriage. A driver and two soldiers accompanied him.

On the afternoon of November 8, 1794, during one of those supervised trips, the carriage stopped by a wheat field, along a stretch of road where Lafayette was routinely allowed a short walk. As he stepped out of the carriage, Huger and Bollmann appeared. Following a scuffle with the prisoner's three escorts, the two managed to free Lafayette. They immediately provided him a horse, and he rode off alone while they dealt with a sergeant putting up a determined resistance. In the village of Hof, about twenty-five miles distant, a carriage with a secret compartment awaited to take Lafayette across the Hapsburg border into Prussian Silesia. However, due to a miscommunication among the conspirators, Lafayette took a wrong turn after riding off.

Soon lost in a rural area, he eventually came upon a local tanner whom he asked for directions to the border. Offering to guide him, the tanner escorted him through forests and fields. As night fell he took Lafayette to a barn, instructing him to wait there until he returned—explaining that he wanted to make sure the route ahead was safe.

In truth, however, the tanner alerted the local bailiff to Lafayette's presence. Possibly the tanner had recognized the famous prisoner; certainly, however, noticing his foreign accent, he was mindful of strict legal directives—backed by draconian punishments—to report all foreigners. Whatever the tanner's reasons for reporting Lafayette, Austrian soldiers soon arrived and returned him to Olmütz prison.

After the botched escape Lafayette's jailers tightened the conditions of his captivity. As for Bollmann and Huger, after being held for seven months and agreeing never to return to Austria, they were released on June 24, 1795. They soon made their way to London. There they met with Angelica Church, who had helped to orchestrate the failed rescue attempt. Amid their conversations a new plot soon emerged—one that required funds they hoped to obtain from the U.S. government. To secure that support Church provided the two young men with letters of introductions to her brother-in-law, U.S. Treasury Secretary Alexander Hamilton. Her letters in hand, Bollmann and Huger arrived in New York in January 1796. Weeks later in Philadelphia—thanks to entrée provided by Hamilton, President George Washington, over dinner at his residence, listened as the two detailed the newly concocted plan to free the Hero of Two Worlds.

Their enthusiasm notwithstanding, however, the young men's description of their conspiracy failed to impress the president. Within weeks a discouraged Huger returned to his medical studies in Europe. Bollmann—for his part, undaunted—continued to call on Washington; and by spring the sixty-three-year-old president had grown weary of—and ended his dinners with—a guest whose visits he had come to regard as an imposition on presidential hospitality.

Adrienne, meanwhile, reacting to her husband's failed escape, decided the time had come for her to travel. In autumn 1795, with her two young daughters in tow, she set off for Vienna to meet with the Austrian Habsburg monarch Francis II—since March 1792, Holy Roman Emperor. Desperate, Adrienne had resolved that if Francis refused to release her husband, she would request permission to—along with her daughters, Anastasie, eighteen, and Marie-Antoinette Virginie thirteen—join Lafayette in his captivity. Her strategy, Adrienne reasoned, would reunite most of the family. And—by rendering Francis II a jailer of women and children—it would place him in an embarrassing position.

The journey of the Lafayette women, crossing multiple borders in war-torn Europe, was perilous. But, with assistance from U.S. diplomats who, in Paris and along the way, provided false passports, ruses, and money, they completed the trip.

Francis II was a nephew of Adrienne's late friend, the queen of France (and namesake of her daughter Marie-Antoinette Virginie). Nonetheless, on October 10, when the two met, Francis declined Adrienne's plea to release her husband. He did, however, eventually grant her permission to join Lafayette in prison—with the proviso that, once inside, she would stay there. And so, on October 15, 1795, the three women did just that—joining a surprised Lafayette in his prison quarters.

As Adrienne anticipated, their imprisonment drew international condemnation. Articles, prints, and poems soon appeared—many exaggerating the direness of their captivity. Indeed, President Washington soon numbered among those writing to Austria's emperor. With George Washington Lafayette still living under his roof, the president—prodded by Alexander Hamilton—in May 1796 took pen in hand and directly addressed Francis II: "I take the liberty of writing this private letter to your majesty," he wrote, arguing that Lafayette's " long imprisonment and the confiscation of his estates" constituted "sufferings, which recommend him to the mediation of humanity."

He thus asked that Lafayette "be permitted to come to this country, on such conditions and under such restrictions, as your Majesty may think it expedient to prescribe."[3]

SIXTY-ONE

Quiet Days in Batavia

Always try to keep a patch of sky above your life.
—MARCEL PROUST, *SWANN'S WAY*
(*REMEMBRANCE OF THINGS PAST*, VOL. 1)

In the end George Washington's May 1796 extreaty to Austria's Francis II seeking Lafayette's release produced no results. Nine months later, on February 16, 1797, John Quincy Adams—by then posted at The Hague as a U.S. diplomat—reflected on the growing futility of such requests: "I have ever since my residence in Europe," wrote Adams, "had applications of various kinds from the friends of M. de la Fayette." But never having received "any instructions from the President, or the department of State . . . I have always avoided an interference in the matter."[1]

Prospects, meanwhile, for pressure from France for Lafayette's release were likewise discouraging. A year after Robespierre's July 1794 execution, public revulsion finally ended the reign of the Committee of Public Safety—the body that had orchestrated his Reign of Terror. By late 1795 a five-man body known as the Directory was governing France. Determined to make a fresh start, the new governnment—radical but less so than the body it replaced—promulgated a new constitution, one whose preamble even drew on Lafayette's Declaration of the Rights of Man.

While receptive to calls for Lafayette's release, the Directory was limited in its options to achieve that end. France's fighting with Prussia had ended, but hostilities with Austria persisted. Moreover, the directors had scant control over a brash young Corsica-born general whose strategic genius had won for France an astonishing run of recent battlefield triumphs.

So impressive were those victories that the general, Napoleon Bonaparte, enjoyed powers greater than his nominal, civilian superiors. Even so, following months of prodding by the Lafayettes' supporters, the Directory's president, on August 1, 1797, wrote to Napoleon of the family's plight, urging him "to end their captivity as soon as possible."

Napoleon was then in Italy, negotiating the terms of his defeat of Austria in the War of the First Coalition. The Treaty of Campo Formio—eventually signed in October 1797—ratified Napoleon's triumphs and French acquisition of former Austrian domains across Europe. With Lafayette in mind, Napoleon also made sure that the treaty included a clause stipulating the release of all prisoners taken during the conflict.[2]

Anticipating that clause, Austrian officials acted before the treaty's formal adoption; and on September 19, 1797, the Lafayettes, Maubourg, and Pusy and their servants left their quarters in dank Olmütz prison. (Lameth, the fourth prisoner of state, had been released due to health concerns in November 1795.) From Olmütz, Austrian officials escorted the freed prisoners to Hamburg. There, on October 4, 1797, they were turned over to John Parish, the U.S. consul in that city.

Unfortunately, however, for Lafayette, Adrienne and their daughters—debilitated by years of confinement and reliant on others for financial sustenance—they were unable to tarry at the North Sea port. As they soon learned, Francis II, setting terms for the prisoners' liberation, had "ordered their release provided the necessary steps be taken . . . to convey them off the territory of the Empire to Holland or America, eight days after their arrival at Hamburgh."[3]

Under other circumstances France or America would have been the couple's first choice of residence. But in France Lafayette still faced possible execution. And Adrienne—after two years in prison unable to walk, suffering from a rash, pains in her teeth and limbs, and with an open wound on her left foot—was too frail for the long voyage to America. Moreover, Franco-American diplomatic tensions further precluded the family's move to America.

Heightening such tensions—and infuriating France's defenders in the United States—U.S. and British diplomats, meeting in London in late 1794, had signed what became known (after John Jay, the chief American negotiator) as Jay's Treaty. Ostensibly resolving festering differences between the U.S. and Britain, the pact was widely viewed as repudiating the American Revolution's Franco-American alliance. Indeed, as war raged between France and Britain, French leaders understandably viewed the pact as an outright betrayal of the country that a few years earlier had come to America's aid and helped to win its independence.

Following their brief stay in Hamburg, the Lafayette family, limited in options, lived for several months on farms in Danish Holstein. There, they were soon reunited with George Washington Lafayette, recently returned from America. Lafayette père, however, soon lost the regular company of his wife and daughters.

In May 1797 Anastasie married the marquis de Latour-Maubourg, the former National Assembly delegate and army officer who had been captured with Lafayette and imprisoned with him at Olmütz. The indefatigable Adrienne, for her part, was soon sufficiently recovered to travel; in the coming months she made repeated trips—often on foot, from Holstein to Paris, and from Paris to Chavaniac—that covered formidable distances and terrain. She also began working to recover the title to a confiscated family estate near Paris. Toward that end she was soon spending increasing amounts of time in France. Moreover, having acquired a passport for herself, she secured two others for the couple's daughters, who began joining her for extended stays in France.

By then Lafayette had moved to the village of Vianen in the Republic of

Batavia—the former Dutch Republic, a client state of France since its capture in 1795 by the French army. In the words of the historian Paul S. Spalding, the French government had "agreed to allow Gilbert himself to move to Holland, but no closer."

In Vianen, Lafayette passed his time reading, gardening, and landscaping. He also found time to reflect upon past days of glory, to correspond with friends, and dream of retiring to a farm in Massachusetts—or even near Mt. Vernon. He also indulged his frustrations over how France's domestic politics and Franco-American tensions were vexing his hopes for a residency in either France or the United States."4

Over the coming years, meanwhile, those growing tensions, continued to frustrate Lafayette's dreams of returning to the United States. John Adams—by then a political adversary of Jefferson—had succeeded Washington as president in March 1797. And in that office Adams struggled to preserve U.S. neutrality in the latest conflict—the War of the Second Coalition—then raging between England and France. Toward that end, Adams, continuing his predecessor's position, claimed that the still unpaid U.S. debts to France from the American Revolution were owed to the kingdom of France, not its successor government.

For U.S. officials those circumstances rendered consideration of an American exile for Lafayette an awkward proposition. By the late 1790s, the two nations were fighting a sustained but undeclared war with each other. Indeed the Quasi-War (July 1798–September 1800), a naval conflict between the United States and France, which erupted during the second year of Adams's presidency, had grown from diplomatic tensions that first flared during the Washington administration.

Compounding Lafayette's frustrations was his awareness that his exile from France—so near yet so far—rendered inapplicable the diplomatic expertise that he might otherwise have offered to reconcile differences dividing the two countries: In May 1799 Lafayette—in his final extant letter to his adoptive father—lamented to Washington (by then two years retired from the presidency) his lack of interaction with current French officials: "How far I am, not only to influence, but Even to ascertain the dispositions of her government."

Further reducing Lafayette's chances of securing his imagined bucolic life in Virginia or Massachusetts was ongoing revulsion among many Americans at the continuing violence of France's Revolution. Emblematic of that predicament was Alexander Hamilton's response, in 1798, to a solicitation for assistance from Lafayette for help in arranging for him an American exile. To his friend, Hamilton frankly admitted that the guillotining of Louis XVI had "cured me of my good will for the French Revolution."

Hamilton knew that Lafayette had opposed most of the Revolution's violence. Even so, he added, American public opinion would nonetheless associate his friend with the king's murder and other outrages—and he could thus envision no prospects for Lafayette's requested American exile in the near future: "No one," Hamilton wrote, "feels more than I do the motives which this country has to love you, to desire and to promote your happiness. . . . In the present state of our affairs with france, I cannot urge you to us—but until some radical change in france I Shall be sorry to learn you have gone elsewhere."

Worsening Lafayette's plight, even as friends in America discouraged his return to the New World, France's five-man Directory discouraged his return to France. On November 9, 1799, that disposition hardened when, through a coup (the "Coup of 18 Brumaire," in the soon-to-be-abandoned republican calendar), Napoleon Bonaparte made himself the country's dictator ("First Consul")—a moment generally regarded as marking the end of the French Revolution. Lafayette, for his part, indignant at what he viewed as the Revolution's betrayal by Napoleon, soon vowed to return to France and restore the rebellion's earlier democratic values.

Shortly after Napoleon's coup, Lafayette—traveling in disguise on a passport inscribed with the name "Motier"—returned to Paris. There he sent repeated notes to Napoleon, informing him of his return. Outraged, Napoleon refused to meet and demanded that Lafayette return to Holland.

Adrienne, however, soon arranged an audience for herself with Napoleon. During their meeting he said that her husband's presence in France could complicate efforts to reestablish the sort of government that both men favored. To that, Adrienne answered that Lafayette shared Napoleon's domestic goals and that he had no desire to challenge the government.

Though unconvinced by Adrienne's argument, Napoleon realized that forcing the Hero of Two Worlds to leave France would reflect badly on his government. Moreover, he was also mindful of the public acclaim he had reaped as Lafayette's liberator. Reluctantly, he thus agreed to permit Lafayette to remain in the country—on the condition that he retire to the countryside and live there quietly. Acting on the terms agreed upon by the First Consul, Lafayette soon established his quiet "country" retirement—at Adrienne's family's estate, the Château de la Grange-Bléneau, forty miles southeast of Paris. Though away from the city, the estate was nonetheless, as the coming years would establish, close enough to Paris for ready access.

The couple were delighted to return to France. But, due to the government's confiscation of most of their wealth and properties, their financial woes persisted. In 1800, they did regain title to La Grange; but there remained the challenge of restoring their new home to its former grandeur—a project that would take decades. Between 1800 and 1834 the couple supervised the reworking of every aspect of La Grange's seven hundred acres—including roads, gardens, arable fields, ponds, irrigation ditches, and streams. They also lovingly selected paintings, furniture, books, and other objects for the château's forty-five habitable rooms.

In March 1803 Congress—aware of the failure of past efforts by the U.S. government to assist Lafayette—authorized a grant of land, to be selected by him, in American territory north of the Ohio River. Jefferson, meanwhile—by then U.S. president—soon learned that all the land in that designated area was already under title to other owners. To redress the error he sought a land grant for Lafayette in the vast territory acquired from France through his recent (1803) Louisiana Purchase.

Moreover, in 1805 Jefferson wrote to Lafayette of his desire to name him governor of the newly created territory of Louisiana. Acceptance of the office would have rendered Lafayette eligible for American citizenship—a designation that had eluded him even as, over the years, he was awarded so-called (but ultimately only honorary) "citizenships" by numerous states.

Lafayette, however, due to a recent injury (a fractured thighbone), was unable to travel and ultimately declined both offers. Ironically, had he accepted Jefferson's offer to serve as governor the Louisiana Territory, Lafayette would have been the titular head of a sprawling region purchased from his old liberator and later—however briefly—nemesis, Napoleon Bonaparte.

On January 11, 1808, Lafayette wrote to a friend whom he knew would understand his anguish: "The Constant Mourning of Your Heart will be deepened by the Grief I am doomed to impart," he wrote to Thomas Jefferson. "Who Better than You can Sympathise for the Loss of a Beloved Wife? The Angel who for thirty four Years Has blessed My Life was to You an Affectionate, Grateful friend—pity me, my dear Jefferson, and believe me for Ever, with all My Heart."

Adrienne, who had never fully recovered from the aftereffects of her Olmütz imprisonment, had died two weeks earlier. After her passing, Lafayette sealed off her room at La Grange as a shrine. And though he would continue to live at the estate for the rest of his life, he allowed no one but himself to enter the room.

In 1815, following Napoleon's passage from France's public life and the restoration of the Bourbon throne—an act Lafayette opposed—he resumed his political career, serving intermittently (1818–24, 1827–34) in France's Chamber of Deputies. During those years—often with his son George Washington, also an assembly member—the old revolutionary found his spirits buoyed by what he viewed as the emergence of a new generation of leaders unbeholden to past alliances.

"The french Youth," he assured Jefferson, was, "Remarkably More Enlightened than You Have known. . . . [T]hey have Risen above the Spirit of faction. . . . [T]here is Now at the Head of public opinion a Sea of men Quite devoted to the Cause of liberty."

During those years Lafayette lent his voice to numerous causes—including press freedoms, the rights of political prisoners and women, nationalist movements in South America, Haiti, Poland, Greece, Spain, Portugal, Germany, Belgium, Ireland, and Switzerland, and abolitionism—the latter often through the French antislavery society Amis des Noirs, founded in 1788. Decades later the stalwart English abolitionist Thomas Clarkson, a Lafayette ally and correspondent, writing in William Lloyd Garrison's *Liberator*, would recall of his friend: "He was decidedly as uncompromising an enemy to the slave-trade, and slavery, as any man I ever knew." Indeed, remembered Clarkson, Lafayette often reflected: "I would never have drawn my sword in the cause of America, if I could have conceived that thereby I was founding a land of slavery."[5]

SIXTY-TWO

Hero's Tour Redux

M. de la Fayette, I must say, has a right to be considered a true republican; none of the vanities of his rank ever entered his head; power,
the effect of which is so great in France, had no ascendancy over him;
the desire of pleasing in drawing-room conversation did not with him
influence a single phrase; he sacrificed all his fortune to his opinions
with the most generous indifference.

—GERMAINE DE STAËL, *CONSIDERATIONS ON THE PRINCIPLE
EVENTS OF THE FRENCH REVOLUTION*, 1818

Separate from all those common principles, which, in themselves,
would unite us to any man, there are ties of a particularly endearing
nature between us and La Fayette. His devotion to our cause was not
only first in point of time, but it has ever been first in all its moral features. He came to bestow, and not to receive.

—JAMES FENIMORE COOPER, *NOTIONS OF THE AMERICANS*, 1828

In the years following Adrienne's death in 1807, Lafayette for the most part
lived quietly as a gentleman farmer at La Grange—until 1824, when he accepted an invitation from President James Monroe to visit the United States. The
eventual tour, conducted at his host government's expense, between July 1824
and September 1825, marked, for the aging general, a triumphant renaissance in
his return to public life. By then, Lafayette was the last prominent living general
from America's War of Independence; and the thirteen-month tour took him to

all twenty-four states and 182 towns. Frustrating abolitionists, his official role as "Guest of the Nation" rendered it awkward for him to publicly criticize slavery during the tour. Lafayette did, however, find opportunities to make symbolic gestures for that cause—meeting in northern states with individual African Americans, and visiting schools and other institutions dedicated to the betterment of their community. Even in southern states, often against the expressed wishes of local officials, he pointedly greeted both free and enslaved African Americans.

Accompanying Lafayette was his son, George Washington Lafayette, and, acting as his secretary, the French writer and diplomat Auguste Levasseur. During the trip he was often escorted and feted by state chapters of the Society of the Cincinnati, a fraternal organization founded in 1783 and composed of commissioned Continental Army officers and their male descendants. More generally during the tour, Lafayette greeted a new generation of American leaders—including Andrew Jackson, Daniel Webster, and John Quincy Adams, the last of whom Lafayette knew from the Adams family's days in Paris; and who, in March 1825, during the second year of Lafayette's tour, was sworn in as the sixth U.S. president.

Other old friends whom Lafayette saw during the tour included James Madison, James Monroe, and John Adams, the latter of whom he visited at the Adamses' Quincy, Massachusetts, home. (John's spouse, Abigail Adams, had died in 1818; their daughter, Nabby—Abigail Adams Smith—in 1813.) In Charlestown, Lafayette even reunited with Francis Kinloch Huger, son of the South Carolina planter Benjamin Huger, who had sheltered *La Victoire*'s weary voyagers in 1777, and who himself had tried to free Lafayette from Olmütz prison in 1794.

In Philadelphia in September 1824, Lafayette was greeted by another man who had tried in vain to win his release from prison—William Short, two days shy of his own sixty-fifth birthday. Impressed, Short soon reported to Jefferson: "I cannot conceive how he has been able to survive the campaign of bustle, confusion & excitement through which he has gone. To him on the contrary it seems to give new life & vigor."[1]

Truth be known, however, most of Lafayette's American friends and colleagues had died years earlier—including John Laurens (1782), Nathanael Greene (1786), Benjamin Franklin (1790), Alexander Hamilton (1804), and Gouverneur Morris (1816). Likewise, his early mentor—the Prussia-born officer Johann Kalb who, in Paris, had helped arrange his Continental army commission, had died in 1780 on a South Carolina battlefield.

Even Jefferson's daughter Polly, whom Lafayette had known in Paris, had died decades before his tour of America. Polly—called Maria after her return from France—had, in 1797, married her cousin John Wayles Eppes. They had two children but, days after the birth of their second child, in 1804, she died—just as her mother had—of complications from her pregnancy.

Patsy, Jefferson's older daughter, whom Lafayette had also known in Paris, remained alive and well when he returned to America: in 1790, Patsy had married her third cousin Thomas Mann Randolph Jr., with whom she had eleven children. Of an intellectual bent, Patsy, by then acting as Monticello's mistress, had long ago become a fierce political advocate for her father. Moreover, her husband, Tom, later served as Virginia governor from 1819 to 1822.

By 1826, however, following her father's death and the sale of Monticello to pay his debts, Patsy and her husband, by then mired in debt and, with Tom dogged by a drinking problem, separated. She reconciled with Tom shortly before his death and spent her remaining years living in Albemarle County, Washington, and Boston. Patsy died in 1836.

During Lafayette's 1824–25 American tour, in homage to his adoptive father, he made two pilgrimages to Mt. Vernon and the tomb of George and Martha Washington—deceased respectively since 1799 and 1802. During the first Mt. Vernon visit, before leaving, George Washington Lafayette—noting that Washington's grandson George Custis had maintained the house exactly "as he saw it twenty-eight years ago"—guided his father to a fondly recalled spot in the house. Recorded Levasseur: "He found in the place where Washington himself had left it, the principal key of the bastile, which was sent him by Lafayette, at the time the monument of despotism was destroyed." (In contrast with Lafayette's abiding affections for Washington's memory, Jefferson's never-close ties to Washington had collapsed in the final years of the latter's presidency.) Among the many poignant moments of Lafayette's tour in 1824 was his brief reunion with James, the enslaved man who, in 1781, had kept him abreast of British troop movements around Yorktown. James had thus contributed mightily to the war's final victory, and with Lafayette's support, he had won his freedom in 1787; still later he was granted a pension and, adopting a surname, changed his name to James Lafayette.

As Lafayette conducted his 1824–25 tour, passions in America stirred by his association with the French Revolution had faded into memory. And because he had spent his past four decades in Europe, far from the contentious issues that roiled the American Republic during those years, he arrived at his various stops—unlike, say, Jefferson and John Adams—as a leader unblemished by partisanship. Lafayette left a lasting impression on people and places: In his wake streets, parks, and entire towns were named, renamed, or even founded in his honor—creating all those Lafayettes, Fayettes, Fayettevilles, and La Granges (after Château de la Grange-Bléneau) that today dot the American landscape.

Typifying the indelible impressions Lafayette left, the adult Walt Whitman would recall the hero's 1825 passage through the Brooklyn of his youth. The future poet was then six years old and numbered among several neighborhood children whom Lafayette—after stepping from his four-horse-drawn carriage—affectionately lifted into the air, one by one.

The stop's nominal purpose was to lay the ceremonial cornerstone for a new library. As Whitman remembered, the visit was accompanied by no fireworks, cannon-fire or other folderol. Indeed, in the poet's memory, the visit "had an air of simplicity, naturalness, and freedom from ostentatious or claptrap—and not without a smack of antique grandeur." On a journey that teemed with poignant moments, however, none would rival the reunion that occurred atop a Virginia mountain.[2]

SIXTY-THREE

Autumn Reunion

[In] idle reveries . . . I have sometimes indulged myself, of seeing all
my friends at Paris once more, for a month or two; a thing impossible, which however I never permitted myself to despair of. . . . [T]he
loss of friends may be the less, as the time is shorter within which we
are to meet again, according to the creed of our education.

—JEFFERSON TO LAFAYETTE, FEBRUARY 14, 1815

It was late afternoon, "about 3'clock," November 4, 1824, when the crowd
outside the mountaintop mansion—later estimated at up to four hundred
persons—spotted the approaching column. Excitement grew as a faint line descended from an adjacent Blue Ridge height. Drawing nearer, the line soon revealed itself to be a train of carriages followed by columns of uniformed men
on horseback.[1]

Then, as abruptly as it had appeared, the procession vanished. But because
all understood that the disappearance meant that the retinue was now on the
two-mile road that spiraled up to where they were gathered, jubilation erupted.
Ending years of separation, Thomas Jefferson and the Frenchman that his
gathered admirers still affectionately called "General Lafayette" would soon
be reunited.

Adding to the occasion's momentousness, since late 1789, when the two men
last saw one another, Jefferson had garnered accolades to match those of the

Hero of Two Worlds. After all, since they last saw one another, Jefferson's role as the Declaration of Independence's principal author had become well known, and he was widely celebrated for that once-anonymous deed.[2] Moreover, since their last meeting, Jefferson had served his nation successively as secretary of state, vice president, and for two terms as president. Attaching still more significance to the event soon to occur, Jefferson's reunion with the American Revolution's last living prominent general was to occur at Monticello—his almost legendary mountaintop estate crowned by its two-story brick mansion.

As the lawn atop the mountain roared with huzzahs, Jefferson, standing in the becolumned mansion's east portico, quietly awaited Lafayette's arrival. At eighty-one, the former U.S. president appeared haggard. By then walking with a cane, he moved slowly and with difficulty. But his mental capacities remained acute. And the Virginian, who had arranged much of the day's pomp himself, had become over the years a connoisseur of such ceremonies.

So, in the meticulous preparations for this moment, Jefferson had instructed his enslaved servants to spare no efforts or fanfare. The barouche drawn by four white horses bearing the visitor through Virginia's Albemarle County had been arranged by Jefferson (the barouche itself belonged to him). Jefferson likewise had arranged the carriage's forty-man mounted military escort, as well as the friends and neighbors gathered to witness the moment.

After more minutes passed, the sound of horse hooves and the clanking of wheels grew clearly audible. As the crowd fell silent, a bugle call as crisp as the Indian summer afternoon sounded, and through boughs of willows overhanging the road leading to Monticello's east lawn, amid patriotic banners hung for the occasion, the entourage streamed into view.

"At length, the first carriage reached the lawn and drew up," one witness later recalled:

A crowd of gentlemen dismounted in eager haste and the Guest of the Nation was handed out: simultaneously Mr. Jefferson had walked to the edge of the lawn hurriedly and bareheaded to meet his guest. They embraced and kissed each other on the cheek in European fashion:—all was so still that we heard the words distinctly—"My dear Jefferson!—My dear Lafayette!"[3]

As they embraced, both men wept. Another witness later described the moment as the only time he saw Jefferson publicly weep. The two then walked toward the mansion's east portico: "The General was led up the stairs by Mr. Jefferson & introduced to Mrs. Randolph"—Patsy Jefferson—whom he remembered as a schoolgirl.

Just sixteen when she last saw Lafayette, Jefferson's only surviving child was now a poised fifty-two-year-old woman. And beneath the house's portico, Lafayette kissed Patsy's hands and uttered "many kind words." She in turn, "with grace and dignity befitting a queen," welcomed their famous visitor "to the hospitality of the home of her father."

Afterward, public ceremonies concluded, the two men disappeared into Jefferson's mansion. Also welcomed inside, having arrived a short time after General Lafayette—were his traveling companions: George Washington Lafayette, now in his midforties, finally making the Monticello visit he had been unable to make as a boy, during his 1790s American exile, and Auguste Levasseur, visibly ill when he arrived but restored by the following morning.

For Jefferson and Lafayette, the intervening decades since they had last seen one another had taken their toll. Recalled Lafayette of his eighty-one-year-old friend, "Mr. Jefferson received me with strong emotion. I found him much aged, without doubt, after a separation of thirty-five years, but bearing marvelously well under his eighty one years of age, in full possession of all the vigor of his mind and heart."

As for Lafayette, at sixty-seven, he remained tall and relatively vigorous—sufficiently fit to endure the grueling tour he was embarked upon. But, added to the normal wear and added girth of age, the hero also bore the ravages of five years of captivity inside Prussian and Austrian prisons. "My old friend embraced me with great warmth," James Madison, who arrived later that day—"just as they were commencing their Desert"—recalled of his own reunion with his old friend. "He is in fine health & spirits but so much increased in bulk & changed in aspect that I should not have known him."

Those who saw the Jefferson-Lafayette reunion that afternoon by rights could look forward to telling others they had witnessed a historical moment. On the hallowed grounds of Monticello—like an electrical charge coursing through the "Leyden jar" fashioned by the two men's late mutual friend Benjamin Franklin—the intellectual and military poles of America's Revolution had symbolically reconnected and thrown off effervescent sparks.

Indeed, with George Washington by then two decades in his grave, Jefferson and Lafayette represented the last major living links to a golden age that had come and gone before most of the four hundred onlookers at Monticello had come into the world. And for those few souls present who *had* been alive during that age, what they knew—or thought they knew—of that age came less from childhood memories and more from the received lore of older relatives.

Jefferson would live another two years, Lafayette another ten. But in fact, long before their reunion, the legends of both men had already been sculpted into marble. Thus for most of those gathered that day, Monticello might as well have been Mount Olympus and the witnessed reunion seemed as real—and as unreal—as it would have for citizens of Periclean Athens winning a glimpse of Zeus or Apollo.

Yes, they were seeing real flesh-and-blood men—and the public achievements of both were matters of recorded history. But on a deeper level, the meeting culminated a more intimate history, largely unknown to those present, shared by two complex individuals.

Offstage over the coming days and during a briefer visit in August 1825, the two men's conversations would include a host of private topics ill suited for statues and monumental paintings—including Jefferson's ongoing strivings to arrange a federal grant recompensing Lafayette's war services and thus stanching his dwindling finances; Lafayette's continuing efforts to persuade Jefferson to free his slaves; and a request by Jefferson, afflicted by an enlarged prostrate, that Lafayette obtain in Paris and send to him superior French catheters.

Moreover, few of the day's onlookers were privy to the ways that, even then, what they thought they knew of both men's public history had been stage-managed. Lafayette's missteps as a military office during France's Revolution, eclipsing his achievements as a legislator, had irreparably tarnished his reputation in his native land. In America, by contrast, his star remained bright. To be sure the American Revolution's gunpowder smoke had barely dispersed when, through conversations and correspondence, Lafayette had initiated exchanges with selected historians intended to ensure that they depicted him prominently and favorably in their published works.

That concern was long standing. Indeed, four decades earlier, during Lafayette's 1784 American tour, even while basking in widespread public acclaim, he was already wondering whether posterity would accord him a similarly high regard. To secure that legacy, during that period on both sides of the Atlantic, he therefore imparted his war stories to or otherwise made them known to various writers—among them Jared Sparks, William Gordon, Jacques Pierre Brissot, Philip Mazzei, and Michel-Guillaume-Jean de Crèvecoeur.

Early Lafayette biographers, particularly chroniclers in the United States, thus asserted that, once in America, he had converted to the republic's dominant Puritanical values. But correspondence unearthed in the mid-twentieth century would make clear that the general's French libertinism robustly survived his Atlantic crossing. Likewise, his early biographers downplayed the degree to which revanchist motives—Lafayette's desire to avenge France for its 1763 defeat by Britain—drove his errand to America.[4]

Buttressing such early image gilding, from the 1830s and throughout his life Lafayette wrote and revised multiple versions of his memoirs. Moreover, although sincere in the causes he espoused, he was also keenly aware of what his biographer Louis Gottschalk called his "Midas touch" for generating flattering publicity.

From Gottschalk's perspective, that touch was evident as early as 1784, when, with James Madison and others, Lafayette, during the diplomatic mission to the Oneida Indians, managed to rhetorically upstage the trip's official American delegation. "The young Frenchman sought publicity from his venture," Gottschalk observed. "He expected his speeches to be printed in the United States and eventually to become known abroad."

Thomas Jefferson, by contrast, published just one book during his lifetime and was not one to court public-speaking opportunities. But the Virginian—particularly in his later years—was not indifferent to how future generations would assay his life. Throughout that life, Jefferson met his critics' harshest barbs with a stony silence—a silence that extended to speculation concerning the as many as six children he allegedly fathered with Sally Hemings.

Still residing at Monticello during Lafayette's 1824 visit, Sally Hemings, though never officially freed by Jefferson, was two years later accorded by Jefferson's daughter, Patsy, "her time." The term referred to a de facto freedom that allowed her to remain in Virginia—in Sally's case, with her son Madison and two of her siblings until her death in 1835.

Sally's older brother James Hemings, who in Paris had served as a chef at the Hôtel de Langeac, eventually accompanied Jefferson to New York and Philadelphia during the early 1790s. After Jefferson granted James his freedom in 1796, he spent the next several years working in, and traveling through, various cities—possibly including Paris; the details remain sketchy.

In 1801 after Jefferson became president, he offered Hemings the chef's position at the Executive Mansion, today's White House. Instead—due to a perceived slight by his former master—he spurned the offer. Although Hemings appeared at Monticello that summer and resumed cooking for the family, the reunion proved short-lived. He left Monticello in September; later that fall Jefferson learned that Hemings, likely from causes attributed to excessive drinking, had committed suicide.

But such personal matters seldom found their way into Thomas Jefferson's public words. Indeed, he rarely wrote for a public audience, and when he did, he measured his words carefully. To be sure, his extant private correspondence, usually often preoccupied with political affairs, largely dodges personal matters. Likewise, during his lifetime he methodically destroyed most correspondence of a personal nature. No known correspondence, for instance, exists between him and his wife, Martha. And long before the early twentieth century's mass media created an entire industry of reputation-managing professionals, Jefferson, for the most part, controlled his image with a steely resolve.

Not until his twilight years, however, did Jefferson consciously begin to burnish that image for posterity. Tellingly, in his final decade—in 1817, during the last year of his friend James Madison's presidency—he relished arranging the commission for John Trumbull to memorialize the Declaration of Independence's creation. In another nod to posterity, as early as 1809 he had begun organizing his massive correspondence. During his lifetime Jefferson wrote about eighteen thousand letters and received around twenty-five thousand, and he eventually made arrangements for their preservation and publication after his death. In those later years Jefferson also drafted a brief autobiography, and though it took his life only up to 1790, it was nonetheless the sole memoir he would ever write. Equally significant, as the historian Francis D. Cogliano has observed, Jefferson in that work detailed—and highlighted—his authorship of the Declaration of Independence. In that retelling the Virginian thus, for himself, "asserted a central place in the history of the American Revolution"—an implicit rebuke to John Marshall "and other critics that Jefferson's contribution to the Revolution had been marginal."[5]

Since their days in Paris, Jefferson and Lafayette had continued to disagree on slavery-related matters. Significantly, in December 1820 Jefferson had defended the policy of allowing slavery to be practiced in the vast lands west of the Mississippi that he had acquired as president. That tolerance, Jefferson predicted, "will dilute the evil every where and facilitate the means of getting finally rid of it, an event more anxiously wished by those on whom it presses than by the noisy pretenders to exclusive humanity."

To that hopeful argument, Lafayette, in 1821, had answered: "Are You Sure, my dear friend, that extending the principle of Slavery to the new Raised states is a method to facilitate the means of getting rid of it? I would Have thought that by Spreading the prejudices, Habits, and Calculations of planters over a larger Surface you rather encrease the difficulties of final liberation."

Lafayette's two Monticello visits would provide the two men occasion to return to the topic of slavery. During both stays, Jefferson's enslaved servant Israel Jefferson took Lafayette, his son, George Washington, and Jefferson on daily carriage rides. On most of those outings, Israel Jefferson recalled, "Lafayette spoke indifferently; sometimes I could scarcely understand him." But on one particular day, "My ears were eagerly taking in every sound that proceeded from the venerable patriot's mouth." Indeed, as Israel Jefferson listened, the two old friends—fleetingly, delicately, yet revealingly—dared to air a topic they generally eschewed:

> Lafayette remarked that he thought that the slaves ought to be free; that no man could rightly hold ownership in his brother man; that he gave his best services to and spent his money in behalf of the Americans freely because he felt that they were fighting for a great and noble principle—the freedom of mankind; that instead of all being free a portion were held in bondage (which seemed to grieve his noble heart); that it would be mutually beneficial to masters and slaves if the latter were educated, and so on. Mr. Jefferson replied that he thought the time would come when the slaves would be free, but did not indicate when or in what manner they would get their freedom. He seemed to think that the time had not then arrived. To the latter proposition of Gen. Lafayette, Mr. Jefferson in part assented. He was in favor of teaching the slaves to learn to read print; that to teach them to write would enable them to forge papers, when they could no longer be kept in subjugation.[6]

Lafayette's November 1824 visit to Monticello lasted ten days. On the day after his arrival, he and Jefferson rode to Charlottesville to visit Jefferson's final public project, the University of Virginia—soon to welcome its first students. At 3:00 that afternoon, in the Roman Pantheon–like "dome room" inside the university's unfinished rotunda, a dinner was held to honor Lafayette.

There and at Monticello, both men remained mindful of their legacies for posterity and their reunion's symbolism. During the three-hour banquet, Jefferson sat between Lafayette and former president James Madison. Too frail for public speaking, Jefferson, when the moment arrived for his tribute to Lafayette, thus handed a text he had composed to the dinner's host, attorney Valentine W. Southall, to read.

Jefferson assumed that his audience knew of Lafayette's deeds at Valley Forge, Barren Hill, Yorktown, and the like. "His deeds in the way of independence you have heard and read," he asserted. "They are known to you, and embalmed in your memories, and in the pages of faithful history." Instead, Jefferson focused on lesser-known contributions made by Lafayette to enhance America's standing in the world. In Paris, after all—during Jefferson's only residency abroad—as he had struggled to find his way as a neophyte diplomat, Lafayette had provided him vital assistance.

Working together, albeit often in vain, the two had sought to advance American commercial interests among European states. Equally—likely more—important, writing to American leaders, they had offered detailed accounts of the Articles of Confederation's weaknesses in advancing America's interests; they thus provided powerful arguments for delegates in Philadelphia aspiring to secure for the United States a new, more practical governing document.

Of his and Lafayette's Paris collaboration, Jefferson recalled: "When I was stationed in his country for the purpose of cementing its friendship with ours, and of advancing our mutual interests, this friend of both, was my most powerful auxiliary and advocate. He made our cause his own, as in truth it was that of his native country also. His influence and connections there were great. All doors of all departments were open to him at all times. In truth, I only held the nail, he drove it."

The tribute would be Jefferson's final public speech.[7]

Epilogue

"A Certain Idea"

Following Lafayette's 1824–25 American tour, Jefferson lived another two years. He died on July 4, 1826, the fiftieth anniversary of his Declaration of Independence and the same day as the death of his friend John Adams, with whom he had reconciled in 1811 after a decadelong estrangement. Jefferson was laid to rest in Monticello's small cemetery in a plot next to his friend from childhood, Dabney Carr.

As for Lafayette, his American tour restored in the United States—and, to a lesser degree, in France—much of his reputation's earlier shimmer. In July 1830 he helped command, though largely symbolically, the National Guard troops that helped to overthrow Charles X and install Louis Philippe on France's throne, restored after Napoleon's fall in 1814.

Indeed, the Hero of Two World's eventual death, in 1834, attested to his renewed popularity in France and growing republican disenchantment with Louis Philippe. Death came to Lafayette on May 20, in a Paris apartment that he had purchased years earlier, in a building still standing at 8 rue d'Anjou. Fearing the forces that would later topple his reign, the king forbade official recognition of Lafayette's passing. By contrast, when word of his death reached

America, President Andrew Jackson ordered official state mourning, equal in pomp and ceremony to that which had followed George Washington's passing.

But it was in France, not America, that Lafayette was laid to rest. Under close guard, he was interred alongside Adrienne, in a marble tomb in Paris's Picpus Cemetery, the same grounds that hold the remains of her sister, mother, and grandmother, along with more than a thousand other martyrs of the Revolution's guillotine.

Each day, during the 1790s Reign of Terror, the remains of those executed at the nearby Place du Trône-Renversé—today's Place de la Nation—were carted to Picpus and cast into two pits in the garden of a recently closed convent, the grounds on which Picpus Cemetery was later established. Fulfilling his wishes, Lafayette was interred in soil that he had asked to be collected at Bunker Hill and shipped to France.

Like Jefferson, whose legacy would be tainted by inconsistencies and personal hypocrisy on matters of race and slavery, so Lafayette's legacy would be complicated by his missteps during France's Revolution. In America the Hero of Two Worlds had helped to establish a state of enduring stability. He died, however, before seeing his own native land under stable republican governance.

Over the years, meanwhile, Lafayette's grave became a shrine for American— and, to a lesser degree, French—patriots. Uttering a soon oft-repeated phrase, U.S. Army colonel Charles E. Stanton, visiting Picpus during World War I, on July 4, 1917, proclaimed: "Lafayette, we are here!" Less well-known is Frederick Douglass's 1886 visit to Picpus. The great abolitionist and orator was no admirer of Thomas Jefferson. Indeed, "What to the Slave is the Fourth of July?" among his most celebrated lectures, indicted Jefferson and his Continental Congress colleagues for a galling hypocrisy. But the former slave took a different view of Lafayette; standing before his grave in Picpus, Douglass reflected: "This spot is doubly hallowed: this patriot had two countries for his own." And today, each year on July 4, the date that commemorates the Declaration of Independence drafted by Lafayette's friend Jefferson, a ceremony attended by American and French officials replaces the grave's American flag.

Only once in his lifetime, as Virginia's governor, was Jefferson, a talented writer and politician, summoned to military-related tasks, duties outside of his established expertises. Lafayette, trained as a soldier, was, by contrast, repeatedly cast into roles of sustained duration in both military and civilian theaters. Pondering those dual roles, the French writer and politician François de Chateaubriand viewed Lafayette as a flawed figure whose well-earned American successes elevated him into leadership roles in his native land in which he proved less adept:

> In the New World, Monsieur de Lafayette contributed to the creation of a new society; in the old world, to the destruction of an old one: freedom invokes him in Washington, anarchy in Paris.
>
> Monsieur de Lafayette had only one idea, and happily for him it was that of the century; the fixity of that idea created his empire; it served to blinker him, it prevented him looking to right or left; he marched with a firm step on a single track; he advanced, without tumbling over precipices, not because he saw them, but because he did not; blindness took the place of genius in him: everything fixed is fatal, and whatever is fatal is powerful.

But then again, France's revolutionaries in general had *all* taken on a challenge more daunting and complex than that faced by their American counterparts. Unlike those of France, America's Patriots never promulgated a new calendar for the ages—never envisioned inventing a new world. To be sure, the project of North America's revolutionaries, compared to those of France, was both strategically less challenging and more limited in scope. America's Patriots, after all, were fighting the army of a distant king—and at that, one unfearful of losing his kingship or life to their rebellion, and thus with limited incentive to invest sustained resources in opposing their efforts.

Beyond that, in fundamental ways, America's Patriots sought merely a restoration of legal rights ("the rights of Englishmen") and governmental structures they prized from earlier years as British subjects. And, unlike their French counterparts, America's revolutionaries had no feudal legacy—except in parts of New York's Hudson Valley—to extinguish. Moreover, relative to the conditions confronting their French counterparts, America's Patriots faced no festering poverty to eradicate—or perhaps more saliently, they never elected to grapple with the poverty that did exist in their Republic. Indeed, most of their early leaders willfully ignored the two main societal inequities that bedeviled the polity they had founded—its system of human-chattel slavery and displacement of native populations.

———

The words of a later French statesman, though not explicitly concerned with Lafayette, perhaps offer a fitting eulogy to his complex legacy. Charles de Gaulle's *War Memoirs*, written between 1949 and 1958, open with a simple declaration: "All my life I have had a certain idea of France," wrote the founder of France's Fifth Republic. But if de Gaulle, born in 1890, enjoyed the luxury of cherishing a "certain idea" of France, surely he and the entire French nation owed Lafayette a debt of gratitude.

During the eighteenth century's waning years, the marquis and his contemporaries confronted a country of varied and dispersed provinces, fiefdoms and state-sanctioned secular and ecclesiastical estates, all tenuously tied to a moribund monarchy at Versailles. And, during those years, they commenced the arduous work of gathering the peoples of those domains into a polity of "citizens"—into what de Gaulle relished as his "certain idea" of France, into what Lafayette and his allies, Jefferson included, dared call *une nation*.[1]

ACKNOWLEDGMENTS

I n Virginia's mountainous Piedmont country, I was privileged, while a fellow at the International Center for Jefferson Studies, to spend four weeks as the sole resident of Tufton Farm. Adjacent to Monticello, Tufton numbered among several farms that Thomas Jefferson owned in Albemarle County. There, when time permitted, I savored long hikes, under slate-gray autumnal skies, in the same upland forests that incited Jefferson's boyhood imagination. And, at each day's close, in a second-floor bedroom, thanks to a window deliberately left cracked-open, I fell asleep to the sea-like whisper of October breezes rustling the leaves of white ash trees planted on the farmhouse's ample grounds.

Two years later, I learned that Tufton Farm took its name from the surname of two sisters who were favorite classmates of Jefferson's daughter Patsy during her days at Paris's Panthémont school. Such random and chance illuminations on matters trivial and great rank among the pleasures of historical research. The narrator Nick Carraway, in F. Scott Fitzgerald's *The Great Gatsby,* remembers, as a young man, being "privy to the secret griefs of wild, unknown men." But while the past's voices—griefs and joys, from men and women, unknown and known—sometimes find their way to the historian's ear, their discovery rarely arrives via solitary enterprise.

In finding the voices that fill this book, I've benefitted from the published works of past and contemporary historians. Likewise, I've been the recipient of direct kindnesses from talented, living historians—scholars of both American and French history, as well as gifted biographers of Jefferson, Lafayette, and other persons who inhabit the narrative. Several of those scholars graciously agreed to read and comment on parts of the manuscript. They include independent historian William H. Adams; Laura Auricchio, of Fordham College at Lincoln Center, in New York City; Rafe Blaufarb, director of Florida State University's Institute on Napoleon and the French Revolution, in Tallahassee; Frank Cogliano, of the University of Edinburgh, in Scotland; Diane W. Shaw, director of Special Collections and College Archives, at Lafayette College, in Easton, Pennsylvania; Lori Glover, of St. Louis University, in St. Louis, Missouri; Mike Fitzsimmons, of Auburn University of Montgomery, in Montgomery, Alabama; Ed Gray, of Florida State University; Kathryn Heleniak, of Fordham University, in New York City; Cynthia Kierner, of George Mason University, in Fairfax, Virginia; independent historian Jon Kukla; Mark Lender, of Kean University, in Union, New Jersey; Rob McDonald, of the U.S. Military Academy, in West Point, New York; Greg Massey, of Freed-Hardeman University, in Henderson, Tennessee; and Paul S. Spalding, of Illinois College, in Jacksonville, Illinois. Among those scholars, special gratitude is owed to Adams, Blufarb, Lender, Fitzsimmons, Shaw, and Spalding, who kindly reviewed and commented on prodigious stretches of the manuscript.

For guiding me to key documents related to Jefferson and Lafayette's interactions in Virginia, I'm grateful to Robert Crout, of the College of Charleston, in South Carolina; Robert's peerless knowledge of Lafayette reaches back to his days as an editor of three of the five volumes—co-editor on the final installment—of the late Stanley J. Idzerda's wonderful five-volume, annotated documents collection, *Lafayette in the Age of the American Revolution*. For other assistance on my paper-chase, I'm grateful to Patrick Joseph Stevens and Hilary Dorsch Wong, of the Division of Rare and Manuscript Collections, at Cornell University, Ithaca, New York.

I also thank Andrew O'Shaughnessy, director of the Robert H. Smith International Center for Jefferson Studies, at the Thomas Jefferson Foundation, in Charlottesville, Virginia. Andrew and his staff welcomed me as a visiting fellow to the Jefferson center. I owe particular gratitude to others associated with the Monticello Foundation: librarian Endrina Tay, curator Emilie Johnson, historian Gaye Wilson, and plants curator Peggy Cornett. For still other kindnesses, I'm indebted to Lafayette biographer and former managing editor of *Time* magazine Jim Kelly; Clay Risen, of *The New York Times*; David Blight, of Yale University, in New Haven, Connecticut; John Inscoe, of the University of Georgia, in Athens; Barbara Bair and Julie Miller of the Library of Congress, in Washington; Janet Bloom, of the William L. Clements Library Manuscripts Division, at the University of Michigan, in Ann Arbor; independent historian, Walt Borneman; Glenn Campbell, of the Historic Annapolis Foundation, in Maryland; John McClure, at the Virginia Historical Society, in Richmond; Mary Wigge, of the Papers of George Washington, at the University of Virginia, in Charlottesville; and Jim Zeender, of the National Archives, in College Park, Maryland. I also thank Steve Hochman, assistant to President Jimmy Carter, at the Carter Center, in Atlanta. An era-straddling historian, Steve, from 1968 to 1981, prior to working with President Carter, assisted Dumas Malone with his six-volume Jefferson biography. For fielding questions related to the South Carolina Low-Country milieu, where Lafayette's *La Victoire,* in 1777, found safe harbor, I thank Lee G. Brockington, of Hobcaw Barony, at the Belle W. Baruch Foundation, in Georgetown, South Carolina; and Tommy Howard, former editor of the *Georgetown Times,* in Georgetown, South Carolina.

In France, I thank Paris friends Ed Goldstein and Dany Allouis. Gratitude is also due to Marie-Alpais Dumoulin-Torcheboeuf, of the Fondation Josée et René de Chambrun, in Paris. Marie-Alpais Dumoulin and her foundation colleagues have proven themselves stalwart guardians of Lafayette's legacy in France. More specifically, they serve as abiding curators of the grounds, buildings, collections, and archives of his and Adrienne's splendid Château de la Grange-Bléneau, outside of Paris. I also thank Jean-François Chuet, the present owner of Lafayette's final Paris residence, on rue d'Anjou, for welcoming me to that elegant space.

In the land of Lafayette's birth, I'm likewise grateful to the Association Hermione-La Fayette, in Rochefort; to curator Delphine Dubois at the Château du Versailles; and to Hélène Charbonneau, of the Centre de Musique Baroque, the performing arts venue that today occupies the Hôtel des Menus-Plaisirs, in the town of Versailles; Patrice Gueniffey, of the École des Hautes Études en

Sciences Sociales, in Paris; Steve Sarson, at the Université Jean Moulin, in Lyon; and Stephen Clay, of the Institut d'Études Politiques de Paris.

For various kindnesses, I thank Hedi Jilani and Nacer Jalloul at the Twelfth Arrondissement's Librairie la Sirène. And for welcoming me back to boulevard de Charonne and my old Twentieth Arrondissement haunts, I thank Karim Zagoud of Le Bar 96, architect Frédéric Rebeyrol, and journalists Sandrine Guioc and Stéphanie Arc; moreover *felicitations* are due Stéphanie on the publication of her first novel.

Mille fois merci to my friend Suzanne Obellianne who, years ago, introduced me to, among other magical places, the Bourbons' Versailles and Monet's Giverny. During my research, friends Bernard Obellianne and Catherine Chatal, with hearty Midi hospitality, graciously hosted me at their home in Toulouse; later, Bernard, with his native son's knowledge of the region's backroads and hidden treasures, proved himself an expert guide to the Canal du Midi and other wonders of the South of France.

For help with the acquisition of visual materials reproduced in this book, I thank the New York Public Library, in Manhattan; and the Library of Congress. More particularly, I'm grateful to Pascale Kahn, of the Bibliothèque nationale de France, in Paris; Vicky Villano, of the Office of Architect of the Capitol, in Washington; Marie-Alpais Dumoulin-Torcheboeuf, of the Fondation Josée et René de Chambrun, in Paris; Meaghan Alston, of the Moorland-Spingarn Research Center at Howard University, in Washington; John McKee, of the Thomas Jefferson Foundation, in Charlottesville, Virginia; David Burnhauser, of the Williams Center Art Galley, and the aforementioned Diane W. Shaw— both at Lafayette College; Dennis P. Buttleman, Jr., of the Masonic Library and Museum of Pennsylvania, in Philadelphia; and Erin Beasley, of the Smithsonian Institution's National Portrait Gallery, in Washington.

During his stellar career, journalist extraordinaire John Huey has earned distinction as a gifted reporter and writer, founding editor of *The Wall Street Journal Europe,* managing editor of *Fortune* magazine, and editor in chief of Time Inc. Since we met in 1972, John, a fellow Atlanta native, has also been, for me, a generous and inspiring friend. Most recently, I'm grateful that he encouraged me to pursue this project and provided editorial guidance as I crafted the attendant book proposal. Beyond that, throughout the research and writing, John has been a source of unstinting good cheer.

I also thank my agent, Alex Hoyt, for finding a home for this book at St. Martin's Press; and, at St. Martin's, I thank my editor, Charlie Spicer, editorial assistant, Sarah Grill, production editor, John Morrone, book designer, Kathryn Parise, book-jacket designer, Danielle Fiorella, publicist Leah Johanson, and marketing director, Danielle Prielipp. I'm also grateful to my copyeditor, Sue Llewellyn, for the care and gifts of erudition that she brought to bear on the manuscript, and to Peter Rooney for the robustly detailed index he created.

Closer to home, I thank friends Tim Ralston; Steve Johnson, Jack Haynes, Dennis Darling, Tommy Archibald, Marysia Harbutt, and Marysia's late husband—my dearly missed friend and fellow historian Fraser Harbutt. At Emory University, Fraser conducted the best history seminar of my doctoral studies there. For help with French language questions, I'm likewise grateful to friend and neighbor, Quebec native, Andrée Germain.

For welcome companionship during the otherwise solitary hours of writing, I thank our dogs Lad and Gracie and our cat Benjamin. Finally, for all her love and support—including reading and commenting on various iterations of the manuscript—I thank my spouse and best critic, Meta Larsson. Our shared journey began with a chance encounter three decades ago. In her native country—on a bridge in Stockholm, outside Riksdagshuset, Sweden's parliament building—Meta answered a visiting stranger's request for directions. All these years later—on matters large and small, with Humboldtian aplomb—she's still giving me reliable directions.

A NOTE ON SOURCES
AND STYLE

This work draws extensively on the National Archives' Founders Online, a splendid resource that offers convenient access to transcriptions of thousands of letters of, and related to, America's Founders. There these documents are presented with the latest emendations and annotations from expert historical documents editors. In most cases documents that appear at Founders Online originally appeared in one of the multivolume printed editions of the papers of various American Founders (e.g., *The Papers of Thomas Jefferson*).

Thanks to Founders Online's ease of use, interested readers may thus readily locate many of the documents quoted and cited herein at that website. But I'm also aware that some may wish to consult those annotated transcriptions in their original printed format. For their convenience, in my endnotes—in cases in which documents appear on both Founders Online and in one of those multivolume sets—I've provided the original publication information (printed volumes and page numbers), instead of citing the Founders site on which I actually accessed the document.

A word on the presentation herein of quoted documents is also in order: eighteenth-century English and French both thrived in an era ungoverned by rules prescribing standardized punctuation, capitalization, spelling, and the like. The name, for instance, of the individual rendered herein as "Lafayette" was also spelled, in his day, as "La Fayette" and similar variations thereof.

In this work, therefore, to avoid undue distractions for modern readers, I've taken the liberty in many, but not all, instances of standardizing such elements— including modernizing place-names. Likewise, in most cases in which I've preserved a quoted document's original (but now nonstandard) spelling, I've resisted—in the interests of preserving textual fluidity—both the impulse to modernize spelling as well as the temptation to insert the (quickly distracting) caveat [*sic*] alongside the word.

ABBREVIATIONS USED IN THE NOTES

Abbreviations for Institutions, Collections, and Published Works

AFC Adams Family Correspendence

"Auto" "Autobiography"

BNF Bibliothèque nationale de France

HOM The Hemingses of Monticello

LAAR Lafayette in the Age of the American Revolution

LOC Library of Congress

MB Memorandum books

MHS Massachusetts Historical Society

POAH Papers of Alexander Hamilton

POBF Papers of Benjamin Franklin

POGW Papers of George Washington

POJM Papers of James Madison

POTJ Papers of Thomas Jefferson

Abbreviations for Individuals

TJ Thomas Jefferson

GW George Washington

GWL George Washington Lafayette

L Michel-Louis-Christophe-Gilbert-Paulette de Motier, le marquis de la Fayette

Adrienne Marie-Adrienne-Françoise de Noailles

NOTES

1. *La Victoire*

1. *La Victoire* dimensions *et al.*, Archive Bordeaux; other details, *LAAR*, 115 n26; L to Adrienne, June 7 and June 15, [1777], *LAAR*, 1:58–60; Gottschalk, *Comes*, 138–39.

2. Gottschalk, *Comes*, 1–5; Auricchio, *Marquis*, 15.

3. Auricchio, *Marquis*, 3–9; Gottschalk, *Comes*, 1–13; "Although my mother," "I recall" *et al.*, L, Auricchio, *Marquis*, 7, 9, 14; Lafayette spelling, Gottschalk, *Comes*, 153–54.

4. Auricchio, *Marquis*, 7, 9–23; Gottschalk, *Comes*, 13–32; "Separated," L, Auricchio, *Marquis*, 9; "One comes away," Louis-Sébastien Mercier, Auricchio, *Marquis*, 15; "Some wise," comte de Ségur, Auricchio, *Marquis*, 30; Wooden Sword, *LAAR*, 1:64 n6. "By the gaucheness," L, Auricchio, *Marquis*, 21; "Danced without" *et al.*, La Marck, quoted in Auricchio, *Marquis*, 22–23.

2. "My Heart Was Enlisted"

1. L., "Memoir of 1779," *LAAR*, 1:3, 6–10; Gottschalk, *Comes*, 32–78; Auricchio, *Marquis*, 3–35; Paul, *Unlikely Allies*, 199–206; Broglie's English invasion, Murphy, *Vergennes*, 268–69; Stillé, "Comte de Broglie," 369–405; "Sparkling eyes," Auricchio, *Marquis*, 24; Broglie in Poland, "De Broglie's 'Secret Du Roi,'" *Nation*, 382–83; "Listened with," L, Auricchio, *Marquis*, 25; "My heart," L, "Memoir of 1779," *LAAR*, 1:7; "When I presented," L, "Memoir of 1779," *LAAR*, 1:8; "Tall, raw-boned," Biddle, *Autobiography*, 148; Kalb's 1768 America visit, Kalb to Étienne-François, Marquis de Stainville, March 2, 1768, Kapp, *Kalb*, 64–65; "On your arrival," "Committee of Secret Correspondence: Instructions to Silas Deane," March 2, 1776, *POBF*, 22:369–74. For Deane, also *Revolutionary Diplomatic Correspondence*, 1: "Chapter 14, Silas Deane,"

159–67; "His considerable," Deane-Lafayette agreement, Dec. 7, 1776, *LAAR*, 1:17; Covart, "Silas Deane"; Gottschalk, *Comes*, 135–42; L, "Memoir of 1779," *LAAR*, 1:3, 6–12; Mauroy, "Memoir," *LAAR*, 1:53–56.

2. Gottschalk, *Comes*, 32–78; Stillé, "Comte de Broglie," 369–405; "We can," *ibid.*, 384.

3. Gottschalk, *Comes*, 32–78; *ibid.*, 161–62; "The secrecy," L, "Memoir of 1779," *LAAR*, 1:8; Brice, GW to Benjamin Harrison, August 19, 1777, *POGW-Revolutionary* [hereafter *"Rev."*] *War Series*, 11:4–5n; *LAAR*, 1:33–34, 50, 84n.

4. "Sluggish ship," L, "Memoir of 1779," *LAAR* 1:10; order to destroy *La Victoire*, L, "Memoir of 1779," *LAAR* 1:10.

5. "I will not," L to Adrienne, May 30 [1777], *LAAR*, 1:57.

6. On-board studies, L to Adrienne, June 7 [1777], *LAAR*, 1:59; "Hasty preparations" and other details of approach to Charlestown, Sparks, *Washington*, 5:450.

7. Sources for chapter's specific quotes noted as they appear. More broadly, account of *La Victoire*'s arrival in South Carolina and Lafayette's travel to and time in Charlestown principally from L., "Memoir of 1779," *LAAR*, 1:3, 10–11; Kapp, *Kalb*, 109–10; Dubuysson (Du Buysson), "Memoir," *LAAR*, 1:73, 75; Sparks, *Washington*, 5:450–52; and L to Adrienne, June 15, 1777, *LAAR*, 1:59–60 and June 19, 1777, *LAAR*, 1:60–61, 63.

8. "The same strong," Sparks, *Washington*, 5:450.

3. Beyond the Reach of Pursuers

1. "Had attained," "beautiful," and "the novelty," Sparks, *Washington*, 5:451; Smith, "The Baronies," 70–74.

2. Five of the twelve officers aboard *La Victoire*—Jean-Pierre du Rousseau de Fayolle and four others—remained on the ship after Lafayette and seven other officers set off in the ship's launch. In turn, Du Rousseau de Fayolle—and apparently some or all of the aforementioned officers—remained aboard *La Victoire* when, days later, it sailed from Winyah Bay to Charlestown; Rousseau de Fayolle, "Journal," *LAAR*, 1:68–69. See also Dubuysson (Du Buysson), "Memoir," *LAAR*, 1:73, 75.

3. "Marauding negroes" and "Some of us" *et al.*; Dubuysson (Du Buysson), "Memoir," *LAAR*, 1:73–75–76. Persistence of rumored slave revolts in that era's South Carolina, Fraser, *Charleston*, 80–81.

4. "Officers," Biddle, *Autobiography*, 148 n.

5. "I even sent," L to Adrienne, June 19, 1777, *LAAR*, 1:61

6. "I miss you" *et al.*, L to Adrienne, June 19, 1777, *LAAR*, 1:63.

7. "Charleston is one," L to Adrienne, June 19, 1777, *LAAR*, 1:61.

8. "A simplicity," L to Adrienne, June 19, 1777, *LAAR*, 1:61; 1790 U.S. census figures, Carolana website; 1771–89, French slave trade, Curtin, *Atlantic Slave Trade: A Census*, 170—and more generally, 163–203.

4. The Pursuit of Happiness

1. June 14, 1777 entry, TJ, *MB*, 1:447; *Journal of the House of Delegates of the Commonwealth of Virginia*, May 20, 1777, 21; Cogliano, *Emperor*, 14–15; Malone, *Virginian*, 287; phaeton and driving arrangement, Isaac Jefferson, "Memoirs," 4; Eric Johnson, "Route to Richmond," Monticello website; Pawlett and Newman, "Route of the Three Notch'd Road."

2. Randolph, *Domestic Life*, 20; "Strong mind," Randolph, *Domestic Life*, 18.

3. Shadwell library, "Shadwell Library Reconstructed (Partial)"—"Thomas Jefferson's Libraries" database at Monticello.org; Jefferson's early readings and formal education, TJ, "Auto," 3; and Randall, *Jefferson*, 1:17–19; achievement of biographer Henry S. Randall, Peterson, *Jefferson Image*, 152.

4. "He, most," TJ, "Auto," 4–5.

5. "Confined to," TJ to Thomas McCauley, June 14, 1819, *POTJ-Retirement Series*, Early Access Document [hereafter "Doc."], Founders Online; TJ as lawyer, Malone, *Virginian*, 118–20; "Exterior grace" comment by marquis de Chastellux, Randall, *Jefferson*, 1:373; "Took the right side," Randolph, *Domestic Life*, 40.

6. Randolph, *Domestic*, 397.

7. Jefferson siblings, Malone, *Virginian*, 430.

8. Burwell, Meacham, *Jefferson*, 23–26; Walker, Malone, *Virginian*, 153–55, 447–51; Meacham, *Jefferson*, 40–42; Kukla, *Jefferson's Women*, 41–63; Jefferson on St. Paul, Meacham, *Jefferson*, 25–26; "You say," TJ to William Fleming, March 20, 1764, TJ, *POTJ*, 1:16.

9. Dabney Carr, Malone, *Virginian*, 160–61; Randall, *Jefferson*, 1:41–42; Malone, *Virginian*, 143–45; Wood, *Friends*, 78.

10. Jefferson's "Memorandum books" transcribed, edited, annotated, and, in 1997, published in two-volume edition—cited herein as *MB*; for Jefferson and Memorandum books, see "Introduction," *MB*, 1:xvii–xxi; "Moved," TJ, *MB*, 1:212.

11. "Meacham, *Jefferson*, 53–57; "A little above," Randolph, *Domestic Life*, 43; Kukla, *Jefferson's Women*, 68–69.

12. Gordon-Reed, *HOM*, 37–76; Meacham, *Jefferson*, 53–56; Kukla, *Jefferson's Women*, 64, 67–68, 117–20.

13. "Spinster," wedding license bond, *POTJ*, 1:86–87; Kukla, *Jefferson's Women*, 64.

14. *Virginian*, 40, 42–45, 162–63; Kukla, *Jefferson's Women*, 67–77.

15. Malone, *Virginian*, 182–90; Meacham, *Jefferson*, 74–75; "Loyalism cut" and estimates of loyalists, Jasanoff, *Liberty's Exiles*, 8, and 364–65, n. 16.

16. Martha Washington Jefferson ("Patsy"), Malone, *Virginian*, 160; "Group statement," McDonald, *Confounding Father*, 7–8.

17. "Our son," June 14, 1777 entry, TJ, *MB*, 1:447.

5. To Philadelphia

1. "Some of our," Dubuysson, "Memoir," *LAAR*, 1:76; Lafayette's overland party, *LAAR*, 1:84 n2; other overland party, Du Rousseau de Fayolle, "Journal," *LAAR*, 1:69, 71.

2. "The farther," L to Adrienne, July 17 [1777], *LAAR*, 1:67; "I have less," L to Adrienne, July 23, 1777, *LAAR* 1:67; "It is safe," Dubuysson, "Memoir," *LAAR*, 1:76–77.

3. "After cleaning," Dubuysson, "Memoir," *LAAR*, 1:76–77; Gaines, *Liberty*, 65.

4. "Induce me," Deane to Committee of Secret Correspondence, Dec. 6, 1776, Elliot, *American Diplomatic Code*, 464; "When I," L, "Imprudent," in Franklin and Deane to Committee of Foreign Affairs, May 25, 1777, Wharton, *Diplomatic Correspondence*, 2:324–25. In early 1777, Committee of Secret Correspondence was renamed Committee of Foreign Affairs. Schiff, *Improvisation*, 14, 15, 21–23; Isaacson, *Franklin*, 321-331-33. Franklin in recent years has been the subject of prodigious studies by gifted historians—notably Walter Isaacson's *Benjamin Franklin, an American Life*; Edmund Morgan's *Benjamin Franklin*; and Stacy Schiff's A *Great Improvisation: Franklin, France, and the Birth of America*.

5. "Had instructions," Dubuysson, "Memoir," *LAAR*, 1:79; Sash described, item #598, *Catalogue of the Loan Exhibition of Historical Portraits and Relics*, 124; July 31, 1777, date of commission, *Journals of Continental Congress*, 8: 592–93; and Sparks, *Writings of Washington*, 5:454; For negative reactions of the twelve men and their desire to return to France, Rousseau de Fayolle, "Journal," *LAAR*, 1:71–72.

6. "He was," Dubuysson, "Memoir," *LAAR*, 1:80.

6. City Tavern

1. First Lafayette-Washington meeting, L, "Memoir of 1776," *LAAR*, 1:91; Sparks, *Washington*, 5:454; "Although he was," L, "Memoir of 1776," *LAAR*, 1:91.

2. "There is a fine," *et al.*, surgeon James Thatcher, Stryker, *Washington*, 5; Washington's hair and other physical characteristics, Chernow, *Washington*, 29–30.

3. City Tavern described, Young, *Philadelphia*, 324, 324n.

4. Washington learns of British army's destination, GW to Horatio Gates, July 31, 1777, *POGW-Rev War Series*, 10:466–67.

5. "Spoke to him," Sparks, *Washington*, 5:454.

6. "That he" and "his joy," Sparks, *Washington*, 5:455. The assumption that Lafayette did not mention the City Tavern dinner to the eleven men of *La Victoire* was deduced from the fact that the event goes unmentioned in any of the men's otherwise often detailed accounts of their Philadelphia stay.

7. "To Learn, and Not to Teach"

1. Troops review, Nolan, *Lafayette*, 10; "About eleven" and Lafayette's account of review, *LAAR*, 1:91; other details, General Orders 8 Sept. 1777, in *POGW-Rev. War. Series*, 10:551–53; "Modest manners," Gottschalk, *Joins*, 33.

2. Moland House—Buck, "Neshaminy," 257–84; "There has," Timothy Pickering to [Rebecca White Pickering], Aug. 20, 1777, Pickering, *Life*, 1:151

3. Fall 1775 French army reforms, Auricchio, *Marquis*, 26; Braddock expedition, Chernow, *Washington*, 52–69; "Merely honorary," GW to Harrison, Aug. 19, 1777, *POGW-Rev. War Series*, 4–5; disposition of officers who accompanied Lafayette to America, *LAAR*, 1:86 n26; for Pulaski, see Pulaski to GW, July 26, 1777, *POGW-Rev. War Series*, 428–29n.

4. "The conduct," GW to Col. Elias Dayton, August 3, 1777, *POGW-Rev. War Series*, 10:491–92.

5. British ships reappearance, GW to Hancock, Aug. 22, 1777, *POAH*, 1:317; Stenton described, General Orders, Aug. 23, 1777, *POGW-Rev. War Series*, 11:19 n1.

6. Massey, *Laurens*, 6–85; John Laurens' appearance, Massey, *Laurens*, 170; Chernow, *Hamilton*, 7–125; "Was slight," Chernow, *Hamilton*, 17; questions persist over Hamilton's birth-date; this work, following Chernow, assumes Jan. 11, 1755, Chernow, *Hamilton*, 16–17; "The drums," GW, General Orders, Aug. 23, 1777, *POGW-Rev. War Series*, 11:19; "Heads adorned," *LAAR*, 1:92; "Much remains" and other parade details, John Adams to Abigail Adams, Aug. 24, 1777, *AFC*, 2:327–28; "With their heads," L., "Memoir of 177[9]," *LAAR*, 1:92.

7. Troop figures, Martin, *Philadelphia Campaign*, 37–39; André, *Journal*, 1:71–72; Middlekauff, *Cause*, 387.

8. Troop movements, *Philadelphia Campaign*, 57, 116, 162; L, "Memoir," *LAAR*, 1:84; and L to Adrienne, Sept. 12 [1777], *LAAR*, 110; for a detailed account of Brandywine Creek, Harris, *Brandywine*.

9. Lafayette at Brandywine, L to Adrienne, Sept. 12 [1777], *LAAR*, 108–110; and "retreating soldiers," etc., L, "Memoir," *LAAR*, 1:95; Harris, *Brandywine*, 310.

8. Renown

1. Lafayette at Brandywine and recovery, L to Adrienne, Sept. 12 [1777], *LAAR*, 108–110; L, "Memoir," *LAAR*, 1:95; Harris, *Brandywine*, 310; "Was about," L, "Memoir," *LAAR*, 1:95; Sash and wound at Brandywine, item #598, *Catalogue of the Loan Exhibition of Historical Portraits and Relics*, 124; McGuire, *Campaign*, 1:269; longest single battle etc., Harris, *Brandywine*, viii.

2. "The ball," L to Adrienne, Sept. 12 [1777], *LAAR*, 108–110; recuperation, Auricchio, *Marquis*, 51–53; "Ttruly touching," "The people" and Lafayette's familiarity with Moravians through Raynal, L to Adrienne, Oct. 1, 1777, *LAAR*, 1:116, 118 n6.

3. "The Marquis," GW to Hancock, Sept. 11, 1777, *POGW-Rev. War Series*, 11:200–01; "No longer," L, *Memoirs* [NY: Saunders and Otley, 1837], 1:26; "Citizens . . . all interested," L, *Memoirs* [NY: Saunders and Otley, 1837], 1:25.

4. "It was not," L quoted in Henry Laurens to John Lewis Gervais, Oct. 8, 1777, Massey, *Laurens*, 75; foundering of *La Victoire*, September 15, 1777, L, "Memoir of 1779," *LAAR*, 1:10, 15 n27; Dubuysson, "Memoir," *LAAR*, 1:75, 84–85 n4.

5. "While I," L to Adrienne, Sept. 12 [1777], *LAAR*, 108–110. Lost letter from Adrienne to Lafayette and Pulaski's delivery of it, L to Adrienne, Nov, 6, 1777, *LAAR*, 1:145 and 145 n1. For Pulaski, GW to Hancock, Aug. 28, 1777, *POAH*, 1:318.

6. "Good Moravian," L, *Memoirs* [New York: Saunders and Otley, 1837], 27; "All the furniture" and Lafayette letter-writing, Auricchio, *Marquis*, 53.

9. "Soldier's Friend"

1. "The Marquis," GW to Henry Laurens, Nov. 26–27, 1777, *POGW-Rev. War Series*, 12:420–22; Grant of command, Laurens to GW, Dec. 1, 1777, *LAAR*, 1:165.

2. "The unfortunate," L., "Memoirs," *LAAR*, 1:170; purchase of clothes etc. and epithet, Unger, *Lafayette*, 58.

3. "My destiny," L to Adrienne, Jan. 6, 1778, *LAAR*, 1:222–26; Anastasie was born July 1, 1777; ref. to Adrienne's now lost letter and its news of Anastasie's birth, L to Adrienne, Dec. 22 [1777], *LAAR*, 1:198.

4. Conway Cabal, Canada *et al.*, Auricchio, *Marquis*, 56–60, and *LAAR*, 1:206n–207n.

5. "I am," GW to L, March 10, 1778, *POGW-Rev. War Series*, 132–33.

6. "Neither of," Middlekauff, *Cause*, 404–05; "The news," *Memoirs* [London: Saunders and Otley, 1837], 1:79; Conway Cabal, Unger, *Lafayette*, 69.

10. Stargazer

1. "Circumstances," *POTJ*, 1: TJ to Hancock, Oct. 11, 1776, 1:524; Paris offer, also Parton, *Jefferson*, 197–98; Malone, *Virginian*, 261; Cogliano, *Emperor*, 14–15.

2. See "Resolution on the Revision of the Virginia Statutes," May 29, 1784—including "Editorial Note," *POTJ*, 8:47–49; Malone, *Virginian*, 261.

3. "If there," "as early," TJ to Giovanni Fabbroni, June 8, 1778, *POTJ*, 2:195–98.

4. Davis, *Phillips*, 99–105; Kranish, *Flight*, 105–113; "May be sent," Harvie to TJ, Sept. 15, 1778, *POTJ*, 2:211–13; "Never shall," Wilhelm de Roi, Kranish, *Flight*, 107; "The British Officers," Phillips to TJ, Aug. 12, 1779, *POTJ*, 3:66; "The great cause," TJ to Phillips [April? 1779], *POTJ*, 2:261.

5. "Somewhat too," Malone, *Virginian*, 291.

6. "America never," GW to Benjamin Harrison, Dec. 18[–30], 1778, *POGW-Rev. War Series*, 18:447–452.

11. "No One Better Situated"

1. "The Artillery," Fisher and "The troops," Tilghman—both in "General Orders," May 5, 1778, *POGW-Rev. War Series*, no pagination, n. 6; Lafayette embrace of GW, Ramsay, *Revolution*, 2:68; white neckerchief, Auricchio, *Marquis*, 62.

2. "Good tidings," GW to Laurens, May 1, 1778, *POGW-Rev. War Series*, 15: no pagination, n. 3.

3. Middlekauff, *Cause*, 405–09.

4. "Will require," GW to L, May 18, 1778, *LAAR*, 2:53–54.

5. "Made a timely," GW to Henry Laurens, May 24, 1778, *POGW-Rev. War Series*, 15:210–11; Unger, *Lafayette*, 74–76; Auricchio, *Marquis*, 62–68; "Like his master," Ségur, *Memoirs*, 89.

6. For Charles Lee and Battle of Monmouth Courthouse, see Lender, Stone, *Fatal Sunday*; and Papas, *Renegade Revolutionary*; Middlekauff, *Cause*, 420–428; Auricchio, *Marquis*, 68–71; and Chernow, *Washington*, 340–47; "Perfect original," Jeremy Belknap, in Papas, *Revolutionary Renegade*, 2; "Cannon fire," Lafayette, in Auricchio, *Marquis*, 70; "Into the maw," Lender, Stone, *Fatal Sunday*, 397; "Passed the night," Lafayette, in Auricchio, *Marquis*, 71.

7. "Conceived their," John Laurens to Henry Laurens, Aug. 26, 1780, Massey, *Laurens*, 116; Gottschalk, *Joins*, 257 269; Massey, *Laurens*, 117–18; Auricchio, *Marquis*, 71–76; "Predicament" and "Would you believe," L to d'Estaing, Aug. 22, 1780, *LAAR*, 2:139–40; Nolan, *Lafayette*, 74–76.

8. "However pleasantly," L to D'Estaing, July 14, 1778, *LAAR*, 2:102–07.

9. "Extreme impatience" and "incalculable slowness," d'Estaing, Auricchio, *Marquis*, 72–73; "No one," D'Estaing to Secretary of Marine, Nov. 5, 1778, Auricchio, *Marquis*, 72; "The French officers," d'Estaing quoted by John Laurens, in Gottschalk, *Joins*, 249; John Laurens and d'Estaing, Massey, *Laurens*, 113–18, 122; "I do most," GW to Gouverneur Morris, July 24, 1778, *POGW-Rev. War Series*, 16:153–55.

10. "I should be," GW to L, Sept. 25, 1778, *POGW-Rev. War Series*, 17:128–32.

11. "As long," L to Pres. of Congress, Oct. 13, 1778, *LAAR*, 2:190–91.

12. "High Esteem," Pres. of Congress to Lafayette, Oct. 24 [1778], *LAAR*, 2:193–95; *Alliance* and return, Gottschalk, *Joins*, 315–21.

12. "À Hunting with the King"

1. Gottschalk, *Joins*, 327–32; Gottschalk, *Close*, 1–6; "I thought only," L, *Memoirs*, *LAAR*, 2:226; Auricchio, *Lafayette*, 80–81.

2. "I wish," Maurois, *Adrienne*, 83–84; also Gottschalk, *Comes*, 13; Voltaire and Madame de Choiseul ref., in Maurois, *Adrienne*, 83.

3. "Loved her husband," Maurois, *Adrienne*, 96.

4. "I have a heart," GW to L, Sept. 30, 1779, *POGW-Rev. War Series*, 22:557–63.

5. "Accept my," Maurois, *Adrienne*, 97.

6. "I am just," L to Franklin [March 20, 1779], *LAAR*, 2:241; Auricchio, *Marquis*, 80–84; "Prisoners Killed" [L and Franklin—partial photo of ms. page, circa May 1779], *LAAR*, 2:266; more on war-atrocities book, L to Franklin, May 19, 1779, *LAAR*, 2:266, 267—particularly, 267 n2;. sword, "A Sword for the Marquis de Lafayette, Four Documents" [before August 24–circa August 24, 1779], *POBF*, 30:257–60; Schiff, *Improvisation*, 207–09; Isaacson, *Franklin*, 385–86, 389.

7. Auricchio, *Marquis*, 81–91; Unger, *Lafayette*, 98–100; "I must leave," L to Vergennes, Feb. 2, 1780, *LAAR*, 2:2:50–352; "Hasten to join," Vergennes order," March 5, 1780, *LAAR*, 2:364–68.

13. Burdens Wrong to Decline

1. June 1, 1779, *Journal of the House of Delegates*, 29.
2. "In a virtuous government," TJ to Richard Henry Lee, June 17, 1779, *POTJ*, 2:298–99; Cogliano, *Emperor*, 14–16.
3. Davis, *Phillips*, 103–111; Riedesel, *Memoirs*, 2:76–94, 105, *Flight*, Kranish, 122; "To the same," TJ to Phillips, June 25, 1779, *POTJ*, 3:14–15; "Not less than," TJ to GW, July 17, 1779, *POGW-Rev. War Series*, 21:534–36; "I must entreat," GW to Bland, July 27, 1779, *POGW-Rev. War Series*, 21:671–72; "Every care," Phillips to Bland, July 3, 1779, Bland, *Papers*, 141.
4. Phillips was born in 1731, but month and date of birth remain unknown, Davis, *Phillips*, 10; Hair etc., *ibid.*, 2; more generally, for other aspects of Phillips's life, also see ibid.
5. Riedesel, *Memoirs*, 2:70–72; Kranish, *Flight*, 124–25; "Forming a caravan" *et al.*, Riedesel, *Memoirs*, 2:75–94; *POTJ*, 3:368–69; "The possibility," TJ to Riedesel, May 3, 1780, *POTJ*, 3:368–69.

14. Blast Like an Earthquake

1. Callahan, "Richmond," 1–5; Kranish, *Flight*, 122–23; Cogliano, *Emperor*, 15–24.
2. "While we are," TJ to Preston, June 15, 1780, *POTJ*, 3:447–49.
3. Middlekauff, *Cause*, 449.
4. "Our intelligence," TJ to GW, June 11, 1780, *POTJ*, 3:432–34.
5. Malone, *Virginian*, 325; "To take," TJ to William Preston, Aug. 8, 1780, *POTJ*, 3:533–34n., re Dudley Diggs's acknowledgment of letter.
6. "The application," TJ to Richard Henry Lee, Sept. 13, 1780, *POTJ*, 3:642–43; Malone, *Virginian*, 328.
7. "Greater abilities," Page to TJ, Dec. 9, 1780, *POTJ*, 4:191–93.
8. TJ, "Diary of Arnold's Invasion," *POTJ*, 4:258–68; "To consider," TJ to Steuben, Jan. 4, 1781, *POTJ*, 4, 308; TJ, "Arnold's Invasion as reported by Jefferson in the Virginia Gazette 13 January 1781," *POTJ*, 4:269–70; "Depredations," Simcoe, *Journal*, 59; Selby, *Virginia*, 222–25; Kranish, *Flight* 134–55; for Benedict Arnold, see also Martin, *Arnold*; Philbrick, *Ambition*; Lender and Martin, "Traitor's Epiphany"; and "The heights," Reed, *Simcoe*, 95; "As soon as," Isaac Jefferson, "Memoirs," 7; Decker, *Steuben*, 20–27; ropewalk and other destruction, Decker, *Steuben*, 26; "Unremitting exertions," TJ to GW, Jan. 10, 1781, *POTJ*, 4:333–35.

15. "The Latitude of His Plans"

1. "In the Uniform of," John Adams to James Lovell, Feb. 29, 1780, *Papers of John Adams*, 8:380; "Universal joy," Abigail Adams to John Adams, May 1, 1780, *AFC*, 3:334.

2. L to Samuel Adams, May 30, 1780, *LAAR*, 3:41–43; letters to Clinton and others described, *LAAR*, 2:42–43n.

3. "It will be proper," GW to L, May 16, 1780, *POGW*, Early Access Doc., Founders Online; "If the French troops," L to Vergennes, May 20, 1780, *LAAR*, 3:26–29.

4. Auricchio, *Marquis*, 87–88; Gaines, *Liberty*, 137; Gottschalk, *Close*, 117.

5. Knapp, *Lafayette*, 5; "Of a perfect whitness" *et al.*, Gottschalk, *Close*, 121–25; L to Matthias Ogden, Sept. 16, 1780, *LAAR*, 3, 173 n1.

6. Kapp, *Steuben*, 345–47; Doyle, *Steuben*, 192–93.

7. "Chiefly," GW to Von Steuben, Feb. 20, 1781, *POGW*, Early Access Doc., Founders Online; "In hopes of finding," GW to TJ, Feb. 21, 1781, *POTJ*, 4:683–85.

8. "Whether General Phillips," GW to L, April 11, 1781, *POGW*-Rev. War Series, Early Access Doc; "I will," L to Nathanael Greene, April 17, 1781, *LAAR*, 4:35, 36–41.

9. Phillips's March and April 1781 movements, GW to L, Feb. 25, 1781, *LAAR*, 3:348 n2; Long, "Green Water Navy," n.p. [on-line]; Kranish, *Flight*, 228–40; Phillips arrival at Portsmouth, Phillips to Clinton, April 15, 1781, in Clinton, *Campaign in Virginia, 1781*, 1:407.

16. "Flattered by the Command"

1. "I Am the More flattered," L to TJ, Feb. 21, 1781, *LAAR*, 2:336, 338.

2. "Of lopping off," TJ to L, March 2, 1781, *POTJ*, 5:43; for the date Jefferson expected Lafayette's arrival at Head of Elk ("by 6th of March at farthest"), GW to TJ, Feb. 21, 1781, *POTJ*, 4:683–85.

3. Jefferson estimate of state assistance for Lafayette, TJ to L, March 8, 1781, *POTJ*, 5:92–93; "Mild laws," TJ to L, March 10, 1781, *POTJ*, 5:113–14.

4. Lucy Elizabeth death, April 15, 1781 entry, TJ, *MB*, 1:508; "The day is so," TJ to David Jameson, April 16, 1781, *POTJ*, 5:468–69.

5. Report of ships on James River, James Innes to TJ, April 18, 1781, *POTJ*, 5:489; "Former experience," TJ to County Lieutenants of Henrico and certain other counties, April 19, 1781, *POTJ*, 5:496–97; removal of state papers, TJ to County Lieutenant of Henrico County, April 19, 1782, *POTJ*, 5:497.

6. Chinard, *Lafayette and Jefferson*, 8–9.

7. L to Greene, April 17, 1781, *LAAR*, 4, 40; "A charge," Phillips to L, April 28, 1781, and other quoted Phillips letter to Lafayette (April 29, 1781), *LAAR*, 4:69, 71–72; Ropewalk quarters *et al.*, Wild, *Journal*, 61-30; Phillips on shore of James River anecdote from firsthand account of American soldier James Johnson, in Dann, *Revolution Remem-*

bered, 399, 405–06; Kranish, *Flight*, 249–50—though erroneous date given for re-counted sighting of Phillips; "The stile," L to Phillips, April 30, 1781, *LAAR*, 4:73. "Rapid March," L to GW, May 4, 1781, *LAAR*, 4:82.

17. Rumours Gone Abroad

1. "Retired," "between 5 & 6 o'clk," "exceeding[ly] warm," "to cut their coats," Wild, *Journal*, 62; "The Arrival," TJ to Members of Assembly, May 1, 1781, *POTJ*, 5:25; Malone, *Virginian*, 349–51.

2. "Rumours gone abroad," TJ to Members of Assembly for Fluvanna and Certain Other Counties, May 1, 1781, *POTJ*, 5:585–86; May 10, 1781, entry, *Journal of the House of Delegates*, 3.

3. Spring 1781 British advantages, Kranish, *Flight*, 270–71; May 8, 1781 Council of State meeting attended by Jefferson and Lafayette, *Journal of the Council of State of Virginia*, 2, 343; and *LAAR*, 4:106 n1.

4. Kranish, *Flight*, 170–71; "Those mutinyous rascals," Samuel Patterson to Davies, May 27, 1781, *Calendar of Virginia State Papers*, 2:126; "The people," Davis Ross to Col. William Davies, May 27, 1781, *Calendar of Virginia State Papers*, 2:124; "A powerful army," Entries for May 28, 29, 1781, *Journal of the House of Delegates*, 4, 5.

5. "This quarrel," "Speech to Jean Baptiste Ducoigne, June [1,] 1781," *POTJ*, 6:60–64 and note on Ducoigne.

6. Malone, *Virginian*, 351; Kranish, *Flight*, 269, 278–79; "Will be the most," TJ to Phillips, June 25, 1779, *POTJ*, 3:14–15.

18. The Enemy at Monticello

1. "I found," Hudson affidavit, July 26, 1805, in Maurer, *Diary*, 326; "Plunged into," "about 18. hours," *et al.*, "Diary of Arnold's Invasion, and Notes on Subsequent Events in 1781: Versions of 1796?, 1805, and 1816," *POTJ*, 4:258–68; "British horse," June 4, 1781, TJ, *MB*, 1:510; Kranish, *Flight* 275–96; Cogliano, *Emperor*, 24–26; "Remained in the dark," Randolph, *Domestic Life*, 56; Wilson, "Jack Jouett's Ride," Monticello website; Malone, *Virginian*, 363; Selby, *Revolution in Virginia*, 281–85; "Sacred care," TJ to William Gordon, July 17, 1788, *POTJ*, 13:362–65.

19. "A Good School for Me"

1. Tucker, *Almanac*, 356–57; Middlekauff, *Glorious Cause*, 481–88; British casualties at Guilford Courthouse, Greene, *Papers*, 7:440; "Until Virginia," "the rivers," Cornwall to Clinton, April 10, 1781, Cornwallis, *Correspondence*, 1:86–87; "Dangerous to," Clinton to Cornwallis, May 29, 1781, *Parliamentary Register, House of Lords, 2nd Sess. 15th Parliament*, 8:159; Cornwallis appearance and biography, O'Shaughnessy, *Lost America*, 247–85; "Dangerous," Clinton to Cornwallis, May 29, 1781, *Parliamentary Register, House of Lords, 2nd Sess. 15th Parliament*, 3:59.

2. "The boy cannot escape me," Gottschalk, *Close*, 431; "I am superior," Cornwallis to Rawdon, May 20, 1781, Cornwallis, *Correspondence*, 1:98; "I shall now," Cornwallis to Clinton, May 26, 1781, Cornwallis, *Correspondence*, 1:100–01; though often attributed to Cornwallis, the "cannot escape me" vow has an uncertain provenance—Gottschalk, *Close*, 431–32.

3. Maass, *Yorktown*, 57; Gottschalk, *Close*, 238–39.

4. Gottschalk, *Close*, 244; Maass, *Yorktown*, 116, 135–40; Wayne's "Mad" sobriquet, GW to Hancock, May 5, 1776, *POGW-Rev. War Series*, 4:209–11 n1.

5. "Lord Cornwallis," L to Luzerne, June 16, 1781, *LAAR*, 4:185–89; Cornwallis's Richmond arrival and departure dates, "Cornwallis Orderly Book," Manuscripts Division, University of Michigan.

6. "What Lord Cornwallis Means," L to Greene, June 21, 1781, *LAAR*, 4:203; distance of Lafayette's camp from Richmond, L to Steuben, June 15, 1781, *LAAR*, 4:185.

7. Date for Cornwallis Richmond departure, Clary, *Adopted Son*, 309; Williamsburg arrival, Maass, *Yorktown*, 135; orders for Cornwallis to find defensible port, Clinton to Cornwallis, June 11, 1781, Cox, *Clinton-Cornwallis Controversy*, 2:18–23; Cornwallis to Clinton, June 30, 1781, and July 8, 1781, in Cornwallis, *Correspondence*, 1:102–05.

8. Green Spring, Clary, *Adopted Son*, 310–12; and Maass, *Yorktown*, 134–39 (latter for cited Green Spring casualties, 138); "The appearance," L to La Luzerne, June 16, 1781, *LAAR*, 4:186; "The Marquis intended," Cornwallis to Clinton, July 8, 1781, Cornwallis, *Correspondence*, 1:105; "This devil," L to Vicomte de Noailles, May 22, 1781, *LAAR*, 4:123.

20. To Do Some Very Good Things

1. Date of GW's learning of de Grasse's sailing to Virginia, GW to L, August 15, *LAAR*, 4:331 n3; Operations of de Grasse's fleet, Selby, *Virginia*, 288–89, 292–95.

2. Gottschalk, *Close*, 294–305; Maass, *Yorktown*, 135–40; "If the French army," L to La Luzerne, August 14, 1781, *LAAR*, 4:321–22.

3. "You will hear," GW to L, Aug. 15, 1781, *POGW*, Early Access Doc., Founders Online; "In the present," L to GW, August 21, 1781, *LAAR*, 4:339.

4. Intelligence from James, L to GW, August 25, 1781, *POGW*, Early Access Doc., Founders Online; Armistead, Clary, *Adopted Son*, 325, and *LAAR*, 5:279 n1; Daigler, "Armistead," online; and Harris, *Old Kent County*, 99–100; until recently the aforementioned spy was often called by historians "James Armistead"; recent scholarship indicates that James never used his master's surname—Flynn, "I Have Been So Long," 13 n9; similarly, recent scholarship disputes past assumptions that James appears in *Lafayette at Yorktown*, a 1782 portrait by Jean Baptiste Le Paon's 1782, Auricchio, "Lafayette at Yorktown," 17–31.

5. Middlekauff, *Cause*, 561–64.

6. Middlekauff, *Cause*, 564; Tucker, *Almanac*, 367; O'Shaughnessy, *Lost America*, 313; Willis, *Sea Power*, 451–55.

21. Yorktown

1. "They are all," Denny, "Diary," 401; "Stealing salt," L to GW, Sept 8, 1781, *LAAR* 4:392; "Have ended up," Luzerne to L, Oct. 8, 1781, Sept. 8, 1781, *LAAR*, 4:39; Gottschalk, *Close*, 303–08; "Try my," Wayne to L, Sept. 11, 1781, *LAAR*, 4:399; "Caught the General," Chernow, *Washington*, 411.

2. "I am no longer," Hamilton to Schuyler, Feb. 18, 1781, *POAH*, 2:563–69; Massey, *Laurens*, 196; Chernow, *Hamilton*, 150–61.

3. Allied vanguard, L to GW, Oct. 16, 1781, *POGW*, Early Access Doc., Founders Online; Cornwallis to GW, Oct. 17, 1781, *POGW*, Early Access Doc., Founders Online; Massey, *Laurens*, 198–99; "Our batteries," Denny, "Diary," 405–06; "You will understand," L to Chevalier de La Luzerne, Oct. 16, 1781 *LAAR*, 4:421; "Owing to," L to GW, Oct. 16. 1781, *POGW*, Early Access Doc., Founders Online; "I propose," Cornwallis to GW, Oct. 17, 1781, Cornwallis, *Correspondence*, 1:523; "An ardent Desire," GW to Cornwallis, Oct. 17, 1781, *POGW*, Early Access Doc., Founders Online; Cornwallis entounters James in Lafayette's quarters, "I Have Been," Shaw, 3.

4. "Finest moments," L to Adrienne, Oct. 22, 1781, *LAAR*, 4:426–27; "He established," L to Prince de Poix, Oct. 20, 1781, *LAAR*, 4:424.

22. Taps

1. "Where is Mason," GW to Benjamin Harrison, Dec. 18[–30], 1778, *POGW-Rev. War Series*, 18:447–52; "I hope," TJ to GW, Oct. 28, 1781, *POTJ*, 6:129–30; horse-riding accident, TJ, "Diary of Arnold's Invasion and Notes on Subsequent Events in 1781: Versions of 1796?, 1805, and 1816," *POTJ*, 4:258–68.

2. "For his impartial," Resolution by the Virginia General Assembly, 12–19 December [12], 1781, *POTJ*, 6:135–37; Cogliano, *Emperor*, 27–29; Malone, *Virginian*, 365–67.

3. Gottschalk, *Close*, 230–31; admitted Phillips's death and "degree of politeness," L to GW, May 17, 1781, *LAAR*, 4:109 n3; "Openly in the field," Dann, *Revolution Remembered*, 399, 405–06; "Made an Apology," TJ to Virginia Delegates, May 10, 1781, *POTJ*, 5:632–34.

4. "A constant sacrifice," TJ to Monroe, May 20, 1782, *POTJ*, 6:184–87; "The Governor does," L to GW, Sept. 8, 1781, *LAAR*, 392–93; Virginia legislature's investigation and exoneration of Jefferson, Malone, *Virginian*, 362–69.

23. More Mortification Than Any of My Life

1. Origins of *Notes on the State of Virginia*, TJ to d'Anmours, Nov. 30, 1780, *POTJ*, 4:167–68, and Malone, *Virginian*, 373–89; "Man not yet," Chastelleux. *Travels*, 228;

decline of Assembly seat, TJ to the Speaker, May 6, 1782, *POTJ*, 6:179; "A family," TJ to Monroe, May 20, 1782, *POTJ*, 6:184–87.

2. Malone, *Virginian*, 396–97; "Never out of," Patsy Jefferson, Randall, *Jefferson*, 1:382; quoted account of Jefferson's alleged deathbed promise to Martha—while comporting with persistent family lore—seems to have originated with Edward Bacon, in Jefferson's later years a Monticello overseer. However, because Bacon was born three years after Martha's death, he could not have personally witnessed the purported exchange and thus (assuming its accuracy) likely drew on the memories of another witness at the scene or other family sources—Pierson, *Private Life*, 106–07. "My dear wife," Sept. 6, 1782 entry, TJ, *MB*, 1:521.

3. *Virginian*, 390–91; "Carried-off, " TJ to William Gordon, July 16, 1788, *POTJ*, 13:362–65; for Elk Hill and disputed damage, Kranish, *Flight*, 292–93; Taylor, *Internal Enemy*, 27–29; Pybus, "Jefferson's Faulty Math," 246–47.

4. Malone, *Virginian*, 398–99, 403–420; Cogliano, *Revolutionary America*, 101–110; "What Office," GW to Robert Livingston, Jan. 8, 1783, *POGW*, Early Access Doc., Founders Online; "You have," L to Hamilton, June 29, 1782, *POAH*, 3:96–97. Acceptance of Paris post renewal, TJ to Robert Livingston, Nov. 26, 1782, *POTJ*, 6:206; Washington, *Writings* [Boston: Russell, Odiorne], 8:372n; "Has given," TJ to L, Aug. 4, 1781, *POTJ*, 6:111–12; "Jefferson's Commission," [Jan. 8, 1783], *POTJ*, 6:213–15; Malone, *Virginian*, 419; for Jefferson-Madison friendship and collaborations, see Burstein, Isenberg, *Madison and Jefferson*.

24. "Your Name Here Is Held in Veneration"

1. Gottschalk, *Close*, 342–47; "Make known," "Report on Lafayette's Return to France [23 Nov. 1781]," *POJM*, 3:313–16.

2. "Grown up," L to GW, Jan. 30, 1782, *POGW*, Early Access Doc., Founders Online. "History records," Vergennes to L, Jan. 23, 1782, in Gottschalk, *Close*, 351. Return to Paris, Gottschalk, *Close*, 348–49, who for "trembling" *et al.* draws on biography of Adrienne by her daughter Marie Antoinette Virginie—Lasteyrie, *Vie de Madame de Lafayette*, 202–03, n. 1; Hôtel de Noailles described, *History of Paris*, 2:212.

3. Gottschalk, *Close*, 349–52; "It is Generally," L to GW, Jan. 30, 1782, *POGW*, Early Access Doc., Founders Online.

4. Gottschalk, *Close*, 350.

5. Gottschalk, *Close*, 353; Gottschalk, *Between*, 39; "[The] Marquis," Franklin to Morris, Jan. 28, 1782, *POBF*, 36:490–92.

6. "Your political," Lafayette to Jay, Feb. 15, 1783, Jay, *Correspondence and Public Papers of John Jay*, 3:29.

7. Lafayette essay, Gottschalk, *Between*, 41–44; Lafayette's scientific interests, Auricchio, *Marquis*, 107–113; Lafayette and Mesmer, Gottschalk, *Between*, 77–78; L to Sec. of

American Philosophical Society, Dec. 10, 1783 [Calendared], *LAAR*, 5:435; "Instructed scholars," L to GW, May 17, 1784, *LAAR*, 4:216, 218 n5; account of Mesmer in Paris also based on account by British physician John Grieve, in Black, *Life and Letters,* 84–85; "Distinguish from," Darnton, *Mesmerism*, 23; "Elastic wooden shoes," *Percy Anecdotes*, Percy, 69–70.

8. "The Instruction," John Adams to James Warren, April 16, 1783, *Papers of John Adams*, 14:417–19.

9. Gottschalk, *Close*, 354–55, 367, 373–74; "But twice," Lafayette to James McHenry, Dec. 26, 1783, *LAAR*, 5:185; philanthropic interests, Gottschalk, *Between*, 18–19, 134, n. 33, 373.

10. "Only rarely" and Lafayette's early readings, Gottschalk, *Close*, 367; Gottschalk, *Between*, 3, 7; Raynal *et al.*, Auricchio, *Marquis*, 123–24.

11. Receipt for purchase of slave, Brice-Jennings Papers, Maryland Historical Society; "Black Servant," Henry Laurens to L, Oct. 23, 1777, *LAAR*, 1:127; for slave see also, in *ibid.*, 128 n3; Lafayette alluded to have read an early edition of *History of the Two Indies*, L to Adrienne, Oct. 1, 1777, *LAAR*, 1:116, 118 n6; Lafayette's ownership of 1780 ed. of *History of the Two Indies* and Raynal's ties to Franklin, "La Fayette, Citizen of Two Worlds," Cornell University website; Wilberforce dinners, Villiers, "Freedom of All," 34.

12. "Let us unite," L to GW, Feb. 5, 1783, *POGW*, Early Access Doc., Founders Online.

13. Nantes and slave trade, Klein, *Middle Passage*, 179, n. 12; Africans transported from French ports during transatlantic slave trade, "French Slave Trade," Slavery and Remembrance website; "The scheme," GW to L, April 5, 1783, *POGW*, Early Access Doc., Founders Online.

14. Auricchio, *Marquis*, 114, 120, 135–37; Gottschalk, *Between*, 15, 53–54; majority age, Villiers, "Freedom of Age," 34; "Chief ornament," comte d'Estaing to GW, Dec. 25, 1783, *POGW*, Early Access Doc., Founders Online; "The most," Lafayette, Gottschalk, *Between*, 53–54; "A belt of feathers" (Comte de Neuilly) and Otsiquette in Paris, Auricchio, *Marquis*, 137–39; "It was intendeded [*sic*]," Smith, *Journal*, 49; Abigail Adams to Mary Smith Cranch, April 15, 1785, *AFC*, 6:82–85.

15. Gottschalk, *Between*, 15–16; Adams, *Paris*, 74–77.

16. "She said," Adams to Mercy Otis Warren, May 10, 1785, *Adams Papers, AFC*, 6, 138–41; Lafayette's extramarital dalliances—Auricchio, *Marquis*, 139–43; Gottschalk, *Close*, 391–92; Gottschalk, *Between*, 16–17; Gaines, *Liberty*, 180–81; Maurois, *Adrienne*, 121–22; "You are too cruel," L to Aglaé, March 27, 1783, Gottschalk, *Lady in Waiting*, 128–29—trans., Auricchio, *Marquis*, 141; "Pretty," L to Prince de Poix, Jan. 13, 1783, Gottschalk, *Lady in Waiting*, 97; "An exalted delicacy," Virginie quoted in Gottschalk, *Lady in Waiting*, 25; Lasteyrie [Virginia], *Vie de Madame de Lafayette*, 194, trans. and quoted, Gottschalk, *Close*, 392; "I shall," "It is more," *et al.*, Lafayette, "Memoir of 1779," *LAAR*, 1:3, 6; "Rumor has it," *Memoires secrets*, March 21, 1783, trans. and quoted, Auricchio, *Marquis*, 142.

17. Gottschalk, *Close*, 381–99; "We shall," L to Poix, Dec. 31, 1782, in Gottschalk, *Close*, 395; Middlekauff, *Cause*, 572; "Beauty" and "English lady," paraphrase of L to Poix, Jan. 28, 1783, in Gottschalk, *Close*, 395.

18. Gottschalk, *Close*, 394–98; Gottschalk, *Between*, 79–108.

19. Packet ships between N.Y. and French ports, Stevens, *Progress of New York*, 48–49; "What my mental and physical," L to Adrianne, June 28, 1784, *LAAR*, 5:231.

25. Paris Autumn

1. "I am now," TJ to Madison, May 8, 1784, *POTJ*, 7:231–35; arrangements for care of Lucy Elizabeth and Mary (Polly), Malone, *Rights*, 12; TJ to Short, May 7, 1784, *POTJ*, 7:229; Malone, *Virginian*, 419–23; Short to TJ, May 14, 1784, *POTJ*, 7:253–56; William Short birthdate, Shackelford, *Adoptive Son*, 3; Gordon-Reed, *HOM*, 160–61; Jefferson's Annapolis departure and travels to Philadelphia, N.Y., and New England, *MB*, 1:548–54; for the biography of Thomas's oldest daughter Martha "Patsy" Jefferson Randolph, see Kierner, *Martha*.

2. Gordon-Reed, *HOM*, 160–61; Malone, *Virginian*, 421–23; Rakove, *Revolutionaries*, 295; "I could," TJ to Elbridge Gerry, July 2, 1784, *POTJ*, 7:357–58; Abigail Adams's sailing plans, June 20, 1784 entry, "Abigail Adams' Diary of Her Voyage from Boston to Deal, 20 June–20 July 1784," *Diary and Autobiography of John Adams*, 3:154–59.

3. Gordon-Reed, *HOM*, 160–61; Malone, *Virginian*, 422–23; Malone, *Rights*, 4–5; Don Quixote claim and Adams skepticism, TJ to George Cabot, July 24, 1784, *POTJ*, 7:383; Boston to Paris, *MB*, 1:544–57; TJ to John Adams, July 24, 1784, Adams Papers, 16:283–84; "I do not," TJ to Madison, June 20, 1787, *POTJ*, 11, 1:480–84.

4. Malone, *Rights*, 5; Rice, *Paris*, 13–14; encyclopedia subscription, *MB*, 1:56 n83.

5. "Religion which makes," TJ, "Tour," *POTJ*, 11, 1:415–64; Hotel St. Jacques, Catlett, *Jefferson*, 73; "Altogether the best," TJ to Mary Jefferson Bolling, July 23, 1787, *POTJ*, 11, 1:612–13. Malone, *Rights*, 5–6; "For the first" and "brightest," Kierner, *Martha*, 54–55.

6. Adams, *Paris*, 47; TJ to Monroe, June 17, 1785, *POTJ*, 8:227–34; Aug.–Sept. 1784, expenditures, *MB* 1:557–64; Rice, *Paris*, 37–41; art purchases, Adams, *Paris*, 43, 83–86.

7. "By Apr. 1786," [TJ to Francis Eppes, Nov. 11, 1784], *POTJ*, 7:500–01; Rice, *Paris*, 40–42; Humphreys, *Life*, 316–17; Gordon-Reed, *HOM*, 156–58, 164–71; Gordon-Reed, Onuf, *Blessed*, 114–15; "I have made," TJ to Paul Bentalou, Aug. 25, 1786, *POTJ*, 10:296, 296n; "Neither simple," Kukla, *Jefferson's Women*, 126.

8. "My family," L to Adrienne, n.d., Maurois, *Adrienne*, 155; "Remarkable person," editor of Marquise de Montagu's memoirs, quoted, L to Madame de Tassé, July 20, 1786, *POTJ*, 10:157–60n; "Madame de Tassé," Monticello website.

9. Malone, *Rights*, 6–12; Adams, *Paris*, 168–77; "Extraordinary Man," "I found," John Adams, [May 27, 1778], *Diary and Autobiography of John Adams*, 4:118–19; "The ten-

der breasts," TJ to Angelica Schuyler Church, Sept. 21, 1778, *POTJ*, 13:623–24; "I am nearly," TJ to Madison, Feb. 14, 1783, *POTJ*, 6:241–44; Wood, *Friends*, 147, 154, 164–65; for Barclay, see also Roberts and Roberts, *Barclay*.

10. "Folly," TJ to Rittenhouse, Nov. 11, 1784, *POTJ*, 7:516–17; "Seasoning," TJ to Monroe, March 18, 1785, *POTJ*, 8:42–45; Rice, *Paris*, 91; Malone, *Rights*, 9; TJ, *MB*, 2:562; Jefferson's French proficiency, Malone, *Rights*, 6; "Instructions to the American Commissioners, May–June 1784, United States in Congress Assembled, May 7, 1784," *Papers of John Adams*, 16:193–202; "Very happy," John Adams to Jay, April 13, 1785, *Papers of John Adams*, 17:16–20; "Mr. Jefferson," Abigail Adams to Cotton Tufts, Sept. 8, 1784, *AFC*, 5:456–59; "Poor Mr. Jefferson," Abigail Adams to Mary Smith Cranch, Sept. 5, 1784, *Adams Family Correspondence*, 5:439–45; "Document of importance," Chinard, *Lafayette and Jefferson*, 83–84; "Papa spoke," Kierner, *Martha*, 50; Short's appearance and age, Shackelford, *Adoptive Son*, 3; "This is the only way," Abigail Adams to Lucy Cranch Smith, May 5, 1785, *AFC*, 6:120–21; "Lowest," TJ to Monroe, Nov. 11, 1784, *POTJ*, 7:508–14.

26. Hero's Tour

1. Post-occupation New York, Stevens, *Progress of New York*, 48–49; and Auricchio, *Marquis*, 105–06; Lafayette's 1784 U.S. trip, Gottschalk, *Between*, 84–150. Gottschalk, however, erroneously states that *Le Courier de l'Europe* brought Lafayette to Manhattan in 1784. That vessel, along with *Courier de New York*, numbered among several packet (mail) ships recently placed in service by the French government, linking U.S and French ports. But it was not the one on which Lafayette returned to America in 1784—August 7, 1784, [New York] *Independent Journal*: "Wednesday evening . . . [of] Le Courier de New-York . . . The Marquis de La Fayette, was a passenger in this Ship."

2. "In the crowd," L to Adrienne, August 13, 1784, *LAAR*, 5:235.

3. "Wonderful effects," August 12, 1784, *Early Proceedings of the American Philosophical Society*, 126–27.

4. Gottschalk, *Between*, 88–89, 126–27; Auricchio, *Marquis*, 116–17; "Never was," L to Adrienne, Aug. 20, 1784, *LAAR*, 5:237; L speech, Oct. 14, 1784, entry, *Journal of the House of Delegates*, 30; Armistead recommendation, Nov. 21, 1784, *LAAR*, 5:277, 279.

5. Gottschalk, *Between*, 89–138; "Fell in with" and "the relation," Madison to TJ, Sept. 7, 1784, *POTJ*, 7:416–18, Auricchio, *Marquis*, 121–22; "It will carry," James Madison, Jr., to James Madison, Sept. 6, 1784, *POJM*, 8:112; "We expressed the desire" *et al.*, "Barbé de Marbois's Journal" Sept. 23–Oct. 6, 1784, *LAAR*, 5:245–53; "Were quite," "my personal," L to Adrienne, Oct. 4, 1784, *LAAR*, 5:260–62; "The Commissioners," Madison to TJ, Oct. 17, 1784, *POTJ*, 7:444–52.

6. Gottschalk, *Between*, 134–38; "More than," *ibid.*, 143–144; "They supposed," TJ to Madison, Sept. 1, 1785, *POTJ*, 8:361–63.

7. Gottschalk, *Between*, 141–142; Otsiquette and Kayenlaha, Gottschalk, *Between*, 433–34; "M. Jefferson will," L to Madison, Dec. 15, 1784, *LAAR*, 5:285.

27. Diplomats

1. "My House," L to TJ, Oct. 11, 1784, *POTJ*, 7:438–39.

2. "Nothing can," TJ to Francis Parkinson, Jan. 13, 1785, *POTJ*, 7:602–03. "Mortification," TJ to Monroe, Jan 14, 1785, *POTJ*, 7:607–08.

3. Lafayette and Washington sculptures, Rice, *Paris*, 57–58; and Malone, *Rights*, 44; "Without hesitating," TJ to Benjamin Harrison, Jan. 12, 1785, *POTJ*, 7:599–601.

4. "You can," TJ to Madison, Dec. 8, 1784, *POTJ*, 7:557–60; "Would you," TJ to Monroe, Dec. 10, 1784, *POTJ*, 7:562–65.

5. "My House," L to TJ, Oct. 11, 1784, *POTJ*, 7:438–39; May 8, 1781, Council of State meeting, *Journal of the Council of State of Virginia*, 2, 343; and *LAAR*, 4:106 n1. Lafayette's Virginia arrival and departure dates, Nolan, *Lafayette*, 168, 204; "This Evening," L to TJ, *POTJ*, 5:564; "Lest any Thing," TJ to L, May 14, 1781, *POTJ*, 5:644–47; "Mr. Jefferson declines," L to Luzerne, Aug. 14, 1781, *LAAR*, 4:322; "I am very sorry," L to Adrienne, Sept. 14, 1784, Archives de la Fondation Josée et René de Chambrun, note 354.

6. Ref. by TJ to "the Marquis Fayette, who arrived here the 26th of Jan."—TJ to Francis Eppes, Feb. 5, 1785, *POTJ*, 7:635–36; notification of Lucy Elizabeth's death in letter from her doctor—James Courie to TJ, Nov. 20, 1784, *POTJ*, 7:538–39; "Mr. J," Jan. 27 1785, Smith, *Journal*, 45; at least four months until Jefferson dined out, Kierner, *Martha*, 57; Rice, *Paris*, 42.

7. Brest arrival and Rennes visit, L to Adrienne, [Jan. 23, 1785], *LAAR*, 5:292–93 n1 and n2; "Breton heart," Gottschalk, *Between*, 151–52.

8. "Large company," Smith, Feb. 14, 1785, Smith, *Journal*, 47.

9. Lafayette's political activities after 1785 return to Paris, *LAAR*, 5:291–92; "Your *character*," TJ to Madison, March 18, 1785, *POTJ*, 8:38–41; "I have struck," TJ to Patrick Henry, Jan. 24, 1786, *POTJ*, 9:212–15; Barbary States, L to American Commissioners, April 8, 1785, *LAAR*, 5:315–17; for Necker, see "has Made [a] Great deal of Noise," L to Madison, March 16, 1785 *POJM*, 8:245–47.

10. "She only once," L to Madame de La Tour Maubourg, Jan. 1808, in Crawford, *Madame de Lafayette*, 322; "You are not," Lasteyrie, *La Fayette*, 408; Gottschalk, *Between*, 170–73; "Marriages are not," L to GW, May 11, 1785, *LAAR*, 5:322–24; "All this new law," Maurois, *Adrienne*, 155; "In such," L to Hamilton, April 13, 1785, *LAAR*, 5:317–318 and n.4.

11. "No one," [Condorcet] to L, Feb. 24, 1785, *LAAR*: 5:299–300; Franklin and Paine influence on Condorcet and Jefferson's translation of his anti-slavery essay, Landes, "His-

tory of Feminism . . . Marquis de Condorcet"; "The want of talents" and Jefferson's
Condorcet trans., "Jefferson's Notes from Condorcet on Slavery," *POTJ*, 14:494–98,
and TJ to Condorcet, *POTJ*, Aug. 30, 1791, *POTJ*, 22:98–99.

12. Dubois, *A Colony of Citizens*, 69–70; Lafayette's plantations, Auricchio, *Marquis*, 120–21;
and Lafayette, *Lafayette and Slavery*, 5–6, 11, 31, 41; "Free my," L to GW, Feb. 6, 1786,
POGW-Confederation [hereafter *Confed*] *Series*, 3:538–47; "The benevolence," GW to
L, May 10, 1786, *POGW-Confed. Series*, 4:41–45; for more details on Cayenne venture,
see Villiers, "Freedom of All," 34–40.

28. *Te Deum*

1. "Mr. Jefferson's Health," L to Madison, March 16, 1785 *POJM*, 8:245–47; "Mr. Jefferson" *et al.*, Smith, *Journal*, 65–68; "In as good a place" *et al.*, April 1, 1785, JQA, Diary, MHS website; "It was nothing," Mauroris, *Adrienne*, 142; "You lost much," TJ to
Short, April 2, 1785, *POTJ*, 8:68; Malone, *Rights*, 13; Gottschalk, *Between*, 160–61.

29. The Patriarch of Passy

1. May 24 Marie-Antoinette procession, TJ to John Adams, May 25, 1785, *POTJ*, 8:163–
64; *Notes on the State of Virginia*, TJ to Madison, May 11, 1785, *POTJ*, 8:147–48; and
Ellis, *Sphinx*, 101–03; "Indeed I tremble," TJ, *Notes*, 289; "We have," Abigail Adams
to Mary Smith Cranch, May 8, 1785, *Adams Family Papers*, 6:118–20; Malone, *Rights*,
13. Versailles credentials, TJ, *MB*, 1:584 and *ibid.*, n56; "The departure," TJ to John
Adams, *POTJ*, May 25, 1785.

2. Malone, *Rights*, 15, 33–35; "Dr F. is at present," John Adams to Arthur Lee, Jan. 31,
1785, *Papers of John Adams*, 16:510–11; Franklin's fur cap, Isaacson, *Franklin*,
306; "Death's wound" and "When he left," TJ to Rev. William Smith, Feb. 19, 1791,
POTJ, 19:112–14.

30. Holy Roman Empire

1. Gottschalk, *Between*, 181–82.

2. "Other states," quotation and variations thereof are often attributed to Honoré Gabriel
Riqueti, count of Mirabeau (1749–91); recent scholarship, however, suggests it originated
with another contemporary—Joerg Muth, H-Net War discussion network, July 12, 2009.

3. Gottschalk, *Between*, 181–82; Rice, *Paris*, 55–57.

4. Childs, *Armies*, 76; "I went," "having the," "highest satisfaction" *et al.*, L to GW,
Feb. 6, 1786, *POGW-Confed. Series*, 3:538–47; "I know," Étienne, *La Fayette*, 122–23;
"I fancy," L to TJ, Sept. 4, 1785, *POTJ*, 8:478–80; "My reception," Cornwallis to
Lieut.-Col. Ross, Oct. 5, 1785, in Cornwallis, *Correspondence*, 1:212; Gottschalk, *Be-
tween*, 181–201; "Altho' I found," L to Knox, Feb. 11, 1786, Gottschalk, *Between*, 187.

5. Gottschalk, *Between*, 188–94.

6. Gottschalk, *Between*, 196–98; "that divides," L to GW, Feb. 6, 1786, *POGW-Confed. Series*, 3:538–47.

7. "The kind Reception," L to TJ, Sept. 4, 1785, *POTJ*, 8:478–80; "I find the," L to GW, Feb. 6, 1786, *POGW-Confed. Series*, 3:538–47.

31. Hôtel de Langeac

1. Malone, *Rights*, 41–49; Gottschalk, *Between*, 207.

2. "Words Cannot," L to GW, Feb. 6, 1786, *POGW-Confed. Series*, 3:538–47; "The Marquis de Lafayette," TJ to Madison, Jan. 30, 1787, *POTJ*, 11, 1:92–97; "I am," TJ to Madison, Feb. 8, 1786, *POJM*, 8:485–89.

3. Adams, *Paris*, 37–38, 52–54; Rice, *Paris*, 51–54; Adams, *Gouverneur Morris*, 172–73; "The building mania," Louis-Sébastien Mercier, in Adams, *Paris*, 38.

4. Rice, *Paris*, 153–54; "I cultivate," TJ to Nicholas Lewis, Sept. 17, 1787, *POTJ*, 12:134–36.

5. "Savage of," TJ to Bellini, Sept. 30, 1785, *POTJ*, 5:568–70.

6. Rice, *Paris*, 52–54; Adams, *Paris*, 19; "There is," Smith, *Journal*, 14; "Manners had," Randall, *Jefferson*, 1:421; "Fastidious adherence," Edward Coles's paraphrase of anecdote attributed to Short, Randall, *Jefferson*, 1:421; "Much of the domestic," Margaret Bayard Smith, paraphrasing Jefferson in Adams, *Paris*, 19.

32. England

1. Malone, *Rights*, 51; for Jefferson and Barbary pirates, see Cogliano, *Emperor*, 42–75; for more general account of U.S. Barbary Wars and their origins, Lambert, *Barbary Wars*; "I immediately," TJ to Abigail Adams, Sept. 25, 1785, *AFC*, 6:390–93.

2. "And let her," Abigail Adams to William Smith, *AFC*, 7:76–77; TJ, "Auto," 57–58; TJ, *MB*, 1:612–13; Malone, *Rights*, 50–51; Nabby to JQ Adams, April 25, 1786, *AFC*, 7:150–56.

3. TJ, "Tour," *POTJ*, 9:369–75; John Adams, "Tour," *John Adams Diary and Autobiography*, 3:184–87; Johnson, "Whose chip?" Monticello website.

4. Malone, *Rights*, 55, 61; "Many very," Abigail Adams to Elizabeth Cranch, April 2, 1786, *AFC*, 7:122–26; "I could write," TJ to Charles Thompson, April 22, 1786, *POTJ*, 9:400–01.

5. Gottschalk, *Between*, 253–53; Malone, *Rights*, 63; TJ, *MB*, 1:623 and *ibid.*, n7; Meschutt, "The Adams-Jefferson Portrait Exchange," 47–54; for an astute account of Jefferson portraits over his lifetime, Wilson, *Jefferson on Display*.

6. "I think," TJ to GW, Aug. 14, 1787, *POTJ*, 12:36–38.

7. George III, O'Shaughnessy, *Men Who Lost America*, 17–46; Malone, *Rights*, 53–58; "Been as gracious," Abigail Adams to TJ, June 6, 1785, *AFC*, 6:169–73; For date of TJ at St. James, see TJ, *MB*, 1:614 n. 48; John Adams to John Jay, June 2, 1785, *John*

Adams Papers, 17:134–45; "More ungracious," TJ, "Auto," 57–58; "Turned his back," John Adams, *Works of John Adams* [print ed.] I:420.

8. Jefferson's return trip, London to Paris, TJ to Smith, May 4, 1786, *POTJ*, 9:447–48; TJ, *MB*, 1:623–64.

33. Historical Scenes

1. May 1–June 26, 1786, TJ, *MB*, 1:625, 630, *ibid.*, n33; meal-costs reductions, TJ, *MB*, 1:646–47; "Designing the capitol," Commonwealth of Virginia website; "She thinks," TJ to Ledyard, August 16, 1786, *POTJ*, 10:258; Hildebrandt, *Airships*, 238; Gottschalk, *Between*, 268–70; "I shall," Ledyard to TJ, Nov. 25, 1786, *POTJ*, 10:548–49; "If I find," Gottschalk, *Between*, 268; above details of Ledyard's life drawn principally from Gray, *Ledyard*; "His flowing," *Ledyard*, Zug, 139.

2. "We have," TJ to Madame de Bréhan, March 14, 1789, *POTJ*, 14:655–56; "Jefferson had a taste," Trumbull, *Auto*, 95; Sizer, "Trumbull's Eyesight," 91–93; Adams, *Paris*, 84–101; Rice, *Paris*, 53–54; Malone, *Rights*, 68–70; "A Painter," John Adams to L, July 8 1786, Adams Papers, Early Access Doc., Founders Online; "He was yesterday," TJ to David Humphreys, Aug. 14, 1786, *POTJ*, 10:250–52; Trumbull, *Auto*, entire book—particularly 6, 68–69, 95–96; also see Hazleton "Trumbull's 'Declaration of Independence,'" 30–33; "John Trumbull" article, National Gallery of Art website; Favata, "John Trumbull," Fordham University website; "His natural talents," TJ to Ezra Stiles, Sept. 1, 1786, *POTJ*, 10:316–18; "I began," Trumbull, *Auto*, 96; "Ought to be," Hazleton, "Value," 37.

34. "No Rose without Its Thorn"

1. "Our charming," TJ to Trumbull, Jan. 10, 1817, *POTJ*, 10:654–55; "A parcel," TJ to Maria Cosway, Oct. 12, 1786, *POTJ*, 10, 443–55; Malone, *Rights*, 70–71; Kukla, *Jefferson's Women*, 92–93; spelling of *Halle au Blé*, Kukla, *Jefferson's Women*, 243, n. 11; Trumbull, *Auto*, 96.

2. Stein, *Worlds*, 176–7; "Maria Cosway (Engraving)," Monticello website; "Mr. Jefferson joined," Trumbull, *Auto*, 118; "Lying messengers," TJ to Maria Cosway, Oct. 12, 1786, *POTJ*, 10, 443–55; Trumbull's Sept. 9 departure from Paris, Trumbull, *Auto*, 120; Kukla, *Jefferson's Women*, 93–95.

3. "The Port de Neuilly," TJ to Maria Cosway, Oct. 12, 1786, *POTJ*, 10, 443–55; Stein, *Worlds*, 176–77; "Maria Cosway (Engraving)," Monticello website; "I am pursuaded," Short to William Nelson, Jr., Oct. 25, 1786, in Rice, *Paris*, 58–59; "Illicit love-making," Malone, *Rights*, 72; Malone, *Rights*, 72–75; Kukla, *Jefferson's Women*, 95–97; Adams, *Paris*, 244–48; Maria Cosway to TJ, [Sept. 20, 1786], *POTJ*, 10:394–95; "It is with," TJ to Cosway, [Oct. 5, 1786], *POTJ*, 10:431–33; "I am very," Maria Cosway to TJ, [Oct 5, 1786], *POTJ*, 10:433; "Having performed," TJ to Maria Cosway, Oct. 12, 1786, *POTJ*, 10: 443–55; while Jefferson admired Sterne's book, he rarely read fiction, Jefferson, *Literary Commonplace Book*, 10–14.

4. Malone, *Rights*, 140–41; Adams, *Paris*, 235–37; Hamilton-Jefferson ties in 1780, 6:206; George Washington, *Correspondence and Miscellaneous Papers*, 372n.

5. Adams, *Paris*, 238–50; Kukla, *Jefferson's Women*, 103–114; "*Je vous*," TJ to Maria Cosway, June 23, 1790, *POTJ*, 16:550–51.

35. Assembly of Not Ables

1. "I hold it," TJ to Madison, Jan. 30, 1987, *POTJ*, 11, 1:92–97.

2. "I trust more," L to Smith, Jan. 16, 1787, in Gottschalk, *Between*, 283.

3. Deficit figures, Gottschalk, *Between*, 287–88; eighteenth-century debt renunciation, Shovlin, *Political Economy of Virtue,* 136; "I shall," Doyle, *Origins*, 51; *Parlements—* Egret, *Louis XV et l'opposition parlementaire*, 11.

4. Gottschalk, *Between*, 274–75; "We talk," TJ to Richard Peters, Feb. 26, 1786, *POTJ*, 11, 1:182–83; "Wicked people," L to GW, Feb. 7, 1787, *POGW-Confed. Series*, 5:13–15.

5. Gottschalk, *Between*, 275–77; "Ardour," Rochambeau to GW, May 12, 1787, *POGW-Confed. Series*, 5:182–84; Gaines, *Liberty*, 221–22; "Actually," Gaines, *Liberty*, 225. For 1780s American "craze" in Paris, as well as ties between Lafayette, Jefferson, Franklin, Raynal, Condorcet, *et al.*, see also Darnton, *Teeth*, 119–136.

6. "That we should turn," *et al.*, L to William Smith, Jan. 16, 1787, in Gottschalk, *Between*, 282; Gaines, *Liberty*, 225; L to GW, Jan. 13, 1787, *POGW-Confed. Series*, 4:514–17.

7. "This shews," TJ to Edward Carrington, Jan. 16, 1787, *POTJ*, 11, 1:48–50; "His education," TJ to Madison, Jan. 30, 1787, *POTJ*, 11, 1:92–97; "When LaFayette," John Adams to TJ, July 13, 1813, *POTJ*, 6:286–88; Wood, *Friends*, 186–87.

8. "A great," TJ to Edward Carrington, Jan. 16, 1787, *POTJ*, 11, 1:48–50; Gottschalk, *Between*, 285–86; "Perhaps, if," Gottschalk, *Between*, 285–86.

9. Hôtel des Menu Plaisirs, opening sessions, quotations from Louis XVI and *Mémoires secret* reports, Auricchio, *Marquis*, 148–50; also Gaines, *Liberty*, 237–40, and Gottschalk, *Between*, 285–97; removal of seating, Friedland, *Political* Actors, 181.

10. "This occasion," TJ to Abigail Adams, Feb. 22, 1787 *POTJ*, 11, 1:174–75; Auricchio, *Marquis*, 151–63; Gaines, *Liberty*, 237–240; and Gottschalk, *Between*, 285–97; "Who shoots himself," TJ to William Short, March 27, 1787, *POTJ*, 11, 1:246–48; "Without metaphor," "Timon" [Vicomte de Cormenin], quoted in Gottschalk, *Between*, 297; "The monster," Lafayette speech, April 24, 1787, and "Now you" *et al.*, Gottschalk, *Between*, 298–300; "It was thought," L to GW, May 5, 1787, *POGW-Confed. Series*, 5:168–70.

36. "To See What I Have Never Seen Before"

1. "I am now, "TJ to Madison, Dec. 18, 1787, *POTJ*: 10:611–13.

2. "The good," TJ to L, Feb. 28, 1787, *POTJ*, 11 1:186; "A journey," TJ to Eliza House Trist, Feb. 23, 1787, *POTJ*, 11, 1:180–81; "Between," TJ to Madame de Tott, April 5,

1786, *POTJ*, 11, 1:270–73; Malone, *Rights*, 114–15; "Post horses," *MB*, 1:655–56 n14; Goss, "Journey through France and Italy (1787)," Monticello website; TJ, *MB*, 1:656–75.

3. "I was quite," "a most excellent," TJ to William Short, March 27, 1787, *POTJ*, 11, 1:246–48; Malone, *Rights*, 117.

4. "Here I am," TJ to Madame de Tessé, March 20, 1787, *POTJ*, 11, 1:226–28; "I took care," TJ to John Jay, May 4, 1787, *POTJ*, 11, 1:348–49; "I have found," TJ to Chastellux, April 4, 1787, *POTJ*, 11, 1:261–62; Malone, *Rights*, 48, 98–99, 98n, 125.

5. "Having taken," TJ to Short, April 7, 1787, *POTJ*, 11, 1:280–81; "Tour," *POTJ*, 11, 1:415–64; Hôtel Saint-Jacques, Shackelford, *Travels*, 83; more generally, for an excellent and copiously researched study of *all* of Jefferson's travels in Europe, see *ibid*.

6. Patsy to TJ, [March] 8, 1787, *POTJ*, 11, 1:202–4; TJ to Patsy, March 28, 1787, *POTJ*, 11, 1:250–52; "I have not," TJ to Cosway, July 1, 1787, *POTJ*, 11, 1:519–20.

7. "I am now," TJ to William Short, March 27, 1787, *POTJ*, 11, 1:246–48.

8. "The Provençale stands," TJ to William Short, March 29, 1787, *POTJ*, 11, 1:253–55. For Provencal dialect and linguistic diversity in that era's France, see Robb, *Discovery of France*, 50–70; Army recruits, Robb, *Discovery of France*, 65; for Provençal dialect and persistence of non-French tongues in France, *ibid.*, 50–70.

9. "Circumstances" ["Hints to Americans Travelling in Europe," recollections and suggestions Jefferson wrote in 1788 for two young American friends with plans to travel in France and Italy"], TJ to Thomas Lee Shippen, June 19, 1778, *POTJ*, 13:264–76; "I have," TJ to Short, March 15, 1787, *POTJ*, 11, 1:214–16; TJ to Madison, Oct. 28, 1785, *POTJ*, 8:681–83; TJ to Short, April 7, 1786, *POTJ*, 11, 1:280–81; "All the oppressions," TJ, "Tour," *POTJ*, 11, 1:415–64; Drayton to TJ, May 22, 1786, *POTJ*, 11, 1:374–75; travel to Rome, TJ to Cosway, July 1, 1787, *POTJ*, 11, 1:519–20.

10. "On arriving," TJ to Thomas Lee Shippen, June 19, 1778, *POTJ*, 13:264–76.

11. "The plan," TJ to Madame de Tott, April 5, 1786, *POTJ*, 11, 1:270–73.

12. "Your head," TJ to L, April 11, 1787, *POTJ*, 11, 1:283–85.

13. "Let my daughter," TJ to Short, April 12, 1787, *POTJ*, 11, 1:287; Malone, *Rights*, 122; "Whenever you go," TJ to Cosway, July 1, 1787, *POTJ*, 11, 1:519–20.

14. Piedmont rice, TJ to Drayton, July 30, 1787, *POTJ*, 11,1:644–50; and Malone, *Rights*, 122–23; "In 3. hours" *et al.*, TJ, "Tour," *POTJ*, 11, 1:415–64.

15. Malone, *Rights*, 121–23; "I calculated," TJ to Cosway, July 1, 1787, *POTJ*, 11, 1:519–20; "Milan was," TJ to Gaudenzio Clerici, Aug. 15, 1787, *POTJ*, 12:38–39.

16. TJ, *MB*, 1:664–65, 665 n56; TJ, "Tour," *POTJ*, 11, 1:415–64; "Mortally sick," TJ to Patsy Jefferson, May 5, 1787, *POTJ*, 11, 1:348–49; Malone, *Rights*, 123–24.

17. "In order," TJ to Patsy Jefferson, May 5, 1787, *POTJ*, 11, 1:348–49; TJ, "Tour," *POTJ*, 11, 1:415–64; TJ, *MB*, 1:664–79; Malone, *Rights*, 124–26.

37. Canal Royal en Languedoc

1. "I dismounted," TJ to Short, May 21, 1787, *POTJ*, 11, 1:371–73; "Tour," *POTJ*, 11, 1:415–64; Shackelford, *Travels*, 112–16. "Stony Mountains" and preoccupation with watersheds and American West explorations, Chaffin, *Pathfinder*, 1–18, 35–74.
2. Malone, *Rights*, 128; "I was alone," TJ to John Bannister, Jr., June 19, 1787, *POTJ*, 11, 1:246–476–77; TJ, *MB*, 1, 675; "Travelling," TJ to Peter Carr, Aug. 10, 1787, *POTJ*, 12:14–19.

38. Bed of Justice

1. Johnson, *Louis XVI*, 51–53; Auricchio, *Marquis*, 159–63; "We have," L to GW, May 5, 1787, *POGW-Confed. Series*, 5:168–70.
2. Johnson, *Louis XVI*, 51–53; Auricchio, *Marquis*, 159–63; "For a fixed," TJ, "Auto," 78.
3. Johnson, *Louis XVI*, 52–53; "The Registration," Louis XVI, *ibid.*, 53.

39. A Parade in Aurillac

1. Charavay, *La Fayette*, 152–53; "One could," *ibid.*, 152; Gottschalk, *Between*, 334–36; Bradshaw, *Travellers' Hand Book*, 229; Garnier, *Notice sur le général baron Delzons*, 236–38; "His noble exploits," Gottschalk, *Between*, 335.
2. Gottschalk, *Between*, 324; "A Convention," GW to L, March 25, 1787, *POGW-Confed. Series*, 5:105–08.
3. "Absolutely incognito," TJ to L, April 11, 1787, *POTJ*, 11, 1:283–85; "He would announce," comte d'Espinchal, quoted in Gottschalk, *Between*, 334.
4. "I Made a Tour," L to GW, Oct. 9, 1787, *POGW-Confed. Series*, 5:358–65; "The fact was," Gottschalk, *Between*, 323; for Lafayette and republicanism, Gottschalk, *Between*, 1–11, 322–24; "The Great Men," L to GW, May 5, 1787, *POGW-Confed. Series*, 5:168–70; Dutch republic constitution influence on U.S. Constitution, Nordholt, "Example," 437–49.

40. Polly and Sally

1. "Is here on," TJ to Benjamin Vaughan, July 2, 1787, *POTJ*, 11, 1:532–53; "A workingman," Kaye, *Paine*, 4; "Beauty and strength," TJ to Paine, Dec. 23, 1788, *POTJ*, 14:372–77; "I have," Abigail Adams to TJ, June 26, 1787, *AFC*, 8:92–93; for an astute study of Paine's fascination with bridges, see Gray, *Tom Paine's Iron Bridge*.
2. "I must have Polly," TJ to Francis Eppes, May 11, 1785, *POTJ*, 8:141–42; "I am sorry," Francis Eppes, Oct. 23, 1786, *POTJ*, 10:483.
3. "I want," Mary Jefferson to TJ, [Sept. 13, 1785], *POTJ*, 8:517; "I should be," Mary Jefferson to TJ [circa March 31, 1787], *POTJ*, 11, 1:260; Kukla, *Jefferson's Women*, 120–21; Malone, *Rights*, 134–35.
4. "At present every thing," Abigail Adams to TJ, June 26, 1787, *AFC*, 8:92–93.

5. "She has a Girl," Abigail Adams to TJ, June 26, 1787, *AFC*, 8:92–93; "The Girl," Abigail Adams to TJ, June 27, 1787, *POTJ*, 11, 1:501–2.

6. "It would reconcile," Abigail Adams to TJ, June 26, 1787, *AFC*, 8:92–93.

7. "A thousand thanks," TJ to Abigail Adams, July 1, 1787, *POTJ*, 11, 1:514–15; "A better reason," Brodie, *Jefferson*, 217–18; for other speculation re Jefferson's not going to London, Gordon-Reed, *HOM*, 204; Petit's London trip, TJ, *MB*, 1:674–77; instructions to Petit [July 2, 1787], *POTJ*, 11, 1:531–32.

8. "Amendments . . . relative to our commerce," TJ to David Hartley, July 2, 1787, *POTJ*, 11, 1:525–26; "I remain in hopes," TJ to GW, Aug. 14, 1787, *POTJ*, 12:36–38.

9. "Your nation," TJ to St. John de Crèvecoeur, Aug. 6, 1787, *POTJ*, 11, 1:692.

10. "All tongues in Paris," TJ to John Adams, Aug. 30, 1787, *POTJ*, 12:66–69.

11. Patsy-Polly reunion and physical descriptions, Kierner, *Martha*, 61–62; Sally "wages," Jan. 1, 1788, TJ, *MB*, 1:690; clothes purchases for Hemings siblings in Paris, Gordon-Reed, Onuf, *Blessed*, 127; Sally Hemings wages, clothes purchases, inoculation, and role assisting Patsy, TJ, *MB*, 1:685–86 n21; inoculation, Gordon-Reed, *HOM*, 215–23; "She had," TJ to Mary Jefferson Bolling, July 23, 1787, *POTJ*, 11, 1:612–13; "I never felt," Abigail Adams to TJ, Sept. 10, 1787, *POTJ*, 12:111–13; date of Polly's return to Paris, TJ to Abigail Adams, July 16, 1787, *POTJ*, 11, 1:592.

12. Gordon-Reed, *HOM*, 205–13, 224–48; Kukla, *Jefferson's Women*, 115–17.

41. The Perpetual Union's Final Days

1. "In the midst," GW to L, September 18, 1787, *POGW-Confed. Series*, 5:334.

2. "You have," GW to TJ, Sept. 18, 1787, *POTJ*, 12:149–50.

3. "I will now," TJ to Madison, Dec. 20, 1787, *POTJ*, 12:438–43.

42. "Our Affairs at Amsterdam Press on My Mind Like a Mountain"

1. Gottschalk, *Between*, 374. "Mr. Jefferson," L to Henry Knox, Feb. 4, 1788, *ibid*.

2. "I was daily," TJ, "Auto," 76; "I received," TJ to John Adams, March 2, 1778, *POTJ*, 12:637–38.

3. Except where noted, all Jefferson quotations concerning 1788 financial crisis and resultant trip to Holland derive from TJ, "Auto," 75–77; "I met," TJ to Short, April 9, 1778, *POTJ*, 13:48–49; other sources, quoted and otherwise, include TJ, "Tour," *POTJ*, 13:8–36; TJ, *MB*, 1:196–704, and the *MB*'s' excellent footnotes thereon. For more on Jefferson's spring 1788 travels, see Shackelford, *Travels*, 121–156.

43. "The Devil, More Cunning"

1. "Associate myself," L, *Mémoires*, 2:183, quoted in Gottschalk, *Between*, 388.

2. "Nothing more," TJ to Madison, Jan. 12, 1789, *POTJ*, 14:436–38; Auricchio, *Marquis*, 166–67.

3. "If you go" and entire Condorcet-Mazzei exchange, Gottschalk, *Between*, 416–17.

44. "To Navigate in Such a Whirling"

1. "Every Thing," Morris to Washington, March 3, 1789, *POGW-Presidential Series* [hereafter *"Pres."*], 1:359–60; "Every body here," TJ to Madison, Jan. 12, 1789, *POTJ*, 14:436–38; Morris notebook, Brookhiser, *Morris*, 101–02; state constitutions, Wood, *Friends Divided*, 183; The Dutch republic's constitution's influence on that era's constitutions, Nordholt, "Example," 437–49.

2. Lafayette learns of Charter, June 2, 1789, Gottschalk, Maddox, *Through the October Days*, 55–56; text and discussion of Jefferson's "Charter," Chinard, *Lafayette and Jefferson*, 78, 127–28; "Sketch," TJ to L, June 3, 1789, *POTJ*, 15:165–66.

3. "I have ventured," TJ to Rabaut, June 3, 1789, *POTJ*, 15:166–67; requested leave of absence, TJ to John Jay, Nov. 19, 1788, *POTJ*, 14:211–17; Apology," TJ to Lafayette, June 3, 1789, *POTJ*, 15:166–67; Gottschalk, Maddox, *Through the October Days*, 55–57; "It is very Hard," L to TJ, [before June 3, 1789], *POTJ*, 15:166.

45. *Vive le Tiers État!*

1. Schama, *Citizens*, 305–07; "The once beautiful," *Cahiers de Paris, en 1789*, 87; "The great mass," Gouverneur Morris to GW, April 29, 1789, *POGW-Pres.*, 2,1:146–48.

2. "Those are the Creatures," Morris to GW, April 29, 1789, *POGW-Pres.*, 2:146–48; "Every scourge," comte de Mirabeau, Schama, *Citizens*, 305.

3. Gottschalk, Maddox, *Through the October Days*, 8, 9; Schama, *Citizens*, 297–98.

4. Gottschalk, Maddox, *Through the October Days*, 11; Schama, *Citizens*, 308.

5. *Cahiers*, Doyle, *Oxford History*, 97; Schama, *Citizens*, 308.

6. Gottschalk, Maddox, *Through the October Days*, 9–10, 19.

7. *Ibid.*, 18–35; "The bishops," Morris, *Diary*, 1:73; "In striking contrast," Morris, *Diary*, 1:70.

8. Gottschalk, Maddox, *Through the October Days*, 46–49; "Grand procession" *et al.*, Morris, *Diary*, 1:74; "Bourgeois in character" and Third Estate statistics, Doyle, *Origins*, 154–55.

9. Gottschalk, Maddox, *Through the October Days*, 49; "The procession," Morris, *Diary*, 1:73; Droz, *Histoire*, 1:402; assembly hall construction, Friedland, *Political Actors*, 181; "Had it been," TJ to Crèvecoeur, May 20, 1789, *POTJ*, 15:139–41.

10. Gottschalk, Maddox, *Through the October Days*, 49.

11. "As it becomes," TJ to L, May 6, 1789, *POTJ*, 15:97–98.

12. "I have not," TJ to GW, May 10, 1789, *POTJ*, 15:117–19.

46. "The Mephitic Atmosphere of Prejudices"

1. Doyle, *Origins*, 147; Schama, *Citizens*, 303–04; "What Is the Third Estate?" Sieyès, in Shusterman, *French Revolution*, 29.

2. "I went away," Lafayette, *Memoirs*, [Saunders and Otley, 1837], 2:293; "Your principles," TJ to L, May 6, 1789, POTJ, 15:97–98; Auricchio, *Marquis*, 177–78; Gottschalk,

Maddox, *Through the October Days*, 46–64; Schama, *Citizens*, 358–61; other details from Morris, *Diary*, 1:72–77; "Was no longer," Schama, *Citizens*, 358; "Nothing can prevent," Auricchio, *Marquis*, 178.

3. Gottschalk, Maddox, *Through the October Days*, 60–71; "Have succeeded," Morris to Jay, July 1, 1789, Morris, *Diary*, 1:108; Doyle, *Oxford History*, 105–07; Unger, *Lafayette*, 233.

4. Auricchio, *Marquis*, 178–81; 25,000 troops surrounding Paris, Price, *Versailles*, 76.

5. French guard, Price, *Versailles*, 96; 3,600 number for French Guard, Crowdy, *French Revolutionary Infantry*, 5; "The eagerness," Young, *Travels*, 153–54; Schama, *Citizens*, 371.

6. Auricchio, *Marquis*, 178–81; Gottschalk, Maddox, *Through the October Days*, 80–82; "To preserve," Morris, *Diary*, 1:112.

7. "If the National Assembly," Paine, *Rights of Man*, 1:27–28; Gottschalk, Maddox, *Through the October Days*, 80–81.

8. "After the levee," Mazzei, *Life and Wanderings*, 414.

47. "Paid at Panthémont in Full"

1. Malone, *Rights*, 203–07; "We are at present," TJ to Nicholas Lewis, Dec. 16, 1788, *POTJ*, 14:362–63; "All out-door labor," TJ, "Auto," 81.

2. "The long continuance," TJ to Short, Dec. 8, 1788, *POTJ*, 14:343–44.

3. Leave of absence, TJ to John Jay, Nov. 19, 1788, *POTJ*, 14:211–17.

4. "Startled," Randolph, *Domestic Life*, 146; Malone, *Rights*, 207–08; Patsy's attraction to Short, Gordon-Reed, Onuf, *Blessed*, 129; "Paid" *et al.*, TJ, *MB*, 730, 730 n47, 731; Kierner, *Martha*, 64–67; "Make it a rule," TJ to Patsy Jefferson, June 28, 1787, *POTJ*, 11, 1:503; Gordon-Reed, *HOM*, 259–60; lease renewal, April 14, 1789 entry, TJ, *MB*, 1:729.

48. "A Catechism of France"

1. "I am returned" L to GW, Jan. 1, 1788, *POGW-Confed. Series*, 6:57.

2. "Good model," TJ to L, Feb. 28, 1787, *POTJ*, 11 *1*:186; "Declaration of rights," L. to [Madame Simiane], "Friday" [circa June], 1789, Lafayette, *Memoirs*, [Saunders and Otley, 1837], 2:295; For TJ and Morris writing of constitutions for France, TJ to Madison, Jan. 12, 1789, *POTJ*, 14:436–38; and Morris to Washington, March 3, 1789, *POGW-Pres.*, 1:359–60.

3. Gottschalk, *Through the October Days*, 80–98; "Will you send," L to TJ, July 6, 1789, *POTJ*, 15:249; "I will bring," TJ to L, July 6. 1789, *POTJ*, 15:250; "To Morrow," L to TJ, [July 9, 1789], *POTJ*, 15:255; Necker-Orléans-Jefferson dispute, Gottschalk, *Between*, 72–82.

4. "Enclosure, Proposed Declarations of Rights Drawn by the Marquis de Lafayette and by Dr. Richard Gem," *POTJ*, 14:438–40; trans. of latter in Chinard, *Lafayette and Jef-*

ferson, 137; discussion of three drafts of Lafayette's declaration, *ibid.*, 79–82, and Gottschalk, Maddox, *Through the October Days,* 84–90; "Declaration of the rights of France," Lafayette, Gottschalk, *Between*, 54; Brookhiser, *Morris*, 125–6.

5. "To Morrow," L to TJ, [July 9, 1789], *POTJ*, 15:255; Gottschalk, *Between*, 72–82.

6. Gottschalk, Maddox, *Through the October Days*, 90–98; quotations from Declaration's second draft, Chinard, *Lafayette and Jefferson*, 140–41; "The noble simplicity," and "it seemed," Gottschalk, Maddox, *Through*, 92–93; "Profession of faith," Lafayette, Gottschalk, *Between*, 97; National Assembly, July 11, 1789 (entire session), *Archives Parlementaires*, 8:219–23.

7. Gottschalk, Maddox, *Through the October Days*, 96–98; "He speaks," comte de Lally-Tollendal, in *ibid.*, 97; "Knowledge of" and "First European" (Lafayette quoted), *ibid.*, 98; "Some usable," *ibid.*

49. *"Aux Armes!"*

1. "Sabres drawn," Morris, *Diary*, 1:120–21; Auricchio, *Marquis*, 184; Schama, *Citizens*, 383–84; Price, *Versailles*, 87–88; Spagnoli, "Revolution Begins," 466–97; TJ, *MB*, 1:738 n70; Jefferson's and Short's July 1789 walks in Paris, TJ to Jay, July 19, 1789, *POTJ*, 15:284–91; "The progress," TJ to Paine, July 13, 1789, *POTJ*, 15:273.

2. Price, *Versailles*, 87–88; Necker and Orléans waxworks, Auricchio, *Marquis*, 186–87; "He is much," Morris, *Diary*, 1:119; "The news," *ibid.*, 1:122; "Daily this great" and "Fêtes and dinners," *ibid.*, 1:119; Auricchio, *Marquis*, 185–86; Gottschalk, Maddox, *Through the October Days*, 100–01; "The palaces," TJ to David Humphreys, Aug. 14, 1787, *POTJ*, 12:32–33; "A beautiful villeta," Mazzei, in Hayes, *Biographical Chronicle*, 75; July 12 attacks on *barrières*, *History of Paris*, 3:179–80; "Barriéres de Paris," *Dictionnaire de la révolution française*, 63.

3. Jefferson's perspective, Chinard, *Lafayette and Jefferson*, 78; "The parties," TJ to Jay, May 9, 1789, *POTJ*, 15:110–13; usage of word "revolution," Hill, *Origins*, 286.

50. Hôtel de Ville

1. "Empowered by," *Histoire des premiers électeurs de Paris en 1789*, 184–86; Auricchio, *Marquis*, 187–88; "Storybook hero," *ibid.*, 188.

2. Gottschalk, Maddox, *Through the October Days*, 101–09; "On another," Lafayette, *ibid.*, 103–04; Auricchio, *Marquis*, 189; "There is nothing," L to [Simiane], quoted and trans. in Gottschalk, Maddox, *Through the October Days*, 104.

3. "On their faces" *et al.*, Auricchio, *Marquis*, 189–90.

51. *Commandant de la Garde Nationale*

1. Auricchio, *Marquis*, 190–91; "The most perplexing," Price, *Versailles*, 89; Schama, *Citizens*, 399–406.

2. Auricchio, *Marquis*, 190–91.

3. Events and quotations, *ibid.*, 189–94; otherwise, unless other sources indicated, Gott-schalk, Maddox, *Through the October Days*, 113–24, and Unger, *Lafayette*, 238–41; "I reign in Paris," L to Madame de Simiane [?], July 16, 1789, Auricchio, *Marquis*, 193.

52. *"Vive la Nation!"*

1. "What the Londoners," "common robbers," TJ to Trumbull, Sept. 24, 1789, *POTJ*, 15:471; "My hotel," TJ to Montmorin, July 8, 1789, *POTJ*, 15:260–61; "Mr. Short," TJ to Jay, July 19, 1789, *POTJ*, 15:284–91; Markovic, "La Révolution aux barrières," 27–48; Adams, *Paris*, 3, 4; more generally, Delvau, *Histoire Anecdotique de Barrières*.
2. *"Grande Peur,"* Lefebvre, *Great Fear of 1789*; also Schama, *Citizens*, 429, 433, 434.
3. "Forty thousand souls," L to Madame de Simiane [?], July 16, 1789, Auricchio, *Marquis*, 193–94.
4. "A committee was held" *et al.*, Campan, *Memoirs*, 2:46–47; Auricchio, *Marquis*, 193–94.
5. Schama, *Citizens*, 422; Auricchio, *Marquis*, 194; Gottschalk, Maddox, *Through the October Days*, 122–31.
6. Schama, *Citizens*, 422–25; "I bring" *et al.*, Auricchio, *Marquis*, 194–95; Gottschalk, Maddox, *Through the October Days*, 159–90; "At least," Morris to GW, *POGW-Pres.*, 3:360–63; "About 60,000," TJ to Jay, July 19, 1789, *POTJ*, 15:284–91; "Our friend," Morris, *Diary*, 1:133.
7. Auricchio, *Marquis*, 195.
8. *"Vive le Roi"* *et al.*, Morris to GW, July 31, 1789, *POGW-Pres.*, 3:360–63.
9. "He had," Morris to GW, July 31, 1789, *POGW-Pres.*, 3:360–63; Lafayette quotations, Auricchio, *Marquis*, 195–96.

53. The Sea Running High

1. Auricchio, *Marquis*, 198–99.
2. "The people," L to GW, May 25, 1788, *POGW-Rev.*, 6:292–95; "The cutting," TJ to Cosway, July 25, 1789, *POTJ*, 15:305–06.
3. Schama, *Citizens*, 437–41; Auricchio, *Marquis*, 200–01; "It would have," "French Na-tion," Auricchio, *Marquis*, 201.
4. Gottschalk, Maddox, *Through the October Days*, 171–76; Schama, *Citizens*, 406–415, 451–55; "Pd. seeing Bastille," TJ, *MB*, 1:738, 738 n70; "I place," Gottschalk, Maddox, *Through the October Days*, 176.
5. "If the clouds," Morris, *Diary*, 1:158.

54. Duties Owed the King

1. Rice, *Paris*, 11, 52; Adams, *Paris*, 52–55.
2. "Have searched," TJ to Trumbull, Aug. 5, 1789, *POTJ*, 15:335; Lafayette request for Jefferson to host dinner—L to TJ, [Aug. 25, 1789], *POTJ*, 15:354–55.

3. Malone, *Rights*, 229; Archbishop to TJ, July 20, 1789, and TJ to Archbishop, July 22, Chinard, *Lafayette and Jefferson*, 143–45; "The only document," Chinard, Lafayette and Jefferson, 83–84; "Obvious considerations," TJ, "Auto," 94–95.

4. Gottschalk, Maddox, *Through the October Days*, 219–28.

5. "We shall be some," L to TJ, [Aug. 25, 1789], *POTJ*, 15:354–55.

6. Gottschalk, Maddox, *Through the October Days*, 219–28; L to TJ, [Aug. 25, 1789], *POTJ*, 15:354–55; "Whatever they should," TJ, "Auto," 96.

7. Serving tables, Adams, *Paris*, 19.

8. "Coolness and candor," TJ, "Auto," 96.

9. "Professedly their model" *et al.*, TJ to Madison, August 28, 1789, *POTJ*, 15:364–69; "Duties of exculpation" *et al.*, TJ, "Auto," 96–97.

10. "I am honoured," TJ to John Jay, Aug. 27, 1789, *POTJ*, 15:356–61.

55. Adieus

1. "Confined me," TJ to Trumbull, Sept. 9, 1789, *POTJ*, 15:407; for William Short, see Gordon-Reed, *HOM*, 254–55; Adams, *Paris*, 208–09; and Kierner, *Martha*, 70–71; "A young man," TJ to Short, March 24, 1789, *POTJ*, 14:694–97; Gordon-Reed, Onuf, *Blessed*, 129–32; "Mr. Jefferson's concubine," and "He desired," in "Life," Madison Hemings; for Sally Hemings' relations with Jefferson and alleged pregnancy in Paris, see Gordon-Reed, *HOM*, 326–75 and Kierner, *Martha*, 66–67, 73; "The extramarital exertions," *ibid.*, 67; "Gordon-Reed, *HOM*, 182; petitions for freedom, Gordon-Reed, "Ways," *New York Times*, Aug. 24, 2017.

2. For Jefferson-Hemings controversy and recent research, Thomas Jefferson Foundation's "Report of the Research Committee on Thomas Jefferson and Sally Hemings" issued 2000, and "Thomas Jefferson and Sally Hemings: A Brief Account," both on Monticello website. Fawn Brodie's *Thomas Jefferson: An Intimate History*, published in 1974, constituted, at the time, a rare instance of a modern Jefferson biographer giving credence to reports of Jefferson's sexual relations with Sally Hemings. Gordon-Reed's *Thomas Jefferson and Sally Hemings: An American Controversy*, generally regarded as having provided convincing evidence of the relationship, appeared in 1997.

3. Adams, *Paris*, 5, 12; "He says," Morris, *Diary*, 1, 156; Gaines, *Liberty*, 319.

4. Paris departure chronology, Sept. 26–Oct. 22, 1789, TJ, *MB*, 1:743–47; Malone, *Rights*, 234–37.

56. "Despotism to Liberty, in a Feather-Bed"

1. "Behold me," TJ to L, April 2, 1790, *POTJ*, 16:292–93; For festival phenomenon, see Ozouf, *Festivals and the French Revolution*; "Defend and maintain," Schama, *Citizens*, 502; *ibid.*, 472–513; Doyle, *Oxford History*, 117, 140.

57. "Cromwell Would Not Have Entered Alone"

1. Gottschalk, Maddox, *Through the October Days*, 329–79; Auricchio, *Marquis*, 204–08; Schama, *Citizens*, 465–70. "There's Cromwell!" exchange, Auricchio, *Marquis*, 207; *Cour de Marbre*, Château de Versailles curator Delphine Dubois, emails to author, Jan. 3, 2019.

2. "His hands," *Revolutions de Paris*, July 17–24, 1790; Auricchio, *Marquis*, 214–21; Schama, *Citizens*, 502–13; Gottschalk, Maddox, *Through the Federation*, 527–55; "Defend and maintain," Schama, "At the elevation," Morris, *Diary*, 1:337; festival phenomenon, Ozouf, *Festivals*.

3. Price, *Versailles*, 167–205; Doyle, *Oxford History*, 151–52; Auricchio, *Marquis*, 223–46; "Auvergnac Cromwell," *ibid.*, 223; "Altho Every Motive," L to TJ, June 7, 1791, *POTJ*, 20:539–41.

4. July 17, 1791, Champs de Mars demonstration and massacre and events (including "perhaps 50,000" and "perhaps 50"), Doyle, *Oxford History*, 152–154. See also Price, *Versailles*, 246–251; and Auricchio, *Marquis*, 245–249. Return to Chavaniac, Auricchio, *Marquis*, 252; "Not a little," GW to L, June 10, 1792, *POGW-Pres.*, 10:446–48; "The monster," TJ to L, June 16, 1792, *POTJ*, 24:85–86.

5. Price, *Versailles*, 289; "Organized like," L to Legislative Assembly, June 16, 1792, Auricchio, *Marquis*, 258; "Strike down," ibid., 259; "Pursued and punished," *ibid.*, 259; "Plotting against," *ibid.*, 262.

58. A Clomping of Approaching Horses

1. Spalding, *Prisoner*, 1, 3–4, 6–8; "Most hated," Staël to comte de Narbonne, Dec. 9, 1792, trans. in Spalding, *Prisoner*, 242n11; "I am making," Adrienne to L, Aug. 21, 1792, *ibid.*, 12, 244 n2; Auricchio, *Marquis*, 265–87; beyond specific citations, account of Lafayette's capture and imprisonment is drawn largely from Paul Spalding's deeply researched *Lafayette: Prisoner of State* and his article "After Seven Years."

2. Spalding, *Prisoner*, 12–21; eventual release of others detained with Lafayette, Spalding, *ibid.*, 16; "To foment," Frederick William II to Duke Albert Saxe-Teschen, Aug. 16, 1792, *ibid.*, 245 n17; "After each," L to Princess Adélaïde d' Hénin, Nov. 15, 1793, *ibid.*, 17; "Not only," Count Friedrich Wilhelm (Frederick William) von der Schulenburg-Kehnert, quoted by Lafayette, L to Princess Hénin, Nov. 23, 1793, *ibid.*, 17–18.

3. Price, *Versailles*, 326; Doyle, *Oxford History*, 195–96; 252–53; Schama, *Citizens*, 657–74.

59. Reign of Terror

1. Price, *Versailles*, 318; Auricchio, *Marquis*, 261, 270–71, 274–76, 309; Crawford, *Madame de Lafayette*, 160; La Petite Force prison, Godfrey, *Revolutionary Justice*, 116; Spalding, *Prisoner*, 140; the names of Adrienne's sister, mother, and grandmother guillotined at La Nation were, respectively, Anne-Jeanne-Baptiste-Louise, vicomtesse

d'Ayen; Henriette-Anne-Louise d'Aguesseau, duchesse d'Ayen; and Catherine de Cossé-Brissac, duchesse de Noailles; Cayenne plantations, Dubois, *Colony of Citizens*, 69–70; Auricchio, *Marquis*, 271; Doyle, *Oxford History*, 412–13.

2. "Under the protection," Adrienne to GW, [April 18, 1795], *POGW-Pres.*, 18:51–54; Spalding, *Prisoner*, 175–76.

3. Spalding, *Prisoner*, 175–77; Chernow, *Washington*, 631–41, 737–39; "Visible distress," GW to Thomas Pickney, May 22, 1796, *POGW-Pres.*, Early Access Doc, Founders Online.

60. "The Unhappy Fortunes of M. de la Fayette"

1. "The satisfaction," TJ to GWL, [June 19, 1796], *POTJ*, 29:126–27; "Although quite young," GWL to TJ, July 29, 1796, *POTJ*, 29:159 60; "My own affections," TJ to Short, Jan. 3, 1793, *POTJ*, 25:14–17; "Greatest illusions," Short to John H. Cocke, Aug. 12, 1826, John Hartwell Cocke Papers, Mss. 640.

2. "It was with," TJ to John Barker Church, Dec. 11, 1793, *POTJ*, 27:502–03; Bollman to Angelica Church, July 9, 1794, Angelica Schuyler Church Papers; Spalding, *Prisoner*, 7, 23–24.

3. Spalding, *Prisoner*, 136–37, 174–75; Hamilton to GW, Jan. 19, 1796, *POAH*, 20:42–43; "I take," GW to Francis II, May 15, 1796, Mack, *Lafayette*, 273–74.

61. Quiet Days in Batavia

1. Account of the final period of Lafayette's imprisonment and post-release life drawn largely from Spalding, *Prisoner;* and Spalding, "After Seven Years"; "I have ever," JQ Adams to John Adams, Feb. 16, 1797, *Adams Papers*, Early Access Doc., Founders Online.

2. "To end their," Aug. 1, 1797, Auricchio, *Marquis*, 280; Treaty of Campo Formio, Spalding, *Prisoner*, 351 n38.

3. Spalding, *Prisoner*, 207–23; "Ordered their release," William Vans Murray to GW, Aug. 26, 1797, in Auricchio, *Marquis*, 280; Lameth release, Spalding, *Prisoner*, 30.

4. "Agreed to allow," Spalding, "After Seven Years," 15; Spalding, *Prisoner*, 207–27; Adrienne's health upon release, Spalding, *Prisoner*, 224.

5. Auricchio, *Marquis*, 280–85; Adrienne regained title to La Grange on April 11, 1800, Marie-Alpais Torcheboeuf, La Grange curator, email to author, March 29, 2018; Spalding, "After Seven Years," 34–36; "How far I am," L to GW, May 9, 1799, *POGW-Retirement Series*, 54–59; "Cured me of my good will," Hamilton to L, April 28, 1798, *POAH*, 21:450–52; offer of Louisiana governorship, TJ to L, Nov. 4, 1803, *POTJ*, 41:665–66. After declining the Louisiana position, Lafayette solicited Jefferson's assistance in securing title to 11,250 acres in Louisiana promised him earlier for his American Revolution service. Lafayette hoped to sell the lands to defray debts in France. Jefferson, however, proved unable to satisfy the request—possibly because of Lafayette's identification by Congressional Federalists with radical Jacobin elements of France's

Revolution, according to historian Paul S. Spalding, email to author, Sept. 9, 2017; "The Constant Mourning," L to TJ, Jan. 11, 1808, *POTJ*, Early Access Doc. For Lafayette's dilemmas during those years, Spalding, "After Seven Years," 13–28; "The "french Youth," L to TJ, July 20, 1820, *POTJ*, Early Access Doc, Founders Online; "He was decidedly," Clarkson letter, Jan. 2, 1846, *Liberator*, Oct. 3, 1846; for more on Lafayette and abolitionism, Stauffer, "Lafayette," 43–53. For more on Lafayette's later political career and, more generally, his political and cultural signficance in the United States and France, see Kramer, *Lafayette in Two Worlds*.

62. Hero's Tour Redux

1. For 1824–25 tour, see Levasseur, *Lafayette in America*; "I cannot," Short to TJ, Nov. 2, 1824, *POTJ-Retirement Series*, Early Access Doc., Founders Online; meetings with African Americans during tour, Shaw, "I Have Been," 8–12.
2. Gaines, *Liberty*, 439–47; Auricchio, *Marquis*, 295–30; Mt. Vernon and Bastille key, Levasseur, *Lafayette*, 1:181–82; Chernow, *Washington*, 801–02; "Where We May try," L to GW, Feb. 5, 1783, Early Access, Founders Online; for Lafayette's late career in France's politics, see Neely, *Lafayette*; For post-Paris life of Martha ("Patsy") Jefferson Randolph, see Kierner, *Martha*; Armistead reunion, "James Lafayette," *Encyclopedia Virginia*; see also L to James [Armistead], Nov. 21, 1784, *LAAR*, 4:279 n1; unblemished by partisanship, Kramer, "Lafayette and the Historians," 375; "Had an air, Reynolds, *Walt Whitman's America*, 33–34.

63. Autumn Reunion

1. "[In] idle," TJ to L, *POTJ-Retirement Series*, 8:261–68; account of Lafayette's Nov. 4, 1824, arrival at Monticello is drawn from multiple sources, all based, directly or indirectly, on eyewitness accounts of the event; crowd estimate and "The General," Kierner, *Martha*, 190–91; while various quoted first-person accounts vary in small details, they comport in the main facts and most details: Smith, "Carysbrook Memoir"; see also transcribed excerpts from multiple sources on "Lafayette's Visit to Monticello (1824)" on Monticello website; Ward, *La Fayette in Virginia*, 90–91; Randolph, *Domestic Life*, 390–91; Israel Jefferson, "Life"; and Levasseur, *Lafayette in America*, 1:212; "My old friend," TJ to Dolley Madison, [Nov. 5, 1824], *POTJ*, 3:425–26.
2. McDonald, *Confounding Father*, 7–8.
3. "At length, the first carriage," Smith, "Carysbrook Memoir."
4. "Arrived a short time," Levasseur, *Lafayette in America*, 1:213; "My old friend," James Madison to Dolley Madison, [Nov. 5, 1824], *POJM-Retirement Series*, 3: 425–26; "Mr. Jefferson received me," L, Chinard, *Lafayette and Jefferson*, 358–59; Auricchio, *Marquis*, 127–28; Gottschalk, *Close*, 437. The referenced Lafayette letters were found in 1956 by a descendant amid a cache of family papers stored in a tower at Château de la Grange-Bléneau, east of Paris, Lafayette's principal residence from 1799 until his death;

the Library of Congress subsequently obtained permission to microfilm the collection; for early biographers and Lafayette's revanchist motives, Gottschalk, *Comes*, 173.

5. "Midas touch," Gottschalk, *Between*, 107; for Hemings siblings' later years, Gordon-Reed, Onuf, *Blessed*, 195, 315–17, and "Sally Hemings," "James Hemings," articles on Monticello website; for Sally Hemings, see also Kukla, *Jefferson's Women*, 119–41; Jefferson's efforts to shape and preserve his legacy, Cogliano, *Jefferson: Reputation and Legacy*, 74–77, and Ellis, *American Sphinx*, 285–96; for tensions of Jefferson during retirement as he struggled to reconcile his public legacy as a "Founding Father" with that of his private life as a literal father, see Glover, *Founders as Fathers*, 161–66; "asserted," Cogliano, *Jefferson: Reputation and Legacy*, 55.

6. "Will dilute," TJ to L, Dec. 26, 1820, Early Access Doc., *POTJ-Retirement Series* Founders Online; "Are You Sure," L to TJ, July 1, 1821, Early Access Doc, *POTJ-Retirement Series* Founders Online. "Lafayette spoke indifferently," Israel Jefferson, "Life."

7. For Jefferson and University of Virginia, Cogliano, *Jefferson: Reputation and Legacy*, 155–59; "His deeds" and other details of Nov. 5, 1826, banquet at University of Virginia, Randolph, *Domestic Life*, 391; see also Nolan, *Lafayette*, 257, and Levasseur, *Lafayette in America*, 219.

Epilogue: A Certain Idea

1. Idzerda, "Lafayette, Apostle of Liberty," 56–61, in Idzerda *et al.*, *Lafayette, Hero of Two Worlds*. Rue d'Anjou apartment, Marie-Alpais Torcheboeuf, La Grange curator, email to author, August 28, 2018; "What to the Slave is the Fourth of July?" Chaffin, *Giant's Causeway*, 170; "This spot," in "Grave of Lafayette," 108; "In the New World," Chateaubriand, book 42, *Mémoires d'Outre-Tombe*, Poetry in Translation website; "All my life," de Gaulle, *Mémoires de Guerre*, 1.

BIBLIOGRAPHY

Manuscript Collections

Adams Papers, Massachusetts Historical Society, Boston.

Archives Bordeaux Métropole: Bordeaux et l'indépendance américaine: une sélection des Archives, Bordeaux.

Archives de la Fondation Josée et René de Chambrun, Paris.

Brice-Jennings Papers, Maryland Historical Society, Annapolis.

Cocke Family Papers, Special Collections, University of Virginia, Charlottesville.

Dean Lafayette Collection, Cornell University, Ithaca, NY.

Various Papers, Bibliothèque nationale de France, Paris.

Silas Deane Papers, Connecticut Historical Society, Hartford.

Marquis de Lafayette Papers, Library of Congress, Washington, DC.

Thomas Jefferson Papers, Library of Congress, Washington, DC.

James Parton Papers, Harvard University, Cambridge, MA.

William Short Papers, American Philosophical Society, Philadelphia.

John Hartwell Cocke Papers, Special Collections, University of Virginia, Charlottesville.

"The Carys of Virginia" [ms. by Jane Blair Cary Smith], Special Collections, University of Virginia, Charlottesville.

Angelica Schuyler Church Papers, University of Virginia, Charlottesville.

"Charles Cornwallis orderly book," William L. Clements Library, Manuscripts Division. University of Michigan, Ann Arbor.

GOVERNMENT PUBLICATIONS

The American Diplomatic Code, Embracing a Collection of Treaties and Conventions between the United States and Foreign Powers; From 1778 to 1834. 2 Vols. Edited by Jonathan Elliot. Washington: Jonathan Elliot, Jr., 1834.

Archives parlementaires de 1787 à 1860. 82 vols. Paris: P. Dupont, 1862–1913.

Journal of the Council of State of Virginia. Vol. 2 (Oct. 6, 1777–Nov. 30, 1781). Edited by H. R. McIlwaine. Richmond: Virginia State Library, 1932.

Parliamentary Register, House of Lords, 2nd Sess. 15th Parliament. Vol. 8. London: J. Debrett, 1782.

Revolutionary Diplomatic Correspondence of the United States. 6 vols. Edited by Francis Wharton *et al.* Washington, DC: U.S. Government Printing Office, 1889.

Journals of the Continental Congress, 1774–1786. 34 vols. Washington, DC: Library of Congress/U.S. Government Printing Office, 1904–37.

Les élections et les cahiers de Paris en 1789; documents recueillis, mis en ordre et annotés par Ch.-L. Chassin. Seine (France): Conseil général, 1888.

Journal of the House of Delegates of the Commonwealth of Virginia [vol. for May 7, 1781–Jan. 21, 1786, sessions]. Richmond: Thomas W. White, 1828.

Journal of the House of Delegates of the Commonwealth of Virginia. [vol. for May 5, 1777–Jan. 1, 1781, sessions]. Richmond: Thomas W. White, 1827.

Calendar of Virginia State Papers . . . April 1, 1781 to December 31, 1781 [vol. 2 in series]. Edited by William Palmer. Richmond: James E. Goode, 1881.

PUBLISHED DOCUMENTS, EDITIONS, AND CONTEMPORARY WRITINGS

Adams, John, *et al. The Adams-Jefferson Letters: The Complete Correspondence between Thomas Jefferson and Abigail and John Adams.* Chapel Hill: University of North Carolina, 1959.

———. *The Adams Papers, Adams Family Correspondence: Vol. 2, June 1776–March 1778.* L. H., Butterfield, ed. Cambridge: Harvard University Press, 1963.

Adams, John Quincy. Diary. MHS website.

———. *Works of John Adams.* Vol. 1. Boston: Little Brown, 1856.

André, John. *André's Journal: An Authentic Record of the Movements and Engagements of the British Army in America from June 1777 to November 1778 as Recorded from Day to Day.* 2 vols. Boston: Bibliophile Society, 1903.

———. *John Major André's Journal, 1777–1778.* 2 vols. Boston: Bibliophile Society, 1903.

["An Officer in the Late Army"]. *A complete history of the Marquis de Lafayette, major general in the army of the United States of America, in the war on the revolution,*

embracing an account of his late tour through the United States to the time of his
departure, September, 1825. Hartford, CT: S. Andrus, 1846.

Biddle, Charles. *Autobiography of Charles Biddle, vice-president of the Supreme executive
council of Pennsylvania, 1745–1821*. Philadelphia: E. Claxton and Co., 1883.

Black, Joseph. *The Life and Letters of Joseph Black, MD*. Edited by W. Ramsay. London:
Constable and Co., 1918.

Bland, Theodorick, Jr. *The Bland Papers*. Vol. 1. Petersburg, VA: Edmund and Julian C.
Ruffin, 1840.

Bradshaw, George. *Bradshaw's illustrated travellers' hand book in [afterw.] to France*.
London: Bradshaw's Guide Office, 1855.

Campan, Madame. *Memoirs of the Court of Marie Antoinette, Queen of France*. 2 vols.
Philadelphia, Parry & McMillan, 1854.

Catalogue of the loan exhibition of historical portraits and relics, Metropolitan Opera
House, New York City, April 17th to May 8th, 1889. New York: Committee on Art and
Education, 1889.

Charavay, Étienne. *Le général La Fayette, 1757–1835: notice biographique*. Paris: Au siège
de la Société, 1898.

Chastellux, Marquis de. *Travels in North America in the years 1780–81–82*. New York,
1828.

Chateaubriand, François de. *Mémoires d'Outre-Tombe* [1848–50]. Poetry in Translation
website.

Clinton, Henry. Charles Cornwallis. *et al. The Campaign in Virginia, 1781: An Exact
Reprint of Six Rare Pamphlets on the Clinton-Cornwallis Controversy*. 2 vols. Edited
by Benjamin Franklin Stevens, London, 1888.

Answer to Sir Henry Clinton's Narrative of the Campaign in 1781 in North America.
Philadelphia : John Campbell, 1866.

Cornwallis, Charles. *Correspondence of Charles, First Marquis Cornwallis*. 3 vols.
London: John Murray, 1859.

Cloquet Jules. *Recollections of the Private Life of Lafayette*. London: Baldwin and
Cradock, 1835.

Dann, John C., ed. *The Revolution Remembered: Eyewitness Accounts of the War for
Independence*. Chicago: University of Chicago Press, 1980.

De Gaulle, Charles. *Mémoires De Guerre: L'appel, 1940–1942*. Vol 1. Paris: Plon, n.d.
[1954].

Deane, Silas. *The Deane Papers; Correspondence between Silas Deane, His Brothers and
Their Business and Political Associates, 1771–1795*. Hartford: Connecticut Historical
Society, 1930.

Delvau, Alfred. *Histoire Anecdotique de Barriéres*. Paris: Libraire de la société des gens de
lettres, 1865.

Denny, Ebenezer. "Diary." In *Letters, Journals & Diaries of ye Colonial America*. Edited by Dan Corbly. Raleigh, NC.: Lulu Press, 2009.

Droz, Joseph. *Histoire du règne de Louis XVI, pendant les années ou l'on pouvait prévenir ou diriger la révolution française, suivie des Applications de la morale à la politque*. Bruxelles: A. Wahlen et compagnie, 1839.

Duveyrier, Honoré, and Charles Duveyrier. *Histoire des premiers électeurs de Paris en 1789*. Paris: A. André, 1828.

——*Early Proceedings of the American Philosophical Society . . . 1744–1838*. Philadelphia: McCalla & Stavely, 1884.

Franklin, Benjamin. *Papers of Benjamin Franklin*. 37 vols. and online. Edited by Leonard Labaree *et al*. New Haven: Yale University Press, 1959–.

Galt, John. *The Life, Studies, and Works of Benjamin West*. London: T. Caddel and W. Davies, 1820.

Gaulle, Charles de. *Mémoires de Guerre. L'Appel, 1940–1942*. Paris: Plon, n.d.

Gérard, Conrad Alexander, Charles Gravier Vergennes, *et al*. *Correspondence of the First French Minister to the United States with the Comte de Vergennes, Despatches and Instructions of Conrad Alexandre Gérard, 1778–1780*. Baltimore: Johns Hopkins Press, 1939.

Greene, Nathanael. *The Papers of Nathanael Greene*, Vol. VII. Edited by Richard Showman. Chapel Hill: University of North Carolina Press, 1994.

Hamilton, Alexander. *Papers of Alexander Hamilton*. 27 vols. Edited by Harold C. Cyrett. New York: Columbia University Press, 1961–87.

Hemings, Madison, "Life Among the Lowly, No. 1." *Pike County* [Ohio] *Republican*. March 13, 1873.

History of Paris, from the earliest period to the present day. 3 vols. London: G. B. Whittaker, 1827.

Jay, John. *Correspondence and Public Papers*. Vol. 3 (1782–93). Edited by Henry P. Johnston. New York: G. P. Putnam's Sons, 1891.

Jefferson, Isaac. "Memoirs." In *Jefferson at Monticello*, edited by James A. Bear, Jr., 3–137. Charlottesville: University Press of Virginia, 1967.

Jefferson, Thomas. *Jefferson's Literary Commonplace Book*. Edited by Douglas L. Wilson. Princeton: Princeton University Press, 1989.

——. *Papers of Thomas Jefferson*. 41 vols. (to date). Edited by Julian P. Boyd *et al*. Princeton: Princeton University Press, 1950–2014.

——. *Thomas Jefferson Travels: Selected Writings, 1784–1789*. Edited by Anthony Brandt. Washington, DC: National Geographic Society, 2006.

——. *Jefferson's Memoranda Books*. 2 vols. Edited by James A. Bear, Jr., and Lucia C. Stanton. Princeton: Princeton University Press, 1997.

——. *Thomas Jefferson's Garden Book, 1766–1824*. Annotated by Edwin Morris Betts. Philadelphia: American Philosophical Society, 1944.

——. "Autobiography." In *Thomas Jefferson, Writings*, edited by Merrill D. Peterson, 1–101. New York: Library of America, 1984.

——. "Notes on the State of Virginia." In *Thomas Jefferson, Writings*, edited by Merrill D. Peterson, 123–25. New York: Library of America, 1984.

Jefferson, Thomas, *et al*. *Jefferson in His Own Time: A Biographical Chronicle of His Life, Drawn from Recollections, Interviews, and Memoirs by Family, Friends, and Associates*. Edited by Kevin J. Hayes. Iowa City: University of Iowa Press, 2012.

Knapp, Samuel Lorenzo. *Memoirs of General Lafayette, with an Account of his present Visit to this country*. Boston: E. G. House, 1825.

Lafayette, Gilbert du Motier de. *Correspondance inédite de La Fayette, 1793–1801; lettres de prison–lettres d'exile*. Edited by Jules Thomas. Paris: Delgrave, [1903].

——. *Lafayette and Slavery, from His Letters to Thomas Clarkson and Granville Sharp*. Edited by Melvin Kennedy. Easton, PA: American Friends of Lafayette, 1950.

——. *Lafayette in Virginia: Unpublished Letters*. Baltimore: Johns Hopkins University Press, 1928.

——. *Mémoires, Correspondance, et manuscrits du général Lafayette, publiés par sa famille*. 6 vols. Paris: Fournier Ainé, 1837–38.

——. *Memoirs, correspondence and manuscripts of General Lafayette*. 3 vols. London: Saunders and Otley, 1837. [Vol. 1, and only vol. 1, published by same firm in a New York edition.]

——, and Thomas Jefferson. *Letters of Lafayette and Jefferson*. Edited by Gilbert Chinard. Baltimore: Johns Hopkins University Press, 1929.

——. *Letters of Lafayette to Washington, 1777–1799*. Edited by Louis Gottschalk. Philadelphia: American Philosophical Society, 1976.

——. *Lafayette in the Age of the American Revolution*. 5 vols. Edited by Stanley Idzerda *et al*. Ithaca, NY: Cornell University Press, 1977–83.

Lasteyrie, Mme de. *Vie de Madame de Lafayette*. Paris: Techener fils, 1869.

Lee, Charles, *et al*. *The Lee Papers*. Vol. 2. New York: New-York Historical Society, 1872.

Lee, Henry. *Memoirs of the war in the Southern department of the United States*. Philadelphia: Bradford and Inskeep, 1812.

LeVasseur, A. *Lafayette in America in 1824 and 1825; or, Journal of a voyage to the United States*. 2 vols. Translated by John D. Godman. Philadelphia: Carey and Lea, 1829.

Mack, Ebenezer. *The Life of Gilbert Motier de Lafayette: A marquis of France; a general in the American and French revolutions; the compatriot and friend of Washington; the champion of American independence, and of the rights and liberties of mankind: from numerous and authentick sources*. Ithaca, NY: Mack, Andrus & Woodruff, 1841.

Madison, James. *Papers of James Madison*. Vols. 3–10 (March 1781–March 1788). Edited by Robert A. Rutland and William M. E. Rachal. Chicago: University of Chicago Press, 1963–77.

Maurer, C. F. William. *Dragoon Diary: The History of the Third Continental Light Dragoons*. Bloomington, IN: Authorhouse, 2005.

Mazzei, Philip. *My Life and Wanderings*. Translated by Sister Margherita Marchione [from 1845 Italian original]. Morristown, NJ: American Institute of Italian Studies, 1980.

Montesquieu, Baron de. *The Spirit of the Laws*. Translated by Thomas Nugent. New York: Hafner Publishing, 1949.

Montrésor, John. *The Montrésor Journals*. Vol. 14. Edited by Gideon Delaplaine Scull. New York: New-York Historical Society, 1882.

Morgan, George. *The True La Fayette*. Philadelphia: J. P. Lippincott, 1919.

Morris, Gouverneur. *The Diaries of Gouverneur Morris, European Travels, 1794–1798*. Edited by Melanie Randolph Miller. Charlottesville: University of Virginia Press, 2011.

———. *The Diary and Letters of Gouverneur Morris*. 2 vols. Edited by Anne Cary Morris. New York: Charles Scribner's Sons, 1888.

Paine, Thomas. *Rights of Man: Being an Answer to Mr. Burke's Attack on the French Revolution*. Part 1. London: J. S. Jordan, 1791.

Percy, Sholto and Reuben Percy. *The Percy Anecdotes*. London: Printed for T. Boys, 1822.

Pickering, Octavius, and Charles Wentworth Upham. *Life of Timothy Pickering*. 2 vols. Boston: Little Brown, 1867–73.

Pierson, Hamilton W. *The Private Life of Thomas Jefferson at Monticello. From Entirely New Materials* [from papers of Edmund Bacon, overseer hired by Jefferson]. New York: Charles Scribner, 1863.

Ramsay, David, *The History of the American Revolution*. 2 vols. Philadelphia: R. Aitken, 1789.

———. *History of the Revolution in South Carolina from a British Province to an Independent State*. Trenton, NJ: Isaac Collins, 1785.

Randall, Henry Stephens. *Life of Thomas Jefferson*. 3 vols. New York: Derby and Jackson, 1858.

Randolph, Sarah N. *The Domestic Life of Thomas Jefferson*. New York: Harper & Bros., 1873.

Raynal, Guillaume-Thomas-François, Abbé. *History of the Two Indies*. Edited and translated by Peter Jimack. Burlington, VT: Ashgate, 2006.

———. *Revolution of America*. London: L. Davis, 1781.

Reed, D. B. *Life and Times of General John Graves Simcoe*. Toronto: George Virtue, 1890.

Riedesel, Friedrich. *Memoirs, and letters and journals, of Major General Riedesel during his residence in America*. 2 vols. Albany, NY: J. Munsell, 1868.

Ségur, Louis-Philippe, comte de. *Memoirs and Recollections*. Boston: Wells and Lilly; New York, 1825.

Simcoe, John Graves. *Simcoe's Military Journal: A History of the Operations of a Partisan Corps Called the Queen's Rangers*. New York: Bartlett & Welford, 1844.

Smith, Abigail ["Nabby"] Adams. *Journal and Correspondence of Miss Adams, daughter of John Adams, second president of the United States. Written in France and England, in 1785*. New York: Wiley and Putnam, 1841.

Smith, John Cotton. *Correspondence and Miscellanies*. New York: Harper & Bros., 1847.

Stevens, John Austin. *Progress of New York in a Century: 1776–1876*. New York: New-York Historical Society, 1876.

Tarleton, Banastre. *A History of the Campaigns of 1780 and 1781: In the Southern Provinces of North America*. London: T. Cadell, 1787.

Thatcher, James. *A military journal during the American revolutionary war, from 1775 to 1783*. Boston: Richardson and Lord, 1823.

[Trist, Nicholas]. *Thomas Jefferson's Library: A Catalog with the Entries in His Own Order*. Edited by James Gilreath and Douglas L. Wilson. LOC website.

Trumbull, John. *Autobiography, Reminiscences and Letters of John Trumbull, from 1756 to 1841*. New Haven: Wiley and Putnam, 1841.

Ward, Robert D. *General La Fayette in Virginia, in 1824 and '25, An Account of His Triumphant Progress*. Richmond, VA: West, Johnston & Co., 1881.

Washington, George. *Papers of George Washington*. Charlottesville: University of Virginia Press, 1985–[Revolutionary War Series. 24 vols. Edited by Philander D. Chase *et al.*, 1985–2016; Confederation Series. 6 vols. Edited by W. W. Abbot, 1992–97; Presidential Series. 18 vols. Edited by Dorothy Twohig *et al.*, 1987–2015; Retirement Series. Edited by W. W. Abbot *et al.*, 1998–99.]

———. *Writings of George Washington*. Vol. 8. Boston: Russell, Odiorne & Co., 1835.

———. *The writings of George Washington: being his correspondence, addresses, messages, and other papers, official and private / selected and published from the original manuscripts with a life of the author, notes and illustrations by Jared Sparks*. Edited by Jared Sparks. 12 vols. Boston: American Stationers' Co./John B. Russell, 1834–37.

Wild, Ebenezer. *The journal of Ebenezer Wild (1776–1781), who served as corporal, sergeant, ensign, and lieutenant in the War of the Revolution*. Edited by James M. Bugbee. Cambridge, MA: John Wilson and Son, University Press, 1891. [Two editions of this work have appeared; the second, published by the Massachusetts Historical Society, has different pagination from the first.]

Young, Arthur. *Travels in France by Arthur Young during the Years 1787, 1788, 1789*. London: George Bell and Sons, 1890.

Young, John Russell. *Memorial History of the City of Philadelphia, from Its First Settlement*. Vol. 1. New York: New York History Company, 1895.

CONTEMPORARY NEWSPAPERS AND JOURNALS

Independent Journal [New York]
Virginia Gazette [Williamsburg and, after 1780, Richmond]
Liberator [Boston]
Niles Register [Baltimore]
Révolutions de Paris [Paris]

PUBLISHED SECONDARY WORKS

Adams, William Howard. *Gouverneur Morris: An Independent Life*. New Haven: Yale University Press, 2003.

———. *Paris Years of Thomas Jefferson*. New Haven: Yale University Press, 1997.

Auricchio, Laura. "Lafayette at Yorktown (1782): Transformations and Interpretations." In Olga Anna Duhl *et al. "A True Friend of the Cause": Lafayette and the Antislavery Movement*, 17–31. New York: Grolier Club/Easton, PA: Lafayette College, 2016.

———. *The Marquis: Lafayette Reconsidered*. New York: Alfred A. Knopf, 2014.

Bailyn, Bernard. *Ideological Origins of the American Revolution*. Cambridge: Harvard University Press, 1967.

"Beaumarchais and the American Revolution." Sept. 22, 1993. Center for the Study of Intelligence. Central Intelligence Agency website.

Boles, John B. *Jefferson: Architect of American Liberty*. New York: Basic Books, 2017.

Bourne, Henry E. "Improvising a Government in Paris in July, 1789." *American Historical Review* 10, no. 2 (Jan. 1905): 280–308.

Brodie, Fawn M. *Thomas Jefferson: An Intimate History*. New York: W. W. Norton, 1974.

Brookhiser, Richard. *Gouverneur Morris: The Rake Who Wrote the Constitution*. New York: Free Press, 2003.

Buck, William J. "Washington's Encampment on the Neshaminy." *Pennsylvania Magazine of History and Biography* 1, no. 3 (1877): 275–84.

Burstein, Andrew. *Jefferson's Secrets: Death and Desire at Monticello*. New York: Basic Books, 2005.

Burstein, Andrew, and Nancy Isenberg. *Madison and Jefferson*. New York: Random House, 2010.

Callahan, Myrtle Elizabeth. "History of Richmond as a Port City." M.A. thesis, University of Richmond, 1952.

Catlett, Lowell. *Thomas Jefferson: A Free Mind*. Victoria, B.C.: Trafford Publishing, 2006.

Chaffin, Tom. *Giant's Causeway: Frederick Douglass's Irish Odyssey and the Making of an American Visionary*. Charlottesville: University of Virginia Press, 2014.

———. *Pathfinder: John Charles Frémont and the Course of American Empire*. New York: Hill and Wang, 2002.

Chartrand, Réne. *American War of Independence Commanders.* Oxford, England: Osprey, 2003.

Chernow, Ron. *Alexander Hamilton.* New York: Penguin Press, 2004.

———. *Washington, A Life.* New York: Penguin Press, 2010.

Childs, James. *Armies and Warfare in Europe, 1648–1789.* Manchester, England: Manchester University Press, 1982.

Chinard, Gilbert. *Thomas Jefferson: The Apostle of Americanism.* Boston: Little Brown, 1929.

Clary, David A. *Washington, Lafayette, and the Friendship That Saved the Revolution.* New York: Bantam, 2007.

Cogliano, Francis D., ed. *A Companion to Thomas Jefferson.* Hoboken, NJ: Wiley-Blackwell, 2011.

———. *Emperor of Liberty: Thomas Jefferson's Foreign Policy.* New Haven: Yale University Press, 2014.

———. *Revolutionary America, 1763–1815: A Political History.* Abingdon-on-Thames, England: Routledge, 2008.

———. *Thomas Jefferson: Reputation and Legacy.* Charlottesville: University of Virginia Press, 2006.

Cooper, Helen A., ed. *John Trumbull: The Hand and Spirit of a Painter.* New Haven: Yale University, 1982.

Covart, Elizabeth M. "Silas Deane, Forgotten Patriot." *Journal of the American Revolution,* July 30, 2014 [online].

Crawford, M. MacDermot. *Madame de Lafayette and Her Family.* New York: James Pott & Co., 1907.

Crowdy, Terry. *French Revolutionary Infantry 1789–1802.* Oxford, England: Osprey, 2003.

Curtin, Philip D. *Atlantic Slave Trade: A Census.* Madison: University of Wisconsin Press, 1972.

Curtis, Michael Christopher. *Jefferson's Freeholders and the Politics of Ownership in the Old Dominion.* Cambridge, England: Cambridge University Press, 2012.

Daigler, Ken. "James Lafayette (James Armistead), American Spy." *Journal of the American Revolution.* Sept. 26, 2017 [online].

Doniol, Henri. *Histoire de la Participation de la France à l'etablissement des États-Unis d'Amérique.* Paris, 1886.

Darnton, Robert. *Mesmerism and the End of the Enlightenment in France.* Cambridge: Harvard University Press, 1968.

———. *George Washington's False Teeth. An Unconventional Guide to the Eighteenth Century.* New York: W. W. Norton, 2003.

Davis, Robert P. *Where a Man Can Go: Major General William Phillips, British Royal Artillery, 1731–1781.* Westport, CT: Greenwood Press, 1999.

Decker, Michael McMillen. "Baron Von Steuben and the Military forces in Virginia during the British Invasions of 1780–1781." M.A. thesis, University of Richmond, 1979.

Doyle, Andrew Beatty. *Frederick William von Steuben and the American Revolution, Aide to Washington and Inspector General of the Army.* Steubenville, OH: H. C. Cook, 1913.

Doyle, William. *Origins of the French Revolution.* 2nd ed. Oxford, England: Oxford University Press, 1988.

———. *Oxford History of the French Revolution.* Rev. ed. Oxford, England: Oxford University Press, 2002.

Dubois, Laurent. *A Colony of Citizens: Revolution and Slave Emancipation in the French Caribbean, 1787–1804.* Chapel Hill: University of North Carolina Press, 2004.

Duhl, Olga Anna and Diane Windham Shaw, eds. *"A True Friend of the Cause": Lafayette and the Antislavery Movement.* New York: Grolier Club/ Easton, PA: Lafayette College, 2016.

Dunn, Susan. *Sister Revolutions: French Lightning, American Light.* New York: Faber & Faber, 1999.

Egret, Jean. *Louis XV et l'opposition parlementaire.* Paris: Armand Colin, 1970.

Ellis, Joseph J. *American Sphinx: The Character of Thomas Jefferson.* New York: Alfred A. Knopf, 1997.

Faragher, John Mack. *Daniel Boone: The Life and Legend of an American Pioneer.* New York: Henry Holt and Co., 1993.

Favata, Daniel C. "John Trumbull: A Founding Father of American Art." Fordham University website.

Fling, Fred Morrow, and Helene Dresser Fling. *Source Problems on the French Revolution.* New York: Harper & Bros., 1913.

Fraser, Walter J., Jr. *Charleston! Charleston! The History of a Southern City.* Columbia: University of South Carolina Press, 1989.

"French Slave Trade." Slavery and Remembrance website.

Friedland, Paul. *Political Actors: Representative Bodies and Theatricality in the Age of the French Revolution.* Ithaca, NY: Cornell University Press, 2002.

Gaines, James. *For Liberty and Glory: Washington, Lafayette and Their Revolutions.* New York: Alfred A. Knopf, 2007.

Garnier, Auguste. *Notice sur le général baron Delzons.* Paris: Librairie d'Eugène Belin, 1863.

Glover, Lorri. *Founders as Fathers: The Private Life and Politics of the American Revolutionaries.* New Haven: Yale University Press, 2016.

Godfrey, James Logan. *Revolutionary Justice: A Study of the Organization, Personnel, and Procedure of the Paris Tribunal, 1793–1795.* Chapel Hill: University of North Carolina Press, 1951.

Good, Cassandra A. *Founding Friendships: Friendships between Men and Women in the Early American Republic.* New York: Oxford University Press, 2005.

Gordon-Reed, Annette. *The Hemingses of Monticello*. New York: W. W. Norton, 2008.

———. "Sally Hemings, Thomas Jefferson and the Ways We Talk about Our Past." *New York Times*, August 24, 2017.

———. *Thomas Jefferson and Sally Hemings: An American Controversy*. Charlottesville: University of Virginia, 1997.

Gordon-Reed, Annette, and Peter S. Onuf. *Most Blessed of the Patriarchs*. New York: W. W. Norton, 2016.

Goss, Betty. "Journey through France and Italy (1787)." *Jefferson Encyclopedia*, 2009 (revised by Anna Berkes, 2011). Monticello website.

Gottschalk, Louis. *Lady in Waiting: The Romance of Lafayette and Aglaé de Hunolstein*. Baltimore: Johns Hopkins University Press, 1939.

———. *Lafayette Comes to America*. Chicago: University of Chicago Press, 1935.

———. *Lafayette Joins the American Army*. Chicago: University of Chicago Press, 1937.

———. *Lafayette and the Close of the American Revolution*. Chicago: University of Chicago Press, 1942.

———. *Lafayette between the American and the French Revolution, 1783–1789*. University of Chicago, 1950.

Gottschalk, Louis, and Margaret Maddox. *Lafayette in the French Revolution through the October Days*. Chicago: University of Chicago Press, 1969.

———. *Lafayette in the French Revolution from the October Days through the Federation*. Chicago: University of Chicago Press, 1973.

Gray, Edward G. *The Making of John Ledyard: Empire and Ambition in the Life of an Early American Traveler*. New Haven: Yale University Press, 2007.

———. *Tom Paine's Iron Bridge: Building a United States*. New York: W. W. Norton, 2016.

Harris, Malcolm. *Old New Kent County [Virginia]: Some Account of the Planters*. Vol. 1. West Point, VA: M. H. Harris, 1977.

Harris, Michael C. *Brandywine: A Military History of the Battle That Lost Philadelphia but Saved America, September 11, 1777*. El Dorado Hills, CA: Savas Beatie, 2004.

Hazleton, John H. "The Historical Value of Trumbull's 'Declaration of Independence.'" *Pennsylvania Magazine of History and Biography* 31 (Jan. 1907): 30–42.

Hildebrandt, Alfred. *Airships past and present, together with chapters on the use of balloons in connection with meteorology, photography and the carrier pigeon*. London: A. Constable & Co. Ltd., 1908.

Hill, Christopher. *Intellectual Origins of the English Revolution—Revisited*. Oxford, England: Clarendon Press, 1997.

Hobsbawm, Eric. *The Age of Revolution: 1789–1848*. 1962. Reprint. New York: Vintage, 1996.

Humphreys, Francis Landon. *Life and Times of David Humphreys, Soldier, Statesman, Poet*. Vol. 1. New York: G. P. Putnam's Sons, 1917.

Hunt, Lynn. *Politics, Culture, and Class in the French Revolution*. Berkeley: University of California Press, 1984.

Isaacson, Walter. *Benjamin Franklin, An American Life*. New York: Simon and Schuster, 2003.

Jaffe, Irma B. *John Trumbull, Patriot Artist of the American Revolution*. Boston: New York Graphic Society, 1975.

Jaffe, Irma B., *et al. Trumbull: The Declaration of Independence*. New York: Viking Press, 1976.

Jasanoff, Maya. *Liberty's Exiles: American Loyalists in the Revolutionary World*. New York: Vintage, 2012.

Johnson, Alison. *Louis XVI and the French Revolution*. Jefferson, NC: McFarland & Co., 2013.

Johnson, Emilie. "History of Jefferson's 1802 Phaeton." Charlottesville, VA: Thomas Jefferson Foundation, 2016.

———. "Whose chip is it anyway?" Monticello website (May 20, 2015).

Kapp, Friedrich. *The Life of Frederick William von Steuben: Major General in the Revolutionary Army*. 2nd ed. New York: Mason Brothers, 1859.

———. *The Life of John Kalb, Major-General in the Revolutionary Army*. New York: Henry Holt, 1884.

Kaye, Harvey J. *Thomas Paine and the Promise of America*. New York: Hill and Wang, 2005.

Kern, Susan A. "The Jeffersons at Shadwell: The Social and Material World of a Virginia Family." Ph.D diss., College of William and Mary, 2005.

Kierner, Cynthia A. *Martha Jefferson Randolph, Daughter of Monticello: Her Life and Times*. Chapel Hill: University of North Carolina Press, 2012.

Kimball, Marie. *Jefferson: The Scene of Europe, 1784–1789*. New York: Coward-McCann, 1950.

Klein, Herbert S. *The Middle Passage: Comparative Studies in the Atlantic Slave Trade*. Princeton: Princeton University Press, 1978.

Kramer, Lloyd S. "Lafayette and the Historians: Changing Symbol, Changing Needs, 1834–1984." *Historical Reflections / Réflexions Historiques* 11, no. 3 (1984): 373–401.

———. *Lafayette in Two Worlds*. Chapel Hill: University of North Carolina Press, 1996.

Kranish, Michael. *Flight from Monticello: Thomas Jefferson at War*. New York: Oxford University Press, 2010.

Kukla, Jon. *Mr. Jefferson's Women*. New York: Alfred A. Knopf, 2007.

Landes, Joan. "The History of Feminism: Marie-Jean-Antoine-Nicolas de Caritat, Marquis de Condorcet." *Stanford Encyclopedia of Philosophy* [online].

Lefebvre, George. *The Coming of the French Revolution*. Translated by R. R. Palmer. Princeton: Princeton University Press, 1979.

———. *The Great Fear of 1789: Rural Panic in Revolutionary France*. New York: Pantheon, 1973.

Lender, Mark Edward, and Garry Wheeler Stone. *Fatal Sunday: George Washington, the Monmouth Campaign, and the Politics of Battle*. Norman: University of Oklahoma Press, 2016.

Lender, Mark Edward, and James Kirby Martin. "A Traitor's Epiphany: Benedict Arnold in Virginia and His Quest for Reconciliation." *Virginia Magazine of History and Biography* 125, no. 4 (October 2017): 314–57.

Long, C. Thomas. "Britain's Green Water Navy in the Revolutionary Chesapeake: Long-Range Asymmetric Warfare in the Littoral." *International Journal of Naval History* 8, no. 2 (August 2009) [n.p., online].

McBride, John David. "The Virginia War Effort, 1775–1783: Manpower Policies and Practices." Ph.D. dissertation, University of Virginia, 1977.

McCarthy, Justin Huntly. *The French Revolution*. 2 vols. New York: Harper & Bros., 1898.

McDonald, Robert M. S. *Confounding Father, Thomas Jefferson's Image in His Own Time*. Charlottesville: University of Virginia Press, 2016.

McGuire, Thomas J. *The Philadelphia Campaign, Volume 1: Brandywine and the Fall of Philadelphia*. Mechanicsburg, PA: Stackpole Books, 2006.

Maass, John R. *The Road to Yorktown: Jefferson, Lafayette and the British Invasion of Virginia*. Charleston, SC: History Press, 2015.

Malone, Dumas. *Thomas Jefferson and His Time*. 6 vols. Boston: Little Brown, 1948–81: *Jefferson the Virginian*, 1948; *Jefferson and the Rights of Man*, 1951; *Jefferson and the Ordeal of Liberty*, 1962; *Jefferson the President, First Term, 1801–1805*, 1970; *Jefferson the President, Second Term, 1805–1809*, 1974; *Sage of Monticello*, 1981.

Markovic, Momcilo. "La Révolution aux barrières: l'incendie des barrières de l'octroi à Paris en juillet 1789." *Annales Historique de la Révolution Française* 372, no. 2 (April–June 2013): 27–48.

Martin, David G. *The Philadelphia Campaign: June 1777–July 1778*. Cambridge, MA: Da Capo, 2003.

Martin, James Kirby. *Benedict Arnold, Revolutionary Hero: An American Warrior Reconsidered*. New York: New York University Press, 1997.

Massey, Gregory D. *John Laurens and the American Revolution*. Columbia: University of South Carolina Press, 2000.

Maurer, C. F. William. *Dragoon Diary: The History of the Third Continental Light Dragoons*. Bloomington, IN: Authorhouse, 2005.

Maurois, André. *Adrienne: The Life of the Marquise de La Fayette*. Translated by Gerard Hopkins. London: Jonathan Cape, 1961.

Maza, Sarah A. *The Myth of the French Bourgeoisie*. Cambridge: Harvard University Press, 2003.

Meacham, Jon. *Thomas Jefferson: The Art of Power*. New York: Random House, 2012.

Merkel, William G. "Jefferson's Failed Anti-Slavery Proviso of 1784 and the Nascence of Free Soil Constitutionalism." *Seton Hall Law Review* 38 (2008): 555–602.

Meschutt, David. "The Adams-Jefferson Portrait Exchange." *American Art Journal* 14, no. 2 (Spring 1982): 47–54.

Middlekauff, Robert. *The Glorious Cause: The American Revolution, 1763–1789.* New York: Oxford University Press, 1982.

Moore, Roy, and Alma Moore. *Thomas Jefferson's Journey to the South of France.* New York: Stewart, Tabori & Chang, 1999.

Morgan, Edmund. *Benjamin Franklin.* New Haven, Connecticut: Yale University Press, 2003.

Murphy, Orville T. *Charles Gravier, Comte de Vergennes: French Diplomacy in the Age of Revolution, 1719–1787.* Albany: State University of New York Press, 1982.

Nelson, Paul David. *General Horatio Gates: A Biography.* Baton Rouge: Louisiana State University Press, 1976.

Nolan, J. Bennett. *Lafayette in America, Day by Day.* Baltimore: Johns Hopkins University Press, 1934.

O'Shaughnessy, Andrew Jackson. *The Men Who Lost America: British Leadership, the American Revolution and the Fate of the Empire.* New Haven: Yale University Press, 2014.

Ozouf, Mona. *Festivals and the French Revolution.* Translated by Alan Sheridan. Cambridge: Harvard University Press, 1991.

Papas, Phillip. *Renegade Revolutionary: The Life of General Charles Lee.* New York: New York University Press, 2014.

Pawlett, Nathaniel Mason, and Howard W. Newman, Jr., *Route of the Three Notch'd Road: A Preliminary Report.* 1976. Revised reprint, Charlottesville: Virginia Highway & Transportation Research Council, 2003.

Peterson, Merrill D. *The Jefferson Image in the American Mind.* 1960. Reprint, Charlottesville: University of Virginia Press, 1998.

———. *Thomas Jefferson and the New Nation.* London: Oxford University Press, 1970.

Philbrick, Nathaniel. *Valiant Ambition: George Washington, Benedict Arnold, and the Fate of the American Revolution.* New York: Viking, 2016.

Pincus, Steve. *The Heart of the Declaration: The Founders' Case for an Activist Government.* New Haven: Yale University Press, 2016.

Polasky, Janet. *Revolutions without Borders.* New Haven: Yale University Press, 2015.

Price, Munro. *Preserving the Monarchy: The Comte de Vergennes 1774–1787.* Cambridge, England: Cambridge University Press, 1995.

———. *The Road from Versailles: Louis XVI, Marie Antoinette, and the Fall of the French Monarchy.* New York: St. Martin's Press, 2003. [Published in UK as *The Fall of the French Monarchy,* 2002.]

Pybus, Cassandra. "Jefferson's Faulty Math: The Question of Slave Defections in the American Revolution." *The William and Mary Quarterly,* Third Series, 62, n. 2 (Apr., 2005): 243–64.

Rakove, Jack. *Revolutionaries: A New History of the Invention of America.* New York: Houghton Mifflin, 2010.

Reynolds, Davis. *Walt Whitman's America: A Cultural Biography*. New York: Vintage, 1996.

Robb, Graham. *The Discovery of France: A Historical Georgraphy from the Revolution to the First World War*. New York: W. W. Norton, 2007.

Roberts, Priscilla H., and Richard S. Roberts. *Thomas Barclay (1728–1793), Consul in France, Diplomat in Barbary*. Bethlehem, PA: Lehigh University Press, 2008.

Schama, Simon. *Citizens: A Chronicle of the French Revolution*. New York: Vintage, 1989.

Scharf, Virginia. *The Women Jefferson Loved*. New York: Harper, 2010.

Schiff, Stacy. *A Great Improvisation: Franklin, France, and the Birth of America*. New York: Henry Holt and Co., 2005.

Schulte-Nordholt, J. W. "The Example of the Dutch Republic for American Federalism." *Low Countries Historical Review* 94, no. 3 (1979): 437–49.

Selby, John E. *Revolution in Virginia, 1775–1783*. Williamsburg, VA: Colonial Williamsburg Foundation, 1988.

Shackelford, George Green. *Jefferson's Adoptive Son: The Life of William Short*. Lexington: University Press of Kentucky, 1993.

———. *Jefferson's Travels in Europe: 1784–1789*. Baltimore: Johns Hopkins University Press, 1995.

Shapiro, Barry M. *Revolutionary Justice in Paris, 1789–1790*. Cambridge, England: Cambridge University Press, 1993.

Shaw, Diane Windham. "'I Have Been So Long the Friend of Emancipation': Lafayette as Abolitionist." In Anna Olga Duhl *et al.*, *"A True Friend of the Cause": Lafayette and the Antislavery Movement*, 1–15. New York: Grolier Club/Easton, PA: Lafayette College, 2016.

Shovlin, John. *The Political Economy of Virtue: Luxury, Patriotism, and the Origins of the French Revolution*. Ithaca, NY: Cornell University Press, 2007.

Shusterman, Noah. *The French Revolution: Faith, Desire and Politics*. Abingdon-on-Thames, England: Routledge, 2014.

Sizer, Theodore. "A Note on Trumbull's Eyesight, a Letter to Benjamin West." *Yale University Library Gazette* 26, no. 2 (October 1951): 91–93.

Smith, Henry A. M. "The Baronies of South Carolina." *South Carolina Historical and Genealogical Magazine* 14 (1913): 61–80.

Spalding, Paul S. "After Seven Years of Prison and Exile, Why Didn't Lafayette Move to America?" In *Symbol in Two Worlds, Essays on Lafayette*, edited by Diane Windham Shaw, 13–28. Easton, PA: American Friends of Lafayette, 2013.

———. *Lafayette, Prisoner of State*. Columbia: University of South Carolina, 2010.

———. "Unwanted Refugee: Lafayette in Holstein, 1797–1799." Paper delivered to German Studies Association meeting, San Diego, Sept. 29–Oct. 2, 2016.

Spagnoli, Paul. "The Revolution Begins: Lambesc's Charge, July 12, 1789." *French Historical Studies* 17 (Autumn 1991): 466–97.

Stauffer, John. "Lafayette and the American Abolitionists." In Anna Olga Duhl *et al.*, *"A True Friend of the Cause": Lafayette and the Antislavery Movement*, 43–53. New York: Grolier Club/Easton, PA: Lafayette College, 2016.

Stein, Susan. *The Worlds of Thomas Jefferson at Monticello*. New York: Harry N. Abrams, 1993.

Stillé, Charles J. "Comte de Broglie, the Proposed Stadtholder of America." *Pennsylvania Magazine of History and Biography* 11, no. 4 (1887): 369–405.

Stryker, William S. *A Study of George Washington*. Trenton, NJ: Naar, Day & Naar, Printers, 1898.

Sutherland, D. M. G. *France 1789–1815: Revolution and Counterrevolution*. New York: Oxford University Press, 1986.

Tower, Charlemagne. *The Marquis de La Fayette in the American Revolution*. 2 vols. Philadelphia: J. P. Lippincott, 1895.

Unger, Harlow Giles. *Lafayette*. New York: John Wiley & Sons, 2002.

Villiers, Patrick. "'The Freedom of All the Blacks on the Plantation': Lafayette and His Fight for Emancipation in French Guiana, 1785–1802." In Olga Anna Duhl *et al.*, *"A True Friend of the Cause": Lafayette and the Antislavery Movement*. New York: Grolier Club/Easton, PA: Lafayette College, 2016, 33–41.

Van Vlack, Milton C. *Silas Deane, Revolutionary War Diplomat and Politician*. Jefferson, NC: McFarland & Company Inc., 2013.

Vowell, Sarah. *Lafayette in the Somewhat United States*. New York: Riverhead, 2015.

Ward, Christopher. *The War of the Revolution*. 2 vols. New York: Macmillan, 1952.

Ward, Henry M. *Richmond, An Illustrated History*. Northridge, CA: Windsor Publications, 1985.

Willis, Sam. *The Struggle for Sea Power: A Naval History of the American Revolution*. New York: W. W. Norton, 2016.

Wills, Garry. *Inventing America: Jefferson's Declaration of Independence*. Garden City, NY: Doubleday, 1978.

Wilson, G. S. *Jefferson on Display: Attire, Etiquette, and the Art of Presentation*. Charlottesville: University of Virginia Press, 2018.

Wilson, Gaye. "Jack Jouett's Ride." *Thomas Jefferson Encyclopedia*. Monticello website.

Wood, Gordon S. *Friends Divided: John Adams and Thomas Jefferson*. New York: Penguin, 2017.

Woods, Edgar. *Albemarle County in Virginia*. Charlottesville: Michie Co., 1901.

Zeender, Jim. "Thomas Jefferson: Governor of Virginia." April 12 and May 16, 2013." "Pieces of History," https://prologue.blogs.archives.gov/about-2/.

Zug, James. *American Traveler: The Life and Adventures of John Ledyard: The Man Who Dreamed of Walking the World*. New York: Basic Books, 2005.

REFERENCE WORKS

Andress, David, ed. *Oxford Handbook of the French Revolution*. Oxford, England: Oxford
    University Press, 2015.

Boursin, Elphège, and Augustin Challamel. *Dictionnaire de la révolution française:
    institutions, hommes & faits*. Paris: Jouvet et cie, 1893.

Tucker, Spencer. *Almanac of American Military History*. Vol. 1 Santa Barbara, CA:
    ABC-Clio, 2013.

WEBSITES AND SOCIAL MEDIA

American Friends of Lafayette, Easton, PA

Ancestry.com

Biographical Directory of the United States Congress

Carolana [www.carolana.com], Little River, South Carolina

Central Intelligence Agency, Langley, Virginia

Chateau de Versailles, France

Colonial Williamsburg, Virginia

Encyclopedia of Greater Philadelphia

Encyclopedia Virginia

Find a Grave.com

Founders Online, National Archives

Papers of Benjamin Franklin, Yale University and American Philosophical Association

French Revolution Digital Archive, Stanford University

H-Net War discussion network

Neil Jeffares, *Dictionary of pastellists before 1800* [online]

"Jefferson and Reading," Jefferson Legacy Foundation

Thomas Jefferson's Monticello

"Thomas Jefferson's Libraries" database at Monticello.org

"Shadwell Library Reconstructed (Partial)," within "Thomas Jefferson's Libraries"
    database at Monticello.org

The Lafayette Society

Special Collections Web site, Lafayette College

"La Fayette, Citizen of Two Worlds," Cornell University

Library of Congress

Marquis de Lafayette Collection, Cleveland State University

Massachusetts Historical Society

[U.S.] National Archives website

[U.S] National Gallery website

Slavery and Remembrance, Colonial Williamsburg Foundation

Commonwealth of Virginia website

INDEX